D0344340

Civic Passions

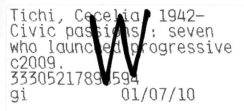

Cecelia Tichi

Civic Passions

SEVEN WHO LAUNCHED PROGRESSIVE AMERICA

(and What They Teach Us)

THE UNIVERSITY OF NORTH CAROLINA PRESS CHAPEL HILL

This book was published with the assistance of the William R. Kenan Jr. Fund of the University of North Carolina Press.

Designed by Courtney Leigh Baker
Set in Whitman and Myriad Pro
by Tseng Information Systems, Inc.
Manufactured in the United States of America

The paper in this book meets the guidelines
for permanence and durability of the Committee
on Production Guidelines for Book Longevity
of the Council on Library Resources.

The University of North Carolina Press has been
a member of the Green Press Initiative since 2003.

Library of Congress Cataloging-in-Publication Data
Tichi, Cecelia, 1942–
Civic passions : seven who launched progressive America
(and what they teach us) / Cecelia Tichi.
    p. cm.
Includes bibliographical references and index.
ISBN 978-0-8078-3300-1 (cloth : alk. paper)
1. United States—History—1865–1921—Biography.
2. Progressivism (United States politics) 3. Political
activists—United States—Biography. 4. Social
reformers—United States—Biography. 5. Leadership—
United States—Case studies. 6. United States—Politics
and government—1865–1933. 7. United States—
Social conditions—1865–1918. 8. Social problems—
United States—History—19th century. 9. Social
problems—United States—History—20th century.
I. Title.
    E663.T53 2009
    324.2732'7—dc22
    2009011634

13 12 11 10 09   5 4 3 2 1

(to Progressives Everywhere)

WE DID NOT ALL

COME OVER ON THE SAME SHIP,

BUT WE ARE ALL IN THE SAME BOAT.

BERNARD M. BARUCH

———

CONTENTS

ILLUSTRATIONS

Two Gilded Ages

A Preface

In July 2007, as the U.S. economy began to sour, the front-page headlines of the Sunday *New York Times* proclaimed, "The Richest of the Rich, Proud of a New Gilded Age. . . . The Nation's Wealthiest Say They Are Proud of New Gilded Age." The wealth of the newest American tycoons, reported the *Times*, "has made the early years of the 21st century truly another Gilded Age." The figures proved it. The new "age of riches" sent 5 percent of the national income to the highest .01 percent of the population. (Eighty-two American billionaires were too "poor" to make *Forbes*'s list of the 400 richest people in America in 2007.) The story of the "new tycoons," said the *Times*, "gives them a heroic role." Their huge fortunes, said the newspaper, grew from business leaders' bold moves that matched the "rough and tumble" of the first Gilded Age of the oil magnate John D. Rockefeller, the steel king Andrew Carnegie, the banking powerhouse J. P. Morgan, and others. *Times* readers saw photos of those titanic grandees mixed with head shots of their successors: Bill Gates of Microsoft, Sam Walton of Walmart, Sanford Weill of Citigroup, Warren Buffett of Berkshire Hathaway, and still others. Proud of their "flair" for business, several of the new titans linked their favorite philanthropies with those of the first Gilded Age tycoons.[1]

Fourteen months earlier, an Ohio man might have welcomed a bit of philanthropy. On May 1, 2006, Timothy J. Bowers, 62, staged a robbery of $80 at the Fifth Third Bank on Broad Street in Columbus, Ohio, then waited for the bank guard to call the police. Bowers was arrested and tried the following October, pleading guilty when his case was heard in the Franklin County Court of Common Pleas. A high school graduate and U.S. Navy veteran, Bowers explained that he hadn't been able to find steady work for almost three years. In a quiet, clear voice, he explained that the only available jobs paid minimum wage and that age discrimination was also against him. Fearing destitution, he hoped to be sentenced to a three-year prison term until he could collect Social Security. His attorney, Jeremy Dodgin, told the court this was "an unusual and unfortunate situation," and Judge Angela White said that the defendant's story "unfortunately made too much sense." She sentenced Bowers, as he wished, to the three-year term that guaranteed him food, shelter, clothing, and medical care.[2]

The case of the bank robber who got his wish appeared nationwide as a humorous feature story in newspapers and on TV. It also struck a deeper chord for a nation sliding toward hard times. The Ohio robber brought up the harsh realities that millions of Americans faced in the late twentieth and early twenty-first centuries. Uppermost for Bowers was age discrimination against workers over forty years of age. His case also tapped a cluster of related troubles: job insecurity, health-care woes, life lived close to the edge from paycheck to paycheck, home foreclosures and evictions, and income too low to meet basic needs. An honorable record of military service and a solid work history now counted for nothing. Bowers had become what one journalist has dubbed the "disposable American."[3]

Timothy Bowers probably did not see the newspaper report on the new Gilded Age "richest of the rich." He was in prison when it appeared. Students of American history, however, could recognize Bowers—and also the new tycoons—as representatives from two historical time zones. They are both déjà vu Americans, mirrored figures from two Gilded Ages.

This book is prompted by the grim similarity of current U.S. conditions to Gilded Age society over a century ago. Not that two historical moments are ever identical. In several ways, the first Gilded Age differs sharply from the second. Massive steel works and factories, for example, marked the industrial capitalism of the first Gilded Age, whereas glass office towers represent computer-driven finance capitalism in the second. Industry and agriculture were primary employers in the first Gilded Age, whereas a service economy has come to dominate employment in more recent times. Gender roles have changed drastically too. Working-class women toiled outside the home in the first Gilded Age, while their affluent counterparts were homemakers. More recent pressures of economic conditions and feminist energies, however, have sent women in unprecedented numbers to the workplace outside the home in the second Gilded Age, including women who span the full range of the middle classes. Ethnic, racial, and sexual identity have also changed, becoming explicit and politicized in ways that continue to evolve in the second Gilded Age. Technology, what's more, has spurred momentous change in material conditions. Americans of the first Gilded Age were well acquainted with the new consumer culture, but few could envision a world of mass electrification, indoor plumbing, appliances, automobiles, supermarkets, highways, commercial aviation, credit cards, television, computers, e-mail, the worldwide web, and so forth. To the first Gilded Age, further, the suburb meant a residence within reach of a streetcar, and the term "subdivision" referred to arithmetic, not houses.

The two eras that are so readily contrasted nonetheless invite comparison. The novelist Mark Twain's 1873 title *The Gilded Age* labeled his era and brands our own. No two historical moments are ever identical, but the points of similarity are eerily close.

A checklist begins with the culture of corruption and Wild West financial schemes that exploded in both Gilded Ages in Washington, D.C., and on Wall Street. Special-interest money lined politicians' pockets and splintered the political system in the first Gilded Age as it has done again in the second. In both eras, elected officials spurned the public that voted them into office while supporting laws and regulations that were custom crafted for the benefit of private interests, notably corporations and the financial services sector. The "Bosses of the Senate" were the powerful monopoly trusts of the first Gilded Age, including oil, metals, banking, and the railroads. The opening years of the twenty-first century saw political favors brokered by K Street, which was shorthand for the powerful lobbying firms that hired politicos, including former members of Congress, to solicit favors from ex-colleagues. Public-interest legislation was kept bottled up or buried in committees. Custom-crafted laws then sucked public monies and gave special interests huge tax breaks that shrank the public treasury and left the favored entities free to seek their own gains. By 2006, according to one researcher, there were sixty-eight lobbyists for each member of Congress (up from thirty-one in 1964). According to one calculation, the average amount spent to lobby Congress for each day of the 2008 congressional session was $16,279,069.[4]

Immigration, too, was a major public issue in the first Gilded Age, as in the late 1900s and early 2000s. In both eras, many native-born Americans worried about an influx of foreigners, whose labor was as crucial for American industry in the first Gilded Age as it later became for the service sector economy. Immigrants, however, have stirred uneasiness and anger. Many have feared that they might drain Americans' money for their health care and the schooling of their children. They might reproduce in great numbers and dominate those in established racial and ethnic categories. Aliens to U.S. culture, they might harbor secret plans for insurrection, hatching cunning, deadly plots in their foreign languages.[5]

At home, Americans of both eras experienced scandals of food, beverage, and pharmaceutical contamination. The first Gilded Age lacked legal protection from toxic medicines and from adulterated and misbranded food, including milk that was preserved with formaldehyde and fruit flavors made with coal tar. Upton Sinclair's 1906 novel *The Jungle* showed the extent of dangerous meat and other food contamination in the packing plants and elsewhere. One century later, governmental inspection of food, drinks, and medicines was nearly nonexistent. Outbreaks of food-borne illnesses prompted repeated (though voluntary) recalls of huge quantities of meat and fresh vegetables, while other food, prescription medicines, and personal care products were found to contain toxic chemicals. Dangerous levels of lead showed up in imported children's toys. As in the past, the industries producing these products were largely left to regulate themselves while the public was left to go it alone.[6]

Similar economic issues also cut deeply in both Gilded Ages. Years of steep economic decline afflicted both eras — post-1873, 1884, 1887, and post-1893 in the first Gilded Age, and 1991–92 and post-2007 in the second. Banks and brokerages failed in both eras. Recession and depression seldom, however, flattened the fortunes of the immensely wealthy. In the depression year of 1897, Mrs. John Jacob Astor was "fairly covered with jewels," according to New York newspapers. Gotham's headlines of the second Gilded Age proclaimed, "Even When Times Get Tough, the Ultrarich Keep Spending." One economics reporter called the world of the new Gilded Age elites "Richistan."[7]

Yet conditions worsened for ordinary people. Millions worked long hours for wages and salaries that barely covered expenses. Charitable food donation programs expanded in both periods. Housing shortages and unaffordable rents forced many into crowded, substandard dwellings, while homeowners who missed mortgage payments faced foreclosure. Whether they were low-income workers, managers, or professionals, Americans in both eras lived in dread of the sudden, massive job losses that rupture lives. Short of labor strikes, the industrial workers in the first Gilded Age had no say in their terms of employment. Employees in the modern workplace are once again rendered "speechless," according to a recent study of workplace behavior and business ethics. In both eras, savings and pensions quickly evaporated, and all adults in a given household felt caught in a time crunch.[8]

Feeling overwhelmed, many tried to escape the pressures by mentally vaulting themselves out of their time and place toward prayed-for states of wealth. "Acres of Diamonds" became a wildly popular sermon in the first Gilded Age, its homilies laced with tributes to merchant princes and capitalists such as Andrew Carnegie and John D. Rockefeller. Similarly, the "prosperity" ministries of certain megachurches of the new Gilded Age attracted millions with messages of heaven-sent real estate, cash, and luxury vehicles.[9]

Organized religion in both Gilded Ages, in addition, offered a theology of divine escape from modern complexities. In the first Gilded Age, speculation about apocalyptic End Times stirred Protestant churches with "millennial fervor." The faithful anticipated their ascension into heaven via a glorious "rapture" while those "left behind" on earth faced "terrible punishment." As of 1995, visions of the Apocalypse returned in force for the tens of millions of readers of the *Left Behind* series of novels, starting with *Left Behind: A Novel of the Earth's Last Days*. In both eras, sinful and unworthy persons would be punished in a world of catastrophic destruction. Believers in the approaching Apocalypse, it goes without saying, are convinced that God has directed them to ignore civic responsibility.[10]

Others have discovered spiritual, if not strictly religious, bases for bowing out. In the first Gilded Age, as the historian Jackson Lears has shown, problems brought on by modern industry seemed to have left "no place of grace." In reaction, many retreated to antimodern ways they considered therapeutic, for example, spiritualized handcrafts and aesthetics of the medieval. In the late twentieth and early twenty-first centuries, the antimodern found expression in the New Age movement. Mystical medievalism now yielded to a mix of paganism and elements of worldwide religions. New Age music drew listeners into meditative states, while its centers typically offered "a more harmonious way of living" in settings of therapeutic springs, spas, and a pristine natural environment removed from civilization. Ironically, the severe stresses of both Gilded Ages can be measured by the strength of spiritual and religious efforts to withdraw from them.[11]

In both eras, sadly, prominent figures in public life have largely offered bromides instead of creative solutions. The real story is "the one most politicians won't even acknowledge," says social critic Bill Moyers. Covering both Gilded Ages, he describes "the reality of the anonymous, disquieting daily struggle of ordinary people, including the most marginalized and vulnerable Americans but also young workers and elders and parents, families and communities, searching for fairness and dignity against long odds in a cruel market world." Said historian Mark Sullivan, "The average American of 1900 had the feeling that . . . his economic freedom, as well as his freedom of action, was being circumscribed in a tightening ring." The millennial year 2000 sparked this reprise from writer Walter Mosley, who lists "poor medical care, job insecurity, the bane of old age, lack of proper education, and the nagging sense of mistrust of a society in which you are a productive member who does not seem to share in the fruit of that production." These issues, says Mosley, "pervade every cultural group, creed, race, and religion." As one American who grew up in the first Gilded Age remarked, "The present time is one in which it requires unusual courage to be courageous. A weary acceptance of apparent defeat is easier."[12]

This book is about seven individuals who are relevant because they neither accepted defeat nor seceded in the first Gilded Age. Working with others, they rejected the scripted lives and attitudes that were prevalent in their day. As fixed and permanent as the first Gilded Age seemed at the time, it gave way under the pressure of their ideas and activism. The result was a renaissance of positive change.

This book concerns innovative leadership in times of grave crisis. In *The Gilded Age*, Mark Twain and his coauthor, Charles Dudley Warner, flayed their America for its greed and political corruption, its business bubble economy, its selfishness, and its daft get-rich schemes. The seven Americans featured here grew up in that era, but in varying ways they achieved a different angle of vision and found practical solutions to seemingly insuperable problems. They acted because they saw great peril beneath the late-1800s golden glitter. Each realized that conventional thought and customs posed a threat to the country as a whole and jeopardized its future.

At a remarkably young age, each of the seven who are profiled here experienced a personal, life-changing moment that crystallized his or her commitment to a career of civic progress. Alice Hamilton, a physician from Fort Wayne, Indiana, found that industrial workers were falling ill and dying from workplace poisons, and she recalled girlhood moments when her mother said, "Somebody must do something about it, then why not I?" As a college student in Ohio, John R. Commons failed at door-to-door sales and began to challenge the orthodox laissez-faire economics that left him sunk in debt. The genteel Julia Lathrop of Rockford, Illinois, ventured to Chicago to Jane Addams's experimental settlement house, Hull House, and was wrenched into action by others' callous disregard for children and the disabled. Similar disregard catapulted the twelve-year-old Florence Kelley into lifetime advocacy for children's (and women workers') rights when she saw little boys toiling past midnight in steel and glass industries in western Pennsylvania. Kelley reached a stunning conclusion: the products took precedence over the lives of the children.

Others experienced equally powerful "lightbulb" moments. The nineteen-year-old law student Louis D. Brandeis committed himself to a career of active citizenship because he knew the havoc of war and economic depression from his family's experience in Louisville, Kentucky. In New York City, a twenty-five-year-old Baptist minister, Walter Rauschenbusch, felt heartsick to find his hardworking church congregation dispirited by their grinding poverty and realized that a radical new theology must fulfill the earthly mandate of the prayer: "Thy kingdom come *on earth*." In Memphis, Tennessee, meanwhile, a young black journalist, Ida B. Wells, was so shocked by the lynching of three friends that she vowed to expose and put a stop to the rampant racial murders of blacks by whites in the post-Reconstruction South, even if it cost her life.

In their own ways, all seven figures in *Civic Passions* understood that the nation's security, economy, and democracy were in jeopardy. Against all odds, they took enormous personal risks to guide the United States toward a better future. In varied ways, these four women and three men brought a renaissance of fresh approaches to U.S. civic life. All of them, that is, turned peril into progress by citizen activism.

A nation that overlooks the leadership of its rank-and-file citizens of the past is apt to overlook the power of such persons in our own day. The seven who are featured here defy the traditional terms of American heroism and fame. None rose to the presidency, led the nation in war, amassed a huge fortune, or glittered as a celebrity. Not one was a star athlete, a scientist, or an inventor. Enduring prominence has come to just one of the seven, Louis D. Brandeis, because of his eventual appointment to (and achievement on) the U.S. Supreme Court, although this book highlights his prior work as an attorney in private practice. All seven won awards and recognition within their lines of work in their own day. Except for academic specialists and a few others, however, their contributions to the national good are largely forgotten, taken for granted, or rejected.

"These are the days when [people] of all social disciplines and all political faiths seek the comfortable and the accepted," wrote a twentieth-century critic in his best-selling analysis of U.S. social and economic arrangements. The late John Kenneth Galbraith's *The Affluent Society* went on to say that controversial individuals are regarded as "a disturbing influence" and that "originality is taken to be a sign of instability." Each of the seven Americans featured here disturbed the status quo of the first Gilded Age and became controversial. Each was accused of being antibusiness, unpatriotic, and radical—in short, un-American. Weathering hostility, they spoke out, wrote books and articles, recruited and joined with others, and involved themselves deeply and without reservation in civic life. Over time, they convinced their fellow citizens (and citizens-to-be) of the rightness of their ideas and of the new policies that were crucial for national well-being. Ultimately, many of their ideas were so fully assimilated and implemented in law that they became the givens of American society and a measure of this nation's decency and humanity. Foregrounding the New Deal legislation of the 1930s, their work came to define human rights in modern America. The stories of these seven come forward now to shed light on the changes that they stirred in the first Gilded Age. Their careers also stand as models of courage, innovation, intelligence, and the power of youthful energy harnessed for a lifetime of positive activism.[13]

Danger and Opportunity

An Introduction

Like a time capsule packed with treasures, the Gilded Age opens on a dazzling fashion show of ladies and working girls in their late-1800s upswept hair and ostrich-plumed hats. They parade in colorful, floor-length, puffed-sleeve dresses and promenade arm-in-arm with whiskered gentlemen and dandies wearing swallowtail coats with fashionable creaseless trousers. They socialize, both men and women, at ice cream parlors, pedal bicycles built for two, and shop at the palatial department stores of Messrs. A. T. Stewart and Marshall Field. They sweep into limelighted theaters in the evenings, vacation at the mountain lake or seashore in summer, and visit the wondrous world's fairs in such cities as Chicago, Buffalo, Nashville, and St. Louis. Gilded Age Americans, all the while, enjoy exciting new consumer products that transform daily life. Their time capsule boasts the "mechanical carriage" or motorcar, the telephone, electric lighting, central heat, indoor plumbing, department stores, and the Sears, Roebuck and Company "wish book" of mail-order items from Kodak cameras to sewing machines and prefab bungalows. At the upper end, the Gilded Age capsule glows with Tiffany glass, Beaux-Arts design, palatial homes and furnishings, private railcars, lavish balls, and portraits by John Singer Sargent. Its sound track rings with Victor Herbert's operettas and John Philip Sousa's rousing "Stars and Stripes Forever."[1]

Other Gilded Age sights and sounds, however, are more somber and disturbing. Queen Victoria reigned, but corporate behemoths now ruled America. The kings were the monarchs of steel, beef, oil, and finance, men like Andrew Carnegie, Philip Armour, John D. Rockefeller, and J. P. Morgan. Their names now became synonymous with big business, its rise more recently dubbed the incorporation of America. Trusts and holding companies signaled the dominant business hyperpower that was supported by legal and judicial maneuvers. "The rise of corporations and trusts inspired both public

Leisure and recreation on two wheels, 1896. (Library of Congress)

celebration and fear," says one writer, adding that "corporations were widely viewed as a force powerful enough to erode democracy itself."[2]

Empire, too, stamped its colossal footprint on the period. Not content with global commerce and with coast-to-coast dominance of the North American continent, U.S. political and military leaders underwrote a two-ocean battleship fleet and "expanded American obligations . . . in regions far removed from American shores and American interests." At a cost of hundreds of thousands of lives, President William McKinley in 1898 took steps to end the Spanish colonial hegemony in Cuba and the Philippines and to project U.S. military and economic power worldwide. On homeland shores, *shame* trademarks the Gilded Age as well, as historians cite the Jim Crow laws, lynchings, and the Chinese Exclusion Act of 1882 as good reason for a rubric of repression and regression. Feminists, for their part, mark the age as the incubation of the independent New Woman and of focused efforts to jumpstart the stalled suffrage movement that denied women the right to vote in national elections until well into the twentieth century.[3]

Behind the stirring Sousa marches and parlor pianos' sweet soulful tunes, the Gilded Age time capsule echoes with wrenching cries. It stirs with the laments of debt-burdened western farmers crushed by years of rock-bottom crop prices and exorbitant railroad shipping rates. It clinks with the meager wages of industrial workers who could not support families on twelve- and fourteen-hour shifts worked seven days a week, many of them immigrant foreigners meeting hostility and violence from the Americans who preceded them in sailing ships that now gave way to steam. It also echoes with the foot-falls of the jobless who pounded pavements and pathways in search of em-ployment in the depression years of the 1870s and 1890s. The capsule, what's more, rustles with the greenback payoffs to politicians, and it resounds with the counterpoint of labor strikers' rage and owner-capitalists' counterforce. It crackles with police gunfire and the deadly explosions of anarchists' politi-cal rage that might be expressed in Albert Nobel's new invention, dynamite. It thunders with the pronouncements of social Darwinists who assert the "law" of the survival of the fittest. It displays, above all, a polarized America of the super-rich and the terribly poor.

The Gilded Age, however, did not last. Thanks to innovators and their energies, it gradually gave way to a renaissance called the Progressive Era. The mutton sleeves went the way of the silk top hat, just as the stock figure of the corrupt machine politician yielded to the election of good-government mayors and governors. In Cleveland, Ohio, the charming Tom Johnson made a fortune on street railways, then became a passionate agent for the public good. As the city's mayor (1901–9), he worked to create a public transit sys-tem with affordable fares, and he wrested city government from "privileged" interests and professionalized Cleveland's government to equip the city for the new twentieth century. Westward, the "Wisconsin Idea" became syn-onymous with Governor Robert La Follette, who served from 1901 to 1906 and fought successfully for equitable taxation, the conservation of natural resources, the direct election of U.S. senators, and the creation of nonpoliti-cal commissions to study hard problems affecting the public good and to propose solutions. As governor, "Fighting Bob" La Follette also championed "the rights of workers, women, and minorities."[4]

The Gilded Age was followed, that is, by an era whose driving ideas and activism moved Americans toward very different ways of life and outlooks in the United States. The change was not easily accomplished. As ever, en-trenched interests and beliefs were powerful. The new outlook required, first, exposing the darker conditions beneath the gold-plate glitter. An exit out of the sordid, baleful conditions required that the Gilded Age be revealed for what it was — a thin plating that hid a host of dangerous social problems that afflicted the middle and working classes and imperiled the country. Be-yond exposé, the new innovators unrolled their practical blueprints for a

better future, but blueprints are only plans, not structures. These archite
of social change worked tirelessly to persuade others that their plans v
workable for the nation as a whole and must be implemented. Over a per...
of years and decades, their effort paid off.

Not that America became a utopia. Social progress is always relative and contingent. Not all groups or individuals benefit equally, and the makeup of society is ever fluid and dynamic. Fear of change is itself powerful, and regression ever a possibility. The Progressives' blind spots have been widely acknowledged. With few exceptions, white Progressives did not sufficiently incorporate African and Asian Americans in their goal of expansive citizenship. Some have seen Progressives as meddlesome, others as naive and nostalgic for a preindustrial world. Still others have criticized them for overlooking the serious class divisions in American society and have questioned who, exactly, belonged on the Progressives' membership rolls and what sort of organization they constituted and commanded.[5]

To be sure, the Progressive agenda did not curb Americans' enthusiasm for the good life of material pleasures, free choice, and geographic mobility from the late nineteenth century and into the 1910s and beyond. The zest for consumer goods and homeownership continued, as did the growth of industrial production, the restless move westward and into cities, the pleasures of leisure activities, and the general enthusiasm for the mechanization that now defined modern life.[6]

Yet bold, unprecedented ideas about civic life steadily took hold at the local, state, and national levels under the guidance of these Progressives, whose agenda centered on quality-of-life issues. They proposed new approaches to childhood, work, health, safety, and security. They pushed for honest and imaginative political leadership, for workplace safety, for municipal services to provide water, electricity, and sewage treatment to the public at affordable prices. They urged protections for children and consumer rights to healthful food, beverages, and medicines. Their efforts gradually moved these and numerous other issues to the forefront of citizens' attention and action. One writer calls this process "reinventing 'the people.'" Thanks to the renaissance of the Progressives, civic concern focused on a range of issues from street sanitation to playgrounds. Over time, the wealth of the new ideas became transformative, and millions of Americans endorsed social change under a broad banner of modern reform.[7]

Progressivism was launched when certain younger individuals and groups began to see personal and social life through a new and different lens. They did not see stock dividends in the smokestack vapors of industrial cities like Buffalo and Cleveland or the cotton dust air of southern mills. They did not calculate fortunes through the blue haze of Havana cigars alight in the gentlemen's clubs and boardrooms of banks and political capitals' inner sanctums. Although Gilded Age urban recreation included sightseeing tours of the working-class slums, these particular individuals did not consider the slum dwellers to be an exotic spectacle staged solely for visitors' amusement. Instead, they saw the slums as a challenge for better living conditions for families trapped in squalid hovels. Middle and upper middle class themselves, they were taught about deplorable conditions by such outspoken working-class activists as Abraham Bisno and Mary Kenney, and they listened carefully and made plans for reform. They saw a future of full-fledged citizenship for the native-born and foreign workers who toiled in New York's sweatshops, just as the counterparts of these workers toiled in the steel mills and coke ovens of Pittsburgh, in the coalfields of West Virginia, in the copper mines of Butte, Montana. They rejected the idea that workers were mere machines to be replaced whenever broken or worn out.

The men and women in this era—in this story—developed a different vision for their times and for the future. Few of their names became bywords of the era, as did those of John D. Rockefeller, Thomas Alva Edison, the prohibitionist Carrie Nation, and the actress Ethel Barrymore. They were known and admired, rather, in medical, religious, political, legal, and cultural circles. Raised in the East Coast, the Midwest, the South, and upstate New York, they spent time in cities and formed a loose confederation of the urban and urbane.

Some of the individuals profiled here knew and worked with one another. The three white women—Dr. Alice Hamilton, Julia Lathrop, Florence Kelley—were the core of Jane Addams's Hull House brain trust in Chicago, and they kept in touch throughout careers that demanded extensive travel in the United States and abroad. They continued to correspond and confer with one another when Hamilton became the first woman professor on the faculty of Harvard University, when Lathrop served as the first chief of the newly formed U.S. Children's Bureau in Washington, D.C., when Kelley became general secretary of the National Consumers' League in New York City.

The Progressive men were their colleagues. From New York, Kelley approached the Boston-based public service–minded attorney Louis D. Brandeis for help in a labor rights case in Oregon. Their meeting resulted in the landmark Brandeis brief filed in the U.S. Supreme Court. Their economist colleague, John R. Commons of the University of Wisconsin, came into their orbit in his research projects in the New York sweatshops, the Chicago packinghouses, and on factory investigation commissions. Though they never met, the Baptist minister Walter Rauschenbusch probably made Commons's acquaintance through the economist's book, *Social Reform and the Church*. Regrettably, Rauschenbusch never met the antilynching journalist Ida B. Wells-Barnett, although she lectured in his home city of Rochester, New York, where she conferred with the city's famous feminist, Susan B. Anthony, on woman suffrage. Wells-Barnett did work with Jane Addams at Hull House on issues of race and public schools, and Kelley may have known of her work in black civic organizations. Both Wells-Barnett and Kelley were active members of the National Association for the Advancement of Colored People.

In all, these individuals were kindred spirits who worked within specific fields of expertise to advance the social, spiritual, material, and physical health of the whole nation. They based their work on solid facts. In 1892, Clarence Darrow declared that the public had lost its appetite for "fairies and angels" and now craved "flesh and blood." Said Darrow, "The world . . . to-day asks for facts." "Ugly facts," the muckraking journalist Ray Stannard Baker called them, while the novelist Upton Sinclair boasted that *The Jungle* was "packed with facts." The new, late-nineteenth-century science of statistics claimed that factual data gained by mathematical precision could achieve precise social analysis. The Progressives demanded, sought, and generated research-based facts in medicine, law, labor, economics, sociology, and criminal justice. Their different fields of endeavor converged to set new terms of civic action and the social order. They became guides, leaders—in fact, Archimedean figures—who moved the United States of America forward inch by inch in what they knew to be positive directions.[8]

These Progressives were not cultists or dropouts from modern America. They traveled in George Pullman's palace and parlor cars, enjoyed beefsteak shipped in Gustavus Swift's refrigerated railcars, and socialized by the light of Tivoli crystal fixtures. They exercised—both men and women—on the new Pope and Monarch bicycles and sat in cushioned seats with "Turkish" fringe as often as on lightweight, portable, Vienna bentwood chairs. Customary for Americans of their comfortable class, they accepted the daily presence of domestic servants—laundresses, cooks, yardmen—as the natural order of things.

In pivotal ways, however, they challenged the social arrangements that seemed to them blatantly unnatural, especially in an era of modern "civilization." The United States was physically metamorphosing as family farms gave way to factories, and villages and towns mushroomed overnight into cities. A shape-shifting nation required new approaches to culture and society. Gilded Age thought and action, these individuals realized, were now dangerously dysfunctional.

*Ice cream soda social, 1901.
(Library of Congress)*

*Fine dining at the Waldorf-
Astoria Palm Garden, 1902.
(Library of Congress)*

To promote a new outlook at the approach of the twentieth century, the young reformers undertook public education on social conditions, rights, and responsibilities in a nation that was demographically identified by industrialization, urbanization, and immigration. Aware that the values of the republic rested largely in the nation's middle classes, they worked to school a broad swath of these middle classes. They knew that the reshaping of America required a reshaping of its public consciousness. They also understood that modern media—advertisements, public relations campaigns, motion pictures, the wireless that became known as radio—were important tools for their work, along with relentless grassroots organizing.

Their efforts, moreover, gave a distinct name—a new brand—to U.S. culture and society in the upcoming twentieth century: the Progressive Era. A full roster of Progressives' names would fill an encyclopedia. This book profiles a select few who typify the Progressives' fresh thinking and action. It includes women and men from varied regions of the country, differing educational backgrounds and temperaments, and a range of racial and ethnic identities. The careers of the four women and three men featured here moved in tandem with the abiding presence of Chicago's Jane Addams of Hull House, as well as the reform-minded presidential paterfamilias, Theodore Roosevelt. Profiles in courage, their lives and work were crucially important for the nation back then, just as they are instructive for the socially and economically troubled second Gilded Age.

To understand the Progressives' achievement, however, we must grasp the extraordinary difficulty they faced in educating the very public whose support was vital to their program. We ought, that is, to take the measure of the adversity, inertia, and resistance these individuals faced. We begin, therefore, in the household of a family—the Clarence Day family—that represents the fixed views of late Victorian, Gilded Age America. The Day family lived comfortably on the affluent Upper East Side of New York City, and they prospered from many of the social and economic arrangements of the Gilded Age. Their interests were served by the status quo, and they represent the very demographic that stood to obstruct the Progressives' proposals for urgently needed change. The senior Days and their son, Clarence Jr., entwine in numerous ways with the work of the seven Progressives profiled here, as we shall see.

IN THE SUMMER OF 1886, a New York City railroad financier named Clarence Day planned a special treat for his son and namesake, Clarence Jr. The young Day, age twelve, dressed in his pepper-and-salt sack suit with short trousers and a white starched Eton collar. His father, who was "solidly built, trim and erect," slipped into his tailed coat, plucked his hat from the hallway rack, and reached for his walking stick. Father and son bid a respectful adieu to wife and mother Vinnie and to the three younger boys. The two then walked — the father striding, the son "hopping" in his black buttoned shoes — past rows of "comfortable-looking" brownstones from their midtown home at 420 Madison and over to Sixth Avenue. They passed milkmen "ladling milk out of tall cans" and chambermaids polishing doorbells, while horses strained at streetcars and sparrows pecked at refuse.[9]

They boarded the "stubby little steam engine" of New York's Sixth Avenue Elevated, which carried middle-class riders between stations of a "dainty green, topped by graceful iron pavilion roofs" resembling charming cottages. This El was just one of the transit lines in operation and extending routes since 1869, "the riding remarkably smooth and easy, and the speed satisfactory" at about fifteen miles per hour, according to the *New York Times*. Mr. Day chose seats in one of the three or four passenger cars, and young Clarence's excitement rose because this was no ordinary Saturday workday in the United States of the 1880s but a "great treat." He was going with his father to "The Office."[10]

En route, a wondrous world unfolded through the Elevated car's plate glass windows whenever the thick locomotive smoke cleared. "Fascinated," the boy glimpsed lives unfolding like images from a set of stereograph views. Workers' families appeared through the windows of "cheap" brick tenements, which were loosely defined as city buildings that housed more than three families. Young Clarence became enthralled by the "Ten Cents a Night" lodging house and envious of the "tramps" inside, for they were never forced to scrub their fingernails or "pull some unwieldy girl around a waxed floor at dancing school." To Clarence, they "looked so easy going, not a thing to do; just tilt their chairs back against the wall, in comfortable old clothes, and smoke." To the boy, they represented leisure and freedom, not an economic system that was hostile to workingmen, forcing them into cycles of unemployment and destitution.[11]

The journey's end near Exchange Place and Broad brought father and son into a "tangle of little streets full of men and boys but no women." They walked past "rickety" stairways, "busy basements," and "dirty" old buildings. The volume of refuse was staggering, for garbage, manure, and dead animals compounded the problem of street sweepings, wastepaper, old shoes, tons of coal and wood ashes, and other assorted rubbish. New York was now two years into the work of the Ladies' Health Protective Association of New York City, founded in 1884 by fifteen affluent women rather like Mrs. Day. Like her, they had ample leisure and took their roles as mothers and good

"Stubby" steam engine of the Sixth Avenue El, New York City, 1899. (Library of Congress)

housekeepers so seriously that the outdoor environment of the city seemed to be their domain. School and slaughterhouse sanitation, refuse disposal, and street-cleaning reform came under their municipal housekeeping, but Wall Street had yet to benefit from their efforts when Clarence and his father walked toward number 38. In this all-male terrain, the occasional "bobbing bonnet" drew all stares, but the whole scene was so dreary that Clarence seemed jolted when the apparently oblivious Mr. Day raised his cane and said, "That's where Great-Aunt Lavinia was born."[12]

Clarence Jr., with his chronicler's eye for detail, sensed certain social frictions pointing to a new era. From prior visits to Father's office, he knew the sound of slamming ledgers meant excruciating frustration roiling the employees, who were denied a half holiday whenever Mr. Day returned to work after lunch on Saturdays. Young Clarence knew his father would never tolerate such insolence as workers' demands for shortened hours, let alone higher wages. Father alone commanded employees' work schedules and pay, as was his sovereign right. He was wary of workers and detested labor strikes.

This morning young Clarence was put to work filling inkwells and setting out steel pens for the clerks. Then it was off to a treat with Father, luncheon at the famed Delmonico's Restaurant, for decades a premier New York spot for social dining. The celebrity author Charles Dickens was feted at a banquet back in 1868, and Thomas Edison and Mark Twain were occasional patrons, as were politicians and businessmen like Mr. Day, who ordinarily kept his brain "clear" by nibbling a bar of chocolate and sipping fizz water in keeping with the New York business lunch custom. Today's French cuisine was prepared "*parfaitement*," and young Clarence's treat was a large chocolate éclair "so delicious . . . [he] forgot where [he] was."[13]

Father and son lingered a bit as gentleman diners lighted cigars. The smoke of fine tobacco hung in the air of the dining room, as did whiffs of the sulfur safety matches that lighted these Havanas and Coronas. The same flaring safety matches were used by Mr. Day's clerks and office boys, who struck them against the seats of their pants to light up when the boss shut the door for good at midday today. Neither the office workers nor the Delmonico diners nor Clarence and his father had a clue about the truer cost of the common "lucifer" matches at their factory point of origin. In the year of young Clarence's birth, 1874, a report was issued from the Day family's ancestral region, New England, warning of "the terrible disorganization of tissues of the body" to those working in the manufacture of phosphorous safety matches. The Massachusetts Bureau of Statistics of Labor found that workers who inhaled and ingested the toxic white phosphorous suffered the painfully disfiguring illness known as "phossy jaw." The report termed it "worse than death." Phosphorous necrosis was just one of several occupational hazards now coming to public attention in this era of booming manufacture, and in 1884 New York's own health inspector issued a report, *Hygiene of Occupation*, which cautioned about the dangers of new substances and processes. Understandably, when the Days left the Wall Street office for a midday lunch and lingered in the restaurant, neither gave a thought to workers' health problems or the origins of cheap and ordinary penny-per-box matches that were sometimes given away free at the foot of the El for advertising purposes.[14]

The afternoon saw father and son on a Staten Island ferry across the "sweet-smelling bay filled with sail-boats and four-masted schooners and tugboats and barges." Surprise of surprises—"Father told me that we were going to see Buffalo Bill. . . . The Wild West spread out before us—dust, horses, and all." The boy thrilled to the live-animal cattle drive, the lariats, the brass band, the stagecoach attacked by Indians, and "the wonderful marksmanship of riders

Boy selling "lucifer" matches, Chicago. (Library of Congress)

who hit glass balls . . . tossed into the air and shot at with careless ease as the horsemen dashed by."[15]

The Wild West show was meant to bond the father and eldest son as they sat on the "splintery benches" in an audience of 31,000 from all walks of life. But the senior Day was uncomfortably aware of the thousands of working-class people in his midst, and his sarcasm bubbled when Clarence Jr., his Eton collar limp and "done for," declared his life's ambition to become a cowboy. Father pitched this dart: that cowboy life was "slummy" and savage and that Clarence "might as well be a tramp." "Put your cap on straight," he added. "I am trying to bring you up to be a civilized man."[16]

This very term — *civilization* — was a keystone word for Mr. Day, as it was for his wife and their friends and counterparts throughout the United States of America. What were family life and child rearing but a rigorous process of civilization? What was proper conduct but civility, speech its signifier, and appropriate clothing its hallmark? What were civilization's landmarks if not banks and churches? Tomorrow, for instance, the entire Day family would settle into their customary pew in the Episcopalian Church of the Peace Everlasting. Sunday attendance was mandatory in the family, even though Mr. Day chafed under Dr. Garden's overwrought sermons about "hard-headed" businessmen who ultimately heed calls to "Far Higher Things." The richly robed minister's chasmic ignorance of business galled Mr. Day.[17]

Young Clarence, who saw his father's face "darken" with disapproval during each weekly sermon, prudently held his tongue in this fraught moment in the wooden grandstand at the Buffalo Bill show when his father equated the site of urban poverty—the slum—with the Wild West and denounced both as depraved. Obediently straightening his cap, Clarence said nothing about the protagonist of a novel published the previous year, 1885, in which a boy with the odd name of Huckleberry "lights out" for the territory under threat of being "sivilized." Clarence, too, lit out at this moment, though solely in his mind. Deferring to his father, he kept alive his private dreams about tramps and cowboys. What good was civilization, he asked himself, with its relentless regimen of "fingernails and improving books and dancing school, and sermons on Sunday"? Civilization was a bad bargain, and he renounced it.[18]

He renounced, of course, boyhood's vision of a straitjacketed adult life of the "better classes," although in due course, perhaps predictably, Clarence would grow up to live exactly the life for which his parents groomed him as a son of the Episcopal Church, prep school, Yale, and genteel New York. He would join his father's brokerage in 1896, become a member of the New York Stock Exchange, then publish the *Yale Alumni Weekly* and write for the *New Yorker* magazine. He was not to become a cowboy memoirist. That role was filled by a New Yorker named Roosevelt, who, Clarence's father complained, "talked too much" and, as a young patrician afflicted with asthma, went West for his health, learned ranch work, wrote *The Winning of the West*, and went on to the presidency. Clarence would, however, publish his best-selling memoir, *Life with Father*, shortly before his death in the throes of the Great Depression, and *Life with Mother* would be published posthumously.[19]

In the early twenty-first century, Clarence Day remains arresting as the diarist of the American better classes of his late-nineteenth-century boyhood. The day-to-day specifics of culinary taste, proper attire, family customs, comings and goings, and domestic dramas make up young Clarence's detailed recollection. The Days were quintessential representatives of the upper middle class. Their name was not synonymous with flagrant excesses and baronial powers of the era. For years, the family summered in rental houses in the countryside outside the city or along the Connecticut shore,

Buffalo Bill Cody, 1903. (Library of Congress)

worlds away from the Astors and Vanderbilts in their marble-and-gold ocean-side Newport palatial "cottages." Mr. Day's career in railway finance did not approach the grandeur or notoriety of those of Jay Gould and Edward H. Harriman. The family reluctantly moved to East Sixty-eighth Street when their midtown residential Manhattan blocks were engulfed by commerce, but they never occupied a mansion on Gotham's Millionaires' Row.

They represent affluence but not great wealth. Their importance lies in their status. They were self-appointed keepers of the flame of their particular version of American civilization, the topmost layer of the social buffer zone between the profligate rich and the desperately poor. They represent the crest of the middle classes—and they are important precisely for that reason. The imminent social changes that were vital to the well-being of the modern nation could be legitimated and adopted only with their tacit or active consent and support. They represent the tipping point for change.

What change? In what direction? Mr. Day was certain that his world needed conservation, not change. "He was by habit and by instinct a methodical man" who dabbed on bay rum after shaving, rammed both arms into heavily starched shirts, and fastened studs and cufflinks that were "strong and handsome but simple," allowing himself a single gold band set with a rectangular sapphire. He expected his family to be punctual at breakfast and at Sunday dinners, where he presided with the carving knife over the piping hot, juicy, "great roast of beef, surrounded by fat potatoes and rich Yorkshire pudding." His zeal for hot coffee, ice water, and vintage claret was theological, and his reading tastes ran to Gibbon and British history. The bedrock of the senior Day's social life was his club. Whether yachting, strolling, or junketing at a board meeting "of some little railroad," the members "all had an air and feeling of enormous authority."[20]

To young Clarence, it was a tyrannical, "imperious" authority projected everywhere, fortified by the senior Day's "powerful and stormy voice" and the certainty that his opponents were wrong. "There was no live and let live," Clarence Jr. recalled. Father "felt that people should be grateful to him for teaching them better." *Them* included not only his family and employees but the public at large. The senior Day was certain his world needed far fewer "weak-natured," "noisy," and "disorderly" people and many more who were strong, dignified, "high spirited," and "resolute." He hated weakness "either in people or in things" and embraced "permanence." He was convinced that the world needed preservation and fortification, not alteration, which is to say that it needed more citizens like him.[21]

The Days typified those who consolidated their class identity through social rituals ranging from piano and violin lessons for the children to ladies' luncheons to dinner parties and evening musicales in their home—with mortgage-free homeownership itself a cornerstone of respectability. The Days were not climbers avid to join the ranks of the fabulously rich and powerful, the Henry Clay Fricks or John Pierpont Morgans. Alighting from horse-drawn broughams, those Olympians might be glimpsed in passing, or encountered over breakfast coffee in newspaper critiques of the "idle rich." In the 1880s, publishers Joseph Pulitzer, E. W. Scripps, and William Randolph Hearst profited handsomely from scathing portraits of the new aristocracy of industry and finance. Americans like the Days, raised in a republican and Protestant milieu, upheld the values of "hard work, frugality, and self-control," and they scorned the ultrarich as decadent and parasitic.[22]

The broad swath of middle-class Americans' lives were, of course, inevitably enmeshed with the actions of these upper-echelon figures. Families of businessmen, professionals, and the newer managerial class suffered in the years of industrial capitalism's financial panics—post-1873, 1884, 1887, especially post-1893. Yet they benefited in flush times as employees and consumers of new manufactured products and services, even as they lighted "kerosene lamps in the parlor." Behind the nostalgia for domestic life lies this fact: the fuels and lubricants of Mr. Rockefeller's petroleum enterprise were fast becoming life's necessities, and Standard Oil a de facto public utility. Hundreds of thousands of families like the Days, moreover, were frequent passengers in Mr. Pullman's comfortable railcars that rolled on track that was itself rolled in Mr. Carnegie's steel mills in a process requiring Mr. Frick's coke. Mr. Day's business was necessarily affected in some way or other by the decisions of the banking house of Morgan, and he ranted, apoplectic, against the tariffs of Presidents Harrison and McKinley. The U.S. middle and upper middle classes were linked in myriad ways to the world of the industrialists and financiers and the political leaders leagued with them.[23]

Other important worlds, however, overlapped and intersected but were invisible to the senior Days as the new century approached. "Sight is a faculty; seeing, an art," said a pioneering New England ecologist, George Perkins Marsh, in the mid-1860s. Typical of the middle classes, the Days had the faculty but not the art, and this apparently included Vinnie, who married Clarence as a debutante just out of school, having been the head of her class who "wrote well and spelled well, and spoke beautiful French, but had never laid eyes on a ledger." Clarence Jr. remembered his mother as a Victorian paradigm, fleeing to her room when the household atmosphere was inflamed, but endearing when she read to her sons on Sunday evenings, concerned for their Christian spiritual welfare, and ever preoccupied with the management of the household staff and felicitous domestic arrangements—and above all with the management of her quick-tempered husband, who controlled the purse strings.[24]

Neither Vinnie nor Clarence Sr. saw the fuller ecological field in which they lived on a daily basis. Their partial vision separated them from the pragmatic visionaries, the Progressives, who charted the new course for American society. It set them apart, that is, from those who were mastering the "art" of "seeing." The Days, in fact, measure how very far the U.S. middle classes needed to travel to conceive of a modern community built on a foundation of civic rights and greater social equality for a broad-based population. Who could or would tell them? In 1886, Edward Bellamy, a Massachusetts newspaper editor who was moonlighting as a utopian romance novelist, put things this way in a manuscript soon to hit the U.S. book market and the best seller lists: "The working classes" of the 1880s, Bellamy wrote, have "become infected with a profound discontent with their condition. . . . On every side, with one accord, they [demand] higher pay, shorter hours, better dwellings, better educational advantages, and a share in the refinements and luxuries of life . . . though they know . . . nothing of how to accomplish it."[25]

The president of the newly formed American Federation of Labor had ideas on accomplishing these goals. Samuel Gompers, a Jewish immigrant from England, started out breathing the dust and fumes of tobacco leaves when he rolled cigars as a boy in his family's tenement apartment in New York's Lower East Side. He joined the Cigar Makers' National Union in 1864, at age fourteen. A short man with powerful shoulders, a square jaw, a thick moustache, and a shock of dark, curly hair, Gompers projected physical power as he rose in union ranks. Here in New York in 1886, a group of unions banded together under an umbrella organization called the American Federation of Labor, founded by Gompers. The AFL was launched with 50,000 members and expected to grow, perhaps into millions. Businessmen and financiers like Mr. Day would watch it closely. "We want more school houses and less jails," Gompers wrote of the union goals, "more books and less arsenals; more learning and less vice; more constant work and less crime; more leisure and less greed; more justice and less revenge; in fact, more of the opportunities to cultivate our better natures, to make manhood more noble, womanhood more beautiful, and childhood more happy and bright."[26]

A novel published in 1873 had etched the times in an acid counterpoint to Gompers's idealism. The title of the novel endured long after readers mostly forgot about the book itself. *The Gilded Age* by Mark Twain and Charles Dudley Warner was the thunderclap of social critique and the challenge to the senior Clarence Day's idea of civilization. It accused America of "money lust" and offered a national motto of breathtaking greed: "Get rich; dishonestly if we can, honestly if we must." *The Gilded Age* signaled the selfishness that fostered want, misery, and chasmic social inequalities. There were certain contemporary voices — Ignatius Donnelly's was one — that described the age in direst terms: as the violent unraveling of the entire social order, the very hastening of the nation's collapse.[27]

Mr. and Mrs. Day, to be sure, had regular close encounters with those accused of fomenting disorder, particularly the working classes, the very people whose situations troubled Bellamy and launched Gompers — and

soon preoccupied the new generation of Progressives. Workers figu[?]
in the Day family's daily routines and provided the infrastructure of th[?]
lives. They included Mr. Day's office workers and the longtime family coo[?]
the "indomitable" Margaret, whom Mr. Day plucked from an "intelligence
office," an employment agency specializing in supplying servants for a fee.
Others included their coachman, O'Dowd, who offended Mrs. Day by his
buffoonish paunch, outsized ears, and hairy red hands. For the Vinnies and
Clarences, there was "our farmer," who tended the dairy cows of the Days'
country house, Upland Farm. There were Tyson the butcher, Flannagan the
news dealer, and Mrs. Tobin the washerwoman. There were, in addition, the
grocers near Grand Central Terminal, who "mixed Father's coffee just to his
taste, and saw to it his cigars were right" (and surely spared him any hint
that the cigars might have been rolled by New York City tenement children
toiling in "stench, filth, and utter wretchedness," according to an 1884 report
of the Bureau of Labor Statistics for New York).[28]

Then there was Jerome, "a taciturn, preoccupied colored man, an expert
at moving," meaning that he could be summoned whenever Vinnie needed
his help for odd jobs. Neither she nor Clarence Sr. nor Clarence Jr. gave a
thought to the predicament that might indeed make an African American
man in late-nineteenth-century America quite taciturn. The racial biases
that restricted employment and housing opportunities and made Jerome a
handyman apparently never entered their minds. The Wall Street employees, the tradesmen and shopgirls, the domestic workers and the others all
impinged on the Days' consciousness solely for utilitarian functions. Neither
Clarence nor Vinnie regarded them as actual human beings within the orbit
of their own American lives.[29]

Why should they? Personhood, as they understood it, was a term applicable only to select individuals, families, neighborhoods, clubs, and
churches. And to select businesses as well. Fortunately for Mr. Day's peace
of mind, there was good news in 1886, for the U.S. Supreme Court issued a
ruling in the case of *Santa Clara County v. Southern Pacific Railroad* that said
corporations were entitled to the rights and privileges of individual persons.
The railroads that Mr. Clarence Day's company financed would now have
full legal rights and protections under the U.S. Constitution, and corporation
lawyers would see to it that the decision was interpreted in a light properly
favorable to business and thereby to American civilization. If necessary, the
Santa Clara County decision would help keep the unions at bay. If workers or
shopgirls got half-baked notions that labor unions could shower them with
higher wages or get them luxurious working conditions, the law and courts
would teach them otherwise.[30]

Yet a glimpse at one vignette in the family drama exposes the larger civic issues that were critical for the U.S. future. At a citizens' meeting one summer evening, Father learned of a proposal to build a new district school to replace the old, "rickety" one. The funds were to be raised through new taxes. As for the pupils? They included the seven children of the paunchy Irishman O'Dowd. "O'Dowd is my coachman," thundered the outraged Mr. Day. "He isn't a citizen. He doesn't pay taxes. I do. What is all this nonsense about? The property owners of this neighborhood don't want a new school. . . . I move that this plan be quashed." And quashed it was. Mr. Day, a father of four young sons, censured the whole lot of O'Dowd children as a fiasco of eugenics, a litter spawned by the coachman's "criminal carelessness." The seven were not to be coddled or indulged. To educate them at his expense was literally unthinkable. The O'Dowds of the world were not on his mental map. They existed for practical purposes, to provide life's infrastructure. Otherwise, their existence was pointless and a drain on civilized society.[31]

It would not occur to Father, therefore, to inquire into the conditions of those who, besides himself, were building America—those men, women, and children far out of sight who mined the coal, sewed the shirts, butchered the hogs, rolled the steel, cast the iron, dug the tunnels, laid the track and the pipe. And who, in addition, sought housing, food, water, recreation, and futures for themselves and their children at work alongside them. It did not occur to Father, as Clarence called him, using the patriarchal capital *F*, to take his son to a "show" at least as colorfully exotic as Buffalo Bill's: the Castle Garden scene of the steerage-class immigrants—up to 5,000 per day—Greeks in slippers and kilts, Arabs in robes, Russian women in babushkas, Jews in yarmulkes. All were processed by officials in navy serge who worked under the terms of the first federal immigration law, enacted in the earlier 1880s.[32]

How circumscribed was the world of the parental Days and their counterparts all over America. Theirs was a well-regulated, affluent, and comfortable world—but self-enclosed and self-mirroring. Their specimen days passed within a kind of haute bourgeois terrarium walled off from a large and dynamic ecological field. Affectionate as it is, Clarence Jr.'s filial portrait reveals something else as well: class-based inertia. The senior Days and their peers would recoil from such a term, protesting that the mantle of social responsibility was borne on their shoulders as they stood, posture erect, starched and steel-stayed guardians of tradition, pillars of civilization, models of rectitude and proper conduct. (Did not Clarence Sr. contribute $1,000 to his church building fund?)

Yet social pressures were intensifying. America was vast, but so were the new foreign populations pouring into the industrial cities and towns along the routes of the rivers and the vast system of rails (788,992 arrivals in 1882 alone). In these later 1800s, the immigrant laborers by definition meant the onset of the detestable labor strikes, and these were not merely irritating but lethal and catastrophically destructive. As a railroad financier, Mr. Day doubtless knew better than most of the horrendous Great Railroad Strike of 1877, brought on by wage cuts. Clarence Jr. was not yet three years of age when the strike engulfed "hundreds of cities and towns from New York to California, leaving in its wake over a hundred people killed and millions of dollars in property destroyed." One reporter described the scene as "the most horrible ever witnessed, except in the carnage of war." A Pittsburgh newspaper warned, "This may be the beginning of a great civil war in this country between labor and capital."[33]

Another rash of strikes beset New York City in the "Great Upheaval of 1886"—with the bricklayers, plumbers, upholsterers, piano makers, quarrymen, street-railway workers, and others agitating for an eight-hour workday. The much-publicized Chicago Haymarket riot in May of that year sent shudders through the middle classes nationwide. A labor rally had erupted when someone threw a bomb that killed seven policemen and injured many others. The nighttime rally was sponsored by anarchists, and the bombing brought the entire labor movement under suspicion and stifled the original rallying cry for the eight-hour workday. Alfred Nobel's 1866 invention of a stable explosive pressed into paper cylinders and set off with a detonator meant that a bomb could be portable. Carried in a valise or sack, it could be exploded at will by one lone political fanatic or conspirator. On Sunday afternoons on the parklike Boston Common, "furrin'" immigrants preached socialism and anarchism. For many in the middle classes, the social disorder and its promoters "raised the specter of a worker-based social revolution like the Paris Commune of 1871, in which enraged mobs chanted, 'Bread or Blood.'"[34]

Here was the bind: the purblind Days and their counterparts nationwide were both powerful and yet inertial in the face of changes swirling all about them. From the Days' vantage point, the immigrant rabble and irresponsible native-born American workers had no compunctions about demanding higher wages and, when refused, walking out on strike, thereby conspiring to restrain trade. Their periodic eruptions seemed endless, their demands insatiable, their cravings for a greater share of wealth delusional. Their behavior, moreover, threatened to make "a sad mess of society."[35]

The immigrants presented other problems to people like the Days. Their own cherished Anglo-Saxon and Nordic ranks shrank with each barge full of swarthy figures ferried from a steamship to the Castle Garden port of

"The Great Strike of the Street-Railway Employees in New York City," March 1886.
Frank Leslie's Illustrated Newspaper. *(Library of Congress)*

Deadly dynamite bombing at the Haymarket, Chicago, May 1886.
Harper's Weekly. *(Library of Congress)*

entry. The Days and their counterparts were people of property and civic authority, city and town fathers and mothers, pillars of their churches, and board members of schools, clubs, and businesses. Their gloved hands rested on the helm of their society. They held sway in civic life even against the plutocratic power of the Goulds and Rockefellers. What did the future hold for them and their leadership? Was the apocalyptic vision of novelist Ignatius Donnelly's *Caesar's Column* coming true? Was their country to become, as a best-selling book of 1885 asserted, "social dynamite," a land of "largely foreign" male "roughs . . . lawless and desperate men of all sorts?"[36]

In 1890, Jacob Riis, the Danish-born newspaperman and photographer, published a searing account of New York City's immigrant population, who were portrayed as criminals by act and inclination, and sick and starving as well. Riis's *How the Other Half Lives* indicted the good citizens of the city for averting their gaze from the open sewers and tenement alleyway warrens and streets occupied by immigrants from east Asia and eastern Europe. His book could have been based on any other East Coast city or Chicago. The issues of his book surfaced in smaller cities from Rochester, New York, to Fort Wayne, Indiana. Riis castigated the slum landlords and politicians for profiteering from their abject misery. He confirmed, nonetheless, the worst suspicions of people like the Days: that the Italian was both a "born gambler" and lightning fast with a stiletto, that the Chinese were stealthy and sneaky, and the Jew compulsively mercenary. Riis warned that in the future, the petty-criminal children — the "street Arab[s]" — were destined, if unchecked and unredeemed, to impose a regime of rampant gang violence on the entire city.[37]

The years ahead did indeed resound with the thwack of cudgels on human bone and the fusillade of firearms wounding and killing many in what became historic strikes — in Pullman, Illinois; Homestead, Pennsylvania; Coeur d'Alene, Idaho. The 1890s were to bring unprecedented and unforeseen social dislocations and turmoil to the nation as a whole. Precipitated by a run on gold, the Panic of 1893 shuttered 500 banks and plunged the U.S. economy into its worst-ever financial crisis. Major railroads went bankrupt, including the Reading, the Northern Pacific, the Union Pacific, and the Atchison, Topeka, and Santa Fe. Over 15,000 companies failed. At one point, over 18 percent of the workforce was unemployed. Those with jobs found their wages cut by one-third to one-half. Small towns saw "the suicides of their bankers and merchants." Against the celebratory moniker "Gay Nineties" were the "heart-breaking nineties" of "hard times, business failures, mortgaged farms, and labor disturbances." In spring 1894, Jacob Sechler Coxey, a wealthy Ohio quarry owner, led a ragtag pedestrian band of several hundred unemployed workmen, dubbed "Coxey's Army," in a 400-mile march from Massillon, Ohio, to the nation's capital to embody — literally, to convey by their bodily presence — their plea to the federal government to provide jobs for them and their counterparts nationwide. Neither "tramps" nor "hobos," as some newspapers called the "army" in the weeks-long front-page national headline coverage, the marchers included skilled workmen and tradesmen, many of them family breadwinners. Focused on Coxey and his army, the movement included other bands of marchers who were organized in almost every western and midwestern U.S. city, from Los Angeles to Walla Walla. Abjuring violence or threats, the "armies" represented something new in U.S. public life: a citizenly "petition in boots" on behalf of the right to work for a living and to insist that the federal government support that right.[38]

By the late 1890s, the middle classes also became increasingly alarmed by the domination of political and economic life by big business and its relentless consolidation into huge monopoly trusts. To cite one example: In the early 1890s, the American Sugar Refining Company purchased stock in four other sugar refineries that previously were its competitors (including the E. C. Knight Company). By 1892, 98 percent of the nation's refineries were owned by American Sugar Refining. The Standard Oil Company similarly typified the ambition for vertical and horizontal control of a single commodity, petroleum. According to the journalist Ida M. Tarbell, Standard Oil was bent on "direct[ing] the course of any particular gallon of oil from the moment it gushed from the earth until it went into the lamp of a housewife."[39]

The journalist Mark Sullivan, not surprisingly, called "irritation" the American mood that was "prevailing" in the years preceding 1900 and for some years thereafter. "The average American in great numbers," he recalled, felt "put-upon" or "crowded" by some intangible force. Clarence Jr. chronicled his father's frequent "rages" prompted by numerous seemingly minor annoyances and by newspaper articles, and he corroborates Sullivan, who recalled that through the 1890s, freedom of action seemed stifled, political liberty thwarted, personal opportunity blocked. Sullivan also recalled the broad range of names personifying the nemesis: Invisible Government, Money Interests, Gold Bugs, Wall Street, the Trusts, and simply "the enemy." The "long depression of the 90s," Clarence Jr. later called these years.[40]

From this bilious atmosphere of the late Gilded Age, however, a new group of younger Americans—Americans closer to Clarence Jr.'s generation—were emerging to rethink the arrangement of society in terms of economic, social, material, and spiritual well-being. They did not simply sing dirges about social ills or rant about the existing order. Thoughtfully they differed from their parents' generation and from other established authorities in business and civic life. Though the United States would produce many more men and women of the exact same mentality as Clarence Sr. and Vinnie, it was from this next generation that useful new ways of thinking about American society emerged.

The change did not happen in a vacuum. And it did not happen overnight. A new generation did not simply evolve, metamorphose, or mutate into a new and different mind-set from that of the hard-shell Clarence Sr. and the genteel but equally implacable Vinnie Day. The younger generation needed to exert powers of persuasion and education—the latter from the Latin *ducere*, "to lead." Younger Americans needed to hear from them about new possibilities, to process what they heard, to talk about the new ideas, to find the new ideas appealing and logical and promising and practicable. The Progressives' potential allies had to absorb data and be moved by anecdotes and by testimonials. They had to see that pilot programs actually did work— a juvenile court in Chicago, a visiting nurse program in New York, a lunchroom and lounge for female knitting mill workers in Fort Wayne, Indiana.

As agents of change, the Progressives had to press on without letup to show the newer generations the fatal flaws of the Gilded Age and mark the pathway out of it. The Progressives who conceived of the new social arrangements that were crucial for modern America could not simply state their views and rest their case. They became advocates and salesmen and saleswoman too. These young Progressives became, in effect, counselors and tutors to their peers (and to some of their elders). They taught ideas on work and leisure and human entitlement across lines of social class in the United States. They opened and focused a conversation on the rights to safe and healthful workplaces, to toil-free childhoods, to decent housing, to adequate education and food, and to the notion that a certain number of hours of a day apart from toilsome work were a human birthright. The right to life itself became the lifelong mission of one of them, a Progressive journalist who tabulated the hundreds upon hundreds of victims of lynch murder, most of them African Americans in the South.

No, Clarence Jr. was not himself to be a leader of this new movement. *Life with Father* and *Life with Mother*, however, show distinct signs of the emergent new consciousness of the younger generation. In some ways, young Clarence signaled the possibilities for new receptivity to change. It was he, not his father, who saw the "whiskery men" in Father's outer office "shaking their heads over some crazy proposal by the Knights of Labor to have an eight-hour day." It was young Clarence who noticed that the seven O'Dowd children had nowhere to play except the paddock and manure pit by the stable. The eldest, a thin and lanky boy named Morris, walked "with a round-shouldered stoop" as if "all youngness had gone out" of him.[41]

Such observations—such insights—across the lines of social class hint at new ways of thinking. They point to members of Clarence Jr.'s generation who were likewise stirred by such moments and prompted to develop innovative ideas about social relationships. They indicate the bases for new approaches to civic life in the workplace, the home, and the community. Young people like Clarence, male and female, were important. Though not themselves social theorists or activists, they listened with open minds to the fresh contemporary voices of those who took the lead. Faithful to many of their parents' beliefs and values, they also gave tacit support to the practicable new ideas they heard expressed in public and read in print. And this support was critical to social viability and momentum as they listened to Dr. Alice Hamilton's reports on the health hazards of industrial workplaces, to Walter Rauschenbusch's message on the new Social Gospel by which the Protestant churches tapped individual and community potential to improve health care, sanitation, and education in cities.

They listened as well to Julia Lathrop, who conducted studies on the institutionalization of the poor and the insane but is best known as the first head of the U.S. Children's Bureau of the Department of Labor, producing new findings on child labor, juvenile delinquency, and nutrition for the formulation of public policy. They listened, in addition, to John R. Commons's message on the role of economics and education in the prevention of "vagrancy, irregular employment, and pauperism." Some of them recognized the work of a young attorney, Louis D. Brandeis, who in the 1900s understood that a major purpose of law was to protect the powerless from the powerful, notably in the Brandeis brief, which successfully defended the constitutionality of an Oregon maximum work-hour law protecting female workers.

At club and church meetings, moreover, younger adults like Clarence Jr. and his friends heard the words of Florence Kelley, whose ability to describe the horrendous working conditions of children as young as three years of age were thought comparable to Charles Dickens's, and who pioneered the use of scientific data to shape public opinion and to promote child labor legislation. Some listened, too, to the voice of a young African American journalist, Ida B. Wells-Barnett, who lectured and wrote widely on the prevalence of the hate crime of lynching in the South and strove to shake the North out of its willful indifference. In 1886, the year Clarence and his father attended the Buffalo Bill show, Wells was horrified to read of the lynching of a young black woman domestic worker, and her newspaper articles and lectures became a "dynamitic" summons to all citizens to obey the laws under the Constitution. From Alice Hamilton to Ida Wells-Barnett, these Progressives helped to foment an American revolution for an upcoming new century. Their lives and work speak to the present as if it were only yesterday.

Alice Hamilton, M.D.
The Dangerous Trades

The last decade of the nineteenth century . . . was simpler in many ways than any period
which followed it. . . . We were far less certain of what was needed to make society over;
we were groping and seeking.—ALICE HAMILTON, *Exploring the Dangerous Trades*, 1943

We faced a world with settled standards.—ALICE HAMILTON, *Alumni Bulletin*,
Miss Porter's School, 1951

It was pioneering, exploration of an unknown field.—ALICE HAMILTON,
Exploring the Dangerous Trades, 1943

The brass cuspidor surely caught Dr. Alice Hamilton's eye when she arrived
at the National Lead Company office on Chicago's Sangamon Street a few
minutes ahead of her scheduled appointment with the company vice president. The cuspidor (or spittoon), a receptacle for spit tobacco juice, signaled
men's territory and the all too common viewpoint that came with it: "Men
knew the world. Women didn't. Women were not fit to deal with the world."
The petite Alice Hamilton, M.D., was unfazed. An alumna of the University
of Michigan Medical School, she had years of experience in primary care
and laboratory research. She had traveled internationally and handled her
own financial affairs. At the moment, she was on the Illinois state payroll
as a medical investigator of health conditions in the lead industry. She was
appointed by the current governor, Charles S. Deneen, who'd named her to
the statewide Commission on Occupational Diseases two years before, in
1908.[1]

Today's visit was no mere courtesy call but a life-or-death challenge.
Hamilton had gathered hard facts that must be faced. At five feet, four inches
tall, she took care to avoid appearing doll-like in the big screw-and-spring
office armchairs that tilted back. She was carefully attired in an ankle-length
skirt, a shirtwaist with a high collar, and a hat—a tailored ensemble for 1910.

Alice Hamilton, M.D., 1895. (The Schlesinger Library, Radcliffe Institute, Harvard University)

Beneath the hat, her carefully combed and parted hair framed a face of cool self-possession. She smoothed her skirt and collected her thoughts as she waited to meet Mr. Edward Cornish. Her rapier wit must be curbed, she knew, and her manner free of sentimentality. Hamilton staunchly rejected all things sentimental, in keeping with her admiration for Jane Addams, the Hull House leader who had no patience with such "interfering affections."[2]

It was injustice that drew Hamilton here. Workingmen were lured to America by labor contractors who promised "a land flowing with jobs and high wages." Instead, the men found themselves weak, crippled, even killed by jobs they clung to in desperate efforts to support their families. Anger at such injustice was a legacy of Hamilton's cherished mother, Gertrude, who angrily "blazed out" over "tales of police brutality, of the lynching of negroes, over child labor and cruelty to prisoners." In this case, modern industry was the source of deadly injustice. Dr. Hamilton was going to tell Mr. Edward Cornish, the vice president of the National Lead Company, that workers at his plants were being poisoned.[3]

Mr. Cornish appeared on the dot, a businessman committed to workday efficiency. He was a first-class man at National Lead, soon to become its president, and he was certain that Dr. Hamilton had come to shower National Lead with compliments on its modern "model plants." He shook her hand as Dr. Hamilton sat forward with both feet together and flat on the floor. The doctor was careful not to sound like an alarmist. She relied on understatement, but facts were facts. Her opening gambit was ingenuous and domestic. "We have not taken enough interest in the subject to find out whether we have any lead poisoning among our workers," she said, adding that industrial lead contamination is "so often . . . simply a matter of bad housekeeping." She then told him of her recent site visits to the local National Lead Company installations in West Pullman and elsewhere. She had "found much dangerous work going on in all of them." She told him frankly that she was sure that "men were being poisoned in those plants."[4]

He was stunned. This petite, brown-haired, hazel-eyed, ladylike woman physician with the nice, low voice utterly blindsided him. His workmen, poisoned? He never heard of such a thing. It could not be true. His indignation rose. This meeting, a goodwill gesture on his part, suddenly turned bizarre and meddlesome. Cornish's company had plants in and around Chicago, and he'd agreed to this meeting for political and business reasons.[5]

Avoiding heated confrontation, Dr. Hamilton now spoke truth to power in a calm, even voice. Her streak of wicked irony, well known to friends and family insiders, was carefully concealed. She met Cornish's gaze and proceeded fearlessly, for Edward Cornish represented the "responsible man at the top," and she understood such men. In Fort Wayne, her paternal grandfather, her father, and her uncle were once prominent in business, politics, and banking. She explained, "Your men are breathing white-lead dust and red lead and the 'roasting oxides' or litharge and the fumes from the oxide furnaces. . . . They are no different from other men; a poison is a poison to them as it is to any man."[6]

Alice paused to let the hard facts sink in. Would Mr. Cornish react like some executives she met, accusing her of exaggeration, malice, and slander? Or would he complain that the lead industry was being singled out unfairly and made a scapegoat?[7]

If so, she would tell him about the work of the economist John B. Andrews, who two years ago, in 1908, had compiled a report on toxins in the match industry, particularly in plants in the South, where phosphorous necrosis, or "phossy jaw," disfigured workers. Many of them were women who breathed the fumes of white or yellow phosphorous and suffered excruciatingly painful infections at the jawbone. Would Mr. Cornish think Dr. Hamilton ghoulish if she told him that the match workers whose jawbones were surgically removed sometimes lived out their lives on liquid diets — or committed suicide? Perhaps it would ease Mr. Cornish's mind if she told him that in order to improve conditions in that industry, the economist, Andrews, had met both with victims and with match manufacturers, just as she spoke with the lead manufacturing vice president at this moment.

Whatever Mr. Cornish said now, including denial or blame, Alice Hamilton was ready. Her very choice of a career in medicine had been an uphill struggle all along. Her revered older sister, Edith, pronounced science "disgusting," and the head of her preparatory school, Miss Porter, thought Alice captive to "an amusing childish whim" and decided that she was "a bluggy-minded butcher" for wishing to observe an appendectomy. As a medical student in the early 1890s, Alice was shocked to find herself among crude young men of the "roughest class." Seated with her female group of fifteen in the medical school amphitheater in 1890–92, she learned to concentrate amid the "din" and the physical "antics of the men," and she vividly recalled the free-for-all scramble for microscopes and lab apparatus.[8]

Yet it was thrilling in medical school to peer into the microscope to discover live microorganisms—healthy versus pathological. The Ann Arbor years had been "happy and exciting," for the school was on the forefront of the new scientific medical education and one of few that admitted women. The ups and downs of internship, postgraduate work in Europe, and practice and teaching here in Chicago had "hardened" but not coarsened her. Politely she awaited Mr. Cornish's response.[9]

A moment passed; then suddenly he rose, went to the door, and shouted "Come in here" to a passing workman.

Alice held her breath. If the lead company executive had the typical laissez-faire business attitude, he would say that each worker was a free agent and that if the job was bad, the workman was free to quit. Alice was ready with a tart reply. She would say, "Mr. Cornish, this is like a captain at sea saying to his sailors, 'If you don't like the ship, get overboard.'"[10]

But Cornish took a different tack. "Did the lead ever make you sick?" he demanded.

"No, me never sick," stammered the badly scared Slav.

"Are any other men sick?" demanded Mr. Cornish.

"No, no, all good."

The worker escaped quickly, and Cornish turned in triumph to his visitor. "There," he exclaimed. "You see!"[11]

But she did not, and she told him so. "No, I do not see." Dr. Hamilton had already learned from numerous industrial site visits that the factory foremen, protecting their jobs, "deny everything." The workmen, living scattered throughout the city, "will not talk." Once again, she explained how toxicity was caused by the inhalation and ingestion of lead dust.[12]

They faced off, the cool, composed lady doctor and the executive whose agitation was visibly rising. Would Edward Cornish now play the last, racial card? Would he meet her gaze as one white gentleman to a lady and say, dismissively, "What can you do with a lot of ignorant Dagoes, Wops, Hunkies, Greasers?" Or would he say that "Negro" workers were naturally shiftless? If so, Alice would lock her gaze on his and reply that she knew otherwise. She would say that she now resided at Hull House on Chicago's Halsted Street. Cornish might recognize that she lived in a neighborhood with the very sorts of families whose husbands and sons worked as laborers at National Lead, the very same Poles, Italians, and Greeks whom he might disparage as "Dagoes" and "Greasers."[13]

It did not come to that.

Perhaps it was something in her voice . . . the tone of quiet insistence, the apparent command of facts? Deeply skeptical, Cornish sensed the lady doctor's obvious sincerity. She was not so readily dismissed. He had an idea. National Lead owned a mine in Missouri, the "Show-Me" state. He snatched that motto now and looked her in the eye. "Now see here, I don't believe you are right, but I can see you do. Very well then, it is up to you to convince me. Come back here with proof that my men are being leaded, and I give you my word that I will follow all your directions."

Leaded. He used the insider's trade term for *poisoned.* Then Cornish upped the ante. If she proved her case, he promised to hire plant doctors.[14]

Cornish thought he'd probably seen the last of Alice Hamilton. After all, National Lead was in full compliance with the 1909 Illinois factory law requiring the use of "ventilating or exhaust devices" to remove "all dust of a character injurious to the health of the persons employed." If a health problem existed in the National Lead works, the inspectors—men with mechanical know-how—would have alerted the supervisors some time ago. The company vice president bid his guest farewell and promptly went about the business of business. National Lead was expanding and would soon boast that every room of the middle-class American home contained its products, from the enamel coatings on bathtubs to the glaze on fine china in the dining room to the electric lightbulbs and the solder in Tiffany-style lampshades of the living room. It owned and operated mines in Missouri and Wisconsin, and its main consumer product was paint—"lead on the walls," as one company advertisement put it. In the previous year, 1909, each family in the United States used an average of 1.5 gallons, and paint was now a $100 million business annually in the nation, thanks to the promotional efforts of National Lead and its competitors. In 1907, the company had begun to market its signature Dutch Boy White Lead Paint, featuring a child on the label,

Before the painters begin work, it is a good idea for
the house-owner to satisfy himself that the painting materials about to go on his building are the *durable* kind.

Cracking and scaling paint is annoying and unsightly. It is more—it is
very expensive, no matter how cheap it may have been by the pound or by the
gallon. Much modern paint—hand-mixed as well as ready-made—has been
skimped on *White Lead*, or else has been deprived of that essential element altogether. No wonder it scales or washes off!

To be sure of getting White Lead—and *all* White Lead—test it with the
blowpipe. We will send the instrument on request, with explanation why it is a
sure test of purity. Try this test on our *guaranteed Pure White Lead* (Dutch Boy
Painter trademark). Ask for test equipment D. Address

NATIONAL LEAD COMPANY

in whichever of the following cities is nearest you:

New York Boston Buffalo Cincinnati Chicago Cleveland St. Louis
Philadelphia (John T. Lewis & Bros. Company)
Pittsburgh (National Lead & Oil Company)

FULL WEIGHT KEGS
The Dutch Boy Painter on
a keg guarantees not only
purity, but *full weight* of
White Lead. Our packages
are not weighed with the
contents; each keg contains
the amount of *White Lead*
designated on the outside.

---

a clever suggestion of the advertising agency. Dutch cleanser was already
successful on the basis of Holland's zeal for spotless homes, and the lead
industry's "Dutch" link was real and historical, for the method of manufacturing white lead pigment was called the "Dutch process." It dated back to
the seventeenth century and involved a chemical curing of lead in a kiln.[15]

Nowadays some workers—immigrant men with unpronounceable
names—manually scraped and pounded lead carbonate from large, buckle-
shaped cast lead forms. They packed the dried lead powder, a major ingredi-
ent in paint, for shipment in barrels. In this modern era, some of the scraping
and packing was mechanized, but workers still shoveled and funneled the
lead powder manually. National Lead had several white-lead and lead-oxide
plants in the Chicago area, and Cornish took great pride in these up-to-date
"model plants," where the foremen made sure that workers washed their

hands and cleaned their nails. That in itself was reassuring to this executive on the move.

Leaving the Sangamon Street office, Alice knew her work was cut out for her. In terms of U.S. workplace health, the dismal fact was that powerful men like Cornish were often sunk in an "ostrich-like" complacency. They believed that workers in America had better working conditions and a higher standard of living than their sorry counterparts in the Old World. The Edward Cornishes of this world were heirs to a full century of foreign visitors' amazement at the "smokeless . . . new and fresh" American factories and to lyrical portraits of New England mill girls, "industry's Angel daughters." Men like Cornish seldom took time to heed the few dire portrayals of U.S. industry that appeared in magazines and books, such as the novel by the mother of the famous war correspondent Richard Harding Davis. Back in 1861, Rebecca Harding Davis's *Life in the Iron Mills* showed a West Virginia foundry as a Dantean inferno, an image reinforced in recent travelogues describing the Iron and Steel City, Pittsburgh, as hell with the "lid lifted."[16]

Hell in more ways than one, thought Alice, who tallied Pittsburgh's grime and soot, its toxic lead works, and its punishing work regimen, "the steel men working twelve hours a day and seven days in the week." And yes, the city of Chicago was still living down the uproar over Upton Sinclair's 1906 novel *The Jungle*. Everybody was revolted by the passages on food contamination, sawdust in the sausage, that sort of thing. Only a few noticed the deadly working conditions of men, women, and children in the meatpacking plants, conditions that the novelist, an acquaintance of Alice, had described graphically and painstakingly. Sinclair's book hastened passage of the 1906 Meat Inspection Act and the Pure Food and Drug Act, two federal laws regulating the interstate commerce of food, beverages, and medicine. This was a step in the right direction, but those laws did nothing to protect workers' safety and health.[17]

Did Alice have second thoughts about the meeting with Cornish just now? Suppose she had told him of the mortifying moment in Brussels this past summer at the International Conference on Occupational Accidents and Diseases. She'd heard a Belgian expert declare industrial health in the United States to be nonexistent. "It is well known," he said, that "*ce n'existe pas*." The match industry was a glaring example, as Dr. Hamilton knew. European countries had banned the use of white phosphorous in their match manufacturing for years, Finland and Denmark leading the way. France, Switzerland, the Netherlands, and Germany had followed, and finally, just the previous year, England had as well. A safe substitute for the toxic phosphorous, called sesquisulfide, was discovered in 1897 by French chemists, then patented and licensed to the Diamond Match Company in the United States in 1898. Diamond Match had briefly produced a nonpoisonous match in 1904, then declared it too expensive to make and inconvenient to strike. The company ceased production. Now, in 1910, it was an open question whether the efforts of the new Progressive activists like John Andrews would succeed in getting a law passed to require the use of the safe new compound. Not even President Taft's backing for the measure guaranteed its passage. Who knew whether, or when, America would outlaw a workplace poison so notorious that it threatened to blemish the reputation of an American business producing over 500 million matches per day.[18]

If Edward Cornish had been with her at the Brussels conference last summer, would he have shared Alice's embarrassment at hearing America dismissed as barbaric in regard to workplace health? Would he agree that "there is nothing admirable in allowing ignorant and helpless people to incur risks which they either do not understand or are compelled to face"? Would Mr. Cornish, like her, determine to do his part to rectify the situation? His mandate rang in Alice Hamilton's ears. *It is up to you to convince me. Come back here with proof that my men are being leaded.* The words stiffened her resolve.[19]

She accepted his challenge. Of course she did. It had a familiar ring. Authoritative men who demanded proof were nothing new in her life. From childhood in the 1870s, the home-schooled Alice and her sister Edith met their father's demands to seek answers to provocative questions. It was a gentleman's library, not a business office or lead works, where she was first dared to produce data-based proofs. The odors of fine leather bindings and rich tobacco, not the fumes of lead oxides, remained in memory along with Montgomery Hamilton's orders to Alice and Edith to seek biblical proof of the Christian doctrine of the Trinity. For the principles of physics, she was sent to her father's *Encyclopædia Britannica*. Medical school and her year of research in microbiology in Germany made a world of difference in her knowledge, of course, but the basic plotline was the same: the senior man defied her to prove a point to his satisfaction.[20]

Alice immediately went in search of the proof that Edward Cornish demanded. It was early in the game, but she was no novice. Starting out just months ago, she had felt "pretty much lost," but no longer. Touring lead factories in England and Europe the summer before, she saw numerous techniques for banishing the deadly lead dust. The stone or iron floors were easily flushed with water, and the sprayers and "baptizings" and centrifuges worked well. The workers' wooden shoes protected feet from the damp. Here in the United States, what's more, she and her eager young assistants had spent months visiting 304 industrial facilities at a breakneck pace in Illinois and elsewhere. They had discovered over seventy processes that exposed workers to lead poisoning, including surprising ones, such as polishing cut glass and wrapping cigars in lead-based "tinfoil." Alice had learned to recognize the workers' symptoms—the extreme pallor, the loss of weight and appetite, "the indigestion, constipation, and gouty pains," and, of course, the giveaway symptom, the limp or dropped wrist.[21]

Challenged by Edward Cornish, Alice proceeded at once with the do-it-yourself "shoe-leather epidemiology" that was fast becoming her routine. It meant "tracking down actual, verifiable cases of lead poisoning among men who came from the Serbian, Bulgarian, and Polish sections" of Chicago, men who were known "to the employment office only as Joe, Jim, or Charlie, with no record of their street number." It meant picking up gossip from labor leaders, pharmacists, visiting nurses, undertakers, charity workers, priests, factory inspectors, and physicians. It meant "digging" into hospital records, often finding them all but useless because doctors scrupulously noted caffeine intake but omitted questions about the workplace.[22]

It also meant going directly to the workers' homes "and talking to them in their own surroundings, where they have the courage to speak out what is in their minds." It meant hearing a "Negro" worker say that the wages at the lead works were "better than any other work a Negro can get," even though such work "sure does break your health." Sometimes it meant passing through the swinging doors of a saloon. Dr. Hamilton knew saloons. As a twenty-three-year-old medical intern in Boston, she treated patients living in tenements above them. She knew the difference between drunkenness and lead poisoning and looked out for symptoms that began with fatigue and the telltale "lead line," a bluish gray discoloration of the gums and teeth. Then she chronicled the other symptoms, the jaundice, the numbness, the palsied wrist, the pain in the extremities, possibly the paralysis, hallucinations, and kidney failure. She asked about the seizures and coma that preceded death.[23]

Dr. Hamilton found twenty-two clear-cut cases of lead poisoning among the National Lead workers. Her notes included a skeletal Hungarian whose eyes were now "expressionless" and a Pole who was hospitalized with "severe lead colic in both wrists," together with a young Italian seized by headaches and convulsions and now, three months later, unable to work a full day. The evidence the doctor compiled pointed to a much larger number of victims, but for the sake of utmost clarity, she would confine her report solely to cases she could fully document.[24]

The report itself would be crucial, a make-or-break document in Mr. Cornish's hands. It would of course be typewritten. Thanks to the widespread use of the front-strike typewriter, no one need confront her impossible "scrawl." Dr. Hamilton never regretted her childhood rebellion against countless hours forming ovals and pothooks in the service of graceful penmanship. To be moved by the "fiery pen" of a forceful writer was one thing, but the "fire" came from the content, not the inked curlicues.[25]

So the report would be in typescript, but the message must be clear and straightforward, understated but airtight. Nothing inflammatory or sentimental. Mr. Cornish sought facts, and facts he would get. Each case should include the nationality of the worker, the duration of his work at the National Lead plant or plants, the date of onset of his symptoms, and a spare description of those symptoms (whether fainting or attacks of severe headache and vomiting or coma). It would also include his record of hospitalization and the outcome of the case, whether recovery, relapse, impairment, or death. Dr. Hamilton would provide an introduction and summary, drawing on the recent medical literature from Britain and Europe.

The doctor moved swiftly. The issue was too urgent for delay. Fingers crossed, she finished her report, sent it to Cornish, and waited, hoping that her effort would not be buried in one of those oak file drawers in the National Lead office. Undaunted by Cornish's authority as a corporate officer, Dr. Hamilton was all too aware that she labored under a hobbling restriction: her sole power was the power of persuasion. Lacking the authority of law or governmental regulation, she and her colleagues on the Illinois commission were on their own. Any action on the part of industry to reduce workplace toxins would be voluntary. Convincing a top executive of serious problems was a crucial first step. Without it, nothing could go forward.

Daily—hourly—she waited for the postal delivery, for the Western Union telegram, for the ring of the candlestick telephone. She did not have to wait long, for Mr. Cornish pronounced himself convinced by her documentation and immediately committed National Lead to eliminate the dangerous dust from all its facilities. He invited Alice, in addition, to deliver an address to the superintendents of the National Lead Company.

It was December 7, 1910, again in Chicago, when she stood before the all-male audience, took a deep breath, and began, "I appreciate very much the opportunity of talking to the men engaged in the White Lead industry in this country." These men before her—Cornish and the superintendents—were the guardians of a dangerous trade. If they heeded and acted on her message, then lead poisoning would cease to stalk legions of workers in the plants, perhaps in the entire industry. It was critical that she persuade these men, that she overcome their suspicion of an outsider physician and a woman. Her title—"The Hygiene of the Lead Industry"—was deliberately plainspoken. "Naturally I do not know much about the technical side of the business," she said to the superintendents in tones of womanly modesty, assuring them she was "very much interested in the hygiene of the trade."[26]

The speech itself was a kind of Trojan horse—chock-full of explosive information. Alice described plants in the United States and abroad in such detail that no listener could doubt her knowledge. She marshaled facts and figures on medical examinations of workers and percentages of affliction. She made it crystal clear that lead poisoning was a matter of inhalation and ingestion, that breathing the dust and "eating" it with lunch were the culprits. Strategically, Alice saved her bombshell for her closing remarks. "All the factories in Illinois and St. Louis are so dangerous to their workmen that they would be closed by law in any European country," she said. "Please do not think that I am exaggerating, for I am not. My figures will bear a very close scrutiny."[27]

She offered flattery too, naming a lead manufacturing plant on State Street in Chicago as the cleanest. Immediately she exhorted the National Lead Company to set a new industry standard. She implied that workers' health in the whole United States might be patterned on the standard established by the company. Holding Cornish to his promise in this open forum, she declared herself supremely "gratified" to hear him say that "the National Lead Company intends to have medical inspection in all its plants." The superintendents gave her a round of applause.[28]

Edward Cornish then rose to affirm National Lead's commitment to "the sanitary conditions of our plants," based on "the intelligent manner" of Dr. Hamilton's presentation. He commended her practical and theoretical grasp of things and called her "the most distinguished expert in the United States." The session concluded with another round of applause both for Cornish and for Dr. Hamilton.[29]

And Cornish kept his word, becoming an ardent reformer of working conditions in his plants. He was soon known as an ideal industrialist committed to a company policy of worker health as a human right, a civil right for workers of all races and ethnicities across social class. He hired engineers to redesign plant operations and called on Dr. Hamilton for further assistance repeatedly over the years, as did executives at other major corporations, including General Electric and DuPont.

Alice knew that this fairy-tale ending did not close the book on the problem. National Lead was only one company among many, and lead dust was not the sole toxin disabling and killing workers. This would be just one chapter in a long, long campaign. There was so much more to do. At age forty, she was just getting started.

TO UNDERSTAND what drove Alice Hamilton, we need to look back to another time. Family photographs from childhood show an Alice who was unlikely ever to take an interest in lead poisoning, mining dust, "phossy jaw," and numerous other industrial-age afflictions. The photos give no hint of her future career in industrial toxicology, for this petite, demure, unfailingly civil, and courteous model of ladylike deportment was known to be "sparkling, amusing, lovely, tireless." None of the photos of young Alice give the slightest hint of her future as the premier industrial toxicologist of the United States. Not one hints of the adventurous Alice who, in 1919, descended into Arizona copper mines, where she took hold of the rock-busting jackhammer to test its violent pulsing, all for her work investigating ergonomic hazards. No facial feature hints of Alice's "walking intrepidly on narrow planks hundreds of feet above the vats of seething sulphuric acid; dropping down vertical ladders into the dense darkness of copper mines; crawling on hands and knees into remote stopes," the steplike excavations in mine shafts. No accessory of clothing suggests her refusal of high-paying jobs for the freedom afforded by contract work for the U.S. Bureau of Labor Statistics, which supported a decade of her work, starting in 1911, to study the diseases and dangers of lead, explosives, pottery, and dyes nationwide. Or that her series of Bureau of Labor Statistics bulletins would succeed in becoming a "quiet but insistent campaign to publicize industrial diseases."[30]

No feature, moreover, foretells Alice Hamilton's future as the first woman professor at Harvard University and the author of numerous popular magazine articles and a landmark book of 1925, *Industrial Poisons in the United States*. Modern industry in the United States, as Alice Hamilton was to learn, was not only the nation's economic engine but a lethal zone of "dangerous trades" in critical need of diagnosis and treatment. Eliminating the toxic dust and vapors that sickened and killed workers in work sites involving lead, benzene, and other dangerous metals and chemicals would become her focus, her mission, her professional life's work as she pioneered the field of industrial medicine in the United States. In due course, she met and overcame resistance and denial. She combated industry's ethnic, racial, and class-based biases, which served the economic interests of the privileged but also crippled and killed those who worked in the foundries, factories, smelters, and mines. None of the early photos give an inkling of the Alice who began this work by gathering clinical data in the Chicago tenements that were similar to those the young Clarence Day saw from the El windows in New York City while en route with his father to "The Office."

Alice Hamilton's youthful Victorian image (b. 1869) reflected exactly who she was: the daughter of a patrician family in late-nineteenth-century heartland America. "I belong," she said, "to Indiana." Alice described herself as the second oldest of five children, including Edith, Margaret, Norah, and the much younger Arthur (known as Quint). In addition to their parents, Montgomery and Gertrude, there were Aunt Phoebe and Uncle Holman and their six children, all living on the family compound, the Homestead. Cousins Agnes and Allen were playmate age, and all the siblings and cousins played and studied together, just as the two families summered together on Michigan's Mackinac Island. The youngsters were so close that they nicknamed themselves the "insiders." Their childhood studio photographs were probably made at Benham's, the daguerreotypy-photography emporium on the corner of Calhoun and Columbia, the busiest commercial streets in Fort Wayne. For each sitting, Alice and her sisters and brother and cousins were carefully groomed, the girls posing in the traditional Gilded Age styles that included floor-length skirts over muslin petticoats, tight sleeves with fitted bodices, high-necked Mother Hubbard collars, and precision-tied bows at the necklines of shirtwaists.[31]

The Hamiltons' relation to the Gilded Age of their own city was complicated, and Alice's pathway to a Progressive state of mind not at all clear cut. The foundation of Alice's life was the grandfather she never knew but allied with as a pioneer. He'd ventured into unknown territory in the American West, just as she was to enter the "new, unexplored field of . . . industrial disease." Allen Hamilton died before she was born, a guiding force in creating modern Fort Wayne, a man who grew wealthy as a land speculator, banker, and canal and railroad financier. Allen had immigrated from northern Ireland in 1823, a shrewd man of driving, ruthless, entrepreneurial energies, a precursor to the Gilded Age tycoons. A great portion of his wealth came from prime Miami tribal lands bought cheaply through his relationship with Chief Jean Baptiste de Richardville (Peshewa, "the Wildcat"), the nephew of Chief Little Turtle. Promoting the Pittsburgh, Fort Wayne, and Chicago Railroad in the postcanal era, Allen Hamilton helped to lay a foundation for the industrial and commercial prosperity of the onetime Indian outpost that Alice recalled as "an attractive little city . . . shaded by elms and maples," with "mellowed red brick" sidewalks and pleasant, uniform shops.[32]

It was much more. By the 1870s, Fort Wayne had its gaslights, horse-drawn streetcars, free mail delivery, and downtown retailers offering everything from cookstoves to dry goods, jewelry, and custom-made shoes. The new courthouse was up; church spires abounded, including the Presbyterian church where the Hamiltons worshipped (a synagogue was established too); and police and fire departments were on duty. Street paving was under way, initially with wood blocks, as pedestrians mixed with horse-drawn wagons, buggies, surreys, and rigs from livery stables.

Immigrants were arriving too, the Amish to farm the cleared fields beyond the city limits, and Germans to work as artisans, mechanics, factory opera-tives, and domestics. The Hamilton family servants—including a "very lovely nursemaid"—were German, and in the frosty predawn hours each Christ-mas, they led the family's children, their hearts pounding with excitement, to the "brilliantly lighted" Lutheran church, whose "great Christmas trees on either side of the altar" each held "hundreds of lighted wax candles."[33]

Typical of Gilded Age America, the society and the economy of Fort Wayne were developing in tandem during Alice's childhood and teens. Industrial-ization was a fact of life in 1886, as the Bass Foundry of Fort Wayne began to manufacture car wheels, castings, and boilers for any of the seven railroads that now ran through the city. Within a few years, the city's heavy industry included the Fort Wayne Rolling Mill; the Kerr Murray Company, makers of steel tanks and gasworks apparatus; S. F. Bowser, a manufacturer of oil tanks and pumps; and the Wayne Knitting Mills, which employed female workers from a large immigrant labor pool.[34]

Society developed apace. Fort Wayne newspapers from 1870 to 1900 chronicled the "brilliant social seasons with as many as eighty receptions, parties, and balls [that] diverted the members of the wealthy and prominent families of Fort Wayne. . . . Merchants, lawyers, doctors, and politicians had then accumulated sufficient wealth . . . to erect and furnish elaborate homes, provide sumptuous entertainments, buy costly gifts and gowns for recep-tions and weddings, and acquired beautiful and expensive jewelry."[35]

In his own day, Alice's grandfather, Allen Hamilton, had also thrown wide the doors of his mansion for lavish entertainment. A family friend wrote down all the specifics so that generations of Hamiltons yet unborn would have the vicarious pleasure of the legendary party of February 1850, when Allen hosted a gala for 350 guests at his mansion, the Homestead. Alice, who spent her first four years living in the mansion, knew every nook and cranny from parlor to library to billiard room. She could readily visualize the grand event. Guests arrived by sleigh to fill the "palatial" and "beautifully furnished" mansion, with its fourteen-foot ceilings and black walnut panel-ing. They socialized amid "tapestry, carpets, splendid curtains and mirrors that reached from the top wall down" to a base of marble. The wood-burning furnace was fully stoked, and every fireplace glowed, with its coal fire tended by a bevy of servants. Allen Hamilton invited every attorney and minister in the city to this winter party. Guests were served "an abundance of everything," including "thirty-five chickens made into salad, besides roast turkey, geese, ham, tongue, and every kind of meat that could be got. . . . The party exceeded all others."[36]

Grandfather Allen Hamilton's career and social life set the stage for the upcoming era of Gilded Age Fort Wayne and for the lives of his descendents. Alice's social life, for instance, surely was meant to include theater parties, since Fort Wayne was known as a good theater town. Laura Keene and Edwin Booth had played in *Hamlet* at Colerick's Opera House. And there was ice skating. The Hamilton children — sisters, brothers, cousins — were physically active, jousting outdoors with wooden swords as they played Robin Hood or King Arthur and the Round Table. In wintertime, didn't they and their friends ice skate at the city rink that held up to 500 skaters? Or did the Hamiltons join the "storm of applause" that greeted "Mr. Samuel L. Clemens . . . known all over the world as 'Mark Twain,'" when he appeared at Fort Wayne's Academy of Music in the winter of 1885, giving "several selections from his latest work, *Huckleberry Finn*"?[37]

No, none of the above. The Hamilton family name is conspicuously absent from the seasonal events recorded in the society pages of the *Daily Fort Wayne Sentinel* and the *Fort Wayne Journal* in the last three decades of the nineteenth century. No Hamiltons appear among the guests and hosts of the various balls, sleighing parties, receptions, and society weddings of the city. Nor is the Hamilton name in the membership rolls of the many social clubs, such as the Hanna House Social Ten and the Fortnightly Club.

Where were they? Where was Alice, if not precociously inspecting Fort Wayne's industrial plants and factories in search of the health hazards of its manual workers? In a queer twist of family history, Alice was prepped for her career largely within the walls and fences of the Homestead family compound. Business was booming in Fort Wayne, but Alice's father largely withdrew from it. Princeton-educated and well-traveled, Montgomery Hamilton was raised to be a gentleman, not a merchant. His partnership in a local wholesale food business dissolved, crushed with debt, in 1885. He joined his wife Gertrude in homeschooling their children, emphasizing literature and languages: he taught them Latin, and Gertrude gave lessons in French and Spanish. The German servants doubled as language teachers in the course of the workday. "Our education," Alice concluded decades later, "was very uneven, with serious omissions."[38]

Loyal and well brought up, Alice kept quiet about the collapse of the family fortune, though in girlhood she planned her exit, climbing trees and carriage-house rafters to talk with her sister about income-producing occupations for women. Sister Edith would become an expert in classical antiquity, teaching Greek and ultimately publishing the hugely successful *The Greek Way*. Alice imagined medicine as a life of service and independence — and a passport to the far corners of the world. "I meant," she recalled, "to be a medical missionary."[39]

Here was a great irony of Alice's life. Like every Gilded Age American city, modern Fort Wayne had its share of social miseries. The Bowser Avenue Irishtown, for instance, was notorious for ramshackle houses, muddy streets, foul water, poor sanitation, poverty, and lawlessness. In the flood-prone Nebraska neighborhood, the immigrant women employees at the Wayne Knitting Mills worked twelve-hour shifts without rest or food. Alice, however, knew little of them and nothing of the health hazards of fine dust cotton fibers lodging deep in the workers' lungs, just as she knew nothing of the local smelters and foundries belching toxic fumes. Fort Wayne offered a case study of the social and industrial ills whose correction became Alice's mission in life. Her pathway to these problems, however, was the printed page and its promise of exotic locales that were far, far away.[40]

In the walled Homestead family compound, Alice closely listened to the voices of the two blunt and provocative British theologians whose writings about "unsocial Christians" were called to her attention by her cousin Agnes. "You may have very ecstatic feelings about the Christian brotherhood at large," she heard Frederick Denison Maurice say in a summons from the page. "But are you ready to help that particular brother, who is lying destitute there, not with feelings, but with a little of the actual food and raiment he is in need of?" The specifics of destitution also filled Charles Kingsley's vivid case study of England's starved, arthritic tailors. In *Cheap Clothes and Nasty* (1850), he calculated that the low-wage tailors numbered over 20,000. He called them England's white chattel slaves who were lashed by a system of subcontracted piecework in which the "sweaters," or subcontractors, colluded with the buyers, including ladies and clergymen. The misers who ducked the "honourable" fair price, Kingsley argued, were nothing short of murderous. To shape enlightened public opinion and policy for the future, Kingsley wrote the immensely popular children's book *The Water-Babies* (1863), which features an abused, orphaned, illiterate, heathen boy who is reborn, that is, bodily and spiritually cleansed, in a reincarnation as a water baby in an aquatic, benevolent Christian utopia.[41]

Alice was never a utopian. The "outside world" she visited vicariously in books was nonetheless irresistible. Thirsting "to explore far countries and meet strange people," she was drawn by the world that the two English theologians put under the Victorian magnifying glass. The teenage Alice envisioned an exotic, yet useful, "life in a big city, exploring the slums. . . . I chose [medicine] because as a doctor I could go anywhere I pleased—to far-off lands or to city slums." By 1888, when she left Miss Porter's, Alice gave her future address as "corner 375 St. & Slum Alley."[42]

By her own admission, the teenage Alice knew nothing whatsoever about the American social pathologies endemic to those slums. Her cousin Agnes introduced her to the essays of Richard T. Ely, the political economist and advocate of social reform, and the two young women taught Sunday school at a mission church in a poor section of town. The pipeline to Alice's career in industrial toxicology, however, was the neighborhood of "slum" dwellers surrounding Hull House on Chicago's Halsted Street.[43]

Alice was won over to Jane Addams's idea of social democracy when she heard the Hull House founder speak at the Methodist church in Fort Wayne in 1895. From that moment on, Alice, cousin Agnes, and sister Norah decided that settlement house life was for them. Among other things, it meant a sociable life with a family of choice rather than the traditional marriage with children. It let Alice stay in close touch with her family while becoming part of a community life that was committed to social goals of engagement across lines of race, ethnicity, and class. Hull House life appealed to Alice as a model of "social democracy," meaning a "much-needed bridge between the . . . well-to-do Americans and the poor immigrants." American democracy, Alice observed, "was concerned mostly with political equality and had little to do with social life." Now it would. This was to be democracy in action as a practice of daily life.[44]

Moving into Hull House felt like coming home. Built in 1846, the house felt much like Grandfather Allen's Fort Wayne Homestead. "There was the same hall and stairway, the same long drawing room with carved white marble mantelpieces, the same French windows at both ends, and the same lofty ceilings with elaborate cornices." Alice appreciated the durable and beautiful "charming furnishings," the paneled dining room, the chandeliers of "Spanish wrought iron," and the breakfast room "coffeehouse built in imitation of an English inn." The year was 1897. Alice had just accepted a professorship in pathology at the women's medical college of Northwestern University when she unpacked her trunks and settled into her Hull House room. She was twenty-eight years of age. She had a new job but not, as yet, her life's work.[45]

The past three years had been at best a mix. Pursuing a career in microbiology after medical school and internships, Alice spent a year of postgraduate work in Germany, which was de rigueur for a serious American medical researcher. She loved the *gutmütigkeit*, or good nature, of the scientists at the German labs and marveled at so much work accomplished in the congenial atmosphere (so unlike the somber, earnest American labs). But sexism in Germany was so oppressive that the women attending classes were ordered to consider themselves "invisible." In the Munich research laboratory, Alice was shunted to a minor project on a bacillus that "turned out to be a big fat nonentity." She called herself a "fourth-rate bacteriologist" and admitted her lack of passion for painstaking and creative research.[46]

The disappointment was all the greater because she already knew in her heart that primary care medicine was not for her. Day after day in the clinic and examining room, on hospital rounds, delivering babies, percussing chests, peering down throats, prescribing ointments and powders—it all was draining and tedious. Her new faculty position in pathology at the women's medical college of Northwestern University was so dismal that she avoided discussing it whenever possible. The pediatric clinic she established at Hull House with its dozen little bathing tubs was a good-works project, and bathing Italian babies each Saturday morning in the Hull House basement was its own reward. But the work of the clinic was routine and repetitive.

Unknown to Alice at the time, her internship years had laid the foundation for the future industrial toxicologist. On house calls in Boston, the former child of privilege found herself in the slums she'd only read about at home in Fort Wayne. She saw directly how the "other half," as the photojournalist Jacob Riis put it, was living "down alleys, in cellars, up attics, over saloons, everywhere in the slums of Boston," including the "Jewish" and "Negro" quarters and the homes of "poor working women."[47]

These years schooled Alice in crucial ways. They stripped away the patrician snobbery that had surfaced in letters to family members when she wrote, for instance, of the "nice red-faced Deutscher," the "rough lumbermen," the obstetrical patient who was "my little negress," and a woman physician whom she dismissed as "Irish and Catholic and rather third class." These clinical years also freed her from the Victorian religious fervor on depravity and sin. No longer would Alice say that "perhaps death" was the "easiest and best solution" for the gravely ill woman whose out-of-wedlock pregnancy had disgraced herself and her family. By 1893, a new Alice was emerging. Her old self, she told cousin Agnes, judged a deathbed family scene as "coarse" and "vulgar." Now she saw through these "externals" to the love and heroism she was privileged to witness as a family gathered at the hospital bedside for final moments with a dying loved one.[48]

The hospital bedside was just one of Alice's life-changing epiphanies. The depression year, 1894, found her seeking food, coal, and bedding for needy patients. "We always used to feel that a family with an able-bodied man in it were poor only from laziness or drunkenness," she wrote to cousin Agnes, then proceeded to describe the intact but desperate families that were headed by unemployed male dry cleaners, waiters, cooks, cab drivers, and fruit venders—all facing destitution from joblessness in these "hard times." When Alice joined her sister and cousin at the Fort Wayne Methodist church to spend the evening at a lecture by Miss Jane Addams in 1895, she was ready both to listen and to hear—and heed—the message.[49]

Alice Hamilton's life work was triggered by Sir Thomas Oliver's 1902 *Dangerous Trades*, a volume as weighty as its subtitle is lengthy: *The Historical, Social, and Legal Aspects of Industrial Occupations as Affecting Health, by a Number of Experts.* The book reached Alice at the perfect moment, about 1907, just when she was facing the dismal fact that her medical career was useful but not fulfilling. She wanted work with clear and measurable objectives, work that gave her autonomy and produced tangible results.

Oliver's *Dangerous Trades* was like a heaven-sent blueprint for her future. It was a springboard for her career and for the field of industrial medicine in the United States. What did Alice Hamilton find on opening this 891-page book? First, a preface proclaiming unprecedented completeness, authority, and breadth—a project befitting the era when the sun never set on the British Empire. Here were sixty chapters on every conceivable workplace hazard and its consequences for the health and welfare of individuals, families, communities, the nation. As a doctor in Newcastle upon Tyne, Oliver had encountered victims of industrial diseases involving white lead, a component of the glazes in the area's pottery industry, which ran the gamut from cheap crockery to fine porcelain. In Newcastle, Oliver examined victims of "potters rot," a pulmonary affliction caused by the inhalation of clay and flint particles that lodge in the bronchial tubes and the lungs of workers, whose hair and clothing turn a thick, dusty white. The pottery workers died, on average, in their mid-forties. He also saw young women dying from lead poisoning just months after beginning work at kilns in which earthenware pots were fired in a process involving plumes of lead dust. Oliver soon headed British Home Office official inquiries into the "dangerous trade." Traveling to France and Germany to study conditions in those industrialized countries, he and his colleagues took leadership roles in the investigation, disclosure, and regulation of various toxic industries in Britain. He successfully spurred reforms and "materially reduced the danger" to workers. The edited volume, *Dangerous Trades*, pooled the knowledge of a cadre of experts in occupational diseases.[50]

Alice was surely struck by Oliver's invitation to a general readership of specialists and nonspecialists alike. He insisted that workplace health hazards were a public concern and freed "the language" of *Dangerous Trades* from unnecessary "technicalities." By design, the book would appeal "to the educated public." Alice Hamilton grasped the crucial point: that a message beamed solely to a band of specialists would not advance the democratic cause of workplace health. That goal could be accomplished only if the broader public were included in the conversation.[51]

In Oliver's preface, what's more, Alice heard a democratic voice. Oliver's endangered workers were "fellow-men and women." This phrase struck a chord. Daily Hull House life had convinced Alice that the split between "the classes" and "the masses" was the falsest—and most vicious—of U.S. social cleavages. Americans' freewheeling ethnic slurs, as she well understood, reinforced a vile class system and devalued workers' lives. Oliver's *Dangerous Trades* avoided that pitfall. His word choices linked readers who worked in safer spheres to those in the dangerous jobs. Oliver and his collaborators avoided such terms as "hands" and "laborers." Readers in white-glove occupations, such as merchants and tradesmen, could not detach themselves from those in dangerous manual labor. Neither could the gentry. Here was a useful lesson for a U.S. author in social work or medicine—a lesson for Alice. As she well knew, Americans' odious top-down slurs abounded, and Hull House life taught her "how deep and fundamental are the inequalities in our democratic country." In *Dangerous Trades*, Alice heard the voice of a Scots grocer's son who grew up in a class-bound British society. As a medical expert and author, he made a clever, deliberate, crucial word choice. *Fellowship* was a do-unto-others mandate. By definition, it made society responsible for the riddance of workplace dangers wherever possible. "Fellow-men and women" was an emphatically democratic term, and its applicability to America self-evident.[52]

Alice Hamilton's "lightbulb" moment happened as she scanned the table of contents of *Dangerous Trades*. The opening chapters "sketched" the history of laws and regulations for "injurious and dangerous industries in England" and in "chief European countries." Here was a trove for anyone concerned about child workers, including chapters titled "Infant Mortality and Factory Labour" and "Child Labour." Here too were analyses of women's "homework" in the garment industry's "No Man's Land of the industrial world." *Dangerous Trades* shattered the charming image of the ivy-covered cottage homes with the kettle on the burnished hob and geraniums flowering in window boxes. It showed, instead, a threat to public health: the workplace home as a disease-infested site of squalor sustained by starvation wages.[53]

Textile workers were here too, and the jeopardy from rags, fur, and fibers (wool workers endangered by anthrax). Mining, quarrying, milling, and railways were just a few of the industries to receive special, separate treatment, and safeguards were urged against the dangers of modern machinery and protection from excessive fatigue and repetitive motion injuries.

Alice Hamilton paid special attention to Oliver's lengthy chapter on "phossy jaw" in the match industry. Recently, the young Wisconsin economist John B. Andrews had stopped by Hull House and told her terrible things about conditions in U.S. match factories. His investigation turned up "cases of phossy jaw quite as dreadful as any reported in foreign literature." The talk with Andrews at Hull House opened Alice's eyes to grim facts. Until now, she'd believed that the American workplace was safe and healthy. Everyone said so, including experts. Young Andrews proved it wasn't true, at least not in match manufacturing.[54]

Which other U.S. workplaces might be toxic?

Dangerous Trades emphasized the perils lurking in numerous inhaled particles. Oliver called them by the simple collective noun "dust." He repeatedly sounded the alarm about lead dust entering the bloodstream through inhalation. His chapter "Lead and Its Compounds" listed some thirty-five "dusty trades," from coal mining to lead smelting. House painters, Oliver warned, were at risk of lead poisoning. So were enamelers, dye workers, makers of porcelain stoves, solderers, printshop workers, and a host of others. While he warned about various chemicals, notably benzene, the mainstay of dry cleaners, it was lead and dust and the toxic combination of the two that captured and held Oliver's attention and became a major theme of the fifteen chapters he wrote for *Dangerous Trades*.

Alice was stunned. Nothing in her medical training or professional work had confronted her with the myriad issues raised in *Dangerous Trades*. Her interest ignited, she hastened to the John Crerar Library of Chicago to read everything available on the subject, a sizable literature — but "all German, or British, Austrian, Dutch, Swiss, Italian and Spanish — everything but American." Eager to speak with her American medical colleagues about the topic, she was met with a "strange silence" by U.S. physicians. They suspected that her interest was "tainted with Socialism or with feminine sentimentality for the poor." She was, in short, smack up against a typical viewpoint of the Gilded Age.[55]

She was also up smack up against the challenge to work for a better, Progressive future. Could Oliver's book, she asked herself, boost this effort? Could it work for America? Suppose she could rouse interest in it here at home — perhaps with extra translations of the European literature on industrial poisons?

Would that work?

No, she realized, it would not. U.S. industrial methods were too different from those abroad. The "foreign literature" was not directly applicable here at home. Oliver and his collaborators opened the topic for America, but the specifics did not transfer one-for-one to these shores. Their book revealed "nothing about the probable incidence of poisoning in American industry."[56]

This meant one thing. If workers in America were to have healthful work environments, the effort to achieve them must be U.S.-based. If American health professionals, business executives, political leaders, plant managers, supervisors, workers, and the public at large were to grasp the importance of the issue — and the extent of workplace health crises across the nation — then they needed a motivational wake-up call.

Who would take on the enormous task of speaking out and writing? Alice surely recalled her mother's dictum on two kinds of people. She could recite it verbatim. Facing a problem, the first kind say, "Somebody ought to do something about it, but why should it be I?" The others say, "Somebody must do something about it, then why not I?"[57]

What to do? Should she publish something? She fretted that a mere "cold, printed report" would move no one and that she lacked "the pen of a ready writer." Certainly she was no Charles Kingsley and no Dickens. But Alice knew one particular kind of writing from practical experience, knew it inside and out as a reader and a writer. She knew that its impact resulted from its very starkness. "Nothing can be more cold-blooded," she said tersely, "than a hospital history." The case history, a narrative based on cold facts, fit the temper of the times. Magazines like *McClure's* captured national attention with crisp, factual exposés of malfeasance in business and government. They roused and educated the public with civic-minded articles on corrupt city machine politics and the brutal practices of the monopoly trusts. Lincoln Steffens and Ida M. Tarbell were practically household names, thanks to their exposés of rotten city machine politics and the Rockefeller oil monopoly. The young journalist Billy Hard was a personal acquaintance of Alice, as was Upton Sinclair. Their good work had hit a nerve with a public fed up with incompetence and corruption in public life. They were so successful that just the year before, 1906, President Roosevelt entered the debate. Growing anxious about an inflamed public, Roosevelt tried to cool things off by tagging these writers with an ugly label — muckrakers.[58]

Suppose Alice joined their ranks. It was tempting. She gave it serious thought. Reluctantly, however, she at last decided against muckraking. The "temporary flurry" of publicity would cost her dearly in the longer term. She

Lead miners, Wallace, Idaho, 1909. (Library of Congress)

*Young men in plumbing class training to use lead pipe,
New York City, c. 1900. (Library of Congress)*

would be blackballed, shut out of work sites everywhere. The hope of "lasting reform" lay in steadily working from the inside, amassing the data that must move state legislatures and Congress to enact the stringent workplace safety legislation. For the sake of workers' health, America must have laws and regulations like those already on the books in England, Germany, Holland, and elsewhere—the industrialized nations on the forefront of progress in industrial health.[59]

Telling herself to write "wisely" and "cautiously," Alice began composing, all the while carefully choosing the periodical for her debut message—and its amplification. She would bypass the medical journals. Their M.D. readers would only "diagnose" socialism and sentimentality, that bane of women's efforts (assuming she could even find a receptive medical journal editor). Besides, Oliver's *Dangerous Trades* showed how vital was the broader public attention and support. In a brilliant stroke, she selected a periodical whose title was not a household name—but it was the perfect choice. Perhaps it was Jane Addams or fellow Hull House resident Florence Kelley who suggested the periodical in which they themselves published. The oddly named *Charities and the Commons* was by now a proven engine of media publicity and public policy. Launched as a magazine of the scientific charity movement of the late nineteenth century, the contributors to *Charities and the Commons: A Weekly Journal of Philanthropy and Social Advance* offered fresh thinking in the early 1900s about the basis of poverty and its disablements. No longer were the poor seen as defectives in need of personal correction by the strict discipline of those who knew best. This had been the idea until quite recently. New studies in the 1900s, however, were reconceiving the basis of poverty, arguing that it resulted from complex interrelationships among corrupt systems.[60]

Alice's Halsted Street Hull House neighborhood abounded with poor workers who sickened and died from poor sanitation and malnutrition—and workplace toxins. Daily she saw how "very black" life became for a family suddenly facing destitution when a husband and father was struck down by accident or illness. These families were especially at risk because, as newcomers to America, they lacked the cushion of "old friends and neighbors and cousins to fall back on as there had been in the old country." Industrial toxicology was thus a topic central to the concerns of readers of *Charities and the Commons*. They included journalists, professionals, and social welfare experts—in short, those in a position to publicize issues and shape public opinion and policy. Her piece would be too alien for broad-based public consumption at this time, but in *Charities and the Commons* it could start a ripple effect, widening to make waves for action. Alice completed her article,

"Industrial Diseases: With Special Reference to the Trades in Which Women Are Employed." This title gave her space to criticize the exhausting work that ruined women's health over "long hours" in overcrowded, dusty, dirty rooms with bad lighting. Published in the issue of September 5, 1908, it urged Americans to become actively involved in the topic of workplace health. It summoned the United States to join "every civilized country" in proving that modern industry need not succeed by "sacrificing life and health."[61]

The article showed something else too, namely, Alice's full knowledge that only new laws could secure workers' rights to a healthy workplace. Her article acknowledged that voluntary compliance was at best a half measure. It was "very improbable," she wrote, "that all American employers would voluntarily take the precautions which stringent legislation has had to force on the foreign employers." Some two years before her meeting with Edward Cornish at the National Lead Company office, Alice knew the severe limits of her best and most successful solo efforts.[62]

Two years after the meeting, however, Alice saw what could be done from a concerted effort by Progressive reformers, political advocates, a U.S. government bureau, and business leaders. On March 28, 1912, the Honorable John J. Esch of La Crosse, Wisconsin, rose to the floor of the U.S. House of Representatives to propose the enactment of a new "phossy jaw" law that would bear his name. At the age of fifty-one, Esch was a colonel in the Wisconsin National Guard and a twelve-year veteran of Congress. A ruddy-complexioned man with a cleft or dimpled chin, he waited while the clerk of the House read the bill to impose a tax on white ("phossy jaw") phosphorous matches. This was a cunning strategy: the tax would be set so high that it would effectively eliminate the toxic compound from the U.S. match industry.

The groundwork for the law had been carefully laid, and a favorable vote was all but certain. The dire effects of white phosphorous match production had become increasingly disturbing to knowledgeable people and organizations. "Phossy jaw" had caught the attention of the U.S. Bureau of Labor Statistics, and in 1909, the bureau agreed to cooperate with an organization focused on working conditions in the United States. Formed in the late nineteenth century, the American Association for Labor Legislation (AALL) was an organization of economists, lawyers, and reformers who were committed to the principle that a democratic society owed its workers the protections guaranteed by law. The Bureau of Labor Statistics cooperated with the AALL, producing a 1910 report that documented the grievous injury to white phosphorous match workers. Momentum built for action by Congress. Wisconsin's Congressman Esch was lobbied and prepped heavily on the matter by economist John B. Andrews, and he became a proponent of the "high tax" strategy, which seemed most likely to survive a constitutional test in the courts.

The match industry had a stake in the law too. For its part, Diamond Match was eager to avoid state-by-state legislative battles that were certain to cloud the company with bad publicity about its role in "phossy jaw." Diamond Match agreed to convene its competitors and offered to release its patent on the safe match-head compound—sesquisulfide—on one condition. Each of the companies must agree to contribute its market share of the $100,000 that Diamond had paid to acquire licensing of the substance. John Andrews helped negotiate the deal. The entire U.S. match industry agreed to it. The congressional hearings were contentious, with one member decrying phossy jaw as a fraud. Finally, in the spring of 1912, Esch brought his bill to the floor.

The congressman began by reminding the lawmakers of recent legislation on national parks. "Congress," he said, "has been engaged in the conservation of natural resources." He now summoned the House to vote for "the conservation of human life." Esch chided members for allowing the United States to fall behind Europe, Japan, and Russia, and he cited President Taft's recent message recommending "stamping out" the "frightful" disease of the match workers. Then Esch urged the House to "adopt this bill" in "the best spirit of the humanitarian nations of the world." The vote was 162 in favor, 31 opposed (190 abstaining). Alice wrote, "So phossy jaw disappeared from American match factories."[63]

The victory was bittersweet. The nicely meshed collaboration of Congress, the business leaders, the federal bureaucracy, the AALL, and the Progressive activist made for a splendid moment—but one unlikely to be repeated in its specifics. The circumstances were exceptional. Unlike most chemicals, the toxic phosphorous was confined to use solely in one industry, match manufacture. The phossy jaw victims, so visible in their suffering, readily evoked public sympathy. And the safe substitute for white phosphorous match heads, sesquisulfide, was quite inexpensive and easy to get. The Esch law was unlikely to be repeated anytime soon in other industries, including lead.

The issue of workplace health, however, had been publicized and shown to be a matter of civic concern and workers' rights. The efforts of one particular activist, John Andrews, who was neither a physician nor a lawyer, had gone far to bring about the Esch law, an achievement that could energize others to similar efforts. The president of the United States, William Howard Taft, had weighed in, setting the example of concern and influence at the highest level of the executive branch of government. Members of Congress, moreover, confirmed the appropriateness not solely of state but of federal involvement in the conditions of work in private industry throughout America. A major corporation, what's more, had shifted from its strict "stick-to-business" posture of autonomy in favor of a move that catered to public opinion.[64]

Alice Hamilton, for her part, realized that she was not alone, that the work of others, such as Andrews, meant that the "voices in the wilderness" were growing. The AALL was committed to workplace safety and health, professional organizations devoted to workplace health were forming, and journals were beginning to analyze the problems and remedies in industrial toxicology. The American Public Health Association organized an industrial health section, and Alice found herself to be a leader and a colleague of others. Now a transatlantic correspondent, Sir Thomas Oliver admired her efforts, as she had admired his. Never an unqualified optimist, Alice Hamilton understood that the proliferation of chemicals in the twentieth century posed continuous challenges to industrial toxicologists—and health hazards to workers. She knew that many workplaces would never be totally without risk. "Where there is lead," she wrote in the mid-1920s, "some case of lead poisoning sooner or later develops, even under the strictest supervision."[65]

Alice refused, what's more, to resort to hollow nostrums on progress when she saw none. At a 1940 conference held at Joplin, Missouri, she refused to pay a "lip service" tribute to industry's position that tremendous improvements had been made over a quarter century to improve working and living conditions by reducing lethal mine tailing dust. "I was here about twenty-five years ago," she began. "I am sorry to say that it seemed a very familiar landscape to me as I looked over it going through today—the heaps of tailings (only they are bigger now), and the housing that I saw reminded me of twenty-five years ago." She pronounced the area "singularly unchanged."[66]

Alice saw her new field of specialization enter the medical school curriculum when she herself was appointed assistant professor of industrial hygiene at Harvard University in 1920. The work that was vital to the well-being of workers throughout the United States and abroad now had institutional legitimacy. As the historian of U.S. industrial health, Christopher Sellers, has said of her, "No individual figures more crucially in the establishment of occupational disease research in this country during the formational period from 1910 to the outbreak of World War I." Alice Hamilton's "great contribution," he continues, was to bring about a fusion of medical and governmental authority in the investigation and mitigation of occupational disease. Sellers adds that Hamilton "laid the groundwork for a historic expansion of the administrative state that would stretch from the Division of Industrial

Hygiene of the U.S. Public Health Service (PHS) to the modern Occupational Safety and Health Administration (OSHA)" and "helped to change the very character of discussion about occupational disease in the United States." As industries employed their own physicians, Dr. Hamilton offered this piece of advice: "Let me beg the industrial physician not to let the atmosphere of the factory befog his view of his special problem. His duty is to the producer (the worker), not to the product." Late in life, she lamented the "instinctive American lawlessness" that prompted opposition to "all legal control." She lived until 1970, a few months before passage of the U.S. Occupational Safety and Health Act.[67]

John R. Commons
The Pittsburgh Survey

Everything seems to be going on as usual, commerce and industry vigorous and expanding, when suddenly there comes a shock, as of a thunderbolt out of a clear sky— a bank breaks, a great manufacturer or merchant fails, and, as if a blow had thrilled through the entire industrial organization, failure succeeds failure, and on every side workmen are discharged from employment.—HENRY GEORGE, *Progress and Poverty*, 1879

The man without an employer is a vagabond and an outlaw.—JOHN R. COMMONS, *Social Reform and the Church*, 1894

I made unemployment the bitterest foe of the capitalist system.—JOHN R. COMMONS, *Myself*, 1934

The unionist who votes as a unionist has taken his first step . . . towards considering the interests of others, and this is the first step towards giving public spirit and abstract principles a place alongside private interests and his own job.—JOHN R. COMMONS, *Races and Immigrants in America*, 1907

Dressed for travel in a coat and tie, John R. Commons, a professor of economics at the University of Wisconsin, stepped onto the railroad platform at the Madison depot, where he met up with his three young men graduate students. It was a hot summer day in 1907, and the four made small talk while waiting for their train.

Nobody on the platform had reason to be especially curious about the professor and three young men. When the pale yellow Milwaukee Road train cars pulled in, the four climbed aboard and stowed their valises on overhead racks of the air-cooled Pullman parlor car before settling on the stiff plush seats. In wildest imaginings, no one would suspect these young men and their professor were off to war. It wasn't to be fought with cannon and cavalry. Theirs was a war of ideas for unprecedented social change in American life, and they were fired with revolutionary fervor. Today's destination—or battlefield — was the smoky industrial city of Pittsburgh, a city known as "hell with the lid lifted."[1]

Who were their enemies in this self-declared war? Were they Pittsburgh's industrial moguls, notably Andrew Carnegie, whose twinkling eyes and snowy beard gave the steel magnate a certain resemblance to Saint Nicholas? Or the cool, polished Henry Clay Frick, the "King of Coke" who won the public's respect when he withstood an assassin's bullets and dagger back in 1892? Or the financier, J. P. Morgan, who'd bought Carnegie Steel and created the United States Steel Company just six years ago in 1901?[2]

Professor Commons knew better than to squander his energy or his students' futures on a frontal skirmish against titans. Besides, he admired the great capitalists. They organized vast, complex plants that defined the industrial age. Their products made this very train trip possible. In Commons's and others' judgment, however, these industrial barons and their followers were dangerously narrow-gauged men. A few fixed ideas had nurtured them, shaped their thoughts, driven their actions. By now, the results of the blinkered ways were plain to see, and the impact was dire. Unchecked, the professor knew, needless suffering, injury, and death lay ahead. Unchallenged, their wrongheaded ideas in action could become a crushing legacy in the new twentieth century.

But who were the adversaries in this campaign, if not the barons of industry and finance? For Commons, the enemy could be found in believers and practitioners of the doctrine of laissez-faire, propounded by the legendary Yale professor William Graham Sumner. Professor Sumner regaled them with brilliant lectures on banking, currency, taxation, and "economic problems and fallacies" and on "strikes, boycotting, and other signs of defects in the organization" of industry.[3]

Yale men had been rock-solid disciples of this professor since 1872, when the wiry, balding figure with the sharp goatee began his teaching career in political and social science. As witty as Mark Twain, Sumner honed his polemics to a fine edge that gleamed with assurance of divine knowledge. "Sumnerology," his students called it. The professor was renowned far beyond the Yale campus as the champion of a doctrine based on the evolutionary principles in Darwin's *Origin of Species* (1859), which emphasized that the struggle for existence was measured by progressively successful adaptations of species. Darwin's theory was revamped by the famed British philosopher Herbert Spencer. Contrary to Darwin, Spencer claimed that creatures struggled incessantly against each other for survival and supremacy. Their constant rivalry, Spencer argued, was the engine of evolutionary progress. Those who stumbled and faltered were best left by the wayside while the

Professor John R. Commons, c. 1925. Photograph by Bachrach. (Records of the National Consumers' League, Library of Congress)

survivors won out. The victors' competitive advantage, measurable by material wealth, proved their superiority as the best specimens of *Homo sapiens*. Spencer insisted that the victors were nature's agents of human advancement and the vanguard of the better future. Human effort to intervene or redirect or expedite the process was simply, as Yale's Sumner declared in 1883, "absurd."[4]

Laissez-faire was the term that Sumner and others used for the industrial culture of Spencerism, otherwise known as social Darwinism. Noninterference in individual action was its sacred precept within industry, commerce, and politics, and it was a bedrock principle of America's Gilded Age bankers, industrialists, and businessmen, including Carnegie, to whom it was the "truth of evolution." Most knew the principle by its shorthand slogan: *survival of the fittest.* "Here we are then," Sumner declared, "once more back at the old doctrine—*Laissez faire.*" Americanized from the French, it meant "nothing but the doctrine of liberty." In "blunt English," said Sumner, it meant, "Mind your own business." The Yale professor's thought was actually far more complex than such simple catchphrases indicate. In his thinking, the term *survival* referred to economic success, while *fitness* meant a moral fitness that was available to all.[5]

The catchphrases in Sumner's speeches and magazine articles, however, branded the professor as a hard-core social Darwinist. The fittest and most self-reliant, he warned, must not be hamstrung by a meddlesome government or muddleheaded philanthropists or reformers. Seeming gifted with certainty, Sumner's force of argument matched his walk: "great strides and the air of self-confidence and power." Sending their sons off to Yale, fathers like Clarence Day Sr. trusted that Professor Sumner's lectern was the best of helms, guiding young minds to an American future that was free of "communists, . . . strikers, . . . and fanatics of sundry roots and sizes."[6]

John Commons (b. 1862) was neither a communist nor fanatic. The Wisconsin professor sought to "save" the United States from partisan "politics, socialism, and anarchism"—but above all to rescue the country from the ruinous effects of laissez-faire. Flanked by his students, he was braced to oppose almost everything that William Graham Sumner and his like-minded political economists stood for. Convinced that laissez-faire corroded the nation's social arrangements and that it blocked civic advance, Professor Commons defined it as the enemy of the people. To his way of thinking, it was a ruse for the enrichment of certain special interests. It served the rich and powerful few at the expense of everybody else. The Wisconsin economist knew that it failed hundreds of thousands—even millions—for every individual who personally gained from it. For every winner, Commons knew, the regime produced countless individuals and families whose lives were needlessly fractured and broken by starvation wages, squalid housing, and volatile cycles of joblessness that alternated with grinding labor of ten, twelve, or fourteen hours at a stretch, both day and night, all week long, including men, women, and children. It was, in short, a ruinous Gilded Age pseudoscience to be exposed and discredited to make way for better social arrangements from the workplace to the household.[7]

The true believers in laissez-faire, however, were everywhere. Like a state religion, it held vast populations of Americans in its grip. Since the closing decades of the nineteenth century, the ideas of Sumner and his fellow social Darwinists had reigned supreme among the nation's businessmen and professionals, numerous economists, politicians, judges, lawyers, teachers, and countless ordinary citizens—all of them convinced that laissez-faire, or social Darwinism, was the God-given natural order of the universe.[8]

John R. Commons understood that he was in for a long, hard, grueling fight. He seemed an unlikely warrior, this skinny forty-four-year-old professor with the sensuous mouth and brown, wavy hair. He cut a figure that was meant for a quiet book-lined faculty office and knew that he was "not fitted for the rough-and-tumble of practical men." His health was iffy, and he struggled to maintain a body weight of 115–120 pounds. Unlike Sumner, he was no orator. His classroom lectures rambled, and his method of teaching was to reject pat answers and stir up doubts. Off campus, he'd become a counselor to high-ranking Wisconsin officials and helped to guide policy and legislation. It was a splendid coincidence that the state's capital and its flag-ship university occupied the same turf in Madison. In good weather, Professor Commons bicycled to the office of Governor Robert La Follette to advise him on a plan to tax railroads that crossed the state. Known as ad valorem taxation, it was based on the value of the railroads' physical property, and it increased Wisconsin's state revenue by 178 percent. Commons also drafted the state's civil service law that had passed two years before, in 1905.[9]

In terms of America's "momentous conflict" of the day—the often violent clash between "capital and labor"—Commons's purpose as an economist was clear and unwavering. He valued capitalists and laborers alike for their respective strengths and worked tirelessly for their mutual advancement. This put him in the crosshairs of the laissez-faire crowd. Depending on his health, he worked on other fronts too. There was so much to be done. For instance, the nation desperately needed the public protection of utilities, such as water and electricity. If Governor La Follette won a seat in the U.S. Senate, Commons hoped to be asked to help draft a law to safeguard public utilities for the American people. The country also needed protections for families that faced destitution in case of the injury, illness, or death of the breadwinner. And businesses, for their part, needed protection against crippling liability lawsuits. As long as his strength held, Commons intended to press hard for workman's compensation, factory safety regulation, and unemployment insurance.[10]

His work schedule? At home in Madison, fueled by weak coffee and to-bacco, Commons got to his desk in the predawn darkness, working ten or twelve hours, often seven days a week. Travel was unavoidable, and this trip to Pittsburgh was typical, wedged in during a university vacation. Grueling winter trips were necessary because he served on national investigative commissions that met in distant cities. Despite the colorful railroad posters that promoted "sumptuous dining" and complete "comfort," Commons sometimes found himself "shivering . . . in cold hotels" and changing trains at icy depots. In a pinch, he'd catch a freight-train caboose before dawn and arrive rumpled and disheveled at a formal hearing, his hair uncombed. Commissioner John R. Commons was once mistaken for a falling-down drunk.[11]

It was for the public, the whole citizenry, that Commons ultimately worked. Yes, professionally he was a labor economist. But his expertise served an evolving democracy. At a high level, this meant honing scientific abilities to develop information that was instrumental in shaping public opinion and policy. Only in this way could superstition be dispelled and "safe progress" promoted. In the big picture, his work meant economic development to promote health, liberty, and equality of opportunity. It meant the "growth in notions of ethics and justice." In the steam-heated classrooms of Wisconsin winters, Commons managed to promote these ideas by deliberately perplexing students with vexing contradictions within economic and social life. Often attacked as a radical, Commons knew he was misunderstood and needed a "thick" skin. John R., as the students called him out of earshot, even used his own intellectual shortcomings as research challenges to his students.[12]

A widening circle of them found him irresistible. They became recruits. They eagerly boarded the train with him to Pittsburgh, where they would join others in this fight for a better future. Specifically, Commons's threesome looked forward to a full month of research training, a boot camp and mission in a strike-torn industrial battlefield. It was a rare opportunity — and a high-stakes risk. The Russell Sage Foundation for the Improvement of Living Conditions had agreed to fund a survey of this "great steel district." Teams of researchers, many as young as their early twenties, were surging to the site to conduct a "rapid, close-range investigation." Their task was to document the conditions of life and work in Pittsburgh. They were to record everything from diet to street paving, recreation, accidents, morale, disease, wages, simply everything. The goal was to "gauge the needs" of a mixed population of immigrants and native-born Americans dwelling in an urban crucible of the modern industrial age. The project was hugely ambitious. It was to create a social "blue print" that must be as accurate as an engineering drawing. The importance of the Pittsburgh Survey could not be overstated. If successful, it could set the stage for material improvement of the lives of hundreds of thousands of area workers and their families. It could be a model for the nation in this new industrial age.[13]

If successful, what's more, the Pittsburgh project could become one victory among the many that were crucial for social progress in the United States. Commons would do everything in his power to overturn the laissez-faire practices that dominated American thought and action for decades.

HOW DID THE SLENDER, quiet John Commons become a relentless foe of entrenched beliefs that so many of his fellow Americans embraced as gospel? What drove him? By temperament, he was no rebel, no iconoclast, no guerrilla, no exile. Commons, on the contrary, started out as an obedient, faithful son of the Midwest, a Hoosier boy who grew up in the southeastern Indiana towns of Union City and Winchester. The son of a churchgoing orthodox Presbyterian mother and a Quaker father for whom he was named, John was the oldest of three surviving children. His boyhood days were as classic as a Winslow Homer painting: diving into "the old swimming hole" and playing seven-up under the apple tree. In the local common schools, he studied textbooks that presented economics in terms fitting snugly with Spencerian laissez-faire. "Riches are the baggage of virtue," said one typical U.S. schoolbook of the 1870s. "Fortune," another proclaimed, favors "the industrious, the self-denying and the prudent." Misfortune in America, including poverty, signifies moral failings and outright depravity, warned the books. Joblessness is a sign of sloth. Child labor on farms and in factories was nonetheless a valuable opportunity for poorer U.S. families, according to the schoolbooks. As for workers who might join with others in a quest for better wages and working conditions, they were nothing but unscrupulous striking rioters who "greatly injured business prosperity."[14]

The drumbeat of this textbook message was amplified tenfold in young John Commons's father's newspaper office, where, at age thirteen, the boy learned the printer's trade, "a sort a handicraft, like carpentering or stonecutting." All year round, summer and winter, the talk of politics, poetry, and social Darwinism filled the air in the "bare and rude" printing office whose walls were "splotched with ink and the floor littered with refuse newspapers." The cases of type were set near the windows to catch all available light, and the inking rollers had to be thawed before use in cold weather, when the compositor spread his fingers, stiffened with cold, before the hot cast-iron woodstove. Odors of type and press, of seasonal woodsmoke and tobacco, mixed with the nasal Hoosier voices extolling social Darwinist philosophy and science, for John's father and his cronies "jawed" for hours in the newspaper offices. "Sprawled back in their chairs, with their feet on the table, squirting tobacco juice and drawling their words lazily," they impressed young John as "funny and keen." Their topics were three: party Republicanism, Protestant Christianity, and the social doctrines of Spencerism.[15]

John Sr.'s *Union City Times* and *Winchester Herald*, however, were not immune to hard times in the United States. Young John learned printing in 1873, the year a severe depression struck. At first, events seemed worlds away from Indiana. European financiers in Vienna suddenly sold off American stocks and bonds, a major eastern U.S. bank collapsed, and the New York stock market closed for ten days. Who knew that Americans would experience widespread bankruptcies and joblessness for the next six years? In the Commons household, the depression hit home when many subscribers to John's father's papers fell behind on their payments. The senior Commons couldn't bring himself to cut them off or to dun the deadbeat advertisers, for his subscribers were mostly "hard-working, hard-thinking folks who dwelt" on "scattered farms." John's father kept faith with them, even when the subscription list was "decimated by delinquents."[16]

Was there a message here for true believers in laissez-faire? Were the farmers, storekeepers, and hard-pressed townspeople in Union City and Winchester, Indiana, blameworthy for their exhausted savings, their deepening debts, their mortgage defaults, and their lack of hard cash money? Survival of the fittest? Were they the unfit? Or were the school textbooks and the cronies somehow wrong, profoundly wrong? As yet, John was in no way equipped to frame such questions. After school, he dug in to help the family. With his younger brother, Alvin, he collected a few of the hundreds of silver dollars owed to their father. Every one of them went to feed and clothe the Commonses, including their parents and little sister, Clara.[17]

To some extent, John Sr.'s notion of economics postponed the day when young John would ask mind-splitting questions about laissez-faire. John Sr., that is, belonged to the bygone pioneer era of old-fashioned American "swapping." He'd bartered brilliantly for farms, horses, and a harness shop—and for the two printshops that made him a newspaper publisher in Union City and Winchester. The modern cash-and-credit economy, however, baffled him. The notion that a newfangled economy could bring hard times halfway around the world from Vienna, Austria, to southeastern Indiana in the 1870s mystified him. He simply paid no attention to it, even though his family lived hand to mouth year after year, avoiding pauperism only because John's mother, Clarissa, watched every penny as she rented out rooms and fed several boarders in the family home. In the newspaper offices, all the while, the cronies gathered and celebrated Herbert Spencer and the doctrines of laissez-faire.

Young John kept faith. Of course he did. Spencerism was a code of conduct, a navigation system for life. The route was clear. He would manfully live as a Hoosier fellow must—under the Spencerian banner. To the marrow of his bones, he swore that "every man and woman in society has one big duty . . . to take care of his or her own self."[18]

The vow surely masked a certain anxiety. The depression of the 1870s exposed a harsh social trend that intensified in America throughout the Gilded Age. The fact was, the new industrial order sharply reduced individuals' ability to shape their own destinies. The independent carpenter, the housepainter, or the metalworker might pose proudly with tools of his trade for the tintype photographer, but the era of the craft worker was rapidly giving way to "the incorporation of America." Ralph Waldo Emerson's call to "trust yourself" rang increasingly hollow and mocked young men whose futures they felt powerless to mold. Impersonal forces of an industrial economy now ruled, and fear of personal failure gnawed at individuals. One yardstick of widespread worry was the skyrocketing sales of success manuals for American young men, each promising the key to a golden future. Such titles as *Getting On in the World* and *Successful Folks: How They Win* distilled the message of Horatio Alger's popular titles like *Cash Boy* and *Strive and Succeed*. All these books "carried the torch of values and virtues of a bygone era to a new generation." The success manuals sold especially well in heartland areas like John Commons's Indiana. The barter era was over, and manhood itself was at stake. What was an earnest young American man without capital to do?[19]

He could try sales. In 1881, shortly out of high school, John answered the call of salesmanship. Union City was a rail hub and drew traveling salesmen, or drummers. They were all dapper fellows with sample cases and trunks full of the newest wares, from dry goods to ready-made clothing, cigars, glassware, hardware. One Hoosier writer, the journalist-novelist Theodore Dreiser, penned an indelible portrait of the drummer, circa 1880, as a "brisk man of the world" in his three-piece business suit and gold plate cufflinks. To see such a man step from a Pullman car onto the Union City platform in the late 1870s was to see a "magnificent being."[20]

By joining the drummers' ranks as a subscription salesman for the *Christian Union*, John believed he could serve both God and Mammon. The founding editor of this bimonthly family magazine was none other than Henry Ward Beecher, at that time the most famous Protestant minister in the United States. Beecher's ministerial years in Indianapolis in the 1840s made him an antebellum adopted Hoosier. John couldn't miss. A week's exciting "intensive training in salesmanship" in Indianapolis, a stronghold of subscription sales, spurred his dreams of "untold dollars per week" earned by the force of his very own "personality." He'd sell magazine subscriptions by selling himself. "Hiking in snow and rain and mud," John shivered at each doorstep, readying his sales pitch on Christian character, church membership, temperance, and the fortifying benefits of the *Christian Union*. The training week promised him a cordial welcome at almost every door and a "sufficient" hearing by potential subscribers. The sight of the young man's muddy boots, however, seemed to sour everyone. He no sooner introduced himself and spoke the magic words, "Henry Ward Beecher," than doors began to swing shut in his face.[21]

Unknown to the fledgling salesman, the ruinous fatal flaw was not wet outerwear or muddy boots but the notorious Beecher-Tilton scandal that broke in 1872 and continued to mushroom, implicating Beecher as an adulterer. As John cryptically said, "'Henry Ward' was suspect by the women and his religion uninteresting to the men." He did not sell one subscription and concluded, "I was a cold, wet failure."[22]

Undaunted, John set out again to prove that he was a self-sufficient, modern American fellow, a social Darwinist's laissez-faire success. By now (1882–88) he was in college, thanks to his remarkable mother's gumption. Clarissa Commons had learned all too well that Hoosier drollery could not support a family. Nor, alas, did her Presbyterian Calvinist faith or zeal for temperance put food on the family table. As her children grew, each new pair of larger shoes measured the shortening distance toward their futures. A graduate of Oberlin College herself, Clara packed up and moved her children to Oberlin, Ohio. By herself, she rented a ramshackle house that she operated as a boardinghouse for poorer students. She hoped that John would enroll in her alma mater and begin the classical curriculum leading to the Presbyterian pulpit. The ministry was a bright prospect in industrial America. It was a profession open to a young man without capital.

John did enroll at Oberlin and answered the siren song of laissez-faire one more time, teaming up with his Oberlin friend and classmate from Japan, Toyokichi Iyenaga. Their scheme was to promote a series of for-profit, Chautauqua-like lectures in Ohio towns throughout the college summer. The depression years of the 1870s were gone, and new moneymaking opportunities hung, they believed, like orchard fruit. "Start a Business of Your Own for a Little Outlay," called Sears, Roebuck and Company in its catalogue. The company offered a complete "money-making lecture outfit" and assured the buyer that "public exhibition work" was proven to be "extremely profitable." It was "ideal" for those with "limited capital." A man of "limited means" could equip himself with a stereopticon, a lecture set, and a series of stereo views. "Experience in public speaking not necessary," crooned the catalogue.[23]

John borrowed $100 from his mother and invested in the equipment. He also bought a proper derby-bowler "plug hat" and a "twelve-dollar suit" that was fitting for an "advance agent" who doubled as the stereopticon operator. Once again, he tried selling door-to-door, this time tickets. But his new suit wilted in the summer heat. Town after town—Wellington, Elyria, Vermillion—the ticket sales were dismal. The tour flopped, leaving Clarissa Commons "ninety dollars in the hole" and John and his partner in her debt. What did this experience say about self-sufficiency? he asked himself. How did debt fit the laissez-faire theory, especially when the debtor and lender lived on marginal incomes? Horatio Alger's luck-and-pluck heroes climbed out of debt and never afterward sank in its quicksand. The success manuals said nothing about owing money to your mother. Perhaps the laissez-faire theories were meant only for those with hefty bank accounts and vaults full of stock certificates.[24]

John's self-sufficiency as a young newspaper printer, nonetheless, remained a mainstay of pride — and income. He spent several college summers as a "sub" printer or typesetter on the *Cleveland Herald*, the forerunner of the *Plain Dealer*. Yet his thoughts sometimes turned to his fellow printers, whose jobs were threatened by "the new invention of photo-engraving." Didn't they, too, try their best to be self-sufficient? The laissez-faire social Darwinists somehow said nothing about these new forms of "technological unemployment," nor about those who were displaced by it. Workers who were left jobless — were they cinders dumped in the evolutionary ash barrel?[25]

What about others, such as the men of "Kelly's Army" whom John was to see and speak with in the years to come? In the depression year of 1894, he was to see a ragtag band of unemployed men on the march. They'd tramped from Southern California and crossed the deserts before coming through the Midwest en route to Ohio to join another such band that called itself Jacob Coxey's "army." These and other "armies" from across the country planned to combine forces in a march on Washington, D.C. They planned to present their "petition in boots," a demand that the federal government involve itself in the solution to the plight of joblessness in yet another devastating depression that stretched through much of the 1890s. In Indiana, John was to talk with one of them, a jobless jeweler from Los Angeles who was chosen by his family to make the trek because "he was the only one physically able to stand the hunger march." As "fine a set of workingmen as [he] had ever known," John was to recall the jeweler and his mates.[26]

Suppose he himself were among them. What then? The hard fact was this: John R. Commons had tried his very best to chart his course according to Spencerian doctrine and the laissez-faire idea put forward by "Sumnerology." He'd plunged ahead in dead earnest as a true believer in a scientific philosophy that was advanced by leading minds and preached by Indiana elders all his life. Like countless others, he'd failed as a self-reliant entrepreneur. Was the failure his? Was it to be the jeweler's? Or the typesetters'? Or was the system itself somehow gravely flawed?

His failures accomplished one thing. They exiled him from the laissez-faire world. Shut out, he was primed for different, unorthodox viewpoints. Yes, he was bound for a future in the newer world that stymied his father, a world of money and markets, credit and debt. However, he would approach that world differently from the social Darwinists. They saw economics as a science solely of wealth. They confined their work to the discovery and explanation of so-called laws that reinforced an industrial business system.

*In their best clothes and proclaiming patriotism with the American flag, the jobless
men of Coxey's Army march to Washington, D.C., to appeal for help, 1894.
(Ray Stannard Baker Papers, Library of Congress)*

Their ideas favored one class, the business class. He, instead, would look
at conditions through a different lens. He would study the actual impact of
work and wages on people in varied life circumstances, including his own.
This was the inductive method. The laissez-faire crowd claimed to uphold
immutable laws, but Commons sought data from the real world. He began
to understand that economic conditions resulted from human actions over
time. What humans created, humans could change.

As for his youthful misadventures, he used them nowadays to amuse and
challenge his students. They made him seem more human too. For Commons himself had struggled as a student and needed eight years to get his
B.A., finally graduating from Oberlin in 1888. He'd failed biology, fixating on
the heartbeat of a water bug when the rest of the class moved on. And he got
preoccupied with the letter omega in Greek class, doubtless drawn to it from
hours spent plucking letters from cases of type in the newspaper offices.
And then came the first of his lifelong periodic breakdowns. It was just after
a Greek exam that he collapsed from an explosive "fierce blow" inside his
head. Yale's own Sumner warned that the "weak" were a "dead weight" on society because they destroyed "the finest efforts of the wise and industrious."
Did John's three months of convalescence "wandering through the woods"

around Oberlin certify him as society's "weakling"? Did rotten "nerves and digestion" disqualify him from Sumner's world of the wise and industrious? Did a lifetime of periodic afflictions of a "mad stomach and neurotic brain" make a person society's Darwinian dead weight?[27]

Commons's school problems didn't end at Oberlin. He was no shoo-in at graduate school at Johns Hopkins University, and he had his troubles at Hopkins. Failing a history examination, he left before getting his doctorate. And he'd desperately needed the lifeline that his former Hopkins professor had thrown out to him. For Commons, it was a fluke, a lucky break that Professor Richard Ely found himself shorthanded and swamped with work once he left Hopkins and settled at the University of Wisconsin. By getting him a job, Ely saved Commons's hide, beckoning his former student to a new faculty position in 1904, just three years before the Pittsburgh venture. However, there was a stipulation: that Commons, like Ely, specialize in the history of the labor movement and help finish Ely's book project. As a husband and father with mounting bills, Commons leaped at the chance.

He refused to let his health or his history of school problems crush him. He did not take social Darwinism to heart when it came time to marry and have a family of his own. Nell—Ella Downey Commons—was his Oberlin classmate and became his wife, the mother of his children, and the social director of the household. Would he have asked Nell to marry a man who was society's dead weight weakling? Could she have traveled the strange route with him, from graduate school in Baltimore to the circuit of his teaching jobs in Connecticut, Indiana, and upstate New York? In those early days of his career, something always went wrong—a rock-bottom salary that wouldn't cover basic expenses, or poor student ratings of his classroom teaching, or political clashes with the administration and trustees. Nell's good cheer steadied him, and it strengthened him during a hiatus of five years out of academic life when he worked amid "the struggles of human beings" in New York City and Washington, D.C., until finally they reached their permanent home, Madison.[28]

He might have told students one particular story, of his short-lived career as a grade school teacher back in Indiana. His Pittsburgh recruits might recognize it for what it truly was: the key to the workings of his mind and a hint of the tasks facing them in Pittsburgh. It was a story with a moral: official doctrines can be poles apart from actualities.

It was back in 1881, when he was fresh out of high school and had already failed at door-to-door subscription sales for the *Christian Union*. As a high school graduate, he was legally entitled by the state of Indiana to teach in a common (grade) school, as many young men did for a year or two before moving into other work. That fall of 1881, John walked the four miles from his Winchester home to his assigned schoolroom. It was filled with country boys, the so-called buckwheats who were raised on fixed doctrines from religion and cracker-barrel folk wisdom. He hadn't grasped the fact that their young minds were closed to anything short of certitude, whether Christian dogma, U.S. history, or the rule that root crops must be planted in the dark of the moon and soap made in the moonlight. These pupils demanded the official, granite-solid Word on all subjects: reading, writing, geography, English grammar, U.S. history, and physiology.[29]

They saw the nineteen-year-old Mr. John R. Commons as a puny schoolmaster who tried to teach things that didn't match up. Physiology was the worst. The textbook illustrations clearly showed muscle layers, valves, and other anatomical innards. They could be seen and memorized. But Mr. Commons complicated things. He brought actual specimens to compare with those in the book. Stopping at a slaughterhouse on the way to school, he got an ox's heart or eye or some other part. He insisted that pupils think over why the actual organs didn't look like those pictured in the textbook. To them, the exercise was not learning but confusion. Why waste good daylight hours in a dim, stuffy schoolroom on hard benches for 136 days of the school year to have your mind filled with doubts?[30]

They rebelled. As John recalled, "The pupils lost faith in me, tumbled me in the grass, pelted me with snow balls, and I had to resign in three months. They wanted something 'for sure' handed down by the great authorities of the past, and I couldn't produce it."[31]

How did anyone honestly "produce" it? What was "for sure"? What was authority—and knowledge? The buckwheats knew. They weren't troubled. They slept like babies. For John Commons, however, the question of authoritative knowledge hovered in ambiguity and contradiction. From the physiology schoolbook to the Sears catalogue lecture tour, John's actual experiences were at odds with the official versions. Something was out of whack.

So it was miraculous that at Oberlin College he found Professor James Monroe, who habitually raised these very issues. Monroe guided him, just as Commons had hoped to guide his students in Pittsburgh. In moments of reverie, he lingered in recollection of his college professor at the classroom lectern, a grandfatherly figure in a black suit with snowy collar and cuffs. Professor Monroe did not appear to be on fire with concerns about dubious sources of knowledge. He did not look like an innovator blazing with modernizing ideas. With his trim white beard and moustache and his ministerial manner, he opened each class with a prayer that came as naturally as breathing.

His appearance was deceiving. Capping his decades-long career with a professorship, James Monroe was an evangelical Christian who had once been a radical abolitionist and later entered the U.S. House of Representatives. At Oberlin, the lawmaker-turned-professor brought political economy, modern history, and the new field of sociology to the classroom. Just as John set the real ox eye against the textbook drawing, the professor opened the academic window onto the contemporary industrial United States. He tested real-world realities against the iron laws propounded in textbooks, such as *Elements of Political Economy*, which promoted laissez-faire doctrines to generations of college students. The textbook taught that a Christian God Almighty had decreed "the exchange" between capital and labor to be one of equals, mutually advantageous to both parties, each of whom enjoyed "the same level of advantage."[32]

Wealthy capitalist owners and low-wage workers at *the same level of advantage*? To believe this, you had to ignore the fact that the average wage for a manufacturing worker was a mere 21.6 cents hourly ($8.37 weekly). You had to accept the notion that the "interests" of workers and owner-operators were aligned. Quite simply, said the textbook, the capitalist is "one blade of the shears," the laborers "the other blade, and it takes two blades to cut."[33]

Professor Monroe had a blade of his own. He found that these so-called laws of God, nature, and political economy were false when tested in real-world terms. Crucial for John's future, the former congressman paid close attention to the new Gilded Age strife, including the miserable conditions of workers. Monroe was a pragmatist. He had seen the power of government to abolish slavery, and he believed that government could be—and ought to be—an instrument for the solution of social problems. "Wages had not increased with the growth of wealth," he found. And the laborer "does not receive his share of the product of industry." Monroe concluded that the wealthy were in dire need of Christian sympathy for labor. He endorsed workers' rights to organize into unions. Christian sympathy for labor, he insisted, ought to be measurable in the tangible, quantifiable form of higher minimum wages.[34]

But would it? Would spiritual motives prevail over and against the orthodoxy of William Graham Sumner and his kind? In New York City and elsewhere in the country, businessmen, industrialists, and financiers like the senior Clarence Day shuddered to think that religion might interfere with the godly world of unrestricted manufacture, trade, and finance. At the same time, younger ministers and theologians such as Walter Rauschenbusch and Washington Gladden insisted that it must. South of Oberlin in Columbus, Ohio, the Protestant Gladden inveighed against "hard-fisted and stony-hearted" corporation officials. In sermons and in print, he called for "determination on the part of individual capitalists to rule their business by the Christian law." This law, insisted Professor Monroe, must prevail for the health of the nation.[35]

John Commons was already veering away from a career in the ministry, but the young man had the great good fortune to read economics textbooks through the corrective lens of Monroe's questions. One book, however, was starkly different. Professor Monroe invited the author to speak at Oberlin. This was Henry George, a California journalist-printer—to think, a fellow printer! Beyond its catchy title, George's *Progress and Poverty* (1879) promised to expose contemporary social-economic crises and provide their remedy. The thick, dense book sold some 2 million copies and was to be translated into several languages by the opening years of the twentieth century. George collared his reader with a jarring statement on America's industrial-era crisis. The "deepest" poverty, the "sharpest" struggle for existence, and the worst unemployment, he said, were located exactly in the nation's wealthiest, most technologically advanced cities. Why, George asked, "*in spite of increase in productive power, do wages tend to a minimum which will get but a bare living?*" Joblessness took center stage as a horrific problem in *Progress and Poverty*, its pages featuring "the strange and unnatural spectacle of large numbers of willing men who cannot find employment . . . vast masses of unemployed men." Modern America was producing serfs and beggars. What had gone so wrong?[36]

At base, George found one explanation: an unearned rise in land values. Whole communities, George reasoned, had developed America's farms, factories, dwellings, and town and city centers. But somehow the whole communities weren't rewarded for their efforts. Elites were enriched to the exclusion of all others. George's solution was seductively simple: impose a single tax on the unearned increment in land values. The tax money would then circulate back to the people and thus put an end to poverty.

Professor Monroe knew a cure-all when he saw it. The Robin Hood–like scheme of future tax revenue returns seemed at best an innocent hoax. Monroe trusted that his enraptured students, such as John Commons, sooner or later would recognize the flaws of *Progress and Poverty*. Indeed, John did look back in amazement at the sophomoric raptures that moved him to form a campus Henry George Club. Yet George's best seller cast a cold light on actual social realities in the United States, and the success of *Progress and Poverty* made a deep impression. The unorthodox book had reshaped people's outlook. It actually changed people's minds. Henry George proved that a book could challenge an entrenched system of thought and open the door to new ideas, to social change.

Progress and Poverty, John came to understand, was one opening salvo in the long war against laissez-faire. To join the battle, Commons gradually realized that he too must speak out in books and articles. In adult life, he must write a great deal and speak tirelessly, making public presentations both in print and in the lecture hall. He must resist jingoistic simple formulas like the single tax. In addition, he must become a *disinterested* party—not *uninterested*, but an impartial expert who was free of self-seeking bias. As such, he must not demonize individuals or organizations, as *Progress and Poverty* had demonized the railroads for land grabs. Commons, instead, knew that he must devise carefully crafted arguments that were backed by depths of historical knowledge, by numerical data, by facts that could stand up to the toughest challenges. He must undertake research in the field, studying actual conditions in factories and mills, including the steel mills of Pittsburgh.

Ultimately, Commons needed a squad of others to amplify the great effort by producing complementary work. As a professor, he was constantly on the lookout for young recruits, handpicking students who showed spunk and brains and streaks of independence. He drilled them in the techniques once drummed into him in graduate school by his own professor, Richard Ely, who was now his colleague at Wisconsin. Ely taught the value of hands-on case work in those days—1880–90—when economics also included political science and sociology too. Ely's look-and-see approach gave Commons a dose of the very same practical politics that he now demanded of his own students. It was the "case system of looking up pertinent documents" that Commons now impressed upon his young charges as fundamental to their own careers.[37]

His students knew their worth. He made certain of that. The generations of student trainees became, in time, colleagues who joined in the fight against laissez-faire. "I am not a person," Commons said repeatedly over the years to his students. "I am a syndicate. I tell the world of you." The students were not isolated hatchlings but a kind of intellectual "seed-bed" to be brought along and cultivated, their thinking shaped by his guidance. Those at his side this summer of 1907 were members of the "syndicate." Changing trains in Chicago, the professor was acutely aware of the crucial role they must play in the weeks ahead in Pittsburgh. Boarding the Tuscan red car of the Pennsylvania Railroad for the last, eastward leg of the trip, the three young men put themselves in John R.'s hands.[38]

Commons's students had prepared themselves as best they could for their

1907 fieldwork in Pittsburgh, starting with the kinds of facts available in a Rand McNally atlas. Pittsburgh, a western Pennsylvania city, was located at the confluence of the Monongahela and Allegheny rivers that joined to form the broad Ohio. Named for William Pitt, it had metamorphosed from a rude river outpost through a half century of heavy industry. A manufacturing center of plate glass and pickles (Heinz's "57 varieties"), Pittsburgh was best identified with iron and steel. The atlas halftone photographs showed a modern city, its "Point" majestic with modern office skyscrapers and fashionable department stores, notably the Joseph Horne Company, which catered to the carriage trade. Promotional literature also extolled the castle-like grandeur of the Frick mansion and celebrated the Carnegie Library with its opulent auditorium and swimming tank. The city boasted the verdant treasure of Schenley Park, the amusement park thrills of Kennywood Park, and the emerald home field of the Pittsburgh Pirates baseball club at Exposition Park, where Honus Wagner played.

Other vital facts about Pittsburgh, however, were difficult to glean. Commons's team learned that one-third of the city's population of some half-million people were foreign born, including southern and eastern European "Slavs," Italians, Germans, Scots, Syrians, and African Americans from the U.S. South. The students scoured the *Pittsburgh Press*, but additional information was sparse. The city, it seemed, could not disclose the most basic information about itself. It was commonly known, for instance, that hundreds of workers died annually in industrial accidents, with uncounted others maimed and disabled by injury. These included the so-called trade diseases that were beginning to be studied by Dr. Alice Hamilton, who almost single-handedly was starting up the field of industrial toxicology in the United States. Yet nobody had hard numbers on this. No one had studied prevention techniques or how families coped when the breadwinner was stricken or died. No one knew the number of school-age children in the city or the state of their health. Or the cost in life and money of those sluicing into the "hospitals, jails, insane asylums, brothels, and orphanages."[39]

Commons and the young men had some knowledge of the grim realities. They possibly knew that the delicate silks and laces sold in Horne's Department Store were kept pristine only by filtering the city's filthy air through an intake of flowing water and cotton batting. They perhaps knew, what's more, that the filtration system operated for the good of the merchandise, not for the health of the salesclerks. They were cautioned in advance that the city's explosive growth came at the expense of the mill workers and their families. The owners had built mansions on Pittsburgh's own Fifth Avenue, and the company-owned superintendent's house was a grand structure of brick and

*Overlooking the homes and steel mills of industrial Pittsburgh,
Pennsylvania, 1903. (Library of Congress)*

stonework with a fine portico. Masses of workers, however, lived crowded
together in airless, "forlorn" clapboard houses, shacks, and shanties on the
"gullied" hill slopes and triangular flats of the river banks and bends. Their
families clustered in the "dirt and ugliness" of cramped alleyway flats. Soot
rained down from "black clouds" that billowed from the smokestacks of the
mills. Plumbing was out of the question. Sewage flowed in some streets, and
when typhoid ravaged the city, politics interfered with a clean public water
supply.[40]

The researchers' tasks were preassigned. Some would analyze work-
related accidents, others household life, still others the role of women, and
so on. The Commons team's task was to survey labor conditions in the blazing steel mills that ran around the clock all year long. It was rumored that
just two legal holidays — Christmas and the Fourth of July — were observed

in the steel industry in 1907, "and even these were denied to the men of the blast furnace crews." Florence Kelley, the children's rights reformer and head of the National Consumers' League, had told Commons a particularly shocking thing. She said that men worked a twenty-four-hour shift in the mills on Sundays, the Sabbath. She said the "water boys" worked the round-the-clock shift too, and that a man occasionally collapsed and died at work or on the way home because of the heat and strain. Was this true? He and his boys would find out, though the time pressures for the work were fierce. Commons prayed not to be knocked flat by one of his god-awful gastrointestinal bouts. He could only hope that his "verve" would ward off the attacks that hit without warning and laid him up for weeks on end.[41]

Commons's tight schedule permitted him to stay in Pittsburgh only for a month—one short month to size up the "smoky" city that he dubbed Andrew Carnegie's "original Sherwood Forest." He must train these fledgling students fast and trust them to carry on there for a full year. They'd be on their own to conduct extensive research and report the results in definitive form. Of the three hand-picked students, two were greenhorns. They must be taught doubly quick to conduct interviews, gather facts, generate and tabulate statistics. Could they do it? Their competence hinged on John Commons's crash course this summer.[42]

The professor kept misgivings to himself as the train at last approached the city. No one needed the Pullman porter to tell them they were entering the "city of tonnage and incandescence." Their gaze shifted from the rivers that were patchy with black fleets of coal barges to the smoky hillsides and valleys seamed with rows of coke ovens. They scanned the gaunt tipples bent above the mouths of mines, then saw the derricks and bull wheels and low-lying mill buildings sided with corrugated iron. They counted the smoke-stacks set like choruses of giant panpipe flutes. Paul Kellogg declared that Pittsburgh was joined in wedlock to the nation: "For richer, for poorer, in sickness and in health, for vigor, waste and optimism, [the city] is rampantly American."[43]

Commons's mind was on the task. He must be tough and poised to confront this city of "mighty Vulcan . . . monarch of all the forges." He must set the example of civility, intellectual inquiry, and stamina. Always struggling with his wretched digestion and body weight, Commons must lead his young men into the heart of the modern steel mill. Faking vigor, he must stand with them at the sides of workers tapping fifty tons of molten steel from the furnace. He must withstand the heat of the Bessemer converter and endure the crash and roar of the blooming mills. He must show a stoic face at the ladling of white-hot molten steel and risk the flying metal and sparks that could lodge in an ear or cost him an eye. At every point, he must appear calm, unflappable, a man in charge. In short, he must be Professor Commons.[44]

Commons faced another challenge. He must show his young men how to navigate a city that was riven with anger and bitterness beneath the surface. A city of "cut-throat competition" and a "Mecca to the immigrant," Pittsburgh smoldered from its past decades of labor wars. A strike had crippled the iron and steel business in the "long and costly" summer of 1882. Rumblings about wage scales erupted in 1889, followed by the bloodiest strike, the "Battle of Homestead." That notorious "war" pitted the owners' hired Pinkertons against armed steel workers in the summer and fall of 1892. Now the unions were broken, disbanded. But memories and anger lingered. The hot, dangerous, and yet efficient mills were now run from a centralized U.S. Steel authority that dictated the working conditions of "vast masses of men." The workers, upwards of 80,000 men, had "no voice" whatsoever in the conditions of their employment.[45]

How did they feel about this state of affairs? The young investigators could find out for sure only if they spoke with the workers off the job, in their homes. Commons must show his students how to use contacts to gain admission to workers' households in order to learn about "the issues of life as seen by the men themselves." Only then, Commons knew, could the students learn of "hopes and plans" and "some half-spoken ambition." Only then could they document the impact of working conditions to the extent required for the Russell Sage Foundation survey. Only in the moment of reflection at home could the researchers hear of the cruel human price of chronic fatigue from long, hard work shifts seven days per week, with the home itself shrunk to two basic bodily functions, eating and sleeping.[46]

Commons knew better than to expect help from the superintendents or owners. Not at this juncture. The so-called expertise of a farm-state professor flanked by his milksop students would only irritate them. The professor's queries about labor unions would raise their ire. They'd suspect that he was soft on labor and its wretched unions. Whatever the workers' union "brotherhood," whether it was the old Sons of Vulcan, or Knights of Labor, or the Amalgamated Association of Iron and Steel Workers, one fact was as plain as daylight to the owners and operators: no friend of the unions could be a true ally of capital.

The professor schooled his young men on this point, knowing that labor strife had hardened the owners and operators against the workingmen, set them dead against unions once and for all. As a labor economist, Commons knew that the mill owners long regarded labor strikes as the chronic Achilles' heel of their industry. The workers claimed that "collective action is the workman's only sure defense against injustice." The owners, however, bridled at such pious moralisms. They had customers to satisfy, contracts to honor, orders to fill, profits to reap. Production was paramount. Rolled steel, wire, tubing, rails—all required a reliably "tractable" workforce. In the owners' view, unionized workers had forgotten who actually owned the steel plants. When mill owners asserted their God-given property rights, the "arrogant" unions forgot their proper place. They behaved as though it were they—the Amalgamated Association of Iron and Steel Workers—who owned and managed the mills. A state militia officer summed up the workers' self-delusion during the Homestead strike: "They believe the works are theirs quite as much as Carnegie's." Over cigars and cognac in the posh, exclusive Duquesne Club, the mill owners might agree that it was a dirty shame that newspapers such as the *St. Louis Post-Dispatch* blamed Carnegie for the strike's bloodshed. But the owners had finally broken the union in 1892. Good riddance.[47]

Commons knew that the iron and steel barons were not alone in their scorn for workers' "justice." Most of the nation's business and banking leaders felt the same way. It was the laissez-faire state of mind. The professor and his young men were among those the laissez-faire forces denounced as society's "meddlers," meaning the "reformers, philanthropists, humanitarians, and would-be-managers-in-general of society." Commons now put himself—and his students—in the line of fire. They were up against vast power, but their cause was as critical as it was just. Commons knew the Pittsburgh Survey was one opportunity to "dig and re-dig" into facts for the greater good of maximal progress for both labor and capital—all to serve the American public interest. The social Darwinist steel magnates were powerful, but the Pittsburgh Survey meant leverage for a "mightier" issue—"democracy."[48]

To maximize efficiency, Commons would try his dangedest to duck any snarling ideological debates in this summer of 1907. A thousand miles from the university lecture hall, his practical Hoosier know-how was needed. For training purposes, he insisted that he and his three students live and eat together for the duration of the fieldwork. The survey grant was modest, so they stayed in a cheap lodging house or hotel. He chose the kind of place where he'd lived while surveying sweatshops in Chicago and New York six years ago for the U.S. Industrial Commission appointed by President McKinley. If the Pittsburgh rented rooms were barely big enough for the beds, so be it. At least there'd be no shivering in a tub bath by an adjacent hot stove in the Chicago winter. That was his vivid memory of the room near Hull House where he'd been a temporary "resident" several years before.[49]

Commons's Pittsburgh team lived by a streetcar line that stopped at the mills, and they ate fairly well, just as his mother had always tried to feed her boarders as best she could. In Indiana, that meant corn bread with pump-kin butter or wild plum preserves, seasonal fruits and vegetables, sometimes wild game or fish, or chicken and dumplings. His mother was skilled at bar-gaining with local farmers. She had to be.[50]

Here in Pittsburgh, the horse-drawn, street-market "huckster" wagon brought the kitchen fresh vegetables from outlying truck farms or the rail-road depot. John R. and the boys breakfasted on eggs and corncakes, potatoes and rhubarb, and coffee. For supper, it was meat or stew, beans, beets and pickles, and bread and butter with every meal. This was an English-speaking establishment, and perhaps the landlady provided each of them with a work-man's dinner bucket for lunch at the mill.[51]

No sooner were they settled and at work than Commons lost a third of his team. A student who was revolted by the notion of working with Slavic "hunkies" fled the city. Commons struck his name from the syndicate, ban-ishing him to anonymity. One of the two still on board was the reliable William Leiserson, a veteran of sweatshop surveys of unskilled and common laborers on New York City's Lower East Side. Leiserson was Commons's kind of man, a bootstrap fellow who worked his way through the University of Wisconsin grilling flapjacks at the One-Minute Coffee Shop. He reminded John R. somewhat of himself and would surely be a quick study, learning the tricks of successful interviewing and entering data on packs of triplicate 4 × 6 cards.[52]

That left Fitch. John A. Fitch was a long shot, and Commons had chosen him on a hunch, as his own professor Ely from the Johns Hopkins days had had a hunch about him and given him his chance in life (saved him, to put it bluntly). A western boy of twenty-six years old, Fitch hailed from the prai-ries of South Dakota. He'd studied at Yankton in his home state, then taught civics and history in Nebraska before enrolling as a graduate student in eco-nomics at Wisconsin. He was feverishly antilabor and imagined labor leaders to be demons with horns. Or maybe saw them as stampeding horned cattle he'd known on the prairie. Commons trusted that firsthand encounters with steelmen would shatter such stereotypes. They would clear Fitch's head and give him a clean-slate outlook. Yet Commons couldn't be sure of that. Field-work was always experimental and messy. You had to be flexible and some-times improvise. Good ideas often lodged in the cracks. You had to be alert and trust your students too. Commons wouldn't have it any other way.[53]

For a full month, he insisted that Fitch and Leiserson simply stay silently at his side to observe him interview the workers. A twenty-year veteran of such interviews, Commons had to show his two students the best examples of his technique. Then he'd help them develop their hypotheses for the Pittsburgh Survey, just as he helped every student who showed spirit. He'd start by speaking to the steelworkers in plain speech, using none of the Hoosier-isms that his wife, Nell, had "weeded" out of him over the years. Who even knew the origins of *Hoosier*? Some said the Indiana state nickname came from "who's here," or from the military "Hussar." Or from eastern Indianans' devotion to a sweet bread produced by a baker named Hoosier.[54]

Commons was always nostalgic for his native state's *lingua rustica*. Yet the steelmen—and his students—would be baffled if he asked them to "wade in" instead of getting started. Or if he said that meeting someone was "lighting upon" him. A chair would be a chair, not a "cheer." And colorful sayings were completely ruled out. No one would hear the Pittsburgh summer compared to an Indiana July that was "so hot that popcorn popped in the fields."[55]

Professor Commons spoke plain, ordinary English when he and his students went to the mill one Sunday night for a scheduled tour conducted by Mahon M. Garland. No one knew a steel mill more intimately than Garland, a man of "fine presence" who had earned his way up in the most physically "back-breaking" jobs in the iron- and steelworks. As a younger man, Garland explained, he was a puddler who began his work shift around two or four in the morning. In those years, he'd faced the full heat of the boiling furnace. It was his job to drive impurities from the molten metal by stirring the liquid mass with a rod through a hole in the furnace door. It was like "churning butter . . . in hell," and it exhausted the best of men by the end of a batch or "spell." Later on, Garland recounted, gangs of men worked under him when he won the highly skilled job of "heater." Less physically punishing, it required a shop-floor man's rule-of-thumb judgment about the temperature of steel ingots.[56]

But this, too, was a "hot job" that soaked a man's work clothes with sweat, summer and winter. No matter how much water they swallowed in the mill, workers like Garland often stopped at a saloon on the way home to quench their thirst and clear their dusty throats with a beer and shot of whiskey. The combination was called a boilermaker. The men swore it was vital to strength and health.[57]

Perhaps the saloon comradeship helped Garland rise in union leadership, for he was elected president of the Amalgamated Association in 1892. It was a fateful moment. He took office at the moment of the Homestead strike, just when the Panic of 1893 was "beginning to show its teeth." This summer night with the professor and his young men brought bittersweet memories of the mill for Garland. He pointed to the very spot where he'd "harangued the workers who for several months had occupied the mills" during the Home-stead strike. He believed in the sacred bonds of a contract, and he disagreed with other union officers who sometimes called unauthorized "wildcat" strikes or work stoppages. Garland regarded them as acts of bad faith that weakened unions by sowing distrust. Several of the now deunionized workmen recognized him tonight, and Garland introduced them to Professor Commons and the two young men. The two kept quiet and listened closely as the professor spoke easily to workers, who in turn talked "freely."[58]

Professor Commons, not surprisingly to Garland, was jolted to meet a worker whose face and arms were "blistered" from the twelve-hour shift by a roaring blast furnace. The man's face was "reddened by the glare of fire and hot steel, his muscles standing out in knots and bands on bare arms, his clothing frayed and grimed." The professor asked many questions about categories of workers, their schedules, the different wage scales, the bonuses and cuts, their relation to tonnage. He was especially interested in the wages of the English-speaking workers versus the others. They all stood close together to hear above the thunder of the mill. The young men scribbled notes on cards but kept quiet as mice, though Fitch seemed surprised to find that a former union leader knew how to behave himself like a gentleman. The professor asked a special question. He'd heard from Mrs. Florence Kelley that steelworkers sometimes worked a twenty-four-hour shift, including Sundays. Was that the case?[59]

Yes, it was. This blistered worker himself had come on this morning at seven. It was now eleven o'clock at night. He had another eight hours to go. He explained that his crew worked the twenty-four-hour shift every other Sunday when the day and night shifts changed places. They worked it — but never got used to it. It meant they could not attend church, a grievous loss for men of faith. The professor thought he'd caught a glimpse of hell. Perhaps Garland had to agree. He'd resigned from the Amalgamated Association presidency in 1898, thankful for the political connections that got him out of the mills. Through friends' help, he'd won President McKinley's appointment as collector of customs for Pittsburgh — and a more recent reappointment by President Roosevelt.[60]

But Garland knew certain hard facts about the mills, the workers, and the management. The two quiet young men dutifully wrote down everything he said, while the professor listened closely. The facts were these: Between 1892 and 1907, a steelworker's wage had dropped by an average of 50 percent, while his work hours had jumped from eight to twelve per shift. Management's saving was 30 to 60 percent greater over the same period. Of all this, Garland was certain.[61]

It would fall to Leiserson and Fitch to verify these numbers and wrestle with the meanings. The task seemed straightforward. Far from it. The two

Pouring molten iron from ladle to mixer, steelworks, Homestead, Pennsylvania, 1903. (Library of Congress)

students, Commons knew from experience, faced the work of deriving theories, hypotheses, so-called principles to help them explain these bare facts. And facts themselves, Professor Commons warned repeatedly, could be slippery and deceptive. The self-styled practical people smugly boasted that two and two always made four—but they were wrong. Commons hammered the point that "two chairs and two beds are not four windows." And "two cats and two dogs are not always four friends." The theory of two and two cannot be true "unless it fits the facts." Time and again, in the lecture hall and in the field, he reminded them that a theory is "empty until it has been filled with facts." And only "good judgment" could fill the theory with "facts that fit." Here in Pittsburgh, he learned, the workers who spoke English averaged two pennies more per hour than those who did not. Language itself had monetary value. "The minimum value of the English language was 2 cents an hour" in Pittsburgh. This was useful information. It was data that an economist could use statistically and perhaps in a hypothesis on race and ethnic identity in relation to wages. The use value of language in the steel industry could be examined in regard to that in other industries, such as meatpacking and textiles. If a close correlation was found to hold true in other industries, then an economic principle could be articulated and other studies could proceed. Caution, however, was always necessary. For those who rode a theory like a hobbyhorse, Commons had one word: beware. Fitch and Leiserson had much work to do.[62]

But Commons was to ask himself some hard questions in the weeks ahead. For starters, "How did this twelve-hour shift and de-unionizing come about" in the steel mills? In research for two books he'd written as a labor economist, he had arrived at certain principles. "The future of American democracy," he learned, was "the future of the American wage-earner." The employer, Commons was certain, was the primary agent of the "Americanization" of the immigrant and of "his children." To numerous immigrants, what's more, "the labor-union was at present the strongest Americanizing force." It weaned the newcomers from their traditional servility to despots. Right here in Pittsburgh, just days before, he had seen this very lesson in a sorry sight right out of the old country. No sooner had he arrived at the Pennsylvania Railroad station with Fitch and Leiserson and the other student than they saw fifty downtrodden Italian laborers ready to be dispatched to a railroad job. Their job was arranged by a labor contractor, a "spick-and-span" padrone with a "huge gold watch." He was fattening his wallet by selling the workers' day labor at a price highly profitable to himself. With the wink-and-a-nod complicity of the business that hired him, he was holding the immigrant workers in peonage. Commons was revolted.[63]

Labor unions, Commons knew, banished the contract labor or padrone system. They taught the worker that his job "belongs to him." It conferred on him his "right to work." The job was not a "personal favor or boss's whim" or based on the extortions of the padroni. The union, in addition, "required every member to be a citizen, or at least to declare his intention of taking out naturalization papers." Commons knew this was tremendously important; it was the very first step toward citizenly identity. He knew that "the American labor movement was the first bulwark against revolution and the strongest defender of constitutional government." He said so to capitalists and to politicians every chance he got.[64]

He did not idealize labor unions. Those who complained of a dominant "employer dictatorship" in the past few decades needed to study the darker facts of unions too. They could find the crooked union boss in league with the company, as Commons had personally seen in the Chicago packinghouses in 1904. The writer Upton Sinclair was showing the reading public exactly this union criminality in his best-selling novel *The Jungle*. In Pittsburgh, investigators could also find that mill workers made corrupt "payoffs to foremen and other supervisors" in order to get promotions and jobs for relatives and friends. A glance into the deeper past would show, what's more, a "labor dictatorship" in the 1850s. Employers, at that time, caved in to the monopolistic unions that disguised their dictatorship as collective bargaining. Commons had learned that "supreme power in the hands of labor means, not the supremacy of labor, but of the labor *politician*."[65]

Neither did Commons sentimentalize immigrants. Their ranks were peppered with hothead anarchists and communist revolutionaries. These zealots robbed their compatriots of their daily bread by promising utopian visions fueled by rage at capitalism. In Commons's view, they believed in "no public purpose," and they treated both individuals and the nation itself as "illusions." In short, they waged "private war" without a "public purpose." In New York City in 1902, Commons witnessed their ruinous intrusion. Their "fiery denunciations" destroyed a good and useful agreement supported by their capitalist employers, including the banker August Belmont, a sportsman in whose honor the Thoroughbred horse race the Belmont Stakes was named. The revolutionaries completely wrecked the agreement. A small knot of hotheads undermined the good-faith efforts of 30,000 Italian subway workers who'd proudly marched in the public street to gain recognition and public support for their union cause—all men with "starved faces, bent shoulders, meager bodies and ragged clothes." Desperate for "bread and butter *now*," the men were twice victimized, first by the laissez-faire system, then by the hotheads.[66]

Commons was adamant that workers' interests were twofold: wages and conditions of work, period. These were the fundamentals. They bound the immigrant with the native-born worker. They were the basics that joined a skilled steel mill "heater" like Mahon Garland to the unskilled ditch diggers who spaded the subway tunnels in New York. These two basic issues—wages and work conditions—must be front and center. The overthrow of the capitalist system was the ruinous fever dream of the anarchists and communists and the fantasy of scores of intellectuals who gravitated to the labor movement to become its "fool friends," in the scathing term of Samuel Gompers, the founder and president of the American Federation of labor. Gompers, as Commons knew, was brilliantly on the mark, for he understood these fools well. They were "class conscious" instead of "wage conscious." Crowd pleasers, they dazzled union members with flaming speeches. Commons tried his best to oust them "from all negotiations between capital and labor, and from the councils of labor." Yes, the unions needed the advice of experts, including economists. Frankly, they needed individuals like him, men steeped in economics and statistical facts.[67]

And free of partisan bias, meaning that his outlook was broader. The best role for an economist, Commons had learned from experience, was advisory. The economist served most effectively as an advisor to the leaders—but only if they sought his advice. He was not to be a propagandist to the mass public. Deep down, the workers might not understand his mentality. Most probably they didn't. Nor, for that matter, did the capitalists. They couldn't. Each side was too heavily invested in its select set of issues to think beyond its own border. Each side could be blinkered, like the horses whose side vision was obstructed. Commons knew that a broad social consciousness was critically important for the mutual benefit of the whole system. Indeed, the broader viewpoint was crucial for the greater good of the U.S. public.

What, then, was sound, principled collective bargaining? What kind of bargaining could possibly have averted the bloody Battle of Homestead, satisfied the owner-capitalists, and saved the Amalgamated Association? Commons knew it must start with the best, most admirable leaders of capital and labor. He knew "many" of them, and they were "honest, aboveboard" capitalists, like the iron and coal shipper Marcus Alonzo (Mark) Hanna. Hanna was precisely the sort of man whom Commons hoped to see ultimately "in control of industry."[68]

At the same time, collective bargaining required "the labor leader who has worked his way up within his own industry by trial and error to leadership." He, too, was admirable. Aggressive yet practical, he knew better than to call a strike for "impossible" goals. And he knew his main mission was preservation of the union. The broad-shouldered, stocky president of the American Federation of Labor, Samuel Gompers, was such a man, for he understood the union's role in a modern world of "interdependence." The eight-hour workday and economic betterment of workers' lives—those were the union goals for which Gompers worked all his life.[69]

As for the mechanics of collective bargaining, Commons thought carefully about it. "Both sides" must be "organized equally. Neither employer or employee acts individually. But the representatives of each draw up a joint agreement, fixing hours, wages, and working rules." The joint agreement should bind all individuals on both sides. Did such model bargaining ever occur? Yes, indeed. Commons was thrilled to be on hand at exactly such a momentous event in the coal industry in 1900. He lectured on it in his University of Wisconsin classrooms and described it to his students who came to the house for informal evening lap suppers in Madison.[70]

Both sides—the owner-operators and miners—had faced each other in a hall at the Italianate-style Chittenden Hotel in Columbus, Ohio, the headquarters city of the United Mine Workers of America. For weeks, "all of the grievances were coldly considered." Then an agreement was hammered out. And ratified by each side. Commons had an epiphany—that he'd seen an updated version of the ancient English parliament. It was the cornerstone of democracy, then and now. It was the modern industrial art of the possible, when the great chieftain capitalists, such as Hanna, faced their counterparts in organized labor, preeminently Gompers. It was partnership "in the public interest."[71]

How, then, had the unions been broken in Pittsburgh? Fitch and Leiserson would examine the specifics, but Commons "traced it out to the union" back in 1889. Carnegie had secured patents for a "new continuous process that carried the molten iron without cooling from the blast-furnace to the finished steel." It required the mill to operate either an eight-hour or a twelve-hour shift. Carnegie proposed an eight-hour workday. The puddlers and heaters, however, had been working nine or ten hours. Suspecting that they faced lowered wages from shorter shifts, they refused. That meant that the Amalgamated Association balked. Nobody budged. Both sides were at an impasse. Three years later, the Homestead strike broke the union. These were the bare facts as he understood them.[72]

It remained for Commons to think through the governing principle within his scientific field of economics. Adam Smith's *Wealth of Nations* would be useless, he decided, and so would the economist David Ricardo's theory of "cost of production." What about the utilitarian Jeremy Bentham? Or David Hume? No, he thought not. Or the American political economists? No, nothing there. Perhaps the philosophers. William James's pragmatism might or might not be applicable. What about Dewey? The Hull House people had alerted him to the work of John Dewey, who made quite a name for himself in Chicago and more recently in New York City. John Dewey thought and wrote about the social psychology of negotiations and transfers of ownership. Once back in his study in Madison, Commons would read what Dewey had to say. Philosopher Dewey's work would help him arrive at an economic theory of negotional psychology. Dewey was his man. He'd work on this through the long Wisconsin winters ahead. So much to do, and the seasons seemed to roll as fast as an express train.[73]

Commons came to represent the group of reformers whose new economic framework discredited laissez-faire to make way for a more equitable society that came about as the twentieth century proceeded. The reformers' achievements included the landmark investigations of the Pittsburgh Survey. The findings were publicized for the general public in national magazines, including *Collier's*, in 1908–9, and then in a cluster of groundbreaking books that richly fused quantitative and qualitative methods. These publications became models for the expanding fields of social work and sociology. The survey director, Paul Kellogg, edited two of them, *The Pittsburgh District: Civic Frontage* (1914) and *Wage-Earning Pittsburgh* (1914). Three of the women investigators published volumes on the household, on women's work, and on legal aspects of workplace safety in Pittsburgh: Elizabeth Beardsley's *Women and the Trades* (1909), Margaret Byington's *Homestead: The Households of a Mill Town* (1911), and Crystal Eastman's *Work-Accidents and the Law* (1910).[74]

As for the steel industry investigation under Commons's direction, it was the North Dakota–born graduate student John A. Fitch who stayed on in Pittsburgh to continue the research through 1908 and then write *The Steel Workers* (1910). His book has been called a "work of unprecedented scope and depth," combining "the research skills of the social investigator" and "the communication skills of the journalist." Reprinted at the end of the twentieth century, it has been judged a "classic."[75]

The objectives of the Pittsburgh Survey were three—investigation, publicity, and reform. For the last of these, Commons's role in Progressivism was perhaps most powerfully felt through the work of his "syndicate" of students. Fitch's fellow student-researcher in the Pittsburgh Survey, William Leiserson, was a Commons disciple who rose to the councils of established authority. Known as a temperamentally genial and highly successful "careerist in mediation and arbitration," Leiserson was appointed, in 1939, to the National Labor Relations Board. He was to serve as well on President Harry S. Truman's Commission on Migratory Labor and was photographed in the White House with the president in April 1951. Another of John R.'s students, John B. Andrews, was to join him to coauthor a book on the principles of labor legislation—but only after Andrews finished a major project. For the time being, the 1910s, he was stage-managing the passage of a federal law to ban the toxic white phosphorous that was used in the manufacture of the "lucifer" matches that young Clarence Day saw flaring into flame to light cigarettes and cigars in the New York of the 1880s.[76]

There were numerous others of the school of John R. Commons, their careers spanning university research and public service. A remarkable number fanned out to teach at U.S. universities, notably Columbia, Chicago, and Stanford. Not all were men. Theresa McMahon got her Ph.D. under Commons and went on to champion minimum-wage legislation and the eight-hour workday for women. Elizabeth Brandeis, the daughter of Louis D. Brandeis, was deeply involved in unemployment compensation. By one count, Commons supervised forty-one doctoral dissertations at the University of Wisconsin. His name was synonymous with the institutional school of economics. Implicit in his reforms were two beliefs: that human beings "will be reasonable if presented with proper alternatives" and that "institutions can be created with incentives built in to ensure behavior consistent with the general interest."[77]

Coincidentally, that same year, 1907, when Commons traveled to Pittsburgh to supervise the steel industry survey, a young Wisconsin farm boy spent his sophomore year of study at the state university in Madison. Edwin E. Witte still had two years of undergraduate work to complete before he, too, joined Professor Commons's syndicate of graduate students in economics at Wisconsin. Eventually Witte went on to administrative posts in the Franklin D. Roosevelt administration. Appointed as executive director of the President's Committee on Economic Security in 1934, Witte was to carry forward the work of John R. Commons in writing a landmark legislative bill. Just as Clarence Day Jr. completed the final editing and proofreading of *Life with Father*, Witte was developing and guiding the Social Security Act of 1935 through the U.S. Congress. The act had three major provisions. A pension fund for retirees was coupled with a federal-state unemployment program and a commitment to public-assistance programs for the disabled and for dependent children. The law helped guarantee survival not only for the fittest but for the people at large. Edwin Witte became known as the father of Social Security, which President Franklin Delano Roosevelt proclaimed to be the New Deal's "cornerstone" and "supreme achievement." From his Arts and Crafts–style bungalow overlooking Lake Mendota in Madison, the now-retired Professor Commons lived to see it happen. Perhaps he took satisfaction in recognizing the lineage that made John R. Commons the grandfather of the most popular public program in U.S. history.[78]

Julia Lathrop
Justice, Not Pity

The justice of today is born of yesterday's pity.—**JULIA LATHROP**, National Conference
of Charities and Corrections, 1912

The parents who came in the cabin of the *Mayflower* and those who sank in the steerage of
the *Titanic* had the same profound impulse.—**JULIA LATHROP**, "The Children's Bureau," 1912

The present time is one in which it requires unusual courage to be courageous.
A weary acceptance of apparent defeat is easier.—**JULIA LATHROP**, quoted in
Jane Addams, *My Friend, Julia Lathrop*, 1935

She [Julia Lathrop] took her citizenship seriously. . . . The nation's children and
their mothers were her own heritage and hope in the American commonwealth.
—**GRAHAM TAYLOR**, quoted in Jane Addams, *My Friend, Julia Lathrop*, 1935

Why do babies die? The lady traveler pondered the question with intense concentration as she crossed the marble concourse of Washington, D.C.'s Union Station in the late spring of 1912. The awful question cut across every category of life in the United States. Hanging unanswered, it shadowed families and communities and darkened the nation's very future. Of the 2.5 million babies born in the United States in 1911, 300,000 did not survive the first year of life. *Why do babies die?* The question itself was tragic. No one could think it political. That, in fact, was its attraction and its promise. The lady traveler knew that was its brilliance.[1]

Julia Lathrop was the traveler. Arriving by rail at the gleaming white Union Station, she was now in the largest passenger depot in the world and architect Daniel Burnham's Beaux-Arts triumph. The slender, well-dressed, sloe-eyed Lathrop, at fifty-four years of age, might have been taken for someone's great-aunt arriving for a visit. No Washington political figures hailed her in the swirl of passengers or in taxicab lines at the terminal entrance. She ap-

Julia Lathrop, c. 1912.
(Library of Congress)

peared to be merely a respectable, well-groomed older lady amid the horse-drawn vehicles jostling with motorcars and electric streetcars. She was little known outside her home state of Illinois, where she'd lived all her life. She cut no figure in this intensely political Washington environment. She knew, for the time being, that was just as well.

Yet Julia Lathrop was poised to become a political force on the national scene. President William Howard Taft had recently appointed her as the first chief of the newly created U.S. Children's Bureau. As chief, she was set to be the human face of a momentous change in federal policy. She felt the weight of opportunity—and risk—at this late-midlife moment in life when many slowed down and eased toward retirement. American life these days was defined by speed. Advertisements gloried in the "speed" of manufactured products from razors to canned food, and pundits called this "the age of hurry" and proclaimed speed the new American religion. Born back before the Civil War, Lathrop felt she needed to prove herself to be a fast-paced twentieth-century professional woman. She couldn't afford to be weary but must guard her health to maximize her energy. To avoid the notorious swamp fevers of Washington, she'd signed a lease for an apartment at the Ontario,

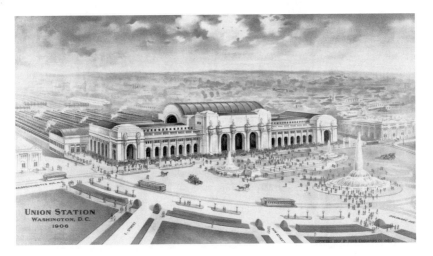

*Union Station, Washington, D.C., the largest passenger terminal in the world.
Artist's projection, 1906. (Library of Congress)*

located in the northwestern Kalorama area, where the building caught the freshest breezes and boasted that its location was "free from malaria." She would need every ounce of strength for the task before her. Not since the founding of the republic had the federal government accepted responsibility for any societal well-being across the nation. The mandate of the Children's Bureau reversed that longstanding, ironclad policy.[2]

How far this reversal went, however, was an agonizing question. New and novel priorities, Lathrop learned from experience, were diabolically difficult to put into place. The gleaming white, classical public buildings of the capital city rose on every side, and this railroad terminal, with its imperial Roman arch and vaults, was the glory of modern capitalism itself—and yet the nation lacked a national birth registry. No one knew for sure how many babies were born in the United States, or where they were born, or who their parents were. The mortality figures were a good estimate, but only an estimate. To Lathrop, this was no mere numbers game. The stakes were literally life-or-death. For social Darwinists, infant deaths simply weeded out those who were unfit to live in a world ruled by the law of survival of the fittest. But this could not explain why annually more babies died per thousand in the United States than in Norway, Ireland, Scotland, and even Bulgaria.[3]

The American mortality crisis was further compounded, Lathrop knew, by high rates of childhood disability. In Chicago and downstate Illinois, she'd seen children who were stunted, chronically sick, and crippled. If they lived, fragile infants became fragile children. She knew that much of this death and disability was preventable. One major cause was sheer human ignorance. In large numbers, mothers across the country knew nothing about prenatal and infant care. Many mothers, for instance, were ignorant of the mortal danger of contaminated or adulterated milk. She wanted the first projects of the fledgling Children's Bureau to be easy-to-read, free advisory pamphlets that blanketed the country. They would be titled, simply, *Prenatal Care* and *Infant Care*.

The new Children's Bureau, nonetheless, was by government standards a small-scale experiment. Her long-range plans were far reaching, but Lathrop knew she had to put them on a back burner for now. Politically, it would be suicide to begin like an ambitious empire builder. Every skeptic and opponent of the new bureau would pounce and attack. Every misogynist would have a field day ridiculing the new lady chief. Besides, Congress had not budgeted enough money for major programs. For now, there could be no close-up field studies of infant mortality in typical American communities. For the time being, there could be no nationwide baby fairs like those staged last year in New York City and Chicago. In these cities, trained nurses offered mothers an afternoon's babysitting while they strolled exhibits and heard short lectures on child rearing in many languages, from French to Chinese. There was also an open-air demonstration school where fresh air could ward off tuberculosis. And there was a model playground to show safe play, off the dangerous streets. A woman like New York City's Mrs. Clarence Day, known as Vinnie, would surely see the playground as a major improvement on the manure pit where the children of the Day family's coachman had spent their open-air hours.[4]

Only if Congress loosened its purse strings could the new bureau sponsor such important fairs across the nation. A bigger budget was also vital for projects such as a national "Children's Year" to reinforce the need for the public protection of maternity and infancy, for healthy recreation, and for free public schooling for all. Lathrop knew that other bureau issues must eventually include children who were orphaned, child labor, and the juvenile courts. What the Children's Bureau needed, at the core, was a professional staff of about seventy-five, organized into five divisions — statistical, library, industrial, hygiene, and social service. Lathrop asked herself, Could she get it done?[5]

Congress had launched the new bureau on a shoestring, only $25,640 for the first year. Lathrop felt the cruel irony that children's well-being was worth a mere fraction of the annual $1 million that Congress spent on the Bureau of Animal Industry in the Department of Agriculture. Cows and pigs fared better than children. She feared that if the budget wasn't expanded in years to come, the Children's Bureau would only limp along, and its clients —

the nation's children—would be victimized by neglect. Her own name would be shorthand for failure and defeat.[6]

Determined to change this state of affairs, Lathrop counted on friends and allies to advise her and a network of supporters to lend her their energies. The Children's Bureau owed its very existence to eleven years of steady effort from "organizations of parents, labor unions, health workers, social workers, and women." This coalition had nominated her to President Taft. Lathrop must not fail them.[7]

Titanic forces, however, were already massing against the nascent bureau. Arriving for her swearing-in ceremony early in the humid, drowsy Washington summer, Lathrop had no illusions about a honeymoon period for the Children's Bureau. Washington was a political minefield, and the bureau was already in jeopardy. Congressional debates had exposed dark suspicions that government officials would invade American families' privacy and usurp parental rights. Some congressmen and senators took the position of a contemporary fictional character: "When the State presumes to teach a mother how to feed her child, . . . the State goes too far." Lathrop knew that doctors suspected that the bureau would encroach on their turf. They could rise up to do battle with intense lobbying. And existing agencies jealously protected their domains. The Department of Education sensed rivalry, as did the Public Health Service. Political timing was dicey. The next election, just two years off, could send a different party to the White House, ousting her in favor of a new political appointee. She'd heard that certain individuals, male and female, already coveted her position and planned campaigns to wrest it from her.[8]

Was she a strong enough leader? Not in the usual sense. Not like the thundering woman labor union organizer in the coal fields, Mother Jones. Not like the political militant Emma Goldman. An appreciative physician in Illinois wrote of Lathrop as a person who does "a tremendously important share of the world's work" through "personality and character." He admired her as someone who "creates a meeting ground" for those who "otherwise could hardly blend." Nearly a century later, a writer named Malcolm Gladwell was to identify persons like Lathrop as "connectors." He was to recognize those like her, past and present, as individuals with a wide and varying circle of acquaintance. Their leadership consisted, he said, of their "particular and rare social gifts." Such connectors, said Gladwell, "manage to occupy many different worlds and subcultures and niches." They lead, he said, by creating a "tipping point."[9]

Lathrop knew for certain that she was about to inflame things by refusing to staff her new agency with political appointees. She insisted that expertise must trump cronyism. She'd seen more than her share of political appointees' incompetence in Chicago and refused to let careless, stupid, lazy sycophants infect the Children's Bureau. No one must mistake her grace and good manners for weakness. No matter who begged her to hire a relative or a political payback "friend," the answer was no, no, and no. On this matter, she was adamant: her fledgling agency needed to be staffed by well-qualified professionals under the merit-based civil service system. She needed, for a start, an expert statistician. It was crucial that the Children's Bureau achieve "the sternest statistical accuracy" because, as she said, "the noblest human passion of pity must never be founded upon anything but truth." The work of the bureau "must guard against the easy charge of sentimentality and must be able to present all its statements dispassionately with scientific candor."[10]

Congress, all the while, would be watching the bureau like a hawk. No group would celebrate its collapse more joyously than certain southern senators and congressmen. Their hostility was the most unforgivable of all. They feared the bureau might crimp the profits of the textile mill owners and cotton planters of Georgia and other Deep South states by stopping the epidemic of cheap child labor in their treacherous mills and fields.

If only Lathrop had more time to allow the bureau to garner support and to placate skeptics and block enemies. There wasn't a minute to lose — which was the reason she used her own money for this trip, for the federal bureau funds weren't yet released. She'd memorized the bureau's mandate. It was dedicated to "the welfare of children and child life among all classes of people."[11]

The phrasing gave her the cue for the first bureau research project, to be launched immediately. She would explain that it was friendly to families. "The only basis for including any family," she'd say, "was the fact that a child had been born in the family during the selected year, thus giving a picture . . . of the whole community." In all honesty she could call it an "entirely democratic inquiry" that overrode all partisanship.[12]

That was the brilliance of the project. It hinged on a question that did not seem one bit political. Having spent over two decades in Chicago in bruising bare-knuckle politics, she'd learned the value of appearing to be above the fray. In her own gracious and ladylike way, she could exploit the low-key, "experimental and tentative" start here in Washington because it served a kid-glove infighter like her.[13]

The huge Capitol dome and the thrusting Washington Monument, however, were a cautionary lesson in power. The very skyline spoke of male authority on a continental scale. Yes, Lathrop's Chicago was a metropolis, and her home state of Illinois a middle-western hub state of the union. But the

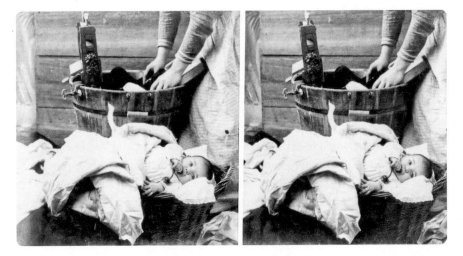

"Why do babies die?" 1902. (Library of Congress)

city was local, the state regional. This was national. The entire United States of America was now Julia Lathrop's provenance. The care of its children was in her hands. Her personal qualifications, such as they were, in no way guaranteed success. What if she became a casualty of good intentions washed down the Potomac? Time was not on her side. The research project was her Children's Bureau lifeline, and the key question hung like a dangling hook: *Why do babies die?*

IF AN INTERVIEWER had asked Miss Julia Lathrop what specific turning point set her on the path to the nation's capital, Lathrop would pause in thought. She'd then reach back to a certain evening lecture in Rockford, Illinois, in the autumn of 1890. Miss Julia Lathrop had no idea, back then, that the lecture she planned to attend at the Rockford Female Seminary would change her life. She couldn't imagine that it would tap into her deep, unspoken discontent. At the time, such negative feelings were a deeply kept secret, even from herself. She had grown up in a hometown of Victorian-era customs and was, to all appearances, well settled in modern Rockford, a thriving northern Illinois industrial city with a census of 23,584, the third-largest Illinois city after Chicago and Galena. Transit was on Rockford's mind in 1890. Construction had just begun on the new State Street bridge, which would have two sidewalks, and the city's horsecars had vanished in the wake of the marvelous new electrified streetcars. A stitchwork of railroad tracks through Rockford carried cargo and passengers to and from every direction of the country.[14]

Rockford's prosperity matched the Lathrops' own, for Julia was the daughter of leading citizens with deep roots in the community. A prominent attorney and U.S. congressman, William Lathrop was a Lincoln Republican who'd come west to Illinois in the mid–nineteenth century. His wife, Adeline Potter Lathrop, was descended from a Rockford pioneering family and was a member of the first class admitted to the seminary in 1844, when it was housed in a converted horse barn. The seminary now symbolized the city's growth, for it occupied an eight-acre campus on the Rock River and was one of the proudest local institutions, soon to be renamed Rockford College. Adeline was an active alumna, and her husband a member of the board of trustees. Of the couple's three boys and two girls, Julia (b. 1858) was the oldest and had studied there for a year—the U.S. centennial year of 1876—before going on to Vassar College for her A.B. Since then, she'd lived at home. With one or both parents, Julia regularly attended educational lyceum lectures at the seminary. The rhythms of her days were the rhythms of her family and community.

This night, however, was special. A capacity audience from the Rockford community was certain to turn out because the speaker, Miss Jane Addams, was a northern Illinois woman who was remembered as a superior student and outstanding debater just a decade ago at the seminary. Addams's topic was to be her new passion, the settlement house movement.[15]

Julia Lathrop had a special incentive to attend. Miss Addams was an acquaintance. Active in drama in her college days, Julia spent part of a school vacation helping the younger Addams and other young women students stage the witches scene from *Macbeth* for a seminary performance. Addams herself well remembered Julia for her "vigor and originality" and recalled being awed by "this brilliant young woman who came from a real woman's college," Vassar. Julia, in turn, was curious about Addams, who was rumored to have suffered a bout of nervous depression in the years following her seminary graduation. Addams then traveled abroad to Europe and England, where she'd become inspired by a new kind of philanthropic organization. It was at Toynbee Hall in London's impoverished East End, where young men of Oxford and Cambridge universities tried to make "the lives of the East End poor more wholesome and beautiful than they could be without such help." Following a visit to Toynbee Hall, Addams returned to the United States and read the current work of American social theorists, especially Richard Ely and Henry Demarest Lloyd. Addams became deeply involved in an American version of the Toynbee Hall venture.[16]

Lathrop, by contrast, had come straight back to Rockford after graduating from Vassar in 1880. She didn't want to teach school, although she adored children, so she'd worked in her father's law office, doing clerical work and reading law, as many apprentice attorneys did at this time. When she passed the Illinois bar exam, she continued in her father's office as a paralegal. People complimented her good humor and easy laughter that never came at others' expense. No young men suitors came her way. Perhaps she didn't expect beaux, for she thought herself rather homely, neither tall nor curly haired. Her enormous brown eyes showed a certain shyness and what one observer called "an almost Italian salience." In her early thirties, she continued to live in the house that her father built.[17]

No one knows whether, on this night, Julia Lathrop felt the bind of an educated, single woman like herself. No one knows whether she felt the yoke of daughterly duty weigh her down as she sat beside her father and heard glowing introductions of Miss Addams in the gas-lighted hall. She could hardly ignore the contrast between Jane Addams's life and her own. She, the former worldly, "brilliant," older woman from the eastern college, sat silently in the audience. The former seminary schoolgirl, who was two years younger than Julia, took her place at the lectern and prepared to speak as an authority. Addams, Rockford people knew, was gaining prominence these days in Chicago. The august Chicago Woman's Club enthusiastically welcomed her into membership. The club was a twenty-year bastion of female civic power and authority in the booming metropolis of the American Midwest, and it adopted Addams's Hull House as an innovative reform project. Addams's reputation was on the rise. The younger woman had become, somehow, Julia Lathrop's senior.[18]

At last, Miss Addams began to speak. At five feet, four inches tall, she could be called "a slip of a girl," and there was nothing dramatic about her appearance on the platform. Julia, who appreciated good clothes, took note of Addams's dark dress of heavy material, her bustle, her sharp and even severe silhouette that was the fashion of the day. With her brown hair pulled back and pinned into a serviceable bun, Addams stood with her head thrown a little forward. Avoiding grand gestures, she simply fingered a string of beads and sometimes clasped both hands behind her back. Truth to tell, she looked rather weary. Her voice, however, was "clear and agreeable," and "she modulated it pleasantly in the lower registers," making certain that it carried to the farthest listeners in the back of the hall.[19]

Everyone was interested. "There was so much freshness and glow of information" that was "gathered at first hand" as she spoke of the goals of Hull House. She eased her audience into the core of the talk rather like a bather who must be eased into icy lake waters in the summertime. It would not do to shock. Addams's speech opened with the sorts of phrases familiar to

*Jane Addams, 1910.
(Library of Congress)*

churchgoing Protestants each Sunday, phrases that circulated in civic clubs and other high-minded gatherings. Listeners heard such terms as "a higher social morality," "established virtues," and "moral energy." Addams spoke their language. Julia had no idea that Addams was on a secret mission. She hadn't the vaguest notion that the speaker had a special target audience in mind, namely, single women who returned to live at home after college. Julia had no clue that this talk was meant for her.[20]

Addams explained that just the year before, 1889, she and her woman friend, Ellen Gates Starr, had founded a settlement house, one of several that would soon spring up in American cities, notably in New York and Philadelphia. The two women partners called their Chicago settlement a "centre for a higher civil and social life." They named it Hull House in tribute to the Charles J. Hull family, who'd built the Italianate-style house back in the 1850s, when Chicago's Halsted Street was a country retreat — that is, before affluent families like the Hulls fled to Lincoln Park and other North Side locations, thereby abandoning their former Chicago neighborhood to industrial development and swarms of immigrants.[21]

Hull House, as Addams carefully explained, was not to be a charity or a Christian mission. The Hull House participants must not be religious zealots. They must, however, make a passionate commitment in a spirit of cooperation. The ethical principle of the house was "egalitarian or democratic social relations" across all social classes. The version of democracy that was embraced at Hull House, Addams emphasized, included economic and social opportunity, even though the audience found her rather vague on this point.[22]

Then the speaker plunged to the heart of the matter, and her message was as pointed as the tip of a hat pin. Addams and Ellen Starr faced a particular challenge right now. They expected other women to join them, and Hull House badly needed new members. The two partners had spent money and elbow grease repairing and freshening up the dilapidated Hull mansion over the past year. With a housekeeper in place, they felt pressed to expand their duo into a community. Eventually, they wanted to include interested men, but for the moment they sought women. The clock was ticking. Hull House needed the energy and vitality that new residents would provide. They needed recruits. Tonight's seminary lecture was one of a number that Addams had scheduled in the northern Illinois area. Julia Lathrop may or may not have made eye contact with Addams in these moments, but the speaker's message reached Lathrop with the impact of a telegram with her name on it.[23]

The homebound, college-educated American woman, Addams said, was by definition a woman filled with discontentment and contradiction. "Perplexities often occur when the daughter returns from college" only to find that her family expects her to "grace the fireside and to add lustre to that social circle which her parents select for her." Quartered in the household, the educated single woman feels eager to assume her "social obligation . . . as a citizen of the world." Thwarted in this, she instead becomes guilt ridden, frustrated, betrayed. The family's grown sons, her brothers, are encouraged to go forth and establish careers and take part in public life, but the daughters are not. They depart with parental blessings only if they marry and continue in traditional domestic life. Otherwise, their futures are blocked. If single and sequestered in the family home, Addams observed, some such women dissipate their energies in "accumulation" or consumerism. Others sicken.[24]

This state of affairs must stop, Addams insisted in her warm voice as the auditorium gas jets slightly hissed. Modern conditions now made change necessary, even imperative, she insisted. The educated woman who has been the "charm and grace of the household" from her infancy must now be set free to assume "duties outside of the family" in order to serve the state and society in the "larger sense." This "larger sense" meant an expansion of democracy in modern America. Educated women must be agents of this expansion.[25]

So far, Addams reminded the audience, democracy had been strictly political, according to the founding fathers' belief that "political equality alone would secure all good to all men." A century of practical experience exposed glaring shortcomings in the political pathway, including election corruption and the denial of voting rights. These problems urgently needed correction, Addams admitted.[26]

But she insisted that the very idea of democracy cried out for a new, expansive definition. "Democracy has made little attempt to assert itself in social affairs," said Addams. Now it must. Basically, it needed to evolve beyond the political and into the social realm of life. The "social function of democracy," Addams said, operates "on the theory that the dependence of classes on each other is reciprocal." To rethink democracy in these new terms was the immediate challenge. The theory of social democracy must be tested and given shape by the hard work of practitioners. Those who were best qualified to work on the newest forefront were the nation's educated women.[27]

Educated women? Julia listened with rapt attention, her mind awhirl. Addams, it seemed, spoke personally to her. The lecture, she realized, outlined her life up to this point—and projected it to a suddenly fascinating future. In Addams's terms, Julia's college years weren't merely a finishing school to burnish her with "delicacy and polish" so that she could serve as an ornamental, "outward symbol of her father's protection and prosperity." Addams showed Lathrop's past as the prelude to a future filled with purpose and usefulness. Framed by Addams, Lathrop's life so far was preparation for the activism of a citizen.[28]

Addams turned to the specifics of Hull House and its neighborhood. She did not sugarcoat the facts. The area's immigrant residents were a poor, polyglot population striving to survive in crammed, filthy tenements without proper sanitation, she said. Many of the surrounding streets were unpaved and littered with trash and garbage. Settlement house life was not for the faint of heart, Addams emphasized, knowing her recruitment effort would fail if candidates for Hull House residency felt misled and fled. Doubtless, some Rockford women in the auditorium at this moment shuddered at her descriptions of "gilded vice." Settlement house life was not their cup of tea.[29]

Not Julia. She grew more intensely interested as Addams vividly described a Hull House neighborhood street "lined with shops of butchers and grocers, with dingy and gorgeous saloons." The streets are "inexpressibly dirty," Addams said, continuing frankly to compile a list of miseries. "The number of schools [is] inadequate, factory legislation unenforced, the street-lighting bad, the paving miserable and altogether lacking in the alleys and smaller streets, and the stables defy all laws of sanitation. Hundreds of houses are unconnected with the street sewer." [30]

Beside her, Julia's father doubtless felt agitated. Knowing his daughter, he could guess the impact of Addams's words. It wasn't the description of the dismal facts of Chicago that bothered him, but the psychology the lecturer set in motion. He'd never call his daughter a sentimental woman, but Julia had a weakness for life's unfortunates, no matter what the circumstance. The picture of human beings trapped in slum life was sure to stir her sympathies. She was vulnerable to appeals like Addams's.

Where this boundless sympathy came from, he could only guess. Maybe it started with Mrs. Stowe's *Uncle Tom's Cabin* and little Julia's childhood in the Civil War years. Perhaps he himself played a part in it, for in court he'd defended a deranged woman client who'd killed her husband and won the landmark case on the grounds that the woman was a victim of emotional insanity. He also knew the work of Dorothea Dix, the crusader for the cause of the mentally ill. Dix lectured in Illinois in the 1840s, and people talked about her for years afterward. Possibly Julia overheard conversations or listened to his household musings on the injustices done to the insane. In the future, William Lathrop was to joke that his daughter was only interested in "someone who was lame or blind or insane." He said that he and Mrs. Lathrop thought that Julia was "only interested in people who are in trouble." In childhood, Julia once spent the night in a stall in the barn for fear that a sick horse was lonely. This evening at the seminary, William Lathrop perhaps saw the color rising in his daughter's cheek in the greenish gaslight as they listened to the lecture. He had reason to worry more and more as Miss Addams went on. She was "not a forceful speaker, but she spoke with conviction and sincerity and held her audience." An attorney and politician like Lathrop had to appreciate that. [31]

"The older and richer inhabitants seem anxious to move away as rapidly as they can afford it," said Addams about the Hull House area of Chicago. "They make room for newly arrived immigrants who are densely ignorant of civic duties." [32]

Julia was indeed fascinated and excited. All her life, she'd heard stories of immigrants' arrivals in primitive Rockford of the 1830s, 1840s, and early 1850s—for instance, the Swedes who brought the scourge of cholera and were quarantined in tents. They were physically exhausted and emotionally wracked from weeks or months of ocean voyaging and overland travel by wagon and rail to Rockford. Infected by cholera, they were sequestered and cared for by kindly but firm American locals who took responsibility for their well-being and for Rockford's public health. She'd also heard of vice-ridden days when pioneer Rockford was a den of cardsharp gamblers. The tales of the early days measured the distance to modern Rockford with its mills, schools, churches, and modern amenities. Yet there was an air of excitement when those old stories were told and retold. A listener could feel that he or she had missed out on the great adventure here in the middle West.[33]

Suppose Jane Addams's Hull House was the new great adventure. Suppose that the numerous miseries that she listed were really opportunities. Suppose that Hull House represented the pioneer moment of the future.

Addams was nearing her conclusion. She called on parents, especially fathers, to recognize that families benefited when educated daughters contributed their talents to the larger world. She then returned to the ideals of the new social democracy, and her phrasing recalled her studies in elocution and debate here at the seminary. A "higher civil life" in a democratic country, she said, must be fostered through "common intercourse." She faced her listeners and made certain to articulate every word. "The blessings which we associate with a life of refinement and cultivation can be made universal and *must* be made universal if they are to be permanent."[34]

Addams paused, then posed a challenge in deliberate, cautionary terms that reminded alert listeners of social turmoil in recent years, especially labor strikes and the deadly Haymarket riot that had erupted so close by, in Chicago, in May 1886. "The good we secure for ourselves is precarious and uncertain," Addams warned. It "is floating in mid-air, until it is secured for all of us and incorporated into our common life."[35]

Julia heard these words as a summons. Addams was recruiting the educated woman to help secure the social "good." Such a woman might be pivotal in turning society's precariousness into stability. The nation's founders, Addams reminded everyone in the hall, had set democracy on its political course. One century later, she was in Rockford to insist that democracy must be rethought and renewed. Couched in veiled terms, her warning was also utterly clear. Americans who failed to act could expect more Haymarket riots that fractured the social and political order.

Suddenly, Julia Lathrop was at a crossroads — or was it the edge of a cliff? Her Rockford life was comfortable and secure. It was also patterned and predictable. She played her part in a family script. Whatever Addams's social democracy was to be, it would take shape from women who joined her project. Was it pure egoism to think that she, Julia Clifford Lathrop, might play this new part in life — in the life of the nation? But how? It would take leadership, and she'd always been "timid and shy." The thought was thrilling—and dismaying, for the likelihood of wounding her parents was horrifying.[36]

Suppose she summoned all the diplomacy she had learned from observing her politically astute father. She would propose a trial residency at Hull House, perhaps comparing it to the length of a college semester, just a season. She'd made a few wise investments in Rockford businesses these last years while working in her father's law office, so money would not be a problem if she spent carefully. And she'd promise to come home to Rockford frequently for visits. Would Addams and Starr accept her on that basis? Would her father and mother approve? It was her most fervent hope. More, it was her rock-solid plan.

"THE BEST 'RESIDENT'" we have had," wrote Addams of Julia Lathrop just after Christmas 1891. The newcomer from Rockford, as Addams and Starr agreed, must have a private room on the third floor of Hull House, where heavily upholstered furnishings were rejected in favor of light-framed and bentwood pieces, potted palms, and scatter rugs. The atmosphere was "wholesome" and "rather Spartan." Julia's room was furnished with a bed, a bureau, a bookcase, and two chairs, one of them armless in order to accommodate a lady's full skirts. Her dresses, skirts, cloaks, and other hanging clothing might have been concealed behind curtains, and a washstand hidden behind a screen. She doubtless brought books, pictures, and a few decorative objects, or "impedimenta," as Addams and Starr had also done. She also had a desk at which she was eventually to sit writing letters, reports, and proposals in the quiet nighttime hours while others slept.[37]

The newcomer from Rockford was no longer "Julia," or "Miss Lathrop," as she had been at Vassar. At Hull House, she answered to "J. Lathrop," a moniker of affection and serious purpose. She began to call Addams "J. A." in return.[38]

But how, exactly, was she to help advance the new social democracy? Addams's advice was reassuring but vague. "Look around," she advised. "See what the neighborhood needs. Then decide what you can do best and do it. If that doesn't work, try something else. You'll find your way."[39]

Perhaps something outdoors needed attention. Addams's description of the neighborhood was on the mark. As winter turned to spring and summer, one saw a seasonal kaleidoscope of wretchedness. There was scarcely a tree or blade of grass in all the Nineteenth Ward, which was now home to some 50,000 people, the most densely packed section in Chicago. Its wooden plank sidewalks became slimy and slippery after a rain, and the cedar paving blocks loosened from the streets and floated about. Drainage was haphazard,

Hull House illustration on cover of Jane Addams's Twenty Years at Hull-House, *1910. (Collection of the author)*

and mud so thick that crossing a street was impossible at certain intersections. And the stench — the alleyway garbage boxes overflowed, and outdoor privies were so close to the houses and to backyard shanties that people had to shut their windows tight on the hottest days. Addams — J. A. — filed complaints, but the City of Chicago replied that garbage hauling was contracted out. The contractor, not the city, bore responsibility. Children, meanwhile, used the garbage boxes as if they were chests of toys, and putrid waste became playthings for street games. City officials seemed not to care one bit. Addams submitted a bid for the garbage contract herself, but her bid was ignored.[40]

The Nineteenth Ward, nevertheless, demanded J. Lathrop's participation as a "social obligation." Living at Hull House, she was committed to a "reciprocal dependence of classes upon each other." That meant going door-to-door on Halsted and the nearby streets—State, Polk, Clark. It meant doing her utmost to meet the foreign immigrants as neighbors instead of "perils." Just last year, 1890, the prominent clergyman and reformer Josiah Strong described the typical immigrant as a European peasant with meager or false training in morals and religion, a narrow horizon, and "low" ideas of life.[41]

J. Lathrop, nevertheless, must venture out to meet these people as neighbors. In snow, in mud, in stench, she must go. Dressed in street wear, she buttoned her shoes and set forth. A proper lady paid calls. That was her strategy at first, to join the women of Hull House in visits required by etiquette. The neighbors were invited to call at Hull House in return. By temperament, Lathrop was a good listener. Almost immediately, she found herself absorbed in the many "piteous recitals" of persecution and hardship both in foreign lands and here in Chicago too. She heard of faraway farmlands so depleted and gullied that whole villages, facing starvation, were forced to emigrate. She heard of eastern European families who fled to save their men and boys from the military conscription that was basically kidnapping by the Russian and Austro-Hungarian armies. She heard Russian and Polish Jews' accounts of flight from mobs of Christians who rampaged at Christmastime against Jewish neighbors they blamed for murdering Jesus Christ.[42]

She heard, too, the travails of American life here in Chicago. Women in shabby black shawls wept in the Hull House reception room as they pleaded for help when their sons or grandsons were arrested for stealing milk or coal. The police took the boys away. Could Miss Addams help?[43]

Often, she could. Her network of Chicago acquaintances was yielding results that were beneficial to the neighbors. Similar pitiful "thefts," however, were doubtless happening all over the city—the nation—without a Hull House to intercede for the children and their families. Those children ought not to be arrested as criminals in the first place, Lathrop knew. Children ought not to have to steal food and fuel to provide for their families. Better-off Americans needed to recognize this and support a fairer system. It was a goal of social democracy, though the task seemed overwhelming. And the role that J. Lathrop might play in it was nowhere in sight.

She had to start somewhere. Hull House, Lathrop had seen at once, was an oasis for neighborhood residents who were drawn to its fast-expanding schedule of readings, classes, lectures, concerts, and club meetings. An impressive group of volunteers conducted and arranged events, including professors from the new University of Chicago. Perhaps Lathrop could launch a new club, something intellectual to use her education and to interest the many Hull House neighbors who hungered for the life of the mind even while earning a living by washing floors or driving an ice wagon. There were

Greeks in the neighborhood, and Addams and Starr had put out classical Greek busts, plaster casts of museum originals. Lathrop started a Plato Club, which attracted "elderly men who had read philosophy of sorts all their lives" and turned out to be closed minded and quarrelsome. The young philosophy professor who occasionally led the club, John Dewey, appeared confounded by their opinionated rants.[44]

For Lathrop, the Plato Club had a certain quirky vibrancy, but it did not advance the cause of social democracy. Professor Dewey's ideas of democracy nonetheless came close to the Hull House idea. He regularly lectured at the house and became good friends with Jane Addams. They had much in common. Like her, he found rigid class divisions to be harmful to democracy. He rejected the "class divisions of industrial capitalism" that gave owners and managers all authority but reduced workers to mere mechanical function, like cogs in a machine. Those at the top were diminished, Dewey argued, by their certitudes, their protocols, and their severance from other human beings, while those who were labeled "laborer" were denied their human "full expression." Intelligence and spirit were quashed in both groups.[45]

Dewey's ideas on education were consistent with his thinking on industrial-era mistakes. The philosopher's theory of education was especially relevant because Lathrop now was a teacher herself, having convened a Hull House class on literature. Dewey rejected the class-based hierarchy of the traditional "scholastic" lecture, in which knowledge was dictated by the expert and absorbed by the mute, passive, regimented student. This flawed system retarded social change because most schools were "designed not to transform societies but to *reproduce* them." Society's so-called expert was a creature of a system that needed reform, the student its virtual prisoner.[46]

Dewey looked to the Hull House children's craft and art studios and workrooms for the "native impulses" that he believed were foundational for human development and thus democratic social change. He hypothesized four "impulses": "to communicate, to construct, to inquire, and to express in finer form." If society was to evolve for the better, he thought, the place to begin was the school. Dewey was able to test his beliefs as a scientific hypothesis in the Chicago Laboratory School, which was organized as a cooperative community. The school was soon called the Dewey School.[47]

What project, Lathrop wondered, was worthy of linkage with her name? The Hull House clubs and classes were important, but the world beyond hadn't beckoned. Frustrated, she forced herself to be patient. The invitation to membership in the Chicago Woman's Club was promising. Acquaintance with so many smart women who worked for the betterment of Chicago was stimulating. And change was stirring in Illinois. In 1892, a new governor,

John P. Altgeld, took office, and civic life began to take a new turn statewide. With his intent stare and his close-cropped hair and beard, the square-jawed, German-born Altgeld looked nothing like Abraham Lincoln. The Lincoln legend that emphasized love and duty to one's fellow men lived on, nonetheless, in Altgeld's vision of governance. He had written a book stating that the U.S. penal system favored the rich over the poor. The chasm between wealth and poverty in the Gilded Age troubled him. In Chicago, a merchant like Marshall Field could spend $75,000 for his son's birthday party, while thousands of women who clerked in his store earned less than a living wage. It wasn't right. Striving to recapture a lost sense of mutual human obligation within society, Governor Altgeld "turned back toward Lincoln's humanism." He planned to exert moral force in ridding Illinois's charitable institutions of "the spoilsmen," those parasites who were rewarded solely for political loyalty, irrespective of competence.[48]

In 1893, in his first months in office, Altgeld appointed Julia Lathrop to the Illinois Board of State Commissioners of Public Charities. It was the state agency charged with the oversight of publicly funded institutions for paupers, the destitute sick, the insane, and dependent children, including orphans.

Lathrop was far from Altgeld's mind on May 1, 1893, when the governor represented Illinois at the opening ceremonies of the World's Columbian Exposition in Chicago's Lincoln Park. Like many officials on hand on this chill and overcast day, Altgeld fretted that a cloudburst might ruin the outdoor procession to the platform and dampen the spirits of thousands of eager fairgoers. He was also mindful of the proper protocol for a governor consorting with his nation's president, Grover Cleveland, and with a Spanish duke and duchess and other dignitaries and officials. He was not thinking about Lathrop, much less about deadly germs—not yet.[49]

The smallpox outbreak that erupted at the fair and swept Julia Lathrop into action did not occur until midsummer. By then, the fair itself was a smashing success, its classical, electrically lighted White City awesome, its famous Midway an irresistible bazaar of worldwide exotic peoples in authentic native huts. Its amazing Ferris wheel rivaled the Eiffel Tower of the Paris Exposition of 1889–90. Another newcomer to Hull House, Florence Kelley, strolled the Midway with her children and declared the Chicago fair "by far the most beautiful thing I've ever beheld." Through the summer months, some 20 million people came to marvel, including the Clarence Day family of New York City. The senior Days were so impressed that they insisted that Clarence Jr., now on vacation from Yale, make a special trip to Chicago to experience the fair for himself.[50]

The closing of the fair, however, brought dual miseries to the city. Suddenly, thousands of workers were stranded, jobless in Chicago, as the nation sank into a severe depression. A more immediate threat, however, was what "the World's Fair bequeathed to Chicago"—a sudden outbreak of smallpox. It started with an undetected case in the Midway in midsummer and spread throughout the city by fall. The health department's monthly statement of mortality tallied the deaths, which steadily climbed to 1,407. Most victims lived in the poorer sections like the Nineteenth Ward, where immigrant families had no notion of germs, vaccination, or quarantine. Two residents of Hull House proved to be "the center of the fight against the smallpox epidemic." One of them was J. Lathrop.[51]

Her Hull House colleague Florence Kelley (affectionately dubbed "Sister Kelley") had a special goal in combating the outbreak. Kelley, too, had received an appointment by Governor Altgeld, who named her the state factory inspector. Her job was to visit factories to make certain that manufacturers complied with Illinois's workplace laws. Everyone knew, however, that much illegal manufacturing occurred outside the factories, in the tenement apartments of poor immigrant families. These were the sweatshops. A Halsted Street child from Poland, Hilda Satt, observed that her playmates' parents, who worked fourteen hours a day in a clothing factory, could not make ends meet unless they brought home "huge bundles of coats, vests, and pants for the family to finish." The mothers would do "the handwork, sewing buttons, and little children would be put to work pulling the bastings."[52]

Sewn, assembled, and finished, this ready-made clothing was shipped all over the United States. A smallpox outbreak among tenement clothing workers gave the deadly disease its own shipping route. One newspaper traced "the smooth path for the feet of the smallpox germ" to the "stores where ready-made clothing is sold" and on to the "home where ready-made clothing is bought." The outbreak threatened to become a national epidemic.[53]

As the pox spread in the city, Kelley requested that tenement residents be vaccinated and that contaminated clothing be burned to prevent further contagion. Chicago city authorities, however, balked at such strict measures, fearing lawsuits from businesses charging loss of trade. The officials urged the useless measure of fumigation. Some denied the existence of smallpox in Chicago.

Kelley and Lathrop went to work. Kelley used her political muscle with the governor to embargo clothing shipments, and Lathrop became her partner in the emergency work of triage. She went into damp basements and climbed the rickety tenement stairs to seek out infected family members. In search of smallpox cases, she breathed the fetid, damp air of small, vermin-infested rooms crowded with bed ticking and cookware, with tables and floors piled with stacks of cloth piecework. Lathrop tried not to alarm adults or children as she scrutinized faces for signs of fever and skin that was mottled with a bumpy rash or pustules or scabs. The victims were to be taken by wagon to the city-operated smallpox hospital, or pesthouse. As Jane Addams described it, "Miss Lathrop went back and forth to the crowded pest house which had been hastily constructed on a stretch of prairie west of the city."[54]

Julia Lathrop surely relished the tribute paid to her and to Florence Kelley by Chicago judge Andrew A. Bruce, who named them as the two women who protected public health by "risking their lives in the sweatshop districts of Chicago." The judge declared that Lathrop and Kelley, "working together, saved hundreds perhaps thousands of human lives." Pleasure at the compliment, however, was offset by Lathrop's anguish at the failure of city officials to safeguard the public during the outbreak. The authorities completely caved in to shortsighted business interests. Once the outbreak was known, they connived with shopkeepers and landlords to hide the yellow quarantine cards that were required by a city ordinance to warn the public to stay clear of infected areas. The cards were to be posted in plain sight at grocery stores, druggists, milk depots, and cigar stores. But city officials did nothing when merchants tacked the cards on rear doors or tore them down. Consumers had no way to know they were at risk of exposure to the deadly disease. In addition, the pest hospital was "scandalously mismanaged." From garbage collection to smallpox, the officials failed the public. In a life-or-death crisis, they went missing. For them, self-interest and money were everything. The middle-class public barely murmured a protest. Civic life was a cruel fiction.[55]

Lathrop was about to find out just how fictional—and how far off was the goal of social democracy. In the winter of 1893–94, she was to see the fate of desperate Chicagoans who were forced to turn to public assistance for their survival. As a member of the State Board of Charities, Lathrop inspected the institutions that were charged with the care of those who had exhausted "all the resources of private charity and neighborly aid." These included men, women, and children who were held in a vast complex just across the Chicago city limits on the northwest side. This was Dunning, founded in 1869, an institution whose name struck fear into the hearts of self-respecting Chicagoans. With its insane asylum, its detention hospital, its infirmary, and its agency of last resort for food relief, Dunning signified utter human failure. "The only place where a person without money or a home can go is Dunning." The very name signified the last, abject stop before death and an ignominious burial in a pauper's grave for "the victims of misfortune, . . . the ineffective criminal, the penniless convalescent."[56]

Dunning included a farm where food crops were raised to defray the costs of operation. The farm fields hid the grim fact, however, of the orphaned children warehoused within, a good many of them afflicted by mental illness or physical disability. In the 1890s, when the U.S. coin of the realm, so to speak, was the five-cent nickel, Cook County, encompassing Chicago, spent $700,000 annually on "the necessities of a great dependent population." This sum provided salaries for over 500 supervisors and staff. As a public charities board member, Lathrop evaluated the effectiveness of the expense and the services provided. As she said, "The comfort, the recovery, the lives of all these thousands of dependent people hang upon the knowledge, the kindliness, the honesty, and good faith of those hired to care for them." She sought to understand the reasons for "the universal dread of the 'County.'"[57]

It was dread mixed with desperation in the fiercely cold winter of 1893–94, which severely strained Cook County because of the nation's "general business depression" and the termination of World's Fair jobs in Chicago. The thousands who had come to the city for job opportunities in the construction and operation of the fair were now abruptly without work. Carpenters, painters, restaurant workers, janitors, unskilled laborers—all were now lumped in one category: unemployed. "Selling our muscular strength in the open market for what it will bring, we sell it under peculiar conditions," observed one spokesman for labor. "It is all the capital we have. We have no reserve means of subsistence. . . . Broadly speaking, we must sell our labor or starve. . . . And for some of us there is other pressure, unspeakable, immeasurable pressure, in the needs of wife and children."[58]

Lathrop saw the pressures mount in those who were suddenly jobless. Reduced to "human *debris*," they now stood outdoors daily by the hundreds in long lines at Dunning's outdoor relief agency in the freezing winter weather. "Shabby men and shawled or hooded women" came from all parts of the vast city and stood "hour after hour with market baskets high above their heads," the police holding them in check. Of mixed ethnicities, their common language was "persistency, weariness, chill, and hunger." "Now and again a woman [in the crowd] was crushed—in one instance reportedly killed, and the ambulance was called to take her away." A posted sign warned of smallpox but deterred no one. Once finally inside the "great dingy waiting-room of the Cook County Agency," one's paperwork and an interview determined eligibility. Approval meant the promise of a delivery of a bag of coal for heating. It also meant that the market basket would be filled with food packets and "one bar of hard soap." Hunger and cold could be kept at bay for a few days.

The system, Lathrop realized, was grueling and stopgap. It was needlessly punishing and barely supportive.[59]

Oddly, the industrial system that turned workers into "debris" was not thought to contribute to their plight. Private charities blamed these victims. Lathrop, along with Jane Addams, saw the flaws in a concept of charity work that was imported from England and took root in the United States through the widely respected and influential Charity Organization Society, headquartered in New York City. The society approached poverty as personal pathology. The poor, by its definition, were lazy, defective, and vice ridden. They needed to reform themselves with stern discipline and very modest help from private charity. The notion of public or governmental involvement was out of the question for the society because it violated the laissez-faire idea in which individualism reigned supreme.

How was it possible, Lathrop asked herself, for democracy based on reciprocal relations among different groups to gain a foothold? How, when jobless, hungry clients of the county were made to feel that destitution was all their fault? And when the more or less well-off public blamed them as well?

Her head spun when Lathrop entered Dunning's steam-heated buildings and saw the rampant neglect and abuse. Inside, the wards of Cook County were spared hunger and frostbite, but men slept crowded on straw ticking in hallways and on floors and mingled with "a melancholy company of feeble and bedridden men and idiot children." Mealtimes meant "very hard" mush and "cheap cuts of meat kept madly jumping in the pot for an hour." Privacy was impossible, and everyone was forced to wear coarse, institutional clothing that stigmatized them as charity cases. The "hideous" clothes of the Dunning children who attended a nearby public school made them the butt of classmates' savage ridicule. Social life was nil because there were no sitting rooms, let alone the "homely comfort" of books or newspapers. The attendants were "too few" to give their charges "proper out-door exercise." Medical care was left principally to interns. The experienced "outside" doctors were seldom seen.[60]

The compulsory segregation by sex was especially distressing because it split couples apart. "Oh—" Lathrop overheard a homeless panic-stricken woman in her nineties exclaim at the suggestion that she and her husband seek shelter at Dunning. "Oh, he'll have to go in with the men; I'll have to go in with the women, and all our own clothes will be taken away from us." Lathrop was dismayed by the "monotony and dullness," the "unutterable dreariness," the "hours of listless idleness" that reduced lives to a state of vegetation.[61]

Or to violence. Some mental health workers, wholly ignorant about insanity, cursed and spit on inmates and sometimes hit them. They treated wards of the state or county as if they themselves were the plantation overseers she remembered from *Uncle Tom's Cabin*. No wonder, Lathrop realized, black residents refused to commit their disabled or mentally ill family members to the state or county, fearing to re-enslave them.[62]

It was all staggering, overwhelming, horrible. The "crudeness of the management" was "shocking." But Lathrop was a witness on official business. She must steel herself and somehow distill this tide of human misery and neglect into data. Pity was easy. It was cheap and passive. Action took work and required efficiency—and hard cold facts. One resource that she brought to her task of evaluation for the charities board was orderliness of procedure. Ten years in her father's law office had instilled the value of proper procedure. Facts were fundamental to law, and she was on a fact-finding mission. Lathrop tabulated the numbers of inmates and their countries of origin, including the United States, Ireland, Germany, England, Sweden, and so on down to the twenty-ninth country. The numbers of admissions in 1893 added up to 5,651. The taxes paid by middle-class people and by businesses ought to be used for good care, for the treatment and rehabilitation for these people. Back on their feet, many could become self-sustaining. Instead, they vegetated while the tax money went down the drain.[63]

Why? In part because the well-off Chicagoans who would never need Dunning closed their eyes and kept their distance from its realities. Out of sight, the place ran on pure politics. The supervisors and staff were not trained health-care workers or qualified support personnel. They got their jobs through "pull." Dunning, in short, was a jobs program fueled by political patronage. "The charities of Cook County," Lathrop concluded, "will never properly perform their duties until politics are divorced from them."[64]

But how could politics be divorced from civic life? Or rather, how could corrupt politics be weakened and civic life made strong and vital? What could a lady from Rockford do? Climbing Chicago's rickety tenement stairs during a smallpox outbreak was one thing, but reforming a whole system—was it remotely possible? Lathrop came to Hull House to help set democracy on a new course. She wasn't a utopian or Pollyanna. The realist in her struggled to find the foothold for change. But America's "high ideals" could seem like so much "sawdust stuffing" in a doll. Sometimes feeling in a "muddle" and sunk in a Bunyanesque pilgrim's "vale of discouragement," Lathrop kept these feelings to herself. Didn't Archimedes say he could move the world if he had a place to stand? Was Hull House that place? It was more and more of a stretch to think so.[65]

She hadn't yet reached bottom. The dismal lessons of Dunning multiplied as Lathrop toured other state institutions as a member of the public charities board. She met a few admirable professionals, such as Dr. Adolph Meyer of Kankakee, who showed what could be accomplished with a high level of professional ability—but who became so discouraged by corrupt politics that he left for the private Johns Hopkins Hospital in the East. Lathrop, meanwhile, was learning another ghastly lesson: there were institutions far worse than Dunning. Dutifully traveling the length and breadth of Illinois as a public charities board member from 1893 to 1909, she visited "every one of the 102 county farms or almshouses." Typical was the Sangamon County Alms House in Buffalo, Illinois, where contracts for "coal, groceries, and supplies" were awarded through cozy deals with local trustees, while the inmates were ignored and sat with hands folded, "staring into space because they had nothing else to do day after day." The annual almshouse report specified the building repairs, livestock, and fencing—but not a word was written about the inmates, who were officially registered as "olde & infirm, pregnant, insane, perlised, destitud, sore eyes, no home, feebel minded, fits, sore gut, pox, child."[66]

What to do? Her reports alone would not guarantee change. Exposing shameful conditions did not, by itself, spur progress, as Lathrop well knew. If it did, the new popular realist fiction would show measurable results by now. Over twenty years before, in 1871, the novelist Edward Eggleston exposed the horrors of a county poorhouse in his well-received *The Hoosier Schoolmaster*. The book was celebrated for its realism. It described local paupers, including children, who were crowded "like chickens in a coop," and it showed scenes of "people slightly demented and raving maniacs in the same rooms." Eggleston wrote the very same phrases that Lathrop could use in her official inspection reports years later: "Shut in these bare rooms, with no treatment, no exercise, no variety, and meager food, cases of slight derangement soon grew into chronic lunacy." Nothing had changed.[67]

What, then, could she do? The mentally ill and the children especially tugged at her heart—the Dunning children who were humiliated in their hideous clothes and the hapless little ones in the many county poorhouses. And what about the older children who were marooned in the so-called industrial schools for "wayward girls or boys"? These were actually prison schools that ruined children's futures by failing to teach basic job skills. Plus countless so-called street Arab children roamed every American city, including the Hull House neighborhood. They lived hand to mouth, yielding to "temptation" without any notion of "orderly living." To her horror, Lathrop found that most were illiterate and unable to do simple arithmetic.

Many never slept in nightclothes or between bedsheets. Instead of blankets, one little girl slept under newspapers. When no tobacco was at hand, boys smoked their own shoelaces. If they built bonfires or played ball in the street or jumped on and off moving railroad cars, the boys were arrested and sent to "lockups" with hardened criminals. The system was grotesque.[68]

She was a witness, but it was time to act. Each boy who was jailed in the lockup and each "wayward" girl who was sent to an industrial school measured the desperate need for a separate court system for juveniles. Since the Civil War, Lathrop knew, the women's organizations in Chicago had worked on the court project. Among others, two wealthy, spirited women leaders had recently decided the moment was ripe for a renewed effort. To head it, they had their eye on Julia Lathrop, judging her temperament just right for the task. Jane Addams's nephew, James Weber Linn, who spent much time at Hull House, spoke for them when he wrote of her sparkle, her laughter that was "as good as an argument," her great wit and humor. "She always kept her head and her temper," he said. "She did what her hand found to do" and "was contented to wait for results."[69]

It was now the 1890s, and the juvenile court was long overdue. The new campaign must succeed. Everyone in Chicago knew that Lucy Flower (Mrs. James M.) was a genius at persuasion, and Louise DeKoven Bowen (Mrs. Joseph T.) was simply indomitable. The formidable pair pressed Lathrop to become president of the newly formed Juvenile Court Committee. Did she have qualms? Yes. She reminded them of her frequent travels over hundreds of miles for the demanding charity board work and of her Hull House duties too. The reputation of the house was growing, and numerous visitors needed hosting in the evenings. J. A. expected residents to dine with visitors and explain the workings of Hull House. It took hours.

Bowen and Flower swept objections aside, knowing Lathrop could charm the officials into cooperation in a pleasant, genteel atmosphere of "harmony" as "a means to an end." They'd doubtless observed Lathrop's exquisite diplomacy, which her friend, Alice Hamilton, the medical doctor from Hull House, found so remarkable when she went along for a site visit to an institution for the insane. As usual, J. Lathrop looked "becoming" and authoritative in her uniform-like "dark blue tailored suit with a Chinese blue shirt-waist."[70]

To Hamilton's amazement, the "sulky and suspicious" hospital superintendent had "thawed" under Lathrop's "skilful handling" and cordiality. Hamilton heard the man then "pour out all his troubles" and turn "mellow" as they concluded their tour of the institution and returned to his office. The doctor expected a "friendly" departure.[71]

Instead, a captivated Hamilton watched Lathrop sit down and "proceed gently but with devastating thoroughness to go over the whole situation." Lathrop, said Hamilton, reminded the superintendent that "if things were rotten it was he who must shoulder the responsibility" because "after all he was the one in authority." J. Lathrop, what's more, "left him no doubt at all as to how rotten things were." Hamilton was braced for the man's icy retort. It didn't come. Despite Lathrop's "severity," the superintendent listened with "amazing meekness" and promised henceforth to "do his best." The episode stiffened Hamilton's own resolve ever afterward to "say the disagreeable things which it is so much easier to leave unsaid." This was the velvet-glove toughness that moved Louise Bowen and Lucy Flower to tap Lathrop for the juvenile court project.[72]

Lathrop knew the power of a lady went only so far. Her power was persuasion. Chicago women had applied it to elected officials on the issue of juvenile courts since the Civil War years, without success. The juvenile court was still a dream.

Yet today's clubwomen were strong, influential, and numerous. This time, they formed a coalition. The Chicago Woman's Club was to be at the forefront, but consolidated with "other clubs of women, other organizations, civic and philanthropic." Lathrop said yes. Allied with them, she pressured the Illinois legislature to create the juvenile court. Success of successes: the Law for the Care of Dependent, Neglected, and Delinquent Children was enacted in January 1899.[73]

Lathrop, like the clubwomen, concealed her shock at the terms of the law. The cunning legislators provided no salaries for the court officers the law required. Undaunted, the wealthy Bowen and Flower spearheaded a drive to raise money to pay probation officers. They knew "absolutely nothing" about juvenile courts and learned that "no literature on Juvenile courts existed." No matter. The women knew that a probation officer must love children and have "the strength of a Samson and the delicacy of an Ariel." They raised the money, and the court opened with a salaried staff in place in the following July.[74]

They taught Lathrop a cardinal lesson about political strength: that a cluster of organizations could band together and multiply power many times over. Social democracy could be advanced through different organizations acting in concert. Coordination and energy and timing could overcome political inertia. Women did not yet have the right to vote in the state of Illinois—and would not achieve that right until 1913. Nevertheless, women's groups joined together and accomplished a political goal that served the most vulnerable population, the children. A coalition could be a juggernaut for progress.

Lathrop learned a discouraging lesson too. Voluntary organizations had a built-in weakness. They were haphazard. Crudely put, a volunteer was an amateur. Lathrop may have recalled an anecdote that was told about Abraham Lincoln by a Rockford man of her father's generation. In 1850, Ralph Emerson, a cousin of Ralph Waldo, remembered the remark of a young lawyer, Lincoln, who said that self-schooled attorneys like himself trusted too much to "the inspiration of the moment." Lincoln vowed to "study law" in order to compete with "college trained men who . . . study on a single case perhaps for months." This was the kind of professionalism that lawyers and physicians and engineers were developing in the latter years of the nineteenth century and anticipating in the twentieth. Leading medical schools within universities were now emphasizing specialization, research, and clinical science. The shop-floor engineer was giving way to the university-trained professional, and attorneys were increasingly trained in university schools of law, not in the offices of local lawyers.[75]

What about those who tried to meet the challenges of modern society—family problems, workplace problems, housing, health care, and so on? They, too, badly needed professional training. Politicians would not provide good leadership on these complex matters. The reeking, overflowing garbage boxes and the smallpox episode were proof of their dangerous laxity. The corrupt Nineteenth Ward alderman, Johnny Powers, was a perfect specimen of the breed. A constant thorn in the side of Hull House, Powers was dubbed the "Gray Wolf" for preying on a defenseless public. Powers "traded votes for favors" and excelled at bribery. As the garbage and horse manure piled up, he wooed the ward's gullible poor with Christmas turkeys.[76]

Well-meaning citizen volunteers, meanwhile, found themselves overwhelmed when faced with complex social problems. Each "solution" opened a Pandora's box. Louise Bowen remarked that the city's problems seemed obvious until the Juvenile Protective Association tried to help; then found they "hardly knew where to begin."[77]

What Julia Clifford Lathrop knew from the Chicago years was that one must record the facts of these lives as hard data, including numbers. The facts, what's more, must speak loudly and clearly to the better-off public as if through a new device, the megaphone. A favorite writer of hers, Mrs. Stowe, wrote that "the muscles are dependent on the brain and nerves for power to move." A progressive movement, Lathrop understood, required the muscle, brain, and nerves of many individuals and groups acting together for a common purpose. The juvenile court movement in Chicago proved that point beyond doubt. The traditional feminine "power of tenderness and sympathy" was important, but taking the reins was everything. These days, the driver's seat belonged to the "sociologist and statistician" and social worker. This was the seat of hard facts and figures, statistics, and careful research. Men had claimed the seat in economics and other fields. As far as Lathrop could tell, hard data belonged to women as well. In this modern moment, a woman ought to know how to seek and get hold of her facts and figures. Jane Addams might rely on wellsprings of hidden wisdom, but Lathrop did not. Some said that this was the age of the engineer. If so, she allied with it. As a social reformer, she was a social engineer. Her mother, Adeline, had long lamented that Julia was not spiritually moved to join the church. At the turn of the twentieth century, Julia had found her intellectual center and her faith. Ever the lady, she gazed at the world as a social scientist.[78]

Lathrop's efforts were now two-pronged in the 1900s and 1910s: first, to help create a modern professional school for social work training and research; second, to help make the volunteer-amateur citizen as effective as possible. For the latter, she went to her Hull House desk late at night, set out pens, and opened her inkwell. Drawing on more than ten years' experience, she composed a training manual for citizen-visitors who evaluated public institutions. It would be a pamphlet, as welcoming as a hot cup of tea and yet coldly scientific as an evaluation tool.

The visitor's encounter must be reliably courteous, she emphasized, and the task approached in a spirit "of friendly co-operation and helpfulness . . . tact and patience." This amounted to a code of conduct. No matter what the mood or temperament of the visitor, he or she would behave in a standardized way. Visitors also needed focus. Left to their own devices, they could be distracted by trivialities and miss the critical factors. A woman like New York's Vinnie Day would probably swipe a white-gloved finger across a surface to check for dust specks yet ignore the drugs and mechanical restraints that subdued patients who ought to be taken out for fresh air and exercise. The visitors also needed to understand the laws that governed the institutions, so Lathrop cited the provisions of the Illinois state statute on "lunacy," trusting that those in other states who might chance to see her pamphlet would research their own laws.[79]

A checklist was also important. Drawn up as a chart, it gave site visitors clear categories for convenient documentation over a series of visits. Under "Buildings," for instance, a visitor could check "Fire-escape" and make a quick note. Under "Care of Inmates," she or he could find "Cleanliness" and jot a comment. There must be practical advice too, for instance, on supplying decks of cards and chess sets for recreation, and ridding bedding of lice and other vermin.[80]

Lathrop concluded her pamphlet with the heading "Need of a Standard."

She urged repeated inspections at sites across Illinois, deliberately making the pamphlet a data file. It could cross-reference information from one visitor to the next, from one county or state institution to the next, until the picture of treatment statewide came clearly into view. The coyly titled *Suggestions for Institution Visitors* represented a newer way of thinking. It moved effective action out of the realm of personalities. Instead of hit-or-miss, it enabled a dependable assessment. It provided the machinery for putting results above political favoritism.

Lathrop glimpsed even greater possibilities for the future. Her *Suggestions for Institution Visitors* was the kind of instrument to cross the boundary line from one state of the union to the next, until the nation had a measured view of its treatment of those who depended on public funding for their lives. This was the mental outlook that belonged to sociology, social work, and statistics. These, in turn, were the components of civic life, of social democracy.

Suggestions for Institution Visitors was published in 1905, just when Lathrop accepted a second charities board appointment that would run to 1909. Her schedule was crammed, and in the freezing Chicago winter, she now shuttled excitedly from Hull House to a building on Michigan Avenue, where a new, irresistible opportunity awaited her. A school for social research and the professional training of social workers was just launched in Chicago, and Lathrop eagerly became a faculty member. The school's founder was himself a settlement house director, a Protestant minister named Graham Taylor who recognized the limitations of settlement houses as educational institutions. They were not meant to sponsor research. They were not created to train practitioners for a new discipline. Only a school could do these things. In 1903, Taylor rented space in a downtown Chicago building and taught a semester-long course to twelve fledgling students in the new profession of social work. Lathrop soon came into his orbit and stepped up to teach a course on public charities, covering the topics dear to her heart and mind: public relief, institutions for the insane, and public responsibility for the disabled and the chronically ill.[81]

Lathrop was afire. The new school could take social work and research in a wholly new direction. If it could survive financially and keep its independence, it was the perfect platform for major breakthroughs in public thinking about assistance to those in need. Above all, Lathrop knew, professional social work must not be a glorified version of the charitable "friendly visit" to the homes of the poor and luckless. The traditional caseworker who treated clients as criminals who had deliberately committed the crime of poverty was a version of the Dunning relief station with its winter food basket. The worker who offered mere palliatives was a distant cousin of Johnny Powers with his Christmas turkeys. The organization that promoted these views was the Charity Organization Society, based in New York City. Dangerously old-fashioned, it impeded social democracy because it pushed low-wage and chronically ill and disabled people to the margins, where they remained social outcasts in the minds of respectable people like the senior Clarence Days.[82]

Gazing eastward, Lathrop would not be surprised to learn that the senior Clarence Day—Father—contributed to the Charity Organization Society, for its notion of charity pleased the true believers in laissez-faire. The soft-hearted Mother—Vinnie Day—tucked envelopes with contributions to hospitals, orphanages, the fresh-air fund. But she gave no thought to social work or its conception, even as the Charity Organization Society gained strength in their city. Lathrop knew it was Chicago's turn to talk back. It was Chicago's turn to set the new reform agenda.[83]

Lathrop became the first director of the Chicago School of Civics and Philanthropy. At her insistence, *civics* was a key term in the name. The school exposed the ways in which the conditions of modern industry contributed to poverty. It taught that the state or government must play a positive role to rectify abysmal social conditions. This role was justified by a merit system—the civil service system—that officially sidelined the spoils system of politics. The horrible assassination of President Garfield by a frustrated office seeker in 1881 had prompted the passage of the Pendleton Act two years later. The waste and graft of the spoils system, it was hoped, would yield to the efficiency and economy of a civil service workforce of professionals who were hired on the basis of competitive examinations. The Pendleton Act did not abolish political patronage, but it set political appointees apart from those placed in the merit service. Oversight of the new system was entrusted to three civil service commissioners. During the Altgeld years, Lathrop had helped put this system in place for the recruitment of physicians at the state hospitals. It worked. It gave her confidence that the high-quality experts within the civil service could be the arm of government best able to strengthen social democracy. "The study of the apparatus of government formed a central component of the Chicago School of Civics and Philanthropy."[84]

Toward these ends, Lathrop knew, the Chicago school must become a leading center for social research in this modern age of fact-based science. Everyone who was involved in the push for the juvenile court in the late 1890s remembered the scramble to make do with anecdotes about street boys and exploited girls. Anecdotes, however, were not data. *Scientific* was now Lathrop's byword, and she worked for rigorous social research that was undertaken by the most sophisticated methods for the collection and analysis of data — and policies then developed from the data. In 1907, a grant from the Russell Sage Foundation let Lathrop create a department of social research at the School of Civics and Philanthropy. It was thrilling to be able to recruit a new generation of professionally trained younger women to undertake it. The Abbott sisters, Edith and Grace, together with Sophonisba ("Nisba") Breckenridge, all with their Ph.D.'s, augured well for the post–Gilded Age future.[85]

The school survived, and Lathrop reluctantly left it as she left Chicago when the Children's Bureau position drew her to Washington in 1912. The irony was palpable: she who had criticized the failings of American politics for years was now to work in its national epicenter. From now on, Lathrop kept her eye on the School of Civics and Philanthropy at long distance from the Children's Bureau headquarters on the fifth floor of the Department of Labor. Finally, in 1920, the school became a part of the University of Chicago. Renamed the School of Social Service Administration, it conferred master's and Ph.D. degrees.

By then, Lathrop had lived in Washington, D.C., for eight years, serving the entire time as Children's Bureau chief. She missed Chicago terribly, and she loved hosting Florence Kelley and Alice Hamilton in her apartment when duty brought them to the capital. The Hull House old friends swapped ideas, plotted strategy, and vented their secret grievances while enjoying Lathrop's homemade omelets or brown buttered oysters.

The eight years — 1912 to 1920 — of her directorship of the Children's Bureau were dynamic, not a minute to spare. The bureau's first small staff of fifteen expanded to seventy-five, and Congress accordingly increased the budget. The chief breathed easier when the prenatal and infant care pamphlets of 1913–14 became runaway successes printed in the multimillions and requested by members of Congress for their constituents. Baby fairs were staged, together with an annual Baby Week and a 1918–19 American Children's Year, all to reinforce the needs for the public protection of maternity and infancy, for wholesome recreation, and for free public schooling for all. The registration of births nationwide was an enormous undertaking, and the bureau enlisted the help of committees of women, mostly members of the General Federation of Women's Clubs, to canvass and organize birth records in all forty-eight states. The pamphlet-manual Lathrop wrote for institution visitors stood her in good stead as the bureau organized the massive birth registration drive.[86]

How did Lathrop weather the constant political storms of Washington? More important, how effective was the Children's Bureau under her direc-

The health of the child is the power of the nation

APRIL 1918   Children's Year   APRIL 1919
UNITED STATES CHILDREN'S BUREAU AND WOMAN'S COMMITTEE OF THE COUNCIL OF NATIONAL DEFENSE

Children's Year poster, 1918–19, cosponsored by U.S. Children's Bureau and Woman's Committee of the Council of National Defense. (Library of Congress)

tion and beyond? One recent historian of the agency, Kriste Lindenmeyer, points out that an ever-expanding Washington bureaucracy tended to lessen the power and influence of the bureau over the course of the twentieth century. She emphasizes a point all too familiar to Lathrop and her colleagues, that "minors are a particularly vulnerable constituency who have little power in a government controlled by adults" and that "the most defenseless children tend to come from socioeconomic groups with little political voice." In the Lathrop era, moreover, the bureau's conception of the "whole child" was the child of a traditional patriarchal family, with its male breadwinner and stay-at-home wife-mother. Neither Lathrop nor the younger researchers and civic groups who worked with the bureau were able to recognize that social democracy must be expanded to include the single-parent family and the mother who worked outside the home.[87]

Lindenmeyer, however, points out that the Children's Bureau "contributed significantly to the growing recognition of childhood as a period of life demanding special attention and direction." She adds that its studies were often "the first 'scientific' investigations into the circumstances of particular groups of children." Its data led to "the nation's first maternal and infant health care program (the 1921 Sheppard-Towner Act), child labor regulation, and the inclusion of children's programs in the 1935 Social Security Act." As another bureau historian has remarked, the Children's Bureau became "the central, and in some cases the sole, source of authoritative information about the welfare of children and their families throughout the United States."[88]

The U.S. Children's Bureau continues today as part of the Administration for Children and Families within the U.S. Department of Health and Human Services. According to its mission statement, "The Children's Bureau seeks to provide for the safety, permanency and well being of children through leadership, support for necessary services, and productive partnerships with States, Tribes, and communities." Inclusive and comprehensive, the statement reflects the continuing legacy of Julia Clifford Lathrop and those who worked with her. Her statement to the National Education Association in Milwaukee on July 5, 1919, speaks clearly to twenty-first-century America and to a globalized world. "We cannot help the world toward democracy if we despise democracy at home," she told the educators. Democracy, she explained, "is despised when mother or child die needlessly. It is despised in the person of every child who is left to grow up ignorant, weak, unskilled, unhappy, no matter what his race or color."[89]

Florence Kelley
The Wages of Work

The old theory was that enlightened self-interest could be trusted to conduct industry, that the sum of all selfish interests would coincide with public interest. Tested in practice, however, this theory has not sustained modern life. Industry conducted for profit and regulated only by the pressure of competition . . . has produced, among its fruits, the maximum cynical disregard of the manhood, womanhood and childhood of the workers, and a loss of moral responsibility in the relation of the owners of industry to the consuming public.—**FLORENCE KELLEY,** *Modern Industry in Relation to the Family, Health, Education, Morality,* 1914

She [Florence Kelley] took a fixed fierce resolution: she would make the salvation of women and children from blind industrial greed the work of her life. . . . Her studies impressed on her the necessity of the *state* to prevent the modern industrial system from destroying its own workers. —**JAMES WEBER LINN,** *Jane Addams: A Biography,* 1935

Mrs. Kelley entered upon her lifelong mission of interpreting the effects of court decisions upon American life.—**JOSEPHINE GOLDMARK,** *Impatient Crusader: Florence Kelley's Life Story,* 1953

We find her tool marks on paving stones all along the road . . . [toward] our nationwide advances in law and administration . . . whether in setting maximum hours or minimum wages, in safeguarding children, in the social insurances or industrial relations.—**PAUL KELLOGG,** "The Living Spirit of Florence Kelley," 1940

January 1899. A New England gentleman, John Graham Brooks, caught a New York Central train for Chicago. The famous Water Level Route sped him along the Hudson River and Lakes Ontario and Erie until he crossed the frozen stubble fields and industrial zone of Indiana and reached Chicago's Union Station. Brooks's destination was Hull House, where he'd lived for a few months in 1896 while teaching a course in the city. At age fifty-two, the former Unitarian minister was well known in Progressive social circles. He traveled and lectured widely, but this January, Brooks came to Chicago for one express purpose only—to persuade Mrs. Florence Kelley to accept a new and untried position in New York. But he had no illusions about recruiting her. It wouldn't be easy.

Brooks thought he had one advantage. He knew that Mrs. Kelley had lost patience with conventional philanthropy and charity. They treated the symptoms of social disorder, she said, but not root causes. "Content to patch and darn, to piece and cobble," they helped a few but "sacrificed tens of thousands." Brooks saw his best chance in Mrs. Kelley's critique. Her well-known "sense of right," he'd say, could now be channeled broadly toward social and economic justice. In their face-to-face conversation, he planned to emphasize that the new position could let Kelley improve the lives of multitudes of working children and adults. He hoped this was true. In fact, Brooks was not at all certain that the high-voltage Florence Kelley would accept the position—or, for that matter, that it was a stage wide and deep enough for her outsize talents.[1]

For herself, Florence Kelley wasn't feeling like a high-voltage woman this January, though she'd agreed to meet with Brooks and find out what was on his mind. Cloaked against the piercing winter wind, she boarded a street railway grip car and made her way nightly from Hull House to work at the John Crerar Library at the corner of Wabash and Washington streets. Each evening, Mrs. Kelley staffed the periodicals room, which held an abundance of journals in science and technology.[2]

She tried to be grateful for the job. The century's end, however, seemed to coincide with the dead end of Florence Kelley's career. At age forty, the former chief inspector of factories for Illinois was now a low-level library assistant. Her life in the last two years had all the earmarks of a melodrama on the old Chicago Opera House stage. Popular titles like *The Dangers of the City* and *The Hidden Hand* could well apply to her shattered career. Two years before, Mrs. Kelley had held an important position as state factory inspector in the administration of the governor of Illinois. These evenings, however, found her in self-confessed "drudgery" while the icy winter wind screamed outside. Attorneys, businessmen, and engineers doffed their hats and heavy mackintosh box coats when they arrived to use the library at the close of their regular workday.[3]

The patrons appreciated Mrs. Kelley's help locating articles they sought in *Iron Age* and the *National Industrial Review* and similar journals. They found the librarian to be a pleasant woman with a "flutelike voice." She was "built on large lines" with a "wide generous mouth," a "squarish jaw," and a dark-eyed, "direct and fearless" gaze. She pinned up her heavy, dark, coiled braids and wore practical clothes instead of the customary women's corsets, high

Florence Kelley. (Records of the National Consumers' League, Library of Congress)

heels, several petticoats, and white gloves. Fashionable in neither dress nor coiffeur, she was the very model of a librarian.[4]

The Crerar patrons otherwise knew very little about her. It would surprise them to learn that she was the daughter of a prominent, late U.S. congressman from Philadelphia and herself a graduate (1882) of Cornell University. It might raise eyebrows to learn that she was fluent in French and German, had pursued advanced study in law at the University of Zurich, and was well known to Chicago's influential women's clubs as a forceful public speaker and writer. There was more. Since arriving with her three children in Chicago in 1891, Florence Kelley had lived at Hull House and had conducted a demographic study of Chicago's slum neighborhoods. She earned a law degree in the city and served for four years as an appointee of Governor John P. Altgeld. As factory inspector, she headed a team of twelve who traveled the entire state of Illinois investigating conditions in its "workshops, factories, and manufacturing establishments."[5]

It might surprise the Crerar Library patrons, further, to learn that Kelley's inspections were conducted under milestone legislation that she herself had helped to create in 1893. The law established a state factory inspection system, and it limited the workday to eight hours for women. To employ a child between the ages of fourteen and sixteen required an affidavit from a parent or guardian certifying his or her age, together with a doctor's certification of physical fitness. Children under fourteen were banned from "any branch of manufacture."[6]

In part, Kelley had helped shape this first Illinois labor law by leading the state's rural lawmakers on a tour of the tenement sweatshops that she knew firsthand from Hull House life on Halsted Street. The legislators had expected a good-time "junket to Chicago." Instead, Mrs. Kelley exposed them to grim "sights that few legislators had ever beheld." She also gave speeches to several labor rights groups and civic organizations in order to encourage them to support the innovative legislation. These groups, in turn, successfully pressed the lawmakers for its passage. Governor John P. Altgeld promptly signed the bill into law. Kelley began her work as factory inspector with a reasonable travel budget and a good, middle-class yearly salary of $1,500. At the time, she was confident that within a year, the new sweatshop law would make "the long hours and unsanitary conditions . . . a thing of the past."[7]

How naive she was back then. What a snare and delusion the road to progress turned out to be. The scenes that she saw as factory inspector haunted her to this day and hadn't changed at all. The annual reports that she wrote and submitted to the governor—including the report that she'd completed in slack hours here in the Crerar Library—gave her no peace of mind. On the contrary, Florence Kelley burned with rage, for Illinois was plagued by child labor and exhausted women workers at this very minute. She was cooped up in this library while little boys in the stockyards sorted animal entrails and "cut the hide from the quivering flesh of freshly stunned cattle." Some of them operated dangerous machinery. In a vicious cycle, boy workers substituted for their fathers who were recovering from injuries from the very machines their sons now manned until the fathers were well enough to return to the risky jobs.[8]

Other industries were equally horrifying. In the glassworks in Alton, Illinois, the managers dismissed the children's tasks as "light and easy," but Kelley saw the reality of "young children, with heads and hands bandaged" from burns "from melting glass." She learned that "children 7 and 8 years old work[ed] until 3 a.m." Their jobs as "blower dogs" required them to run constantly over dusty pathways strewn with broken glass. In winter, the "scantily

Boy workers stuff sausages in meatpacking plant, 1893. (Library of Congress)

clad," fatigued children risked pneumonia when they dashed from "the hot air beside the furnaces out over the ice [on] the frozen [Mississippi] river." Kelley learned that when a poor mother with a small son applied for public assistance, Alton's mayor sent them "to the glass works together." Both mother and son were employed there, and the mother now bore the costs of new clothes and shoes to replace those that were burned by hot cinders or by "fragments of cooling glass."[9]

In the steam laundries, what's more, Kelley's team found children operating mangles and other treacherous machines. "Exhausted from overwork in the heat and steam," the children risked infection from handling "soiled clothing on its way to the washing machine." Kelley noted that at one laundry, children had "worked last Saturday from 7:30 in the morning until Sunday morning at 3 o'clock."[10]

All this work brutalized the children. The stockyard boys were injured in both "body and mind," and the youngsters in the glassworks, as Kelley wrote in her report, were "ill-fed, ill-clothed, profane, obscene, and in many cases unable to work without stimulants." Many were illiterate. Many had never seen the inside of a school, where they all belonged. As a mother of two sons and a daughter, Kelley personally knew that the children's futures and the nation's own depended on education.[11]

She also knew how entrenched and formidable was the opposition to their schooling. The poor parents who lived hand to mouth took their children out of school and sent them to work so the family could supposedly get ahead in America. This "false ideal" was ignorantly shortsighted. Yet the middle class supported the system too. Well-off employers profited from cheap child labor, and affluent Americans believed that grinding toil instilled "the habit of industry, which cannot be acquired too young." Notions of charity were also involved. By truly "perverted" reasoning, many Americans thought poorer children ought to earn income to help support widowed mothers and disabled fathers. They failed to see that the public ought to take responsibility for the well-being of these families.[12]

The double standard across class lines was the height of hypocrisy. The well-off would never dream of permitting their own children to go to work, and yet they swore that constant toil instilled discipline and character in the children of the poor. A gentleman like Mr. Clarence Day had this very attitude. His four rambunctious, red-headed boys, including Clarence Jr., were enrolled in prep school near the family's Madison Avenue brownstone in New York. The seven children of his coachman, O'Dowd, were another story. As we have seen, Mr. Day denied the O'Dowd children the tax dollars needed to construct a decent new school. He was not alone. Many public schools in New York, Illinois, and elsewhere lacked enough places for the children who tried to enroll. They were turned away at the door.[13]

What would it take to change the minds and prompt progressive action by men like Mr. Day? What would get the attention of ladies like Vinnie Day, a woman in "prosperous circumstances," a woman "to whom leisure has come unsought, a free gift of the new industrial order"? Mrs. Day enjoyed "flowing water, gaslight and electricity, modern facilities for heating and cooking, foods prepared outside the home, garments bought ready-made or made to order." All such "contrivances" gave Mrs. Day an expansive "leisure" that she accepted as "an unqualified right." It was the same right enjoyed by her friends up and down Madison Avenue and elsewhere. A recent best-selling book by the economist Thorstein Veblen had bitingly explored the topmost reaches of their world: *The Theory of the Leisure Class*.[14]

Yet women like Vinnie Day seemed blind to the need for restful leisure for wage earners like the textile and garment workers who made her cloaks and other clothing. The Vinnie Days of America must be made to understand that a guarantee of health-giving rest for body and mind wasn't to promote laziness or sloth. A Saturday half holiday and a summer vacation would do a world of good. Restorative rest and personal time would surely increase efficiency in industry and cut the injury rate for factory and mill workers too. "The establishment of reasonable daily leisure in the lives of working people" was a moral and practical matter. Why didn't people like the Days understand the terrible toll that ignorance and relentless toil took on the whole country? Why, Florence Kelley asked, wasn't it obvious to everybody?[15]

The "everybody" included her own late father. He too had a baffling blind spot. An ardent abolitionist who had struggled as a poor boy himself, Congressman William "Pig Iron" Kelley railed against the injustice of slavery. He championed the rights of workers. After the Civil War, he spoke eloquently on the floor of the U.S. Congress about the human cost of an unschooled population of southern poor whites, the "dirt-eaters." He called for "common schools" to "offer shelter and culture to the laborer's child." He was a man of conscience. The family had Quaker roots. When Florence was a little girl, her father gave her a "terrible" picture book showing child laborers in an English brickyard, their legs so crooked and their frames so splayed that the children "looked like little gnomes." The father-to-daughter lesson was clear: child labor was horrid, and no group in America should be degraded and kept ignorant.[16]

William Kelley, however, faltered when he took twelve-year-old Florence to view the spectacle of modern, post–Civil War American industry. In 1871, father and daughter saw a blazing steel mill and a glass factory. William Kelley was dazzled by the new Bessemer converter, a giant cauldron of white-hot liquid fire. The high-volume production of bottles bewitched him as well. Entranced, he failed to notice that his daughter's eyes were on the child workers. Boys smaller than she hauled heavy pails of drinking water for the men in the steel mill, just as the glass plant boys, "blower dogs," cleaned and scraped bottle molds and crouched with their heads near the furnaces of molten glass. No adult in sight thought this abnormal. Florence got the "astonished impression of the utter unimportance of children compared with products." At home in Philadelphia, it was she, not her father, who was troubled by the sight of "pasty-faced little working children in jail-like textile mills" in the Manayunk area of the city. The scenes haunted her. State by state, Kelley was convinced, modern labor laws must be enacted. Legislation and education must go hand in hand. The new Illinois sweatshop law of 1893 was meant to be a big step toward changing hearts and minds—and children's and women workers' lives.[17]

At first, factory inspector Kelley was sure the law would work. She had no doubts. She was unfazed by the first sign of trouble in 1893, when she took a child labor case to a "brisk young politician" in Chicago's Cook County prosecutor's office. Kelley presented him these facts: An eleven-year-old boy was hired to gild picture frames with a "poisonous fluid" that paralyzed his right arm. The employer had violated the provision banning workers younger than sixteen. On that basis, the case was clear cut.[18]

The young prosecutor, however, stared at Kelley with "impudent surprise." Mildly astonished, he asked, "Are you calculating on *my* taking the case?"

Armed with the new law, Kelley retorted, "I thought you were the district attorney."

"Well," he said, "suppose I am." Then he flaunted his disdain for the case—and for the woman factory inspector. "You bring me this evidence this week against some little two-by-six cheap picture-frame maker—and how do I know you won't bring me a suit against Marshall Field next week?"

A chasm opened between them. The name of Chicago's powerful premier retailer was a taunt. It meant the boy with the paralyzed arm was to be sacrificed for the prosecutor's political ambition. In truth, Kelley was fully prepared to bring suit against any violator, including the department store titan Marshall Field. Why, Field set a terrible example. He paid a sweatshop "home" worker a meager $9.37 for thirteen weeks' hard work. Field showed shameless hypocrisy in a long, face-to-face interview with Kelley. He portrayed the woman worker as one of the "worthy widows working at home with their children." Piously, Field said he would not bring himself to "deprive" her of such an earnings opportunity.[19]

Deprive? Kelley had other words for the starvation wages and exploitation.

"Don't count on me," sneered the cocky young prosecutor. "I'm overloaded. I wouldn't reach this case inside of two years."

It was a splash of cold reality. The boy with the paralyzed arm was dismissed by an official who despised the public he had sworn to serve. Kelley was about to learn—to her sorrow and fury—that countless officials like him ignored violations in the factories where young girls "contracted permanent disability from operating the heavy foot-power machine." Mere children, they handled cloth "that was heavy, stiff, and dyed with injurious dyes." These young workers wrestled with serge and worsted, taffeta and whipcord, and a host of other difficult fabrics. Production mattered, not the young girl workers.[20]

Chicago's netherworld of sweatshops was another horror that officials like the prosecutor seemed loath to deal with. From the wilting summer heat to subzero winters, adults and children staggered under back-breaking bundles of ready-made clothing to be finished with hand-sewn buttons or trim work for pittances in their tenement dwellings. The foul, airless living quarters became workshops—sewing sweatshops—that sapped a family's energy, leaving adults and children exhausted and sickened.

Middle-class women who bought fashionable clothing with the labels of "large and widely known companies," such as Joseph Beifeld and Company, would surely be shocked to learn that their cloaks and capes and shirtwaists came from a "low-ceilinged and dirty" home "shop" over a stable at 159 West Taylor Street. Inside, the workers hunched over tables or mattresses to trim cloaks and other garments with beading, sequins, fur, and lace. Straining their eyes, they cramped their hands as they sewed on the fasteners, including toggles and smoked pearl and horn buttons. The shop on West Taylor consisted of one room with a "dirty" sink that gave off rank odors that mixed, in turn, with manure smells from the stable and also with vapors from the gasoline used in pressing. Kelley's factory inspector report described "a stench unbearable alike in winter and summer."[21]

What kind of person knowingly profited from such conditions? Kelley's deputy factory inspector, Abraham Bisno, had tutored her on this point. Bisno, a Jewish immigrant and labor organizer, knew the story personally. He knew to his very marrow the kind of man who succeeded in these terms and became a clothing magnate like the cloak maker Joseph Beifeld. Bisno abhorred the type. Beifeld-style success, Bisno told Kelley, required a level of extreme human iciness that most men could not summon. A man like Beifeld, of immigrant stock, first saw the opportunity to exploit his fellow immigrants by hiring them "very cheaply." He typically began with a loan of a few dollars for a used sewing machine, press irons, and rent for a small, cheap space. He thus became a contractor who "manages to get help cheaper than the manufacturer can." Bisno explained the situation to his boss, Mrs. Kelley. "Men efficient at that class of enterprise," he said, "must be able to bargain for the very last sou [cent]. They must completely dispossess themselves of normal human sympathy." They thus employ "the poorest of the poor and the most helpless." They necessarily "drive them to get work out of them, and next, pay them . . . barely enough for their living." The working men and women, said Bisno, "suffered great hardship in the industry."[22]

The "rush" season was especially brutal. "When a girl in a sweatshop is unable to ply her machine, by foot power, from seven in the morning to four the next morning, the sweater tells her . . . that there are others who will take her place and do his work on his terms." The union leader, Samuel Gompers, an acquaintance of Bisno, knew how cunning the clothing manufacturers could be. Some of them deliberately cast their eyes on the old country to seek out Russian Jewish victims of political "oppression" and "cruelty." They then encouraged them to come to the United States. Pretending to take an interest in their welfare, the manufacturers put the newcomers to work in sweatshop bedrooms "where they worked from early morning to late at night" for "miserable low wages."[23]

Once he became successful as a manufacturer, Bisno said, a man like Beifeld did not change, not even with a fine modern factory blazoned with his name and pictured on seasonal catalogues. In the early 1880s, Bisno told Kelley, Beifeld and Company employed about 350 workers in its seven-story factory at Jackson Boulevard and Market Street, in the heart of Chicago's apparel industry. Eleven years later, in 1893, the company severely shrank its workforce while expanding its business 600 percent. How? By outsourcing its cloak making to subcontractors and sweatshops.[24]

Was this the hallmark of success? Unchecked, did the Joseph Beifelds own America strictly on their terms? And the Marshall Fields? And the stockyard meat packers, Augustus Swift and Philip Armour? And the Illinois Glass Company? And the lackey prosecutors and their ilk who were always willing to grease the way—all while the Clarence Days and William Kelleys wrapped their wives in sweatshop cloaks and ignored the fate of whole populations of unschooled child workers?

These were the issues that deviled Florence Kelley month in and month out in the Crerar Library reading room. How deceptively easy it had seemed, at first, to bring the malefactors to justice under the new law. She relished her first flush of success as factory inspector in 1893. She'd boasted to Governor Altgeld of the victory against Beifeld, one of many women's apparel firms that prospered in Chicago after the disastrous fire of 1871. The court ruling was especially sweet because Beifeld had become one of the nation's major manufacturers of cloaks, a mainstay of women's wardrobes. Year-round, the classic "up to date" and "distinctive" cloak (or the shorter cape) was essential for the respectable American woman who was careful to reveal little of herself in public. As one 1890s etiquette manual put it, "The true lady walks the street wrapped in a mantle of proper reserve so impenetrable that insult and coarse familiarity shrink from her."[25]

The pivotal moment began modestly. Two underage children were found working for a Beifeld subcontractor, and a jury trial found the subcontractor, or "sweater," guilty as charged and imposed a fine of three dollars and court costs. To the new factory inspector, the verdict and the three-dollar fine proved that the legal system could work. They showed that not all prosecutors, judges, and jurors were as cynical as the corrupt official who dismissed the boy with the paralyzed arm. The case showed that law enforcement eventually could eliminate child labor and the horrible sweatshops. It could curtail the work shifts of ten, twelve, sixteen hours at a stretch. An optimist by nature, Kelley began to plan the next step — new laws to require workplace safety. And new rules penalizing employers whose workers were injured by toxins or hazardous, unguarded machinery. She would strive to outlaw the "poisonous fluid" that paralyzed the boy's arm and the exposed naked blades that sawed off a hand or an arm in the blink of an eye. Getting it done was a matter of civic organization and legislation.[26]

The future seemed so bright, and Kelley did everything to get ready, even squeezing in night school at Northwestern University's Union College of Law. Fortunately, it welcomed women. In the high-ceilinged lecture hall, she studied alongside men who were bound for corporate careers in insurance, real estate, railroads, brewing, and the city's new communications industry, notably the company that became Western Union. Like her classmates, Kelley learned to draw up legal documents. Unlike the corporate careerists, however, she meant to use the law as an instrument for social progress. Chattel slavery had ended with the Civil War, but the vile slave labor system that took its place must be smashed. The law would soon do its work for justice.[27]

If only she'd heeded Bisno's warning that their team's victory against the "sweater" was only a token win. How naive of her to trust that businesses would simply comply with the new law. Instead, they swiftly got organized and marshaled their forces against her. They too grasped the far-reaching implications of the little court case that they lost. If Mrs. Kelley wasn't stopped, their business practices could be crippled. Joseph Beifeld wasted no time joining with others to form the Illinois Manufacturers' Association. It spared no expense. It exerted political pressure and commanded a battery of top lawyers. It filed suit against the sweatshop law and challenged it all the way to the Illinois Supreme Court.[28]

The case of *Ritchie v. People* was the test. W. C. Ritchie and Company, a paper box manufacturer, challenged the eight-hour provision of the sweatshop law. The legal brief on Kelley's side focused on the need to protect women's reproductive biology. The Illinois Supreme Court decision, however, ruled that the law was discriminatory. The court said the law arbitrarily restricted "the fundamental right of the citizen to control his or her own time." The court said it "took away the right of private judgment as to the amount and duration of the labor to be put forth in a specific period." The court, in

Elegant script on seasonal catalogue of Joseph Beifeld, women's clothier, 1892–93.
Note detailing of jacket. (Amador Collection, Archives and Special Collections Depart-
ment, Rio Grande Historical Collections, New Mexico State University Library)

Tenement sweatshop labor, 1912, photographed and described by Lewis W. Hine: "High up on the top floor of a rickety tenement, 214 Elizabeth St., N.Y., this mother and her two children, boy 10 years old and girl 12, were living in a tiny one room, and were finishing garments. The garments were packed under the bed and on top of it and around the room. Said [she makes] from $1 to $2 a week, and the boys [sic] earns some selling newspapers." (Library of Congress)

short, presumed that a worker on the job for twelve or fourteen hours daily had freely agreed to such a schedule. The supreme court unanimously upheld the laissez-faire philosophy of the Gilded Age. Worse, as Kelley realized, a good many women workers took the side of the box maker. They were eager to work themselves to the bone and to an early grave for a few extra, precious pennies. Until a living wage could be earned in a reasonable work week, Kelley knew, a worker was basically a slave.[29]

As if to rub salt in an open wound, the noxious sweatshops she'd tried to shut down as the state's factory inspector now thrived in Chicago, more virulent than ever at the end of the century. And child workers were toiling everywhere because the required medical certificates were dispensed "to all comers" with "reckless" abandon by company-employed physicians and were sold on the street for as little as twenty-five cents. Everything she'd worked for in the mid-1890s had collapsed like a house of cards. Governor Altgeld lost his reelection bid in 1896, and the new governor was an ally of the industries that Kelley had successfully fought in court. He fired her. The new factory inspector came from the Illinois Glass Company. It was back to business as usual, and she was suddenly jobless.[30]

They'd slapped her down. They'd penned her in. At first, the setback seemed temporary. Shocked by the firing and wretched without a salary, she sprang into action. As a single mother with three young children to support, she had no choice. Thanks to Hull House, she'd had a home ever since the wintry day in late December 1891, when she'd rung the bell, unannounced, at the thick oak front door with her children at her side. Jane Addams—who was Hull House itself—opened the door and "welcomed" Kelley and her brood of three as if they were "invited." Kelley's third-floor bedroom "cell" overlooking the little courtyard with its fountain was the very dearest home space of her entire life. The residents' footsteps were the sounds of social action on the rise. Hull House meant vitality, spirit, intellectual spark, and drive.[31]

It also meant help for her job search. Jane Addams networked on her behalf, and powerful women in Chicago made helpful inquiries. Prospects at first seemed bright. Openings for factory inspectors were announced at the national and state levels. President William McKinley had a position to offer, as did the governor of New York, Theodore Roosevelt, whose state had a wretched record of factory child labor. Little ones of eight and nine years old worked day and night in mill towns like Utica, while four-year-olds rolled cigars and toiled in button works in the city.[32]

Who better to appoint than Florence Kelley? She was experienced, superbly well qualified, and nationally known from years of speaking and writing on the topic of labor. She'd researched and written on labor law since her senior thesis days as a Cornell undergraduate in the late 1870s and early 1880s. She was respected by the U.S. commissioner of commerce and labor, Carroll D. Wright, who'd named her to survey the square-mile slum around Hull House in 1892. This became the *Hull House Maps and Papers* fieldwork project that yielded pathbreaking color-coded grid maps. The maps showed, block by block, the concentrations of immigrant workers by race, ethnicity, and income. The project proved that African Americans' wages were lowest, and those of immigrant workers from English-speaking countries highest. This was precisely the kind of fact-based research that legitimated the new discipline of social science and gave policy makers the tools necessary for progressive action.[33]

Did President McKinley appoint her the nation's factory inspector? He did not. Nor did Governor Roosevelt name her factory inspector for the state of New York. Instead, Roosevelt chose an elevator operator from the state capital, Albany. It was disgraceful. Friends from Hull House and the Chicago women's clubs had tried valiantly to help. Nothing worthwhile worked out.

Kelley didn't sulk, but the long evenings in the Crerar Library gave her hours to ponder her sudden, staggering fall.[34]

Could her sex be the problem? It was galling to think that she was by-passed as a woman who dared to operate in public life in the late 1800s. Besides, a good many women had achieved public prominence in this waning century. Just two years before, Kelley's acquaintance, Frances Willard, the prominent temperance leader, had published a hefty book, *Occupations for Women*, which devoted whole chapters to successful women in banking, advertising, real estate, medicine, business, the pulpit, lecturing, photography, and a host of other fields. If those women could succeed, surely Kelley could too.[35]

Was her temperament possibly the problem? Her "flutelike voice" with reserves of "deep organ tones" was perfect for conversation and public speaking. But there were moments when her own son thought that her anger approached a "hurricane." Some found her to be "a little frightening." A close friend and colleague, Alice Hamilton, thought her merciless in the face of "foolish questions, half-baked opinions, and sentimental attitudes." Suppose Kelley's employment problem was personal. Suppose her "bursting vitality," her "dismaying energy," her "fierceness" worked against her.[36]

Or was her politics the sticking point? In her mid-twenties, she'd abandoned the Republican Party politics of her late father and embraced socialism. His generation, he said, built up "great industries in America so that more wealth could be produced for more people." The duty of her generation was now to see that "the product be distributed justly." To Florence, socialism was best suited to meet that goal.[37]

The Honorable William Kelley did not foresee that his Florrie's idea of justice would move her to become a socialist. Yes, he was proud of his daughter's Cornell bachelor's thesis, "The Law and the Child." And he'd gladly paid for her postgraduate study in Europe, where "the new wildfire of Socialism [was] spreading over the whole Continent." It was splendid that Florence learned German, but William Kelley doubtless considered it extreme that she translated the German Friedrich Engels's tract on the conditions of the English working class in 1844, *Die Lage der arbeitenden Klasse in England, nach eigener Anschauung und authentischen Quellen*. Did she have to go so far as to join the Socialist Labor Party? His daughter's conversion to socialism dealt the congressman a blow. In Florence's case, the "wildfire" did not burn itself out. She resigned from the strife-ridden party in 1888, but her heart always belonged, politically speaking, to socialism.[38]

Her politics wasn't at all bizarre, Florence always insisted. The movement was gaining serious attention in the United States. Socialist themes were mainstreamed in Edward Bellamy's 1897 best-selling American novel *Looking Backward*, and such themes were topmost in the highly respected William Dean Howells's 1894 novel *Traveler from Altruria*, its title implying a state of altruism across lines of social class. Jack London, a rising literary star, also proclaimed himself a socialist and had a copy of Kelley's translation of Engels in his own library. Meanwhile, certain leading intellectuals, notably Richard T. Ely of Johns Hopkins University, were showing how religion, politics, and economics could help move society into a more just balance. And the public had begun to elect socialist mayors and city councilmen across the country.[39]

In 1896, what's more, the prominent New England reformer John Graham Brooks taught a course in Chicago titled "Modern Socialism at Work." Kelley looked forward to seeing him this very month of January 1899, for he'd notified her of his travel plans and asked her for ample time for an important conversation. They had many mutual friends and acquaintances. No flaming radical, Brooks came from an affluent, well-connected New England family and was educated at Oberlin College and Harvard Divinity School. He was fondly remembered at Hull House, where he'd lived while teaching his course. Everyone thought him charming. Socialism, Kelley always said, was a peaceful process that must proceed within the law. Social and economic justice was its goal. She realized that some feared that it meant "dynamite warfare." They were so wrong.[40]

Whatever the problem was, Kelley was well into her second year at the Crerar Library with nothing better in sight. And the job paid so little — sixty dollars monthly, less than half her former salary—that she couldn't make ends meet. For herself alone, the money wouldn't much matter. She once said that she wouldn't leave her Chicago Hull House "slum" for "a thousand dollars an hour." She wasn't a spender. Deeply invested in conditions in the garment industry, she had ceased to care about women's fashion. She dressed each morning with a "negligence of appearance," as Jane Addams's nephew, James Linn, observed. She simply coiled and pinned up her braids, washed, pulled on her skirt and stockings that might or might not match, and she was off. By herself, Kelley could get by.[41]

Because she was the sole supporter of her three young children, however, the money problems were monstrous, and child care was a constant shuffle. Hull House was residential, but the settlement house was not a suitable full-time home for children. During her travels as factory inspector, the three Kelley "chicks" stayed with the Henry Demarest Lloyd family in Winnetka and also boarded with Anna Wright, whose son, Frank Lloyd, was drawn to architecture. Kelley shuttled to spend weekends with her "brood" in the outlying Chicago suburbs or gathered them to her in the city. For one trial season, she'd rented a cheap flat near Hull House when her mother, Caroline, came to stay with her and the children. But Caroline Kelley was not strong, and that winter Florence's firstborn, Nicholas ("Ko"), romped with the Hull House neighborhood "street Arab" boys, jumping heedlessly onto the runners of horse-drawn sleighs. He reveled in his dirty clothes, but Kelley worried that her son might fall into bad habits from the ruffians who smoked cigarettes and cursed and sometimes snorted cocaine "dust" they got from neighborhood apothecaries.[42]

On the other hand, she fretted just as much that Ko was a perfectionist in his schoolwork. A mother worried, period. Right now, 1899, she faced heavy expenses. The children's school bills loomed, and her twelve-year-old daughter, Margaret, craved pretty things. All three children, including little John, who was now ten, outgrew their clothes and wore out their shoes, needed winter wear and surely a few treats . . . and what about college? Ko would soon be fourteen. Kelley managed to eke out her income by writing freelance articles for German magazines, but it still wasn't enough. Her mother and the wealthy Hull House benefactors, especially Mary Rozet Smith, wrote generous bank checks to keep her afloat, but Kelley was too proud to become their charity case. Where did the money go?[43]

One thing was certain: the Crerar Library was too small. In idle moments, she could do research and writing, but the Crerar was only a job. Kelley's life work was elsewhere — and it was far from finished. The anguished pleas from her factory inspector years rang out inside her head and called her to action. She heard the clamor of the mothers driven "wild" by their daughters' overwork in the steam laundry. And the civic-minded businessman's outrage on behalf of "little girls" who were "forced" to work over seventy hours weekly operating folding machines. And the terror of the mother who feared for the safety of her thirteen-year-old daughter who walked home after work at night "through a most dangerous section of the city, where midnight brawls, assaults, and police raids are of frequent occurrence."[44]

Kelley owed her best fight to the distraught mothers and child workers and concerned citizens. She owed it to futures otherwise doomed to the sweatshops and packing plants and glassworks. As a mother, she owed nurture and protection to all children. If she looked inward and far into her past, Kelley also saw her duty as a sister. Of the eight children born to her parents, Florence was one of three who survived—and the only girl. Still in infancy when the first of her sisters died, she vividly remembered the four other little girls who succumbed when Florence was four years of age, then six, then nine, and finally twelve. "No sisters escaped this cruel winnowing." She herself suffered long bouts of childhood illness, but her five little sisters probably had died of preventable diseases. Her brothers lived, the older Will and younger Albert, but their mother, Caroline Bonsall Kelley, was a figure of "entrenched sorrow" who developed a "permanent terror of impending loss" and constantly conveyed a certain "melancholy" that suffused the household. Florence owed her life's energy to women like her mother, who otherwise walked the earth in a kind of living death.[45]

Now she herself was in limbo, desperate to break out of the Crerar Library. Could she? How? For now, she was sidelined, but more angry than discouraged. Righteous anger fueled and stoked her resolve. A setback was not a defeat, she told herself. On the contrary, it could be a lesson learned, a necessary step toward progress. She believed in the future, but where was it?

JOHN GRAHAM BROOKS had the grappling hook for Kelley's future—or so he hoped. This was not a rescue mission. Florence Kelley was nobody's damsel in distress. The train out from New York gave him the chance to reread her publications, including her influential 1889 pamphlet, *Our Toiling Children*, which appeared under her married name, Wischnewetzky. As a gentleman, Brooks would not refer to Mrs. Kelley's divorce during their conversation in Chicago. It was well known that she preferred not to speak of her difficult past. As a divorced woman, she was properly addressed as Mrs. Florence Kelley.

Her article "Hull House," in a back issue of *New England Magazine*, was helpful. It brought him up-to-date since he'd taught his socialism course in 1896 and lived at the house. Mrs. Kelley wrote that the garbage-choked alleys in the Halsted Street neighborhood were cleaned up, the kindergarten programs expanded, and five new rooms added for men residents. Illustrated with photographs, Kelley's article showed the Hull House Coffeehouse, a spacious room with stout oak tables and spindle back chairs where they could begin their pointed conversation. Brooks was currently writing a book to be titled *The Social Unrest*. It was just the sort of title to interest Kelley, and when their meeting began, the New Englander described it as a guide to a more equitable American future and perhaps added that he planned to give copies to reformers such as his friend and regular dinner companion Theodore Roosevelt.[46]

The two got down to the business at hand. Brooks was on a mission to uproot Mrs. Kelley, and the closing paragraphs of her magazine article gave him the perfect opening. Kelley had mentioned that two Hull House residents were "active members" of Chicago's Consumers' League. One of those two was, of course, her.

It was true. Kelley had joined the local consumer education organization to raise awareness of the hideous conditions of manufacturing. She was certain that most ladies, if educated, would reject purchases they knew to be tainted by child labor or foul workplace conditions. As it was, the ladies were oblivious. They weren't to blame. The gorgeous displays of merchandise in the department stores somehow obscured the realities of manufacture. So did the thousand-plus pages of catalog items pictured for sale in the Sears, Roebuck and Montgomery Ward catalogs. The consumer thought only of selection and purchase, not of people toiling somewhere at pounding machines to make the products. "Wherever one bought it, that was where it came from."[47]

Once consumers were taught to think about the origins of products, the situation would change. Consumers would pressure manufacturers to undertake improvements in working conditions and wages. Profitability would depend on doing so. Kelley also enthusiastically endorsed the recent linkage among all local leagues. The previous year, 1898, the Illinois Consumers' League had joined with those of the Northeast in a federation that named itself the National Consumers' League. The very name sounded strong and expansive. It reached far and wide. The name was a bold stroke that Kelley could only applaud. It was typical of her ambition for the future.

The reality, however, was different, more like the facades of buildings in the towns out West, showy from the front but actually small and hastily knocked together. Brooks pressed the point as they spoke. To succeed, the National Consumers' League must be truly nationwide, he said. Its name must become reality. The moment was ripe for a large and long-lasting organization. Life in America was now tied to the pleasures of consumerism. Americans' habits of penny-pinching frugality were on the wane in a new retail environment. Brooks noticed that even working-class wives avoided old-fashioned, "stuffy" stores in favor of a free, "exhilarating" trolley ride to the department store, where shopping was "like going to a theatre." Even the longtime Bostonian doyenne of American charity work, the genteel Josephine Shaw Lowell, remarked that "it will be a good thing for the American nation when a piano and a bicycle are regarded as necessaries of life by everybody." Wasn't the moment ripe for the National Consumers' League?[48]

Kelley knew how ripe. In her father's childhood in the late 1810s, a typical list of salable goods featured commodities such as paper, wine, coal, hay, cheese, and goose quills. Everything today was different. Products were branded (Pears Soap, Quaker Oats). Retail was booming in Chicago. The Crerar Library was housed in a building named for Marshall Field. Other department stores in the city had sprung up like mushrooms after rain. There were Mandel Brothers, the Fair, and Schlesinger-Mayer in its new building designed by Louis Sullivan. In Chicago, it seemed "as if the trolley cars were made for . . . these emporiums of trade."[49]

Kelley and Brooks were well aware that cities all over America had their own version of Chicago's retail Loop. New York had Macy's, while Bostonians shopped at Jordan Marsh, and Pittsburgh had its Joseph Horne. Kelley's own hometown, Philadelphia, had Wanamaker, and San Francisco the Emporium. These stores were America's new palaces. They dazzled customers with displays featuring plate glass, mirrors, and electric lighting. Between 1870 and the end of the century, the output of American manufactured goods quadrupled, and much of the output appeared, as if by magic, in the department stores.[50]

The clerks seemed cheerful and stylish behind the counters, but appearances were deceiving. A Chicago woman, Annie MacLean, had recently gone undercover to work as a saleslady and reported horrific working conditions in department stores—long, crippling hours standing on hard floors without a sit-down break, sadistic managers, rude customers, and wages so low that some desperate shop girls resorted to prostitution. They could hardly be blamed. These inexperienced young women from the tenements were engulfed in disorienting, "poisonous" luxury not seen since the days of the court of Louis XVI. Frances Willard warned young women against taking jobs in department stores because they were "killing places." Marshall Field paid his clerks at most twelve dollars for a fifty-nine-hour work week. Kelley doubted that Macy's or the Emporium did better. The clerks, too, were a facade.[51]

It was high time for the National Consumers' League to be smart and muscular, Brooks told Kelley. To connect shoppers with the workers who made and sold the goods, the league must plan effective strategies. Factories must be persuaded to cooperate and to submit to inspection. The league must set the standard. The National Consumers' League needed a full-time corresponding secretary, he said at the opportune moment. This was why he had come all the way to Hull House to meet with her. It wasn't for himself alone that he'd traveled so many hours across the frozen landscape in January. He also came on behalf of three women reformers who knew her work. They were friends, and friends of friends, including Josephine Shaw Lowell, the renowned founder of the Charity Organization Society, and Mary Jacobi, the prominent physician. The third was Kelley's friend Helen Campbell, the activist author of a book on women wageworkers, *Prisoners of Poverty*. All three had kept abreast of her work, read her published writings, and heard her speak. They knew of her successes as chief Illinois factory inspector. She was their unanimous choice for the new position. It would pay $1,500 per year, equal to her factory inspector salary, plus funds for travel and other expenses.[52]

There was one stipulation. To accept, she must agree to move to New York City.

Kelley was speechless. It was the city where she'd spent two miserable, heartbreaking years, 1888–91. It was a sealed chapter in her life. She'd then lived in an apartment on East Seventy-sixth Street as Mrs. Lazare Wischnewetzky, the wife of a Russian émigré physician who was struggling, and failing, to establish a medical practice in New York. She'd met and married Lazare in 1884 in Zurich, when he was a medical student and she was studying law at the university, one of few to admit women for advanced study. Lazare knew no English, Florence no Russian, so they spoke German together.

Perhaps Zurich had cast a spell that was certain, in time, to be broken. The Swiss city was so charming, with its curved and narrow old streets, its groomed forest and Zurich Sea, its Limmat and Sihl rivers, its winter garden and backdrop of snow-capped Alps. Perhaps the socialist intellectual ferment in the peaceable, prosperous, cosmopolitan European city lulled the young couple into fantasies about the future. They made common cause as avid socialists, and Lazare pursued Florence until she envisioned a future with him in New York City, where he would treat patients while she translated Engels and furthered the socialist cause.[53]

These days, she was tight-lipped about the New York years, how she tried to make a go of it in the cramped apartment with a toddler and, in due course, two more babies. She did not discuss the financial strains, the mounting debts, the loans from her father, or her husband's violent temper. She did not describe the collapse of her marriage and sudden flight with the children to Chicago in the last days of 1891, her face still purple from her husband's blows. She'd researched the state laws on divorce and learned that Illinois was more lenient than other states. If she ever wrote her autobiography, readers would hear of the supreme happiness of her undergraduate years at Cornell and the pleasures and excitement of Zurich. The dark time would be cropped to two sentences. Kelley promptly reclaimed her maiden name after the divorce that gave her custody of her children. They too were Kelleys.[54]

Brooks made it clear that he wouldn't dream of pressing Mrs. Kelley for an immediate answer to the National Consumers' League offer. A gentleman instinctively respected the "delicate shade of difference between civility and intrusiveness." Brooks knew that Mrs. Kelley would give the league idea the utmost consideration in the weeks, perhaps months, ahead. Misses Lowell and Campbell and Dr. Jacobi were eager, though patient.[55]

Brooks emphasized, nonetheless, that the National Consumers' League represented a quite new set of possibilities for the American future. It opened the opportunity for fresh thinking and innovative action. This was the moment to seize the initiative. Otherwise, as Mrs. Kelley herself had written, the lion's share of society's wealth would remain in the hands of the lions. In Chicago, Kelley had entered their dens as factory inspector, but they'd roared on, unfazed. She could name a particular lion for the list, his lair a mansion on Calumet Avenue, the "Gold Coast" of the industrial and mercantile barons of the late nineteenth century. Like the others, Joseph Beifeld amassed a fortune through deadly disregard for adult and child workers. His company catalogues masked sweatshop work and hid the smallpox that Kelley and her friend Julia Lathrop found in the Chicago outbreak of 1893, when the labeled cloaks and capes could have infected customers all over the country. She'd stopped Beifeld then. Perhaps it was time to take him on again.[56]

Yet questions swirled, questions that the genial Brooks could not possibly appreciate. No matter how far he traveled, Brooks's family's "rambling farmhouse," the "Ledges," was his lifelong anchorage and summer retreat. If Kelley left Hull House, could she return? The late-night debates with Julia Lathrop and Alice Hamilton and others over steaming cups of hot chocolate here in the Hull House "Oval" suddenly seemed precious beyond words. Was the National Consumers' League her best opportunity? If she uprooted herself and went to New York, what awaited her? Back in 1843, long before she was born, the feminist writer Margaret Fuller said that women needed "a platform on which to stand." Fuller meant a public space from which to speak out and be heard, a public space to which a woman was entitled as a birthright. Was the new league the platform Kelley yearned for and desperately needed? Would the platform support the weight of her ideas and ambitions? Or could it collapse like a trapdoor and leave her stranded a thousand miles from Chicago and the best home she had ever known?[57]

NEW YORKERS remembered Sunday, May 1, 1899, for its record-breaking heat and "summer-like sunshine" in the city. The mercury hit eighty degrees, and picnickers carried "baskets of cold victuals and beer." According to the *New York Times*, the whole city "staid out all day," and "every breathing spot . . . was populous with Sunday idlers."[58]

Children at play near horse hooves and metal wheels of delivery wagons in Lower
East Side street scene, New York City, 1907. (Library of Congress)

Never an idler, the new general secretary of the National Consumers'
League was headed for her new home on New York's Lower East Side. Determined to approach her new position with zest and vigor, Kelley fought
homesickness for Hull House as she and the children found themselves surrounded by the Russian, Italian, and central European voices of immigrants
while their horse-drawn cab navigated Lower East Side streets crowded with
"pushcart dealers" who sold "anything from pickles and damaged eggs to
suspenders and hernia trusses." The Kelley children wrinkled their noses at
the open-air "odorous fish-stands" and vile "uncovered garbage-cans."[59]

In the thick of this "dense industrial population" was their new home at
265 Henry Street. The three-story Federal-style brick house was best known
as the Nurses' Settlement. Its director, Lillian D. Wald, was a pioneering
public health nurse who was currently at work to establish an innovative

school nurse program in the city. Wald and her settlement-house partner, Mary Brewster, told Kelley a story echoing Jane Addams's. As a trained nurse, Wald was so moved by the conditions of a Lower East Side woman patient whom she'd treated that she "proposed to move into the neighborhood; to carry on volunteer nursing, and contribute our citizenship to what seemed an alien group in a so-called democratic community."[60]

Wald showed the newest Henry Street residents several area landmarks that were blessedly different from the New York of Kelley's turbulent years on East Seventy-sixth Street a decade ago. Looking west across Henry Street, they saw the "roofs and masses" of high-rise municipal buildings, and to the east a century-old church "with the last slave gallery left in New York City" and windowpanes scratched by "Boss" Tweed's diamond ring.[61]

The Lower East Side neighborhood, however, was as wrenching as it was familiar. As in Chicago, the street scenes made Kelley's new challenges plain to see—and just as urgent. Here too were the "dirty tenements, cluttered airshafts and fire escapes, crowded schools, corner saloons." Here were the sweatshops where parents kept little children home from kindergarten so that their tiny fingers could twist paper around wire to make artificial flowers for sale. Here also were daughters turned into "little mothers." This sentimental term, cherished by the U.S. middle class, hid the reality of the lives of girls who were sacrificed to "the baby, the washtub, the scrubbing brush." The sentimental mush about the "little mothers" was infuriating. In fact, the girls grew up to be illiterate drudges—that is, if they escaped death by tuberculosis.[62]

And the streets? The photojournalist Jacob Riis exposed tenement miseries in his 1890 *How the Other Half Lives*, as did other illustrators and writers, but some popular magazines assured middle-class Americans that Lower East Side residents were "the happiest people," their streets a "kindergarten," and the nearby East River a swimmer's delight.[63]

It was an outrage. Only a blind sentimentalist could call these streets a playground and ignore girls and boys trapped in endless "premature employment" of boot blacking, hawking pencils and chewing gum, peddling newspapers, or working all night long as telegraph messengers or delivery boys. Why couldn't the well-off public see that these children were not cherubs, nor their families the disinherited? All were entitled "to become enlightened self-governing citizens." They deserved "to participate in new standards of comfort and of dignity." Achieving this standard for all of America was, of course, a primary goal of the National Consumers' League.[64]

The task was huge, for fear and hostility toward invasive immigrant "aliens" were everywhere. Here in New York, the senior Clarence Day—

Father—railed against the notion of personal contact with "Russians . . . down in the slums," while the writer Henry James visited the new U.S. immigration center at Ellis Island and glimpsed a "million or so immigrants annually knocking at our official door" to "feed the mill" of industry. James was appalled by the "aliens." But he understood, deep down, that people like him "must go . . . *more* than half-way to meet them," and he foresaw the necessary "colossal" social and political "machinery" for the work ahead.[65]

The National Consumers' League was a motor of that machinery, even if its Lower Manhattan office at Twenty-second Street and Fourth Avenue was merely two connecting rooms measuring 760 square feet of space in a renovated Victorian church that was now called the United Charities Building. Kelley's private office barely held her desk and an extra, small chair "squeezed" in for visitors. The partition separating her from her secretary was too thin to be called a wall, but so what? She'd learned to type and could fire off her share of letters. The clack of typewriters would be the sound of production. Mighty oaks from tiny acorns, as the proverb went. Yet professional office standards must be met, and as the league grew, each member of the staff was to be "thoroughly presentable and reasonably attractive" to pass muster with visiting state league officers and wealthy donors, such as the New York socialite and political activist Mrs. J. Borden Harriman, who must eventually chair the league board. It was pleasant to have light pour in through five windows, and the in-house neighbors were the best, including *Survey* editor Paul Kellogg, who was to direct the Pittsburgh Survey in 1907. Professor John R. Commons came in whenever work brought him to the city. Commons's former student John B. Andrews was also in the building, working on the project to ban the poison that caused phossy jaw in the match industry.[66]

Kelley wasn't starting from scratch. Her predecessors' efforts in New York City gave her a running start, for the National Consumers' League was rooted in thirteen years of prior civic energy. It began in 1886, the year when Kelley's daughter, Margaret, was born and Clarence Day Jr. saw the Buffalo Bill show with Father. It was also the year of the Great Upheaval of labor strikes and the national trauma of the Haymarket riot, which was triggered by workers' demands for an eight-hour workday. That same year, the working conditions of department store "salesgirls" caught the attention of the woman whose name was synonymous with Gilded Age charity for the poor. A labor activist invited the esteemed Josephine Shaw Lowell of the Charity Organization Society to hear the harrowing testimony of female department store clerks. Lowell's "loving face" hid the shock of the deplorable working conditions that moved her to act. She went to Macy's department store to see for herself the physical stress on young women salesclerks forced to stand without rest for hours on end with no customers in sight. Lowell then joined other "society ladies" to launch a plan of action that was up and running by the time Florence Kelley and other Chicago women became involved.[67]

The plan of the Consumers' League of New York City was based on the principle of a "Standard of a Fair House." Simply put, a business whose labor practices were certified as humane by league inspectors was to be named a "Fair House." League members knew the certification needed a catchy name, something like a brand. "Blacklisting" was a word of censure and exclusion, but the league sought a positive, progressive phrase and chose "White List." The list was published in league ads in the leading newspapers. Consumers reading the *New York Times* or *New York Herald* at the breakfast table would confront the ethics of their favorite retail stores. Their "dormant" sense of responsibility would be awakened and they'd shop accordingly. The merchant of children's toys F. A. O. Schwarz soon was on the White List, as was one of Vinnie Day's favorite stores, Lord and Taylor.[68]

New York City's consumer league also flexed political muscle. In 1895, just as the Illinois Supreme Court struck down the sweatshop law that Kelley worked to craft, Josephine Shaw Lowell led a delegation to Albany, the state capital, to lobby for a bill meant to strengthen workers' rights and protect their health in New York. Her testimony helped to pass New York's Mercantile Act of 1896. Attacked as "socialistic" by business and the newspapers, it set the workday at ten hours and the workweek at sixty hours. Some New York consumer league members knew these were excessive hours, but the principle of legally capping a person's workday and workweek was an important step in protecting his or her health in a major manufacturing state of the union. The swirling publicity out of Albany backfired on the hostile businesses and media when consumer leagues suddenly blossomed all over the state. Within a year, leagues were also formed in Philadelphia and Boston.[69]

And in Chicago too, with Florence Kelley at the forefront. She herself had already proposed an idea to bolster the White List: a National Consumers' League clothing label. In this era of national advertising and trademarks, U.S. manufacturers proudly labeled their products, while the garment industry's labor unions sewed their labels on goods to signal production in union shops. A sewn-in National Consumers' League label—a White Label—would instantly identify a garment. The label would signify that the clothing was made and offered for sale under "fair" management-employee relations, together with living wages for workers and safe workplace conditions free of child labor. These were the cardinal issues the National Consumers' League would fight for in the new twentieth century.[70]

A graphic designer shortly produced the White Label logo for the national league. It resembled the outline of a plain and serviceable bow tie. Shoppers could read the words "made under CLEAN AND HEALTHFUL conditions" and be assured that the label was "AUTHORIZED after INSPECTION." If it worked as planned, the label could promote a boycott of goods *not* produced under fair conditions. Kelley cherished the memory of her dear Quaker antislavery great-aunt Sarah Pugh, who boycotted sugar and cotton cloth as an act of conscience against slave labor. Kelley meant to turn Aunt Sarah's conscience into modern civic action by making the label as familiar as Ivory Soap or Uneeda Biscuit. Her strategy was already in mind. Women were the principal shoppers in American families, and the White Label would start in a foundational way, with foundation garments. The first clothing to bear the new label would be women's and children's white cotton underwear. By 1907, sixty-one manufacturers in thirteen states were "authorized" to use the label. It was especially satisfying that one listed company was none other than Chicago's Marshall Field and Company.[71]

Kelley braced the league and its allies for the intense, constant opposition that the White Label was sure to arouse. The scalding loss to the Illinois Manufacturers' Association in the *Ritchie* case in 1895 was a league challenge for the future. Fair labor laws were certain to be enacted by other states in the years ahead—and certain to face fierce court challenges. The National Consumers' League must make heroic efforts to help such laws pass the judicial test. Kelley learned a hard lesson in Illinois, and the league must learn it too: a law was only a draft document until it survived court challenges. Yes, the league was getting nationally organized, but so were the deep-pocketed American manufacturers. They'd gathered in Cincinnati in 1895 to form the National Association of Manufacturers. They were now at work on a "Declaration of Principles" that defied most of the projects the National Consumers' League would work for in the new twentieth century. To them, the White Label would be a red flag in a bullring.[72]

The label, of course, was just one of many tactics to press on all fronts without a second's delay. Kelley had chafed to get going ever since John Graham Brooks's visit to Chicago the previous January. Her "mental machinery" hummed with "vital energy in gear," as the American philosopher William James (Henry's older brother) put it in an essay he was writing on the subject of human energy. Kelley's well-intentioned supporters seemed to think the new general secretary would spend her days inspecting factories and other work sites. Kelley saw no need, just now, to startle them with a grand vision that reached beyond the horizons of their imaginations. There was no need to trouble them about budgets either. In truth, money would probably be in chronically short supply. She made up her mind at the beginning: league work was too important to be hindered by the shortage of mere cash.[73]

First off, she must organize. A slate of officers must be elected, including a president, no doubt John Graham Brooks, whose sterling reputation and heavy travel schedule could help publicize the league nationwide. The league also needed a board of directors chosen from every region of the United States. For intellectual heft, college and university professors must be on board, and the chair a marquee name. Every sheet of official National Consumers' League stationery was blazoned with the names of these notables, her own appearing directly beneath the board chair's: Mrs. Florence Kelley, General Secretary. She carefully appointed a small executive committee as an inner circle she could speak with freely, often in full-throttle sarcasm.

Hard work was expected from the league committees assigned to investigate urgent issues and "promote" progressive labor laws at the state and federal level—and worldwide. The Committee on International Relations was charged to develop links with individuals and groups abroad for an interchange of ideas, ventures, and the promotion of European leagues. Close to home, a large membership was crucial. The Young Men's and Young Women's Christian associations had a well-tested model, so the league copied it. Each member was asked to recruit others, while chapter secretaries prodded the delinquent with a barrage of personal letters. Kelley herself suggested the appropriate membership for any given city. Portland, Oregon, she said, ought to have 500 members.[74]

For muscle, the league must link up with like-minded organizations. Kelley carved out half days and evenings for meetings of the Women's Trade Union League, the American Association for Labor Legislation, and other allied groups. With organized labor, it was touch and go. At times, she felt the wrath of unions that accused the league of encroaching on their territory with its White Label. It helped to have a thick hide, especially to fend off the cheap racist attacks when she joined a new organization that was vital to the goals of the league: the National Association for the Advancement of Colored People. The founder, the Harvard-trained sociologist W. E. B. Du Bois, welcomed Kelley to the board in 1911 as one of the rare (white) social workers who "dared to see the plight of the American Negro as an integral part of the problem of American democracy." Some board members, Du Bois said, lent their names and put in an occasional appearance, but he prized the meetings that drew "drowsily" toward "conventional conclusions"—at which point Kelley "galvanized" the room by a burst of incisive questions. She could pose them only because she faithfully attended NAACP meetings, worked on its committees, and seized each opportunity to learn new facts and launch investigations.[75]

Provocative or seductive, Kelley knew a thing or two about human motivation. To keep spirits high, the league must rally at an annual convention in a major U.S. city. Her annual report would cap a "grand" banquet dinner, and delegates from all over the country would hear such speakers as John Dewey and Walter Lippmann. Yearly galas, however, were no substitute for grassroots work from the New York headquarters, where each staff member must have an "investigator's nose for facts" and the skill to marshal them into pamphlets with "punch and piquancy." Printed at low cost and mailed in bulk for distribution by branch leagues all over the country, the publications could be slipped into pocket or purse — portable, punchy instruments of social change: *What Price Children?*; *The Working Child*; *Labor, Law, and Life*; *Women in Industry: The Eight Hours Day and Rest at Night*; *A Legal Minimum Wage*. The league must also blanket the country with articles on child labor and the conditions of work, especially in magazines with large middle-class circulations and influential readerships. Each article glorifying the charms of tenement life must be met with caustic rebuttal. The *Century* and *Atlantic Monthly* were stuffy yet prestigious, and *McClure's* was a sparkplug of exposé or, as Theodore Roosevelt called it, the journalism of the "muck rake." Titles such as "This Matter of the Eight-Hour Day" and "Toilers of the Tenements" were tools for the education of well-off readers enjoying their leisured hours in parlors and dens.[76]

Kelley insisted on one bedrock principle: all league projects must be grounded in hard-rock facts. Jane Addams's nephew thought Kelley used any tactic that came to mind — "evidence, argument, irony, or invective." The young man was likeable, but so wrong. If he read her 1889 pamphlet, *Our Toiling Children*, he'd see that every foot-pound of her energy was driven by the facts that she carefully dug out of libraries. From her childhood reading in her father's home library at the "Elms" to her college years in Cornell's McGraw Hall library and the Library of Congress, then to Zurich's university and Polytecknicum libraries, and lately the Crerar — in all of them Kelley spent hours deep in the documents that yielded a mother lode of facts. The British, European, and U.S. government reports were the ore that she milled into iron-clad argument for the abolition of child labor and the promotion of safe and healthy working conditions for women and for men. Others offered artful, "Rembrandtesque" social sketches or brayed in airy "abstract discussions of abstract freedom." Not Kelley, who knew factual data were the bones of argument.[77]

She faced a bemusing paradox. To hasten progressive social change, the league must operate in harmony with the customs of the moment. It must glide in the very currents it worked to redirect. The big corporations hired public relations specialists to persuade a skeptical public that they were not cold-hearted, greedy behemoths but had "souls." The National Consumers' League also must campaign for the American "soul." Kelley understood that public opinion was not random, and she saw to it that the league's constitution required it "to educate public opinion." People must be taught to reject child labor and the notion that newcomers to U.S. shores were "aliens." They must become convinced that crushing toil was abhorrent and intolerable everywhere in civilized society. They must learn that leisure was not slothful but regenerative for individuals and the nation too. In short, people must change their minds to make progressive changes.[78]

The stakes couldn't be higher. The American Federation of Labor leader, Samuel Gompers, said that the Haymarket riot of 1886 set back the eight-hour workday for decades because the public was revolted and frightened and turned against the workers. This must become a new day for a new conscience, especially for the success of new workplace laws. Kelley struggled to curb her sarcasm on the dismal recent record of the courts and labor law. The courthouse, she thought, had become a mildewed, haunted house. The Fourteenth Amendment to the U.S. Constitution, the very amendment meant to "guarantee the Negro [freedom] from oppression" in post–Civil War America, was instead perverted by state supreme courts to protect business and industry and to hold workers in a state of wage slavery, including women and children and African Americans too.[79]

Recently, however, new attitudes were stirring. Change was in the air. Utah passed an 1895 eight-hour law to safeguard miners' health, and the Utah Supreme Court upheld the law—as did the U.S. Supreme Court, in the case known as *Holden v. Hardy*. True, the more recent (1905), adverse *Lochner v. New York* decision dismayed all Progressives when the U.S. Supreme Court declared unconstitutional a maximum workday of ten hours set for bakers. The majority of the justices thought of cozy home kitchen bakeries, not the damp basement warrens where bakery workers contracted chronic respiratory diseases. Kelley nonetheless saw reasons to be hopeful. The burden of proof was on the defendant to show beyond all doubt that workers' health was imperiled by overwork—the key phrase being that an occupation must be "proven injurious to the health." *Proven*—that was the flashpoint test. The league would arm itself to supply proof of workplace peril beyond human doubt when the next case surfaced.[80]

And it would. New test cases on the workplace could pop up anytime, anywhere, and new judges would hear them in the context of new public thinking. Ideally, the judges themselves would be a part of the newer, progressive public mentality. In Portland, Oregon, at this very moment, a man named Curt Muller, the owner of Grand Laundry, was appealing his conviction and ten-dollar fine for requiring his employee, Mrs. Elmer Gotcher, to work longer than the ten-hour day as limited by the Oregon state law that governed women workers in factories and laundries. Mr. Muller was challenging the Oregon law. The league was alert and vigilant, ready for action on the case.[81]

Not that reactionary judges would simply vanish. The courts would continue to seat obstructionist judges who would do everything possible to thwart progressive new laws. But the legal system had the virtues of its own vices, as the *Survey* editor, Paul Kellogg, saw so brilliantly. He recognized that the best weapon of the law school–trained Progressive like Kelley was the very "structural bent" of the legal mind. Law school training, Kellogg observed, gave "the creative lawyer or jurist an engineer's talent in . . . [under]mining such barricades and opening the way for progress."[82]

The league, meanwhile, took advantage of traditional and new media for its educational campaigns. Seasonal holidays became opportunities; for instance, Christmas card pictures reminded well-off Americans to shop early because holiday pleasures cost agonizingly long shifts worked by the retail clerks and the candy and giftware factory workers. Everyone knew the modern public was "eye-minded" and that people beelined to visual displays featuring "charts, maps, photographs and even samples of goods." Small "suitcase exhibits" of league projects could be sent for display at conferences, colleges, clubs and Chautauquas all over the country. And two world's fairs were coming up in the United States, one in St. Louis in 1904 to commemorate the Louisiana Purchase and another in San Francisco in 1915 to celebrate the completion of the Panama Canal. Tens of thousands of visitors were going to be awed by exhibitions and describe them to friends and family back home. The league must mount visually gripping billboard-type displays to illustrate the benefits of decent wages and the human costs of workplace exhaustion. The newest experimental technologies could also be important in the near future. If the wireless (as some called it, radio) achieved public broadcast status, the league must reach the public with appealing short broadcasts, Kelley herself stepping up to the microphone.[83]

What were the unique strengths Florence Kelley brought to the league, and how could she maximize them? Writing was crucial, and public speaking too. People said she was gifted with "a beautiful clear speaking voice and an extraordinary capacity for imparting moral earnestness in everything she said." Listeners, it was true, grew quiet as her sentences sang out, and they

Facts for the consumer: tenement sweatshop labor produces clothing for middle-class children and adults. National Consumers' League Exhibit, c. 1908. (Library of Congress)

laughed at her pointed but merry wit. She had a feel for timing and tempo. A speech was something like a musical composition with an overture, a theme and variations, a resolute finish. She could take any stage to address men and women in groups large or small, from a lecture hall to a parlor.[84]

Style served the content, the message. She pitched statistics and figures like action verbs. Her phrases showed flair. Kelley sharpened her wit on the whetstone of Dickens's prose. Children who were hastened from elementary school to factory work were, she said, in "educational steerage." The best way to turn child workers into schoolchildren was to "deprive them of their immediate cash value." Those who thought children ought to work to support widowed mothers or disabled fathers might have a sudden change of heart when seeing the image that she drew like a charcoal sketch: "the burden of the decrepit adult's maintenance upon the slender shoulders of the child."[85]

She was also quotable. In this age of advertising, brands and slogans vied for public attention. "Ask the man who owns one" was the advertising catchphrase of the Packard Motor Car Company. "You press the button, we do the rest," was Eastman Kodak's come-on for its new snapshot camera. Karo corn syrup was "a spread for bread," while Coca-Cola "relieves fatigue." Surely the league could do as well on behalf of banning child labor. A slogan must be clear, simple, and grasped immediately. It must appeal to people everywhere, male and female, from a Wyoming ranch to a New York brownstone. It must capture the needs of children in words as clear and winning as those that promoted car and camera sales, because Kelley, too, was selling. The consumer was a citizen, and Kelley appealed to civic identity to sell her ideas. A vote was a purchase of sorts, and children's rights would require votes for officials eager to enact the crucial new workplace laws.[86]

What, then, was the right phrase? The best slogan? Across the country at every hour of the day, children were wronged. These wrongs must be put right. The Constitution included a Bill of Rights. She brainstormed, and it came to her: "The Right to Childhood." That was it. It was to be the signature slogan for all children's entitlement to schooling and to their "immunity" from toil.[87]

All this was well and good—but it wasn't enough; it was never enough. The vast work yet to do was a summons and a rebuke to the present for its shortcomings. As the voice of the league, she was its presence, its embodiment. The league, however, could not be a one-woman performance. No matter how buoyant the general secretary's energy, how fierce her purpose, how stirring her speeches and writings, how clever her turns of phrase and fervid her drive toward goals of social justice—beyond all these, she must inspire others to join with her. She must somehow multiply her efforts.

Kelley thought about her acquaintance the economist John R. Commons. At the University of Wisconsin, Professor Commons cultivated cadres of devoted students for what George Alger called the "long warfare against the bloodless and inhuman *laissez faire* economics." Commons's recruits lined up to join his "syndicate." The university was a magnet, and they came to him in Madison, a new crop with each school year.[88]

The league depended on recruitment too. Kelley's Hull House years put her in a nationwide network of women's organizations, and these must be tapped for active participation. And a roster of eager young people like Professor Commons's "syndicate" was obviously crucial. Young people were the league's future: "There should be an active Consumers' League in every college in the country."[89]

The philosopher William James's modern ideas about human energy were key. He described the different kinds of human energy, "some outer and some inner, some muscular, some emotional, some moral, some spiritual." James understood the multiplier effect of energy that was "set loose," doubled and redoubled from a single human source. His notion of freeing the latent or dammed-up energies could be a secret to the league's success. James's notion of the "enlargement of power" for social progress was her mandate. By energizing others all over the country, the ideas radiating from the league office could break the dammed-up Gilded Age "social convention" and propel society forward. The *"excitements, ideas, and efforts"* that she exerted and released in others would carry the day.[90]

This task required Florence Kelley *in person*. Telegram requests would fail. U.S. Postal Service letters of invitation would fizzle. The "energy-releasing ideas" could not be generated solely from the New York headquarters. Josephine Goldmark, who was Kelley's coworker at the league and was becoming an expert in the perils of workplace fatigue, said that "everyone who associated with [Kelley] felt the power of her personality." The message was clear: to "sell" the league, she herself must be the sales agent. There was no choice. Like the traveling salesmen and saleswomen, she had to go on the road.[91]

Was timing on her side? Years ago, in the early 1870s, Mark Twain spoofed the figure of the woman lecturer in *The Gilded Age*. He called "the lecture platform" the "final resort" of "disappointed" women. Perhaps Twain, a popular lecturer himself, was a bit jealous and rivalrous. In any case, today was the modern moment. Frances Willard lectured everywhere, and her *Occupations for Women* included a chapter titled "In the Lecture Field." Willard mapped the vast territory of the woman lecturer appearing in every "town in the United States . . . even in the most remote backwoods district."[92]

Remote backwoods? Kelley knew what that meant: catching pokey milk trains that stopped at every hamlet, then idling away hours on hard benches in drafty or stifling depots in the dead of night waiting for express trains. It meant sleep reduced to catnaps and meals on the go. It meant life on the run. Sprint and marathon, tortoise and hare . . . Could she do it? She must. Superabundant energy was one of her major strengths. Everyone said so. Jane Addams said Sister Kelley "galvanized us all." Behind her back at Henry Street, they called her "the Niagara Falls," and Jane Addams's nephew said something similar, that she was "a power . . . [with] bursting vitality . . . the finest rough-and-tumble fighter for the good life for others." Linn thought of Kelley in Homeric epic terms, as a modern "daughter of Minerva and Mars sallying forth to war."[93]

From her first year as general secretary, Kelley boarded train after train to promote the league idea at meetings of established organizations in Minneapolis. In Eau Claire, Wisconsin. In Pittsburgh. In Providence, Rhode Island. She addressed the American Association for the Advancement of Science in Columbus, Ohio, and the American Social Science Association at Saratoga Springs, New York. She spoke to young people at Wellesley College, at the University of Chicago, at Brown and Syracuse universities, at Vassar. She made presentations to thirty-six clubs and church groups that year, from the Sewickley Women's Club in Pittsburgh to the Far and Near Club in New York.[94]

Kelley dismissed her fifty-five speaking engagements as far too few. Traveling salesmen and saleswomen met ever-higher annual quotas, and so would she. By 1905, she addressed 108 meetings, and over 200 in each of several subsequent years, rallying branch leagues from Grand Rapids, Michigan, to Detroit, to Meadville, Pennsylvania. She went to Miss Dana's School in Morristown, New Jersey, that year, and to Miss Botford's School on Staten Island. She spoke at "parlor meetings" in Philadelphia and the Commercial Travelers' Fair in Boston. If one group paid her travel expenses for a speech, say, to a women's club in Vermont, Kelley then booked as many additional talks in the area as possible, from Brattleboro to Bellows Falls to Northfield to Barre to Burlington, all in a span of five days. Two or three talks per day were best, as many as she could cram in. Audience size was not important. Better ten young college women who would become lifelong league activists than a hundred who were merely titillated for an hour. The payoff? Two years into Kelley's league work, there were thirty league branches in eleven states, and three years later, sixty-four branch leagues in twenty states.[95]

Invaluable in the near term were the many new face-to-face acquaintances and friends who were suddenly worth their weight in gold in a lawsuit that popped up and could possibly—just possibly—become "a turning point in American social and legal history." The case of Curt Muller, the Oregon laundry owner, was proceeding through the courts. Mr. Muller was challenging the constitutionality of the law that was passed to protect the women factory and laundry workers in his home state of Oregon. Unknown to Muller, the National Consumers' League general secretary had already put her footprint on Mr. Muller's turf. "Not for nothing" did Kelley "travel the length and breadth of the land year after year, preaching Consumers' League doctrine," including ten days in Portland, where she "spoke daily at public meetings and private houses" and "formed lasting friendships" with Portland league officers and key members of the clergy, Catholic, Jew, and Protestant.[96]

In 1907, the Oregon league alerted the New York headquarters of the impending *Muller* case, and Kelley leaped into action. The arena was to be the U.S. Supreme Court. When a prestigious New York attorney advised Kelley that he saw no reason why "a big, husky Irishwoman should not work more than ten hours in a laundry if her employers wanted her to," the league general secretary hastened to Boston for legal counsel. The brilliant young Boston attorney Louis D. Brandeis agreed to act as counsel for the National Consumers' League. Brandeis, however, stipulated two conditions for his defense of the Oregon ten-hour law for women. First, he required that the Oregon state attorney who headed his state's defense must extend an invitation to Brandeis to participate. No problem. Kelley tapped her network of Oregonians and got Brandeis the prized invitation.[97]

His second demand was dicey. The league must provide the young lawyer a file of facts for his brief. What did this mean? It meant published, factual documents by experts who were knowledgeable about women's work in industry. Factory inspector reports? Kelley had a file drawer from her Altgeld years in Illinois. But Brandeis wanted physicians' reports too, and data from social workers, trade unions, economists. The American record on all this was dismally thin, even if British records went back to 1833. And other international reports were published in Italian, German, French. Who would, or could, make sense of such a polyglot mix, even if Kelley and the league staff could somehow get it together? Brandeis agreed to work on the Oregon case only if he judged the league's fact file to be sufficiently authoritative. Time was so short, a mere fortnight.

Sprint and marathon. Kelley canceled all speaking dates and dug in. The New York Public Library and Columbia University's library opened "every facility," and copyists and translators produced "a mounting pile of handwritten pages." A "few" typists hammered away at sixty or eighty words per

Women laundry workers, c. 1905. Heavy baskets must be lifted and carried by hand. (Library of Congress)

minute, and the league team proofread and dispatched the bundle to Boston in the nick of time. Brandeis "immersed himself in the conglomerate." If Kelley paused to await his verdict on the strength of league documents, she might imply weakness — absolutely the wrong message, so she fired off more documents to Boston. Brandeis declared himself "well satisfied" and went to work. Kelley resumed her hectic schedule, kept her eye on the Court in Washington, and held her breath.[98]

Brandeis's contribution to the 1908 triumph of *Muller v. Oregon* before the U.S. Supreme Court became known as the path-breaking "Brandeis brief." Kelley didn't care a fig that her own name wasn't featured in the Oregon victory for working women. What mattered was the brief itself, a sword and shield to fight and win battles in a series of labor law state court challenges over the next several years, including in Illinois. League connections got Louis Brandeis a sheaf of invitations from the states involved. A second *Ritchie* case — *Ritchie v. Wayman* — was won in a rematch in 1910, and Kelley glowed with deepest satisfaction. The Chicago clothier Joseph Beifeld and his ilk would now feel the teeth of the law. The dark period of judicial backwardness was ending, and the "fatigue" of thousands of women and girls was now "reduced" by law. And the health of the family was strengthened, too, since exhausted women who worked nightlong and spent their days in cooking, child care, and household chores lost stamina, sickened, and died—and orphaned their children. All credit for the judicial triumph belonged to the league, Kelley proclaimed. Its eleven years of existence to date was "justified" by this decision alone.[99]

Other monumental issues, however, cried for attention—for one, a living wage for all workers, including men. Low-priced "cheap goods" were all the rage—so much so that "men and women who would shrink in horror from buying stolen goods will congratulate themselves on buying cheap goods." These "hungry passions for the lowest price," however, were powers that "crushed the life out of the working people." The consumer league movement identified this urgent issue from the beginning, when Josephine Shaw Lowell advised that "honest hard work" ought to raise the whole nation's "standard of living." Lowell warned that for the health of the "nation as a whole," American consumers "must not demand products priced so cheaply that they send the workers who make them into poverty." The minimum wage, a living wage, was the check against the plunge into poverty. It must be a right secured by law—although Kelley feared that a sloppily drafted law might be struck down by the courts and set the movement back for decades.[100]

Americans, as usual, needed schooling on the matter. The payroll, they must learn, was not a trade secret but a matter of "the highest public importance, the gravest public concern." Meager wages produced "human wreckage" and cost the public dearly, including a prison system that housed those who "avenge themselves upon society" by criminal acts. League pamphlets kept up a drumbeat with punchy titles through the 1910s and 1920s: *American Minimum Wage Laws at Work*; *Minimum Wage Laws Are Good Business*; *A Living Wage for Women Wage Earners*. Meanwhile, as always, Kelley tracked the status of the issue in the states. Massachusetts, as usual, was "at the head of the procession"; Utah was in a push-pull struggle; and New York, Michigan, Indiana, and Missouri were beginning to address wages via state commissions.[101]

And what about the South? In 1915, Kelley announced that the mid-South states, notably Kentucky, were making progress toward investigating workplace conditions, but the Deep South hadn't budged from its primitive practices. Apart from branch leagues in North Carolina and Louisville, Kentucky, there was not one consumers' league from Virginia to Florida. Child workers picked cotton in blistering hot fields and went into the southern mills without setting foot in a school. Photographer Lewis Hine captured the woeful

*Child laborers in cotton field, 1899, photographed for home entertainment, with
the caption "We's done all dis s'mornin." (Library of Congress)*

figures of southern textile mill children tending the industrial looms and
bobbins, and a notable sociologist remarked that "in certain cotton-raising
districts of the South there is a strange saying that cotton and ignorance go
naturally together." The child, he continued, "is for exploitation and profit,
rather than for nurture." "So little has been accomplished," Kelley wrote,
that "in the near future" the league "might well concentrate our effort largely
upon that [southern] region, and upon Congressional measures applied to
the whole country." She insisted, "We must have a league in every educational institution in the Southern States, in order that the young generation
there may return eager to take their part . . . in three principal goals — a short
working day, minimum wage legislation, and prolonged education for working boys and girls."[102]

The "whirligig of time" spun on. Kelley's sixth decade became her seventh,
and still she traveled, spoke, wrote, and lobbied Congress. Few knew of the
heartbreak she harbored from two hard blows. The first was the sudden
death of her adored daughter Margaret from a heart attack just when the
young woman enrolled at Smith College in 1905. Yes, her sons had since
graduated from college, married, and made her a grandmother of delightful
children, but the wound of a child's loss never healed.[103]

Anguish also became her companion in the 1920s, when the insurgent
Women's Party mounted a campaign for an equal rights amendment. Kelley
saw the naivete of the well-meaning younger women who felt so empowered
now that the Nineteenth Amendment secured the vote for women nation-

wide. To legitimate women's equality, the new party proposed an equal rights amendment to the Constitution. Kelley was filled with dread. The nightmarish days of woman's workplace exhaustion would return in a heartbeat. Equality would be the excuse for a disastrous rollback of working women's rights that were achieved inch by inch, through hard years of legislation and fierce court tests. The women in the canneries, in the candy factories, in the mills—Kelley knew politicians and business interests too well to think they'd resist temptation to sink into the dark past. But the young women of the Women's Party wouldn't compromise, and Kelley launched a battle she would never remotely have imagined in her wildest dreams: the league waged war against a political party of, by, and for women.[104]

She fought on, although she scheduled vacation time at the urging of friends, who knew Kelley must recharge her batteries in the bracing salt air of coastal Maine in the summertime. But so much remained to do. As the old adage went, beyond the mountains were still more mountains. The constitutional amendment to secure children's rights had stalled, and the minimum wage law of the District of Columbia was nullified by the courts—nullified in Washington, D.C., the very backyard of Congress! A friend who hadn't seen Kelley since the Chicago days relished the old "vigorous ring" of the voice that "carried conviction to followers and put the fear of God into her opponents." But the old friend missed Kelley's sparkling humor and sensed her weariness from "the constant struggle against stupidity and selfishness and entrenched forces."[105]

Suppose it took a 100-year lifetime for the states of the union to act on the progressive measures the league fought for. Suppose 100 years were needed for Congress and courts to legitimate the terms of an authentic civilization. If so, Kelley would live for a century. "I expect times will be better for ideals by then," she said, "and I want to see the world made safe for idealism." Easing up was impossible. If Kelley slacked off, as some hinted that she ought, there would be no Sheppard-Towner Act of 1921 to provide federal money for the "public protection of maternity and infancy." Her league colleague Josephine Goldmark thought it striking that Kelley "spent herself as though aid to mothers and babies had sole claim upon her time, her sympathies, and her philosophy." Whole-hearted effort, body and mind—that was the only way to live! Her Hull House friend and Children's Bureau chief, Julia Lathrop, called her "q.c.," meaning "quintessentially courageous," but Kelley preferred a simpler, humbler term: service.[106]

The Scots anthropologist James George Frazer, author of the popular 1890 *The Golden Bough*, spoke of superstitious magical thinking in societies and individuals. Was the 100-year life plan Kelley's own magical thinking?

For her, the matter was simple. She needed a century's worth of health and stamina, so she'd have them.[107]

Her correspondence from the mid-1920s, however, told another story, of lameness, pain and exhaustion. A former league president and Cleveland mayor, Newton Baker, spoke of "people like you who wear yourselves out in good work." In her early seventies, "her face and figure," said an observer, "bore all the scars of a lifetime of heroic battle for the weak, downtrodden, and oppressed."[108]

Florence Kelley died in February 1932, at age seventy-two, six years before the passage of the landmark federal legislation that bore her "tool-marks" in craftsmanship: the Fair Labor Standards Act, which provides minimum standards for wages and overtime entitlement and includes provisions related to child labor and equal pay. It is currently administered under the U.S. Department of Labor by the Wage and Hour Division of the Employment Standards Administration. The late-twentieth- and early-twenty-first century battles for higher minimum ("living") wages, for the abolition of offshore sweatshops and child labor, for broad-based health care and education are Kelley's legacy to her country and her world.[109]

Louis D. Brandeis
Citizen

Those who won our independence believed that the final end of the State was to
make men free to develop their faculties. They valued liberty both as an end and as
a means. They believed liberty to be the secret of happiness and courage to be the
secret of liberty.—LOUIS D. BRANDEIS, *Whitney v. California*, 1927

The most important political office is that of private citizen.—LOUIS D. BRANDEIS,
dissenting opinion, *Olmstead v. United States*, 1928

True human progress is based less on the inventive mind than on the conscience
of such men as Brandeis.—ALBERT EINSTEIN, *The Jewish Advocate*, 1931

In the heavy heat of July 1905, Adolph Brandeis of Louisville, Kentucky,
looked carefully at the several neatly folded newspaper clippings enclosed
with letters from his adult son, Louis. Stuffing envelopes was a longtime
father-son custom and a mainstay of conversation between the eighty-three-
year-old father and his forty-nine-year-old son. The excellent U.S. postal
service helped. It helped bridge the 1,000-mile distance from Kentucky to
Boston, Massachusetts, where Louis, a highly successful attorney, lived with
his wife and two young daughters. Louis looked forward to the editorials
and articles from the hometown *Louisville Courier-Journal*. In turn, his father
received current news covering a range of national and international topics,
from zoning rules in Germany to politics in czarist Russia.

Adolph, a retired wholesale grain merchant, saw one particular topic appearing repeatedly in his son's clippings this summer. As the blades of a high
ceiling fan stirred the sultry Louisville air, he read Louis's latest news on the
scandals that were currently rocking the life insurance industry. Newspaper
accounts of the business crime provoked his son's acid irony. Louis was never
witty for the sake of humor alone, so his verbal barbs were a sure signal of
serious involvement in the issue. The New York newspapers, especially the
New York World, provided a scrapbook's worth of clippings on the misman-

agement and graft running rampant in America's life insurance industry. Charges and countercharges flew thick and fast. Editorials blasted the "licensed prodigals of other people's money" and the "neglect or worse of . . . sworn public officials."[1]

Louis's father could sense within his son's letters a growing special interest. The scent of insurance fraud was the "odor of sanctity," Louis wrote. Its creatures were "Guinea Pigs" and "dummy directors" of insurance company boards of directors. Knowing his son, Adolph guessed the phrases meant only one thing: Louis Brandeis was joining the fight in the intensifying insurance battles.[2]

Adolph worried about his son. He feared that he'd fall ill from overwork or once again injure his sensitive eyes. His concerns didn't stop there. His son was ready, it seemed, to risk everything for the sake of this case—both his reputation and the good life he'd earned for himself in Boston. Why, Adolph asked, would his son do this? Why not be satisfied with the traditional life of a prosperous attorney in a premier U.S. city? Louis had first shown a streak of independence when he turned down a professorship at Harvard Law School at the age of twenty-five. He rejected the secure, prestigious position because he wanted to take his chances as a "practicing attorney." From the start of his career, what's more, an odd notion of public service gripped him with the force of religious devotion. Other lawyers were content to help the less fortunate by joining boards of charities, hospitals, or orphanages, as so many attorneys in Louisville did. Louis's adopted home, in New England, had the finest tradition of such service.[3]

But Louis D. Brandeis's idea of service was starkly different. In the last several years, starting in the late 1890s, he'd fought the giant Boston city transit system and the municipal gas utility too, as if he saw himself as a knight in arms for everyone in the whole city of Boston. Louis's middle name given at his birth in 1856 was David—the boy who fought the giant Goliath. Was the Goliath insurance business next? It was a powerful, multibillion-dollar group of companies, and Louis could easily overreach and suffer defeat. He could lose what he'd worked for. And what about his wife, Alice, and the two little girls? Why take that risk? One thing Adolph knew: he couldn't stop him. His fatherly influence on Louis's life was a thing of the distant past, and he could only pray that God would protect his son.

Adolph was correct; Louis Brandeis was not merely watching the insurance mess from the sidelines and clipping newspapers for his father's diversion. He'd been tracking the unfolding scandal since the previous spring, when the newspaper stories broke and a small group of policyholders came to seek his help. Since then, he'd given himself a crash course in the insur-

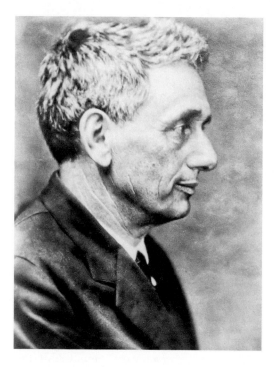

ance business. For weeks he hauled heavy satchels of insurance and banking documents and state commissioners' reports to his Beacon Hill home to study them after dinner, when his two daughters were asleep, with his wife reading in lamplight near his side. He could see a dire picture emerging from these assorted documents, and he began to gear up for a fight that would take years of his time and challenge his bulldog determination.

Brandeis was tough. Warm and loving within his family circle, the slim, dark-haired, olive-complexioned attorney had earned his sterling reputation by never squandering a minute of his professional time. He'd built a highly successful practice in Boston from the day he entered partnership with Samuel Warren, a law school friend and classmate from a prominent New England family. Their specialty was business and commercial law. They'd climbed their career ladder as they climbed the stairs to their fledgling firm, Warren and Brandeis, which opened in 1879. It was located two flights up at 60–62 Devonshire Street—and boldly modern with its telephone and stenographer. Success followed and prompted a move to more spacious quarters at 220 Devonshire a decade later. Louis, meanwhile, traveled a good deal, winning cases in trial courtrooms from Rhode Island to Wisconsin. He found trials as exciting as law school had been, and he'd argued before the U.S. Supreme Court. For Brandeis, it was a sad day when Sam Warren's family called him to work full-time in their paper business, but the newer partnership of Brandeis, Dunbar and Nutter at 161 Devonshire continued to flourish. By 1905, Louis D. Brandeis had a national reputation and sufficient wealth from careful investing to give him ample time for the pro bono work of his choosing.[4]

Was the insurance fight a choice? Or did his passion for citizenship leave him no choice in the matter? In Judeo-Christian specifics, Brandeis was not religious. But if citizenship in the United States of America could be called a patriot's religion, Brandeis practiced it with zeal. In Boston, the life insurance scandals came to his doorstep when a group of five men calling themselves the New England Policy-Holders' Protective Committee asked to meet with him. Edwin H. Abbot was one, as was William Whitman, the head of Arlington Cotton Mills. They came as nervous policyholders and investors in the Equitable Life Assurance Society (the "Protector of Widows and Orphans"). Like many Americans, they too read the morning papers and worried over breakfast about their money and the worth of the policies in the midst of the widely reported waste, fraud, and abuse in the industry. Brandeis's excellent secretary, Miss Alice H. Grady, ushered them into his sparsely furnished office. Looking about, they saw no rug and no easy chair. This lack of comfort was deliberate on Brandeis's part. Clients were here to state their business, not to lounge about and waste his time and their own.[5]

The committee members were seeing a frightening story unfolding from articles and editorials in the New York World and other papers. Six years before, in 1899, the founder of the Equitable Life Assurance Society had died, and the controlling interest passed to the deceased's young son, James Hazan Hyde. Indifferent to his father's business, the twenty-three-year-old Hyde was a luxury-loving fop who promptly spent lavishly to import barbers and chefs from Paris to trim his beard and tempt him with dishes worthy of the French court of Louis XIV. Hyde built a chateau on Long Island, hosted French costume dramas and masked balls, and was reportedly seen in New York City "driving jauntily downtown in his private hansom cab" with "a bunch of violets nodding at the side of the horse's head." Representing a business that purported to serve policyholders and investors with sobriety and good judgment, the flamboyant Hyde became a scandal.[6]

In order to "see that the young man did things right," several men of high finance stepped in to woo and discipline the young insurance heir. One of them was Jacob Henry Schiff of the firm of Kuhn, Loeb and Company. The competing financiers' real goal, however, was the potential control of the half-billion-dollar treasury of the Equitable Life Assurance Society for such projects as railroad ventures. Schiff, who was allied with the railroad mogul

E. H. Harriman, was put on the board of the Equitable in 1900. But the erratic young Hyde made a sudden move. He abruptly sold all his Equitable stock to "a lone wolf speculator" named Thomas Fortune Ryan for a disturbingly small price, $2.5 million, and fled to Paris.[7]

"Why?" cried the *New York World*. "What is the real motive?" The public was aroused and suspicious. The April 1905 issue of the *Life Insurance Independent* spoke for the responsible interests of the insurance business, especially the policyholders, who had a direct and personal stake in its affairs. A political cartoon in the *World* showed a policyholder being mugged on the street by a trio of top-hatted businessmen labeled "Equitable" and "New York Life." Writing in vivid images of disease and blood poisoning, the *Life Insurance Independent* demanded an investigation and a cleansing of the business ("that this matter not be hushed up").[8]

Brandeis knew that policyholders in Massachusetts pumped close to $1 million yearly in premiums to the New York company. Policyholders in other states, including his home state of Kentucky, also funneled large sums to New York. This meant that a huge population of ordinary people were probably being cheated in their good-faith efforts to protect their families with insurance. In his Beacon Hill home, Brandeis pored over documents spanning several companies, including New York Life and Mutual Life. Along with the Equitable, they constituted the big three. The reports in the satchels were chilling, as Brandeis realized the vast power that insurance companies wielded over the nation's economy.

He recognized that insurance was a unique business. Unlike the Boston department store merchants the Filenes, insurance companies were spared the cost of inventories of goods and the expense of maintaining and updating a large, fashionable department store and providing services to customers who liked to have purchases sent to their homes in horse-drawn delivery wagons. Unlike the paper-manufacturing family of his former partner, Sam Warren, the insurers were not required to maintain production plants and replace expensive worn-out or outdated machinery. For insurers, "home" offices with desks, managers, clerks, and field agents were the basic costs of doing business. Insurance companies mainly collected policyholders' premium payments. The companies were cash rich. Financiers like Schiff and the railroad titan Harriman wanted to get their hands on the Equitable. No wonder Schiff suddenly appeared on its board of directors. It seemed that "the staid and conservative financiers of the Equitable . . . used policyholders' money . . . to buy railroads, trusts and banks."[9]

Reading in soft light to cut the glare on his eyes, Brandeis realized that the powerful insurance industry was a vault full of money and, in that way, a source of loans for other businesses. Holding the loans, the insurers held the power. Behind the scenes, the insurance industry thus wielded "monstrous" power. The policyholders, meanwhile, paid twice. The premiums they dutifully sent to the company were bundled as loans to businesses that, in turn, hiked the prices of goods and services in order to pay the interest on the loans. As consumers in everyday life, the policyholders paid the interest. The price that Americans paid for consumer goods, train tickets, and even coal to heat their homes might well include hidden "taxes" to the insurance industry. The insurance business, like some other enterprises, was adept at using "other people's money."[10]

Three investigations were under way, the first by the Equitable directors and chaired by the steel and coke magnate Henry Clay Frick. Its focus was the safeguarding of investors, not policyholders. A second was led by New York insurance commissioner Francis Hendricks. The third was scheduled for the following fall, 1905. It was to be a thorough, months-long investigation of the industry, chaired by new state senator William Armstrong, its chief counsel the future U.S. Supreme Court justice Charles Evans Hughes. The committee in Brandeis's office wanted to know: Were the premiums being misspent? Did the Equitable have sufficient reserve funds to cover claims? Were stockholders in the company receiving fair dividends? Did legal safeguards protect them as policyholders and investors? Was the Equitable sound?[11]

Brandeis listened carefully. One particular name at the center of the scandals had special resonance for him, as for his father, Adolph, and all the Brandeis family. Jacob Schiff of Kuhn, Loeb and Company was a high-profile financier on par with J. P. Morgan and Harriman. Unlike them, he was a Jew, and the Brandeises, as Jews themselves, always took note of those identified with scandal and of possible anti-Semitism. So far, no one in the Brandeis family could identify any particular, overt anti-Semitic act committed against them personally in the United States. Still, a certain vigilance was wise. If a Jewish businessman was exposed nationally for criminal connivance, it was well to pay attention.

The committee poured out their fears and grievances, as clients always did, while Brandeis asked a few questions and listened closely. Seated in the spartan office, the committee had no notion of Mr. Brandeis's thoughts as they faced the conservatively dressed attorney with the thick shock of hair, the slightly pouty, full mouth, and the intense gray eyes that revealed nothing of his thoughts. As always, Brandeis kept his own counsel. Wrapped up in their problems and anxieties, clients were often blind to the full legal implications of their concerns. Monumental issues of law and society often eluded them. Larger legal conceptions bored or baffled them. Or irritated them as off the point.

To be sure, issues of citizenship in a democracy were nowhere near the concerns of the committee in the spring of 1905. They did not realize that these issues were close to Brandeis's heart and mind, the precise issues that moved him to take or decline a case. The committee worried about an industry whose executives were overpaying themselves, fleecing policyholders, and falsifying their financial data, but they wanted legal advice for themselves alone.

Brandeis, however, saw the insurance debacle in darker terms, as a mounting threat to American civic life. Ordinary people were outraged by the Frenchified young Hyde and the gaggle of thieving corporate executives. They were affronted by bad behavior and furious about the misuse of their money. Brandeis agreed, but he could see ahead to more dangerous trends and practices. Beyond the pocketbooks of committee members and those like them, he could see monopoly power that suffocated the vibrant American free enterprise system and sapped the energies of democracy. He saw himself as a friend of capitalism and capitalists, but as a citizen Brandeis was an archenemy of monopoly, of "trusts," and of "tycoons." He was coming to fear the courts' support for unchecked corporate power wielded by the trusts. Trusts, he saw, incurred no penalty in the courts for their wanton destruction of competing businesses. He saw that the courts appeared prepared to give pseudo-constitutional protection to the trusts' "vested wrongs." As a citizen, he was obliged to act.[12]

In this particular case, Brandeis feared additional jeopardy to the nation and its future. In the use of the single insurance term—industrial—he detected a vicious exploitation of vast populations of laboring men and their families who tried to avoid pauperism by buying life insurance. Through his self-education in insurance, he saw them being cheated on a massive scale. Workers who signed up for industrial insurance paid too much for scant coverage by policies that seldom paid out. Once again, as in the Boston transit and gas company cases, he knew he must fight for the greater public good. Let others think, if they wished, that he was simply spoiling for a good fight. Let them think that the gas and transit struggles were personal addictions. Let them think, at best, that the wealthy "People's Lawyer," as the newspapers called him, was taking up the cause of workers' finances as a rich man's hobby.[13]

Others might insist, too, that "industrial insurance" of the working class had no possible connection to the grim prospect of massive poverty in America—or to the distant threat of a socialist revolution. They might say that the peculiar industrial policies of some 15 million workers had no relevance whatsoever to an American "living wage" or to civil unrest.[14]

Brandeis knew otherwise. He could foresee a destitute population that would threaten the nation's economy and its well-being. Aggrieved people, in addition, could turn violent and fracture civic life. For him, this was no textbook lesson; he'd lived the reality of a shattered world as a boy when the Union split and turned his hometown of Louisville into a monolithic military occupation and a target of armies and predators. And a site of human misery. In Union army–occupied Louisville, he rode horseback along the Ohio River and walked the city streets, glimpsing the large "number of maimed men" among the thousands of Union troops quartered in the city. At eight years of age, he could have seen the "sad sight" on his own family street, the fashionable Broadway with its "profusion" of fine shade trees, where a detachment of Confederate prisoners was allowed to rest for a few moments. The men were "thin, emaciated, half-starved," some of them too weak to eat the corn bread and drink the coffee offered by the Brandeises' neighbors. During and after the war, what's more, orphaned and neglected children and youths, white and black, roamed the streets of Louisville to "obtain a living any way, by driving carts, blacking boots, or by begging." Louis had seen the ravages of social disorder on a daily basis.[15]

Boston, like all the North, couldn't know what it had meant to live in daily dread of the lawless element on the loose in Louisville and throughout the state during and immediately after the war—as some Kentuckians called it, the War of Secession. The Brandeis family doubtless were blindsided by the virulent anti-Semitism that erupted in 1862, when General Henry Halleck accused Jewish merchants of corrupt war profiteering, prompting General Ulysses Grant to issue an order prohibiting trading transactions with Jews. The episode reeked of the oppression of Jews in the old country. Safety wasn't guaranteed. Like all Kentuckians, what's more, the Brandeis family were on the lookout for wartime and postwar guerrilla bands of "unsoldierly rubbish, deserters, and outlaws of both armies" who raided, stole, and terrorized neighborhoods and communities, inflicting "grievous hardships." The "dreaded bands" included Confederate soldiers whose sole livelihood was "brigandage." "Fierce, uncouth men," they called themselves "captains," "majors," and "colonels." Their numbers sometimes swelled with "stragglers, deserters, and draft-jumpers" from the Union army. They came to be known as the Regulators.[16]

Boston escaped other wars too—of labor and capital. None of Brandeis's classmates at Harvard Law School found themselves, as he did, in the midst of one of the worst labor strikes in U.S. history, the railroad strike of 1877, so destructive that newspapers called it a war. At home from law school for a vacation in Louisville, he'd shouldered a rifle to join the militia to help keep order in the city as the strike raged nationwide. Playing a small part in a war between workers and capitalists, he knew that sooner or later social upheaval could erupt from grievances that were stored and stoked, grievances arising from the injustice he recognized in the insurance industry. Brandeis feared, most deeply, that a revolt by U.S. workers could bring on a regime of socialism, which he regarded as a form of oppressive monopoly. By taking this insurance case, he could perhaps help to ward it off.[17]

As a citizen, he had to try. He knew the case was bigger and far more important that his clients dreamed. Not that they were dreamers. Hard-headed businessmen, the committee of five sought Brandeis because he was the shrewdest, smartest commercial lawyer in the city and possibly the nation. They expected to pay handsomely for his services. It took them by surprise to hear Brandeis insist on taking the case pro bono, for no fee. He needed the freedom, he said, to act as he must. They objected. They were neither a charitable organization nor a quintet of reformers. If Brandeis couldn't come to terms, they might bolt. Hereafter, as he knew, they'd caution their friends and associates that the principal partner of Brandeis, Dunbar and Nutter was not reliable.

Brandeis knew exactly what the stakes were. An attorney in public life needed allies, and he'd already lost some friends in the Boston transit and gas fights. He had also alienated powerful Boston temperance leaders by upholding the right of taverns and liquor dealers to operate on strict business principles. Could he now afford to lose such clients as these, a prominent merchant, a manufacturer, a financier—men whose help he might need for various projects in the years ahead? Then again, how could he shirk his civic duty to the country itself? Their legal fees, he explained to the committee, would unduly restrict his field of action. He assured them that they needn't have qualms about their interests being served to the fullest. They objected and urged him to reconsider. But his terms were pro bono. Take it or leave it. His gray eyes met their gaze directly. They balked. He did not blink. The moments passed before they finally agreed, and their reluctance was palpable.[18]

This was not a moment of victory, Brandeis knew, but a necessary first step. The work ahead would be costly in time and require enormous effort. Looking ahead, Brandeis perhaps saw other costs too—of certain longtime friends turned into bitter enemies and his good name assailed by opponents who fought fiercely, as boys did in the snowy winters on the parklike Boston Common. Sometimes their snowballs were packed hard as cannonballs. Sometimes they had rocks inside.

LEADING CITIZENS of Boston would never say it aloud, but they regarded Louis Brandeis as their own creation. His Jewishness was a fixed identity, but they thought his unfortunate Kentucky origins could be corrected. The Bluegrass State, they knew, was ideal for racehorses, for fine tobacco, and for bourbon whiskey, which Brandeis helped supply to those Bostonians who had a taste for his home state's signature distilled spirits. Boston, however, regarded itself as the nation's sole seat of civilization, its center of intellect, art, and serious purpose. Individuals from outlying areas might gravitate to the city, show the right spirit, serve a probationary period, and become adopted sons or daughters. They could do so, that is, if they put themselves into the capable hands of the "best" of Boston and its kindred city, Cambridge, the home of Harvard. Accidents of birth—such as being born in Louisville— could thus be remedied. A "social thaw" was possible.[19]

Louis Brandeis didn't necessarily understand that he was a prime candidate for adoption from the minute he enrolled in Harvard Law School in the fall of 1875. He was eighteen years old, going on nineteen, and just back from a three-year European sojourn with his parents, his two sisters, and his older brother, Alfred. His father, sensing a coming business downturn, had decided to ride it out by taking the family to Europe in 1872. Louis was glad to come home to America at last, free from the rigid prep school he'd attended in Dresden. As for Europe, he would treasure the family experience forever. Hiking in the Swiss Alps was spectacular (even though Alfred nearly wore him out searching for the source of every "damned" river on the continent). The cities were amazing too, though he doubted that the music of the leading orchestras of Europe would inspire him to new effort on his violin, as his mother hoped. He'd brought his instrument with him to New England, mostly to please her, but couldn't practice much. Law school would demand most of his time—that, and making himself acquainted with the new surroundings. Just as his parents had immigrated from Prague to Kentucky a quarter century ago, so now he too was an immigrant to New England.[20]

Boston and Cambridge detected an Old World "suavity" about him. Better suavity than raw youth, for his classmates were college graduates with the advantage of full manhood. Many of them were already friends or acquainted through family connections. He was the newcomer, the stranger. His hometown of Louisville had a law school, and he could have stayed and studied among friends and family as the New Englanders were doing here at Harvard. He chose Cambridge instead, knowing he'd be a stranger in a strange land. The personal traits he'd need to succeed were two, and he called them by name: "bulldog perseverance & obstinacy." He asked himself, Would these be enough? In his notebook he copied Ralph Waldo Emerson's aphorism "They can conquer who believe they can." [21]

In one crucial way, his timing was perfect. The Harvard Law School dean, Christopher Columbus Langdell, was ready to launch a new curriculum: the innovative case-study method. No longer would law students memorize legal principles from textbooks, as in the past, but they would learn the law by dissecting individual cases from every conceivable approach until a case was as fully "eviscerated" as a cadaver on a medical student's slab in anatomy class. [22]

Brandeis appreciated the term *eviscerate*. It suggested a sharp scalpel, as if the human mind were a scientific instrument of tempered steel. From the first, he caught the attention of students and faculty alike when he analyzed cases in old Dane Hall. The classroom fell silent as he spoke, his soft southern voice of Louisville, Kentucky, analyzing the conceptual bases of contracts, torts, property, or constitutional law. Some thought that he'd developed a photographic memory. He didn't disagree. But it wasn't all smooth sailing here. The sudden, blinding eyestrain from reading at night in the greenish gaslight almost ruined his plans. Unable to read, he knew his future hung in the balance, even when he hired classmates to read to him. The New York City oculist who urged him to read less and think more gave him the best advice a young man could receive. [23]

Brandeis never boasted of his record as a precocious cum laude law school graduate of 1877. He knew stellar grades didn't necessarily guarantee a brilliant future. The law, nevertheless, was the only career he ever thought worthwhile, not because it was a gentleman's profession (which it was), but because of the powerful influence of his beloved and brilliant uncle, the Louisville-based lawyer Lewis Dembitz. Brandeis proudly had taken Dembitz as his middle name while in high school in Louisville. It replaced David, for his uncle proved that a man could be a legal scholar and participant in community affairs. His uncle was an immigrant himself, a five-foot-tall religiously observant Jew from central Europe who practiced law, raised a family, wrote a landmark legal code of the Commonwealth of Kentucky, and enjoyed astronomy as a hobby. Every day Uncle Lewis Dembitz lived the ideal combination of work, civic duty, family life, and fun. His career choice was never once disappointing. Neither was Louis Brandeis's. He was determined to make every moment a positive one and said so in his many letters home.

Law school, he wrote, was "splendid," and he was "pleased with everything that pertains to the law."[24]

Career success required that Boston and Cambridge, in turn, be pleased with him. Of his two identities—southerner and Jew—the racial one found more favor with Boston. He learned that an intriguing relation joined Jews with Bostonians from New England's colonial days. The Puritan and Pilgrim ancestors had called themselves the New English Israel because they believed themselves to be a chosen people tested by God in the wilderness, just like the Israelites of the Old Testament. Their descendents were dubbed Boston Brahmins by their kinsman the physician and writer Dr. Oliver Wendell Holmes, who wrote that they "were very aware of their colonial descent, which, they believed, imbued them with both superiority and responsibility."[25]

Brandeis blended easily with Brahmin Boston gentiles. Thanks to his parents, his vocabulary and manners mirrored theirs. His mother, Frederika Dembitz Brandeis, made certain that her two girls (Frances and Amy) and two boys (Alfred and Louis) were well acquainted with European history, literature, art, and music. She and Adolph shipped their two pianos along with sheet music and cases of books when they immigrated to Kentucky from Prague in 1849. An educated couple, they were Forty-Eighters, German Jews who immigrated to America when the European democratic revolutions of 1848 failed, leaving them once again to face the centuries-long restrictions and special taxes levied on Jews. In America, the Brandeis children were bilingual, moving easily from their parents' native German into English and back again.[26]

Beyond the untold hours devoted to law school and, later, law practice, the social and cultural scene was intoxicating. Brandeis enjoyed outdoor summer concerts on Boston Common, whereas colder weather found him in the Boston Music Hall and, after 1900, in the new Symphony Hall, with its incredible acoustics. The theater was splendid too, especially Shakespeare. The invitations to tea and dinner parties signaled the acceptance of the immigrant from Kentucky, as did his welcome into the home of the grande dame of the literati, Mrs. James T. (Annie) Fields. Brandeis could measure his inroads into Boston with each step up her "deeply carpeted stairs into the long, narrow, heavily curtained drawing room, looking out across a garden to the Charles River." Surely such Bostonians as Mrs. Fields were relieved to learn that back in Kentucky, the Brandeis family lived as secular Christians, exchanging holiday gifts at Christmas and dining without dietary restriction. Bostonians were especially gratified to know that the Brandeis family were ardent abolitionists well before the Civil War.[27]

There were other treats. Brandeis heard the awesome Emerson read his essay "Education" at one private home, and at another rubbed elbows with Henry Wadsworth Longfellow and Oliver Wendell Holmes, the nation's premier poets of the day. Coming and going, there were luminaries everywhere, and Louis tried to be cool and casual when he wrote to Alfred that "celebrities are so numerous here [that] one cannot take the trouble to look at all of them." In his notebook, nevertheless, he made lists of the important people he met. An immigrant needed contacts and networks, and Boston and Cambridge together were his New World.[28]

Social evenings, admittedly, could be tedious. Brandeis got his fill of social chitchat, and the New Englanders seemed overly fond of "pencil-and-paper games," charades, and "the lightest of suppers." He joined in to be a good sport—and to cultivate the society of the people he must get to know. For career and social success, he needed to understand their "inclinations" and "habits" so completely that his knowledge of them became "instinctive."[29]

He was not merely camouflaging himself in New England customs. Like Louisville, Boston was a river city, and horsemanship was a favorite pastime in both locales. Despite the war, he'd loved riding along the Ohio River when he was younger, and also playing on the city's riverfront wharves, sometimes near his father's river freighter, the *Fanny Brandeis*, a grain boat. Once in law practice, he'd be in the saddle almost daily on the bridle paths of Boston and its nearby leafy suburbs. For convenience, he'd stable a horse on Brimmer Street, within easy reach of his office and home. Vacationers in nearby Dedham and Cape Cod saw him ride by in the summertime. Or they glimpsed Brandeis rowing or, more often in Boston, paddling a canoe, his "birch," on the Charles River among thousands of other canoe enthusiasts, for the river provided "the most remarkable canoeing water in the world." On warm weekends, he paddled among the "three thousand canoes side by side . . . filled with young people in white, and gay with colored cushions and flags." In winter, he skied and went snowshoeing. Or he laced up his bootskates and joined Bostonians gliding and speeding on the frozen Charles. Like all of New England, he seemed to go in for what one "son of Harvard" called "the love of nature and the healthy sports that bring body and spirit together."[30]

He didn't tell many New England friends or acquaintances that sport, to him, meant something far beyond recreation. Life and good health were not givens in his family history. "In Louisville malaria had been such a constant companion that Brandeis always remembered the bowl of antimalaria pills that stood on the dining-room table throughout his childhood." He remembered the malarial wracking chills and recalled his sister Amy's struggle with typhoid fever in Europe and the death of his nephew and his sister Fannie in 1890. His eyesight always worried him, and during law school days, the director of Harvard's Hemenway Gymnasium gave him a real shock, saying that his muscles were dangerously weak. Brandeis immediately scheduled daily exercise as a lifelong must. The two-pound iron dumbbell was recommended for "students" and "brain-workers," especially those whose "arms are thin and weak and soft." He took up the dumbbells. His well-being was at stake in the gym, on the bridle path, on the snow and ice, on the hiking trail, and on the calm or roiling waters of the Charles and the salt tidal Massachusetts Bay. Vigorous exercise, he believed, was also crucial for an attorney whose mind must be kept fresh and nimble. Once in law practice, no matter how heavy his caseload, he left the office daily by five o'clock and scheduled annual long vacations. "I soon learned that I could do twelve months' work in eleven months," he said, "but not in twelve." The twelfth month, usually August, found him on vacation. He joined the Union Boat Club and, for stabling privileges, the Dedham Polo Club.[31]

In New England, it was easy to spend money sparingly, both as a student and later as a professional. His wardrobe was good quality, but limited, which was fine with him. Ornate styles left him cold, whether it was a woman's "burden of precious stones" or the "abundance of plush and tapestry" in food, dress, and furnishings. He was so much better off in Boston than its upstart rival, New York City. Gotham of the 1890s was to go mad for diamonds, a sure sign of "success in city life." Boston shuddered at such vulgarity, and so did he, rebelling "against the accepted American belief that life consists largely in the abundance of possessions." A stranger would never guess at the wealth of certain New Englanders, who hid their huge inherited fortunes behind the "simple life" in which "dressing up" was an unpardonable sin. In winter, a person wore "what one *had*," while the informal summer wardrobe meant "washed-out khaki and cotton." Whatever Boston spent money on, "it was not on status symbols."[32]

The deliberate simplicity served Brandeis in a special way. It kept his expenses down and let him save and invest every possible cent of his income. For thrift, he endured dreary boardinghouse life well after a flat with maid service was affordable. Fearing risky, wild stock market rides, he warned Alfred to keep clear of Wall Street, as he did. Financial certainty lay with bonds and mortgage investments. There would be no high-risk gambles on stocks but a slow, steadily rising fortune over a good many years.[33]

Never a miser, Brandeis saved and invested for a larger purpose. Unlike the first families of Boston, the Putnams and Lees, the Cabots and Lowells, he had no inherited wealth. And wealth meant one thing: freedom. Not for gaudy luxury or self-indulgent hobbies like yachts or the new craze of auto-mobiling. A wastrel like the young insurance heir Hyde was contemptible. Brandeis wanted financial independence for public service, and he under-stood personal finance in stark terms. "In this age of millions," he said, "the man without some capital can only continue to slave and toil for others to the end of his days."[34]

He never spoke the word *slave* casually. It echoed from his childhood among slaveholders in prewar Louisville. Brandeis was clear about life lived free — or in shackles. To be a hireling and dependent on an employer was to be denied a life of freedom. Sad to say, that was the hobbled life of a cor-poration attorney who was enslaved to the dictates of the railroads or the manufacturers. It was not to be Louis Brandeis's life. Financial autonomy was a rock-solid foundation to build on. With it, he could fulfill his "deep sense of obligation," meaning the citizenship that defined him at the very center of his being. In 1890, he revealed this sense of self to a young woman named Alice Goldmark.[35]

Boston was delighted (and perhaps relieved) to learn of his engagement and marriage in spring 1891 to the lovely young woman to whom he confided his sense of civic "obligation." The bride, Miss Goldmark of New York City, was charming and cultivated. Boston thought it was high time that Bran-deis, at age thirty-five, settled down. Never mind what Boston thought; he was deeply in love. He'd told Alice his story, and she understood him. Their tastes and sense of life's purpose were perfectly in harmony. If Bostonians noticed that Brandeis's wife was a Jew (and a distant cousin, as were many of their own spouses), they were not so crude as to comment for the record. He married within his lineage. So did they.[36]

Peering from parted curtains or opened "Indian" shutters, the neighbors on Mount Vernon Street on Beacon Hill saw a crew of "carpenters, plaster-ers, and paperhangers" descend on the narrow brick townhouse, number 114, the new home of Mr. and Mrs. Louis D. Brandeis. They perhaps saw deliveries of furnishings that the couple received as wedding gifts, the Ori-ental rugs, the dining room table and chairs, the grandfather clock. Soon two babies would be born and become charming little girls, Elizabeth and Susan, and the Brandeis family would move to a larger Beacon Hill home at 6 Otis Place. Like Mrs. Fields's drawing room, Brandeis's Otis Place library was to have a fine view "overlooking the widening of the Charles River and the Back Bay."[37]

Neighbors who watched the very first afternoon visitor arrive at the Mount Vernon Street home in the spring of 1891 knew immediately that the attorney's long probationary period in New England had officially ended. Ida

(Mrs. Henry Lee) Higginson, the caller, represented the "best" of the Boston Brahmins. Her husband, Major Higginson (from his Civil War service), was a paragon of Boston civic and financial authority, the founder of the Boston Symphony Orchestra and the principal of the powerful banking firm of Lee, Higginson and Company. Celebrated for his "genius for friendship," Higginson was revered as a beloved comrade, citizen, and public servant. He'd hosted Brandeis at a Fourth of July holiday on Lake Champlain in 1890, and Mrs. Higginson's visit to Mrs. Brandeis at her newly furnished home a year later was the ultimate Boston stamp of approval. To Boston, Brandeis had come of age. The immigrant from Kentucky was now a certified citizen of the city that regarded itself as the Hub of the Universe.[38]

The adopted son was expected to follow the tried-and-true New England reformist commitment to "do-good and *do-right*" in a proper "critical spirit." For a while, all was well. He did "right" in sponsoring the Harvard Law School's alumni association and helping raise an endowment for a faculty position for Oliver Wendell Holmes. Boston's "best" people, the Higginson circles, applauded his support for the numerous charitable causes that long distinguished the city — institutions for the aged, the poor, the young, and the jobless. There were the Home for Aged Men, the Home for Aged Women, and the Home for Aged Colored Females. There were an infant asylum, several institutions for orphans, and the Industrial Temporary Home for those who were unemployed but willing to do manual work. Brandeis drove his horse and buggy to committee meetings and wrote checks to the Municipal League of Boston, the Associated Charities of Boston, the United Hebrew Charities, and others. He became a member of the "citadel of Brahmin nobility," the Union Club.[39]

To outward appearances, all was well. No Bostonian heard a storm warning bell when Brandeis repeatedly spoke of the duties of a "citizen." Until the late 1890s, the young attorney led an exemplary Boston Brahmin life. He was their made man.[40]

So they thought. What did they miss noticing about him? The Brahmins must have asked themselves that question as events unfolded. They must have asked how he could turn on them and bite the hand that fed him. They must have asked, as his own father did, why Brandeis would risk so much for ventures that gained him no money or glory from the right people. Why throw away the life he'd achieved from law school days in Brahmin Boston? Was it something to do with his idolized Uncle Lewis Dembitz of Louisville? Perhaps it was about Brandeis's immigrant mother Frederika's ideas — that humane and even self-sacrificing conduct toward those in need was godly, that it brought "God nearer to us."[41]

If Boston's elite rummaged for answers in Kentucky, they were half right. Brandeis's wartime boyhood and postwar adolescence marked him in ways they could not begin to grasp. They failed, in addition, to see that a certain Kentuckian in their very midst had captured young Brandeis's full attention from his law school days. Somehow they overlooked a particular person whose message was so powerful that it muted theirs and became the guiding principle of Louis D. Brandeis's future conduct. This individual became Brandeis's alchemist, for he showed how the wartime and postwar baseness could be transmuted into a Progressive future.

Nathaniel Southgate Shaler (b. 1841) was a Harvard faculty geologist and paleontologist—and a Kentuckian who hailed from a backwoods Ohio River town and literally spoke young Brandeis's language. He understood the young law student's boyhood years in a city of mixed Confederate and Union sympathies, for he had served as a Union army artillery captain of the Fifth Kentucky Battery, his dark blue Union uniform severing him from lifelong Bluegrass State friends who'd donned the Confederate gray. The geologist was a favorite of New England friends and Harvard colleagues, who liked his "racy wit, homely shrewdness, persuasive wisdom and poetic feeling." Mindful of his distant student days, the geologist from Kentucky did not burden young Brandeis with tales of his own arduous rite of passage into Harvard's intellectual tribe of "cold and super-rational" New Englanders. The region could be wintry in more ways than one, and young Brandeis could use a measure of "human sympathy."[42]

Professor Shaler understood how fragile were the bonds of the social order. He knew the tensions underlying young Brandeis's seemingly offhand remark on the "times when the rebels came so near that we could hear the firing." He understood the near panic of the families of Louisville, including the Brandeis family, who feared an all-out Confederate attack on their city in October 1862. The Louisvillians crowded the decks of every kind of boat to flee across the broad and turbulent Ohio River to seek safety on the opposite shore, in Indiana, where they camped for two weeks, uncertain what lay ahead if the city was attacked as winter approached. Brandeis was then six years old, an impressionable age.[43]

Shaler knew of the grim aftermath of war and its devastating impact on families of the South. Through the war years, Adolph Brandeis maintained his flour mill, his tobacco trade, and the wholesale grain business that was his mainstay. The family's home of limestone-front brick was large and staffed by servants, and no expense was spared. On return from Europe, however, the Brandeis family was caught in the undertow of the post-1873 national depression that compounded the problems of Reconstruction. In the mid-

1870s, the Louisville city directory, *Caron's*, opened with warnings about the cessation of building growth, the "business depression" and "hard times." Louisville writers referred to "crippled" industries and to others that "disappeared entirely."[44]

Few could find work in those years. With southern homes and towns in ruins, ex–Confederate officers flooded into Louisville to restart their lives but overwhelmed the local economy. Emancipated blacks, too, descended on Louisville in hopes of living decently from now on. Skilled and unskilled, they competed fiercely with immigrant whites. The president of Louisville's House of Refuge, which was a combination orphanage and vocational school for wayward children, called for a local philanthropist to help find jobs for the young graduates. At eighteen, "after they have to leave us," he asked, "what then? It will not do to turn them out without home or friends, dependent on the cold charities of a selfish world." The official's frustration was audible. What good was the House of Refuge's training in shoe repair or furniture upholstery or sewing if the newly skilled young graduates could find no work? The editor of the *Louisville Courier-Journal*, Henry Watterson, lamented the "ruin" of the "bankrupt" South that was now held captive by bombastic politicians leading the public to "blind alleys, circles, and ruts." The editor called for fiscal responsibility as the "highway to relief."[45]

Adolph Brandeis searched in vain for that highway, as the young Louis learned from the many letters from home during his first year of law school. Each envelope postmarked "Louisville" brought reports of grinding struggles. He didn't tell his Harvard classmates that his father was suddenly too broke to provide the money for his first semester at law school, that his brother Alfred loaned him the money—Alfred who had come back home before the rest of the family and gone to work and saved just enough. In his Cambridge room in the autumn of 1875, Louis read and reread the letters that described the plight of his father, who was now a clerk in others' firms, while his brother hired out as a bookkeeper. At this time, Adolph's sole source of income was the collection of old, prewar debts. "Misery likes Company," he wrote, remarking on the "respectable" widening circle of "miserable merchants" like himself. Louis Brandeis detected the tone of deepening despair in his father's admission that he now lived "like a real proletarian."[46]

This was the shattered world that Professor Shaler understood. The older man surely sympathized with young Brandeis's eagerness to flee it for the settled order of Boston. Shaler, however, knew something the young Brandeis was yet to learn—that a fresh start in a new place didn't erase powerful, long-term memories. The trauma of war was an inescapable legacy, and Brandeis would face it sooner or later. Shaler wrestled with it himself in

The six-year-old Louis Brandeis and his family were in the Louisville, Kentucky, crowd rushing to the Ohio River to escape to the Indiana shore in October 1862, "preparatory to the expected bombardment by the [Confederate] General Bragg." Frank Leslie's Illustrated Newspaper. *(Library of Congress)*

these days of the mid-1870s. He was now pondering the complex problem of social order and ways to counteract such cataclysm in the future. As a Union military veteran, Shaler certainly agreed with young Brandeis that the slave system was medieval and "the Federal Union" essential "for uniting [the] states for protection and interchange."[47]

Boston surely glimpsed—yet was too myopic to really see—Shaler's hold on the young man whom they regarded solely as their own. The seeds of Brandeis's independence, however, were planted in a soil that Shaler tilled, and the seeds germinated in the definition of the word *citizen*. Brandeis came into Shaler's world at a prime moment, just when the senior scientist's intellectual life took a sharp new turn. In 1861, the year the war broke out, Shaler began to shift his attention from fossils to philosophical reflections on the self and civic life. Confronting the trauma of war as an evolutionary scientist, he became convinced that the term *citizen* provided the key to the Progressive social, political, and economic future. Framing his thoughts through United States history, the senior man was making notes for a long-term project, a book to be titled *The Citizen: A Study of the Individual and the Government*. The topic dominated his thought and made its way into his tutorial conversation with Brandeis. Shaler may not have recognized, at first, how crucial the term was for Brandeis. It was, in fact, key to turning a young man's memory of war and postwar devastation into a cogent plan of action for the future.

The professor outlined a topic that the young law student had not studied in any class: the history of the United States of America. His conversation became a tutorial. Shaler's concept of U.S. history was evolutionary, echoing Darwin, whose theory he had gradually accepted. The most advanced species of *Homo sapiens*, Shaler concluded, was the citizen. Two centuries of England's American colonies, he said, provided the first "great experiment in individual freedom" and gave rise to the Declaration of Independence and the U.S. Constitution. In turn, the democratic principles set forth in these documents created an environment of opportunity and obligation for each free modern person—specifically, for each citizen.[48]

Civic life, however, meant serious challenges. Americans, Brandeis heard Shaler say, were now poised at a critical moment between two materialistic eras. Chattel slavery—the ownership of human beings for profit and power—defined the immediate past, just as an emergent consumer era of manufactured goods cast a shadow over the future. In a republic, Shaler insisted, "the plain citizen has to . . . direct the course of events." If citizens failed to do so, the evolutionary forward movement would "descend" into "oligarchy." To prevent such backsliding, a "man must persistently act for the good of his people." That civic goal must be first and foremost.[49]

Brandeis listened intently as Shaler emphasized the crucial role of civic leadership. Holding elective office was not necessary, but citizenly action was imperative. Brandeis must have asked, Who were these civic activists, these "valuable helpers to their fellow-citizens"? They might be schoolmasters, said Shaler. Or men of business. Or farmers. Or lawyers.[50]

Lawyers? Did Brandeis flush to hear his own profession named as key to the health of the republic—more, as key to his relation to the worlds of his past, his present, and his future? The failure of citizenship fractured the country and ruptured families. He knew this personally. Suppose, however, that active citizenship could so well fortify society that it would not backslide again, but advance. Was he thrilled at the idea? Sobered? More likely, Shaler's message sank deep inside and embedded itself as an embryonic mandate for the future, when *citizen* became a key term of Louis Brandeis's identity and a theme in his speeches and writings. Brandeis copied his mentor's observations in his notebook, along with aphorisms from Ralph Waldo Emerson, poetic lines from Tennyson and Oliver Wendell Holmes, and the wisdom of various law school professors. It was, however, Shaler whose "'persuasive wisdom' struck young Brandeis most forcibly." He "would continue to cite Professor Shaler throughout his life."[51]

Shaler's specifics were crucial when, in 1897, Brandeis learned of a scheme involving public transportation in Boston. A cozy deal with state lawmakers greased the way for the Boston Elevated Railway to monopolize the city's transportation system and to lock in high customer fares for decades to come. This, surely, was a Shaler moment. The citizen, said Shaler, must act on issues "which are of immediate importance to ordinary needs—the care of schools and libraries, of roads and bridges, of paupers, of police, public halls, burial places . . . [and] matters relating to health [and] water supply." The professor did not list public transportation or utilities. He didn't have to. Brandeis knew he must step up to challenge the Boston Elevated Railway scheme.[52]

Some asked how one man could go up against a major company and the Massachusetts legislature too. How, Brandeis rejoined, could a citizen do otherwise—especially when he was committed to act for the good of the public? For him, the very idea of monopoly was revolting. It was detestable, contrary to everything America stood for. Like all monopolies, the Elevated plan was hostile to the people, who deserved to commute for reasonable fares. Like all U.S. cities, Boston was growing. Only a relative few lived within walking distance of home, workplace, schools, and shops, as Louis and his wife and daughters did. Only a few stabled their own horses, let alone owned the new and novel gasoline automobile. After researching the facts of the matter, Brandeis wrote a stern letter to a leading Boston newspaper and chaired a committee of businessmen to oppose the Elevated scheme. Knowing that one individual acting alone could not possibly win the anti-monopoly fight, Brandeis mounted a campaign. With the secretarial help of Miss Grady, he "poured out letters to supporters," providing them "facts by which to argue." He brought department store merchants into his alliance. They joined him from fear that shoppers would stay home or buy little if streetcar or El fares ate into their pocketbooks. Brandeis also "solicited support from prominent citizens, legislators, and friendly journalists."[53]

It was a hard, tough fight against the cunning moves of the Elevated and its political enablers in the legislature, but finally the Brandeis side — the citizens' side — won out. No sooner had the new century turned, however, than the gas company tried its own version of monopolistic price gouging. Using self-taught accounting skills, Brandeis penetrated the smokescreen of the Boston Consolidated Gas Company balance sheet and waged another battle along similar lines. In the end, he showed how the company could earn more revenue if it operated more efficiently, a kind of "profit sharing between consumer and share holder." The Brandeis compromise that settled the gas fight protected both the public and the investors. It was win-win. Some began to think that Brandeis hated the capitalist system, but they were completely in error. It was monopoly that he hated. It smacked of the oligarchy that signaled the decay of democracy, as Shaler warned. Monopoly by government became the vile socialism that he detested, while business monopoly was just another name for the trusts. He was on the record: "Monopolies, however well intentioned and however well regulated, inevitably become oppressive, arbitrary, unprogressive, and inefficient." Open competition, on the contrary, was vitality itself, and a close look at the gas case showed how deeply Brandeis was committed to the private enterprise business system. Win-win.[54]

Or was it? Those who had groomed Brandeis since he arrived from Kentucky suddenly had serious doubts about him. In Boston, opposition to the banking interests of august figures like Henry Lee Higginson was enough to brand one as radical — that, and the insistence that "control remain vested in the people." The local newspapers began to call Brandeis the "People's Attorney." The "best" people of Boston and Cambridge grew alarmed. They were watching him closely for signs of radicalism. Some crossed Mr. and Mrs. Brandeis off their guest lists. Now, in 1905, came the insurance corruption scandals. If he joined the fight in earnest, Brandeis would alienate Boston for good. The life he'd sought and earned would wash away like sand in a coastal storm. A Beacon Hill neighbor, Mark DeWolfe Howe, cautioned that someone with "the critical spirit" was "seldom a popular member of society."[55]

Popularity? What was it worth? Years earlier, it measured his acceptance into Boston's social circles. His uncle Lewis Dembitz, however, cared nothing for popularity when he kept the Jewish Sabbath weekly in Louisville with a full day of prayers and reflection. And Brandeis's parents taught their children a lesson about popularity in the family home on Louisville's fashionable Broadway, where abolitionism was clearly disliked by slaveholding neighbors. Popularity did nothing for the public good. What harm, then, could Brahmin Boston do him? His law practice was flourishing, and he was nearing the point of financial independence, thanks to years of careful spending and investment. This year, 1905, he was just two years shy of becoming a millionaire. He had his family, both here and in Kentucky, and other friendships to ward off the chill of the Brahmins' "glacial drift." There were many other interesting people in the city. The *Boston Globe* reporter John O'Sullivan was a good man to know, as was his wife, the labor organizer Mary Kenney, who'd come from Chicago and knew Jane Addams and worked with the other fascinating Hull House women, including Florence Kelley. They'd surely accept invitations to join the Brandeises for dinner on Otis Place. So would particular, loyal friends, notably the widowed Elizabeth Glendower Evans, who was active in Boston's juvenile court system and other reform issues. She was to widen Brandeis's circle of friends by insisting that he meet Wisconsin's Progressive governor, Robert "Fighting Bob" La Follette, who was about to become a U.S. senator.[56]

What, then, could Brahmin Boston do to Brandeis? Call him names? Or vent a hateful anti-Semitism lurking just beneath the surface? One "established" Boston lawyer was to remark that Brandeis offended Boston as "an outsider, successful, and a Jew." Brandeis could shrug it off. "Sticks and stones . . ." as the jingle went.[57]

Suppose, however, that powerful Brahmins were to lie low and wait for their chance to rise up to try to defeat and humiliate him for once and all at some future point? They had allies. In business as in families, they were entwined root and branch. The insurance war probably wouldn't be his last fight. There were other public service battles yet to come, other campaigns for a committed citizen. A railroad case might surface here in New England, with consolidation issues hinting of monopoly and inflated stock. Or a case needing his fight for land conservation when public land in Alaska was sold to private capitalist interests. Or a case testing whether a law that restricted a woman's hours of manual work was constitutional. Suppose, what's more, that he took Professor Shaler's advice to counsel politicians and candidates for public office, even the nation's highest office, the presidency. This was citizenly duty. Could the Brahmins hurt him? If so, it was a chance he'd have to take. One thing he knew: retreat was out of the question.

Brandeis's first shot? His insurance clients, the New England Policy-Holders' Protective Committee, were watching closely. They expected prompt, robust action. They must be assured that he served their interests, that pro bono did not mean their issues were on a back burner or that he'd veer off into legal atmospherics. His letter of July 12, 1905, to the trustees of the Equitable Life Assurance Society was to go out in the names of the committee members. They'd need to sign the letter he drafted. It must be clear, crisp, civil, and hard-hitting. He organized it in a nine-point plan that censured the Equitable Life Assurance Society for "deplorable management" and promised legal "radical action" to bring about "reform." The "test of success" in the life insurance industry, Brandeis wrote, was "absolute safety at the smallest possible cost." Merely changing one cast of executive officers for another, he made clear, was a useless game of musical chairs. He demanded the end to "lavish payments" for agents and a cessation of the seduction and "deception" by advertising. The insurance industry, he asserted, "should not be used as an investment company or as a means of gambling on the misfortunes of others."[58]

The investments of the Equitable, what's more, must be surrounded by "legal safeguards." Among these, Brandeis insisted, were prohibitions against any Equitable "executive officers from engaging in any other business or holding office in any other corporations." This prohibition would stop a man like Schiff or Harriman from using one company for the advantage of another, which is to say, it would both expose and prohibit acts of collusion and conflicting interest. The company, finally, "should be brought under the absolute control of the policy holders." Working pro bono, Brandeis made every Equitable policyholder in the United States and abroad his client. (The renamed committee, accordingly, was now to be the Protective Committee of Policy Holders of the Equitable Life Assurance Society.) Policyholders with other companies might well become his clients too, for Brandeis thirsted for all facts of a case and claimed the broadest domain. The committee of five, meanwhile, was pleased. For now, pro bono was no longer alarming.[59]

On his own, Brandeis also wrote to one of the New York investigators to express a growing concern—that big business, such as insurance, was getting too big. Although it was not "fashionable" to suggest that "anything

Miniature Uncle Sam faces the Trusts, whose trophy belt includes skulls of the Small Grocer, the Small Merchant, and Honest Labor. Artist: Homer Davenport. (Library of Congress)

can be too large" in this day and age, he said, it was his "inclination . . . to think that the evils which inhere in and surround the life insurance business cannot be fully met" without "some limitation upon the size of an insurance company." It was his customary formal and courteous language that stopped short of saying bluntly the business was out of control because it had become monstrously bloated to elephantine proportions. The insurance case, among others, heightened Brandeis's concern about an American mythology of business size and efficiency. The public seemed to accept the notion that gigantic size guaranteed maximal efficiency and low costs. The notion was taking hold as a national creed. Depending on the particular business, Brandeis realized, huge size could actually become a disadvantage. A business could become too big to be well managed, especially the trusts. Their promoters' prospectuses on fine bond paper promised hugely increased efficiencies at every level if several businesses were combined into trusts.[60]

Brandeis was convinced, "on the contrary," that "the purpose of combining has often been to curb efficiency or even to preserve inefficiency." All too often, he realized, the trusts maneuvered to shut off competition. Their "conspicuous" profits were earned "mainly through control of the market—through the power of monopoly to fix prices." The insurance business tended this way. So did other trusts, oil and sugar and steel. A good case in point was Andrew Carnegie's superefficient and competitive Carnegie Steel, which made and sold steel "several dollars a ton cheaper than any other concern." Its competitors failed to match its "remarkable efficiency" and so shut Carnegie down in 1901 by buying him out. The new trust was U.S. Steel. It was created, Brandeis said bluntly, through a "bribe" paid to send Carnegie into retirement. The steel for bridges and buildings and rail lines would cost more now that the trust had its monopoly. The insurance industry, too, had the makings of a trust. Brandeis was soon to ask, Was there a money trust? The question was far from preposterous.[61]

One red flag—the word *industrial*—caught his eye in those spring 1905 evenings when Brandeis immersed himself in insurance documents. A special kind of life insurance was sold by these companies: industrial insurance. It was entirely different from ordinary insurance that policyholders paid quarterly, semiannually, or annually, often by mail. He'd never heard of industrial insurance. The committee who'd sought his help were unconcerned about it. They weren't directly affected by it. He grew interested. From the insurance papers Brandeis toted home nightly in the heavy satchels, it seemed that industrial insurance was enormously profitable. Indeed, it was the most profitable part of the business.

What, exactly, was it?

If Brandeis had been in New Haven, Connecticut, a year earlier, 1904, he might have heard a definition. It was given to the Yale senior class in a lecture by John F. Dryden, the president of the Prudential Insurance Company and a U.S. senator. "*Industrial Insurance*," Dryden told the college seniors, "is primarily designed to meet the needs of wage earners employed in manufacturing industries." Its premiums "coincided" with paydays and cost as little as five cents. The coins were conveniently collected weekly by agents at policyholders' homes. The main purpose of the program was to "provide for the burial expenses of the insured." For as little as 5 cents weekly, the deceased poor worker could be saved from burial in a paupers' grave. Industrial insurance, in sum, sounded like a benevolent social service program.[62]

Perhaps the satchels that Brandeis toted home nightly contained the insurance industry's promotional materials for industrial policies. If so, he learned a good deal more about the operation of the business. Just three companies had a near monopoly: the Metropolitan of New York, the Prudential of New Jersey, and the John Hancock of Massachusetts. Together they controlled 94 percent of the business in the United States. Each of the three recruited an "army" of young men agents, to whom the companies furnished advice manuals that sounded remarkably like Horatio Alger novels, such as *The Store Boy, or The Fortunes of Ben Barclay* (1887). Ben is a scrupulously honest rural lad, sociable, energetic, and mathematically quick. He fits the mold of the young men sought by the companies for their "exceptional ability" and "individual talent." The Bens of the industry literally entered every nickel of premiums in neat script in a ledger-like debit book. They were to be cheerful and well groomed. "Seem to be prosperous," the manuals urged, and "people will like you all the better for it." A hearty work ethic was imperative. Never discouraged or fatigued, the agents were to "make the most of every day" all year long. Rapid "promotion to higher positions" was promised, especially to those who liked "outdoor life" and "contact with different elements of the population."[63]

The army of agents was not merely chasing commissions but building "the poor man's estate" and taking "a step toward the abolition of poverty." Industrial insurance, the companies emphasized in their literature, was "family insurance." It tapped into "domestic affections" and must be sold "in the midst of domestic surroundings." A stock of free gifts made the agent welcome in workers' homes. For her children, a housewife might be given an illustrated booklet of patriotic stories, *The Signers of the Declaration of Independence*. For herself, there was an inspirational pamphlet, *Household Words*. Or perhaps a package of sewing needles such as Stork brand Gold-Eyed Sharps. Or a wall calendar with touching scenes of mothers and of rosy-cheeked children at play—a reminder of the family's vulnerability if the breadwinner were to die.[64]

Where did the agents canvass for clients? Door-to-door cold calls in working-class neighborhoods and tenements could yield new policies, but "often, a pastor will furnish a list of the members of his parish most likely to insure." Funeral undertakers also promised a rich harvest of new industrial policies, for "sudden deaths" served as "a warning against the neglect of life insurance." If the agent was at a loss for words when facing the man of the house, his company gave him a script. He was to look the workman in the eye and ask, "What will the family do when you and your earnings are cut off by the hand of death? Will they not then wish you had been insured?"[65]

Industrial workers throughout the nation needed no statistics on the "hand of death." It lay on their shoulders daily. Brandeis had industrial workers' perils in mind at this time because of a project of his sister-in-law,

Josephine Goldmark. A colleague of Florence Kelley at the National Consumers' League, Josephine was preparing to go to Pittsburgh to study the causes of deadly industrial accidents and their relation to workers' fatigue. Her work was part of the Russell Sage Foundation's Pittsburgh Survey project. In the years ahead, she was to write a landmark book on the topic, *Fatigue and Efficiency*. Meanwhile, a young journalist was counting the fingers of death's hand in this year, 1905. One of the new muckrakers, William Hard, visited a Chicago steel mill and chronicled the year's accidental deaths—the twelve men killed by blast furnace mishaps, the three electrocuted, the four who died from blows by falling objects, the four others who burned to death from molten metal, and so on to a tally of forty-six men.[66]

These were Chicago workers, but the forty-six could have been paper or textile mill or shoe factory workers in nearby Lowell or Lawrence or Lynn right here in Massachusetts. For that matter, they could be workers in the new industrial Louisville that emerged in the 1880s. Brandeis saw its development with every visit back home—the Louisville Bridge and Iron Company, the Hackett Company foundry, the Louisville Chemical Works, Louisville Steel, the Louisville Mining and Manufacturing Company. Or the textile mills that turned out jeans clothing of coarse cloth that wrinkled in the legs. In downtown Louisville, in fact, Metropolitan Life opened an industrial insurance agency at 252 West Main Street. Agents gave out full-color picture cards showing a sweet little girl gardening in a white dress with a red sash. She was watering roses under the headline "INDUSTRIAL INSURANCE." On the reverse side, a policyholder could calculate in multiples of a nickel the cost of insuring a family member up to the age of seventy.[67]

From New England to Louisville and beyond, industrial insurance sounded like an important service to America's working-class families. A policyholder could be thankful knowing that if he became fatally ill or was killed on the job, he could "avoid the ignominy of burial in a Potter's Field." "Deep at the root of the problem of life insurance for the poor," said Prudential's Dryden, "lies their abhorrence of a pauper burial." The dreaded pauper's potter's field (from Matthew 27: 5–7) referred to a place where potters dug clay, leaving trenches and pits for the burial of strangers. The term was now synonymous with extreme poverty and shame, for anyone who died penniless would be interred in an unmarked grave at public expense in such a field. One New York writer offered a glimpse of New York City's "common trench of the Poor Burying Ground [where] they lie packed three stories deep, shoulder to shoulder, crowded in death as they were in life."[68]

Workers who bought industrial insurance policies believed that if they died, their families could pay for a burial plot, an undertaker, and a casket, even if they must select "a cloth-covered wooden casket in a somewhat cheaper style." They could afford a viewing in a funeral parlor and a hearse driven by a liveryman to the cemetery. Thanks to the promptly paid industrial insurance claim, the surviving family members could gather at the gravesite marked by a modest stone, perhaps carved with a bit of scrollwork. Insurance money that was left over could help settle debts.[69]

The business seemed like a public service. It protected workers and their families, provided good jobs for over 10,000 energetic, young sales agents, and was backed by three longstanding companies with billions of dollars in resources promptly paying valid claims.

To Brandeis, however, the documents told another, terrible story of predatory corporate greed that jeopardized social stability. Unchecked, he realized, the industrial insurance practices could do great harm to American society. The companies, as he learned, paid nothing if death occurred within three years of purchase of the policy. Also, they paid nothing if the policy was cancelled in less than twenty years. Actual payment to the survivors was made in only one-eighth of the cases. In all others, "no money was paid out by the insurance companies." On any given week, the agent might be told at the door that the family could no longer afford the nickels and dimes of the weekly premium. After four missed payments, the agent scratched the family from his debit book. They had their calendars and other trinkets but were no longer covered. They also lost the money already paid out. "Two-thirds of the industrial life insurance policies . . . could be counted on to lapse in this manner within three years."[70]

Brandeis focused on the average amount paid out from a claim—$140— and contrasted an industrial policy with an ordinary policy. The finding was startling. A twenty-one-year-old man, perhaps an office clerk working for the senior Mr. Clarence Day, would pay $16.55 yearly for an ordinary policy worth $1,000. A twenty-one-year-old meatpacking plant worker who signed up for an industrial policy, however, would pay nearly twice as much, $31.20 yearly, for a $984 policy. Or suppose a forty-year-old middle-class man, perhaps a hotel manager, bought a regular policy for $1,000 of coverage. His yearly cost would be $27.03. If a house painter of the same age bought an industrial policy that cost $26 per year, however, his benefit would be only $500—half as much.[71]

Brandeis dug deeper into the figures. Last year, 1904, 87 percent of the industrial policies issued by the three companies lapsed in the first year. Something else leaped out as he cross-checked facts and figures. For ordinary policies, management costs ran to about 20 percent of the cost of a premium. For industrial policies, however, the amount ballooned to 40 percent.

An advertisement for industrial life insurance combines five minutes with the suggestion of the nickel, c. 1890s. (Warshaw Collection, Smithsonian Institution)

For every hard-earned dollar that a workingman's family spent for industrial life insurance, forty cents came off the top for management expenses. The "army" of 12,000 to 14,000 agents, what's more, were not earning a middle-class living. The average income of an agent was all of $11.64 per week, about $100 less per year than that of a glass furnace worker. Brandeis was horrified. The system was so wasteful it was "disastrous" and "vicious," and he called it a "shocking fraud perpetrated on the working class." Stopping this fraud was imperative for the longtime health of U.S. society.[72]

Brandeis saw no freedom ahead for the workers trapped in the system of industrial insurance. It was unlikely that the Armstrong Commission would take up their cause when it met in Albany to hold investigative hearings. The commission would be too preoccupied with the "exorbitant salaries" of executives, the "unjustifiable dividends," and the "use of policyholders' money . . . for private profit." Yet the country's workers needed insurance protection. Nearly three-quarters of all insurance policies issued in the nation this year, 1905, were industrial policies.[73]

Brandeis recognized that workers weren't merely dazzled by agents' salesmanship. They proved how deeply they cared about coverage by voting for protection with their hard-earned money. Working twelve- and fourteen-hour shifts, they hadn't time to investigate the insurance business on their own, and many were immigrants who spoke little English. No one told them about ordinary policies, and they didn't think to ask about them. Brandeis owed them more than a muckraker's exposé. The issue, he saw, was a time bomb for American society. Sooner or later, the workers would find out about the theft of their hard-earned money. Political radicals could then stoke their anger to a boil. Riots and repression were sure to follow. Industrial insurance could thus trigger two dire long-term outcomes: workers' mass poverty and social upheaval. Both echoed from Brandeis's wartime boyhood and postwar youth. He owed the country and the workers a solution to this problem.

And he saw one. It was right in front of him, so to speak, on Massachusetts Avenue: the Boston Five Cents Savings Bank. Chartered by the state in 1853, it promised to "induce the young and industrial classes to save, by encouraging deposits as small as five cents." Nowadays, in 1905, the bank was one of 189 such institutions for savings in Massachusetts. Many had "five cents" in their names—the amount later to hold the same meaning in the public mind as the dollar. Just as the industrial policies relied on multiples of the nickel, so in name did the Plymouth Five Cents Savings Bank, the Stoneham Five Cents Savings Bank, the Webster Five Cents Savings Bank, and many others. Their depositors were low-wage workers who were trying to build nest eggs to stave off pauperism. In fact, these banks were created specifically to serve "the poor . . . those who gain their living by their own labor of hand or brain, with no accumulated capital yielding an assured income." Years of steady, small deposits in a savings bank account helped a low-wage person accumulate capital and avoid becoming a charity case in an institution for the destitute. The theory of savings banks was "that *some*, *many*, perhaps a majority of mankind would prefer honest independence . . . to beggarly dependence."[74]

Brandeis compared the savings bank plan with industrial insurance. His starting point was that both plans were promoted as hedges against pauperism. The difference between the two businesses, however, was galactic. The savings banks paid interest on their accounts, currently 3.83 percent annually. A person who deposited money in the Boston Five Cents Savings

Bank saw the account grow, and much of the growth came from interest that was steadily compounding. If "the day of adversity" should come, the savings bank depositor could withdraw money from his or her account at any time without penalty. If an industrial policyholder was laid off and couldn't make the premiums, however, his family lost the amount already paid out. It simply vanished. And the management fees? The insurance companies skimmed 40 percent of an industrial policyholder's premium for management fees, but the savings banks administered their accounts for a mere 1.47 percent. The savings banks, what's more, had a rock-solid record of financial responsibility. They invested conservatively and prevailed even in times of economic stress.[75] Could the low-wage workers of America somehow get their insurance through the savings banks? Could they get insurance coverage at low cost through interest-bearing insurance policy accounts at the very banks created to serve people like them? Could such insurance yield pension-like annuities and prevent poverty in a policyholder's later years? How could it work? What were the mechanics?

Brandeis was not out to destroy the insurance industry; his aim was to reform it. If he could devise a workable alternative plan and get it up and running in Massachusetts, then the big insurance companies would feel the fires of competition. They would react. They'd modify their policies, streamline their operations, bring discipline to their accounting systems, lower their rates, cut back on their lavish advertising—in sum, serve the policyholders as valued customers instead of victimizing them from greed. The companies would still make good, reasonable profits. Brandeis's plan would act as a lever for reform.

Working on facts and figures, he enlisted Miss Grady's help. His secretary put on her spectacles and worked with all her concentration. Devoted to her boss and fond of Mrs. Brandeis and the girls, Miss Grady nonetheless sensed the overwhelming odds against Mr. Brandeis if he pursued this insurance plan. With his self-confessed "bulldog determination & obstinacy," he never dodged a worthy fight, but this one could be especially brutal—and could test his endurance in ways he couldn't yet imagine. To succeed, the savings bank plan must be approved by both houses of the highly political Massachusetts legislature and signed by the governor. Only public pressure would move the elected representatives to act, and that required rallying support from every quarter, from business to civic and church groups to the labor unions. Fortunately, Miss Grady and her office colleague, Miss Louise Malloch, had learned this drill in the Boston transit and gas company fights. Once again, they'd be called on to dispatch a blizzard of fact-filled letters and booklets soliciting support from business and civic leaders, attorneys, industrialists, financiers, welfare workers, clergymen. Miss Grady would type the letters and articles that Mr. Brandeis was certain to write, and she'd help prepare accompanying graphs and tables too, for she foresaw a monumental publicity campaign in newspapers and national magazines, perhaps *Collier's Weekly*. For the foreseeable future, she'd spend her nights, her Sundays, and her holidays on insurance. Best to stock up on postage stamps and typewriter ribbons.[76]

Mr. Brandeis's packed schedule would be tighter than ever, she knew. He'd probably bring a dinner suit to hang in an office closet for a quick change of clothes, because he'd make evening speeches to civic groups four or five nights each week. He'd certainly address the city's leading business executives in October at a dinner meeting of the Commercial Club of Boston, which met at the elegant Algonquin Club on Commonwealth Avenue. She could foresee the title, "Life Insurance — the Abuses and the Remedies." Miss Grady knew how winning was Mr. Brandeis's speaking style. He never grew red in the face, never blustered, never became bombastic. He'd "calmly build up his case" in a "slow, conversational," and "tranquil" voice, standing with "his left hand in his trouser pocket and the other on the desk" or speaker's stand. Most listeners fell under the "spell" of his "magnetic voice."[77]

As ever, she and Miss Malloch would stick with him every inch of the way, although the obstacles were almost unimaginable. The savings bank men were ultraconservative and terrified of innovation. Opposed to change of any sort, they'd be as hard as the New England granite of their bank buildings. The insurance men, for their part, would play the hand they already held. Once past the storms of the current scandal, they would count on the public's short attention span and forgetfulness. They'd launch new advertising campaigns with fetching slogans, like the Metropolitan's "The Light That Never Fails" and "Mother Metropolitan." The insurers, meanwhile, would court the politicians at the statehouse on Beacon Hill and in every other state capital. They would see a Brandeis-supported insurance bill as a chance to insert tricky language that was advantageous to them, or else certain to scuttle the plan for good. Or they'd work behind the scenes to cue up rival legislation favorable to their own interests. Major Henry Lee Higginson would promote such a rival plan. Boston called him "Uncle Henry" for his good works, but recently he'd turned against Mr. Brandeis and tried, spitefully it seemed, to block his every move.[78]

For certain, as Miss Grady knew from the gas and transit fights, the insurance men would accuse Mr. Brandeis of a "most dangerous experiment" that promised "disastrous failure and permanent injury" to the cause of "sound investment." They'd sneer at him for lacking "the necessary knowledge and experience." And they'd play a waiting game, trusting that delay was on their side as the sands of the hourglass ran out. And who would educate the workers themselves? Once they understood how the industrial scheme had cheated them, how and why would they possibly believe in the savings bank plan? Mr. Brandeis was a student of the classics. The Greek myth of Sisyphus might fit here and now, for Sisyphus was doomed forever to try to push a rock up a steep hill. Each time, the rock slipped and rolled back down, and the cycle started over again. Miss Grady had to hope that the savings bank plan was not Mr. Brandeis's rock and he was not a modern-day Sisyphus.[79]

Brandeis was not thinking about Greek myths or ancient history. His mind was alive with the memory of epic, horrible battles fought on American soil within his lifetime—and the odds of their happening again. He was thinking, too, of the economic downturns and slack periods when workers were laid off in droves, had no source of income, and ultimately faced old age in poverty. He was thinking, that is, of the jeopardy to democracy. His family history held a particularly grave lesson in that cost, and the lesson drove him now. No one need know the specific, deepest roots of his savings bank campaign. Boston wasn't interested in motives, and personal life was private.

Echoing from his law school days of the mid-1870s, however, Brandeis could still hear the tone of deepening despair in his father's confession that he lived like a proletarian. This was no joke. Louis's father likened himself to Louisville laborers living hand to mouth in shotgun cottages or the 1820s-era Walnut Street townhouses that became tenements or the tin-roofed "ramshackle cottages" by the Louisville and Nashville railroad tracks.[80]

That crisis wasn't only about material things. The human spirit suffered. Battered by economic storms, Adolph Brandeis lost his former "joy in fighting." In his fifties, an age when most Americans were considered to be old, Adolph looked inward and found "cowardice." A coward lived in fear and had no freedom. A coward could not be a citizen. Without citizens, democracy was doomed. One lesson was plain to see: a man at the mercy of outside forces could be crushed, his vitality sapped, his citizenship snuffed out. Democracy could be buried in its own potter's field.[81]

Professor Shaler's reflections on laborers' plight in times of financial distress hit home in the insurance fight. In times of financial panics, Shaler wrote, "the wage-earner is likely to use up his savings and fall towards pauperism." In a capitalist system, their "only chance in life is to earn steadily, put aside all they can," and gain "some share in the wealth that earns money." The wage earner who could not "share in the wealth that earns money" was to face squalor, destitution, and life in the bleak poorhouses as a ward of the state. Was a person such as Brandeis's own father among this group? It was possible to think it could happen.[82]

Or, in desperation, might the wageworker heed the anarchists or demagogues who urged dynamite as the solution to his problems? The strikers in Louisville and throughout the nation took that destructive path in 1877. Grievances and despair over wage cuts spurred the horrific railroad strike. Suppose that while patrolling his hometown during his law school vacation, Brandeis had faced a striker and been ordered to pull the trigger of his militia rifle. He'd since joked about the nocturnal military mission, for he was no rifleman. In fact, it was a deadly serious matter. This year, 1905, Brandeis began a newspaper clip file on the enmity between capital and labor, for the two sides shelled one another in the press. Labor leaders asserted the unionists' "rights as workers and citizens" to organize "in modern industry." They threatened to bring industry to a halt with their strikes. In turn, the breakfast cereal magnate C. W. Post bought space to accuse organized workers of being a "riotous, arrogant and lawbreaking . . . labor trust," while the inflammatory *Boston Herald* charged that "labor unionism . . . seems to turn peaceable citizens to demons." This very year, 1905, the former U.S. commissioner of labor Carroll D. Wright delivered several lectures on labor strikes, including a description of the "riots, many acts of violence, intimidation, and the destruction of a great amount of property" in the strike of 1877. Wright also described the Battle of Homestead, the steel strike of 1892, when the mill owners turned a hired army of Pinkertons against their own steelworkers. The warlike terms of that strike had sickened Brandeis. Wright's lectures were to be published the following spring in a book whose title captured the bellicose reality of strikes: *The Battles of Labor*. Democracy could die on the strikers' battlefield.[83]

It need not, however, if Americans of every class were helped to be citizens. The savings bank plan was meant to provide one foundation for citizenship of the working class. To Brandeis, this meant "sufficient . . . surplus" saved to "provide for the contingencies for the future." It meant savings beyond basic expenses for food, shelter, clothing, and recreation. It meant money left after the rent was paid and the food bought, money remaining after haircuts and ice cream and the nickelodeon. Brandeis mulled the problem, studied savings bank records, gathered facts, enlisted the help of the notable actuary Walter Wright, and made calculations through the summer and early autumn of 1905. A hunch was worthless, and a trial balloon could burst. All relevant data must be sought and verified. Miss Grady, his gem of a secretary, helped tremendously. She had a head for figures. Her intelligence, and that of Miss Malloch, and also his wife and sisters-in-law and his good friend Elizabeth Glendower Evans, and so many bright women in the working class—they were persuading him that the vote must be extended to women. He no longer doubted the suffragist cause. He'd support the proposed Nineteenth Amendment while attending to insurance and other matters. Now, at last, the savings bank facts were in, and he saw the solution in focus as sharp as a photographic print emerging from a developing tank. He wrote it up in a memo to the devoted Miss Grady, who recalled her boss's tone of triumph in the message: "We've found the answer. The savings banks *can* be adapted to the writing of life insurance."[84]

The message sounded low key and logistical. Rightly so. A law office was no place for theatrics. Miss Grady, however, heard it as loud and clear as a herald trumpet for a very long campaign. As she foresaw, it was endless and grueling in every way imaginable, including an effort to bribe Brandeis to back off. In Albany, meanwhile, New York's Armstrong Commission took testimony from insurance executives, cross-examined them, exposed their shady and illegal dealings, and in April 1906 published a scathing report that prompted new legislation and industry-wide reform. Brandeis's clients, the committee of five, were pleased. The Armstrong Commission, as he predicted, cited industrial insurance as a problem in need of further study and possible action. He was miles ahead of them. By 1907, three Massachusetts banks had instituted his savings bank insurance plan, and through the 1910s and 1920s, other banks joined. Miss Alice H. Grady served as the state deputy commissioner of Savings Bank Life Insurance from 1919 until her death in 1934.[85]

Until late in his career, "Brandeis considered savings bank life insurance his greatest achievement." As he hoped, the savings bank insurance plan became a lever for industrial insurance reform. It was the tool Brandeis intended to forge and wield, a pry bar to move the insurance companies to reform. "Its greatest success by far," Brandeis said, "has been its effect upon the industrial insurance companies." They reduced their premium rates and paid the full amount if death occurred after six months. Policyholders also received remittances if they cancelled their policies. In 1906, Brandeis estimated that "the reforms would save American workers between $10 and $15 million annually" (the equivalent of about $24 million to $36 million in 2007, according to the consumer price index). "The early success of savings bank life insurance," as one historian remarked, "is to be measured largely by the reforms it forced upon the most reluctant industrial companies."[86]

In the years ahead, high-profile cases continued to bring Brandeis fame as the nation's "People's Lawyer." Democracy was always his key issue, although the specifics of various cases — and causes — ranged far and wide. Though never a devoutly religious Jew, Brandeis became engaged in the Zionist movement, the idea of a home country for the world's Jews. His family history was a powerful incentive, as were discussions with prominent Zionists in the 1910s. He doubtless remembered Professor Shaler's praise for the strength and resilience of a long-oppressed people who amazingly achieved "dominance" in Western civilization without modern armies or the control of the capitals of commerce and art. Perhaps Brandeis was also moved by the representation of Jews in charts of world religions and geography. For instance, the popular Rand McNally U.S. and world atlas of 1911, a publication meant for the American consumer marketplace, featured the adherents of religions of the world as a full-page colorful pie chart. Christians, Buddhists, "Mohammedans" (Muslims), and "Brahminists" (Hindus) took up nearly the whole pie, with the world's 10 million Jews as a thin sliver. Brandeis began to think of a Zionist Palestine based on his classical schooling on the democratic nation-state of Athens. He conceived of a small, democratic Jewish state that would bridge the Christian and non-Christian world. He began to speak and write in its support and became the U.S. leader of the Zionist movement.[87]

Immigrant Jews whom Brandeis met in the New York garment industry labor strike negotiations of 1910 reinforced his ideas on Zionism and also brought him deeper into issues of labor-capital relations. The power of capital, he was more than ever convinced, must be counterbalanced by the power of labor. "The cause of unionism is one which must advance," he was to write in 1912. "It is an essential part of our present industrial system." He added, "Without unions the cause of democracy in America would have suffered far more than it has from the abuse of power and the oppressive methods of the great financial and industrial interests." Brandeis regretted that industrial democracy made very little headway in the United States, for he understood that workers belonged at the table when management decisions were being made.[88]

Elsewhere, the "Brandeis brief" became a landmark document in the legal and social history of workers' rights in America. Brandeis said yes when Florence Kelley and his sister-in-law, Josephine Goldmark, begged him to take the lead in the 1908 *Muller v. Oregon* case scheduled for argument before the U.S. Supreme Court. At issue was whether the state could constitutionally restrict a woman's work hours. Brandeis distilled his argument into a mere two pages. In them, he stated that the right to "liberty," which is guaranteed in the Fourteenth Amendment to the Constitution, has "a real and substantial relation to public health, safety, or welfare." The innovation of the Brandeis brief was its thick, book-length file of documentation on pub-lic health, safety, and welfare in workplace health reports from the United States, Europe, and Britain. All proved consistently that onerous labor led to illness, disability, and harm to a woman's reproductive capacity (and there-fore had an adverse impact on the nation's well-being). Regulated hours and safe workplaces, on the other hand, promoted personal and public well-being. It was as simple as the light and the darkness. The boldness of the brief was its data. Instead of mounting a case based on legal precedent, Brandeis relied on the authority of in-the-world social facts. Brandeis believed deeply in "the living law," and the Supreme Court's favorable *Muller* decision cemented his belief that the courts would recognize and respond positively to the realities of social change.[89]

Well known within the legal profession, the name Brandeis became a household word in 1911 when newspapers from New York to San Francisco put his name on the front page in coverage of a transit case known as the Eastern Rate case. For Brandeis, the case echoed from the Boston Elevated fight, and yet again he went to work pro bono, for he'd learned that finan-ciers, mainly J. P. Morgan, attempted to control the New Haven and Boston and Maine railroads with no concern for the rights of passengers and ship-pers. Ignorant of rail transport, they wanted to wring maximal profits by watering the stock via falsified financial reports. Brandeis won the case on behalf of the shippers by exposing the dishonesty and featuring the testimony of the efficiency expert, Frederick Winslow Taylor, who claimed that the rail-roads could be run so efficiently that they could save $1 million per day. Brandeis's role in the Eastern Rate case infuriated the financiers—including, it seems, the senior Clarence Day. Young Clarence recalled his father, the financier of small railroads, "thumping his hand with a hammer-like beat on his newspaper" as he "thought of the New Haven Railroad" and "roared" out, "*Damned* heavy losses!"[90]

Brandeis's involvement in national politics came to seem inevitable. Pro-fessor Shaler called it a citizen's duty to guide the work of elected officials, and Brandeis regularly counseled the governor of Massachusetts, Curtis Guild Jr., during the insurance fight. In 1910, he found a new friend in a Pro-gressive midwestern U.S. senator in the Ballinger-Pinchot affair, a political-legal case concerning the sale of Alaskan wilderness public lands to private interests. Brandeis had much in common with Wisconsin's Fighting Bob La Follette, the man who'd risked his health to lead the successful reform of Wisconsin's Republican Party, which La Follette saw as captive to the rail-road and timber corporations. Governor La Follette was now U.S. Senator La Follette, and in 1912 Brandeis supported his candidacy for president until it became clear that New Jersey's governor, Woodrow Wilson, was to be the Democratic Party's nominee. Having left the Republican Party, which he saw as the party of the monopolistic trusts, Brandeis had become a registered Democrat, according to Shaler's principle that "the citizen clearly owes an allegiance to the party which represents his ideals of government," but owes this allegiance as "a freeman," not as an indentured servant.[91]

Brandeis became a counselor to Woodrow Wilson in the campaign of 1912, when former president Theodore Roosevelt mounted a vigorous third-party candidacy to regain the White House. Roosevelt's Progressive (or "Bull-moose") Party platform called for the federal government to oversee and regulate the gigantic trusts. Roosevelt called his plan the New Nationalism. Its flaw, Brandeis saw, was the presumption that the wasteful, monopolist trusts were a permanent fixture of American economic life. Brandeis advised Wilson, on the contrary, to propose new rules to open up competition, force the trusts to adhere to a tough new set of business rules, and thereby reduce their hold on business by letting new competitors into the marketplace. The Wilson campaign called the plan the New Freedom.[92]

When Wilson won the presidency, many expected Brandeis to be named secretary of commerce or appointed to another high office. He was not. He was bypassed, further, when Wilson nominated James C. McReynolds of Tennessee for the U.S. Supreme Court, for Wilson was advised that Brandeis's enemies were too many and too powerful. A Brandeis nomination, Wilson was warned, would harm the president politically in a vicious confirmation fight. Brandeis had enraged the bankers with his work on the Eastern Rate case and with his indictment of the money trust in *Other People's Money and How the Bankers Use It* (1914). Henry Lee Higginson declared that "Brandeis and his gang have misrepresented and misused every indecent means to corrupt the public mind and deceive people." The Higginson Brahmins stood ready to do battle whenever their former protégé was nominated for any powerful office. Brandeis, meanwhile, remained a principal advisor to the president. He assisted in drafting key legislative measures, such as the Federal Reserve Act of 1913 and the Clayton Antitrust Act and Federal Trade Commission Act of 1914.[93]

When a second Supreme Court vacancy occurred in 1916, the People's Attorney won the nomination; Justice Louis D. Brandeis served on the Court from 1916 to 1939. His confirmation, as many predicted, was a bruising affair in which he was declared to be "unfit" and "an insult . . . to the business interests of the country," and also "delinquent" and "dishonorable in his professional conduct." Once on the Court, he joined his older friend, Justice Oliver Wendell Holmes, with whom he served for sixteen years. "The two men differed greatly in temperament and sentiment: the Boston Brahmin distrusted the people but let them have their way; the Jewish reformer placed his trust in the people and let them have their way."[94]

Brandeis "taught judges that it was their duty to undertake independent fact-gathering before they rendered constitutional judgments." His opinions (notably in *Myers v. United States* in 1926) reinforced the doctrine of the separation of powers among the branches of government. The doctrine, he emphasized, was designed "not to promote efficiency but to preclude the exercise of arbitrary power," especially by the president. Brandeis's reputation as a defender of civil liberties came from his dissenting opinion in *Olmstead v. United States* and his concurring opinion in *Whitney v. California*, the former involving government entrapment and invasion of privacy, the latter upholding the right to free speech. Brandeis's biographer, Philippa Strum, remarks that "together, they constitute the clearest and most eloquent explanation of the importance of civil liberties in a democratic society."[95]

Strum writes that Brandeis "avoided the simplistic right-left political spectrum common among most Americans" and that he "did not believe laissez-faire capitalism was possible in an industrialized society." She goes on, "He deplored the centralization of power that accompanied socialism. He wanted the equality of power that would come from balancing organizations of disparate interests; he wanted the individual to have the liberty of leisure and the equality of economic partnership; he wanted the central government to use its power, and particularly its taxing power, to break up concentrations of power elsewhere and to ensure that society's underdogs would be treated fairly. He did not want substitution of the power of Washington for the power of the trusts; neither did he want a return to nineteenth-century economics and government."[96]

As for the individual, Strum adds, "Two strands run through Brandeis's thought: possibilities and limitations. . . . The most important thing individuals could do for themselves was to fulfill their own possibilities. For that, they needed the freedom to read and hear and think and speak. 'I believe that the possibilities of human advancement are unlimited,' Brandeis said. 'Liberty is the greatest developer.'" Brandeis, says Strum, worked for "the beginnings of economic liberty through regularity of employment, freedom of speech and assembly, minimum wages, and maximum hours." One admirer labeled him "a serenely implacable democrat" who was "secure in his faith in democracy and tireless in fighting for it." In honor of his achievement, Brandeis University is named for him, as is the Louis D. Brandeis School of Law at the University of Louisville, where his and his wife's ashes are interred.[97]

Walter Rauschenbusch

The Social Gospel

The Gospel, to have power over an age, must be the highest expression of the moral and religious truths held by that age. If it lags behind and presents outgrown conceptions of life and duty, it is no longer in the full sense the Gospel. Christianity itself lifts the minds of men to demand a better expression of Christianity.—WALTER RAUSCHENBUSCH, "The New Evangelism," 1904

Walter Rauschenbusch was the most influential and important religious public intellectual in early-twentieth-century America.—CORNEL WEST, "Can These Dry Bones Live?" 2007

In the early 50s I read Walter Rauschenbusch's *Christianity and the Social Crisis*, a book that left an indelible imprint on my thinking.—MARTIN LUTHER KING JR., quoted in *Christianity and the Social Crisis in the 21st Century*, 2007

In the autumn of 1908, the Baptist Protestant minister Walter Rauschenbusch arrived at the entrance of New York City's lavish Waldorf-Astoria Hotel at Fifth Avenue and Thirty-fourth Street. The doorman who ushered in the tall, slim, "physically commanding" figure probably did not know he was the best-selling author of a controversial new book titled *Christianity and the Social Crisis*. Nor could the gold-buttoned doorman guess that the hotel threshold was Rauschenbusch's version of the Rubicon River of the ancient Roman Empire—a point of no return. As someone who was classically educated, Rauschenbusch himself surely knew the story of Julius Caesar's bold move across the boundary of the Rubicon in 49 B.C. Crossing the river was prohibited under Roman law, and Caesar's deliberate defiance of that law made armed conflict inevitable. Once Caesar crossed the Rubicon, there was no turning back.[1]

The Baptist minister and theologian did not think in pagan military terms, but the reference was fitting. By the 1900s, the phrase "crossing the Rubicon" referred to anyone committing to a risky or revolutionary course of action. Like Caesar, Rauschenbusch was fighting entrenched powers that had their

Walter Rauschenbusch, c. 1917. (Library of Congress)

own stake in the status quo with its prohibitions and boundaries. He too was waging a public campaign that put him on the side of revolution.

This Christian revolution was called the Social Gospel. It called Christians to create a "new social and political order" that was instituted on the earth by Jesus Christ. It focused on the words of the Lord's Prayer: "Thy kingdom come, thy will be done on earth . . ." Everyone must take an active part for the kingdom to come, not solely in the divine afterlife but here on earth. Rauschenbusch's campaign was to be an all-out effort. If successful, it would transform Christian thought and practice and redeem society both spiritually and materially. Rauschenbusch knew the moment was critical and the need urgent, for the modern era of industrial capitalism was catastrophic for vast numbers of men, women, and children. The wondrous industrial machinery that could improve life for so many had instead "submerged a large part of the people in perpetual want and fear." Modern extreme capitalism, he said, "swept the bread from men's tables and the pride from their hearts." Today's Christian duty was to lift all humanity from the ravages of a system that enriched a few and left others in desperation. Only a new Christian evangelism could hasten desperately needed equitable arrangements along social, political, and economic lines. The scale was vast, the challenge monumental.[2]

And the opposition was entrenched and powerful. The church pews of the well-to-do were filled each Sunday with those who profited handsomely from the Gilded Age's extreme capitalism. They thought God was their divine benefactor and regarded those in dire straits (if they regarded them at all) as chastened or punished by the Lord. Still others insisted that religion had no legitimate role to play in the secular world of business and finance, and their blood boiled at the very suggestion that the Gospel ought to influence those worlds. The status quo, by their logic, was divinely ordained, and the doctrine of laissez-faire was the economic expression of religious truth.

Rauschenbusch was well aware that ministers who challenged the status quo risked swift dismissal by church committees. Clergy and other church and seminary officials often sided with the rich and powerful. The trustees and faculty at the upstate New York seminary where Rauschenbusch taught and earned his living, the Rochester Theological Seminary, included such a bloc. To them, the Social Gospel smelled of heresy. Some had Rauschenbusch under surveillance and suspicion, and they frowned on the reform message of his new book. They suspected that he thought like a common laborer, not a member of the better classes. Rauschenbusch knew the power of their opposition. A good friend who shared his commitment to the Social Gospel had been fired from the faculty of another seminary. Word of a provocative speech in New York City at a hotel that was designed to resemble a French chateau could reach Rochester at telegraph speed. Consequences could be dire. For the minister-theologian, however, there was no retreat. This elite space of "mobility, transience, and anonymity" was about to become the site of an urgent summons to transform the social order of America. As Caesar reportedly said, "The die is cast."[3]

No guest who passed Rauschenbusch in the "mirrored and amber marble corridor" known as the Waldorf-Astoria's Peacock Alley could sense that fires burned within him. Some who awaited him in the ballroom could say this much: for the past decade, Walter Rauschenbusch had been a servant of the Lord and solid citizen of the city of his birth, Rochester, which was now a bustling industrial metropolis on the Genesee River at the western edge of New York, by Lake Ontario. He'd spent a good many of his younger years in Europe and elsewhere in the United States but returned permanently to his home city in 1897, when an offer of a professorship at the Rochester Theological Seminary proved timely and fortuitous. As a notable figure in Rochester church and civic affairs, Rauschenbusch was happily married to

The Peacock Alley of the Waldorf-Astoria Hotel, c. 1897. (Library of Congress)

the former Pauline Rother and was the father of five fine children. Until this past year, his days had been filled with rounds of family duties, faculty obligations, civic functions, and writing articles for Protestant Christian magazines.[4]

During summer months at a family vacation cottage in Canada, however, Rauschenbusch at last found his truest and most commanding voice—the voice of the Social Gospel. That is, he finally wrote the book—the manifesto—that had taken him years to develop. *Christianity and the Social Crisis* did not open with a trumpet clarion call. Bombast was never Rauschenbusch's style. Readers found in the opening pages a survey of social ethics that began with the Hebrew prophets as exemplars of ethics of service, morality, righteousness, and justice. Rauschenbusch called them "the beating heart of the Old Testament," and his book then proceeded to the New Testament life of "the Jesus who had walked from Galilee to Jerusalem doing good—curing lepers, giving sight to the blind, feeding thousands, and raising the dead to life." This Jesus, said Rauschenbusch, provided "the template" for "the early church" and for "the entire Christian life."[5]

Thus far in the book, Christian readers would find traditional points with which they were familiar. The waters began to stir, however, in the pages ahead. The Christian life, Rauschenbusch wrote, became concealed and distorted through centuries of church practices that emphasized ceremony and false doctrines. The promising Protestant Reformation had its own failings and led, finally, to a modern nineteenth century that was stained by social crisis and human misery.

By this point, Rauschenbusch's readers were tossing in a tempest of the author's making, especially when he emphasized that "personal religion" was not the focus of Christianity. A renewal of Christian compassion, insisted Rauschenbusch, depended on a *social* awakening. The personal, he insisted, was "chiefly a means to an end," and "the end was social," as Jesus himself was social. Christian salvation was thus "devotion to the common good," a matter of great urgency in this modern moment, when the common good was so often reduced to mere lip service. The Gospel, Rauschenbusch proclaimed, was a Social Gospel. The very term was both a declaration and a summons to hasten a profound reform movement.[6]

Drafting his book in the cottage in the Canadian woods, Rauschenbusch never dared to dream that it would catapult him to speakers' platforms all over the United States, much less to the Waldorf-Astoria. He expected a small circle of readers, mainly clergymen and theologians who would debate his message based on Christian doctrine and dogma. Some would be hostile, he knew, but he persisted "for the Lord Christ and the People." In his darkest moments, he'd feared that the book's message on social reform would seem "dangerous" to the seminary trustees and cost him his job. *Christianity and the Social Crisis* arrived from the publisher just as he sailed with his family to Germany in April 1907. The year of sabbatical leave granted by his seminary was a blessing, and it put him out of touch with America. Perhaps he hoped that whatever hostility his book aroused would diminish by the time he returned.[7]

When Rauschenbusch returned to U.S. shores, he was greatly relieved to learn that for now the seminary trustees stood behind him—and he was astonished to find that he was famous. During his absence, his book sold out and was reprinted and reprinted again. Suddenly he was a nationally acclaimed author of a book that summoned Christians to create a new social order. The Rochester postman brought sackfuls of mail from admiring readers and numerous invitations to speak to audiences throughout the United States— including the gathering at the Waldorf-Astoria. American Christians wanted to see and hear this figure with a "wide forehead, heavy eyebrows, deep-set hazel eyes," and "a full head of dark-brown hair and trim auburn beard." Many detected "a trace of a smile" at the mouth. Some noticed a similarity to Abraham Lincoln.[8]

But Lincoln was nowhere in Rauschenbusch's thoughts as he made his way to the electrically lighted hotel ballroom. Those who anticipated a fire-and-brimstone performance with a fist pounding the lectern were to be disappointed. Still others probably hoped for the stirring oratory of a legendary evangelist like Dwight Moody, whose late 1800s sermons held thousands rapt in halls all over the world. Or they might anticipate a sermon like Russell Conwell's famous "Acres of Diamonds," with its promise of twinned spiritual and material riches. Instead, listeners must pay close attention to hear every word spoken in his rather high, thin voice. Some may have heard the rumor that Rauschenbusch suffered from a disability, a loss of hearing, although no one could suspect his deafness from his speech or appearance. They saw a properly dressed professor-clergyman whose formal dark suit was carefully brushed, his linen collar starched, the knot of his silk four-in-hand necktie accented with a pearl stickpin.

Formality did not mean remoteness. Rauschenbusch planned to beckon listeners with heartfelt, self-deprecating humor that wove its way through all his talks and always drew hearers close to him. En route to the ballroom, he perhaps noticed the velvet rope that flattered the elite and reminded outsiders of their exclusion. He was here to warn that a society that roped off large numbers of fellow human beings was inhumane, anti-Christian, and deadly. He was to speak with authority because he knew to the depths of his soul that another New York—another America—struggled to survive just blocks away, in slum neighborhoods with names like Rag Pickers' Row and Hell's Kitchen. City residents and visitors sometimes took actual nighttime guided tours of these slums. They deluded themselves into thinking "that an individual could do his bit for a social problem by *looking* at it."[9]

Few educated, middle-class Americans knew such people or places from intimate personal experience. Walter Rauschenbusch was one of the few. Before moving to Rochester, he'd lived in the gang-infested, saloon- and prostitute-riddled slum at the edge of Hell's Kitchen. For over a decade (1886–97), he'd served as the minister of the Second German Baptist Church, a small congregation of struggling workers and their families. In those years he baptized, married, and buried parents and children whose squalid living conditions left them prey to cholera, diphtheria, tuberculosis, and a host of other diseases and fatal temptations. He knew that the plight of those who were victimized by American "social wrongs" was destructive and disgraceful. For the sake of their future, for the future of America, Rauschenbusch came to the Waldorf-Astoria to underscore the message of his book. He'd challenge the entrenched idea that salvation was strictly a privatized relation between the individual and God and that extreme wealth proved God's blessings on the rich. He was here, that is, to challenge the lethal idolatry of gold and dollars in the American religion of laissez-faire.[10]

Sightseeing in the slums, New York City, 1885. Frank Leslie's
Illustrated Newspaper. *(Library of Congress)*

Today's social crisis was real, he said. His were not the words of a misan-
thrope, Rauschenbusch assured his 500 listeners, many of them "rich, famous, beautiful, and fashionable men and women" in their "bright hats and
splendors of costume." "I am not a despiser of my age and achievements,"
he told them. "There is no other age in which I should prefer to have lived."
Today's duty, however, was to lift all humanity from the ravages of a system
that enriched a few and left others in desperation. To do so required a revi-
val of Christianity, a new Christian evangelism. "The moral power generated by the Christian religion is available for the task of social regeneration,"
Rauschenbusch insisted. "It is needed, fully and immediately, if our Christian civilization is to stand and advance."[11]

As the ballroom electric lights blazed, the terms of the Social Gospel
filled the air. "Thy kingdom come, thy will be done on earth . . ." Everyone
must take an active part for the kingdom to come. Would they? Rauschenbusch's words were blunt, forceful, and direct. They came from years of biblical scholarship and experience. Could his words stir his audience to action?
Could he and like-minded brethren of the clergy move others actually to
try to love their neighbors as themselves? Would America's Christians rouse

themselves and answer the call at this critical moment? Would they meet the challenge? Or would the country's churchgoers prove that it was not Walter Rauschenbusch but they themselves who were deaf?

ROCHESTER, NEW YORK, was a horse-and-buggy city when Walter Rauschenbusch's father arrived with his pregnant wife and their five-year-old daughter in 1858. At the intersection of North Main and Buffalo streets, idlers lingered in the afternoon sun, and "occasionally a man puffing a cigar would stop to stroke the nose of a horse hitched to an awning post." Already numbering over 6,000, industrious German immigrants were contributing to a faster pace of life in a city whose population approached 45,000 and was growing. Some worked for the railroads that eclipsed the slower Erie Canal boats. Some owned and operated the factories that turned out textiles at a good clip. A good many others came to work in the industry that gave the city its proud nickname, the Flower City. Rochester's flowers and orchard fruit graced the tables of homes all over America, and its shrubs and young trees shaped the country's lawns and gardens.[12]

August Rauschenbusch loved to garden. He did not, however, move his family to Rochester to grow roses or tulips for the market. He was here to cultivate souls for the Baptist ministry in America. A "formidable" figure, August was a sixth-generation Protestant theologian and minister. He knew American pioneering life firsthand, for he'd served as a missionary in a German settlement in far-off Missouri, where he "grafted Baptist principles on Lutheran antecedents" and preached that slavery was an abomination under God. In the Missouri hinterlands, August was baptized by immersion in the "Father of Waters," the Mississippi River. His Baptist piety and pledge of allegiance to America were both signified in that one sacred act. A much-respected theologian in his native Germany, he was called to Rochester to help rescue its tiny Baptist seminary. Like the city's university, the Rochester Theological Seminary was struggling for survival in the 1850s. August agreed to chair the Department of German. He installed his wife, Caroline, and little daughter, Frida, in a rented house on Charlotte Street and was thankful when his wife delivered a baby girl, Emma. He prayed fervently, however, that God would bless him with a son to carry the Rauschenbusch name for the future in the New World.[13]

August's prayers were answered. Born in 1861, the infant Walter represented the prospect of a seventh generation of Rauschenbusch theologian-ministers. The route to the baby's eventual ordination was immediately mapped. Predictable to some, it did not appear in Walter's sightline for many years. When it did, not everyone rejoiced at the career that followed. Some were alarmed. Certain dark suspicions grew that the young Rauschenbusch's theology was heretical, that he committed the sin of apostasy—that he was a black sheep of a son.[14]

The boy's earliest memories of the church were revealing; he remembered "the baptisms and communion services" solely because "they spoke to the eye and the imagination." Walter's eye for nature and a hand for the sketchbook made him think, deep down, that he had the makings of an artist. Long into adulthood, he could still recall the boyhood feel of his colored pencils that brought "gardens and houses" to life on drawing paper. He recalled, too, his cherished teenage student days of European travel in the early 1880s, when he spent long evenings in artists' studios and refined his "artistic taste" in German art museums. His practical-minded aunt suggested that he become an architect.[15]

It was not to be. Perhaps the novelist was right: "Father was Fate" and "his will controlled [the] universe." August Rauschenbusch kept his son on a tight rein. A purebred American upbringing was out of the question for the boy whose father was baptized in the Mississippi. Before the age of four, Walter sailed with his mother and sisters to Germany, where he remained until 1869, attending nursery and primary schools and proudly waving the Prussian flag. With Protestant playmates, he learned to regard the Catholic children as "bad and dangerous, quite different from us." Frau Rauschenbusch and the three children lived mostly in the town of Barman, just a few houses away from the Wupper River, where they occupied a suite of rooms over a bakery. Industrial Germany surrounded Walter, for the Wupper River was "dyed an inky black by the effluvia of the countless factories and dyeing establishments." In Europe, nevertheless, Walter found the love of beauty that fostered his poetic expression. Traveling in the Swiss Alps in his teenage high school years, he felt "so intensely happy" to "drink in . . . the beauty that God has poured with a prodigal hand over this earth of ours."[16]

Visits from his father were spaced far apart in Walter's earlier years, for August was busy in Rochester and in demand in German churches and centers of learning when he traveled in the United States and abroad. The boy's warmest memories were summertime swimming excursions at lakeside and along the Rhine. Father "took me swimming and made me swim across a deep pond," he remembered. A "bathing beach" in the Black Forest was a treat, and so was a brook where he caught a fish by hand. In the Rhine, he bathed with other children in the nude ("à la Adam and Eve"), which was delicious. His "great love for swimming" was a paternal gift. August Rauschenbusch proudly swam once across the Rhine, but in a bold show of strength, Walter secretly swam both across and back—without touching. Some would think that particular swim signaled a future of limits pushed to extremes.[17]

Prematurely, Walter always thought, his father warned him about "sexual morality." It was a useless lecture because he had nothing to do with girls. Nature, not Fraüleins, absorbed his erotic feelings, although the two sometimes merged. The Swiss lakes between two mountains struck him as "a jewel on the breast of a fair girl."[18]

His father enrolled him in the all-male Evangelical Gymnasium of Gütersloh in Westphalia for a German classical high school education. Proud of his academic achievements, Walter made good friends with classmates. They marched together in Prussian-style field drills, and he spent time at their homes on weekends. Girls were another matter. Shut away in the gymnasium, he turned "green" when a girl only looked at him. The fragile ones frightened him, and the bold ones were repulsive. Confused, he could only blush "violently." Yet Lord Byron's erotic poetry was irresistible, and in his gymnasium years, Walter took license to write his own Byronesque sensual yearnings in verse ("How I long thy lips to press / On thy mouth, oh sweet caress").[19]

Men and women, however, could repel one another. He knew it deeply and personally from his own family household. As far back as he could remember, his parents waged domestic warfare. It was the family secret. Fearful and distressed, little Walter was sent into another room while his parents stormed at one another. They never called a truce, neither in Germany nor in Rochester, not even when the family lived in Rochester's upscale Arnold Park, with its exquisite lawns and fine trees. The senior Rauschenbusch expected "absolute submission," which was "not natural" to his wife. He accused her of malice and dealt the cruelest blow when he charged that she was "no Christian." Walter's mother fought back by refusing to cook her husband's lunch, thus rebelling against a sacred duty of a German hausfrau. "Poor Mrs. Rauschenbusch," the president of the seminary wrote privately, suspecting the couple's "total alienation" from one another. Walter sympathized with his mother. Those who thought he was unduly "solemn" never guessed the family sorrows he held deep inside. His sisters suffered too, Emma the "wild bumble bee" and Frida, who felt she'd "never been young." If he ever were to marry, Walter vowed to be different from his father. He resolved to give his children the happier home lives denied to him and his sisters.[20]

For his peace of mind, it was good fortune that his father traveled so much and sent him away from home for farm work in Pennsylvania during the German school vacation months. Each summer in the 1870s, a German farmer of Lycoming County put a hoe and a horse rake, a toothed sickle, in Walter's hands and taught him fieldwork. He learned to bind sheaves of wheat and to butcher the occasional sheep for fresh meat. On market days he took butter, eggs, and berries to the nearest town and sold them house to house and at curbside. He was thankful for the experience on an "old-fashioned farm."[21]

But this, too, was probably part of August Rauschenbusch's plan. Why else would Walter look back on his religious conversion experience as a rebellion against a farm laborer's life? "I am out in the far country . . . and I don't want to tend the hogs any longer." At seventeen, he experienced his conversion, a "tender, mysterious experience." It carried overtones of secular life. An inner voice spoke, saying, "I want to become a man; I want to be respected." He called it "right living and good citizenship." And he identified the calling that confirmed his destiny as the son of August Rauschenbusch: "Very soon the idea came to me that I ought to be a preacher, and help to save souls."[22]

Four more years under the stormy parental roof in Rochester was the price he knew he'd pay when he enrolled at the Rochester Theological Seminary in 1883. The paternal family tradition dictated that he also earn a university degree, so he registered at the University of Rochester, where his A.B. was conferred in 1884. As always, his academic work was excellent, his study of theology intense. One theological tenet concerned the era known as the Millennium, the thousand peaceful years during which Jesus Christ was foretold by scripture to return to earth. After it, God would destroy the world with catastrophic power. This was the Apocalypse.

From his study of church history, Rauschenbusch knew how avidly Christians debated the timing and terms of Jesus Christ's return and the End Times, the Apocalypse. The Old and New Testament Books of Daniel, Isaiah, and Revelation seemed to foretell a series of cataclysmic events to culminate in the Day of Judgment. Strenuous efforts were made to locate an exact calendar date for the Apocalypse. From the Protestant Reformation to the present, theologians studied particular symbols in the New Testament book of Revelation (such as the ten-horned beast and grapes of wrath) in order to match them up with particular wars, plagues, floods, years of drought, and so on in recorded history. By this method, they tried to locate a precise moment for the final events of human life on earth. On that date, God's wrath would send all non-Christians, evildoers, and the unrepentant to the flames of hell, while his gracious mercy elevated the saved souls to heaven to dwell with him for all eternity.[23]

Rauschenbusch recognized the potential pitfall in apocalyptic thinking, which reached deep into U.S. history from the era of the Pilgrims and Puritans. Some could use it to justify doing nothing in the face of monumental worldly problems. Obsessed with the Apocalypse, they could decide that the clock and calendar pointed to an imminent end and that human effort was therefore futile, wasteful, or even contrary to God's plan. They might privately repent and pray—and wait for Judgment Day, perhaps secretly relishing the prospect of their foes writhing in the fiery furnace of damnation.

Rauschenbusch was having none of it. He saw the phrase "heavenly catastrophe" as a contradiction in terms. He concluded that the early church had absorbed too much of the Jewish apocalyptic literature and "spilled a little of the lurid colors of its own apocalypticism over the loftier conceptions of its Master." Just suppose his own father had surrendered to apocalyptic ruminations and hunkered down in Germany to await the End. Suppose he'd refused missionary service in Missouri and missed his calling to preach the urgency of abolition of slavery in God's name. Multiply this one example, and the outcome was clear. No, the Judeo-Christian tradition was of a people with "a great past and a greater future." It was now for young Walter Rauschenbusch to claim the contemporary moment in the name of Jesus and the Gospel.[24]

Suppose, however, that the greatest Christian cause in America—the emancipation of slaves—had bypassed him by one generation. Suppose he was left in its wake, deprived of a great opportunity. He couldn't bring himself to think about it. Rauschenbusch had his graduate degrees, but the son's silhouette was barely outlined under the broad shadow cast by his father. The senior Rauschenbusch's effort for God was self-evident in the success of the seminary, its bricks and mortar and increased enrollments. The growth of the Baptist church in America was itself in part a tribute to *Vater* August. No greater work of God for one's fellow man could be imagined than the anti-slavery cause in pre–Civil War America. Now it was Walter's turn. The young man who'd hoed and mowed from dawn to dark in Pennsylvania farm fields knew what hard work meant. He knew the meaning of his words when he resolved "to do hard work for God." This meant going out, as his father had, "as a foreign missionary."[25]

Louisville, Kentucky, wasn't foreign enough. In 1884 and 1885, Walter spent summers ministering to a small German Baptist church in the Ohio River city. The features of Louisville did not interest him, but he discovered his counseling skills amid a congregation that was split in dissension and backbiting. He smoothed the waters, learning as much as he taught—perhaps more, for the Louisville congregation awakened him to the reality of living in imitation of Christ. He visited homes, heard personal stories, preached, and organized youth groups. Conforming to the "image" of Christ was a humbling and profound experience of "unselfishness and self-sacrifice." Spiritually, the experience was transcendent. He doubled the size of the congregation in three months and "rejoiced in a number of conversions."[26]

Missionary work beckoned in faraway India, where his sister, Emma, served as a missionary. There was talk of Walter's heading a seminary there under the sponsorship of the American Baptist Foreign Mission Society. For a time, there was also the possibility of a post at a church in Springfield, Illinois. Neither worked out. Certain Rochester seminary faculty perhaps ruined his chances. All along, the son of Herr Professor Doktor Rauschenbusch was expected to be a favorite "nephew" of the seminary faculty. In turn, the faculty were to be "uncles" to the young man. Some of them surely took notice—and offense—when young Rauschenbusch found his honorary uncle outside the seminary. In fact, Rauschenbusch's most cordial, challenging, and helpful teacher was not a theologian but a geology professor, Harrison Webster, who spent many campus hours with the young man and impressed him with his "breezy and geniusy" style and "utterly fearless" mind. The geologist called himself a "Christian evolutionist" who reconciled Darwin with the Bible. This was exactly the sort of heretical notion that was certain to rile particular seminary faculty. It confirmed suspicions that young Rauschenbusch veered toward the unorthodox. The Baptist elders would be watchful. A day of reckoning might come. For his own part, the new seminary and university graduate could not foresee, at the time, that Webster the geologist was most influential for recommending a book on economics.[27]

The call that Walter Rauschenbusch answered came in the form of a letter written in German from the Second German Baptist Church in New York City. At first, the church and its location seemed far removed from missionary service. How wrong that first impression turned out to be. Rustic, pioneering, antebellum Missouri was his father's missionary scene, but Walter was about to experience its modern counterpart—the urban, immigrant world on the edge of New York's Hell's Kitchen.

Arriving in the city on June 1, 1886, he found his church building on West Forty-fifth Street near Tenth Avenue to be "old-fashioned, inconvenient and rather ugly." A poor neighborhood, he learned, didn't mean low-cost housing for its minister. A "decent flat" was $25 per month, one-half of his annual salary of $600, but he relished independent living as his "own master." Yet the small church had severe problems. As a student in Germany, Walter had traveled in fourth-class railcars with "peasants, men and women, carrying butter, chickens, etc., to market." The peasants were as spirited as his New

York flock was downtrodden. He was now the pastor of a demoralized and fractious congregation of about 125 persons, mostly laborers and their families — "a homeless, playless, joyless, proletarian population." There was much to be done. There was everything to be done.[28]

Worship services were just the beginning. A church like his must provide "a day-nursery or kindergarten, a playground for the children, a meeting place for young people, or educational facilities for those who are ambitious." Most churches in large cities had some of these institutional features, but those serving the poor were terribly burdened. A "large plant and an expensive staff" were required. Time and again, Rauschenbusch saw the problems and felt his hands were tied. No matter how eager and willing, no matter how filled with the Christian spirit, church workers quit because few could stand the strain for long. And he learned how scarce were sturdy volunteers. A man who was exhausted by deafening, dangerous, fast-paced machinery on the job lacked the "physical and mental elasticity" for volunteer church work. A saleswoman on her feet in high heels behind a department store counter close to midnight on Saturday night was an "impaired" Sunday school teacher.[29]

An unforgettable stream of human desperation appeared on the church threshold in the years ahead: a "procession of men out of work, out of clothes, out of shoes, and out of hope." Rauschenbusch recalled, "They wore down our threshold and they wore away our hearts." "Buried at times under a stream of human wreckage," he began to ask questions. What was the source of such abject misery? Who was responsible for "unloading this burden of poverty and suffering" on so many "bruised" human beings? How could he begin to think constructively about the lives surrounding him?[30]

For answers, Rauschenbusch reached back to the words of the University of Rochester geologist Professor Harrison Webster, who discussed new approaches that the church could take amid current hard social realities. The geologist perhaps reflected on the church's long, lingering complacency from its past successes. Protestants' pre–Civil War abolitionism—August Rauschenbusch's own mission—hastened the emancipation of slaves, and many Christians harbored a spiritual nostalgia for that shining moment. The postwar years of economic prosperity, what's more, had their own dark shadings. At the time, they seemed to prove that God showered his blessings on deserving Christians of the Gilded Age. "God has need of rich Christians, and He makes them," declared a typical Protestant magazine. Church publications celebrated the captains of steel and rail as exemplary Christian businessmen. Blessed with superabundant worldly success, they surely reflected God's glory.[31]

Meanwhile, those mired in poverty were sunk in sloth and depravity of their own making, according to countless sermons and Christian publications in the post–Civil War decades. Professor Webster and the Rochester seminary faculty doubtless knew that "over and over religious writers insisted that poverty, like riches, was generally deserved." New York's Charity Organization Society, which gentlemen like the senior Clarence Day supported with contributions, reinforced this outlook. Mr. Day, a financier of small railroads, approved of the rigorous discipline the society imposed on its impoverished clientele. For the poor, he and his friends believed that "incessant toil was useful and good." Others expressed a less punitive view of their "heavily-burdened neighbors," but they sounded more smug than concerned. The poor were routinely exhorted on all sides to raise themselves up by working harder.[32]

Workers' self-help through labor organization, however, prompted hostility. Across the board, the Protestant churches censured the labor union movement for abetting laziness ("ten hours' pay" for "eight hours' work") and for stratifying society along class lines. Labor strikes and "disturbances" provoked "the sternest condemnations."[33]

The power of traditional religious revivals had waned, Professor Webster cautioned young Rauschenbusch. So had exhortations that echoed scripture. They were faint calls and empty rituals in the face of today's massive urban poverty and labor strife. The church needed fresh, vigorous approaches to society. Webster "talked with Rauschenbusch about the economic dimensions of these issues and commended the author Henry George's provocative new analysis to him." Just as a professor at Oberlin College introduced young John R. Commons to the ideas of Henry George, so did Webster recommend that Rauschenbusch become acquainted with George's 1879 *Progress and Poverty*.[34]

Rauschenbusch may have tracked the expanding reputation of the author of *Progress and Poverty* while he completed his studies, became ordained, and prepared to answer the call to the church in New York City. All the while, Henry George was becoming a national figure. He lectured widely across the United States and abroad to promote his idea of an innovative single tax on unearned increases in land values. The single tax, George's admirers believed, was certain to bring an end to economic injustice and to poverty. It would accomplish these goals simply by recirculating tax money back to the ordinary people whose energies had developed America's farms, factories, dwellings, and town and city centers. At last, those who built America would be justly rewarded for their efforts. Workingmen in the early 1880s bought cheap editions of George's book, discussed it in their workshops, and embraced the author as a true friend of the workingman. They began to support Henry George for elective political office.[35]

In 1886, just as the young Rauschenbusch moved to his new church, a hotly contested mayoral campaign was rolling in New York City. Nominated by the United Labor Party, the author of *Progress and Poverty* was proving to be a strong candidate for mayor. Rauschenbusch already found his church duties in the city to be all-consuming. After one month on the job, his only reading was the Bible and "Anderson's [sic] Fairy Tales while waiting in a doctor's ante-room." But Rauschenbusch also remembered Professor Webster's advice to pay attention to the self-taught California-based economist who linked modern progress with chronic poverty. On October 2, two days before his twenty-fifth birthday, Rauschenbusch took time out to join other New Yorkers at a mayoral campaign rally for Henry George. It was held downtown at Cooper Union, the institute that provided free classes for workers and a great hall where civic issues were debated. The weather was unseasonably cold, the thermometer hitting a record low at 39 degrees Fahrenheit, but the crowd was large and enthusiastic.[36]

The candidate was not the opening speaker. As was customary at a rally, preliminary speeches boosted everybody's spirits, and a prayer was scheduled. The Lord's Prayer was to be recited by a locally prominent advocate for the poor, Father Edward McGlynn, a Catholic priest. Overcoming suspicion of a Catholic wasn't easy for Rauschenbusch. From his Baptist, Protestant perspective, the Catholic doctrine of the mystical body of Christ was the epitome of misunderstanding of Jesus. To the Baptist minister, the Catholics' "amulets, vows, oracles, festivals [of saints], incense, candles, pictures, and statues" were holdovers from paganism. Rauschenbusch, however, heard favorable things about Father McGlynn. Besides, the Lord's Prayer belonged to all Christians. Growing up with the prayer, most of the faithful couldn't possibly count the times they had recited it. Its familiarity sometimes worked against the impact of its message, which made close attention all the more necessary.[37]

Whatever his expectations on this chill, early autumn day, Rauschenbusch did not anticipate a life-changing epiphany. Certainly not by way of a Catholic priest reciting a familiar prayer at a political rally. The Lord's Prayer on this occasion nonetheless proved to be wholly different—and radically new. It wasn't simply that Rauschenbusch let himself be led in prayer by a Catholic priest. Rather, it was his own unique moment of receptivity, his openness to complex issues that faced him in this new city life. So far in New York, his "idea was to save souls in the ordinarily accepted religious sense." He worked, that is, according to his training and studies, guiding each and every "poor and downtrodden" parishioner "into living and personal relations with our Lord Jesus Christ." This was traditional. The individual's own personal relation with God was key to salvation and thus to his ministry.[38]

Prepared to hear Henry George, Rauschenbusch had no inkling that the priest's prayer was about to change his life — and his theology. Everyone at the rally bowed their heads at the familiar words "Our Father who art in heaven, hallowed be thy name . . ." McGlynn's celebrated eloquence was audible in every syllable. Non-Christians were respectful. Jews in attendance were patient. Then came the words that split the air like a bolt of lightning. "Thy kingdom come!" exclaimed the priest. "Thy will be done *on earth* . . ." The familiar words suddenly burst forth as new as the sunrise. Rauschenbusch was thunderstruck. So were those around him. It was as if everyone heard the prayer for the first time. The kingdom of God was meant to arrive not only in the afterlife but here on earth. Rauschenbusch sprang to his feet. Everyone did. The "great audience" at the political rally "realized for the first time the social significance of the holy words," and "it lifted them off their seats with a shout of joy."[39]

Rauschenbusch's life spun in an instant. The meaning of the Social Gospel was outlined in broad strokes. Others were writing and preaching about the idea. It meant, basically, that Christian principles were directly applicable to social problems here on earth, from labor to health and housing and schools. ("Thy will be done on earth . . .") The idea wasn't entirely new with Rauschenbusch. He had encountered it in the writings of a number of theologians, especially in Washington Gladden of Columbus, Ohio, and in Shailer Matthews, Josiah Strong, and several others. The idea was stated and elaborated in their many books and articles.[40]

This October, 1886, however, marked the moment when Walter Rauschenbusch absorbed the true meaning of the Social Gospel. It required a new evangelism ("Thy kingdom come!"). Its foundation was based in social relations. It joined Christians with the social and political world of their daily lives. Yes, the church and the state were properly separated in America, but they were closely linked. "The State is the representative of things as they are; the church is the representative of things as they ought to be." The church must thus ever show the state its shortcomings — but motivate positive change. The Social Gospel affirmed a bond between Christianity and sociopolitics.[41]

So far, Rauschenbusch had taken only a moderate interest in U.S. politics, supporting the candidacy of Grover Cleveland for president in 1884. The campaign of Henry George for mayor of New York was different. He felt its spiritual and political energies. Rauschenbusch probably ventured into the cold rain of October 31 to see the parade of workers from the ranks of his own

Second German Baptist Church, "a human river, two miles long, of tailors, plumbers, painters, brass workers, street railway workers." They marched with "Cuban cigarmakers, Italian fruit handlers, Bohemian single taxers, and German cooperationists (pushing a huge broom with which to sweep the election)." As the rain became a drenching downpour, Rauschenbusch could read the campaign signs in the light of sputtering torches and calcium lights: "HONEST LABOR AGAINST THIEVING LANDLORDS AND POLITICIANS — THE LAND BELONGS TO THE PEOPLE! GEORGE! HEN-RY GEORGE!"[42]

George's respectable second-place finish behind Abraham Hewitt in the election was disappointing. It did not for one minute, however, dampen Rauschenbusch's commitment to the issues of *Progress and Poverty*. Beyond the keen social observation and idea of the single tax, Rauschenbusch knew he must seek a broader range of social theory to help him understand why his parishioners and others in Hell's Kitchen were so badly damaged by the circumstances of their lives — and what he must do to help.[43]

Rauschenbusch couldn't guess how many other troubled kindred spirits were turning, as he was about to do, to the writings of Richard T. Ely. Numerous thoughtful Gilded Age Americans who felt enormous frustration at the status quo listened to the words of the young Johns Hopkins University professor of political economy. Far and wide, people were reading Richard Ely in the later 1800s. In New York City, Rauschenbusch met Ely through Leighton Williams, a mutual friend, and heard him speak at a meeting of Baptist ministers in 1888. Nowadays, said Ely, Christians were teaching a "one-sided half-gospel" that emphasized individual salvation but ignored "a social . . . Gospel." The political economist elaborated on this point: "What we need is the whole truth, and that includes a social as well as an individual Gospel. . . . The Gospel of Christ is both individual and social regeneration, individual and social salvation."[44]

The Johns Hopkins professor had a head start on many of America's Progressives. Just seven years older than Rauschenbusch, Richard T. Ely was one of the half-dozen junior faculty who were recruited to infuse the new university in Baltimore with intellectual brilliance and youthful vigor. In boyhood in rural upstate New York in the 1850s and 1860s, Ely absorbed lessons in contrarian ethics from his civil engineer father, a man who was so passionate about setting the world "right" that he once wore farmer's overalls to church to affirm God's welcome of rich and poor alike. Ely attended Columbia College on a scholarship, won a postgraduate fellowship upon graduation in 1877, and sailed for Germany for doctoral study in economics at the University of Heidelberg. The newly minted Dr. Ely returned to the United States in 1880 and was revolted while "tramping the streets of New York." Instead

Labor Day Parade, New York City, 1886. Frank Leslie's
Illustrated Newspaper. *(Library of Congress)*

of Berlin's "clean and beautiful streets," he found a "dirty and ill-kept" New York City, its "pavements poor," and "evidence of graft and incompetence on every hand." The ink was barely dry on his monograph on the excellent administration of the city of Berlin, and now Ely was face to face with the crisis of Gilded Age America, which he diagnosed in the Manichaean terms of the stage melodramas that played nightly on Broadway: "I became aware that our country was experiencing a crisis in which the potentialities for good or for evil were beyond precedent." "Optimism or pessimism" was equally easy, he thought, "but both dangerous."[45]

No facile optimist, Ely saw a "crisis" that was centered in "the labor movement." A "faulty" and "iniquitous" industrial system, he realized, posed extreme danger. "World-wide," masses of working people were stirring with deep desires for changes "in the very foundations of the social order." What they craved was not vengeance or anarchy but adequate personal time for themselves and a decent living wage — "more leisure and larger economic resources." Neither greedy nor materialistic, they sought "ethical aims," meaning "the development . . . of whatever capabilities of good there may be in us." They sought, that is, "the ethical aim expressed in that command which contains the secret of all true progress: 'Thou shalt love thy neighbor as thyself.'"[46]

Yet how could America's middle and upper-middle classes come to this recognition when they viewed workers as a terrifying half-criminal class and labor unions as a criminal conspiracy? Ely's father's occupation — engineering — was useful here. Its mission was practical problem solving through new design and its implementation. The mandate of the engineer was progress. The Episcopalian Ely never used the chilling term *social engineering*, speaking instead in a heartfelt vocabulary of Christianity. But a new social structure was needed, and Ely vowed "to do whatever was in my power to bring about better conditions." By 1888, he was a prolific writer and researcher and founding member of the American Economic Association (chartered in 1885). Adopting research techniques of his German "master" at Heidelberg, Karl Knies, he practiced and taught the "case system of looking up pertinent documents."[47]

His "master," what's more, showed the young Ely the fallacy of laissez-faire, a fallacy at the core of economics. Heidelberg's Knies rejected the idea that economics was a science. Instead, he showed the young American that it was a discipline for "the study of man in society in terms of its historical growth." In other words, it was human activity, not the operation of impersonal laws, that determined economic outcomes. The supposed absolutist "laws" of economics, Ely had learned from Knies, were often merely policies perpetuated in the guise of laws because they served the interests of particular groups. In that regard, laissez-faire was not an immutable law but a human contrivance that was subject to change.[48]

But how? Today's ministers were the blind leading the blind, Ely reported, because the seminaries concentrated solely on theology and excluded the social sciences. In this modern moment, said the young Johns Hopkins professor, the social sciences were critically needed to give the clergy a new lens on scripture and on society. "Half of the time of a theological student should be devoted to social science," said Ely, "and theological seminaries should be the chief intellectual centers for sociology." Otherwise, he warned, spiritual leaders would flounder in the face of child labor, public corruption, and crushing work schedules that put personal and family time out of reach for millions. As for Sunday labor—call it by its real name, "Sunday slavery."[49]

The political economist pulled no punches, and Rauschenbusch confronted a cruel irony: years of advanced schooling certified him as officially educated—yet left him ignorant. He must somehow find time for self-education. What he learned he must pass on to his parishioners so they too could know the facts. It would be an uphill effort because his flock came from a population whose human initiative was stunted. Like their counterparts who poured into America's cities, they were conditioned to "take orders," to "use their muscles almost automatically," to be "employed or dismissed at a word." Their habitual on-the-job submission meant they had "no voice in the conduct of their own shop." Despite it all, they must be shown how to help themselves toward better lives. They must be fortified. In the workplace, labor leaders like Samuel Gompers were helping workers to focus the issues of wages and working conditions, but Rauschenbusch knew the church must also take the lead. The church must find a way.[50]

Bolstering the wageworkers, Rauschenbusch also realized, was not enough. The church must also exert itself in the realms of those who controlled business and industry. The church must reach the owners and managers whose "habits of mind" were "bred by the exercise of authority." They routinely issued orders, and "an army of men obeyed." Their habits of total command and control, however, were creating grave problems. The business class wedged itself comfortably apart from others by its wealth, Rauschenbusch knew, and was thus "paralyzed" when it came to feeling for others. "That is the charm of riches," he realized, and also its "curse."[51]

But the business class was also caught in an economic system that could cause the country severe damage. Unchecked, extreme capitalism could drag the nation backward. As a man of European roots, Rauschenbusch saw that if current trends continued, America would become a society of aristocrats and serfs. The wonderful New World of freedom and opportunity would sooner or later replicate the feudal system of the past. The modern age could become the medieval. And a "class struggle" was by no means out of the question, as recent violent labor strikes proved.[52]

For the love of God and all human beings, the church must step in. Theologian Washington Gladden said that "the first and foremost function of the church is that of teaching." Pastors were teachers. Countless lives on the margins could be bettered if employers, managers, and public officials gained new knowledge and understanding from the pulpit—and took action for the sake of others as well as themselves. Above all, for the sake of Christianizing modern society. Those of the business class were churchgoers. A minister had their ear weekly on the Sabbath. The pulpit must be the agent of change.[53]

Easier said than done. Pastors of well-off congregations, Rauschenbusch knew, often settled comfortably in the rarified world of their parishioners. He had no illusions on this score when he accepted the call to the church in Hell's Kitchen in 1886. "Water seeks its own level," he said, "and so do men." The U.S. caste system was on display in America's churches. "The wealthier families . . . gravitate toward churches composed in the main of their own class." The Clarence Day family, for instance, joined the elite St. Bartholomew's Episcopal Church when the family became considerably wealthy. According to Father, the congregation "were all the right sort . . . bank directors and doctors and judges—solid men of affairs." Mr. Day regarded the church as "a good club," and the sermon "like a strong editorial in a conservative newspaper." Each Sunday, as Rauschenbusch knew, boys like Clarence Jr. and his brothers heard the "mellow chants" of "a choir of men and boys in surplices" and raised their heads to see the "high vaulted roof that rang with the organ music, and stained glass with deep colors."[54]

Pastors like the Day family's Rev. Dr. Owen Lloyd Garden were privileged to enjoy "the artistic side of the church interior," including stained glass perhaps ordered from the studio of Louis Comfort Tiffany. Their churches had the grained hardwood (not pine) for the chancel, pulpit platform, and pews, and a baptismal font of marble and mosaic tile, not a cement imitation. Rauschenbusch loved a beautiful church. The Cologne Cathedral remained in his memory as "the nearest approach to the sublime that the hand of man has erected." In due course, he was to raise the funds for the new Second German Baptist Church and secure a donation from America's best-known Baptist, John D. Rockefeller, who was approached through connections at the Rochester seminary. The aesthetic beauty of a church, however, must not distract the worshipper from the Gospel.[55]

Rauschenbusch probably never met Dr. Garden, but he knew his type. The Owen Lloyd Gardens of America echoed their parishioners' views with the "courtly grace and smoothness" that guaranteed a "warm berth . . . in the right stratum of society." They paid genteel pastoral calls, raised funds for missions in distant lands, and supported select church-sponsored charities. Their churches enjoyed the help of volunteers from business, medicine, and education, all people with the leisure and the physical and mental strength to boost the energy of the church like a tonic.[56]

At the same time, most ministers in Dr. Garden's position avoided issues that were likely to challenge their parishioners' set views, so they steered clear of social reform. They might denounce drunkenness and profanity but yet hide America's "actual dangers" in the boosterish bunting of "spread-eagleism," which was the nation's "deadly" optimism.[57]

No one who worshipped at the Church of the Peace Everlasting heard Dr. Garden lead his flock in prayers for workingmen or immigrants or the women who toiled. Yet those were the crucial prayers to break the barriers of class and advance the Social Gospel. The consciences of the well-off could be stirred if prayers were framed as Christian approaches to social problems. A prayer "For Women Who Toil" would ask God to save women workers "from the strain of unremitting toil that would unfit them for the holy duties of home and motherhood." A prayer "For Children Who Work" would ask God's blessing on "young lives whose slender shoulders are already bowed beneath the yoke of toil." A prayer "For Immigrants" would seek blessings on "the people of other lands who are coming to our land, seeking bread, a home, and a future." This prayer would remind worshippers that they too "are the children of immigrants, who came with anxious hearts and halting feet on the westward path of hope."[58]

Other prayers ought to resound in churches like Dr. Garden's all over America, and Rauschenbusch foresaw a prayer "For Employers," those who "hold power over the bread, the safety, and the hopes of the workers." Countless men seated in the pews on Sunday needed to be summoned in God's name to "wield their powers justly and with love" and not to "sin against the Christ by using the bodies and souls of men as mere tools to make things." "Men in Business" would also have a special prayer. It would acknowledge that "the wealth and welfare of our nation are controlled by our business men." The prayer would beseech God to help businessmen "realize that they serve not themselves alone, but hold high public functions." It would warn businessmen not to betray "the interests of the many for their own enrichment," lest "a new tyranny grow up in a land that is dedicated to freedom." Yet another prayer for "the lords of industry and trade" would implore God to help these powerful men "not to waste the labor of the many for their own luxury" and to "save them from the terrible temptations of their position."[59]

The ladies in the church pews would hear a prayer meant for them as well, especially since they shopped for their family homes. A prayer "For Consumers" would seek God's blessings on "all the men and women who have toiled to build and warm our homes, to fashion our raiment, and to wrest from the sea and land the food that nourishes us and our children." It would ask the consumer to remember that "the comforts of our life are brought to us from afar, and made by those whom we do not know or see." The prayer would urge the worshipper to take responsibility for conditions of work in faraway places. It would go something like this: "May the time come when we need wear and use nothing that is wet in thy sight with human tears, or cheapened by wearing down the lives of the weak."[60]

These were the prayers that congregations like Dr. Garden's urgently needed to hear on Sunday and take home in printed form to read and reread so their consciences would be stirred to a state of repentance and a resolve to take action. If the prayers struck true in the depths of the soul, they would advance a "social awakening." Rauschenbusch was to compose these very prayers years from now, although they were desperately needed at this moment.[61]

In the meantime, if only he could put a copy of a certain best-selling novel into the kid-gloved hands of every churchgoer. Edward Bellamy's time-travel romance, *Looking Backward, 2000–1887*, was Rauschenbusch's best textbook because it was a Christian blueprint for a socially awakened America. The novel showed an industrial America of the near future. It portrayed a society that lived at every level in a cooperative state of abundant food, housing, medical care, ample personal time, and accessible transportation. It showed what the world of the Social Gospel might look like in its secular arrangements if people only let themselves think and act on "a new moral and religious synthesis."[62]

Perhaps Rauschenbusch recalled Ely's *Social Aspects of Christianity*, which pinpointed a problem that echoed in the novel. Ely criticized the Christians of Montreal for failing to stop a private monopoly of street railway transportation. The result was "public robbery," meaning high fares for the low-wage people who must pinch every penny, together with high taxes for everybody. By failing to block the monopoly, Ely wrote, the churchgoers of the city failed in their municipal civic duty as Christians. Ely posed the question that Bellamy raised in his novel: "What safety is there for the property of the masses, for public property?"[63]

Public property was a constant in Rauschenbusch's thoughts in New York

City. He did his Christian duty in the public interest—for public property—by prodding city hall to truck in sandpiles for safe play for the children of Hell's Kitchen. Every stroll in Central Park, what's more, reminded him of the blessed civic-minded New Yorkers of the past who overrode partisan feuds to secure the public park, which was completed in 1873. Initially, some were revolted by the notion of a city park that was to be freely accessible to the "vicious" lower classes ("jewels in the snouts of swine," said one newspaper). The greensward design of Calvert Vaux and Frederick Law Olmsted, however, showed what could be done for the public at large. On every afternoon that was free of rain and snow and church duties, Rauschenbusch refreshed his spirits with a walk along the pathways and charming bridges of Central Park, an oasis for the public and "the lungs of the city."[64]

Property held in common for the public was an immediate Christian matter in other ways. Water, for instance, ought not to be a privatized, for-profit commodity but a public utility. Bellamy's novel presumed abundant safe water for bathing, cooking, drinking. Water, in fact, was much in the news from the 1880s as New York authorities confronted the problem of supplying safe drinking water to some 3.5 million city residents who used "nearly 370 million gallons per day." Rauschenbusch doubtless knew of the massive, much-publicized Croton Aqueduct project, a system of dams, reservoirs, and conduits being built to pipe water from the upstate Catskill Mountains to the city. Legal and political wrangling was to resolve itself in the creation of the public New York Board of Water Supply, but the supply of pure, healthful water was crucial for the health of everyone. No one would die from being unable to afford the price of clean water. No one would sicken or fall fatally ill from drinking contaminated water.[65]

Public utilities and property were basic to the America of Bellamy's *Looking Backward*, and Rauschenbusch never overlooked its Christian meanings or its possibilities for the future. The "predatory interests" of extreme capitalism that sought to privatize everything could be kept at bay if—and only if—Christians were mobilized to protect and promote public property. Americans had taken a few encouraging steps in this direction in the pioneering days of homesteading, when communities set land aside "for the support of the public schools." For the sake of a healthy society, they must again be inspired to do so in this modern urban era of piped water, gas, drainage and sewerage, paved roads, electricity, and rail transport.[66]

What was legitimately private, and what public? The questions were debated and debatable. In practical terms, Rauschenbusch framed his outlook in terms of the life span of a little child, perhaps a poor child, since "even the child of a poor man in a civilized community is a large property holder."

The child in his infancy was a "part owner of a great network of streets" that were available when adults took him outdoors in a baby carriage. The baby could "enjoy the panorama of wonders in peace," and Rauschenbusch mentally filled in the scene with "shade trees and lawns, with swings and see-saws, with lakes and swans, and possibly with a zoo." Public health services came into the picture too, for "in some cities skilled hands [were] working to eliminate microbes from his milk bottle." Should he "get seriously sick, great institutions are open to receive him—if they are not too full." It was a public responsibility to see to it that the hospitals would not be "too full" or understaffed.[67]

Rauschenbusch followed the infant into childhood and to the free public school system. "When he begins to trudge about, the Kindergarten, once the privilege of the rich, teaches him games, songs, and stories." And if he should somehow lose his way home, "an army of blue-coated giants [the police] hunt for him, wipe his nose, and take him home to his mother." Firefighters, too, were best understood to be service workers in the public domain. "If he has played with matches," the child is rescued by "another set of giants [who] swarm up ladders and risk their lives to save him from his own naughtiness." Rauschenbusch was utterly clear about the child's entitlement to every service that safeguarded his life and guaranteed him the best possible future. "All this is not charity," he was to write. "It is his right. He is part owner of a great corporation."[68]

The corporation could be organized through outright municipal ownership. Or it could be organized through private ownership that was subject to legal, rigorous public supervision and regulation. Or a mix of the two. What mattered above all was public control of the well-being of the public. Americans must not sleepwalk like the Montreal Christians who let a thieving company steal their transit system and pick their pockets too. Could the church awaken them to their duties in municipal affairs?[69]

It could do so only if U.S. Christians were persuaded, first, to reject the entrenched and pernicious individualism that so many cherished both in secular and religious life. From the printed page, Rauschenbusch heard Ely denounce the "negative, narrow, individualistic Protestantism" that was a selfish misreading of scripture. This individualistic Protestantism bypassed the Golden Rule of the Gospel: "Whatsoever ye would that men should do to you, do ye to them; for this is the law" (Matthew 7:12).[70]

The notion of salvation as private, however, had wormed its way into every aspect of Christian life. Even the best-loved hymns were rife with the self-centered pronoun *I*, and home Bible study became an exercise solely in individual salvation. Well-intentioned persons who learned the Twenty-

Angelic young lady in prayer, seeming oblivious of the Social Gospel, c. 1902. Artist: Charles Gibson. (Library of Congress)

third Psalm ("The Lord is *my* shepherd") to the exclusion of verses from the Gospel of Luke, for instance, reinforced this focus on the individual self.[71]

From the start, the Second German Baptist Church congregation heard Rauschenbusch "talk about needed changes in the world around them." Preaching both in German and English, he urged them to "accept their responsibility as Christian citizens," to work through the ballot box to bring public life under the control of "Christian ideas and Christian men." He prodded his parishioners to minister to one another.[72]

And he organized youth groups because children and young people were the future and must be nurtured spiritually and taught how to be citizens. Older youth must take part in mock legislatures so they could practice debating as citizens whose lives were impacted by such issues as tariffs and prohibition. For young boys, Rauschenbusch formed a marching brigade, recalling the friendships he enjoyed in the outdoor marching drills in his German gymnasium days. It was also good to cooperate with the reform-minded newspaper editor Jacob Riis to get the city to create a playground park in the notorious Mulberry Street "Bend" and to deliver wagonloads of sand for safe sandpile play.[73]

Rauschenbusch hatched a plan for a monthly magazine to extend his ministry from the pulpit to the printing press. He and a few others decided to publish stories and informal short pieces, written in a simple style, to help awaken the minds of men and women who were habituated to taking orders in mute silence for hours on the job. The Christians of Hell's Kitchen could absorb social facts and good advice for healthful living. The Social Gospel could reach them from the printed page, and literacy would be upgraded. His friend Leighton Williams joined him, as did two other Baptists. *For the Right* debuted in November 1889, promising to "reflect the needs, the aspirations, the longings of the tens of thousands of wage-earners who are sighing for better things." For the eighteen months of the magazine's publication, the small group struggled to meet deadlines and sell advertisements, sometimes pasting in pieces from other sources. A sampling from the novel Rauschenbusch so admired, *Looking Backward*, appeared in one issue. The typewriter he bought did double duty.[74]

Other church projects were under way. The day nursery was welcomed by parish women who were desperate for child care, and the training program for women for the care of the sick and needy had some success. On Rauschenbusch's tenth anniversary as minister of the Second German Baptist Church, the tribute that he most prized was spoken by a parishioner, a butcher named Julius Dietz, who commended Brother Rauschenbusch as "Christ-like" and "fearless."[75]

Thank God, he was not alone. From childhood, Rauschenbusch was nourished by companionship — of playmates, schoolmates, and fellow seminarians. He traveled regularly to regional meetings of Baptist organizations and had a wide circle of acquaintances. In spring 1892, another circle was ready to form. Six years into his ministry in New York, Rauschenbusch joined with a band of brothers to stake his generation's claim for the present and future.

The Hell's Kitchen minister knew to the depths of his soul that the era of God's great cause had not ended with the emancipation of the chattel slaves. He lived in a new era of slavery — industrial slavery. With God's help, it too must be brought to an end by human effort. Rauschenbusch was not alone in this realization. In the ministry, other younger men like him were equally horrified by the situation of the wageworkers and their families. Like Rauschenbusch, they were profoundly disturbed by the huge wealth gap that violated Christian principles. They too were working in slum neighborhoods and knew the social crisis intimately. They were also troubled, as Baptists, to find that the vast majority of workers' churchgoing families were Catholics. Equally troubling, they learned that countless wageworkers avoided the Protestant Christian church because they saw it as the servant of the business owners and managers ("spiritual lackeys of capitalism," one labor union organizer said). Worse still, they felt the workers were correct: the church was now "under the spiritual domination of the commercial and professional classes" and thus failing hundreds of thousands of God's children.[76]

This was a moment not to surrender to the status quo but to fight with new missionary zeal. Rauschenbusch determined to seize his opportunity at a Baptist convocation in Philadelphia in spring 1892, when he called for the kingdom of God as the focus of new missions in urban America. It was a bold proposal on the part of the young minister. Some in attendance doubtless saw Rauschenbusch step out of his father's shadow when he spoke — and they were offended by this upstart about whom they'd heard disturbing rumblings from Rochester.

Others, however, were thrilled when they heard Rauschenbusch speak of "the sanctification of all life, the regeneration of all humanity, and the reformation of all social institutions" under the divine mandate of the kingdom of God. Gripped by the new possibilities, several younger men eagerly scheduled a meeting in Rauschenbusch's tenement apartment. They wanted to make plans. In secular terms, they'd be called Young Turks, but they thought of themselves as a new society of Jesus. A young Baptist pastor of a church in the Philadelphia slums, Samuel Zane Batten, was on hand, as were Leighton Williams and Nathaniel Schmidt and others. Everyone knew the Catholics had their own potent Society of Jesus, the Jesuits, a brain trust of their faith and its theology. Batten proposed the name for this new group: Brotherhood of the Kingdom. By the end of the year, there were nine founding members, and the next summer they gathered for several days at Williams's family's summer home, "a spacious Victorian house with ample accommodations and bracing hilltop views" of the Hudson River. They read prepared papers to one another, listened closely, gained confidence in mutual strengths, and talked endlessly into the evening as dusk settled and fireflies twinkled. Within two years, the brotherhood "widened to include women and non-Baptists," and attendance rose to some fifty participants. The Brotherhood of the Kingdom was to be a mainstay of Rauschenbusch's life and work for the next twenty years. It meant strength in numbers and the social gospel for an era marked by social crisis.[77]

In 1893, church members learned, to their delight, that their young pastor was nearing the end of a three-year, long-distance courtship of a lovely schoolteacher from Milwaukee. Miss Pauline Rother was the daughter of immigrants from Germanic Silesia and had broken off a prior engagement to enter an intense correspondence with Walter Rauschenbusch. He'd met her while on a church errand to her city. Once they were engaged, he wrote Pauline poetry of "yearning" for the touch of her arms and "hunger" for her presence and of her "rich and constant love . . . the greatest thing that any being can give to another." Soon Rauschenbusch wrote his seminary classmates that "the proud and independent bachelorhood of the bachelorest one of us all" was about to end.[78]

He and Pauline were married in the spring of 1893, and two children soon followed, Winifred and Hilmar. They were blessed when a widowed member of the church, Tante Schaefer, volunteered to help the young couple and stayed with them as nurse, maid, and cook. At this point, Rauschenbusch had served his church for nearly eleven years. He loved his work. He'd twice turned down offers to return to Rochester as a member of the seminary faculty. Despite reservations about him, it was acknowledged that no one was better qualified to teach in the German department. Now a third seminary invitation arrived just as Rauschenbusch faced a personal crisis that made the new offer irresistible. The healthy, robust young minister of the Second German Baptist Church had gone permanently deaf.

IT CAME ON STEADILY, the deafness that also afflicted Thomas Edison and the amazing young woman Helen Keller. Rauschenbusch recalled that his grandmother, the "lovely old lady" with the "sweet smile," was "completely deaf and had a little slate on which people wrote for her." He too needed a helper to write him notes and messages to which he could respond. He didn't hide his disability from the church. His congregation hired an assistant minister to help him. But the day-to-day duties were difficult, and Pauline worried about their children growing up on the New York city streets. The offer of a faculty position at the Rochester Theological Seminary seemed providential. In the classroom, he could lecture to students and respond in writing to their papers. The structure was formal and manageable. In 1897, Rauschenbusch bid a wrenching farewell to the Second German Baptist Church and prepared to return to the city of his birth.[79]

The historian of Rochester, Blake McKelvey, has written that Walter Rauschenbusch came back "as the scholarly son of Dr. Augustus Rauschenbusch" and that "his post was a humble one at the start and like many new appointees he was expected to fill a wide schedule." The historian added that "there was no hint in this assignment of his interest in social Christianity."[80]

The moment of return was not ripe for such a hint. Other ministers in Rochester were experimenting with Social Gospel approaches in the late 1890s, but for now, Rauschenbusch watched from the sidelines. He was guarded. And wary. He'd been warned that certain seminary trustees had a "great horror of socialism" and had doubts about his appointment. He was suspected of "think[ing] like a workingman." For now, he wisely allayed their suspicions. His position was probationary for the first year, and a permanent post was no guarantee for the long run. He learned just how precarious his own job was when his friend Nathaniel Schmidt was fired from the Colgate Theological Seminary for unorthodox ideas about biblical authority. It was a shock—and a warning. Rauschenbusch had a family to support, bills to pay. Each week the Rochester neighborhood iceman brought a dripping block to the Rauschenbusch's newly rented frame house on Avondale Street. The fruit and vegetable huckster stopped his horse-drawn rig too, and in winter the coal deliveries for the furnace were frequent. Everyone must be paid. The home was comfortable but not secure. A faculty job could be as unsteady as a church ministry, for the deacons had no qualms about "sacking" a minister these days. The "long line of applicants" for ministerial jobs let the churches operate in a buyer's marketplace. All too often it gripped pastors "in bondage through fear."[81]

In good weather Rauschenbusch bicycled from home to the seminary, where he lectured in fluent German. Over the span of two years, he was told, his teaching schedule required preparation in English literature, American literature, physiology, physics, civil government, political economy, astronomy, and zoology. In the theological section of the German department, he was to teach courses on the life of Christ and on separate books of the New Testament. He accepted this barrage of courses without complaint, although the Social Gospel pressed at every moment. He emphasized to his students that in the book of Revelation, the message of John (of Patmos) is that "the rich are the oppressors, and the poor are the heirs of the Kingdom."[82]

The students knew how deeply he cared about them, both as trainees and as persons. Rauschenbusch was anxious about the shape of the future that would rest one day in their hands. Ministers rarely came from the ranks of the "very rich or very poor." They grew up in the families of farmers, of small business men and skilled artisans in the smaller towns and the countryside. He worried that America's rapid urbanization was shrinking the pool of the ministry's best prospects. Rochester itself typified the new urban America of the late 1890s. The population of the city approached 200,000, many of whom came from surrounding rural counties. From the granite tower of the Powers Building at the corner of State and Main streets, one saw a panoramic view of the city's commercial buildings, warehouses, and factories extending across the Genesee River. Columns of dark smoke from the locomotives of the New York Central, the Erie, and other rail lines meant freight cars carrying Rochester's shrubs and flowers and manufactured products, from tobacco to stoves to shoes. On the streets directly below the Powers Building tower, one saw the bustle of businessmen, workers, shoppers, and commercial travelers coming and going.[83]

The current "fierce competition for wealth" was everywhere apparent. Rauschenbusch worried that it siphoned off good men who otherwise might enter the ministry but instead chose careers in advertising and business. They could hardly be blamed. Clergymen's salaries (his own a case in point) were deplorable, and most ministers lived from "hand to mouth." The consequences were profoundly troubling. To protect their jobs, some of the future ministers in his seminary classes would doubtless tailor their Sunday sermons to minimize the risk of upsetting church committees.[84]

Rauschenbusch yearned to share his wealth of experience and to thrust into every student's hand a list of readings to help equip him for the modern era—Ely, Bellamy, Leo Tolstoy, Giuseppe Mazzini. One of Ely's former students, the economist John R. Commons, had published a useful short book titled *Social Reform and the Church* (1894). He too urged "the preacher" to become "a student of social science," to "study persons and families" by "personal contact" and to acquaint himself with "the police court, the jail, the workhouse, and the almshouse." The economist recommended that each minister acquire "a small library" of social science books, "wisely selected for him by some sociologist, and costing from thirty to fifty dollars." He reiterated Ely's message. "Sociology has rightly been said to be one half of religion," wrote Commons. "Theology is the other half."[85]

To teach the seminarians through the lens of social science, however, Rauschenbusch needed intellectual freedoms that were denied to him in his seminary post in the German department. In effect, he was muzzled. And his expanding family made the stakes ever clearer, for he and Pauline became parents of three more children, Paul, Karl, and Elizabeth. The family would soon need a larger house. At every moment, Rauschenbusch chafed under the institutional repression of a church that opposed the social Christianity that defined his mission, the mission of Jesus.[86]

Rochester, meanwhile, was in the throes of the same problems that beset New York City. It too had slums and brothels and schools that needed reform. It too had an aging infrastructure that begged for modernization. Rochester, like New York City, also needed new sources of drinking water, more paved streets, more affordable housing for workers and their families, more parks and recreational facilities. It needed a modern snow removal system and modern methods of sewage treatment for the sake of public health.[87]

Rochester, moreover, was subject to monopolistic practices of private corporations eager to control gas, electricity, and transportation. By the mid-1890s, "almost before anyone realized what was happening," two private utility companies monopolized gas and electricity in Rochester. In a bid to eliminate competition, local businesses tried to monopolize coal and milk in a price-fixing scheme. Outside capitalists had managed to lock in long-term franchises for street transit, and the railroads dictated schedules and rates of speed through the city. Rochester's city fathers, who took pride in the city's traditional competitive vitality, found themselves helpless to intercede when speeding trains caused "an appalling number of fatalities." The "courteous cooperation among rival firms" that characterized Rochester's past had given way to "a relentless struggle for monopoly position." The city was increasingly roiled by labor struggles, especially in its shoe and clothing industries.[88]

Rauschenbusch was drawn into these conflicts, which became a forum for the actual practice of the Social Gospel. He began to take part in civic affairs and to gain the respect of Rochester's leaders, including reform-minded businessmen such as Joseph Alling. As a parent, Rauschenbusch became active in school reform. He joined the advisory board of the Labor Lyceum, which sponsored Sunday afternoon discussions on topics of interest to wage-workers. He promoted the Federation of Churches to seek common ground among the various denominations. He enthusiastically supported the social Christianity of the Salvation Army and the Young Men's and Young Women's Christian associations for their development of Christian citizens, and he promoted programs for affordable housing and better wages. He was active in the development of parks for cost-free recreation in Rochester. He also led the effort to lower gas rates by pressuring the monopolistic Rochester Gas and Electric Company to lower its rates by 20 percent, lest the company lose its franchise. In this effort, "Rauschenbusch tasted victory in his first pubic skirmish with big business."[89]

In 1902, things changed for him at the seminary. The death of a professor in the English department opened a position that Rauschenbusch vied for successfully. He was now to join the English department as the Pettengill Professor of Church History. The burden of courses lightened. The time had come to write his book, the one he'd planned and deferred after three previous abandoned attempts. It was to be a book "on social questions for the Lord Christ and the People." The annual Rauschenbusch summer family vacations in the Canadian woods became his writing time. Swimming with his children, fishing, hiking, and canoeing were interspersed in the summers of 1905 and 1906 with drafting the manuscript and preparing it for publication.[90]

Near the end of his New York ministry, Rauschenbusch told the congregation that his goal was always to "preach Christ . . . simply, clearly, and boldly." This was the governing principle of *Christianity and the Social Crisis*, the book that propelled him to the ballroom of the Waldorf-Astoria Hotel in the autumn of 1908. After his lecture in the hotel, Rauschenbusch would linger to answer questions submitted in writing and passed to him at the lectern. Listeners appreciated his thoughtful answers and conversational style of response.[91]

He knew, however, that the talk at the Waldorf-Astoria was only the beginning of a new, momentous campaign. From now until his illness and death from cancer in 1918, almost every weekend was consumed with travel all over the country, and his readers and publisher would press him for another book, and yet another. He remained on the seminary faculty and taught a full schedule, but his time was not to be his own, and his family bore the burden of his frequent absences. The invitations to speak all across America must be accepted, for they were vital to the Social Gospel. Rauschenbusch kept close sight of his mission: to help "to elevate the aims, ennoble the motives, and intensify the affections" that manifested "the spirit of Christ working in the human spirit." He knew that the "process is never complete," that "the Christian is always but in the making" and the kingdom of God "always but coming."[92]

Leaving the Waldorf-Astoria to catch his train for Rochester, Rauschenbusch could not foresee that Europe was to erupt in war and the United States to be drawn in, a time of particular anguish for any American with roots in Germany. He suffered accordingly. Though he authored other books, *Christianity and the Social Crisis* was Rauschenbusch's landmark statement. In reflection in 1913 he said, "The social movement got hold of me, just as the social awakening was getting hold of the country. The book came out at a psychological moment, and was taken as an expression of what thousands were feeling. People told me that it gave them a new experience of religion and a new feeling about Christ."[93]

The legacy of the Social Gospel was not solely Rauschenbusch's, and his work was criticized as naive in the new century of unprecedented social violence, from Fascism and Nazism to nuclear weaponry. The opening of the twenty-first century, however, has brought a reappraisal of Rauschenbusch's relevance as America's "most influential and important religious public intellectual" in the Gilded Age era of "imperial extension, corporate greed, and massive immigration." Rauschenbusch's rich legacy in U.S. history is voiced by his editor (and great-grandson), Paul Raushenbush, who captures the profoundly wide-ranging influence of the Social Gospel movement that is synonymous with the family name: "The Church's new enthusiasm for the kingdom of God powered many of the reform movements that swept the nation over the next century, including the fight for child labor laws, a manageable workweek with a minimum wage, FDR's New Deal, the Great Society, and the civil rights movement." These are the benchmarks to measure the kingdom in terms of "a theology and politics of the common good," according to the evangelical theologian and churchman Jim Wallis, who is one of a new generation of evangelical leaders who are redirecting their followers toward the message of the Social Gospel. As Rauschenbusch wrote, "At best there is always but an approximation to a perfect social order. The kingdom of God is always but coming. But every approximation to it is worthwhile."[94]

Ida B. Wells-Barnett
Lynching in All Its Phases

The anchor of my [African American] race is grounded on the Constitution, and whenever our privileges are taken away from us or are curtailed, we must point to the Constitution as the Christian does to his Bible. It is the great source and Magna Carta of our rights, and we must know it in order to defend the boon that has been given to us by its amendments. It is the certificate of our liberty and our equality before the law.—LUTIE LYTLE, quoted in *Occupations for Women* by Frances Willard, 1897

The flower of the nineteenth century civilization for the American people was the abolition of slavery and the enfranchisement of all manhood. . . . The reproach and disgrace of the twentieth century is that the whole of the American people have permitted a part [of the public] to nullify this glorious achievement, and make the fourteenth and fifteenth amendments to the Constitution playthings, a mockery and . . . an absolute dead letter in the Constitution of the United States.—IDA B. WELLS-BARNETT, "How Enfranchisement Stops Lynching," 1910

With no sacredness of the ballot there can be no sacredness of human life itself, for if the strong can take the weak man's ballot when it suits his purpose to do so, he will take his life also.—IDA B. WELLS-BARNETT, "How Enfranchisement Stops Lynching," 1910

There is no educator to compare with the press.—IDA B. WELLS, *Southern Horrors: Lynch Law in All Its Phases*, 1892

Ida Wells-Barnett was the pioneer of the anti-lynching crusade in the United States. . . . She roused the South to vigorous and bitter defense and she began the awakening of the conscience of the nation.—W. E. B. DU BOIS, *Crisis*, 1931

The two-story family brick home was quiet when Ida B. Wells-Barnett sat down at her dining room table and reached for the *Chicago Daily Tribune* on November 10, 1909. So far, it was an ordinary day in the Wells-Barnett household. The four children, ages five to fourteen, were at school. Their father, the attorney Ferdinand L. Barnett, had taken the streetcar to his downtown law office. The sky was overcast in a November of unusually high temperatures in Chicago. Inside, the forty-seven-year-old Wells-Barnett, a wife and mother, lingered at a table that was piled at one end with the papers and magazines that were crucial to her work as a writer and civic activist. For now, the papers lay untouched as she opened the *Tribune* and began to enjoy a late-morning breakfast of her favorite tea and toast.[1]

Her pleasant morning instantly ceased when she reached page 7 of the *Tribune* and saw the headlines that stopped her cold: "GIRL MURDERED; BODY MUTILATED . . . Bloodhounds Capture Four Negroes." The dateline was Cairo, Illinois, a city settled by southerners, at the southernmost tip of the state. The naked, strangled body of a twenty-four-year-old white woman, a department store clerk named Anna Pelley, had been found on a rubbish heap in a Cairo alley. Bloodhounds reportedly led the police to "a negro shanty," and four negroes were under arrest and in custody. "The authorities are taking extraordinary precautions," said the *Tribune*, adding that "excitement is high in all parts of Cairo" and that "the arrest of the four negroes already has engendered some race feeling in connection with the case."[2]

"Race feeling" meant only one thing to Wells-Barnett. To an African American writer and activist like her, it meant mortal danger to blacks and the breakdown of the rule of law. The paper printed day-old news, so perhaps a Cairo mob had already taken the law into its own, homicidal hands. A sickening sense of déjà vu overcame her. Wells-Barnett had worked diligently and risked life, limb, and reputation to teach the U.S. public the facts about the crime of lynching that overwhelmingly victimized black Americans. She had spoken out, written, traveled, lectured, and organized to bring the "civilized" public to its senses and put a stop to the racial murders that had burgeoned in the closing decades of the nineteenth century and continued into the twentieth. No one, male or female, had so extensively and relentlessly publicized the issue to audiences of blacks and whites throughout the country and abroad. Wells-Barnett had published, at personal expense, fact-packed pamphlets documenting the specifics of the racial hate crime of lynching in America: *Southern Horrors: Lynch Law in All Its Phases* (1892), *A Red Record* (1895), *Mob Rule in New Orleans* (1900). She knew the moment was ripe for lynching in Cairo.

The crisis in the southern Illinois city surely triggered a flashback memory. Seventeen years ago, at age thirty, Ida B. Wells was a single young newspaper reporter and publisher in Memphis, Tennessee, when she exposed the major pretext for lynching. In an editorial of May 1892, she dared to expose "the old threadbare lie that Negro men assault white women." Wells's words were taboo to whites. They ignited a firestorm in that Mississippi River city. Fortunately, Wells was in Pennsylvania when the office of her Memphis newspaper,

Ida B. Wells, c. 1894. (Courtesy of Special Collections Research Center, University of Chicago Library)

the *Free Speech and Headlight*, was trashed and her life threatened. She did not return to Memphis but worked in New York as a reporter for T. Thomas Fortune's *New York Age*, her articles widely syndicated in the robust African American press. She also became a sought-after public speaker, making her mark in lectures to black and white audiences in the United States and England, where she raised awareness of the injustice of lynching—and worked to put a stop to it. She was driven to do this in the years of Jim Crow laws and regulations that so tightly restricted African Americans that they found themselves nearly reenslaved.[3]

Chicago became Wells's hometown in 1893, when she joined the staff of the *Chicago Conservator*, a paper edited by Ferdinand Lee Barnett, whom she married in a formal wedding in June 1895. He was by then a widower with two sons. The Lord God blessed the new couple with four children: Charles A., Herman K., Ida B., and Alfreda M. The family now lived at 3234 Rhodes Avenue, in a mostly white section of Chicago. Wells-Barnett's work with civic organizations and with a settlement house for her own race led some to call her "the Jane Addams among the Negroes," a flawed comparison, if well meant. Feeling fairly safe in the Rhodes Avenue home and neighborhood, the Barnetts nonetheless encountered a certain "consternation" on the part of white neighbors when they moved in, and they kept a Winchester rifle in the house just in case. Ida once brandished it to chase away a gang of white boys who harassed her sons. (She and Ferdinand made sure the rifle was hidden from the children.)[4]

The news of November 10 from Cairo was shocking but not surprising. As reported, Anna Pelley's death fit the "threadbare lie." It was a myth that refused to die. Various respected U.S. writers had inscribed the idea of volcanic black male lust for white women as far back as the year of Ida B. Wells's birth, the Civil War year of 1862. In that year, Rebecca Harding Davis, a white writer, published a story titled "John Lamar" in the prestigious *Atlantic Monthly* magazine. Readers relished Davis's fictional brawny slave-manservant named Ben. Reading by parlor lamplight, they could picture the "gigantic fellow, with a gladiator's muscles." The *Atlantic Monthly* readers were doubtless horrified to read that Ben, stealing a knife, kills his master and escapes, perhaps to go back to the Georgia plantation where the murdered man's defenseless sister awaits the war's end. Her "creamy whiteness of the full-blown flower" telegraphed to every reader the message of her white racial virginity, just as her "thin little hands" signaled her inability to "hold sway" over the presumably vengeful slaves who vastly outnumbered her. The magazine readers grasped the chilling implication: the slaves threatened her virginity and her life, both equally precious.[5]

Decades later, the same story was being told and sold across the country, much to Wells-Barnett's dismay and fury. The white supremacist Thomas Dixon's pro–Ku Klux Klan novel of 1905, *The Clansman*, featured the rape (or "outrage") of an aristocratic young white woman by a freed black man. Here in Chicago the novel was advertised in the *Tribune* alongside department store ads for Marshall Field and Company's men's vests and ladies' embroidery flouncing. *The Clansman* became a national best seller, and a stage version was presented around the country, despite efforts by the Colored Citizens Protective League to stop the production. In this very year of 1909, a young filmmaker named David W. Griffith was honing his craft and soon would bring Dixon's racist novel to the screen, where it was to be retitled *The Birth of a Nation*. When the film appeared in 1915, Wells-Barnett was to denounce it and support those who sought a judicial injunction to bar it from being shown in Chicago. She knew how dangerous the dramatization of the "threadbare lie" could be. Just as *The Clansman* had incited at least one actual lynching, so could the feature-length film rouse a mob to murder people of color.[6]

The citizens of Cairo needed no motion picture to stoke their racial hatreds this November, 1909. Described in the *Chicago Daily Tribune* as "a country girl" who "fought desperately" against her assailants, the murdered Anna Pelley typified white womanhood that was preyed on and victimized by rapacious black men. The old formula made her death an open invitation to a lynching. Reading the *Tribune* account, Wells-Barnett was surely braced for the sequel to the Anna Pelley story in the days ahead. Her many years of investigation into the facts of hundreds of lynchings revealed a model or paradigm to these killings. With a few variations, the lynching at Cairo would prove as horrendous as it was predictable.

The *Tribune* front page brought gruesome details to the Wells-Barnett home in the following days. The newspaper accounts were so graphic that a reader virtually relived the events. Of the arrested African Americans, William "Frog" James was identified as the murderer. For his legal protection, the law required that he be put in the county jail and guarded by deputies who were sworn to protect him. Instead, the accused man was taken by train into the countryside, some twenty-five miles north of the city, by Sheriff Frank Davis of Alexander County. The sheriff was reported to be apprehensive about a possible Cairo mob and hoped to hide the prisoner. Telephone and telegraph links to informants along the way, however, let the Cairo vigilantes easily track down James, overpower the sheriff and his one deputy, and haul the accused murderer back to Cairo. In the early evening of November 10, a mob of about 20,000, including 500 women (some of them mothers pushing baby carriages), dragged James to the center of the city and heard a "refined" and "elderly gray haired woman" cry out, "Men, men. . . . Will you see your daughters murdered by a black fiend?"[7]

James supposedly confessed to the crime "almost as the hangman's noose tightened about his neck." He was hanged after sundown from the electrically lighted steel gateway arch that spanned the city's main commercial street. Some 500 bullets were then fired into his body, which was cut down, "mutilated," and set on fire. The body was then decapitated and the head impaled on a nearby pole. The *Tribune* omitted one detail: James's heart was cut from his body, and slices were "handed out as souvenirs." Crowds gathered the next morning to gawk at "the little pile of charred bones which marked the ghastly end of James . . . [until] the charred fragments were shoveled into a wagon and carted away." No expressions of remorse were recorded in the aftermath. The mob reportedly included the city's "best citizens," and a newspaper editorial declared that "lynchings were simply the popular cry for justice."[8]

Wells-Barnett's circle of friends and associates were not idle as news of the lynching reached Chicago. Strength in numbers served political goals, and the group immediately called a meeting and telegraphed Illinois governor Charles S. Deneen to demand the dismissal of Sheriff Davis of Cairo's Alexander County. Their telegram reminded the governor of the Illinois Mob Violence Act of 1904, which was shepherded through the legislature by an acquaintance of the Barnetts, the African American assemblyman Edward Green. It stated, "If any person shall be taken from the custody of the Sheriff or his deputy and lynched, it shall be prima facie evidence of failure on the part of the Sheriff to do his duty. And upon that fact being made to appear to the Governor, he shall publish a proclamation declaring the office of Sheriff vacant." Reminded of his duty under the law, Governor Deneen promptly dismissed Sheriff Frank Davis. According to the law, the sheriff was not thereafter eligible to be elected or reappointed to the office.[9]

But he could appeal. If Sheriff Davis persuaded the governor that he had done everything in his power to protect the life of Frog James, the governor could reinstate him. The decision of the governor was final.

Everyone in Wells-Barnett's circle understood the stakes. The sheriff's probable reinstatement posed extreme danger to African Americans everywhere in Illinois and beyond. Since 1893, there had been sixteen lynchings in the state, some by rope noose, others by firearms and other means. Race riots had occurred in the capital, Springfield. "With each repetition," Ida Wells-Barnett was to write, "there has been increased violence, rioting, and barbarism." Cairo, she said, "was one of the most inhuman spectacles ever witnessed in this country." But Cairo was not necessarily the last of it. Or the worst. Depending on the outcome of the sheriff's appeal, Cairo could incite others to commit the same heinous crime. If Sheriff Davis got his job back with the governor's blessing, then the Klan and their ilk would know that they had a free pass to murder. The sheriff's reinstatement would be their "all-clear" signal for homicide by lynching.[10]

Sheriff Frank Davis, in fact, had already scheduled his appeal for the next Wednesday in Springfield. He would demand reinstatement and be represented by a prominent lawyer from the Cairo area. Here in Chicago, Ferdinand Barnett was working hard to enlist prominent Chicago-based African American men to go on a fact-finding trip to Cairo and on to the hearing in Springfield. He appealed to members of the Appomattox Club, an important black political organization in Chicago. He used all the persuasion and pressure that an attorney of his senior stature and experience could summon. It was now Saturday evening, just days before the hearing, and Barnett was forced to admit failure and frustration. He'd done his best, but the effort proved "fruitless." One of the Barnetts' friends expected "a whitewash."[11]

At the family dinner table, flanked by the children, Ferdinand Barnett recounted his efforts, admitted his frustration, and turned suddenly to his wife. She could hardly believe her ears when he said, "So it would seem that you will have to go to Cairo and get the facts with which to confront the sheriff next Wednesday morning. Your train leaves at eight o'clock."

Her train? *Hers*? How preposterous. She objected "very strongly." The family finished dinner, the meat stew and hash that Mr. Barnett so enjoyed. Her own appetite vanished. Why should she be asked to walk the streets of an "inflamed" Cairo? The *Tribune* reported that the city was still "at the mercy of the mob" and its "blind wrath." Governor Deneen had declared martial law and sent ten companies of National Guard troops to keep order, but "a crowd of vengeful men and women kept watch and waited," and "little knots of men gathered all about the city and planned further vengeance." The quiet of Cairo was reportedly "ominous," and public order was maintained only with "triple ranks of soldiers, with rifles loaded with ball cartridges and gleaming bayonets held menacingly breast high."[12]

Why should Wells-Barnett enter the racial war zone by herself? For all practical purposes, her days of single-handed investigation in far-flung locales were a thing of the past. The former Miss Wells was a sweet-voiced but feisty and independent woman journalist who crossed ocean and continent to lecture and dispatch reports. Mrs. Ferdinand L. Barnett, however, stayed close to home. Hyphenating her name to keep her identity, she was ahead of her time, but Wells-Barnett was now a Chicago matron and club woman who turned her formidable energies to social service organizations that included the Negro Fellowship League, the National Association of Colored Women, and the club that bore her name, the Ida B. Wells Club. She sought to unite African Americans for the "arduous work" of social, legal, and economic justice, believing that these goals were best achieved by organized effort. She'd arranged a symposium, "What It Means to Be a Mother," and was active in promoting kindergartens. She wrote articles and letters for various publications, all the while maintaining a home and bringing up four spirited children. Her busy schedule did not have space for an impromptu investigative side trip some 350 miles away. Besides, who would care for the children if something happened to her in Cairo?[13]

For that matter, why not urge the leading men of the newly organized National Association for the Advancement of Colored People to go to the hearing? The NAACP had male leadership under the sociologist W. E. B. Du Bois and others. The organization was about to take on the mantle of Wells-Barnett's longtime antilynching crusade. Let Du Bois or the association's first

Ida B. Wells-Barnett and children Charles, Herman, Ida, and Alfreda, 1909.
(Courtesy of the Special Collections Research Center, University of Chicago Library)

president, Moorfield Storey, take a turn in Cairo. Why should she "do the work that others refuse"?[14]

Ferdinand Barnett only repeated how "important" it was "that somebody gather the evidence." He knew his wife's skills as a fact-finding reporter were still as sharp as forged steel scissors. She was a veteran of similar missions and knew how to take care of herself. He added that if she was unwilling to go, "there was nothing more to be said." He picked up his evening paper, and Ida took little Alfreda up to bed and sang her to sleep, dozing off herself until she was stirred by the voice of her older son, Charles, who said, "Mother, Pa says it is time to go . . . to take the train to Cairo." Drowsy, she demurred. The boy paused, then challenged his mother in terms that awoke Wells-Barnett and shredded her defenses: "*Mother, if you don't go nobody else will.*"[15]

It was a moment out of scripture, "out of the mouths of babes." She was summoned to yet another mission by her firstborn child, the voice of Christian and civic duty. Across centuries, the lone heroic figure of Joan of Arc also echoed in the moment. The fearless female, a figure in arms, arose and found the courage to fight against terrible odds. Wells-Barnett too must answer the call. Perhaps she would take the modern-day arms, the handgun she'd bought years ago in Memphis for protection. Indeed, she must make this solo journey as a mother and a wife. She must do it, what's more, as a citizen striving to secure constitutional rights for the black Americans who were often denied their rights. Those who thought that she had retired to domestic life and "deserted the cause" were about to be silenced, for she promised to go. Not tonight (she needed a decent night's sleep), but next morning, Sunday. The entire family came to the Romanesque railroad station with the clock tower at the southern end of Grant Park to bid her farewell. They sat on the oak benches in the barrel-vaulted waiting room with pale light filtered through a wall of stained glass. The inset glass mural on the wall depicted a team of horses driven by a charioteer. The railroad's own emblem could symbolize her mission to drive hard and fast in full control.[16]

Awaiting the Illinois Central train, Wells-Barnett doubtless recalled a moment firmly linked to the campaign in Cairo. Central Station, she knew, was built for the traffic of Chicago's 1893 World's Columbian Exposition. Thousands of visitors poured into this very rail station from all over the United States and abroad. They were awed by the fair's classical structures, called its White City. Ferdinand Barnett, who was at the time her husband-to-be, sardonically called it "literally and figuratively a *White* City." Although African Americans constituted a full tenth of the nation's population, they were systematically excluded from the planning and the exhibits. In effect, they were effaced from the story of America as told by the fair.[17]

Action was demanded back then in 1893 too, especially when the fair commissioners proposed a special "Colored People's Day" with free watermelon, the very fruit linked to cartoon stereotypes of blacks. Many in the black community, however, felt grateful instead of furious. Many remained passive as the fair celebrated white Anglo-Saxon America. Not Ida B. Wells. She quickly worked to put a pamphlet together. A bombshell of a pamphlet, it was a free handout souvenir to expose the brutal facts behind the patriotic pomp of the racially savage and exclusionary White City. It proclaimed the contributions that blacks made to the nation, ranging from agriculture and artisanship to law, literature, and medicine. Her future husband, as F. L. Barnett, contributed a chapter that documented the extensive—but futile—efforts of black citizens to take part in the fair planning and staffing and the exhibitions. The esteemed Frederick Douglass, one of Wells's longtime supporters and mentors, was a marquee name for the pamphlet. His chapters spanned the era of slavery and of the promised post–Civil War freedom under the Constitution and the amendments to the Bill of Rights. Douglass's rhetoric scalded white America for its failure to fulfill the terms of its founding documents. He also exposed the southern neoslavery of black men arrested on trumped-up charges, convicted and imprisoned, then leased as cheap labor to the coal, timber, and steel industries.[18]

Wells herself contributed a chapter, "Lynch Law," which included a drawing and a photographic reproduction of two black men hanged by the neck while crowds look on. Perhaps after their visit, the white fairgoers who tucked the pamphlet among their souvenirs would look at the images of hangings and be properly horrified. They might see that the onlookers in the pictures mirrored them, a crowd of spectators who gaze at exhibits of mob murder in the land of the free. Perhaps their consciences would be stirred to corrective action.

The fair's officials, of course, would not permit the pamphlet to be given out at the White City. Haiti had an exhibit building, however, and Frederick Douglass had served as the U.S. ambassador there, so Wells "manned a desk at the Haitian Building." She handed out copies for two months, until the fair closed. Titled *The Reason Why the Colored American Is Not in the World's Columbian Exposition*, the pamphlets circulated in the world at large, winged words dispatched to tell the truth and guide the nation progressively toward the authentic civilization that met the standards of its founding documents.[19]

The Illinois Central train for Cairo steamed into Central Station, and Wells-Barnett hugged her children and said goodbye to her husband. Boarding for the daylong journey on a drab, rainy day, she perhaps recalled Frederick Douglass's words in the introduction to the pamphlet. Douglass wrote of his yearning to report truthfully that in America "Negroes are not tortured, shot, hanged or burned to death, merely on suspicion of crime and without ever seeing a judge, jury, or advocate." She too yearned to live in that America. Only aggressive action could make it a reality. Dressed for travel, with her upswept hair tightly pinned, and with her own fiftieth birthday less than three years off, Wells-Barnett girded for one more battle.[20]

THE TICKET TO CAIRO was inevitably a ticket toward Wells-Barnett's past. Minus the magnolias, the gently rolling landscape of southern Illinois was reminiscent of the rural Mississippi region where she grew up. Her birthplace, the town of Holly Springs, Mississippi, was the seat of plantations when Ida Belle Wells was "born into slavery," as the opening chapter of her autobiography was to proclaim. She was ever aware that her career was made possible, first, by the legacy of her parents. As grim as life became under the post-Reconstruction Jim Crow laws, her parents' slave times had been far worse. Whenever her domestic and public roles in Chicago conflicted, Wells-Barnett needed only to recall that her father James Wells grew up trapped in two snarled identities. He was the "son of a plantation master and his slave woman," Peggy, and his paternity protected him from two "cruelties of slavery," the auction block and the whip. But his legal status as mere property denied him the self-possession necessary to plan for his own future. His body was not his own.[21]

Wells-Barnett's practical skills as a writer and speaker echoed certain terms of her father's occupation. Taught carpentry for work on the plantation, James Wells used his abilities to express his rights when freedom came. Carpentry was crucial to the rebuilding of postwar Holly Springs. It gave James Wells the power to issue his own declaration of independence when his former master, a partisan Old South Democrat, tried to punish him for voting for the party of Lincoln, the Republicans. After the vote, Wells found his plantation carpentry workshop locked up tight, with his tools shut inside. Loath to apologize to his former master and beg for the key, Wells simply went into town, bought a new set of tools, rented a house, and moved his family off the plantation property for good. Perhaps relishing her father's grit during the daylong train ride, Wells-Barnett could find an important link to his story: that marketable skills were the cornerstone of independence. Her father's hammer and saw, his drawknife and mallet and square nails were the tools of independence, just as her articles and speeches were useful to the building of a more just and equitable America.[22]

The legacy of Wells-Barnett's Virginia-born mother, Elizabeth, was also present in this Pullman car to Cairo. Elizabeth (Lizzie) Wells's life underscored her husband's lesson on freedom and independence. Elizabeth's own parents and six siblings were lost to her in childhood, when she and a sister "were sold to slave traders . . . and were taken to Mississippi and sold again." Plantation life meant physical and emotional pain, and Elizabeth Wells made certain that Ida Belle and the other children knew their mother "had been beaten by slave owners and the hard times she had as a slave." The point was not pity but instruction. Elizabeth taught her children they must never again permit the hell of slavery to overcome God's blessing of freedom. Enduring plantation cruelties, Elizabeth nonetheless learned her way around the big house kitchen, mastering the long-handled frying pans and heavy iron skillets with tight-fitting lids. Culinary secrets of spices and herbs readied her for a better future when freedom came and she had a family and household of her own. All Holly Springs knew her as "a famous cook."[23]

Her children, however, knew her best as a deeply spiritual mother who instilled ironclad habits of discipline. Except for the baby and for Ida's disabled sister, Eugenia, all six children—three girls and three boys—were mustered for the tasks of housework. They were taught how to clean and launder and iron clothes, skills that Wells-Barnett insisted her own children learn in Chicago. Each Sabbath, Lizzie Wells marched her brood to nine o'clock Sunday school, come rain or shine. Most impressive, their mother "went along to school" with Ida and the other children "until she learned to read the Bible." Her Christian faith became Ida B. Wells-Barnett's anchorage. On the train this Sabbath day in Illinois, she surely prayed to God for strength, support, and protection in the hard days to come in Cairo.[24]

Faith in God always fueled Wells-Barnett's mission for civil rights. Back in 1866, when Ida Belle was four years old, Congress passed the Civil Rights Act, which declared that "all persons born in the United States and not subject to any foreign power" were citizens entitled to "full and equal benefit of all laws." By the time she was a child of six, the U.S. Congress in faraway Washington, D.C., clarified the meaning of the act when it passed the Thirteenth and Fourteenth amendments to the Constitution. The Fourteenth Amendment was intended to be extremely important for black Americans. As historians have emphasized, "It reaffirmed state and federal citizenship for persons born or naturalized in the United States, and it forbade any state . . . to abridge the 'privileges and immunities' of citizens" or "to deprive any person 'the equal protection of the laws.'" Ida Belle was eight years old in 1870 when Congress passed the Fifteenth Amendment, which gave black men like her father the right to vote and to hold elective public office. Yet the little girl remembered "the anxious way [her] mother walked the floor at night when [her] father was out at a political meeting." She remembered, too, that she "heard the words Ku Klux Klan long before [she] knew what they meant."[25]

In 1878, she learned the meaning of another deadly term—yellow fever—which swept the Mississippi Valley and within twenty-four hours killed both of her parents. The sixteen-year-old Ida got the news while staying with her grandmother Peggy in the countryside, and she caught a freight train for Holly Springs as soon as it was safe to go home. James Wells had been making coffins for the dead, and now he himself was laid to rest, while the kitchen rhythms of Elizabeth were forever stilled. The baby, Stanley, had died too. Neighbors and members of the local Masonic lodge discussed exactly which relatives and neighbors might accept a particular Wells child (the youngest only two years of age) into their home to raise. The crippled Eugenia, they agreed, might need to be institutionalized in a county poorhouse. The Masons decided that Ida, now age sixteen, could fend for herself.[26]

"When all this had been arranged to their satisfaction," Ida "calmly . . . announced that they were not going to put any of the children anywhere." James and Elizabeth Wells would "turn over in their graves to know that their children had been scattered." If the Masons would help her find work, she promised to take care of the children. A self-described "butterfly" and "light-hearted schoolgirl" now asserted herself as "the head of a family."[27]

She never glorified her new role. The Masons found her a position teaching in a country school. She lengthened her skirts and began a weekly routine that merged duty and drudgery. An old friend of her mother agreed to "stay at the house with the children" during the week, and Miss Ida Belle Wells mounted the big, "long-eared, balking, braying mule" that meant transportation in the rural South. Mules pulled plows, hauled crops to market, built levees, and carried riders. Ida rode muleback six miles to the country school every Sunday afternoon, returning to Holly Springs on the same mule on Friday afternoons. The weekends were "for washing, ironing, and darning the children's clothes." She was ever grateful for the good country folks' gifts of eggs and butter. This went on for over two years. She didn't complain.[28]

The most painful sacrifice was withdrawing from school. Both James and Lizzie Wells laid down the law: the children's "job was to go to school and learn all [they] could." Slaves had been forbidden by law to learn to read and write, and the Wells parents prized literacy and learning as key to their children's future. Ida was enrolled at Holly Springs's Shaw University (later renamed Rust College), and James served on its board, while Elizabeth closely monitored the children's scholastic progress. Their deaths and Ida's teaching schedule meant that she could attend school only part-time, in the summers.[29]

A turning point came some two years later, when her aunt offered Ida the chance of a lifetime—to leave rural Holly Springs for one of the "Queen" Mississippi River cities, Memphis. City life was an irresistible opportunity. Wells-Barnett later called herself "a young, inexperienced girl" who knew "nothing whatever of the world's ways." She meant this in terms of male-female relationships, but she also implied ignorance of city life. Yet she was better prepared than she realized when she moved to Memphis in 1881–82, at the age of nineteen. Her middle-class code of conduct was as firmly shaped as a Victorian corset. The faculty at Shaw saw to it during her school days in the postwar years of Reconstruction. First of all, the school was staffed and administered in a "missionary spirit" under the jurisdiction of the Methodist Episcopal Church. Ida's teachers were mainly white women from the North. Their emphasis on "daily chapel, weekly prayer meetings, and church on Sunday" were in harmony with the views of the Wells parents, who doubtless applauded the goals of the curriculum: to lay "a foundation for a broad, thorough and practical education."[30]

Ida, however, absorbed other attitudes that came specifically from white, northern teachers who enshrined and transmitted to their female pupils the concept of "ideal womanhood" and "Victorian codes of propriety." The codes emphasized habits of refinement in every aspect of life, from grooming and dress to proper table setting, for the very placement of the knife, fork, and spoon was thought to be an index of "delicacy" and "taste." Victorian good manners were not to be considered pretentious or snobbish but a moral and godly expression of Christian virtue. For Ida's parents, Christianity provided the hope of salvation and the faith that God would one day "let my people go," according to the African American spiritual. For the Shaw teachers, the practice of Christianity also meant deportment, the refinement of manners, and the belief that "the refined virtues were rooted in Christian principles and improved with compliance to God's law." From the chapel to the luncheon table and parlor, a young woman was to demonstrate her mastery of the codes of propriety.[31]

Above all, "no matter what other personal gifts a woman had, she was not complete without a 'mental culture' achieved through study." Books and reading stood at the pinnacle of this effort, for books identified "cultivated people." Victorian-era America believed that books and reading "ingrained refined habits into the minds, hearts, and speech of readers, making books the purest symbols of true refinement." Owning books "implied sensibility, taste, even polish."[32]

A proper young lady, according to the codes of Wells's teachers, must also show refinement in her penmanship, for Victorians believed that handwriting revealed "the solidity and integrity of the writer's character"—or lack of it. Each pen stroke of Wells's "large, well-formed letters" expressed her refinement, and when a prominent New York newspaper publisher complimented her as a woman reporter "who handles a goose quill with diamond point," the tribute echoed back into the classroom days at Shaw.[33]

The Victorian young lady was well prepared to move to Memphis, where her Aunt Fannie was widowed with three children in the aftermath of the yellow fever epidemic. Fannie Wells invited Ida Belle and her two youngest sisters, Annie and Lily, to come stay with her. Ida's brothers, Jim and George, were now apprenticed to carpenters, and Aunt Belle welcomed the disabled Eugenia to live with her on her farm. With her sisters, Ida Belle packed up and made the move. It was a step toward the career that eventually sent her to Cairo.[34]

Memphis of the early 1880s was dazzling. With a population of 33,592, it was ten times larger than Holly Springs and spread out regally on high bluffs over the vast Mississippi River. Like Holly Springs, however, Memphis was still recovering from the Civil War and the recent yellow fever epidemic that decimated the population. It was nonetheless a vibrant city. One historian's description captures the scene that awaited Wells and her sisters: "Up from the dock were several blocks devoted to black-owned businesses—groceries and saloons, clothing stores, doctors' offices, photographers, insurance agents, pawnshops and barbers. An open-air market offered vegetables and fruits sold from stalls, as well as goods laid out in blankets and hawked by vendors." The major thoroughfare was Beale Street, "the Main Street of Negro America."[35]

Ida Wells was awed by the magnificence of the churches where she now worshipped every Sunday. The Romanesque-style Beale Street Baptist Church held some 2,000 congregants, nearly two-thirds the population of Holly Springs. On any given Sabbath, Wells was also drawn to services at Avery Chapel, at the African Methodist Episcopal Church, and especially at the Vance Street Christian Church. For the first time in her life, she saw a black bishop and black ministers, together with black businessmen and professionals—and black ladies too. Memphis African Americans were obviously economically prosperous. Ironically, the yellow fever epidemic had helped make this possible, for in its aftermath, many properties of the departed whites were purchased at good prices by enterprising blacks. A flourishing black middle class sponsored cultural, educational, charitable, and artistic organizations. Observing the customs, manners, and dress of her fellow worshippers, Wells was also "excited by the glitter: the gaslight theaters, cobblestone streets, railroad terminals, department stores, churches and synagogues, schools and hospitals." There was a men's crack military drill team, too, the Tennessee Rifles. For African Americans, she learned, Memphis of the early 1880s was "Mecca."[36]

Soon enough, Miss Ida B. Wells would join in the social and cultural life of this urban black mecca. But not right away. At church and in public, she "watched the crowds" and worried about her future, for once again she was a rural county schoolteacher. The mule gave way to the railroad train for travel from the city, but her job took her into the countryside of the surrounding Shelby County. Off-hours were crammed with the care of her sisters, plus preparation for classes and for the dreaded teacher's examination that she must pass to keep her job and raise her salary. The exam was especially worrying because she had not completed her program at Shaw. She had no guarantees here in Memphis. Except for one black member, the school board was white, and teachers' contracts were up for annual renewal—or cancellation without warning. Her salary (fifty dollars per month) barely covered expenses and often arrived a month or two late. When payment came, a hefty portion went to Holly Springs for her family, and ten to fifteen dollars went to the landlady of whatever boarding house she temporarily called home, once her aunt moved permanently to California. As seasons passed, the month outpaced the money every time.[37]

Wells also faced a grim fact about teaching: for her, it was a "distasteful" grind. The famous temperance leader Frances Willard extolled the ideal female teacher as one who "guides, inspires, and elevates . . . thousands of little souls." As conscientious as she was, Wells could not recognize herself or her pupils in Willard's words. True, the school board assigned her to crowded classrooms of seventy or more pupils and restricted her to the primary grades. And the board had no qualms about depriving the black schoolchildren of ample supplies and up-to-date textbooks. The basic fact, however, was this: Ida B. Wells "never cared for teaching."[38]

Yet the classroom provided one key advantage: it was a respectable position. It gave her entrance into the middle class. By definition, a teacher was a member of the Memphis black elite. The diary that Wells began in 1885 chronicled her debut in her new social world. It recorded her rounds of evening parties, teas, dances, concerts, theater, and other entertainments.

It also showed her struggle to maintain a fashionable wardrobe on a teacher's meager salary. The young teacher slipped into consumer debt, for the five-story Menken's Palatial Emporium on Main Street happily opened a charge account for Miss Wells, who grazed its counters on Saturdays and discovered the pleasures of dressing well. The fabrics were sumptuous: the velvets and cashmeres, the fine cottons and silks in vibrant colors that set off her coffee-and-cream complexion. Menken's extended credit for her purchases of shoes, gloves, dress goods, hats, and shirtwaists. In her boardinghouse rooms, she regularly sewed and mended and ironed, as a proper Christian young woman ought to do, but she also splurged to have her hair styled and hired a dressmaker to fashion a delectable dress that cost almost half a month's salary.[39]

She joined a literary group that met at the Vance Street Christian Church on Friday afternoons—the Memphis Lyceum, which featured "recitations, essays, and debates interspersed with music . . . and some choice poetry." Wells was thrilled to become the "editress" of the group's newsletter, *Evening Star*, when its founder moved away. Writing for publication was soon a serious hobby. The minister of the Beale Street Baptist Church, the Reverend Robert N. Countee, invited her to write for his *Living Way*, an established religious weekly serving African Americans. Other periodicals soon provided space for her writing, and she began to portray herself as a newspaperwoman with a pen name: Iola. Composing the "letters," Wells discovered, was far more satisfying than classroom teaching. At her writing desk in her room, she could draw from the familiar, uplifting Victorian fiction and advice literature. She urged black women readers to attain "a standard of earnest, thoughtful, pure, noble womanhood." Iola was mistress of the Victorian keyboard of nouns and adjectives.[40]

Iola, however, lived solely on the page, while a public speaker enjoyed actual bodily presence in society. Wells began to take lessons in elocution. Each lesson, at fifty cents, was the cost of a day at her boardinghouse, but public speaking skills were surely a wise investment. Her teacher assigned her to memorize the speeches of Shakespeare's Lady Macbeth. This was self-study, a life commitment whose importance she'd learned from her teachers in Holly Springs.[41]

Suitors came calling. Numerous young men were drawn to this attractive, five-foot-tall, "rather girlish looking" young woman "with sharp regular features, penetrating eyes, firm set thin lips and a sweet voice." By the mid-1880s, Miss Wells socialized and corresponded with Messrs. Carr, Avant, Mosely, Morris, and Taylor, among others. According to the custom of the time, she exchanged photographs with them (another expense) and expected these gentlemen to write her letters, as she wrote to them on good stationery at her writing desk. To gauge their character, she scrutinized their words and the quality of their penmanship. Her life seemed on course toward the Victorian ideal of marriage and a family and home of her own.[42]

Marriage, for one thing, would stop the rumors that inevitably dogged her as a single black woman. The sexual baggage from slave days haunted every African American woman. She, Ida B. Wells, was heir to the twisted tradition of sexual license that male slave owners allowed themselves with enslaved women in the pre–Civil War South. Her own dear grandmother Peggy was a woman whose bondage required submission to her married white master. Since emancipation in 1865, a poisonous racial and sexual double standard prevailed. No one impugned the character of a white man for his presumed erotic appetites, but a black woman was regarded as nature's own slut. Whites were not the sole culprits firing up this caldron of lies. It was unforgivable that some African Americans stirred the brew. In Wells's case, Holly Springs neighbors started rumors about a liaison when they saw her in public in a conversation with a white man. Here in Memphis, some people thought that her sister Lily was actually her daughter. Some thought her a manipulative coquette and spread "base slanderous lie[s] that blackened [her] life." The rumor that she was the mistress of a prominent minister filled her soul with "iron."[43]

But marriage, for starters, meant the "inevitable baby . . . with the habits peculiar to all babyhood." The elder child of a large family knew too well the rigors of infant and child care, the Saturday night baths, the laundering. For now, she enjoyed "the society of the gentlemen" but did not "wish to be married."[44]

Turmoil, what's more, was a frequent companion. Despite the social whirl, Wells could not shake off the blue bouts of isolation and "fits of loneliness." In vibrant inks, she admitted dark thoughts to her diary: "I don't know what's the matter with me, I feel so dissatisfied with my life, so isolated from all my kind." Friendships seemed difficult, and her future murky. The few dollars earned for her Iola articles in newspapers and magazines were nowhere near enough to support her as a journalist. Her elocution lessons were progressing, and she loved the theater, so maybe the stage was a possibility. Then again, actresses had an overall unsavory reputation. Perhaps she could become a novelist, but Wells had never read a black-authored novel. The issue was unsettled.[45]

Her own mind was unsettled. Rogue thoughts surged. The codes of "ideal womanhood" taught the importance of virtuous sentiments, but the lined pages of her diary flashed like the knife blade of the critic. She well understood, for instance, that a proper lady was meant to praise an amateur performance of *Macbeth* for the actors' worthy good-faith effort. Wells, however, dipped her pen in ink to shed blood: the play "was extremely dull & tiresome & some of the pronunciation was execrable in the extreme." A minister who failed to meet her expectations opened the critical sluice gates: "Went to service yesterday morning & found a very slender, puerile-looking, small specimen of humanity occupying the pulpit."[46]

If she confined these observations solely to a private diary, as countless ladies managed to do, Wells could live a life of accepted social norms. She prayed to God for help, searching for "consolation" in the faith that "my Heavenly Father will reward and bless me for doing what is right and just."[47]

The fact was, Ida Belle Wells could not lace her whole self into the steel-boned foundation garment of the Victorian lady. Her "sweet voice" concealed the temper of a spitfire. When it erupted, she faced the consequences. Her departure from schooling at Shaw, to cite one grievous example, was not solely prompted by the Wells children's sudden orphanage. The "darkest days" in Holly Springs referred, instead, to a confrontation with Shaw president W. W. Hooper, who expelled her. She was not suspended from school but permanently exiled. To her lifelong regret, her "tempestuousness, rebelliousness, hard headed willfulness" got the best of her. If only James and Elizabeth Wells had lived, they might have helped her, protected her—persuaded President Hooper to give her another chance. No more. She was on her own.[48]

Memphis, too, had a horrific—but momentous—trap set for Wells one fine May morning in 1884, when she boarded the commuter train to go to work in the county school. Wearing a lightweight linen travel coat, a duster, over her dress, she took her seat in the ladies' car. That spring day became a turning point that linked directly to this Cairo mission. She opened a book as the commuter train pulled out and the conductor began collecting tickets "as usual." Trouble started when the conductor refused her ticket and ordered her to the forward car, a smoker that was thick with men's tobacco smoke and grimy with locomotive soot and dirt. The terms of another African American young lady who underwent a similar experience on a train a few years earlier now applied to Wells: "My hands were clean and so was my face. I hadn't mussed my hair. . . . I hadn't soiled my dress a single bit. I was sitting up 'straight and proper'. . . . I wasn't talking out loud. . . . In short, I was behaving 'like a . . . lady.'" By definition, a lady belonged in a ladies' car. Wells refused to budge.[49]

The conductor "caught hold" of her arm, a flagrant violation of a lady's right not to be touched by a stranger. When he tried to "drag" her from her seat, Ida reacted: "I fastened my teeth in the back of his hand."

A fight was on. The "badly bitten" conductor yanked at Wells, and two other train crewmen ganged up on her. Things got more physical. Wells gripped the seatback and "braced" her feet against the seat in front. Passengers stirred, but not one came to her defense or aid. Instead, the so-called white ladies and white gentlemen began cheering—for the conductor. "Some of them even stood on the seats so they could get a good view and continued applauding the conductor" and his gang of two "for the brave stand" in man-handling a petite woman. At the first stop, Wells agreed to exit the train rather than be forced bodily into the smoker, "which was already filled with colored people." In moments she stood on the platform alone, roughed up, the sleeves of her duster "torn out."

Physically she was not injured, but ladylike manners had proven worth-less. She was smack against the barrier of race—the color line—in the new Jim Crow South. The constitutional rights that she had grown up with were being dismantled, the very rights that defined her parents and all the Wells children as full citizens and also granted her father the vote. At best, these rights were honored in the breach. At worst, they were nullified, as she was to discover when an angry, indignant, confident, and assertive Miss Ida B. Wells, now twenty-two years of age, crossed the railway platform and re-turned to Memphis without incident. This time, her anger was targeted. She marched into a law office and hired a black attorney to file suit against the Chesapeake, Ohio and Southwestern Railroad Company.

"A Darky Damsel Obtains a Verdict," headlined the racist *Memphis Daily Appeal* the following December. The circuit court awarded Wells $500 in damages. The victory, however, proved short-lived. The railroad appealed to the Tennessee Supreme Court, which decreed in 1887 that Wells's intention was mere harassment with an eye to financial gain ("We think it evident that the purpose of the defendant in error was to harass with a view to this suit."). The court refused to address the charge that Wells's civil rights were denied to her, that banishment to the smoker car of all paying, ticketed passengers of color was a step back toward the slave days.[50]

Separate was not equal, despite the court ruling. Where, then, was the civilized America of James and Lizzie Wells's faith and commitment? The nation was suffering the erosion of civilization and betraying its newly freed people. It wasn't supposed to be this way. But in 1883, the year before Wells's humiliating incident on the train, the U.S. Supreme Court had nullified the Civil Rights Act, declaring it unconstitutional. The Court ruled that the Fourteenth Amendment did not protect black people from discrimination by private businesses and individuals, only from discrimination by states. Southern states began to pass sweeping segregation legislation. Tennessee required railroads to maintain separate first-class cars for blacks and whites in a law passed in 1881. Then came more restrictive such laws in Mississippi and Louisiana. These Jim Crow laws (named for the African American song-

and-dance caricature, "Jump Jim Crow") used racial identity to segregate public accommodations. This meant railway cars, and also theaters, hotels, and public eating places. Jim Crow separated black from white children in public schools and playgrounds. White supremacy was also proclaimed in antimiscegenation laws, which prohibited marriage between blacks and whites.[51]

Within a few years, racial segregation was to be certified by the U.S. Supreme Court in the infamous 1896 case of *Plessy v. Ferguson.* Railroads, once again, were at the center. In specific, the *Plessy* decision upheld a Louisiana law that prohibited a person of African American ancestry from riding in any railroad car that was reserved for whites. The court endorsed the principle that police powers were the province of the state legislatures. The larger principle was the authorization of racially "separate but equal" facilities under state and local law throughout the South. The Supreme Court, in short, gave its blessing to the official reinstatement of white rule throughout the South. The color line became a racial stockade fence. Jim Crow effectively nullified the Fifteenth Amendment by imposing poll taxes and literacy tests on black voters. Threats and violence by the Ku Klux Klan and other terrorist gangs became whites' rule by blunt force and murder. The new "brand of justice" was no justice for blacks.[52]

Memphis did not show Wells its deadly racist face when she arrived and settled in. Or perhaps she failed to take full notice. Iola became her passion, and Iola was rewarded. The African American press enthusiastically sought Wells's articles. Periodicals from the *Cleveland Gazette* to the *Indianapolis Freeman, Christian Index, Chicago Conservator,* and *New York Age* welcomed her "letters." Iola urged her race onward toward social, economic, and civic uplift. She advocated exemplary conduct and leadership as the pathway toward self-respect and social acceptance. Wells also took a big step into professional journalism in 1889, when she joined the Memphis *Free Speech and Headlight* and became a partner because the business required so very little capital. Advertisers and subscribers covered the printing bills. When her teaching contract was not renewed, she found that she could earn a living in journalism. She attended a meeting of the National Colored Press Association in Louisville, Kentucky, and was proclaimed "the Princess of the Press." Iola could now call herself a newspaperwoman without a blush or a blink.[53]

The racial climate of the 1880s South, however, was "hardening," and black Memphis felt the impact. In 1886, "the black community lost its representative on the local school board" and in city government too. In the black community, "ridicule, harassment, and threats plagued independent leaders." The white press smeared a local black man whose name was proposed for appointive federal office. A married couple was tried in court under local antimiscegenation laws. Wells read an insightful, white-authored novel of 1889, Albion Tourgee's *Bricks without Straw*, which exposed the perils that freed blacks faced from racist, resentful whites in the Reconstruction-era South. The 1887 Tennessee Supreme Court decision in her railroad case was a crushing blow of biblical proportions. She felt "utterly discouraged" and confided to her diary, "I had hoped such great things from my suit for my people. I have firmly believed all along that the law was on our side and would . . . give us justice." "O God," she asked, "is there no redress, no peace, no justice in this land for us?" In sorrow, she yearned to "gather my race in my arms and fly far away with them."[54]

Flight, however, was not the Ida B. Wells way. It was fight, not flight, that she owed to her parents' memory, to herself, to her people — and under the rights guaranteed by the Constitution of the United States of America. Her weapons of choice were the pen and printing press. Sweet, sentimental terms had their place, but she must marshal facts and couch them in biting irony and scathing indictment. The social critic inside her — the spitfire — claimed primacy. The moment demanded it. She began to conceive her newspaper articles in terms of the most terrifying and powerful explosive substance in existence: dynamite. Her own court case was only one of the racial outrages on her mental map. Her diary listed others. In 1886, in Jackson, Tennessee, "a colored woman accused of poisoning a white one was taken from the county jail and stripped naked and hung up in the courthouse yard and her body riddled with bullets and left exposed to view." The evidence against the lynched woman was utterly flimsy. Wells wrote a self-styled "dynamitic" newspaper article about the case.[55]

Then came the traumatic episode in Memphis. It was the "southern horror" that changed Wells's life, and it started at the corner of Walker Avenue and Mississippi Boulevard known as the "Curve." The lynching of her three friends thrust Wells into full "dynamitic" journalism and into a new social role that ultimately drove her to Cairo. Back in 1885, she'd written an article that urged enterprising black men to open "business establishments" and to hire "young colored men and women" to provide them training and employment." Three of her good friends did just that: Thomas (Tommie) Moss, Calvin McDowell, and Henry Stewart, who formed a corporation to open a grocery store at the corner where the streetcar line curved "sharply." Wells was "best friends" with Moss and his wife, Betty, and their little girl, Maurine, who was her goddaughter. Moss had steady income as a federally employed mail carrier. He owned his home and had savings and taught Sunday school at Avery Chapel. A grocery store in the black Curve neighborhood was a smart move for him and his two partners. They would staff the store by day, and he'd take over most evenings. The store was well situated, close to the Moss family's church and to Tommie's fraternal lodge.[56]

The People's Cooperative Grocery Store opened its doors in 1889 and quickly became a popular social center in the neighborhood. The black grocers sold sugar, flour, spices, tea, coffee, and canned foods in cheap steel coated with tin. Their trade was mostly with blacks, but also with some white folks. The store gave customers a choice of grocers, and many preferred the People's Grocery to the established rival, W. H. Barrett's. At the time, the new grocers weren't concerned about the white-owned grocery that was located diagonally across the intersection. American business favored competition. The longtime white grocer, Barrett, no longer had a monopoly, but his "hostility" in the face of new competition appeared unimportant.[57]

Barrett, as Wells came to understand, smoldered in fury as his competitors succeeded. His receipts were down. Every customer who crossed the threshold of the People's Grocery felt like a personal rebuke to him and an insult to the white race. The social conversation and jokes that went on just outside the blacks' store were, to Barrett, intolerable. Even though some neighborhood whites called his store "a crap den and a gambling hell," the situation was outrageous to a white southern man who felt his racial superiority mocked. He swore that something must be done. Both groceries were located just outside the city limits and beyond the range of police protection. Barrett doubtless saw the potential advantage in this. He kept an eye out for his chance, which came in spring 1892, when an outdoor neighborhood game of marbles between black and white boys broke up in a quarrel. One white boy's father whipped the victorious black boy, whereupon the black father and his friends "pitched in to avenge the white man's flogging of a colored boy." Feelings ran high on both sides of the racial divide.[58]

The black grocers were not involved, but Barrett surely knew how to tap local whites' fury in these Jim Crow days—and how to set a trap for the black grocers. A trap needed bait. Word went out that the People's Grocery was to be raided. In the darkness of a Saturday night, a menacing, shadowy band of men approached the store. They were not customers. The rumored raid was about to take place, and deep inside the store, a crew of black men were armed and ready to defend the People's Grocery against the assault. As the band advanced on the store, the crew opened fire. Three white men were wounded. The black customers and the armed black men who'd fired all fled, but deputized white men and boys soon swarmed the neighborhood. They raided "over a hundred black homes" and arrested and rounded up over a dozen black men—as the white Sunday newspaper called them, "a nest of turbulent and unruly negroes." Grocer Thomas Moss was in his home and nowhere near the store at the time of the shooting, but he was identified as the "ringleader." He was charged with shooting the most seriously wounded man, who turned out to be a white deputy who'd worn civilian clothing to take part in the unlawful nighttime raid on the store. The People's Cooperative Grocery Store was looted of its entire inventory. The three grocers were jailed. Four days after the shoot-out, a group of whites entered the jail, seized the three men, dragged them to a field north of the city, and shot them dead. At the time, Moss's wife was pregnant with their second child. His dying words were these: "Tell my people to go west—there is no justice for them here."[59]

These were the facts that Ida B. Wells sorted out as a reporter and editor of the *Free Press and Headlight*. The lynching, as she wrote, "changed the whole course of my life." She'd been in Natchez, Mississippi, when it all happened. The funerals were concluded when she returned to join black Memphis in its anger and mourning. At first, the episode made no sense. Her good friends suddenly murdered . . . fellow Christians, responsible citizens, family men killed in an unforeseen eruption of homicidal white rage. The white Memphis newspapers blamed the victims. They smeared the People's Grocery as "a low dive . . . a resort of thieves and thugs." The white *Memphis Appeal-Avalanche* published an illustration of the three bodies lying in an open field. Tommie Moss lay on his back in a pool of blood. He was "murdered," Wells wrote, "with no more consideration than if he had been a dog." If a well-liked man like Moss could be murdered on a pretext, so could an outspoken black woman newspaper editor. Wells bought and carried a pistol, probably a used .32 caliber snub-nosed black powder pistol as used by the navy. Known as a pocket pistol, it was wildly inaccurate at long range. Aimed carefully at short range, it was deadly. If a lynch mob came after her, she'd take at least one of them down.[60]

The *Free Press* demanded that the lynchers be brought to justice in "the name of God and in the name of the law we have always obeyed." The judiciary of white Memphis barely responded. Some were questioned, no one indicted. Throughout that springtime, as the grass turned green and the flowers bloomed and the Mississippi currents quickened, "Wells filled the columns of the *Free Press* with antilynching tirades." She published *Free Press* articles and editorials in support of black citizens' exodus westward from the city, as Tommie Moss urged with his last breath of life. Hundreds left, including entire church congregations. The *Free Press* also supported a black boycott of the white-owned businesses and the city transit system. White merchants and capitalist investors must learn that black Memphis had muscle. An economic punch by African American citizens got the attention of the white powers-that-be. *Free Press* articles also recounted "the contributions of African Americans to the city and the aid they provided during the yellow fever epidemic." All the while, Wells mourned with the community and felt the fires of its rage. Perhaps she was not surprised when no one was held responsible for the lynchings.[61]

Above all, she asked, Why?

The *why* of it gripped Wells to her depths. No charge of black male lust for a white woman was involved. The grocers had been entrapped by the raid on their store. Wells traced the sequence of events back from the lynchings to the boys' game of marbles. At last, the lynchings showed her exactly why whites in the post–Civil War south murdered blacks, especially black men. It was not about vigilante punishment for sexual transgressions against white women. That was the cover story, the myth. The truth lay elsewhere. Lynching, she found, was terrorism against blacks' economic, political, and social success. It was homicide targeted at blacks' steps toward equality. Lynching was intended to keep a people cowering in fear, systematically reducing that people to subservience as in the days of slavery. Lynching, as she said, was "an excuse to get rid of Negroes who were acquiring wealth and property and thus keep the race terrorized and 'keep the nigger down.'"[62]

The lynchings at the Curve "opened" her "eyes" in a blazing moment of clarity, and journalism itself suddenly metamorphosed from her occupation to her mission. From that moment on, it was more than her livelihood and profession. From this springtime of 1892, the princess of the press became a crusader, for journalism was now synonymous with the title of her autobiography—a crusade for justice.[63]

That year, Wells published the "dynamitic" editorial that exiled Iola from Memphis. Her single-minded investigation of other lynchings exposed another lie when she discovered evidence of cross-racial romances between white women and black men. She found accounts of mutual attraction that ended in tragedy for the men. "In whites' minds these relationships were as bad, if not worse, than rape." Five lynched black men were accused of raping white women, but Iola set the record straight in the *Free Press*: "Nobody in this section believes the old threadbare lie that Negro men assault white women. If Southern men are not careful they will over-reach themselves and a conclusion will be reached that will be very damaging to the moral reputation of their women."[64]

The editorial was the last straw for white Memphis. The brazen Iola and the *Free Press* must be destroyed. Wells was traveling to Philadelphia when her editorial appeared. She was in the Northeast when word came of the smashing of the *Free Press* office and the white *Evening Scimitar*'s editorial threat to lynch the author. Within days, she was in New York City, working full-time for the African American T. Thomas Fortune's *New York Age*. She was no longer Iola"; her byline was "Exiled." The newest *Age* reporter "has no sympathy for humbug," as Fortune had already learned about Miss Wells. This crusading "princess of the press," he knew, was "smart as a steel trap."[65]

Wells's mission was now clearly charted: to investigate and publicize the facts about lynch murder everywhere in America. Her "array of facts" would "stimulate this great American Republic to demand that justice be done." Statistics was a popular new tool of science, and she would present the "Tabulated Statistics . . . of Lynchings in the United States." She cited "lynch law statistics" by place, date, and names of victims. No state or region would escape her exposure of racial homicide of African Americans by whites, be it in Georgia, Alabama, Virginia, Ohio, or New York—all the while she emphasized that "there is little difference between the Ante-bellum [slave] South and the New South."[66]

Wells wielded all the tools of newspaper journalism of the era. Writing about lynching, she deliberately used and quoted the popular sensational language to give readers the ghoulish, voyeuristic satisfaction they craved. She, however, meant to turn such language against the readers' consciences. She'd force them to relive the horrific lynch murders so they'd see that homicide was sanctioned by their silence and buoyed by their craven racism. She'd be accused of racial bias, so she'd cite evidence as published in the white press—the "news gathered by white correspondents, compiled by white press bureaus and disseminated among white people." The white South, in effect, would show itself convicted of genocide, and the white North, of criminal complicity.[67]

But only if she kept her composure in print and in person. She must be seen as having "attractive manners and a pleasant voice." She must brace herself for the inevitable personal attacks. She'd be reviled as a troublemaker and a black harlot. Some blacks opposed her efforts, but she spoke and wrote to rally her own people to step up and assert themselves. African Americans must not keep quiet in the false hope that subservience to whites would protect them. The ideas of Booker T. Washington, she believed, were dangerous for her people. Washington's conception of education for blacks was centered on industrial training to the exclusion of intellectual and professional schooling. Popular with whites, Washington's ideas meant an accommodation to whites and second-class citizenship for blacks. It meant a racial and social structure of deference — "trying to be first-class people in a jim crow car [rather than] insisting that the jim crow car be abolished."[68]

Black men and women must insist upon full equality — *now*. When necessary, African Americans must use the economic power of the boycott against the white merchants and faraway capitalists whose profits depended on black labor and black purchasing power. A white man like the senior Clarence Day of New York City must be made to understand that he was linked to the system of racial repression in the South. As a railroad financier, Mr. Day was complicit in the system that penned paying passengers in filthy "colored-only" railcars — and left Wells alone on the station platform for asserting her right to travel in comfort and dignity. Her own people must call the Clarence Days of America to account. For their very survival, her people must realize that "the more the Afro-American yields and cringes and begs, . . . the more he is insulted, outraged and lynched." She filled the black press with these ideas, for her *New York Age* pieces were syndicated nationally.[69]

But the white press? The white public? She was up against the racial slander of "legislators, preachers, governors and bishops" who portrayed black Americans as "a race of cut-throats, robbers and lustful wild beasts." Yet Wells must somehow cross the color line to awaken white America to its complicity in these genocidal crimes. Comfortable, affluent white America must recognize its collusion in the race war of whites against blacks. White southerners who remained silent in the face of these outrages must be exposed as "accomplices and accessories before and after the fact, equally guilty with the actual law breakers." White Christians who failed to protest these crimes must be revealed as "cowards," for they provided "tacit encouragement" and "silent acquiescence" to "the black shadow of lawlessness in the form of lynch law . . . spreading its wings over the whole country." Lynching would stop only when white society condemned it and brought the perpetrators to justice — that is, when the criminal justice system prosecuted the culprits and juries brought verdicts of guilty and judges sentenced accordingly.[70]

White America, however, was largely insulated and oblivious at this time. Or worse. Families like the Clarence Days apparently gave no thought to racial oppression in post–Civil War America. Or they believed the "threadbare lie." The much-respected Frances Willard boasted of her abolitionist heritage, but she typified whites' worst racism when she publicly remarked in 1890 that "the colored race multiplies like the locusts of Egypt," adding that "the safety of womanhood, of childhood, of the home, is menaced in a thousand localities." Willard perpetuated the myth of black men rapists, and she was one of the most authoritative white women in U.S. public life.[71]

White Americans on the cutting edge of Progressive change were hardly better. "Many of the settlement workers decided that special segregated facilities would best serve the interest of the Negroes." Certain individuals who were positioned to speak out against lynching and the segregationist Jim Crow laws kept silent. Louis D. Brandeis's family were abolitionists, but evidently the citizenship that Brandeis cared so passionately about as a Jew did not extend to African Americans, for Brandeis's "civil liberties record was disappointing with regard to the rights of black . . . citizens." Perhaps Brandeis's mentor, Nathaniel Shaler, was responsible, for Shaler excluded African Americans from his grand design of citizenship. American blacks, wrote Shaler, risked lapsing into the "old African savagery" because they lacked "the great virtues of the superior race."[72]

Other Progressives were equally absentminded when it came to African Americans. The Reverend Walter Rauschenbusch's father was an ardent abolitionist, but the younger Rauschenbusch's long list of prayers for the "social awakening" had no prayer for God's justice for blacks. Instead, the leader of the Social Gospel movement grouped African Americans with the "belated races." Nor did the economist Professor John R. Commons cross the color line in his book *Races and Immigrants in America*. Commons's own favorite college professor had helped slaves escape on the Underground Railroad before the Civil War, and yet Commons now urged a prohibition on racial "amalgamation," meaning intermarriage. Nor did gender necessarily help Wells's cause. Dr. Alice Hamilton was outraged by disregard for immigrant workers, including African Americans, who were poisoned at toxic work sites, but she did not follow the lead of her mother's outrage at "the lynching of negroes." Only Jane Addams and Florence Kelley recognized that the country could not be democratic unless all citizens were protected by the Constitution.[73]

Wells took to the lectern. Public speaking was oral publication. The Memphis elocution lessons paid off. She'd done some lecturing in Memphis and spoken at press association meetings. Now posters and newspaper announcements advertised "A Lecture" on "SOUTHERN MOB RULE" by Miss Ida B. Wells. Admission was twenty-five cents. She lectured from Washington, D.C., to Boston. The meager turnout, however, was disappointing. Only Boston showed interest. Reaching out to the preeminent African American Frederick Douglass, Wells gained a mentor. White America respected the elderly Douglass, who represented the emancipation from slavery and the Civil War vindication of the North. But Douglass's endorsement alone was not enough to gain her the ears of the white public.[74]

Newspaper articles, what's more, were scattershot and gone in a flash. A more focused and forceful forum was the pamphlet. In advance of the American Revolution, Tom Paine's pamphlet *Common Sense* was revered for its political power. In the early 1890s, social activists fired off pamphlets to support a range of causes. The National Consumers' League, led by Florence Kelley, was to publish a barrage of pamphlets on industrial wage slavery of women and children. Wells saw opportunity. When she was honored at a testimonial dinner in New York City in 1892, she was awarded a gift of $300 — which she spent for the printing of her first of her series of pamphlets, *Southern Horrors: Lynch Law in All Its Phases*. The pamphlet, she trusted, could have the leverage of a crowbar — a crowbar to fight Jim Crow.[75]

Wells's immersion in the culture of media and publicity was a huge advantage. The dynamics and mechanics of the press were second nature to her. Among themselves, she knew, newspapers operated like a chamber of echoes, and they scavenged off each other for news columns. What's more, the undersea telegraphic cable shrank the world, and a U.S.-British relation could be crucial to her mission. Privileged American whites, Wells knew, harbored feelings of inferiority in relation to Great Britain. Americans' servile deference reached back to colonial days. British culture and tradition were thought to be superior, just as its writers were assumed to be more sophisticated than American authors. British voices and views on virtually every subject were presumed to be more authoritative than American ones. The British, if roused, could powerfully shame white America in regard to lynching. Making no headway with the U.S. white public, Wells took Douglass's advice to lecture on lynching in England and Scotland in 1893 and 1894. It was a strategic move. As she said, on the "Negro question," the "great bulk of white Americans . . . are all afraid to speak out, and it is only British public opinion which will move them." British news reports of Wells's speeches could boomerang back to America and shame it and prompt action.[76]

In addition, if Wells could become a correspondent for one of the few white U.S. newspapers that "persistently denounced lynching," she could dispatch a series of reports of her lecture tour and thus amplify the antilynching message. She knew exactly the paper to approach, the daily *Chicago Inter-Ocean*, whose sympathetic editor made her "a regular paid correspondent." To lecture in Britain was "an open door in a stone wall," and Wells marched through it to break the "silent indifference."[77]

She made progress. The *Edinburgh Evening Gazette*, the *Edinburgh Scotsman*, the *Manchester Guardian*, and other British papers reported extensively on her lectures. U.S. northern and midwestern newspapers soon followed suit. The *Detroit Plaindealer* praised her work, as did the *Cleveland Gazette* and the *St. Paul Appeal*. Her statements came to public attention. "The London correspondent to the *New York Times* frequently mentioned her activities," and the *Chicago Inter-Ocean* published her accounts. Its headlines were blunt: "British Emigrants Warned Away from the South Until Negro Lynching Ceases." The inevitable attacks came, both racist and misogynist, but so did appreciation and credibility. The British press abhorred lynching, and Wells's portfolio of British press clippings became her cache of weaponry. British activists, what's more, became involved in the issue. The London *Times* of August 1, 1894, cited the aim of the newly formed English Anti-lynching Committee: "to obtain reliable information on the subject of lynching and mob outrages in America, to make the facts known, and to give expression to public opinion in condemnation of such outrages in whatever way might seem best calculated to assist humanity and civilization."[78]

The Cairo trip of November 1909 was yet another battle in what had become a lifelong, incessant antilynching campaign. Wells-Barnett surely dreaded the racial "weather" that awaited her that Sunday night when the rain-spattered Illinois Central train arrived in the city that had just staged a lynching. Two days hence in Springfield, the governor was to hear the suspended Cairo sheriff Frank Davis's appeal for reinstatement. The *Chicago Daily Tribune* reported the "ominous" mood of Cairo's whites, but Wells-Barnett was especially shocked by the stance of the Cairo black community. The lynching of Frog James didn't trouble them. Cairo's blacks, she learned, denounced the lynch victim as a "worthless sort of fellow" who might well commit murder. Several had written to Governor Deneen to urge that Sheriff Davis regain his position. Petitions in support of the sheriff were also circulated and signed in the city's black barber shops, and these petitions were obviously "typewritten and worded" by parties who were interested in promoting the sheriff's reinstatement. Inviting the notable journalist-activist Wells-Barnett into their homes, Cairo's blacks explained to the visitor that they supported the sheriff because he put black deputies on his payroll. The black citizens forgave him for disobeying the law when he failed to put the accused man in protective custody in the county jail following Anna Pelley's murder. Unanimously, they hoped to see Sheriff Davis back on the job in Cairo's Alexander County.[79]

Wells-Barnett was horrified. The local black professionals—the druggist, the ministers, the teachers—failed to grasp the consequences of their endorsement of lynching. They couldn't see that if they condoned one lynching, they themselves might become the next victims. Time was short for a major tutorial on racial mob murder, but Wells-Barnett marshaled her skills from longtime political work and public speaking. Over two days, she made Cairo blacks understand the gravity of the situation and won them over in a voice ranging from sweet to "blistering." She drafted a resolution urging the governor to deny the sheriff his reinstatement—and got black Cairo's signatures.

In the nick of time, she won the consent of black Cairo to be its "mouthpiece" at the hearing in Springfield, then caught the train that put her in the state capital at midnight.[80]

It was ten o'clock on Wednesday morning when she entered the hearing room of the domed French Renaissance state capitol building of Illinois. In her bag were the signed resolution and a legal brief that Ferdinand had prepared from newspaper accounts and sent ahead for her use here today. She looked around the hearing room. "Not a Negro face was in evidence!" The sea of whites included the suspended sheriff, his "big" lawyer, his parish priest, the state's attorney of Cairo's Alexander County, the U.S. land commissioner, and about half a dozen representative white men ("who had journeyed from Cairo to give aid and comfort to Frank Davis in his fight for reinstatement"). A blizzard of documents from Cairo was produced in support of the sheriff's reinstatement—letters and telegrams from white politicians, bankers, lawyers, doctors, newspaper editors, heads of women's clubs and men's organizations. "The whole of the white population of Cairo was evidently behind Frank Davis and his demand for reinstatement."[81]

Especially galling were the fawning letters from Cairo's "Negro ministers and Colored politicians," who commended the sheriff's exemplary character. Their letters were read aloud, and "special emphasis was laid upon them." Then came the barbershop petitions bearing the signatures of "nearly five hundred Negro men." Wells-Barnett felt the burden of the moment and the weight of the issue when the governor turned to say, "I understand Mrs. Barnett is here to represent the colored people of Illinois."[82]

How could she? She had no legal training. Ferdinand's brief would help, and the newly signed resolution could bolster her case if she introduced it at an opportune moment. But could she find such a moment when the suspended sheriff's "big," swaggering lawyer was ready to run the show? Fortunately, a black Springfield attorney who came to invite her to his home for dinner agreed to stay at her side to keep her from falling into legalistic traps. Fortunate, too, was the customary long midday dinner hour that gave her time to prepare her presentation while the others enjoyed their meals. When they reconvened, she was ready—ready to underscore the fact that the sheriff had broken the law that required him to incarcerate the murder suspect and provide the accused with armed protection from the mob. She explained, too, that Cairo's black citizens now withdrew their previous support for the sheriff's reinstatement. She presented her resolution with all the fresh signatures.

It was late afternoon when, finally, she turned to Governor Deneen, a stocky figure with full features and close-cropped, wavy hair. She addressed him directly. This was the wind-up moment. "Governor," she said, "the state of Illinois has had too many terrible lynchings within her borders within the last few years. If this man is sent back it will be an encouragement to those who resort to mob violence and will do so at any time. . . . I repeat, Governor, that if this man is reinstated, it will simply mean an increase in lynchings in the state of Illinois and an encouragement to mob violence." Noncommittal, the governor requested a fact file on the case and took the matter under advisement. Leaving the state capitol, the white officials at the hearing tipped their hats to Wells-Barnett, commended her "wonderful speech," and even shook her hand. Was their gentlemanly courtesy to a black woman real grounds for hope? She doubtless asked this on the train homeward to Chicago, aware that the Cairo whites' pressure on the governor was nonetheless "terrific." She had done her best under the circumstances. "Angels could do no more."[83]

Six days later came the verdict: Governor Deneen proclaimed that Frank Davis was *not* to be reinstated because "he had not properly protected the prisoner within his keeping." The governor ratified Wells-Barnett's argument, and the case ramified to the furthest borders of the state: from now on, "lynch law could have no place in Illinois."[84]

The victory was decisive, but the campaign unrelenting, as Wells-Barnett knew it must be. Ever vigilant, she made her Chicago home the engine room of her dual causes of antilynching and socioeconomic racial justice in America. The years ahead saw her "dig dig dig" for the facts that underlay the lethal race riots, illegal imprisonment, and murder of blacks in East St. Louis, in Arkansas, and in Chicago too. Her work in civic organizations was based on the recognition of all Progressives that individual effort must be magnified by the strength of organized groups. In *A Red Record*, she laid out the plan of civic action:

1. to disseminate the facts of lynching to the public via the media and all religious and civic organizations
2. to bring economic pressure by boycott or blocking investment in states where segregation, codified in law, thwarts economic advancement of Afro Americans and fosters lynching
3. to press Congress for resolutions and for legislation guaranteeing all Americans their full rights of citizenship.

No such legislation existed at the time of her death in 1931, when W. E. B. Du Bois, the preeminent African American scholar and founder of the NAACP,

U.S. citizen, lynched, 1925.
(Library of Congress)

memorialized Ida B. Wells-Barnett as "the pioneer of the anti-lynching crusade in the United States" and the woman who "began the awakening of the conscience of the nation."[85]

The Progressive racial agenda that was inaugurated by Wells-Barnett has proven crucial through the twentieth (and now twenty-first) century that bears repeated scars of continuing lynchings and institutionalized racial violence in the United States. Some of the lynchings have been actual, as in the case of Emmett Till, the fourteen-year-old boy who was abducted in August 1955 from his great-uncle's home in Money, Mississippi, tortured, and murdered, his mutilated body dumped in the Tallahatchie River. The lynching of young Till is widely credited with spurring the civil rights movement, just as the rope noose dangling from a schoolyard tree in Jena, Louisiana, in 2007 drew nationwide attention to continuing racial bias in the educational and criminal justice systems and to the ways in which the signifier of lynching—the rope noose—periodically appears in workplaces and schools to intimidate individuals and groups.[86]

Wells-Barnett's work nonetheless ramifies powerfully in legal and social progress in the United States. Her refusal to give up her seat on the Memphis train in 1884 anticipates the African American Rosa L. Parks's refusal in 1955 to obey the Montgomery, Alabama, bus driver who ordered her into the rear, "black" section. Parks's act of civil disobedience in the segregated South prompted the successful boycott of the transit system by Montgomery's blacks—the very economic leverage that Wells-Barnett urged to combat socially structured racism. Wells-Barnett's club work and fervent Christianity also anticipate the Reverend Martin Luther King Jr.'s organization of the Southern Christian Leadership Conference to promote civil rights activism. Her work augurs King's campaign to marshal black Americans to nonviolent resistance and thereby to challenge the heart and conscience of white America to meet its obligations under the U.S. Constitution.

Wells-Barnett's public lectures and writings were crucial, too, for the eventual reshaping of U.S. public opinion on racial violence. Her efforts underlie the shift that is measurable in "before" and "after" images separated by just a few decades. Early-twentieth-century postal card images show festive crowds of whites enjoying the spectacles of lynchings as if on holiday. The era of TV images, however, prompted a different racial response. The white public was not amused but largely revolted by the 1963 video footage of black citizens assaulted by high-pressure fire hoses and police dogs as they walked in public streets to express their claim to full citizenship.[87]

The public revulsion marks a distinct change in public consciousness, a change that must be credited substantially to the pioneering Wells-Barnett. Her efforts from the 1890s became the platform that underlay the passage of the Civil Rights Act of 1957 and the Civil Rights Act of 1964, "the most far-reaching civil-rights measure ever enacted by Congress. The act outlawed discrimination in hotels, restaurants, and other accommodations. . . . The attorney-general could now bring suits for school desegregation," and "federally assisted programs and private employers alike were required to eliminate discrimination. An Equal Employment Opportunity Commission administered a ban on job discrimination by race, religion, national origin, or sex." It is significant that shortly before King's murder in Memphis, he delivered his last presidential address to the Southern Christian Leadership Conference urging focused attention on "questions about the [U.S.] economic system, about a broader distribution of wealth" and economic opportunity across lines of class and race. The Memphis murders of her friends opened Wells's eyes to the economic motives behind lynching, and the commemoration of King's birthday as a national holiday, together with the annual Black History Month in February, serves to remind Americans of the distance traveled—and the work that lies ahead.[88]

Progressive Encore?

A Postscript

We are now in a second Gilded Age. Instead of taking steps that
would strengthen our democracy, we are heading back to the
wealth inequalities of a century ago.
—BILL GATES SR. AND CHUCK COLLINS, *Nation*, 2003

Progress . . . depends on retentiveness.
—GEORGE SANTAYANA, *The Life of Reason*, 1905–6

"All progress is experimental," declared the American essayist John Jay Chapman in 1900. The success of the Progressives' experiment became clear as the twentieth century unfolded. Their "experiment" persuaded the American people as a whole to reject child labor and to support education for children in all socioeconomic groups. It encouraged the public, in the main, to endorse human and financial services for the disabled and for dependent minors. The Progressives' work, in addition, showed the public that impoverished elderly Americans ought not to be shunted off to poorhouses but sustained through a work-related contributory retirement program (Social Security). The ideas of a legal minimum wage and a financial safety net for the unemployed are also their continuing legacy. So are the beliefs that workplaces ought to be safe and consumer products reliable and not dangerous. The Progressives, in addition, successfully promoted the idea that municipal services such as water, electricity, and transportation ought to be provided to everyone at reasonable cost. The Progressive campaign to put a stop to racialized murders has been the cornerstone of the guarantee to the right to life, liberty, and the pursuit of happiness in modern America.[1]

The Progressives' work is codified in laws and in agencies at the state and federal levels. The U.S. Department of Education and Department of Health and Human Services testify to the Progressives' success, as do the

Civil Rights Commission, the Social Security Administration, the Consumer Product Safety Commission, the Occupational Safety and Health Administration. The seeming alphabet soup of agencies (FAA, FDA, FCC) can best be understood as centers of professional expertise committed to the benefit of the public, from air transport safety to effective drugs to media broadcasting serving the public interest.

None of the above would have been possible in the first Gilded Age—the era in which the individuals who became Progressives were born and raised. At the start, their ideas seemed outlandish. Over decades, their otherworldly, utopian ideas became worldly realities. The long-range achievement of the Progressives who are represented in *Civic Passions* cannot therefore be measured solely by the years that textbooks officially allocate to the Progressive Era. The cutoff point of the movement is often dated at World War I (1914–18) or else the Roaring Twenties or Jazz Age. These, in turn, are often regarded as preludes to the stock market crash of 1929 and onset of the Great Depression and New Deal. A new era is said to commence with World War II, post–World War II, and so on. The longer trajectory, however, finds the Progressive ideas put in place along a timeline that includes child labor and workplace safety legislation, civil rights laws, clean air and water legislation (1963–72), and automobile safety legislation too.

The philosopher George Santayana cautioned, however, that "progress . . . depends on retentiveness." On that score, the U.S. public has lost much ground in civic, social, and financial terms. Indeed, the term *citizen* has largely given way to *consumer*, *taxpayer*, and *investor*, and the shift is powerfully suggestive of a radically different outlook. In a back-to-the-future scenario, late-twentieth-century America steadily slid into a second Gilded Age that would mystify and horrify the Progressives. The onset was marked by the 1981 inaugural address of President Ronald Reagan, who repudiated publicly funded services when he declared, "Government is not the solution to our problem. Government *is* the problem." Public funds for public purposes—taxes—were no longer seen as civic membership dues but as theft. Neediness was redefined as dependency, which justified repeated budget cuts in a range of social services. The Reagan administration proposed that a condiment—catsup—be considered a vegetable in the national school lunch program.[2]

The new Gilded Age deepened as benefits such as unemployment insurance diminished in amount and availability. (By 2008, a mere 37 percent of jobless U.S. workers qualified for unemployment insurance, and the few who qualified found the benefit covered only a small fraction of their lost wages.) In addition, agencies that were created to ensure public safety, to protect the food supply, water, and consumer products ranging from medicines to toys instead became hollowed out, starved of the professional staff, funding, and regulatory tools necessary to do their work. They now became "captive" agencies because those appointed to lead them were political cronies who served the businesses they were sworn to regulate. Safety rules and regulations were said to be "eased" or "relaxed," meaning seriously weakened. In an oft-quoted analogy, the fox now guarded the henhouse. The failure of the Federal Emergency Management Agency (FEMA) following the devastating 2005 hurricanes Katrina and Rita on the Gulf coast showed the human costs of political cronyism.[3]

Watchdogs failed in other ways. The subprime mortgage financial crisis of 2007 that plunged millions of households into foreclosure and gravely weakened the economy showed the results of the years-long deregulation of banking under the blessing of leaders of both major political parties. Responsibility for the crisis lay with mortgage companies, banking executives, the Securities and Exchange Commission, financial ratings agencies, congressional committees, the Federal National Mortgage Association (Fannie Mae), the Federal Home Loan Mortgage Corporation (Freddie Mac), and other agencies entrusted to oversee the financial system. All these were exposed as feckless at best and predatory at worst. By early 2009, U.S. citizens' money was sought in hundreds of billions of dollars to shore up a financial system that verged on collapse from what two business journalists termed a years-long "pyramid scheme" that "required all sorts of important, plugged-in people to sacrifice our collective long-term interests for short-term gain. . . . Rather than expose financial risk they systematically disguised it."[4]

The term *public*, all the while, had become pejorative, whether it was applied to schools, hospitals, or recreational facilities. *Private* became the new accolade, and the sole measure of worthiness was now a marketplace measure. Venues that previously belonged to the citizens of a city or town now sprouted corporate logos as baseball fields and sports stadiums became privatized, just as annual events bore corporate names for electronics and processed snack foods. In a twist that would have baffled the Progressives, citizens in the new Gilded Age looked to corporations as virtual public service agencies. Research money for possible cures for dreadful afflictions was often sought not from public funds but from corporations, which sponsored runners' and bicyclists' fund-raising marathons. The term *corporate sponsorship* became a seal of approval and legitimacy of purpose.

Private philanthropic foundations, the legatees of corporate wealth, also were now seen as primary sources of funding for various humanitarian causes, as the new Gilded Age titans followed their forebears in creating charitable foundations and identifying worthy causes to support. Just as Andrew Carnegie donated libraries all over America and John D. Rockefeller supported medical research, the philanthropists of the new Gilded Age continued to donate impressive sums to medical science, to HIV/AIDS treatment, to literacy and many other causes. Behind these gifts, nonetheless, is the fact that philanthropy is personal. The causes that are supported are those of the personal preferences of the donors. These may coincide with the interest of the public at large but need not do so. The sums involved, while impressive, are small fractions of the monies needed for important public purposes—purposes that otherwise are identified through democratic processes. Meanwhile, a gap in life expectancy widened across the nation, according to government research that found "'large and growing' disparities in life expectancy for richer and poorer Americans, paralleling the growth of income inequality in the last two decades."[5]

Democracy itself in the new Gilded Age was reduced in many Americans' minds solely to the casting of a ballot on election day. Understandably so. At the national level, elected officials succumbed to the same Washington rhythms that Mark Twain savagely satirized in his late-nineteenth-century *The Gilded Age*. Campaign fund-raising now proceeded nonstop, and members of Congress were once again continuously courted by special interests in rounds of fine dining and resort junketing that one journalist terms the "Beltway Bacchanal."[6]

As in the first Gilded Age, the ideology of individualism and laissez-faire economics was once again dominant. "Free market" and "free trade" became the mantra of a supposed emancipation from civic bondage. The term *marketplace democracy* became commonplace, and those who used it seemed oblivious of any internal contradiction between the two terms. Corporate globalism, which has been called "supercapitalism," meant that products bearing long-esteemed U.S. brand names, from tools to clothing to toys, were now manufactured in sweatshops located in the poorest countries. Far-off workers now toiled as their first Gilded Age immigrant predecessors did—working a staggering number of hours at bare subsistence wages, and lacking the workplace protections of labor union contract agreements and government labor and safety regulations that John R. Commons and Dr. Alice Hamilton fought for in the first Gilded Age.[7]

Indeed, Commons would be as horrified as Louis Brandeis and Florence Kelley to learn the fate of American labor unions in the second Gilded Age. The unions, which the Progressives understood to be pathways to good citizenship, fair earnings, safe workplaces, and a decent standard of living, had flourished in the mid-twentieth century—but then became ghosts of their former hearty selves, as the unionized U.S. workforce shrank from 30 percent to about 12.1 percent, while workers' efforts to organize unions became a legalized obstacle course.[8]

In the United States, meanwhile, stable jobs with health care and other benefits that afforded a middle-class way of life became scarcer. "Between 1979 and 1996, the U.S. Department of Labor statistics show more than 43 million jobs lost in the U.S." Workers learned that companies had failed to fund their pension plans and cancelled or cut back their health care. Some companies were found to tap pension funds in order to fund lavish executive benefits. By the turn of the twenty-first century, the United States had become the most unequal of the industrialized nations. (The subtitle of one economist's book warned that "rising inequality harms the middle class," in part by triggering excessive personal spending.) A major research center found that middle-class Americans now felt "stuck in their tracks" in the "most downbeat short-term assessment of personal progress in nearly half a century of polling." One journalist identified contemporary American work and family life as a financial "high wire" act, and millions who sought full time work in the new Gilded Age were instead "pushed" into part-time employment, many working two or three jobs at low wages for upward of sixty hours weekly. The number of hours worked, of course, was now the same as in the first Gilded Age. The healthful leisure hours promoted by the Progressives Florence Kelley and Louis D. Brandeis over a century ago for personal and national well-being were now out of the question.[9]

In addition, the personal finance of ordinary people was subject to legalized predatory practices on par with the insurance company scandals that Louis D. Brandeis exposed in the first Gilded Age. Brandeis would surely locate the new predation in the credit card industry, for retail banks of the new Gilded Age profited enormously from draconian fees and penalties on cardholders, starting with "a 1978 ruling that allowed banks to override state usury laws and offer whatever rate was allowed in the banks' home state." In 1996, "the court cleared the way for even higher fees." As the first decade of the twenty-first century drew toward a close, Americans' credit card debt ballooned to 9,000 percent of the 1968 level (adjusted for inflation), and "struggling borrowers" were now "the industry's bread and butter."[10]

Just as families like the Clarence Days of the first Gilded Age were insulated from the critical issues of their time, so the U.S. middle class of the new Gilded Age was kept largely ignorant of equally grave matters demanding citizenly action. Television news under the ownership of powerful corporations now provided more amusement than information. The network news divisions were no longer regarded as a public service but as profit centers catering to advertisers, and they stopped producing eye-opening documentaries on nationally urgent topics, such as the prevalence of hunger and environmental destruction. In the late 1900s and opening years of the twenty-first century, the celebrity TV news anchors did not reveal stark facts about the rise of poverty and infant mortality in the United States. According to the Center on Budget and Policy Priorities, however, the number of children living in families with cash incomes below half the poverty line increased by 774,000 in the first four years of the new century. The first Children's Bureau chief, Julia Lathrop, would be stunned to learn that the United States now had a higher rate of infant deaths per 1,000 births (6.9) than Canada, France, Australia, and Britain.[11]

Viewers of network and cable TV and online news, further, learned nothing about the "missing class" who barely eked out a living in America and, when ill, relied on over-the-counter painkillers because health care was an unaffordable luxury. Nor did news organizations disturb viewers with accounts of an imperiled group that doubtless would command the attention of Ida B. Wells-Barnett and John R. Commons. These were the "nobodies," the trafficked and enslaved workers in the United States, most of them illegal immigrants whose lives depended on labor contractors and bosses—who sometimes murdered the workers and evaded justice.[12]

The TV and Internet viewing public, moreover, knew little of the growth of the U.S. "prison nation," in which 1 percent of the public was incarcerated, many for nonviolent drug offenses—and most from racial minority groups. Listed on the stock exchange, the prison industry's shares were traded daily, but the public was not asked to think about the conflicting identities of investors and citizens (the former profiting from the expanding market in prisoners, while the citizenly interest lay in prisoner rehabilitation and mainstreaming into society). Those striving to create public school systems that might help children overcome racial barriers and avoid involvement in the criminal justice system could not necessarily find support from the courts. The U.S. Supreme Court that once legitimated the racist "separate but equal" doctrine in the first Gilded Age seemed to reemerge in a 2007 decision of the John Roberts Court. In a case involving two school districts' efforts to achieve racial balance, the Court used language of democracy to reinstate what many consider to be a racist policy. Wrote Chief Justice Roberts in a statement worthy of Orwellian doublethink, "The way to stop discrimination on the basis of race is to stop discriminating on the basis of race." In short, school districts were now prohibited from considering race as a factor in the assignment of children to public schools. The racial criterion, the court decided in a five-to-four vote, was not constitutional.[13]

The Supreme Court's pattern of other decisions indicated a retreat to the norms of the first Gilded Age. According to one analyst, the Court has undergone "an ideological sea change," and one that would horrify the public service–minded Louis D. Brandeis. Relinquishing its concern for the welfare of the public, the court now showed remarkable unity "in cases affecting business interests." Its "pro-business jurisprudence" now meant a "relatively laissez faire . . . vision of the economy," which was hastened by the appointment of Associate Justice Samuel Alito and the 2005 appointment of John Roberts as chief justice. The Court has increasingly "cut back on consumer suits" and "by and large . . . defers to agencies that refuse to regulate public health and safety." Two federal governmental agencies, the Justice Department and the Internal Revenue Service, have also proved increasingly friendly to large corporations. The IRS has sharply curtailed audits of large firms, according to a university research group. The Justice Department, meanwhile, has adopted a policy of so-called deferred prosecution in cases of business crime. Rather than prosecute through criminal indictments and trials, the department now arranged fines and appointed outside monitors to impose internal reforms. "In many cases, the name of the monitor and the details of the agreement are kept secret."[14]

Hiding—or gilding—the myriad societal problems has not, fortunately, hidden them from everyone. Public education is key to change, and signs of renewal began to appear at the approach of the twenty-first century, when a new group of investigative writers produced compelling, well-received, and fact-packed narratives of the dark side of the new Gilded Age. Their predecessors—the muckrakers of the first Gilded Age—had proven the power of exposé to school the public. The new group had the precedent of Ida M. Tarbell's 1902–4 dissection of the Standard Oil trust and Lincoln Steffens's 1902 account of pervasive political corruption in U.S. cities, *The Shame of the Cities*. Indeed, a timeline of outstanding muckraker-activists must include mid-twentieth-century figures whose work also sparked positive change. In *Unsafe at Any Speed* (1965), the young Ralph Nader exposed deadly design flaws in a General Motors car, and his cadre of young attorneys, dubbed Nader's Raiders, successfully pushed for auto safety, consumer rights, and corporate responsibility. Elsewhere, a nature writer with scientific training, Rachel Carson, documented the poisoning of the environment by pesticides and other chemicals, and her blockbuster book *Silent Spring* (1962) launched a new era of ecological thinking that resulted in the Clean Water and Clean Air acts. Also in the Cold War 1960s, Randall Forsberg, then a typist at a peace institute in Sweden, became alarmed by the documents she was typing because they showed the threat of nuclear weapons. Going on to doctoral study, Forsberg founded the Institute for Defense and Disarmament Studies in order to campaign against the nuclear weapons that threatened the planet (and threaten it still). Forsberg's grassroots campaign—to "freeze and reverse the nuclear arms race"—gained traction in ballot initiatives across the country and brought her to armament advisory roles for two presidents.[15]

By 2000, the baton of exposé was passing to others. In 2001, Eric Schlosser's *Fast Food Nation* exposed the disgraceful (and deadly) working conditions and lethal contamination of meat products in the very industry that Upton Sinclair dissected in *The Jungle* a century earlier. As Schlosser's book rose to the best-seller lists, so did Barbara Ehrenreich's *Nickel and Dimed: On (Not) Getting By in America*, an account of the author's harrowing experience struggling to meet basic expenses as a worker in a series of minimum-wage jobs. (Both best sellers made their way to book club selections and college course syllabi.)

Other titles were equally instructive about the new Gilded Age, from Joseph Hallinan's account of the U.S. prison industry, *Going Up the River: Travels in a Prison Nation*, to Laurie Garrett's *Betrayal of Trust: The Collapse of Global Public Health*. A young Canadian, Naomi Klein, revealed that slave labor in east Asia, the Philippines, the Mariana Islands, and elsewhere underlay the modern Western world consumerist era of prestigious corporate branding, especially of shoes and clothing. Klein's *No Logo: Taking Aim at the Brand Bullies* brought affluent consumers face-to-face with the grim reality that the fabric of their lives, quite literally, meant sweatshop labor. Shortly after these titles appeared, HBO brought viewers of *The Wire* a sense of the depth of structural social injustice (sometimes called structural violence) in government, in the media, and in the drug "war" zones in the poor inner cities, where nonwhite Americans are left in a world that the educator-specialist Jonathan Kozol calls one of apartheid "savage inequalities."[16]

The new muckrakers' diagnoses of social ills did not take place in a vacuum. The crises they revealed began to gain attention and action. Investigative reporters' Pulitzer Prize–quality exposés of corruption and scandal (a good many cited in this discussion) began to rouse public sentiment in favor of new regulatory protections. In a move that Louis Brandeis would surely applaud, the Rockefeller Foundation in 2008 announced a $70 million effort to "help build a new safety net for the nation's workers, especially the poorest and most vulnerable," including the economically insecure American middle class.[17]

Young Progressives were once again moving to the vanguard of social change, seeking new facts and organizing initiatives for social betterment and pressing Congress for new protective regulation. In numerous ways, the new Progressive generation occupies a different world from their predecessors — a truly global one that is far more vast than that of the first generation. Theirs is a planetary outlook that is focused on their own country and the larger world. Just as Florence Kelley would surely applaud Naomi Klein for exposing the globalized sweatshop, so John R. Commons (and his college mentor, Professor Monroe) would be pleased to hear of the "green conscience" at work at Commons's alma mater, Oberlin College, where the campus "sustainability house — SEED, for Student Experiment in Ecological Design," is "a microcosm of a growing sustainability movement on campuses nationwide." The *New York Times* reports that, whereas "previous generations focused on recycling and cleaning up rivers, these students want to combat global warming by figuring out ways to reduce carbon emissions in their own lives, starting with their own colleges." The colleges include liberal arts schools such as Berea in Kentucky, Oberlin and Middlebury in Vermont, Lansing Community College in Michigan, and Morehouse in Atlanta, as well as public universities like the University of New Hampshire. The students, reports the *Times*, "view the environment as broadly connected with social and economic issues."[18]

As in the first Gilded Age, new Progressives are also helping those at the margins to secure better material conditions, principally higher wages and improved conditions of work. The Student/Farmworker Alliance, in conjunction with the Coalition of Immokalee Workers, to cite one example, has successfully pressured leading corporations of the fast-food industry to improve working conditions and wages for Florida tomato field workers who were trapped for decades in peonage. Similar campaigns internationally have been mounted for fair-trade coffee, cocoa, sugar, tea, bananas and other fruit, honey, cotton, wine, and flowers. A complementary organization, United Students against Sweatshops, with chapters on over 200 campuses in the United States and Canada, "works with NGOs [nongovernmental organizations], human rights groups, and local labor unions or federations, in countries where collegiate apparel is produced," to determine that no sweatshop labor in the United States or abroad has produced the insignia clothing and other items bearing emblems of member colleges and universities.[19]

One important link binds the two generations of Progressives, bridging the first to the second Gilded Age. Both have understood that they operate within the deep-seated governing or "dominant myth" of their eras. This is "the economic myth," according to Betty S. Flowers, and its "hardiest expressions" are "varieties of capitalism." Its advantage, she emphasizes, is a certain egalitarianism. It allows the nineteenth-century immigrant son of a Scots lace maker to become a steel industry chieftain. It also lets a twentieth-century college dropout start a revolutionary computer software business. Both Andrew Carnegie and Bill Gates are the blessed sons, so to speak, of the economic myth. They are its winners.[20]

The Progressives' attention in both Gilded Ages, however, is focused on the citizenry as a whole. They know that the economic myth is severely numerical and quantitative, its vocabulary the "bottom line." They understand, in addition, that "we live in an economic myth the way the fish swim in the sea—unconsciously." Those who would set new directions must thus realize that, in order to reroute culture and society for a better future, Progressives must work with full consciousness of the ambient dominant myth. The Progressives' challenge was—and is—clear: in order "to create a future that is different from the past," one must "tell a better story about who we are and what we might become." The story must nonetheless accord with its historical moment.[21]

The Progressives who came forward in the first Gilded Age of extreme industrial capitalism understood the necessity of shaping their stories in accordance with the economic myth of their time. Alice Hamilton, John R. Commons, Florence Kelley, and Julia Lathrop argued vigorously that an industrial economy benefited from a citizenry that was healthy and educated. Louis D. Brandeis and Ida B. Wells-Barnett insisted that open and fair competition paved the way for personal and business success and, in turn, promoted a strong economy. Walter Rauschenbusch's prayers for a social awakening sent pointed messages to those at the center of modern capitalism.

One phrase that sometimes identifies the new generation of Progressives—*social entrepreneurs*—indicates the awareness of twenty-first-century Progressives that they, too, live in a world governed by the economic myth. Their projects seek to adapt the approaches and practices of business entrepreneurship to community building, a living wage, health care, microfinance, cooperative farming, eco-responsible practices, and a host of other causes. The highly acclaimed (and highly competitive) Teach for America program, for instance, places young college graduates in classrooms in rural areas and inner cities for two-year periods of commitment (an impressive 10 percent of the new graduates' lifetimes). Indeed, some 10 percent of the graduating classes of some of the nation's most select colleges and universities applied for these positions in 2007, and in the following year upward of 4,000 young men and women accepted classroom assignments in the nation's lowest-performing schools from South Dakota to New York City. Alumni of the program are serving on school boards across the country and see education as the domain and platform for major social change. The founder and director of Teach for America, Wendy Kopp, together with her partner, Richard Barth, have been acclaimed as "school entrepreneurs."[22]

The outcome of the new Progressives' work will reveal itself in the years ahead. Some may enter government service, as did Alice Hamilton, Julia Lathrop, and Louis D. Brandeis, all of whom respected careers based in service to the public. The work of the new generation will be no easier than that of their predecessors, but emboldening words resound to this era from the first Progressive age. As Julia Lathrop remarked, "The present time is one in which it requires unusual courage to be courageous." Like Lathrop and her peers of the first Gilded Age, the new Progressives must refuse "the weary acceptance of apparent defeat." They, too, will—and must—make every effort to leave their "tool marks on paving stones all along the road" to a better world.[23]

SUGGESTED READING

Interested readers are encouraged to explore in greater detail the complex lives and careers of the figures profiled in *Civic Passions*. The single volumes available on John R. Commons and Julia Lathrop provide broad outlines of their contributions to Progressive thought and action. The richly detailed published work on the others will reward anyone interested in the complex dramas of the lives and times of Louis D. Brandeis, Alice Hamilton, Florence Kelley, Walter Rauschenbusch, and Ida B. Wells-Barnett. The list below is a tribute to those who put these public figures on the public record.

LOUIS D. BRANDEIS
Alpheus Mason, *Brandeis: A Free Man's Life* (1946)
Philippa Strum, *Louis D. Brandeis: Justice for the People* (1984) and
    Brandeis: Beyond Progressivism (1993)
Melvin I. Urofsky, *Louis D. Brandeis and the Progressive Tradition* (1981)

JOHN R. COMMONS
Lafayette G. Harter Jr., *John R. Commons: His Assault on Laissez-Faire* (1962)

ALICE HAMILTON
Barbara Sicherman, *Alice Hamilton: A Life in Letters* (1984)

FLORENCE KELLEY
Kathryn Kish Sklar, *Florence Kelley and the Nation's Work: The Rise of
    Women's Political Culture, 1830–1900* (1995)

JULIA LATHROP
Jane Addams, *My Friend, Julia Lathrop* (1935; reprint 2002)

WALTER RAUSCHENBUSCH
Christopher H. Evans, *The Kingdom Is Always but Coming: A Life of Walter
    Rauschenbusch* (2004)
Paul M. Minus, *Walter Rauschenbusch: American Reformer* (1988)

IDA B. WELLS-BARNETT
Paula J. Giddings, *Ida: A Sword among Lions* (2008)
Linda O. McMurry, *To Keep the Waters Troubled: The Life of Ida B. Wells* (1998)
Patricia A. Schechter, *Ida B. Wells-Barnett & American Reform, 1880–1930* (2001)
Mildred I. Thompson, *Ida B. Wells-Barnett: An Exploratory Study of an American
    Black Woman* (1990)

NOTES

ABBREVIATIONS

BL   John J. Burns Library, Boston College, Boston

BP   Louis Dembitz Brandeis Papers, Louis D. Brandeis
        School of Law, University of Louisville, Louisville, Ky.

FHS   Filson Historical Society, Louisville, Ky.

HP   Alice Hamilton Papers, Schlesinger Library,
        Harvard University, Cambridge, Mass.

IBW   Ida B. Wells Papers, Joseph Regenstein Library,
        University of Chicago, Chicago

NCL   National Consumers' League Papers, Manuscript Division,
        Library of Congress, Washington, D.C.

WC   Warshaw Collection, Smithsonian National Museum
        of American History, Washington, D.C.

PREFACE

1   Louis Uchitelle, "The Richest of the Rich, Proud of a New Gilded Age," *New York Times*, July 15, 2007, 1, 18–19. Douglas, "Forbes 400."

2   "Personal Account," *Harper's*, 16 ("unusual and unfortunate situation . . . too much sense").

3   See Uchitelle, *Disposable American*.

4   Tindall and Shi, *America*, 862, 863 ("Bosses of the Senate"). On lobbyists, see Continetti, *K Street Gang*, 16. On the average sum spent to lobby Congress for each day of the 2008 session, see "Harper's Index," *Harper's*, 13.

5   A survey of anti-immigrant sentiment from the nineteenth century appears in Tichi, *Embodiment of a Nation*, 36–47. Typical nativist sentiments of the first Gilded Age appear in Strong, *Our Country*. See also Gerstle, *American Crucible*. Early twenty-first-century groups variously advocated the restriction of immigrants into the United States, the deportation of immigrants who lacked authentic documentation, the denial of health care or education to them or to their children, and the denial of processes of legalization (denounced as "amnesty") or of U.S. citizenship to such immigrants. The groups include the American Immigration Control Foundation, Californians for Population Stabilization, the Federation for American Immigration Reform, NumbersUSA, Americans for Legal Immigration, and the Immigration Reform Law Institute. For a summary of the activities of some of these groups, see Nicole Gaouette, "An Immigration End Run around the President," *Los Angeles Times*, June 23, 2008, A9.

6   See Walt Bogdanich, "F.D.A. Is Unable to Ensure Drugs Are Safe, Panel Is Told," *New York Times*, Nov. 2, 2007, A17: On Nov. 1, 2007, Marcia Crosse, director of health care for the Government Accountability Office, testified before the House Energy and Commerce Subcommittee on Oversight and Investigations, "F.D.A.'s [Food and Drug Administration] effectiveness in managing the foreign drug inspection program continues to be hindered by weaknesses in its data systems." According to Crosse, Bogdanich reported, "At the current rate, the agency would take more than 13 years to inspect each foreign establishment once — and those are just the factories it knows about."

See also Walt Bogdanich, "Chinese Chemicals Flow Unchecked onto World Drug Market," *New York Times*, Oct. 31, 2007, A1, which reports that "because the [Chinese] chemical companies are not required to meet even minimal drug-manufacturing standards, there is little to stop them from exporting unapproved, adulterated, or counterfeit ingredients." The food supply was also found to lack regulatory protection. One recall in the summer of 2007 involved nearly 22 million pounds of ground beef from the now-bankrupt Topps Meat Company. See Christopher Drew and Andrew Martin, "Many Red Flags Preceded a Recall," *New York Times*, Oct. 23, 2007, C1. In February 2008, in response to undercover video showing the slaughter at the Hallmark/Westland Meat Packing Company of "downer" cows linked to the fatal neurological disease known as mad cow disease, the U.S. government issued the largest beef recall in history, 143.4 million pounds shipped principally for school lunch programs. The recall dated to cattle slaughtered two years previously, and the USDA acknowledged that most of the recalled beef had been consumed. The agency's chief inspector stated, "We don't know exactly where all the product went" but will "cast a wide net to make sure that we can find all the product that we can find" (James R. Healey and Julie Schmit, "U.S. Issues Largest Beef Recall in History," *Tennessean*, Feb. 18, 2008, A1). See Ilan Brat, David Kesmodel, and Thomas M. Burton, "Humane Society Sues USDA," *Wall Street Journal*, Feb. 28, 2008, A4, which reports that in February 2008 the Humane Society of the United States filed a lawsuit in federal court against the federal agency tasked with inspecting livestock at slaughtering plants, charging "inadequate U.S. Department of Agriculture regulations designed to protect the nation's food supply from being contaminated from cattle at a higher risk of carrying mad cow disease." For an account of legalized toxic substances in consumer products in the United States, see Schapiro, *Exposed*.

7   Dunlop, *Gilded City*, 13 ("fairly covered with jewels"). Christine Haughney and Eric Konigsberg, "Even When Times Get Tough, the Ultrarich Keep Spending," *New York Times*, Apr. 14, 2008, A1, A17. Frank, *Richistan*. See also Greg Ip, "Income-Inequality Gap Widens," *Wall Street Journal*, Oct. 12, 2007, A3, and the editorial "Corporate Croesus," *New York Times*, Apr. 7, 2008, A26: "This polarization [of incomes of chief executives in contrast to those of "the bottom 99 percent"] is producing a pattern . . . unheard of in the United States, at least since the gilded age." See also Claudia H. Deutsch, "A Brighter Spotlight, yet the Pay Rises," *New York Times*, Apr. 6, 2008, Sunday Business sec., pp. 1, 7, and "C.E.O. Pay: The Tables," *New York Times*, Apr. 6, 2008, Sunday Business sec., pp. 10–11. See also Erik Eckholm, "As Jobs Vanish and Prices Rise, Food Stamp Use Nears Record," *New York Times*, Mar. 31, 2008, A1, which states that "driven by a painful mix of layoffs and rising food and fuel prices, the number of

Americans receiving food stamps is projected to reach 28 million in the coming year [of 2009]" and that "federal benefits costs are projected to rise to $36 billion in the 2009 fiscal year from $34 billion" in 2008.

8 Barry, *Speechless*. Two early-twenty-first-century novels corroborate Barry's findings that the corporate workplace of the second Gilded Age became an environment of oppression and fear: Joshua Ferris's *Then We Came to the End* (2007) and Ed Park's *Personal Days* (2008).

9 See Conwell, "Acres of Diamonds." Prosperity ministries in the late 1900s were often anchored in interpretations of an obscure prayer of Jabez in 1 Chronicles 4:9. For reassurance that this prayer endorses material wealth on earth, see Wilkinson, *Prayer of Jabez*.

10 Qtd. in Evans, *Kingdom Is Always but Coming*, 48 ("millennial fervor"). See also the chapter on Walter Rauschenbusch in this volume. See LeHaye and Jenkins, *Left Behind*. The *Left Behind* books have been critiqued by theologians and ministers as a travesty of the Christian message of the Gospels; see "Controversies and Criticisms," *Wikipedia*, < http://en.wikipedia.org/wiki/Left_Behind >.

11 See Lears, *No Place of Grace*, chaps. 2, 5. For "experiential learning," see < http:// www.avalonsprings.org/indexhome.htm >. For "a more harmonious way of living," see *Alpha Farm*, < http://www.pioneer.net/~alpha/ >. See also Oppenheimer, "Queen of the New Age."

12 Moyers, "For America's Sake," 12 ("one most politicians . . . cruel market world"). Sullivan, *Our Times*, 137 ("average American . . . tightening ring"). Mosley, *Workin' on the Chain Gang*, 11 ("poor medical care . . . religion"). Julia Lathrop qtd. in Addams, *My Friend, Julia Lathrop*, 149 ("present time . . . easier").

13 Galbraith qtd. in Lytle, *America's Uncivil Wars*, 54 ("These are the days . . . sign of instability").

INTRODUCTION

1 Matteucci, *History of the Motor Car*, 23 ("mechanical carriage"). See also *Sears, Roebuck and Co. Catalogue*.

2 See Trachtenberg, *Incorporation of America*. McGovern, *Sold American*, 88 ("The rise . . . democracy itself").

3 Kagan, *Dangerous Nation*, 357–58 ("expanded . . . interests"). See also Tindall and Shi, *America*, 898–933.

4 On Johnson's career, see Mackin, *Americans and Their Land*, 114–22, and Howe, *Confessions of a Reformer*, 113–45. Johnson's conversion to public service was brought about by his reading of Henry George's *Progress and Poverty*, recounted in Johnson, *My Story*, 48–58. On La Follette, see Unger, *Fighting Bob La Follette*, 1–5, and Ely, *Ground under Our Feet*, 209–18. Unger, *Fighting Bob La Follette*, 4 ("rights . . . minorities").

5 On Progressives' racial obtuseness and its consequences, see Luker, *Social Gospel in Black and White*, 317–20, which takes special notice of Walter Rauschenbusch's equivocation in terming blacks one of the "belated races." Progressives' statements on race, which were intended to be supportive of minority rights, often reveal racial bias. See Baker, "Problem of Race," 91–92:

Shall the Negro vote? . . . The vast majority of Negroes (and many foreigners and "poor whites") are vastly ignorant, and have little or no appreciation of the duties of citizenship. It seems right that they should be required to wait until they are prepared before being allowed to vote. A wise parent hedges his son about with restrictions . . . because it seems the wisest course for him, for the family, and for the state. . . . So the state limits suffrage; and rightly limits it, so long as it accompanies that limitation with a determined policy of education.

The Progressives' officiousness is instanced in the normative (and unwittingly biased) outlook on spending practices of the working classes as documented in Horowitz, *Morality of Spending*, 13–108, which discloses the terms by which statistical studies from 1875 through the 1910s were premised on moralistic bases.

The complexity of the term "middle class" cannot be overstated, as historians and sociologists have exhaustively demonstrated. The lines of argument over one-half century ago from Richard Hofstadter's *Age of Reform* are most usefully recapitulated in Johnston, *Radical Middle Class*, 18–19, which states, "Insofar as scholars have focused on one main foundation for Progressivism, they have targeted the middle class." Johnston joins other revisionists in critiquing such a monolithic, normative term as one suppressive of congeries of conflicts. See also Johnston, *Radical Middle Class*, 10–16. This project finds it useful to regard the occupational and income categories in data compiled in 1875 and in 1909 and elucidated in Horowitz, *Morality of Spending*, which locates a central group whose earnings and occupation can be correlated: "Earning high incomes were professional and white-collar people — most of the fathers employed in 'professional service' and several of those who worked as 'agents, clerks, salesmen' and merchants and dealers." Horowitz continues, "In terms of total family earnings, those with the highest incomes (above $1500) were also professionals and white-collar workers: families headed by clergymen, dentists, barbershop proprietors, railroad inspectors, and telegraphers" (52). Acknowledging the intraclass dynamic that further complicates the issue, Horowitz states,

> *Middle class* is a problematic concept, partly because the groups it covered
> hardly remained constant. In the years between 1890 and 1920, the
> composition of the middle class became even more diverse than previously.
> Those committed to prudence and self-restraint — frequently but not always the
> old middle class of farmers and small entrepreneurs — became less numerous
> and powerful. At the same time, there emerged a new middle class, composed
> of salaried professionals, managers, salespeople, and office workers employed
> in bureaucratic organizations. . . . Writers from a variety of backgrounds argued
> for a combination of prudence and pleasure but most of them felt that what was
> at stake was the soul of the middle class, especially its urban and professional
> members. (68–69)

Scholars who have critiqued and challenged the validity and duration of the Progressive movement in recent years include Shelton Stromquist, Glenda E. Gilmore, Richard McCormack, Arthur S. Link, David Kennedy, Daniel T. Rodgers, John D. Buenker, Peter Filene, and Alan Dawley. For citations, see Stromquist, *Re-inventing "the People,"* 205–6. See also Milkis and Mileur, *Progressivism and the New Democracy.* Three recent book-length studies assess the Progressive Era in highly skeptical terms: Danbom, "*World of Hope*"; Diner, *Very Different Age*; and McGerr, *Fierce Discontent.*

6 For consumerist practices of the era, see Schlereth, *Victorian America*; McGovern, *Sold American*; and Strasser, *Satisfaction Guaranteed.*

7 Stromquist, *Re-inventing "the People."*

8 Darrow qtd. in Davis, *Life in the Iron Mills*, 14 ("fairies and angels," "flesh and blood," "The world . . . for facts"). Baker and Sinclair qtd. in Tichi, *Exposés and Excess*, 69 ("ugly facts," "packed with facts").

9 Day, *Best of Clarence Day*, 58 ("solidly built, trim and erect"), 42–43 ("hopping . . . tall cans").

10 Ibid., 51 ("stubby . . . engine"). Burrows and Wallace, *Gotham*, 1055 ("dainty green . . . pavilion roofs"). "The Elevated Railway," *New York Times*, Sept. 7, 1869, qtd. in Burrows and Wallace, *Gotham*, 1055 ("riding . . . satisfactory"). Day, *Best of Clarence Day*, 51 ("great treat," "The Office").

11 Day, *Best of Clarence Day*, 51–52 ("Fascinated . . . and smoke"). For the socioeconomic status of tramps, see DePastino, *Citizen Hobo*, 3–29.

12 On the Ladies' Health Protective Association, see Melosi, *Garbage in the Cities*, 40, 35–36. See also Hoy, "'Municipal Housekeeping.'" Day, *Best of Clarence Day*, 52 ("tangle of . . . was born").

13 On Delmonico's, see Burrows and Wallace, *Gotham*, 723–24, 878–79. On the banquet for Dickens, see Kurlansky, *Big Oyster*, 211–13. According to Commons, *Myself*, 23, Wall Street financiers at every level believed that abstemious lunches of chocolate and "fizz water" kept the brain "clear" for the "strenuous forenoon and afternoon on the Stock Exchange or in the banks or commercial houses." Day, *Best of Clarence Day*, 56 ("so delicious . . . where [he] was").

14 For "lucifer" matches to the 1874 Massachusetts Bureau of Statistics of Labor report on "phossy jaw" and the 1884 New York report, *Hygiene of Occupation*, see U.S. Department of Labor, Office of the Assistant Secretary for Administration and Management, "The Job Safety Law of 1970," <http://www.dol.gov/oasam/programs/history/osha.htm>. See also Hamilton, *Exploring the Dangerous Trades*, 116, for a description of this "very distressing form of industrial disease" and a recollection that, in the 1880s in London, Jane Addams "went to a mass meeting of protest against phossy jaw and on the platform were a number of pitiful cases, showing their scars and deformities."

15 Day, *Best of Clarence Day*, 56 ("sweet-smelling bay . . . horsemen dashed by").

16 Ibid., 56–57 ("splintery benches . . . civilized man"). DePastino, in *Citizen Hobo*, 4–5, writes that "Americans in 1873 coined the word 'tramp' to describe the legion of men traveling the nation 'with no visible means of support'" and that this Gilded Age designation "served as a convenient screen onto which middle-class Americans projected their insecurities, anxieties, and fantasies about urban industrial life." See Schlereth, *Victorian America*, 77, which quotes an 1887 study by Wisconsin's Department of Labor, Census, and Statistics reporting "an average yearly figure of sixty-one days of unemployment per man in all trades."

17 Day, *Best of Clarence Day*, 18–23 ("hard-headed . . . Higher Things").

18 Ibid., 56–57 ("darken," "fingernails . . . sermons on Sunday").

19 See Coyne and Moran, *Bio-bibliography of Clarence S. Day, Jr.*, 12–13. Clarence Day Jr.

served also in the U.S. Naval Reserve. His move from finance to slower-paced publishing was prompted by the onset of rheumatoid arthritis. Day, *Best of Clarence Day*, 316 ("talked too much").

20 Day, *Best of Clarence Day*, 156 ("He was . . . methodical man," "strong and handsome"), 25 ("great roast . . . pudding"), 187 ("some little railroad . . . enormous authority").

21 Ibid., 103 ("imperious"), 103–4 ("powerful and stormy voice"), 188 ("no live and let live," "felt that . . . better"), 191 ("weak-natured"), 317 ("noisy," "disorderly"), 6 ("high spirited"), 8 ("resolute"), 341 ("either in people or in things"), 171 ("permanence").

22 On mortgage-free homeownership as the cornerstone of the Days' respectability, see Day, *Best of Clarence Day*, 341. On the Days' republican and Protestant ethos of "hard work, frugality, and self-control" and scorn for the ultrarich, see Ponce de Leon, *Self-Exposure*, 145.

23 Day, *Best of Clarence Day*, 342 ("kerosene lamps").

24 Marsh, *Man and Nature*, 15 ("Sight . . . an art"). Day, *Best of Clarence Day*, 108 ("wrote well . . . ledger").

25 Bellamy, *Looking Backward*, 42 ("The working classes . . . to accomplish it").

26 For the origins of the AFL under Gompers, see Cashman, *America in the Gilded Age*, 121–24, 131–32. On Gompers, see Mandel, *Samuel Gompers*, 13, 88. Gompers qtd. in Mandel, *Samuel Gompers*, 64 ("We want more school houses . . . happy and bright"). Gompers's unionist philosophy is set forth in his miscellany *Labor and the Common Welfare*. See also Montgomery, *Fall of the House of Labor*, 6: "Before the 1920s the house of labor had many mansions. Although most of its leading officers endorsed Samuel Gompers's vision of 'pure and simple unionism,' its ranks teemed with socialists, Catholic activists, single taxers, and philosophical anarchists. All of them agreed that their hopes of reshaping the American republic in accordance with the aspirations of its working class could best be achieved by working within labor's own, self-legitimizing federation. . . . After 1909, strikes and union membership grew rapidly both inside and outside the bounds of legitimacy defined by the AFL."

27 *Gilded Age* qtd. in *Who Built America*, 61 ("money lust . . . if we must").

28 Day, *Best of Clarence Day*, 86 ("indomitable"). Schlereth, *Victorian America*, 72 ("intelligence office"). Day, *Best of Clarence Day*, 339 ("our farmer"), 337 ("mixed Father's coffee"). Report qtd. in Wischnewetzky, *Our Toiling Children*, 19–21 ("stench . . . wretchedness"). For the history of New York state legislation regarding the tenement house cigar law, see Fairchild, "Factory Legislation of the State of New York."

29 Day, *Best of Clarence Day*, 200–201 ("a taciturn, preoccupied colored man"). Ray Stannard Baker's chapter "The Negroes' Struggle for Survival in Northern Cities," in *Following the Color Line*, 131, emphasizes the limitation of economic opportunity for blacks: "As a Negro said to me, 'There are always places for the colored man at the bottom.'"

30 On the *Santa Clara County* decision, see Marchand, *Creating the Corporate Soul*, 7.

31 Day, *Best of Clarence Day*, 305–7 ("rickety . . . criminal carelessness").

32 On federal immigration laws, see Thernstrom, Orlov, and Handlin, *Harvard Encyclopedia of Ethnic Groups*, 490–91. See also Montgomery, *Fall of the House of Labor*, 48: "Not only did immigrants flood into the United States every time business revived [from a recession], but also they moved quickly to all corners of the land, creating enclaves of foreign-born factory or railroad workers that stood out sharply against the

native-born population of the adjacent shops, offices, and farms. . . . From New England's mill towns to Rocky Mountain mining camps—immigrants and their children provided the overwhelming majority of industrial wage workers."

33 Qtd. in Tindall and Shi, *America*, 794–95 ("hundreds of cities . . . labor and capital").

34 On labor strife, see Schocket, *Vanishing Moments*, 73. On the Haymarket riot, see Green, *Death in the Haymarket*. Morison, *One Boy's Boston*, 20 ("furrin'"). Tindall and Shi, *America*, 795 ("raised the specter . . . 'Bread or Blood'").

35 On the nativist views of those like the Day family, see Nord, *Communities of Journalism*, 135–36. Bellamy, *Looking Backward*, 42–43 ("a sad mess of society").

36 Strong, *Our Country*, 132 ("social dynamite . . . men of all sorts").

37 Riis, *How the Other Half Lives*, 44 ("born gambler . . . and very frequently his knife is in it too before the game is ended"), 78 ("stealth and secretiveness are as much part of the Chinaman in New York as the cat-like tread of his felt shoes"), 86 ("Money is their [Jews'] God"), 153 ("street Arab").

38 Beer, *Mauve Decade*, 80 ("suicides of . . . merchants"). Schwantes, *Coxey's Army*, 13 ("heart-breaking nineties . . . labor disturbances"), 1–48 ("petition in boots"). See also McMurry, *Coxey's Army*, 3.

39 Tarbell, *History of the Standard Oil Company*, 2:31 ("direct[ing] the course . . . of a housewife").

40 Sullivan, *Our Times*, 137 ("irritation . . . crowded," "enemy"). Day, *Best of Clarence Day*, 148 ("long depression of the 90s").

41 Day, *Best of Clarence Day*, 53 ("whiskery men . . . eight-hour day"), 305 ("with a round-shouldered stoop," "all youngness had gone out").

CHAPTER 1

1 See Sicherman, *Alice Hamilton*, 22. Day, *Best of Clarence Day*, 192 ("Men knew the world . . . with the world"). See also *Boston Daily Globe*, Feb. 25, 1959, HP, A-22, box 2, folder 1. My presumption is that the National Lead Company office furnishings in Chicago matched those in the National Lead office in New Orleans in 1917. See *Early Office Museum*, <http://www.officemuseum.com/IMagesWWW/1917_Accounting_Dept_National_Lead_Co_New_Orleans_vertical_file_Covert_LSU_cc000784.jpg>.

2 Hamilton, *Exploring the Dangerous Trades*, 61 ("interfering affections").

3 Ibid., 125–26 ("a land . . . wages"). Sicherman, *Alice Hamilton*, 21 ("blazing out . . . to prisoners").

4 Hamilton, *Exploring the Dangerous Trades*, 8–9 ("model plants . . . in those plants." For background on the impetus for the investigation of occupational disease in Illinois, see Beckner, *History of Labor Legislation in Illinois*, 272–82: "Upon recommendation by the Industrial Insurance Commission of 1906, the General Assembly of 1907 passed a joint resolution, drafted by Chief State Factory Inspector Davies, creating a commission of nine members appointed by the governor to investigate the problem of occupational diseases in Illinois. . . . In its preliminary report of April, 1909, the Commission stated that the problem of occupational disease was so large and complex as to require at least two years' additional study, and urged the General

Assembly to appropriate the sum of $15,000 to defray the costs of this investigation. . . . The 1909 General Assembly granted a two years' extension of time and made the necessary appropriation."

5 See Hamilton qtd. in *Boston Daily Globe*, Feb. 25, 1959: "I often found a half-amused interest. The industrialists thought it queer that a woman should be engaged in such work."

6 Hamilton, *Exploring the Dangerous Trades*, 8 ("responsible man"), 9 ("Your men . . . furances"), 129 ("They are . . . any man").

7 See John B. Andrews to A[lice] H[amilton], Feb. 1913 (copy), HP, A-22, box 1, folder 29.

8 Hamilton qtd. in Sicherman, *Alice Hamilton*, 34 ("disgusting," "amusing childish whim," "bluggy-minded butcher"). Ibid., 35 ("roughest class"). Hamilton, *Exploring the Dangerous Trades*, 38, 40 ("din," "antics").

9 Hamilton, *Exploring the Dangerous Trades*, 38 ("happy and exciting"). Hamilton qtd. in Sicherman, *Alice Hamilton*, 53 ("hardened").

10 Hamilton, "Industrial Diseases," 659 ("like a captain . . . get overboard").

11 Dialogue qtd. in Sicherman, *Alice Hamilton*, 8–10.

12 Hamilton qtd. in ibid., 157.

13 Hamilton, *Exploring the Dangerous Trades*, 5 ("What . . . Greasers?"), 131 ("Negro").

14 Cornish qtd. in Hamilton, *Exploring the Dangerous Trades*, 9–10 ("Now see here . . . your directions").

15 See "Gospel of Paint," *McClure's*. See also Illinois Acts of 1909, sections 11 and 12 (*Bulletin of the Bureau of Labor Statistics*, no. 85), 202, 547, 548: "In every room or apartment of any factory, mercantile establishment, mill, or workshop, where 1 or more persons are employed, at least 500 cubic feet of air space shall be provided for each and every person employed therein, and fresh air, to the amount specified by this act, shall be supplied in such as manner as not to create injurious drafts. . . . And all dust of a character injurious to the health of the persons employed, which is created in the course of a manufacturing process, within such factory, mill, or workshop shall be removed as far as practicable by either ventilating or exhaust devices." These Illinois statutes are summarized in Commons, *Principles of Labor Legislation*, 332–33.

16 Alice Hamilton, "Industrial Medicine," 9 ("ostrich-like"), HP, A-22, box 6, folder 2. On the presumption of superior U.S. workplace conditions, see Hamilton, *Exploring the Dangerous Trades*, 115. Qtd. in Boorstin, *Americans*, 25 ("smokeless . . . new and fresh"). Boorstin, *Americans*, 25, also quotes a French economist of the 1830s who described American factories as "like an opera scene," with New England female mill workers as "industry's Angel daughters," while yet another visiting economist rhapsodized about "a smokeless factory town canopied by the sky." See also "Factory Life—Romance and Reality," in Davis, *Life in the Iron Mills*, 169–72, and Watson, *Bread and Roses*, 50–52. Glazier, *Peculiarities of American Cities*, 332 ("lid lifted").

17 Hamilton, *Exploring the Dangerous Trades*, 132–33 ("steel men . . . week"). On her acquaintance with Sinclair, see ibid., 73.

18 Qtd. in ibid., 128 ("It is well known"). On the match industry, see Moss, "Kindling a Flame under Federalism," 249–53.

19 Qtd. in Hamilton, "Industrial Diseases," 658–59 ("there is nothing . . . to face").

20 See Detzer, *Myself When Young*, 53 ("old leather bindings"). On *Encyclopædia Britannica* usage, see Sicherman, *Alice Hamilton*, 18–19.

21 Qtd. in Sicherman, *Alice Hamilton*, 156 ("pretty much lost"). On Hamilton's inspection of English and European factories, see Alice Hamilton, "The Hygiene of the Lead Industry" (typescript), 2, 6, 10, HP, A-22, box 2, folder 29. Sicherman, *Alice Hamilton*, 157 ("tinfoil," "indigestion . . . pains").

22 Hamilton, *Exploring the Dangerous Trades*, 10 ("shoe-leather epidemiology," "tracking . . . number"). On Hamilton's sources, see Sicherman, *Alice Hamilton*, 157. See also Hamilton, *Industrial Poisons in the United States*, vi.

23 Hamilton, *Exploring the Dangerous Trades*, 125 ("and talking . . . minds"), 131 ("better than . . . can get," "sure does"). On Chicago saloons, see Duis, *Saloon*, 91.

24 Hamilton, *Exploring the Dangerous Trades*, 123–24 ("expressionless," "severe lead colic," young Italian).

25 Ibid., 115 ("fiery pen").

26 Hamilton, "Hygiene of the Lead Industry," 1, 17, 18.

27 Ibid., 14.

28 Ibid., 12.

29 "Rising Vote of Thanks," HP, A-22, box 2, folder 29, 4.

30 See James Weber Linn, draft of *Jane Addams* (typescript), HP, 22-A, box 6, folder 6 ("sparkling, amusing, lovely, tireless"). See typescript of manuscript in progress for essay in *Industrial Medicine* for Aug. 1935, HP, A-22, box 1, folder 3, 22 ("walking intrepidly . . . remote stopes"). Sicherman, *Alice Hamilton*, 169 ("quiet . . . diseases").

31 Hamilton, *Exploring the Dangerous Trades*, 18 ("I belong to Indiana"). Qtd. in Sicherman, *Alice Hamilton*, 13 ("insiders"). Note: Benham's became D. H. Hamilton, Photographer (no relation to the Hamilton family profiled here).

32 Hamilton, *Exploring the Dangerous Trades*, 3 ("new, unexplored field of . . . industrial disease"). Sicherman, *Alice Hamilton*, 18 ("an attractive little city . . . mellowed red brick").

33 On immigrant ethnicities in Fort Wayne, see Bates and Keller, *Columbia Street Story*, 75. Hamilton, *Exploring the Dangerous Trades*, 33 ("very lovely nursemaid," "brilliantly lighted," "great Christmas trees . . . wax candles"). On Christmas decor and custom in Fort Wayne, see Detzer, *Myself When Young*, 210, 56.

34 On industrial Fort Wayne, see Hawfield, *Fort Wayne Cityscapes*, 21; Ankenbruck, *Fort Wayne Story*, 102; and Violette, *Images of America*, 63.

35 *Gilded Age in Fort Wayne*, 1 ("brilliant social . . . expensive jewelry"). The brewer, Charles Centlivre, erected a Queen Anne–style mansion in 1888, while John Bass of the Bass Foundry built the turreted pile he named "Brookside."

36 *A Conversation with Edith Hamilton*, Indiana Collection, Allen County Public Library, Fort Wayne, Ind. ("palatial . . . all others"). See also Peter Certia album, Fort Wayne Historical Society, Fort Wayne, Ind.

37 See Bates and Keller, *Columbia Street Story*, 59: Colerick's Opera House was "the theatre that introduced Fort Wayne to the fine arts." See also Hawfield, *Fort Wayne Cityscapes*. On sports and recreation, see Angue Cameron McCoy, "The Streets of Fort Wayne" (bound typescript), 31–32, Allen County Public Library, Fort Wayne, Ind. See also Allen County Public Library vertical file "Fort Wayne History, 1850–1899."

On the performance by Mark Twain, see *Fort Wayne (Ind.) Daily Gazette*, Feb. 6, 1885, Allen County Public Library vertical file "Fort Wayne History, 1850–1899."

38 Hamilton, *Exploring the Dangerous Trades*, 29 ("Our education . . . omissions").

39 Ibid., 26 ("I meant to be a medical missionary"). Tehran was Hamilton's imagined destination, inspired by reading *The Merv Oasis*, Edmond O'Donovan's account of his 1879–81 travels.

40 On Fort Wayne slums, crime, sewage, and impure water, see Detzer, *Myself When Young*, 54, 187. See also Diana L. Hawfield, "Commencements: Agnes Hamilton of Fort Wayne" (typescript, 1986), 18, "Hamilton Family" folder, Fort Wayne Historical Society, Fort Wayne, Ind.

41 Maurice, "Loving in Deed and in Truth," in *Reconstructing Christian Ethics*, n.p. ("You may have . . . in need of"). On the influence of Maurice and Kingsley, see Hamilton, *Exploring the Dangerous Trades*, 26. Kingsley, *Cheap Clothes and Nasty*, n.p. ("honourable"). Note: Hamilton read Kingsley's *Hypatia* (1853) while in medical school at the University of Michigan (Sicherman, *Alice Hamilton*, 43–45).

42 Hamilton, *Exploring the Dangerous Trades*, 37 ("outside world"), 26–27 ("to explore . . . meet strange people"), 38 ("life in a big city . . . to city slums"). On Edith Hamilton's observation that her sister was "very anxious to talk to other people and to have friends," see Diana L. Hawfield, "Spades and Silver Spoons: The Life and Work of Edith Hamilton" (typescript, 1986), 7, "Hamilton Family" folder, Fort Wayne Historical Society, Fort Wayne, Ind. Hamilton qtd. in Sicherman, *Alice Hamilton*, 33 ("corner 375 St. & Slum Alley").

43 On Fort Wayne's notorious Irishtown slum, see Detzer, *Myself When Young*, 54, 187.

44 Alice Hamilton, "Jane Addams of Hull House, Chicago," HP, A-22, box 1, folder 6 (typescript, 1952), 1 ("social democracy . . . social life").

45 Hamilton, *Exploring the Dangerous Trades*, 68 ("There was the same hall . . . elaborate cornices"), 69 ("charming furnishings . . . English inn").

46 Sicherman, *Alice Hamilton*, 89 ("invisible"), 90 ("turned . . . bacteriologist").

47 Ibid., 78 ("down alleys . . . Boston"), 80 ("Jewish," "Negro"), 76 ("poor working women").

48 Qtd. in ibid., 44 ("nice red-faced Deutscher"), 57 ("rough lumbermen"), 68 ("my little negress"), 50 ("perhaps death," "easiest . . . solution"), 63 ("Irish and Catholic," "coarse," "vulgar").

49 Qtd. in ibid., 80 ("We always . . . hard times").

50 See the obituary of Sir Thomas Oliver, *British Medical Journal*, May 30, 1942, 681–82. See also *Oxford Dictionary of National Biography*, <http://oxforddnb.com/view/printable/35308>.

51 Oliver, *Dangerous Trades*, vii–viii ("the language . . . educated public").

52 Ibid., vii ("fellow-men and women"). Hamilton, *Exploring the Dangerous Trades*, 72 ("the classes" versus "the masses"), 75 ("how deep and fundamental . . . country").

53 Oliver, *Dangerous Trades*, 98–99 ("injurious and dangerous industries in England," "chief European countries," "Infant Mortality and Factory Labour," "Child Labour," "home-work," "No Man's Land of the industrial world").

54 See *John B. Andrews Memorial Symposium*, 196 ("cases of phossy jaw").

55 Hamilton, *Exploring the Dangerous Trades*, 115 ("all German . . . the poor"). As of 1901, at least one U.S. printed source reported workplace lead poisoning in the United

States. In *Report of the Industrial Commission on the Relations of Capital and Labor Employed in the Mining Industry*, 308–9, the testimony of John R. Wright of the Smeltermen's Union (Denver, Colorado) indicated that "if a man works longer than twenty-two days per month at 12 hours per day in the smoke of the [lead] works, he will ruin his health."

56 Hamilton, *Industrial Poisons in the United States*, vi–vii ("foreign literature," "nothing . . . American industry").

57 Qtd. in Hamilton, *Exploring the Dangerous Trades*, 31–32 ("Somebody ought . . . why not I?").

58 Qtd. in Sicherman, *Alice Hamilton*, 154 ("cold, printed report," "the pen of a ready writer"), 167 ("Nothing . . . a hospital history").

59 Hamilton, *Exploring the Dangerous Trades*, 135 ("temporary flurry," "lasting reform").

60 Sicherman, *Alice Hamilton*, 163 ("wisely," "cautiously," "diagnose"). General interest magazine publications on poverty and working conditions include Low and Ely, "Programme for Labor Reform"; Stimson, "Democracy and the Laboring Man"; and Riis, "Children of the Poor." In years to come, Hamilton published in these and other magazines. See her "State Pensions or Charity," "Nineteen Years in the Poisonous Trades," and "Cost of Medical Care."

Hull House residents' contributions to this literature include Kelley, "Congestion and Sweated Labor," and Addams, "Chicago Settlements and Social Unrest."

61 Hamilton, *Exploring the Dangerous Trades*, 115 ("very black . . . old country"). Hamilton, "Industrial Diseases," 657 ("long hours"), 658 ("every civilized country," "sacrificing life and health").

62 Hamilton, "Industrial Diseases," 655 ("very improbable . . . employers").

63 Qtd. in *Congressional Record*, 62nd Cong., 2nd sess., Mar. 28, 1912, 3976 ("Congress . . . nations of the world"). See Moss, "Kindling a Flame under Federalism." Hamilton, *Exploring the Dangerous Trades*, 118 ("So phossy jaw . . . factories").

64 See Marchand, *Creating the Corporate Soul*, 3–4: "The great business giants of the earlier twentieth century were not only seeking to legitimize their newly amassed power . . . but also constantly renegotiating their position along a series of increasingly fuzzy boundaries within business. . . . The quest of large corporations for enhanced social and moral legitimacy went forward with an almost evangelical ardor."

65 Hamilton, *Exploring the Dangerous Trades*, 118 ("voices in the wilderness"). Hamilton, "What Price Safety," 333 ("Where there is lead . . . strictest supervision").

66 Hamilton qtd. in Rosner and Markowitz, *Deadly Dust*, 161 ("lip service . . . singularly unchanged").

67 Sellers, *Hazards of the Job*, 70 ("No individual . . . World War I"), 101 ("great contribution . . . United States"). Hamilton qtd. in Markowitz and Rosner, *Dying for Work*, 160–61 ("Let me beg . . . the product"). Hamilton, *Exploring the Dangerous Trades*, 13 ("instinctive American lawlessness . . . all legal control").

CHAPTER 2

1 Glazier, *Peculiarities of American Cities*, 332 ("hell with the lid lifted").

2 See Holbrook, *Age of the Moguls*, 143–52, and Standiford, *Meet You in Hell*, 13, 62. Morgan bought Carnegie Steel for $492 million, then created a steel trust, the United

States Steel Corporation, a behemoth capitalized at over $1.4 billion. The new steel trust included, in addition, American Steel and Wire, American Tin Plate, American Steel Hoop, American Bridge, Federal Steel, National Steel, and National Tube.

3   See Bellomy, "Molding of an Iconoclast," 720ff, for a reprinting of the chronology and descriptions of Sumner's courses from the Yale catalogue. Ibid., 723 ("economic problems . . . organization").

4   See ibid., chaps. 5–13, for a detailed account of Sumner's academic career at Yale. Sklansky, *Soul's Economy*, 131 ("Sumnerology"). Sumner, *War and Other Essays*, 197 ("absurd").

5   Carnegie qtd. in Standiford, *Meet You in Hell*, 42 ("truth of evolution"). Sumner, *What Social Classes Owe*, 112–13 ("Here we are . . . *Laissez faire*"), 120 ("nothing . . . business"). See also Sumner, *War and Other Essays*, 197. Over decades, Sumner sought to understand human motivation and action through knowledge of the social sciences, and he was a staunch advocate of free speech in the academy. Sumner opposed U.S. imperial wars but, toward the end of his long career, conceded the need for federal intervention in cases of social and financial emergency. For a full explanation of Sumner's concepts of survival and fitness, see Bellomy, "Molding of an Iconoclast," chaps. 9–10. See also Bannister, *Social Darwinism*, 105: "At a speech before the Free Trade Club in 1879, and on several other subsequent occasions, [Sumner] noted that in the struggle for existence there were but two alternatives. 'The law of survival of the fittest was not made by man,' went the argument. 'We can only, by interfering with it, produce the survival of the unfittest.'"

6   Arne, "William Graham Sumner," n.p. ("great strides . . . power"). Baltzell, *Protestant Establishment*, 102 ("communists . . . sizes").

7   Commons, *Myself*, 170 ("save . . . anarchism"). See Lippmann, *Preface to Morals*, 226, which states that adherents to laissez-faire thought that human rights meant "freedom of contract, freedom of trade, freedom of occupation," all such freedoms meaning the employer's right "to buy and sell, to hire and fire without being accountable to anyone."

8   See Commons, *Institutional Economics*, 843: "Herbert Spencer's philosophy is not only the laissez faire *political* philosophy of [Adam] Smith, [Jeremy] Bentham, and [David] Ricardo; it is also the philosophy underlying their opposition to *all forms of collective action* as well as state action. Private collective action, the individualist economists claimed, was always monopolistic and opposed to the common welfare."

9   Commons, *Myself*, 170 ("not fitted . . . men"). On ad valorem tax, see Unger, *Fighting Bob La Follette*, 129, 134. On Wisconsin civil service law, see Harter, *John R. Commons*, 60.

10 Harter, *John R. Commons*, 89–129, 255 ("momentous conflict"). Commons, *Myself*, 170 ("capital and labor").

11 Stilgoe, *Metropolitan Corridor*, 68 ("sumptuous . . . comfort"). Commons, *Myself*, 165 ("shivering . . . hotels").

12 Commons, *Myself*, 87–88 ("safe progress," "growth . . . justice"). See also Stromquist, *Re-inventing "the People*," 89–92, 175–76, 181–87. Commons, *Myself*, 153 ("thick").

13 Kellogg, "Pittsburgh Survey," 517 ("great steel . . . blue print"). Commons's American students were about to encounter the American version of Germany's industrial Ruhr Valley with its coal mines, iron foundries, and steel mills. The Commons team knew

that the University of Wisconsin economist Richard T. Ely (formerly Commons's graduate school professor at Johns Hopkins University) had studied conditions in the Ruhr as a student at the University of Heidelberg, where a professor named Karl Knies directed Ely to "the aspirations of the workingman," his "privations," and his "excessive toil." Ely, in turn, focused Commons's attention on U.S. workers "in a way that would have stirred the ire of the Old Guard of the United States" (Ely, *Ground under My Feet*, 44).

14 Commons, *Myself*, 13–14 ("old swimming hole"). Textbooks qtd. in Elson, *Guardians of Tradition*, 252–54 ("Riches . . . the prudent"), 248–49 ("greatly . . . prosperity"). Horowitz, in *Morality of Spending*, 50–66, calculates that child labor in poor families increased income by as much as one-third.

15 Howells, "Country Printer," 33 ("a sort a handicraft . . . stone-cutting"), 7–8 ("bare and rude"), 10 ("splotched . . . newspapers"). Commons, *Myself*, 11 ("jawed," "Sprawled . . . lazily"), 8 ("funny and keen"). For this description of the typical country newspaper office, I rely on Howells, "Country Printer," a memoir of boyhood experience in his father's rural Ohio newspaper that closely resembles that of the senior Commons.

16 On the post-1873 depression, see Tindall and Shi, *America*, 727. Howells, "Country Printer," 5 ("hard-working . . . dwelt"), 17 ("scattered farms"), 22 ("decimated by delinquents").

17 Coinage of Liberty Seated silver dollars was suspended after 1873 and resumed with the Morgan silver dollar in 1878, although Liberty Seated was still in circulation.

18 Sumner, *What Social Classes Owe*, 113 ("every man . . . self").

19 Hilkey, *Character Is Capital*, 8–9 ("carried . . . new generation"). See ibid., 9: "In the success manual, 'manhood' and 'manliness' signify the man who is dominant over all other men by virtue of behaviors and attitudes that are consistent with legitimation [*sic*] the new industrial order."

20 Dreiser, *Sister Carrie*, 10–11 ("brisk man"). Don Marquis, qtd. in Spears, *100 Years on the Road*, 13, recalled the "magnificent" drummer: "My memory still retains a picture of myself, as a barefoot, freckle-faced boy of twelve, standing on a plank sidewalk in a prairie town . . . and looking up at one of these magnificent beings." Items named for sale in the late nineteenth century appear at "Indiana—Randolph County," *National Register of Historic Places*, <http://www.nationalregisterofhistoricplaces.com/IN/Randolph/state.html>.

21 Commons, *Myself*, 28 ("intensive training . . . sufficient"). For an analysis of the malleable persona of the sales agent, see Spears, *100 Years on the Road*, 106, 143. See also Hochschild, *Managed Heart*. The dollar outlook seemed especially bright, for Commons intuited the fact that, from 1870 until the end of the century, a salesman earned an average of $1,200 to $1,800 per annum. (By contrast, a skilled worker earned between $500 and $800 per year.) See Spears, *100 Years on the Road*, 55.

22 Commons, *Myself*, 28 ("I . . . failure"). On sales techniques, see Hilkey, *Character Is Capital*, 22–23. The Beecher-Tilton scandal erupted when Victoria Woodhull published a story in her weekly newspaper revealing that Elizabeth Tilton, a married woman, had had an affair with the nation's most renowned minister, Beecher (who, she averred, advocated free love outside the bounds of marriage). The scandal grew with Woodhull's arrest for sending obscene materials through the mail, and it con-

tinued through the 1875 trial in which Mrs. Tilton's husband, Theodore, sued Beecher for adultery. The timing could not have been worse for John as he tried selling subscriptions to the *Christian Union*. Though the minister had left the editorship in 1878, Hoosier memories lingered of the mistrial that was declared after the days-long jury deliberations and of the publicized board of inquiry proceedings at Beecher's Plymouth Church—and of Elizabeth Tilton's repeated confessions to the adulterous relationship. See Applegate, *Most Famous Man in America*, 395–468.

23 *Sears, Roebuck and Company. . . . Consumers Guide*, 208–13. The publication of this catalogue postdates Commons's summer venture by nearly ten years, but the terms of its appeal are consistent with advertising of the 1880s.

24 Commons, *Myself*, 41 ("plug hat . . . in the hole").

25 Ibid., 35 ("sub"), 16 ("new invention of photo-engraving," "technological unemployment").

26 On the Coxey's (and Kelly's) Army movement, see McMurry, *Coxey's Army*, and Schwantes, *Coxey's Army*. Commons, *Myself*, 189 ("he was . . . had ever known").

27 Commons, *Myself*, 26 ("fierce blow"). Sumner, *What Social Classes Owe*, 20–21 ("weak," "dead weight," "finest . . . industrious"). Commons, *Myself*, 31 ("wandering . . . woods," "weakling"), 33 ("nerves and digestion"), 38 ("mad . . . brain"). See also Sumner, *What Social Classes Owe*, 80, 182, 191.

28 Commons, *Myself*, 60 ("struggles . . . beings").

29 Byington, *Homestead*, 6 ("buckwheats"). For the Indiana common school curriculum, see *Indiana*, 118.

30 See Thornbrough, *Indiana in the Civil War*, 501: "Miserable pay and short school terms and the greater financial rewards offered in other occupations caused many persons to regard teaching as a temporary vocation." See also ibid., 480, 476. See also Eggleston, *Hoosier Schoolmaster*, 37, which offers advice to the rural schoolmaster who is slight of build: make the school's best fighter your ally, or the boys will "pitch you out of doors, neck and heels, afore Christmas."

31 Commons, *Myself*, 27 ("pupils . . . produce it").

32 Photos of James Monroe as an Oberlin professor are reprinted in Rokicky, *James Monroe*, 176, 194. My discussion of Monroe is drawn from this study, which includes much information on Commons's work under Monroe and their postcollegiate relationship. Perry, *Elements of Political Economy*, 160–61 ("exchange," "same . . . advantage").

33 Perry, *Elements of Political Economy*, 148 ("interests"), 160 ("one blade . . . to cut"). Perry asserted that the driving force in the economic world, namely, the capitalist's "self-interest," was expressed in terms benefiting the laboring "masses of men" (ibid., 160–61, 164). Perry also assured readers that the laws of economics prohibited no man from becoming rich but asserted that "most men are unwilling, some are unable, to fulfill the moral conditions of getting rich" (ibid., 202). See also Greenwood, *Gilded Age*, 57, and Schlereth, *Victorian America*, 77–81, in which annual budgets of laborers and middle-class families are itemized, the latter showing laborers' families to earn at most one-half of those of the middle class. Wrote Perry in *Political Economy* (1888), 196, "The natural laws of Production are *inexorable* in their operation. . . . If custom or legislation thwart these laws, they will take their revenge without pity, and lapse of time will only exhibit transgressors more clearly as firmly held in the grip of violated law." See also Harter, *John R. Commons*, 14, 33.

34 Monroe qtd. in Rokicky, *James Monroe*, xii–xiii ("Wages . . . of industry"). Writes Rokicky in ibid., 184–85, "Monroe covered a wide range of subjects, including Malthusian economics, but he spent most of the class discussing contemporary affairs such as the tariff, labor, currency, and taxation . . . moving from classical orthodoxy to concern with immediate social afflictions." Supporting education in his years in Congress, Monroe urged that workers, who were hobbled by ignorance, seek formal schooling because he saw it as the best path to promote their interests in the workplace. See also ibid., 131–48, 186.

35 Gladden, *Working People and Their Employers*, 174–75 ("hard-fisted . . . law"). See also Furner, *Advocacy and Objectivity*, 35–58.

36 On sales of *Progress and Poverty*, see Tindall and Shi, *America*, 846. George, *Progress and Poverty*, 6 ("deepest," "sharpest"), 270–71 ("*in spite* . . . unemployed men"). George also exposed a system of usurious interest rates and high rents that vastly inflated land values. See Johnston, *Radical Middle Class*, 160: "Henry George's vision helped inspire some of the most substantial challenges to industrial capitalism during the Gilded Age. His picture of a nation riven by classes and exploitation and saturated with illegitimate wealth and power proved crucial in forging working-class movements as well as cross-class alliances." Rejecting preindustrial life, George, in *Progress and Poverty*, 285, called civilization "the enfranchisement, elevation, and refinement of all his [mankind's] powers."

37 Ely, *Ground under My Feet*, 58 ("case system . . . documents").

38 Commons, *Myself*, 130 ("I am not a person . . . of you"), 132 ("seed-bed").

39 Serrin, *Homestead*, 122–23 ("Slavs"). Kellogg, "Pittsburgh Survey," 525 ("hospitals . . . orphanages").

40 On department store air, see Kelley, *Modern Industry*, 58. On the company-owned superintendent's house, see caption in Byington, *Homestead*, 23: "The purpose in providing it is, of course, to make it practicable for the responsible executive to be within call of the works." Fitch, *Steel Workers*, 151–52 ("gullied," "forlorn," "dirt and ugliness"), 46–47 ("black clouds").

41 Fitch, *Steel Workers*, 177 ("and even these . . . furnace crews"). Kelley, *Modern Industry*, 62–63 ("water boys"). Commons, *Myself*, 38 ("verve"). For Commons's recurrent references to his health problems and weight, see Commons, *Myself*, 28, 38, 78, 80.

42 Commons, *Myself*, 140 ("smoky," "original Sherwood Forest").

43 Kellogg, "Pittsburgh Survey," 521 ("city of tonnage"), 525 ("For richer . . . rampantly American"). This description of Pittsburgh draws substantially from ibid., 520–21. The cities of Allegheny and Pittsburgh merged into greater Pittsburgh in December 1907.

44 Richard Realf, "Hymn of Pittsburgh," reprinted in Kellogg, "Pittsburgh Survey," n.p. ("mighty Vulcan . . . forges"). On the danger of injury in steel mills, see Fitch, *Steel Workers*, 10, 13.

45 Kellogg, "Pittsburgh Survey," 5 ("cut-throat competition"), 9 ("Mecca to the immigrant"), 87–88 ("long and costly"), 4 ("vast masses of men"), 9 ("no voice"). See Montgomery, *Fall of the House of Labor*, 274, which reports that the Pittsburgh area was riven by labor strikes and discord in 1907 "as the region was flooded with private eyes and state constabulary" involving "U.S. Steel, the Pressed Steel Car Company, and the Mesta Machine Company."

46 Fitch, *Steel Workers*, 10–11 ("the issues . . . themselves"), 10 ("hopes and plans," "some half-spoken ambition"), 14–15 (home shrunk to eating and sleeping).

47 Ibid., 124 ("collective action . . . injustice"). On the "tractable" workforce, see Byington, *Homestead*, 6, which quotes a letter by the Carnegie loyalist Captain Jones of the Edgar Thomson Steel Works on judicious mixing of Germans, Irish, Swedes, and "buckwheats" to create "the most tractable work force you can find." *Who Built America*, 133 ("arrogant," "They believe . . . Carnegie's"). See also Fitch, *Steel Workers*, 123, and Serrin, *Homestead*, 66–95.

48 Sumner, *What Social Classes Owe*, 113 ("meddlers . . . of society"). Commons, *Myself*, 3 ("dig and re-dig"). Fitch, *Steel Workers*, 6 ("mightier," "democracy").

49 On Commons's sweatshop survey in Chicago and New York, see Bisno, *Union Pioneer*, 211–12: "Congress had appointed a commission to investigate the kind of immigrants coming to America and their motive for coming, their economic and cultural levels at home, their manner of adjustment to conditions in America, their economic conditions here, the influence they had on American life and the way they were influenced by American life, their cultural level here in America, the way they became Americanized, etc, etc. The head of the organization was John R. Commons . . . [who] asked me to join him in the investigation." On the immigration report for the U.S. Industrial Commission appointed by President McKinley and Commons's Hull House residency, see Commons, *Myself*, 67, 68.

50 On Indiana foodways, see *Indiana*, 120.

51 For typical meals in an English-speaking household in Pittsburgh during the survey, see Byington, *Homestead*, 63–64, 73.

52 Commons, *Myself*, 133 ("hunkies"). On the career of William Leiserson, see "Two Nice Men," *Time*, 17.

53 On Fitch, see Commons, *Myself*, 141, and Lubove, "John A. Fitch," vii.

54 See Commons, *Myself*, 7: "It required some years for my wife, Ella Downey, to weed out my Hoosierisms. Yet I often think how Indiana created an indigenous American school of letters." For the dispute on the origins of *Hoosier*, see Nicholson, *Hoosiers*, 29–35.

55 For vernacular "Hoosierisms," see Eggleston, *Hoosier Schoolmaster*, 6, 7, 37, 39, 42, 47, 60, 64, and 97. See also *Indiana*, 121.

56 Fitch, *Steel Workers*, 107 ("fine presence," "back-breaking"), 33–35 ("churning butter . . . in hell"), 46 ("spell").

57 Ibid., 46 ("hot job"), 154, 226–27 (steelworker culture).

58 Ibid., 107 ("beginning . . . teeth"). Commons, *Myself*, 143–44 ("harangued . . . mills," "wildcat," "freely").

59 Fitch, *Steel Workers*, 10 ("blistered," "reddened . . . grimed").

60 On working conditions in the mill, see Commons, *Myself*, 144. For an undercover journalist's first-person account of the twenty-four-hour shift in a steel mill, see Walker, "Twenty-Four-Hour Shift."

61 On workers' wages and hours, see Fitch, *Steel Workers*, 105–7, 155, and Commons, *Myself*, 143–44.

62 Commons, *Industrial Goodwill*, 62–63 ("two chairs . . . fits the facts"), 126 ("empty until . . . cents an hour"). Commons, in *Races and Immigrants*, 160, writes that, in the study of "social subjects, it is only statistics that tell us the true proportions and

relative importance of our facts." The financial advantage of speakers of English in the later-nineteenth-century U.S. workplace is discussed in Horowitz, *Morality of Spending*, 14, 56.

63 Commons, *Myself*, 144 ("How did this . . . come about"). Commons, *Races and Immigrants*, 112 ("The future of . . . American wage-earner"), 219–22 ("Americanization," "his children," "the labor-union . . . force"). Commons, introduction, xi ("spick-and-span . . . huge gold watch").

64 Commons, *Races and Immigrants*, 222 ("belongs to him . . . naturalization papers"). Wrote Commons, "The unionist who votes as a unionist has taken his first step . . . towards considering the interests of others, and this is the first step towards giving public spirit and abstract principles a place alongside private interests and his own job" (ibid., 222). Commons, introduction, xvii ("American labor movement . . . government"). See also Montgomery, *Fall of the House of Labor*, 74–75: By 1909, "the Irish-Americans and Irish immigrants [in the U.S. Northeast] together held virtually all the jobs paying more than two dollars per day. They were all literate, and most of the Irish-born workers who were eligible had become citizens. Only 10 percent of the laborers of this region were whites of native parentage, and 6 percent were Afro-Americans. Almost half were Italians in their twenties, and the rest were Slavic or Hungarian. Less than one-third of the latter groups of immigrants had been in the United States as long as five years, and hardly any were citizens."

65 Commons, introduction, i ("employer dictatorship"). Serrin, *Homestead*, 166–67 ("payoffs . . . supervisors"). See also Commons, introduction, i–iii, and Commons, *Industrial Goodwill*, 175. Commons, *Institutional Economics*, 757 ("labor dictatorship . . . labor *politician*").

66 Commons, *Industrial Goodwill*, 30 ("no public purpose," "illusions," "private war," "public purpose"). Commons, introduction, ix–x ("fiery denunciations . . . butter now"). See Montgomery, *Fall of the House of Labor*, 60: "The demand for portable muscle power had by no means been eclipsed by the much-heralded triumph of 'labor-saving' machinery. On the contrary, the nineteenth-century expended human physical exertion more prodigiously than any other epoch in the country's history. . . . Common laborers were not an archaic vestige of preindustrial society. In fact, their largest employers included the most highly capitalized industries: railroads, steel, chemicals, mining, and metal fabricating."

67 Gompers qtd. in Commons, *Myself*, 87 ("fool friends"). Commons, *Industrial Goodwill*, 139 ("class conscious," "wage conscious," "from all negotiations . . . councils of labor"). Commons wrote, "No class can be trusted to decide for itself. No class, either aristocrats, capitalists, educators or workers, can see the needs, or rights, or duties, of others as vividly as its own" (*Industrial Goodwill*, 139).

68 Commons, *Myself*, 82–83 ("many . . . control of industry").

69 Commons, *Industrial Goodwill*, 175 ("labor leader . . . to leadership," "impossible"). On union preservation as the main goal of union leaders, see ibid. Gompers, *Labor and the Common Welfare*, 158–59, 12 ("interdependence").

70 Commons, *Institutional Economics*, 758 ("Both sides . . . working rules").

71 Commons, introduction, xiii–xvi ("all of the grievances"). See also Commons, *Myself*, 82–83, 86. Commons, *Industrial Goodwill*, 43 ("in the public interest").

72 Commons, *Myself*, 144–45 ("traced it . . . steel"). Commons erred in this assessment

of the reasons for the strike. Fitch's subsequent research, published in *Steel Workers*, together with that of later historians, indicates that Carnegie and Frick maximized profits by conspiring to break the Amalgamated Association and dictate the lengths of shifts. See Standiford, *Meet You in Hell*, 109–74.

73 Commons, *Myself*, 52 ("cost of production"). On the application of Dewey's theory, see Commons, *Institutional Economics*, 90–93.

74 The paradigm of the Pittsburgh Survey evidently also motivated Epstein's *Negro Migrant in Pittsburgh* (1918).

75 Lubove, "John A. Fitch," viii ("work of unprecedented scope . . . of the journalist," "classic").

76 "Two Nice Men," *Time*, 17 ("careerist in mediation and arbitration"). For appreciation of Commons's work in impacting legislation and court decisions, see Schneider, *Three Economics Professors*, 85–110. For the academic context of Commons's work, see Fink, *Progressive Intellectuals*, 64–79. Commons's preeminent status in institutional economics is challenged by Bernstein in *Perilous Progress*, 44: "While John R. Commons of the University of Wisconsin and [Thorstein] Veblen himself were often regarded as two of the most significant founders of an 'American school of institutional economics,' it was [Wesley Clair] Mitchell most of all, with the crucial support and commitment of [Edwin F.] Gay, who set much of the methodological agenda for which the school would long be known." See Bernstein, *Perilous Progress*, 7–72, for a full discussion.

77 For an account of the careers of Commons's "syndicate" of graduate students, see Rutherford, "Wisconsin Institutionalism, 15–20. Harter, *John R. Commons*, 255 ("will be reasonable . . . general interest").

78 Roosevelt qtd. in Tindall and Shi, *America*, 1122–23 ("cornerstone," "supreme achievement").

CHAPTER 3

1 For estimated mortality figures, see Lindenmeyer, *Right to Childhood*, 35, 43.

2 Qtd. in Tichi, *Shifting Gears*, 231–40 ("speed," "age of hurry"). Goode, *Best Addresses*, 59 ("free from malaria"). See Lindenmeyer, *Right to Childhood*, 31: "In the wider spectrum of public policy history, the 1912 Children's Bureau Act set the stage for a reversal of previous guidelines generally denying federal responsibility for social welfare."

3 On Union Station, see Mitchell, *Washington Then and Now*, n.p. On international birth rates, see Lindenmeyer, *Right to Childhood*, 43.

4 See *Child in the City*, 18, 43.

5 On "Children's Year," see Tobey, *Children's Bureau*, 8–9. On the range of issues important to children, see Bradbury, *Five Decades of Action for Children*, 4. On the structuring of the Children's Bureau, see Lindenmeyer, *Right to Childhood*, 51.

6 On the initial budget of the Children's Bureau, see Lindenmeyer, *Right to Childhood*, 34.

7 Bradbury, *Five Decades of Action for Children*, 2–3 ("organizations . . . women"). On January 31, 1912, the bill sponsored by Senator William E. Borah was passed by the

Senate, and the House of Representatives passed its version two months later, on April 2. See Lindenmeyer, *Right to Childhood*, 9–29.

8   Rice, *Calvary Alley*, 37 ("When the State . . . the State goes too far").

9   Qtd. in Addams, *My Friend, Julia Lathrop*, 62 ("a tremendously . . . hardly blend"). Gladwell, *Tipping Point*, 46–88 ("connectors," "particular and rare . . . niches," "tipping point").

10   Lathrop, "Children's Bureau," 319–20 ("sternest . . . scientific candor)."

11   Qtd. in Costin, *Two Sisters for Social Justice*, 182 ("the welfare . . . people"). See Lindenmeyer, *Right to Childhood*, 33–34: "Appointed on April 17, 1912, Lathrop went to work almost immediately. Because the agency's operational funds would not be available until August 23, Lathrop traveled at her own expense gathering support and soliciting opinions from women's organizations, prominent child welfare reformers, and social workers."

12   Lathrop qtd. in Bradbury, *Five Decades of Action for Children*, 5–6 ("The only basis . . . whole community," "entirely democratic inquiry").

13   Lindenmeyer, *Right to Childhood*, 34 ("experimental and tentative").

14   See Goode, *Best Addresses*, 61. The tall ceilings and elegant birch woodwork of Lathrop's apartment were as pleasing as the convenience of a downstairs dining room, where she could take all her meals for thirty dollars per month, or, if she chose, she could have meals served in her apartment for an extra charge of twenty-five cents. Her fellow tenants included U.S. senators, military officers, various government officials, and professionals. For the history of industrial Rockford, see Nelson, *Sinnissippi Saga*, 58–59, 61.

15   See Knight, *Citizen*, 86–87, 197. Addams, newly wealthy following her father's death, was appointed to the Rockford Female Seminary board of trustees in 1889.

16   Addams, *My Friend, Julia Lathrop*, 27–28 ("vigor and originality," "this brilliant . . . college"). Addams qtd. in Knight, *Citizen*, 154 ("the lives . . . such help"). See also Knight, *Citizen*, 166–76.

17   Qtd in Ruegamer, "'Paradise of Exceptional Women,'" 52 ("an almost Italian salience"). On Lathrop's adult life in Rockford, see Addams, *My Friend, Julia Lathrop*, 17.

18   See Ruegamer, "'Paradise of Exceptional Women,'" 146–82.

19   Waugh, *Unsentimental Reformer*, 227 ("slip of a girl," clothing description). Linn, *Jane Addams*, 115–16 ("clear and agreeable . . . lower registers"). See also Knight, *Citizen*, 74.

20   Linn, *Jane Addams*, 116 ("There was so much . . . at first hand"). Addams, *Democracy and Social Ethics*, 35 ("higher social morality . . . moral energy").

21   Qtd. in Kelley, "Hull House," 550 ("centre for . . . life").

22   Knight, *Citizen*, 190 ("egalitarian . . . relations"). See also ibid., 183–87. See also Elshtain, *Jane Addams and the Dream*, chap. 3.

23   On men's relation to Hull House, see Deegan, *Jane Addams and the Men*.

24   Addams, *Democracy and Social Ethics*, 40–41 ("Perplexities . . . citizen of the world"), 42 ("accumulation").

25   Ibid., 39 ("charm and grace . . . larger sense").

26   Ibid. ("political equality . . . all men").

27 Addams, "Subjective Value of a Social Settlement," 1–3 ("Democracy has made . . . reciprocal").

28 Addams, *Democracy and Social Ethics*, 40 ("delicacy and polish . . . protection and prosperity").

29 Addams, "Objective Value of a Social Settlement," 27 ("gilded vice"). For the location and number of U.S. settlement houses until 1911, see Woods and Kennedy, *Handbook of Settlements*.

30 Addams, "Objective Value of a Social Settlement," 29 ("lined . . . sewer").

31 On Stowe, William Lathrop's defense of a client on the grounds of insanity, and Dix in Illinois, see Addams, *My Friend, Julia Lathrop*, 18–20. See also Gollaher, *Voice for the Mad*. Lathrop qtd. in Addams, *My Friend, Julia Lathrop*, 33 ("someone who was lame . . . in trouble"). Polacheck, *I Came a Stranger*, 102 ("not a forceful speaker . . . her audience").

32 Addams, "Objective Value of a Social Settlement," 29 ("The older and richer . . . civic duties").

33 On Rockford's decades of early settlement, see Addams, *My Friend, Julia Lathrop*, 21–22. See also Nelson, *We, the People of Winnebago County*, 62.

34 Addams, "Subjective Value of a Social Settlement," 7 ("higher civil life . . . to be permanent").

35 Ibid. ("good we secure . . . our common life"). For an account of one early recruitment speech to members of the Chicago Woman's Club, see Knight, *Citizen*, 219–21.

36 Addams, *My Friend, Julia Lathrop*, 25 ("timid and shy").

37 Addams qtd. in Ruegamer, "'Paradise of Exceptional Women,'" 190 ("The best 'resident'"). Hamilton, *Exploring the Dangerous Trades*, 61 ("wholesome," "rather Spartan"). Glowacki and Hendry, *Images of America*, 17 ("impedimenta"). The inventory of Lathrop's room is reprinted in Stebner, "Women of Hull House," 166. For customary furnishings of the era, see Schlereth, *Victorian America*, 122, 129. See also Cromley, "History of American Beds."

38 See Stebner, "Women of Hull House," 173.

39 Addams qtd. in Polikoff, *With One Bold Act*, 86 ("Look around . . . your way").

40 For a description of Chicago's Nineteenth Ward, see Polacheck, *I Came a Stranger*, 30.

41 Addams, "Subjective Value of a Social Settlement," 1 ("social obligation"), 3 ("reciprocal dependence . . . other"), 7 ("perils"). Strong qtd. in Davis, *Life in the Iron Mills*, 247 ("low").

42 Addams, *My Friend, Julia Lathrop*, 37 ("piteous recitals"). See Kraut, *Huddled Masses*, 22–23. See also Polacheck, *I Came a Stranger*, 1–24.

43 See Polacheck, *I Came a Stranger*, 70.

44 Addams, *My Friend, Julia Lathrop*, 37 ("elderly men . . . their lives").

45 Dewey qtd. in Westbrook, *John Dewey and American Democracy*, 50–51 ("class divisions," "full expression").

46 Dewey qtd. in ibid., 109 ("designed . . . them"). See also ibid., 94.

47 Dewey qtd. in ibid., 98 ("native impulses," " to communicate . . . finer form"). For a description of the principles and curriculum of the Chicago Laboratory School, see ibid., 104–11. For a fuller account of Dewey's relation to Addams and Hull House, see Knight, *Citizen*, 237–40, and Menand, *Metaphysical Club*, 285–333.

48 Ginger, *Altgeld's America*, 8 (Marshall Field), 10 ("turned back . . . humanism"). See also ibid., 1–14. Browne, *Altgeld of Illinois*, 223 ("spoilsmen"). See also Addams, *My Friend, Julia Lathrop*, 48–69.

49 See Badger, *Great American Fair*, xi–xiii.

50 Kelley qtd. in Sklar, *Florence Kelley*, 242 ("by far . . . beheld"). See *Encyclopedia of Chicago*, 898–902. See Day, *Best of Clarence Day*, 147–55.

51 Addams, *My Friend, Julia Lathrop*, 83 ("the World's Fair bequeathed . . . smallpox epidemic"). For the number of smallpox cases (1,407), see Sklar, *Florence Kelley*, 265.

52 Polacheck, *I Came a Stranger*, 51 ("huge bundles . . . the bastings").

53 Qtd. in Sklar, *Florence Kelley*, 266 ("the smooth path . . . is bought").

54 See Kelley, *First Special Report*, 7: "We obtained from the city board of health a daily list of cases of infectious disease, compared these addresses with our office lists, and made immediate inspections of shops in and near the infected premises. In the course of these inspections we found so many cases of small-pox which had not been reported to us that we soon ceased to depend on the city hall lists alone, and supplemented them with the daily lists of diagnoses of the district physicians, of which the number varied . . . from 30 to 47 in a single district in a day." For "Record of Illustrative Cases" found by Lathrop and Kelley, see ibid., 10–40. Addams, *Twenty Years at Hull-House*, 162 ("Miss Lathrop went . . . the city"). Note: Because she was not an employee of the Illinois factory inspector group, Lathrop's name does not appear in the above-quoted report.

55 Bruce qtd. in Addams, *My Friend, Julia Lathrop*, 83 ("risking their lives . . . human lives"). On Chicago officials' connivance, see Kelley, *First Special Report*, 42. Miller, *City of the Century*, 458–59 ("scandalously mismanaged"). For a fuller account of the smallpox episode, see Sklar, *Florence Kelley*, 266–68.

56 Lathrop, "Cook County Charities," 144 ("all the resources . . . aid"), 156 ("only place . . . penniless convalescent").

57 Ibid., 160–61 ("necessities . . . care for them"), 148 ("universal dread").

58 Wyckoff, *Workers*, 2:61–62 ("general business depression . . . and children").

59 Lathrop, "Cook County Charities," 158–59 ("human *debris* . . . hard soap").

60 Ibid., 147 ("melancholy company . . . children"), 150 ("very hard"), 153 ("cheap cuts . . . an hour"), 149 ("hideous . . . homely comfort"), 153 ("too few . . . exercise").

61 Ibid., 149 ("Oh— . . . away from us," "monotony and dullness"), 153 ("unutterable dreariness"), 146 ("hours of listless idleness").

62 On blacks' aversion to the institutionalization of family members, see Addams, *My Friend, Julia Lathrop*, 66.

63 Lathrop, "Cook County Charities," 160–61 ("crudeness of the management," "shocking").

64 Ibid., 153 ("pull"), 160–61 ("charities . . . divorced from them").

65 Lathrop qtd. in Addams, *My Friend, Julia Lathrop*, 63 ("high ideals . . . vale of discouragement").

66 The large public institutions included Jacksonville State Hospital, which the Illinois legislature built in 1851 when Dorothea Dix persuaded it of the public obligation to care for the insane. There were also Elgin in northern Illinois and Anna State Hospital to the south, as well as Kankakee and the new Chester State Hospital for the criminally insane. Addams, *My Friend, Julia Lathrop*, 59 ("every . . . almshouses"), 66 ("coal

. . . supplies"). Lathrop qtd. in ibid., 59–60 ("staring into space . . . day after day"). *Sangamon County Alms House*, 136 ("olde & infirm . . . pox, child").

67 Eggleston, *Hoosier Schoolmaster*, 204–5 ("like chickens . . . chronic lunacy").

68 Lathrop, *Suggestions for Institution Visitors*, 35–36 ("wayward," "temptation," "orderly living"). On children's sleeping provisions and boys' smoking, see Bowen, *Growing Up with a City*, 72, 107–8. Lathrop, introduction, 1–2 ("lockups"). Other criminalized juvenile offenses included "building bonfires, playing ball in the street, and 'flipping trains,' that is, jumping on and off moving cars. . . . The offences of Chicago children were dealt with under the same laws and in the same courts as were the offences of adults" (Lathrop, Introduction, 1–2).

69 Virtually everyone who had dealings with Julia Lathrop lauded her graciousness, charm, good humor, patience, and tact. Linn, *Jane Addams*, 134 ("as good as . . . wait for results"). Tributes to the social efficacy of Lathrop's personal qualities appear from diverse sources in Addams, *My Friend, Julia Lathrop*, 42, 45, 61, 63, 107.

    See Spears, *Chicago Dreaming*, 193–98, for an analysis of a 1914 novel, *The Precipice*, that may indirectly critique Lathrop and the Hull House social work tradition.

70 Addams, *My Friend, Julia Lathrop*, 66 ("harmony . . . shirtwaist").

71 Hamilton qtd. in Addams, *My Friend, Julia Lathrop*, 61 ("sulky and suspicious . . . friendly").

72 Hamilton qtd. in ibid. ("proceed . . . unsaid").

73 Lathrop, "Background of the Juvenile Court," 291 ("other clubs . . . philanthropic"). Lathrop cited the support of judges; prison wardens; public-spirited physicians, lawyers, and clergymen; the State Board of Charities; the State Federation of Clubs; and the Bar Association (ibid., 293).

74 Bowen, *Growing Up with a City*, 104–5 ("absolutely nothing . . . delicacy of an Ariel").

75 Emerson, *Abraham Lincoln*, 7–9 ("inspiration . . . for months").

76 *Encyclopedia of Chicago*, 360 ("Gray Wolf," who "traded votes for favors").

77 Bowen, *Growing Up with a City*, 119 ("hardly knew where to begin").

78 Beecher and Stowe, *American Woman's Home*, 111–12 ("muscles . . . to move"). Costin, *Two Sisters for Social Justice*, 100 ("power . . . sympathy"), viii ("sociologist and statistician"). See Schocket, *Vanishing Moments*, 132–33. Costin, *Two Sisters for Social Justice*, viii, links Lathrop with the Progressives Edith and Grace Abbott as a newer type of social reformer, "the professional expert who took on the role of social engineer." It is significant that, toward the end of her career, Josephine Shaw Lowell, whose Charity Organization Society long operated on the principle that the poor were morally defective and must be taught discipline, now recognized that the plight of the poor was "not due usually to moral or intellectual defects" but to "economic causes over which they had no control, and which were as much beyond their power to avert as if they had been natural calamities of fire, flood, or storm" (qtd. in Burrows and Wallace, *Gotham*, 1187–88).

79 Lathrop, *Suggestions for Institution Visitors*, 6 ("friendly co-operation and helpfulness"), 8 ("tact and patience"). See also ibid., 44.

80 Ibid., 9 ("Buildings," "Fire-escape"), 15 ("Care of Inmates," "Cleanliness").

81 See Shoemaker, "Jane Addams and the Settlement House Movement," 134. In 1894, Taylor had started a settlement house that he modeled on Hull House. Committed

to applied Christianity, he opened his Chicago Commons in an immigrant neighborhood in the northwest part of the city. By 1901, the commons operated a five-story building comparable in facilities to Hull House (see *Encyclopedia of Chicago*, 133).

82 For the origins and basis of this newer approach, see Devine, *When Social Work Was Young*, 21–66. See Sinclair Lewis's indictment of the Charity Organization Society in the novel *Elmer Gantry*, 372.

83 Day, *Best of Clarence Day*, 293.

84 During the Altgeld years in Illinois (1893–97), Lathrop had helped put a civil service system in place for the recruitment of physicians at the state hospitals, which gave her confidence that the high-quality experts within the civil service could be the arm of government best able to strengthen social democracy. Shoemaker, "Jane Addams and the Settlement House Movement," 148 ("study of the apparatus . . . Philanthropy"). See Van Riper, *History of the United States Civil Service*, and Johnson and Libecap, *Federal Civil Service System*.

85 On the Abbott sisters and Breckenridge, see Costin, *Two Sisters for Social Justice*.

86 The bureau was forbidden to provide medical services or direct aid, so public education was key. See Bradbury, *Five Decades of Action for Children*, 9: In her first annual bureau report, Lathrop announced the "first series of pamphlets . . . with the questions affecting the youngest lives of the Nation." Available free of charge, *Prenatal Care* (1913) called for women to take care of themselves while pregnant. Seventy percent of the infants who died within the first month, the bureau found, were the casualties of poor prenatal care and birth injury. *Prenatal Care* promoted personal hygiene and provided tips on nursing and caring for a newborn (see Ladd-Taylor, *Raising a Baby the Government Way*, 34–35). The reception of *Infant Care* (1914), the follow-up pamphlet, measured Congress's support for the bureau as members began to request copies for their constituents, who found advice on sunshine, pure air, pure water, and milk that was certified to be clean. Once again, Lathrop navigated the treacherous waters between the bureau and the doctors, assuring readers that *Infant Care* was not meant to "substitute for the care and advice of a physician" (qtd. in Ladd-Taylor, *Raising a Baby the Government Way*, 33). *Infant Care* became a runaway success, with nearly 3 million copies in circulation over the next decade, and a hefty series of other pamphlets followed, all free of charge. See Tobey, *Children's Bureau*, 15.

87 Lindenmeyer, *Right to Childhood*, 2 ("minors . . . little political voice"). Lathrop, like Florence Kelley, evidently continued to follow the demographic paradigm set by the pioneering labor statistician Carroll D. Wright, who in 1875 conducted what Horowitz, in *Morality of Spending*, 13, calls a "path-breaking study of laborers' household budgets." For Wright, says Horowitz, the ability of the male head of the household to provide decent conditions for his family was the linchpin, since he objected to the employment of young children and opposed wives' working outside the home, finding that alternative "baneful in its effects, and a false economy in the end" (Horowitz, *Morality of Spending*, 16).

88 Lindenmeyer, *Right to Childhood*, 2–3 ("contributed . . . Social Security Act"). Trattner qtd. in ibid., 3 ("central . . . United States").

89 "About the Children's Bureau," *Administration for Children and Families*, <http://www.acf.hhs.gov/programs/cb/aboutcb/about_cb.htm> ("Children's Bureau . . . commu-

nities"). Lathrop qtd. in Bradbury, *Five Decades of Action for Children*, 13 ("We cannot help . . . his race or color").

CHAPTER 4

1   Kelley, "Need of Theoretical Preparation for Philanthropic Work," 94 ("Content to . . . thousands"), 92 ("sense of right").
2   Kelley, *Some Ethical Gains through Legislation*, 23 ("grip car"). Bay, in *John Crerar Library*, n.p., reports that in 1899, the library housed about 11,000 volumes and 171 periodicals. See also Bay, *John Crerar Library*, 105, 107.
3   Kelley qtd. in Sklar, *Florence Kelley*, 287 ("drudgery").
4   Kelley, "Early Days at Hull House," 427 ("flutelike voice"). Goldmark, *Impatient Crusader*, 72 ("built on large lines," "direct and fearless"). Blumberg, *Florence Kelley*, 89 ("squarish jaw").
5   Beckner, *History of Labor Legislation in Illinois*, 263 ("workshops . . . establishments").
6   Blumberg, *Florence Kelley*, 134 ("any branch of manufacture").
7   Goldmark, *Impatient Crusader*, 34 ("junket . . . ever beheld"). See Kelley, *Third Annual Report*, 49: "The tenement house shop may be . . . in a basement so low, damp and dark that its walls drip slime." On middle-class salaries of this period, see Schlereth, *Victorian America*, 82–83. Kelley qtd. in Blumberg, *Florence Kelley*, 135 ("the long hours . . . a thing of the past").
8   Kelley, *Third Annual Report*, 10 ("cut the hide . . . cattle").
9   Qtd. in ibid., 14 ("light and easy"). Ibid., 15–17 ("young children . . . cooling glass"). The danger and physical exhaustion of young girls at work in glass factories is represented in Alice Hegan Rice's novel *Calvary Alley*, 147–53: "Girls were crowded at machines and tables, filing, clipping and packing bottles. [Nance's] task was to take the screw-neck bottles that came from the leer [conveyer belt], and chip and file their jagged necks until all the roughness was removed. It was dirty work, and dangerous. . . . It was a blow to find that . . . the cleverest girl in the finishing room had been filing bottle necks for four years. [Nance] stole a glance at her stooped shoulders and sallow skin and the hideous, empty socket of her left eye that was lost to flying glass."
10 Kelley, *Third Annual Report*, 19 ("Exhausted . . . washing machine"), 20 ("worked last Saturday . . . 3 o'clock").
11 Ibid., 26 ("body and mind . . . stimulants").
12 Kelley, *Some Ethical Gains through Legislation*, 50 ("false ideal"). Rice, *Calvary Alley*, 37 ("habit of industry . . . young"). Rice's fictional character voices the position of those believing child labor to be basic to the formation of character. Kelley, *Some Ethical Gains through Legislation*, 12 ("perverted"). See also Kelley, *Some Ethical Gains through Legislation*, 63: "The insistent plea that children must work in order that they may acquire habits of thrift and attain prosperity for themselves and their families is uttered with greatest persistence by the employers who profit by the labor of the children."
13 Lack of space for working-class public school children is emphasized in Rice, *Calvary Alley*, 62: "The truant officer said she must go [to school] every day, yet when she got there, there was no room for her."

14 Kelley, *Some Ethical Gains through Legislation*, 112–13 ("prosperous circumstances . . . unqualified right").

15 Ibid., 106 ("establishment . . . people"). See ibid., 105–26 ("The Right to Leisure").

16 *Speech of Hon. William Kelley*, 24 ("dirt-eaters . . . laborer's child"). Florence Kelley qtd. in Sklar, *Florence Kelley*, 29 ("terrible . . . gnomes").

17 See Sinclair, *Jungle*, 197, for a description of the Bessemer steel process. Florence Kelley qtd. in Sklar, *Florence Kelley*, 45–46 ("blower dogs . . . with products"). In 1882, William Kelley also took Florence to the "Black Country" of the English Midlands, where she visited the cottage of "a poor woman working in a lean-to at the back of her two-room cottage, hammering chains on an anvil." Kelley learned that the woman could not earn enough money making chains to send her three children to school and thereby broke the mandatory school laws and was arrested and fined: "Her tears fell on the anvil as she told us" (qtd. in Sklar, *Florence Kelley*, 66–67). *Autobiography of Florence Kelley*, 71 ("pasty-faced . . . mills").

18 For the full exchange between Kelley and the prosecutor, see *Autobiography of Florence Kelley*, 86.

19 Qtd. in Blumberg, *Florence Kelley*, 130 ("home," "deprive"). See Sklar, *Florence Kelley*, 219.

20 Levine, *Women's Garment Workers*, 513 ("contracted . . . machine"). Beckner, *History of Labor Legislation in Illinois*, 258–60 ("that was heavy . . . dyes").

21 Levine, *Women's Garment Workers*, 20 ("large . . . shop"). On fabrics and trim, see Snyder-Haug, *Antique and Vintage Clothing*, 35. Kelley, *Third Annual Report*, 67 ("dirty . . . and summer").

22 Bisno, *Union Pioneer*, 207–8 ("very cheaply . . . their living"), 221 ("suffered . . . industry").

23 Kelley, *Third Annual Report*, 19 ("When a girl . . . his terms"). Gompers, *Seventy Years of Life and Labor*, 1:278–79 ("oppression," "cruelty," "where they worked . . . low wages"). Note: No matter how poor Bisno was or how severe his own family's straits, he could never bring himself to take the Beifeld path to prosperity. Exhausted and unemployed, he turned to his skilled trade, tailoring. See Montgomery, *Fall of the House of Labor*, 116–70, for an account of the rise of the specialized worker, including garment industry operatives.

24 Bisno so testified before the Illinois investigative committee in 1893, according to Sklar, "Hull House in the 1890s," 674.

25 See Sklar, *Florence Kelley*, 248: Kelley wrote to Governor Altgeld, "We won our first jury case today. . . . There was a certain pleasure in beating them today." Schorman, *Selling Style*, 47 ("up to date"), 49 ("distinctive"), 47 ("true lady . . . from her").

26 On the "sweater," see Florence Kelley, *First Annual Report of the Factory Inspectors of Illinois* (1894), excerpted in "Florence Kelley and the Illinois Sweatshop Law," *Women and Social Movements in the United States, 1600-2000*, <http://womhist.alexanderstreet.com/teacher/DBQfactory7.htm>.

27 On the early days of the Northwestern University law school, see *Encyclopedia of Chicago*, 656. See also Williamson, *Northwestern University*, 49, 57, and *Autobiography of Florence Kelley*, 86: "Credit was given for my reading law with father in Washington in 1882, my study in Zurich, and one year in the senior [law] class in Chicago. The lec-

tures were given in the evening and did not interfere with my administrative work." Kelley's law degree entitled her "to practice before the Supreme Court in Illinois."

28   See Sklar, *Florence Kelley*, 248, 255. On the national market for Beifeld products, see Howard, "Beifeld Cloak."

29   Beckner, *History of Labor Legislation in Illinois*, 188–90 ("fundamental right . . . specific period"). The court saw a restriction of contractual rights, meaning the freedom of a woman to enter freely into an agreement to work as many hours as she wished in order to "acquire and possess property of every kind," meaning wages (ibid.).

30   Kelley, *Third Annual Report*, 23 ("to all comers," "reckless").

31   *Autobiography of Florence Kelley*, 77 ("welcomed," "invited"). Goldmark, *Impatient Crusader*, 48 ("cell").

32   See Sklar, *Florence Kelley*, 286. See also Fairchild, "Factory Legislation of the State of New York," 110–11.

33   See Goldmark, *Impatient Crusader*, 32: "In writing her Cornell thesis she [Kelley] had discovered how to use the British Factory Inspectors' Reports, the best research material on her subject." Kelley's undergraduate senior thesis was published as "On Some Changes in the Legal Status of the Child since Blackstone."

34   See Nathan, *Once upon a Time and Today*, 134–35, which recounts a conversation in which Roosevelt, as New York governor, explained that although the labor unions and the Consumers' League of New York City urged him to appoint "a certain experienced woman" of "splendid qualifications," i.e., Kelley, his male "constituents would expect him to appoint a man." See also Riis, *Making of an American*, 382: "I saw how faithfully [Theodore Roosevelt] labored. I was his umpire . . . in the enforcement of the Factory Law against sweaters, and I know . . . he had no other thought than how best to serve the people who trusted him."

35   See Piepmeier, *Out in Public*, on Victorian women in the public sphere.

36   Goldmark, *Impatient Crusader*, 72 ("deep organ tones," "little frightening"). Kelley, "Early Days at Hull House," 427 ("hurricane"). Hamilton, *Exploring the Dangerous Trades*, 61–62 ("foolish . . . attitudes"). Linn, *Jane Addams*, 139 ("bursting vitality"), 140 ("dismaying energy"), 137 ("fierceness"). Goldmark, in *Impatient Crusader*, 72, wrote, "No other man or woman whom I have ever heard so blended knowledge of facts, wit, satire, burning indignation, prophetic denunciation."

37   William Kelley qtd. in Sklar, *Florence Kelley*, 29 ("great industries . . . distributed justly").

38   *Autobiography of Florence Kelley*, 62–63 ("new wildfire . . . Continent"). On Kelley's translation of Engels, see Sklar, *Florence Kelley*, 100–104. See Goldmark, *Impatient Crusader*, 17: "The force of [Engels's] book lay mainly in the evidence of the official British reports quoted by Engels, such as the Children's Factory Commission of 1833 and the Factories Inquiry of 1842. Doctors, factory inspectors, poor law and sanitary visitors, all painted a dreadful picture of misery and degeneration following the incredibly long hours of work, starvation wages, and other hardships of men, women, and little children employed in the early factory period." On Kelley's resignation from the Socialist Labor Party but commitment to socialist principles, see *Autobiography of Florence Kelley*, 73–74, which recounts a socialist meeting in Zurich at which she grasped the flaw in her father's U.S. tariff policy: "Before midnight every aspect of the tariff that I had ever heard or read of was presented, plus one that was utterly new to

me, as a serious middle-aged Swiss railroad man argued: 'There is an objection that has not been mentioned. We are internationalists; we are intimately acquainted with the textile industries; we should not fail to consider the effect on the producers of raw silk in the Orient that the [proposed German] tariff will involve, if prices of silk products in Germany are to be raised. . . . As internationalists, should we give our assent to this lowering of the standard of fellow workers on the other side of the globe?'"

39 The Jack London Collection at the Huntington Library, San Marino, California, includes a copy of Kelley's translation of Engels. See Chace, *1912*, 182–83: "By 1912 the Socialists were seen as an increasingly reasonable alternative to the two major parties. In the 1911 elections, American voters elected some 450 Socialist officials, including 56 mayors and 3065 aldermen and city councilmen, and 1 congressman."

40 Sklar, *Florence Kelley*, 307 ("Modern Socialism at Work"). See Mooney, *John Graham Brooks*, 26: "Brooks treated of the charities, of the danger of great city life, of the tramp question, and of the criminal indifference of society and of the poor." Sklar, in *Florence Kelley*, 154–55, 108–9, 162, documents the extent to which Kelley criticized Bellamy and Ely for doctrines she considered, respectively, too authoritarian and insufficiently rigorous. Sklar, *Florence Kelley*, 108 ("dynamite warfare").

41 Kelley qtd. in Sklar, *Florence Kelley*, 274 ("slum . . . an hour"). Linn, *Jane Addams*, 139 ("negligence of appearance").

42 See Kelley, "Early Days at Hull House," 426 ("chicks"), 427 ("street Arab"). Kelley repeatedly referred to her children collectively as "chicks," "bairns," and "brood." Hamilton, *Exploring the Dangerous Trades*, 100 ("dust").

43 See Sklar, *Florence Kelley*, 287. The Kelley children were sometimes enrolled in boarding school; Margaret's fees were paid by Smith.

44 Qtd. in Kelley, *Third Annual Report*, 22 ("wild"), 26 ("little girls," "forced"), 217 ("through . . . frequent occurrence").

45 Sklar, *Florence Kelley*, 27 ("No sisters . . . winnowing"), 27–28 ("entrenched sorrow," "permanent . . . melancholy").

46 See Brooks, *Social Unrest*, 101: An ordained minister, Brooks had resigned from pastoral duties, discouraged by a "slow decay of authority in religion" and the belief that churches too often used their power "to quiet the masses and reconcile them to their lot." Brooks saw the conditions of working-class life while serving churches in Boston's Roxbury section and in working-class Brockton, Massachusetts. Both churches exposed him to families trapped in the same grinding struggles as the residents of Chicago's Nineteenth Ward. The well-traveled, cosmopolitan Brooks became a reformer, joining reform groups and studying issues of labor and capital, housing, health care, and social policy in western Europe. In 1899, he was writing *The Social Unrest* to give a clear picture of U.S. labor-capital strife and increasing machine automation. He was also intrigued by the problems of cities and towns trying to decide what was in the public interest and what belonged separately to entrepreneurs and to business—such as water, electricity, gas, and transportation services. Brooks was to put *The Social Unrest* into the hands of other reformers, such as Theodore Roosevelt. See Mooney, *John Graham Brooks*, 11–12: "The Boston into which Brooks had emerged . . . was the locale of active movements in reform . . . [including] the New England Reform League . . . the Eight Hour League . . . the Knights of St. Crispin and the Massachusetts Labor Union."

47 Cronon, *Nature's Metropolis*, 340 ("Wherever . . . it came from"). For a discussion of the mail-order business centered in Chicago and the ways in which merchandise obscured its sources, see ibid., 336–40.

48 For an account of preliminary National Consumers' League activities, see Goldmark, *Impatient Crusader*, 51–55. Brooks, *Social Unrest*, 2 ("stuffy . . . theatre"). Lowell qtd. in Waugh, *Unsentimental Reformer*, 201 ("it will be . . . by everybody").

49 On commodity bulk merchandise, see Cornell, *Traders Ready Reckoner*, 184–85. Brooks, *Social Unrest*, 267–68 ("as if the trolley . . . trade").

50 On department store displays and lighting, see Strasser, *Satisfaction Guaranteed*, 209, 211.

51 See MacLean, "Two Weeks in Department Stores." Kelley, *Modern Industry*, 129 ("poisonous"). See Willard, *Occupations for Women*, 94: "Many of the department stores are killing places: killing not only because of the work, which keeps a girl for almost the entire time on her feet, but . . . because of the sightless corners in which clerks are confined, the inhumanly small wages which afford only mean lodgings, poor food and tawdry clothing; killing because [there is] . . . nothing to give dignity of feeling or stimulation of thought." See also Sklar, *Florence Kelley*, 306–7. See also Waugh, *Unsentimental Reformer*, 197–98, on the investigation of working conditions in department stores by the Working Women's Society of the City of New York: "The Society's secretary, Alice Woodbridge, had worked in department stores herself and became an expert in eliciting testimony from frightened salesgirls." On wages paid by Field, see Urofsky, "Louis D. Brandeis, Progressivism," 2.

52 On sponsors of Kelley's nomination to head the National Consumers' League, see Sklar, *Florence Kelley*, 310.

53 For Kelley's account of the Zurich years, see *Autobiography of Florence Kelley*, 69–72. On Zurich, see also Brooks, *Social Unrest*, 29–30, 52, 213, 216; Sklar, *Florence Kelley*, 82–86; Baedeker, *Switzerland and the Adjacent Portions*, 32–38; and Blumberg, *Florence Kelley*, 36.

54 On Kelley's mention of her marriage, see *Autobiography of Florence Kelley*, 45–53. See also Goldmark, *Impatient Crusader*, 18: "Only once or twice in the course of our long intimacy did she speak to me about [her marriage, indicating that marriage] was worth all the cost" and adding, "Let no one wish to undo what satisfied the deepest of human instincts." For a detailed account of these years, see Sklar, *Florence Kelley*, 93–139.

55 Wells, *Manners*, 25 ("delicate . . . intrusiveness"). See also ibid., 36.

56 See *Beifeld Catalogue*, n.p.: "Do not confuse these summer skirts with the cheap, trashy, ill-fitting sweat-shop skirts that usually flood the market this season of the year." During the 1893 smallpox outbreak, Kelley discovered a case of smallpox in the sweatshop of a Beifeld subcontractor. See Kelley, *First Special Report*, 46: "723 Severson St., M. Belinsky, contractor for Joseph Beifeld & Co." A multimillionaire clothing manufacturer, Beifeld was emerging as a power in Chicago real estate development. He was a major investor in—and soon president of—the Midwest's largest amusement park, White City, which opened on Chicago's South Side in 1905 and featured a water chute ride and an electric tower designed to echo the famed Beaux-Arts White City of the World's Fair of 1893. Beifeld invested millions of dollars, in addition, in the renovation of the venerable Sherman Hotel, whose "famed restaurant, the Col-

lege Inn," became "the talk of the town, increasingly frequented by local celebrities and members of high society" ("Hotel Sherman," *Jazz Age Chicago*, June 20, 1998, <http://chicago.urban-history.org/ven/hls/sherman.shtml>). See also *Encyclopedia of Chicago*, 176–78. Beifeld also supported Jewish causes, becoming a patron of the Jewish Publication Society of America.

57 Mooney, *John Graham Brooks*, 43 ("rambling farmhouse . . . Ledges"). Fuller, *Great Lawsuit*, 1190 ("platform . . . stand"). Fuller, *Great Lawsuit*, 1190, continues, "But how to get the platform, or how to make it of reasonable access is the difficulty."

58 "A Fine Sunday Outdoors," *New York Times*, May 2, 1899 ("summer-like sunshine . . . Sunday idlers").

59 Hired as corresponding secretary, Kelley promptly renamed the position "general secretary," today's equivalent of the title "executive director." Kisseloff, *You Must Remember This*, 5 ("pushcart dealers . . . trusses"). Wald, *House on Henry Street*, 5 ("odorous fish-stands," "uncovered garbage-cans").

60 Wald, *House on Henry Street*, 3 ("dense industrial population"). Woods and Kennedy, *Handbook of Settlements*, 205 ("proposed to move . . . democratic community"). See also Burrows and Wallace, *Gotham*, 1175–76: "Wald, raised in a comfortable bourgeois Rochester family, came to study at New York Hospital's School of Nursing in 1889. After graduating in 1891, she worked for a year at an orphan asylum, enrolled for a time in Elizabeth Blackwell's Women's Medical College, then taught a course in home nursing at an East Side program. With financial backers, she was joined by her nursing classmate, Mary Brewster, in establishing a visiting nurse service operated from an apartment on Jefferson Street, then expanding in 1895 into the Henry Street Settlement, called the Nurses Settlement."

61 Wald, *House on Henry Street*, 5 ("roofs and masses"), 3 ("with the last slave gallery," "'Boss' Tweed's"). See also Wald, *Windows on Henry Street*, 12–13, 18, 21.

62 Wald, *Windows on Henry Street*, 18 ("dirty tenements . . . saloons"). Kelley, *Some Ethical Gains through Legislation*, 12 ("little mothers . . . scrubbing brush"). See also Kelley, *Some Ethical Gains through Legislation*, 9, 16.

63 Oppel, *Tales of Gaslight New York*, 93 ("happiest people"), 129–37 ("kindergarten" conditions), 187–98 (on swimming). See Kisseloff, *You Must Remember This*, 19, for the oral history of Dr. Robert Leslie (b. 1885) of Lower East Side life in the 1890s: "There were no parks at the time. . . . The only recreation was to go down to the East River where the barges were. The people would swim in it, but they also moved their bowels there."

64 Wald, *House on Henry Street*, 149 ("premature employment"). See also ibid., 135–68. Kelley, *Some Ethical Gains through Legislation*, 3 ("to become . . . citizens"). Wald, *Windows on Henry Street*, 15 ("to participate . . . dignity").

65 Day, *Best of Clarence Day*, 164 ("Russians . . . down in the slums"). James, *American Scene*, 84–86 ("million . . . machinery").

66 See Waugh, *Unsentimental Reformer*, 176, describing the United Charities Building in 1893 as occupied by the Charity Organization Society, the Association for the Improvement of the Conditions of the Poor, the Children's Aid Society, and the New York City Mission and Tract Society. See also Goldmark, *Impatient Crusader*, 68–69: After 1900, the building housed "a variety of new social movements," such as the National Child Labor Committee and the editorial office of the *Survey* under the leader-

ship of Paul Kellogg. See Kelley, *Some Ethical Gains through Legislation*, 10, for the possibility that moving into her office in the former church "secular temple" prompted Kelley's thought that "in the Republic, childhood must be sacred to preparation for citizenship." On the description of Kelley's National Consumers' League office, see Mary Dewson to Florence Kelley, Mar. 27, 1923, NCL, reel 25. See also Kellogg, "Living Spirit of Florence Kelley," 8. On Kelley's typing skill, see Sklar, *Florence Kelley*, 284. The National Consumers' League was to relocate several times in New York City in the years ahead. By 1915, it occupied offices in the Craftsman Building at 6 East Thirty-ninth Street, and in 1918 it was located at 289 Fourth Avenue. In 1920, the league address was 44 East Twenty-third Street, and in 1925 it moved to Fifth Avenue. On the "thoroughly presentable and reasonably attractive" staff, see Florence Kelley to Grace Abbott, Apr. 7, 1927, NCL, reel 23.

67 Waugh, *Unsentimental Reformer*, 197–99 ("loving face . . . society ladies").

68 Ibid., 199 ("Standard of a Fair House," "White List"). Consumers' League of New York City, *Annual Report* (1897), NCL, reel 112 ("dormant"). See also Consumers' League of New York City, *Annual Report* (1897): "Being on the White List was considered by many businesses [at first] as a punishment, not a reward, for good labor practices. . . . Yet the [league] women persevered, and in a relatively short time they were pleased to announce that thirty-one establishments had made the White List. . . . The businesses named were among the most prominent, and it was hoped that they would set a shining example for the others." See also Sklar, *Florence Kelley*, 308–11. See also U.S. Bureau of Labor Statistics, *Conciliation, Arbitration, and Sanitation*, 33: "One of the new features of the dress and waist industry, as distinguishing it from the protocol in the cloak and suit industry, is the provision for the introduction . . . of the so-called white label. Whenever complete and regular inspection of the entire industry is fully under way and certificates are issued to the shops maintaining adequate standards, the chain of evidence is to be carried one link farther—the garment itself is to be certified by the board, so that the consumer will know the condition under which the garment was made."

69 See Waugh, *Unsentimental Reformer*, 100–101.

70 See U.S. Bureau of Labor Statistics, *Conciliation, Arbitration, and Sanitation*, 35–39: In 1915, the Bureau of Labor Statistics of the U.S. Department of Labor reported that a labor-management settlement "in the dress and [shirt]waist industry in New York (as distinct from the cloak and suit industry) included provisions for the inspection of manufacturing sites and certification of garments by the sewn-in white label."

71 For Kelley's label idea, see Sklar, *Florence Kelley*, 309. See also Goldmark, *Impatient Crusader*, 56–57. For a list of manufacturers authorized to use the White Label as of March 1907, see NCL, reel 3. On Kelley's great-aunt Sarah Pugh, see Sklar, *Florence Kelley*, 22.

72 See Florence Kelley, "Minimum Wage Laws" (1913), 3–4, NCL, reel 100: "In this country a statute is only a trial draft until the Supreme Court of the United States has passed upon it." On the National Association of Manufacturers' "Declaration of Principles," see Steigerwalt, *National Association of Manufacturers*, appendix C, 186: The association "is unalterably opposed to boycotts, blacklists and other illegal acts of interference with the personal liberty of employer or employe [*sic*]." For Kelley's

expression of suspicion that the National Association of Manufacturers might subvert the league by "posing as a friend," see Florence Kelley to Mrs. Cushing, June 29, 1928, NCL, reel 24.

73 James, "Energies of Men," 230 ("mental machinery"), 228 ("vital energy in gear"). See Holbrook, "Florence Kelley," 34: "With one of the smallest annual budgets of any of the national social service organizations (never more than $35,000), the National Consumers' League under Mrs. Kelley's leadership from its organization in 1899 has been a medium for . . . services that could never have been paid for." See *Summary Statement of the Work of the First Year of the National Consumers' League, 1899* (May 1, 1900), NCL, reel 113, in which Kelley announced the formation of the Finance Committee: "As the work of the National Consumers' League expands, its expenditures naturally increase with the growing demand for literature, lectures, organizing leagues in states previously not organized and especially for visiting and revisiting factories for purposes of inspection." See also Florence Kelley to Miss Susan R. Gillean, Dec. 13, 1913, NCL, reel 25, proposing assessment of each league quarterly to offset the "deficit." See also "The Eighth Annual Session of the [National Consumers' League] Council, 1907," NCL, reel 3: "Mrs Kelley . . . stated that the League is rapidly outgrowing its finances." For a summary overview of the National Consumers' League, see Storrs, *Civilizing Capitalism*, 13–90.

74 Josephine Goldmark's *Fatigue and Efficiency* began with her chairmanship of the National Consumers' League Committee on the Legal Defense of Labor Laws in 1908 (see ibid., vii). Kelley also appointed a Committee on Legislation. See National Consumers' League, *Sixth Annual Report* (1905), including article II of the league's constitution, 3, 6, NCL, reel 4.

75 On the history of women's labor unions, see Kessler-Harris, *Gendering Labor History*. W. E. B. Du Bois, "Memorial Meeting in Honor of Florence Kelley" (Mar. 16, 1932), 19–20, NCL, reel 118 ("dared . . . galvanized").

76 Kelley to Abbott, Apr. 7, 1927 ("investigator's nose . . . piquancy"). For Kelley's plan to motivate league members with annual meetings, see Florence Kelley to Miss K. L. Trevett, Oct. 3, 1917, NCL, reel 34. For the menu and venue for a banquet honoring Kelley's work, held on November 29, 1927, see program for National Consumers' League meeting, NCL, reel 5. The National Consumers' League compiled annual extensive international bibliographies of publications relevant to its goals. See, for instance, the bibliography compiled by Margaret L. Franklin, NCL, reel 114.

77 Linn, *Jane Addams*, 139 ("evidence . . . invective"). Stead, *If Christ Came to Chicago*, 25 ("Rembrandtesque"). See Kelley, *Modern Industry*, 72: "Instead of abstract discussions of abstract freedom, the [proper] procedure is, to-day, to ascertain the exact facts, to show what the existing working hours [of employees] are, what other nations and states have done about it, and what the medical profession has to say about it. The final deciding factor is not [employees'] 'freedom' but health." See also Mrs. Ramona T. Mattson to unknown recipient, Apr. 1, 1954, NCL, reel 25: Florence Kelley "knew the facts from A to Z."

78 Marchand, *Creating the Corporate Soul*. Kelley, *Some Ethical Gains through Legislation*, 33 ("to educate public opinion"). See also article II of the league's constitution in National Consumers' League, *Sixth Annual Report* (1905), 3.

79 On the Fourteenth Amendment, see Tindall and Shi, *America*, 707–8. National Con-

sumers' League, *Third Annual Report* (1902), 6, NCL, reel 7 ("guarantee . . . oppression").

80 See Kelley, *Modern Industry*, 71: "The Court was not acquainted with the trade life of bakers. It did not know that in American cities, thousands of bakers work underground, almost like miners." See Irons, *People's History of the Supreme Court*, 254–58, for the deliberate strategy by which the Court was encouraged by the plaintiff's lawyer to associate the work of bakers with home kitchens.

81 For a thorough account of the background of *Muller v. Oregon*, see Johnston, *Radical Middle Class*, 18–28.

82 Kellogg, "Living Spirit of Florence Kelley," 6 ("structural bent . . . for progress").

83 For the league's holiday campaign strategies, see Consumers' League of New Jersey, *Fiftieth Anniversary Booklet*, NCL, reel 113. *The National Consumers' League, First Quarter Century, 1899–1924*, 7, NCL, reel 113 ("charts . . . of goods," "suitcase exhibits"). For examples of National Consumers' League visual displays, see NCL, reel 114, which includes the records of Kelley's five noontime radio talks on WAHG in April–May 1925: "The Importance of Fathers," "Keeping Fathers Alive," "Next Steps in Social Work," "Social Work as It May Be in 1950," and "A Romance of Industry in California." The broadcasts were sponsored by A. H. Grebe and Company.

84 Goldmark, *Impatient Crusader*, 208 ("beautiful . . . she said"). From her teens, Kelley had an ear for her father's oratory in Congress. His rolling cadences in the House chamber and on the printed page became her own. Some sentences in her 1889 Philadelphia speech on patriot Thomas Paine could be mistaken for Congressman Kelley's. See Wischnewetzky, *Address in Memory of Thomas Paine*, 2: "The Great American Desert of Paine's day is the wheat-field of the nation, struggling with India and Russia for the mastery of the market of the world."

85 For Kelley's reading of Dickens, see Sklar, *Florence Kelley*, 34. See also Kelley, *Modern Industry*, 29 ("educational steerage"), 99 ("deprive . . . cash value"). See Kelley, *Working Child*, 4. See Kellogg, "Living Spirit of Florence Kelley," 5: "What she wrote was sheer joy . . . crisp, fact-riveted copy, with clarity, grasp and vigorous thrust to it [and editing] that buttressed some point or a turn of phrase that packed a surprise." Kelley, *Some Ethical Gains through Legislation*, 13 ("burden . . . the child").

86 "Retirement Community Slideshow," *Terpening Terrace*, 2001, <http://www.terpeningterrace.com/slide03a.htm> ("Ask the man . . . one"). "Kodak Music," *American Experience*, <http://www.pbs.org/wgbh/amex/eastman/sfeature/music.html> ("You press . . . the rest"). Basten, *Great American Billboards*, 7 ("spread for bread"), 8 ("relieves fatigue").

87 Kelley, *Some Ethical Gains through Legislation*, chap. 1 ("The Right to Childhood"), 34 ("immunity"). See also Mattson to unknown recipient, Apr. 1, 1954: "Figures of speech that listeners could not forget were one of Mrs. Kelley's greatest strengths. Wherever she talked she was at home. Delivery and voice were gold."

88 Alger qtd. in Goldmark, *Impatient Crusader*, 208 ("long warfare . . . economics").

89 "Eighth Annual Session of the [National Consumers' League] Council," 16 ("There should be . . . the country").

90 James, "Energies of Men," 230 ("some outer . . . some spiritual"), 228 ("set loose"), 220 ("enlargement of power"), 232 ("social convention"), 236 *"excitements, ideas, and efforts,"* 236). See also ibid., 222.

91 Ibid., 223 ("energy-releasing ideas"). Goldmark, *Impatient Crusader*, 208 ("everyone . . . her personality").

92 Twain, *Gilded Age*, 295 ("lecture platform"), 272 ("final resort," "disappointed"). Willard, *Occupations for Women*, 277–78 ("town in . . . district").

93 Addams qtd. in Goldmark, *Impatient Crusader*, 208–9 ("galvanized"). See also Kellogg, "Living Spirit of Florence Kelley," 7, and Louis Lyons, "Florence Kelley Labored Constantly for Welfare Legislation—First Woman Factory Inspector," *Boston Globe*, Feb. 18, 1932, NCL, reel 119. John Howland Lathrop, "Memorial Meeting in Honor of Florence Kelley" (typescript, Mar. 16, 1932), 3, NCL, reel 118 ("Niagara Falls"). Linn, *Jane Addams*, 139 ("power . . . for others"), 140 ("daughter . . . war"). See also Florence Kelley to John A. Fitch, Mar. 25, 1925, NCL, reel 25, in which Kelley considers herself a "raging furnace, consumed with burning indignation."

94 See *Summary Statement of the Work of the First Year*.

95 Ibid. Kelley's first annual league report admitted that "a severe attack of diphtheria contracted during a visit to Cleveland rendered all public speaking impossible for the space of two months." To appreciate Kelley's strategic multiple speaking engagements, see Florence Kelley to Mrs. [J. Borden] Harriman, Apr. 14, 1925, NCL, reel 26: "I am extremely happy to report that the California State Conference of Social Work has invited me to come (at its expense for the entire tour) to Sacramento for the whole term of its meetings, May 26th, 27th, and 28th, and to be principal speaker on the evening of the 28th. This enables me to attend, also, the national Conference of Social Work in Denver on the way back, almost without expense." On the growth of the league, see *National Consumers' League, First Quarter Century*, 4.

96 Goldmark, *Impatient Crusader*, 143 ("turning point . . . history"), 150–51 ("Not for nothing . . . lasting friendships").

97 Qtd. in Todd, *Justice on Trial*, 57 ("big, husky . . . wanted her to").

98 Goldmark, *Impatient Crusader*, 151 ("every facility"), 153 ("mounting pile . . . pages"), 152 ("few"), 157 ("immersed . . . conglomerate"), 159 ("well satisfied"). For an account of the league's appeal to Brandeis in the Oregon case, see ibid., 151–59.

99 On the second *Ritchie* case, see Beckner, *History of Labor Legislation in Illinois*, 198–201. National Consumers' League, *Annual Report* (1910), qtd. in Goldmark, *Impatient Crusader*, 162 ("fatigue," "reduced," "justified").

100 Brooks, *Consumers' League*, 18 ("cheap goods . . . working people"). Lowell qtd. in Waugh, *Unsentimental Reformer*, 201 ("honest hard work . . . poverty").

101 Kelley, "Minimum Wage Laws," 6 ("highest public . . . upon society"), 3 ("at the head of the procession"). For a listing of National Consumers' League pamphlet publications, see "Publications of the National Consumers' League," NCL, reel 114. See Kelley, "Minimum Wage Laws," 3, on Kelley's travel to Geneva for an international meeting of consumer leagues and allies in 1908, when she was heartened by the English Anti-sweating League summons to "agitate for the creation of official minimum wage boards."

    Attacks on Kelley, especially during the anti-red hysteria of the 1920s, prompted a spirited exchange with feminist Carrie Chapman Catt, who became alarmed at Kelley's apparent indifference to newspaper attacks on her as an anti-American socialist. The press used Kelley's translation of Engels as a smear tactic to impugn her patriotism, and she mostly ignored the attacks, believing her time better spent on behalf of children and women exploited by industry. Catt took up the defense of Kelley (and Jane Addams) against charges of sedition by the Daughters of the American Revolution and other groups, but she found Kelley less than appreciative of her efforts. See Carrie Chapman Catt to Florence Kelley, May 27, June 3, June 11, 1927, and Florence Kelley to Mrs. Catt, June 4, June 15, 1927, NCL, reel 24.

102 Devine, *Social Forces*, 25 ("in certain cotton-raising . . . for nurture"). *Consumers' League Bulletin*, Jan. 1915, NCL, reel 113 ("So little . . . working boys and girls"). See also National Consumers' League, *Annual Report* (1913), 10–11, NCL, reel 3.

103 Goldmark, *Impatient Crusader*, 48 ("whirligig of time"). On the death of Margaret Kelley, see ibid., 69–70.

104 On Kelley and the Women's Party, see ibid., 180–88.

105 Bertha Payne Newell to Miss Roche, Nov. 11, 1939, NCL, reel 118 ("vigorous ring . . . entrenched forces"). Written seven years after Kelley's death, this letter is a recollection.

106 Kelley qtd. in Lyons, "Florence Kelley Labored Constantly" ("I expect times . . . for idealism"). Goldmark, *Impatient Crusader*, 106 ("public protection . . . her philosophy"). Julia Lathrop to Florence Kelley, May 28, 1923, NCL, reel 28 ("q.c.," "quintessentially courageous").

107 Louis Lyons recounted, "A year ago [1931], she [Kelley] told me that she expected to live to be 100" (Lyons, "Florence Kelley Labored Constantly").

108 Newton Baker to Florence Kelley, Dec. 25, 1925, NCL, reel 23 ("people like you . . . good work"). John Haynes Holmes, Taylor Society Necrology, "Mrs. Florence Kelley" (1932), NCL, reel 118 ("her face . . . oppressed"). Correspondence from the mid-1920s registers Kelley's health problems. Baker hoped that Kelley "profited" from treatment for painful arthritis (Baker to Kelley, Dec. 25, 1925). See Florence Kelley to Grace Abbott, June 11, 1928, NCL, reel 23: "I came home sick, and am still demoralized, hobbling round like a lame old cow, feeling greatly exhausted by continuous pain. . . . I have developed such severe phlebitis that I shall have to keep my right leg up through the whole of my vacation, beginning by staying in bed a fortnight." See Kelley to Cushing, June 29, 1928: Kelley admitted being "below par as to my supply of vitality."

109 The Fair Labor Standards Act is published in sections 201–19 of title 29, U.S. Code. In a retrospective essay, "The Living Spirit of Florence Kelley," 6, *Survey* editor Paul Kellogg wrote of her "tool-marks" on the landmark legislation "in setting maximum hours or minimum wages, in safeguarding children, in the social insurances or industrial relations." See U.S. Supreme Court justice Felix Frankfurter, qtd. in Storrs, *Civilizing Capitalism*, 15: Florence Kelley "had probably the largest single share in shaping the social history of the United States during the first thirty years of this century," particularly in "securing legislation for the removal of the most glaring abuses of our hectic industrialization following the Civil War."

CHAPTER 5

1 Qtd. in Mason, *Brandeis Way*, 95–96 ("licensed prodigals . . . public officials").

2 Louis D. Brandeis to Adolph Brandeis, July 9, 1905, *Letters of Louis D. Brandeis*, 1:334 ("odor of sanctity"), 335 ("Guinea Pigs"). Louis D. Brandeis to Adolph Brandeis, July

15, 1905, *Letters of Louis D. Brandeis*, 1:338 ("dummy directors"). Note: A reference by Louis to "Marse Henry" as being a "poor prophet" in a letter of Sept. 3, 1905, indicates that he received editorials and articles from the *Louisville Courier-Journal*, since "Marse Henry" was the nickname of Henry Watterson, the editor and publisher of the Louisville newspaper.

3 Strum, *Louis D. Brandeis*, 35 ("practicing attorney"). For an account of the offer by Harvard Law School dean Christopher Langdell, see ibid., 36–37. See also Aldritch, *Old Money*, 62: "The Old Rich [by the late nineteenth century] had established nuclear and extended (private and quasi-public) patrimonies in every city of New England's sphere of influence. . . . Hospitals, museums, symphony orchestras, clinics, boarding schools and colleges, asylums, and 'charities' of every variety were flourishing."

4 On Brandeis's law firm locations, see Strum, *Louis D. Brandeis*, 30–31. See also Lief, *Brandeis*, 24.

5 For the roster of the committee, see Lief, *Brandeis*, 94. Mason, *Brandeis Way*, 90 ("Protector . . . Orphans"). Strum, *Louis D. Brandeis*, 38 (description of Brandeis's office).

6 Birmingham, *"Our Crowd,"* 299 ("driving jauntily . . . horse's head"). On J. H. Hyde and the Equitable Life Assurance Society, see Mason, *Brandeis Way*, 84–87.

7 Mason, *Brandeis Way*, 86 ("see that . . . right"). Birmingham, *"Our Crowd,"* 300 ("lone wolf speculator").

8 *New York World*, Apr. 1905 ("Why," "What . . . motive"). Qtd. in Mason, *Brandeis Way*, 88 ("that this matter not be hushed up"). My discussion of the insurance business and Brandeis's involvement in it is indebted to Mason's book, which is devoted in its entirety to the topic. The cartoon, captioned "The Easy Cop," appeared in the *New York World* on Dec. 23, 1905, and is reprinted in Mason, *Brandeis Way*, 90.

9 Mason, *Brandeis Way*, 86 ("the staid . . . banks").

10 Lief, *Brandeis*, 97 ("monstrous"). See Brandeis, *Other People's Money*.

11 See Mason, *Brandeis Way*, 89–93. The Equitable directors sponsored the investigation headed by Frick; its report was submitted on May 31, 1905. The report of the second investigation, led by Hendricks, was submitted on June 21.

12 Strum, *Louis D. Brandeis*, 69 ("trusts"), 58 ("tycoons"), 153 ("vested wrongs").

13 The full account of Brandeis's involvement in the Boston Consolidated Gas Company episode is found in ibid., 67–72. Strum explains that in 1911, the Supreme Court held Standard Oil to be in restraint of trade but gave no redress to those businesses destroyed by the trust. She quotes Brandeis: "You will realize the danger of letting the people learn that our sacred Constitution protects not only vested rights but vested wrongs."

14 Qtd. in ibid., 91 ("living wage").

15 Qtd. in Yater, *Two Hundred Years*, 87 ("An English visitor to Louisville in 1863 noted 'that what first struck a stranger was the number of maimed men'"), 92 ("sad sight . . . half-starved"). *Annual Reports of the House of Refuge*, 20 ("obtain . . . by begging").

16 See Ely, *Jewish Louisville*, 46–47. Union general Henry Halleck condemned "Jews and other unprincipled traitors," and in December 1862, General Grant issued General Order 11, which stated, "The Jews, as a class violating every regulation of trade established by the Treasury Department . . . are hereby expelled from the Department within twenty-four hours from the receipt of this order." In Paducah, a city to the west

of Louisville, thirty Jewish families were ousted from their homes, and the Jewish community of Louisville organized protests. Adolph Brandeis had contracts to supply Union troops with food and fiber agricultural products and was able to continue wartime business through his gentile partner, Charles W. Crawford, in the firm of Brandeis and Crawford.

Autobiography of Nathaniel Southgate Shaler, 223 ("unsoldierly rubbish . . . grievous hardships"). Webb, *Kentucky in the Reconstruction Era*, 9 ("dreaded bands . . . colonels"). Tapp and Klotter, *Kentucky*, 5–6 ("stragglers . . . draft-jumpers"). The complexities of sociopolitical conditions in postwar Louisville and Kentucky at large are beyond the scope of this discussion, and readers are referred to Tapp and Klotter, *Kentucky*, an extensive study of postwar Kentucky that begins, "The end of the Civil War found Kentucky in a deplorable condition. During the conflict the state had sustained heavy human and economic losses, and the internecine strife had left violent antipathies. The people were in a mood to hate, retaliate, and destroy. It seemed that a black cloud hung over the 'dark and bloody ground'; there was little joy in the land" (1). For an extensive discussion of African American conditions in postwar Louisville, see Wright, *Life behind a Veil*.

17 On Brandeis in Louisville during the 1877 rail strike, see Lief, *Brandeis*, 15. Wage cuts and a backlog of workers' grievances erupted and shut down rail service everywhere across the country. In 1906, the former U.S. commissioner of labor Carroll D. Wright published *The Battles of Labor*, a title meant to capture the bellicose reality of labor strikes, including that of 1877, which Wright summarized as "riots, many acts of violence, intimidation, and the destruction of a great amount of property" (115).

18 Footnotes identify committee members in *Letters of Louis D. Brandeis*, 1:345–46. Of the committee, William Mather was president of the British Textile Guild and the British Science Guild; George P. Field was a senior member of a large fire insurance underwriting firm; Arthur Amory was a partner in a Boston investment firm.

19 On Kentucky bourbon, see Louis D. Brandeis to Alfred Brandeis, Mar. 23, 1889, *Letters of Louis D. Brandeis*, 1:79, in which Louis, on behalf of three Boston gentlemen (and through his brother's agency), requests two gallons of "Short Horn," a nickname for bourbon whiskey distilled in barrels with designated owners (the term "short horn" possibly referring to the appearance of the tap). Howe, *Boston*, 42 ("social thaw"). See also Howe, *Boston*, 375: "The term ["Boston Proper"] . . . distinguish[es] the core and center of intellectual Boston from its more or less vulgar and outlying dependencies."

20 Qtd. in Strum, *Louis D. Brandeis*, 11 ("damned").

21 Qtd. in ibid., 18 ("suavity"). Louis D. Brandeis to Charles Nagel, July 12, 1879, *Letters of Louis D. Brandeis*, 1:37 ("bulldog . . . obstinacy"). Brandeis refers to his "bulldog perseverance & obstinacy which brought me here," meaning New England and the new partnership with Samuel Warren. Emerson qtd. in Strum, *Louis D. Brandeis*, 23 ("They can conquer").

22 Qtd. in Strum, *Louis D. Brandeis*, 19 ("eviscerated" as the term of a law school professor, repeated by Brandeis). See Mason, *Brandeis Way*, 28: U.S. Supreme Court chief justice Charles Evans Hughes said of Brandeis, "No keener blade has ever been used, but it is the knife and skill of the surgeon exploring the operations of the social organism with the purpose of cure."

23 Strum, *Louis D. Brandeis*, 19 (the sequence of courses in the Harvard Law School curriculum was "contracts, property, torts, civil procedure, criminal law, evidence, equity, trusts, and constitutional law"), 23 ("photographic memory," Brandeis's visual problems). For an account of Brandeis's family's immigration, first to Indiana in 1849, then to Louisville in 1851, see ibid., 4–6.

24 On Lewis Dembitz and European Jews' immigration to the United States, see Goldmark, *Pilgrims of '48*. See also Friedman, *Jewish Pioneers and Patriots*; Handlin, *American Jews*; and Wiernik, *History of the Jews in America*. Louis D. Brandeis to Otto A. Wehle, Mar. 12, 1876, *Letters of Louis D. Brandeis*, 1:5–6 ("splendid . . . to the law").

25 See Strum, *Louis D. Brandeis*, chap. 2, "The World of the Boston Brahmin." For the naming of Brahmins by Holmes, see Menand, *Metaphysical Club*, 6. Holmes qtd. in Strum, *Louis D. Brandeis*, 16 ("were very . . . responsibility").

26 See Strum, *Louis D. Brandeis*, 3: "The German-Jewish middle class took the world's literature and history as part of its legacy." Beethoven, Goethe, and Shakespeare were mainstays of Brandeis's heritage and education. Like the Brahmin New Englanders, he could also quote lines from poets and historians of ancient Greece and Rome, for he too had a classical education. In Louisville's Male High School, he studied Latin, Greek, French, and German, along with science and mathematics, and he pursued these same subjects in Dresden in the Annen-Realschule during his family's European sojourn (see ibid., 9, 12). See also Goldmark, *Pilgrims of '48*. Scholars debate the extent to which Brandeis was assimilated into New England gentile society. Strum argues for maximal assimilation, whereas Gal, in *Brandeis of Boston*, states that Brandeis entered Harvard Law School only after securing patronage from Boston-area Jews known to his family and that Brahmin Boston always set him apart as a Jew.

27 On Brandeis at the theater and at concerts, see Louis D. Brandeis to Alfred Brandeis, July 5, 1878, Mar. 24, 1890, *Letters of Louis D. Brandeis*, 1:25, 88–89. Howe, *Gentle Americans*, 74, reprints a letter to her mother suggesting that "Professor Thayer and Brandeis might think it odd if they were not informed of it [a theatrical production]." Howe, *Gentle Americans*, 74 ("deeply carpeted . . . Charles River"). Brandeis's parents, Adolph and Frederika Brandeis, must have been aware, in 1851, of four slave markets operating in Louisville. See Coleman, *Slavery Times in Kentucky*, 167: "Men, women, and children [were] sold like sheep—[at] Garrison's Powell's, Arteburn's and one other." The Arteburn brothers advertised in the *Louisville Democrat*, Jan. 1, 1859, "100 NEGROES WANTED." Their office was located in Louisville's central business district at 12 First Street, between Market and Jefferson.

28 Louis D. Brandeis to Alfred Brandeis, June 28, 1878, *Letters of Louis D. Brandeis*, 1:24 ("celebrities . . . of them"). See also Louis D. Brandeis to Alice Goldmark, Oct. 13, 1890, *Letters of Louis D. Brandeis*, 1:93.

29 Howe, *Gentle Americans*, 40–41 ("pencil-and-paper . . . suppers"). Strum, *Louis D. Brandeis*, 21, reports Brandeis's account of one parlor game. In Louis D. Brandeis to Amy Brandeis Wehle, Nov. 25, 1880, *Letters of Louis D. Brandeis*, 1:58–59, Brandeis remarks on a "really pleasant . . . most unBostonian" social evening that ended at 11:15, which he described to his sister as shockingly late for New England. Louis D. Brandeis to William Harrison Dunbar, Feb. 2, 1893, *Letters of Louis D. Brandeis*, 1:106–10 ("inclinations," "habits," "instinctive"). The often-cited letter of advice that Brandeis

wrote to a junior attorney, urging him to gain full knowledge of clients, is applicable to Brandeis's approach to the Boston social milieu as well.

30 Cruikshank, *Canoeing*, 20–21 ("most remarkable . . . and flags"). On Brandeis's recreation, see Strum, *Louis D. Brandeis*, 43. On winter sports, see Louis D. Brandeis to Alfred Brandeis, Mar. 18, 1906, *Letters of Louis D. Brandeis*, 1:411. Howe, *Gentle Americans*, 42 ("son of Harvard"). Howe, *Boston*, 387 ("love of nature . . . together").

31 Strum, *Louis D. Brandeis*, 37 ("In Louisville malaria . . . childhood"). O'Reilly, *Athletics and Manly Sport*, 133–35 ("students . . . soft"). Brandeis qtd. in Strum, *Louis D. Brandeis*, 42 ("I soon learned . . . not in twelve"). For Brandeis's concern about his health, see Strum, *Louis D. Brandeis*, 27, 42–44.

32 Louis D. Brandeis to Alice Goldmark, Dec. 29, 1890, *Letters of Louis D. Brandeis*, 1:97–98 ("burden . . . tapestry"). Dunlop, *Gilded City*, 11 ("success in city life"). Dunlop, *Gilded City*, 11, adds that in New York City, "diamonds were no luxury; they were a necessity for the presentation of self." Howe, *Boston*, 387 ("against the accepted . . . possessions"). Howe, *Gentle Americans*, 165 ("simple life . . . status symbols").

33 Brandeis to Wehle, Nov. 25, 1880, 1:59 ("The Best of Boarding House life is mitigated misery").

34 See Aldritch, *Old Money*, 29–69. Brandeis qtd. in Lief, *Brandeis*, 200: "Some men buy diamonds and rare works of art. Others delight in autos and yachts. My luxury is to invest my surplus effort . . . to the pleasure of taking up a public problem and solving, or helping to solve it." Brandeis qtd. in Strum, *Louis D. Brandeis*, 47 ("In this age . . . his days").

35 The term *slave* appears in numerous of Brandeis's statements. Qtd. in Lief, *Brandeis*, 205 (in reference to monopoly trusts: "Our democracy cannot endure half free and half slave"), 233 (in ironic reference to the treatment of workers who had no say in their conditions of work: "A horse was a valuable asset [in prewar Kentucky]. So was a slave"). See Strum, *Louis D. Brandeis*, 22 (copied from Tennyson: "Drink deep until the habits of the slave / . . . die"). See Stafford, "Slavery in a Border City," 24–29, for an account of pre–Civil War slavery in Louisville indicating "a less inhumane form of slavery practiced in Louisville than in many other cities" because the diversification of labor led to slaves' living and hiring out as carpenters, stevedores, ropewalk workers, liverymen, blacksmiths, painters, wheelwrights, laundry workers, cooks, porters, coachmen, waiters, etc. It is inconceivable that Brandeis did not encounter hired-out slaves in the course of daily life in Louisville. Brandeis qtd. in Strum, *Louis D. Brandeis*, 44 ("deep sense of obligation").

36 See Howe, *Boston*, 165, on New England wealth secured in relationships "thoroughly inbred and crossbred."

37 Ibid., 47 ("carpenters . . . paperhangers," items listed as inventoried from the Brandeis estate). Note: Number 114 Mount Vernon Street was previously owned by Mark DeWolfe Howe, whose *Boston* is cited elsewhere in this chapter and whose daughter Helen Howe's memoir, *Gentle Americans*, is also a useful source of information here. Goldmark, *Impatient Crusader*, 143 ("overlooking . . . Back Bay").

38 On the significance of this home visit, see Katz, "Henry Lee Higginson vs. Louis Dembitz Brandeis," 74. Perry, *Life and Letters of Henry Lee Higginson*, 408 ("genius for friendship"). See Perry's chapters "Comrade and Citizen" and "Public Servant." On Brandeis as Higginson's guest, see Mason, *Brandeis*, 103 (Brandeis and Higgin-

son "communing . . . with the great and the good"). Note: Oliver Wendell Holmes's coinage of Boston as the Hub referred specifically to the Massachusetts statehouse as a center of authority, but it was widely interpreted as a reference to the status of Boston.

39 Howe, *Gentle Americans*, 164 ("do-good and *do-right*"). Howe, *Boston*, 374 ("critical spirit"). For the background of the region's reformist identity, see Mintz, *Moralists and Modernizers*. See also *King's Handbook of Boston*, 189–204, which identifies "the Heart of the City" as "Benevolent and Charitable Organizations, Homes, and Asylums." On charities to which Brandeis contributed time and money, see Lief, *Brandeis*, 54. Katz, "Henry Lee Higginson vs. Louis Dembitz Brandeis," 72 ("citadel of Brahmin nobility").

40 Numerous statements on citizenship appear in Brandeis's letters, newspaper articles, and speeches. See Mason, *Brandeis*, 111 ("My only interest in the matter [of the Boston traction dispute] was as a citizen"), 122 ("What I have desired to do is to make the people of Boston realize that the most important office which all of us can and should fulfill, is that of private citizen. The duties of the office of private citizen cannot under a republican form of government be neglected without serious injury to the public"), 125 (to physicians: "Your professional success can be attained only through good citizenship"), 149 (on the role of unions: "The community at large has to have unions 'to raise the level of the citizen'"), 151 ("The citizen should be able to comprehend among other things the great and difficult problems of industry, commerce, and finance, which with us necessarily become political questions").

41 Qtd. in ibid., 28 ("God . . . us").

42 Shaler's was a slaveholding family, and in *Autobiography of Nathaniel Southgate Shaler*, 26–27, he recalled the "rough talk of the slaves" in his antebellum household. See Shaler, *Citizen*, 221 ("It is the duty of every true [white] citizen to see what should be done to help this [black] people, so that they may be set upon the way of advancement to the dignity of citizenship"), 225 (on slavery as deplorable but giving "primitive man" the opportunity to rid himself of "savagery"). Scholars in recent years have denounced Shaler as a temporizing racist. See Goldsby, *Spectacular Secret*, 56 (on the "malleable" discourse of the "southern gentleman," typified by Shaler and one "legitimating lynching's violence" in post–Civil War America). Shaler headed the Kentucky Geological Survey of 1873–80 and became chief of the Atlantic Coast Division of the U.S. Geological Survey. For his professional reputation, see *Biographical Dictionary*. Mason, *Brandeis*, 42–43 ("racy wit . . . feeling"). *Autobiography of Nathaniel Southgate Shaler*, 93 ("cold and . . . sympathy"). For Shaler's genealogical links to New England, see *Autobiography of Nathaniel Southgate Shaler*, 68–69.

43 Brandeis qtd. in Mason, *Brandeis*, 23–24: "I remember helping my mother carry out food and coffee to the men from the North. . . . There were times when the rebels came so near that we could hear the firing. At one such time my father moved us across the river. Those were my first memories."

44 *Caron's Directory*, 13 ("business depression," "hard times"). Johnston, *Memorial History of Louisville*, 277–78 ("crippled," "disappeared entirely"). The *Louisville Courier-Journal* and other Louisville newspapers referred in these depression years to charity fundraising by churches and other groups, and the city distributed coal by the bushel.

45 On conditions in postwar Louisville, see Stafford, "Slavery in a Border City," and

Wright, *Life behind a Veil*. See also Yater, *Two Hundred Years*, 115: "The hard times fell most severely on the blue-collar [white] workers, and particularly those thrifty [black] freedmen who lost most of their savings." For an account of the success and failure of the Freedmen's Savings Bank, see Webb, *Kentucky in the Reconstruction Era*, 52–54. *Annual Reports of the House of Refuge*, 6–7 ("after they . . . selfish world"), 19 (on the House of Refuge's return of $5,000 to the City of Louisville in consideration of its depressed condition). *Editorials of Henry Watterson*, 46–47 ("ruin . . . highway to relief").

46 The Brandeis file at FHS chronicles the struggles of Adolph and Alfred Brandeis, as indicated in city directories from 1874 to 1878. Adolph J. Brandeis was listed in 1875 as a clerk with C. G. Tachan and Company and the following year as a clerk with Woolner Brothers, after which he appeared (in 1877) in the partnership of Brandeis, Sanders and Company. In 1878, he was registered as a merchant. Alfred Brandeis was listed from 1875 to 1878 as a bookkeeper for the firm of Reed and Ferguson, Wholesale Fish Dealers and Commission Merchants. Alfred wrote letters to Louis on the letterhead stationery of the firm. See, for example, Alfred Brandeis to Louis D. Brandeis, Mar. 3, 1877, BP, reel 11. Adolph Brandeis qtd. in Strum, *Louis D. Brandeis*, 13 ("Misery likes . . . proletarian").

47 *Autobiography of Nathaniel Southgate Shaler*, 210–11 ("Federal Union . . . interchange").

48 Ibid., 29 ("great experiment in individual freedom"). See also ibid., 31.

49 See Shaler, *Citizen*, 38–39, on chattel slavery's sometimes concealing the "enslaving influence of prejudices and greeds," which the "ideal freeman" foreswore, while the free citizen's vitality, instead, came from "an intelligent affection for his fellowmen." True liberty, Shaler insisted, required resisting all-consuming "greeds" for "personal ends." Material cravings only yielded "transitory things" that trivialized life. They wearied and satiated a person but never afforded true satisfaction. The citizen must ignore the siren song of false values and instead focus energies on behalf of the people's "good." Ibid., 47–49 ("plain citizen . . . his people"). See also ibid., 64, in which Shaler asserted that liberty has ever "rested upon the right and duty of the man to exercise the higher qualities of his intelligence for his own development, and ever for the benefit of those who may be bettered by his thoughts and deeds." On political party affiliation, see ibid., 95, in which Shaler stated that "the citizen clearly owes an allegiance to the party which represents his ideals of government," but owes this allegiance as "a freeman," not as an "indentured servant."

50 Ibid., 80–81 ("valuable helpers to their fellow-citizens").

51 Mason, *Brandeis*, 42 ("'persuasive wisdom' . . . forcibly"). Strum, *Louis D. Brandeis*, 45 ("would continue . . . his life"). See Strum, *Louis D. Brandeis*, 20: Brandeis and Shaler became "sufficiently intimate for Brandeis to consult Shaler about his post–law school plans." See also Strum, *Louis D. Brandeis*, 22.

52 Shaler, *Citizen*, 69 ("which are . . . water supply"). See also ibid., 76–77.

53 Strum, *Louis D. Brandeis*, 59 ("poured out . . . to friendly journalists"). For the full account, see ibid., 57–66.

54 Ibid., 71 ("profit sharing . . . share holder"). Brandeis qtd. in Lief, *Brandeis*, 123 ("Monopolies . . . inefficient").

55 Lief, *Brandeis*, 56–57 ("control . . . people"). Howe, *Boston*, 374 ("The critical spirit

. . . renders [the Bostonian] sometimes a useful, sometimes an obstructive, seldom a popular member of society"). See Howe, *Boston*, 377, for the question that echoed Shaler's advice: "How does the Boston state of mind express itself in the twentieth-century city? [With a] keen sense of civic responsibility," especially for "public works" rather than "private undertakings?"

56 On Jewish Sabbath rituals and customs, see Dembitz, *Jewish Services in Synagogue and Home*. On Brandeis's finances, see Lief, *Brandeis*, 107: "A millionaire by 1907, he was earning more than fifty thousand dollars a year from his practice and had his investments placed where anxiety did not need to follow them." On Bostonian suspicions of Brandeis's radicalism, see Strum, *Louis D. Brandeis*, 63. See also Lief, *Brandeis*, 56–57: "It did not take much in Boston to be called a radical. . . . To oppose banking interests . . . and insist that control remain vested in the people was enough to earn this stamp. . . . By stepping out of line a man might witness a glacial drift. Boston's better people, unable to understand how one of their own could challenge society's charming etiquette, froze up to Mr. and Mrs. Brandeis." On Brandeis's friendship with Elizabeth Glendower Evans, see Strum, *Louis D. Brandeis*, 43.

57 Qtd. in Strum, *Louis D. Brandeis*, 23 ("established," "outsider . . . Jew").

58 Louis D. Brandeis to policyholders of the Equitable Life Assurance Society, July 22, 1905, *Letters of Louis D. Brandeis*, 1:341–42 ("deplorable management . . . misfortunes of others").

59 Ibid., 342 ("legal safeguards . . . policy holders").

60 Louis D. Brandeis to trustees of stock, Equitable Life Assurance Society, July 14, 1905, *Letters of Louis D. Brandeis*, 1:342–44 ("fashionable," "anything can be too large"). Strum, *Louis D. Brandeis*, 76 ("inclination . . . insurance company"). See also Clarke, *These Days of Large Things*, which examines the American culture of largeness from the post–Civil War period to 1930.

61 Brandeis, *Business*, 206–9 ("on the contrary . . . bribe"). See also ibid., 205–24, and, Brandeis, *Other People's Money*, an analysis of investment banking and numerous other banking activities.

62 Dryden, *Addresses and Papers*, 65–66 ("*Industrial* . . . manufacturing industries"), 69–70 ("provide . . . insured").

63 Dryden, *Careers for the Coming Men*, 3–6 ("exceptional ability," "individual talent." Miller, *Art of Canvassing*, 49 ("Seem to be . . . better for it"), 23–25 ("make . . . every day"). Dryden, *Careers for the Coming Men*, 3–6 ("promotion to higher positions"), 13–14 ("outdoor life," "contact with . . . population"). See also Miller, *Art of Canvassing*, 143 (on insurance agents as "the working bees who bring honey to the hive" and soldiers who do "the hardest work on the insurance battlefield"), 117–18 (on agents discouraged from identifying themselves as salesmen but as counselors called to prevent "the hard lot of destitution"), 54 ("A good face and a fine coat help in making a good impression").

On agents' compensation, see Ackerman, *Industrial Life Insurance*, 44: "The agents of an industrial insurance company are compensated by a stated salary based on the size of their debit and also by an increase made in the debit." See also Stalson, *Marketing Life Insurance*, 469: "The American companies [recognized that] salaries alone were discovered to be inadequate—they did not encourage the men to produce new business, did not sufficiently stimulate them in retaining old business—and so a system of rewards for added business and penalties for lost business was set up in association with salaries."

64 Miller, *Art of Canvassing*, 100 ("poor man's estate . . . poverty"), 99 ("family insurance . . . domestic surroundings"). On agents' stock of free gifts to potential clients, see Metropolitan Life Insurance, John Hancock, and Prudential company files, WC, folders 3, 4.

65 Miller, *Art of Canvassing*, 36 ("often, a pastor . . . insure"), 86 ("sudden deaths . . . life insurance"), 104–6 ("What will the family . . . been insured").

66 On steel mill deaths, see Hard and others, *Injured in the Course of Duty*, 11, 14. See also Eastman, *Work-Accidents and the Law*, especially the prefatory "Death Calendar in Industry for Allegheny County" (which includes Pittsburgh) and the day-by-day chronicling of 526 workers' deaths, July 1906–June 1907.

67 On Gilded Age industrial Louisville, see *Louisville Past and Present*, 37–38. On textile mills and jeans clothing, see Tapp and Klotter, *Kentucky*, 68. The picture card advertising industrial insurance in the Louisville Metropolitan Life Insurance office is in the collection of the author.

68 Ackerman, *Industrial Life Insurance*, 47 ("avoid . . . Potter's Field"). Dryden, *Addresses and Papers*, 75 ("Deep at the root . . . pauper burial"). Riis, *How the Other Half Lives*, 136 ("common trench . . . in life").

69 Habenstein and Lamers, *History of American Funeral Directing*, 400 ("cloth-covered . . . style"). See also ibid., 408–9. See also Steiner, *Study of the Intellectual and Material Culture*, 131: "Clustered dwellings especially (urban tenements and apartments, for example) made home displays of the deceased inappropriate, if not impossible. In response, funeral directors offered their own 'parlors' or 'funeral homes' for the purpose." A related but separate and controversial matter of sales of industrial policies to cover children is beyond the scope of this discussion; the issue is thoroughly addressed in Zelizer, *Pricing the Priceless Child*.

70 Strum, *Louis D. Brandeis*, 74 ("no money . . . within three years"). See Horowitz, *Morality of Spending*, 53, on a 1909 study in which "families [of the working class] purchased a variety of insurance policies. Slightly less than half had property insurance. The most common kind of protection provided money for burial costs."

71 On Brandeis's calculations, see Strum, *Louis D. Brandeis*, 75, and Brandeis, "Wage-Earners' Life Insurance," 314–15.

72 Brandeis, "Wage-Earners' Life Insurance," 315 ("disastrous," "vicious"), 317 ("shocking . . . working class"). See ibid., 315: "Of the 2,761,449 industrial insurance policies in these three great companies which terminated by death, surrender, and lapse during the year 1904, aggregating in amount $422,633,987, payment was made to insured on only 347,072, or about one-eighth of the policies. In other words, the holders of 2,414,377 policies, with aggregate insurance of $379,708,958, made a total loss of all premiums paid." For the wage scale of the average glass factory worker in 1907, see table in Schlereth, *Victorian America*, 81.

The Armstrong Commission's report corroborated Brandeis's findings on ordinary and industrial insurance. The commission concluded its hearings in December 1905 and published its report on February 22, 1906. Its main focus was on the fraud and abuse of the insurance companies; for conclusions on industrial insurance, see New York Legislature, *Report of the Joint Committee*.

73   Brandeis, "Wage-Earners' Life Insurance," 316 ("exorbitant salaries . . . private profit"). The Armstrong Commission did earmark industrial insurance for further study but, as Brandeis predicted, focused principally on the abuses reported in the press. See New York Legislature, *Report of the Joint Committee*. The Armstrong Committee elicited testimony from insurance executives, such as John R. Hegeman, president of the Metropolitan Life Insurance Company, who admitted that industrial insurance was the sole source of his company's profit. For excerpts of this testimony, see Mason, *Brandeis*, 156–57. See Brandeis, "Wage-Earners' Life Insurance," 312, which finds that of the nearly 21 million insurance policies in effect in the United States on January 1, 1905, over 15 million were industrial policies.

74   Keyes, *History of Savings Banks*, 101 ("induce . . . five cents"), 5–7 ("poor . . . assured income"), 13 ("that *some* . . . dependence").

75   Ibid., 12 ("day of adversity").

76   On solicitation of support, see Mason, *Brandeis Way*, 162–63. On the *Collier's Weekly* article, see Strum, *Louis D. Brandeis*, 90.

77   On Brandeis's address to the Commercial Club at the Algonquin Club, see Commercial Club secretary Dwight to Arthur Amory of the Equitable Life Assurance Society of Boston, Oct. 11, 1905, BL: "The 334th Regular meeting of the Commercial Club of Boston will be held in the New Algonquin Club, Thursday, Oct 26th, at six, dinner being served at seven o'clock. Mr. Louis Brandeis will talk on the topic 'Life Insurance—the Abuses and the Remedies.'" Lief, *Brandeis*, 86 ("calmly build . . . on the desk"). Mason, *Brandeis Way*, 153 ("spell," "magnetic voice").

78   See Marchand, *Creating the Corporate Soul*, 183–89, on the campaign of the Metropolitan Life Insurance Company to win public favor in advertising based on a good-health initiative that included the participation of Lillian Wald of the New York Nurses' Settlement and included these slogans. For specifics of the Higginson plan, see Mason, *Brandeis Way*, 193–96. Howe, *Gentle Americans*, 106–7 ("Uncle Henry"). For Higginson's antipathy to Brandeis, see Katz, "Henry Lee Higginson vs. Louis Dembitz Brandeis."

79   Mason, *Brandeis Way*, 135–36 ("most dangerous . . . and experience").

80   Rice, *Mrs. Wiggs of the Cabbage Patch*, 4–5 ("ramshackle cottages"). This was the social class that the Louisville author Alice Hegan Rice nostalgically represented in her popular novella with the jaunty title. See Yater, *Two Hundred Years*, 108, on the "poorest of blacks and the cast-offs of white society" as occupants of the Oakland (Louisville) area that became the setting for Hegan's novella. See also *Views of Louisville since 1766*, fig. 122.

81   Adolph Brandeis qtd. in Strum, *Louis D. Brandeis*, 13 ("joy in fighting," "cowardice").

82   Shaler, *Citizen*, 161 ("wage-earner . . . that earns money").

83   *Boston Post*, July 23, 1906 ("rights as workers . . . modern industry"). *New York Times*, May 7, 1905 ("riotous . . . labor trust"). *Boston Herald*, July 11, 1905 ("labor unionism . . . demons"). The foregoing appear in Brandeis's newspaper clippings file, BP, reel 31. Wright, *Battles of Labor*, 122–23 ("riots . . . property"). On the 1877 labor strike, see also Wright, *Battles of Labor*, 112–24.

84   Brandeis qtd. in Paper, *Brandeis*, 85 ("sufficient . . . the future"). Brandeis qtd. in Strum, *Louis D. Brandeis*, 79 ("We've found . . . life insurance").

85   See Mason, *Brandeis Way*, 230–31. See also Brandeis, *Business*, 203–4, for the 1924

summary statement of Deputy Commissioner Grady on the development of the Massachusetts Savings Bank Life Insurance system.

86   Strum, *Louis D. Brandeis*, 90 ("Brandeis considered . . . achievement"). Brandeis qtd. in ibid., 90–91 ("Its greatest . . . annually"). Mason, *Brandeis Way*, 246 ("early success . . . industrial companies"). See Louis D. Brandeis, "Life Insurance" and "Successes of Savings Bank Insurance," in Brandeis, *Business*, 116–203.

87   Shaler, *Citizen*, 306 ("dominance"). See *Rand McNally & Co's*, 93. See Strum, *Louis D. Brandeis*, 224–90, for a fuller account of Brandeis's Zionism and his efforts in its support.

88   Brandeis, "What Labor Can Learn," 237 ("cause of unionism . . . industrial interests"). On Brandeis's advocacy of worker participation, see Strum, *Louis D. Brandeis*, 174–90. See also Mason, *Brandeis*, 141–52.

89   Brandeis, *Women in Industry*, 9 ("liberty . . . or welfare"). Louis D. Brandeis, "The Living Law," in Brandeis, *Business*, 344–63.

90   For specifics of this intricate case, see Strum, *Louis D. Brandeis*, 159–65. See also Mason, *Brandeis*, 315–51. Day, *Best of Clarence Day*, 16 ("thumping . . . losses").

91   See Strum, *Louis D. Brandeis*, 139–46, for an account of the complex Ballinger-Pinchot affair. See also Mason, *Brandeis*, 254–89. Shaler, *Citizen*, 95 ("citizen clearly . . . a freeman"). Brandeis withdrew his support from the sitting president, William Howard Taft, because he did not consider Taft a reformer.

92   See Chace, *1912*. See Urofsky, *Mind of One Piece*, 72–92, for Brandeis's advice to Wilson on trusts.

93   Katz, "Henry Lee Higginson vs. Louis Dembitz Brandeis," 75 ("Brandeis . . . deceive people"). See Irons, *People's History of the Supreme Court*, 262, on McReynolds as "a judicial reactionary, with a violent temper and a vicious streak of anti-Semitism."

94   U.S. Senate, *Hearings before the Subcommittee*, pt. 1, p. 123 ("unfit"); pt. 2, pp. 149–50 ("insult . . . of the country"), 160 ("delinquent," "dishonorable in his professional conduct"). See ibid., pt. 4, pp. 172–89, and pt. 5, pp. 189–261, for testimony by Sidney W. Winslow attempting to impugn Brandeis's work as a trustee of the estate of the deceased father of his first law partner, Samuel Warren. Brandeis was confirmed by the U.S. Senate on a mainly party-line vote of forty-seven to twenty-two. Irons, *People's History of the Supreme Court*, 262 ("two men . . . their way").

95   Strum, *Louis D. Brandeis*, 311 ("taught judges . . . judgments"), 315 ("not to promote . . . power"), 322–23 ("together . . . society"). On *Whitney v. California*, see ibid., 306–8. See also ibid., 323–30. Irons, *People's History of the Supreme Court*, 262 ("traveling . . . in dissent").

96   Strum, *Louis D. Brandeis*, 413.

97   Ibid. ("Two strands . . . maximum hours"). Alvin Johnson qtd. in ibid., 407 ("serenely . . . for it"). Brandeis's involvement with the University of Louisville and its law school is documented in Flexner, *Mr. Justice Brandeis*. Strum, in *Louis D. Brandeis*, 151–52, poses specific sociocultural concerns raised by Brandeis's career:

> His focus today would be on two series of questions. The first would begin, how much creativity has been suppressed through the centralization of economic power? . . . What has been the cost to the consumer? What are the implications for "efficiency" of cars that must be recalled because of serious

defects; electrical appliances that appear to be programmed to fall apart within a relatively short time; the financial collapse of [major corporations]; the polluting of the environment, the production of foods that have a profitable shelf life only through the inclusion in them of chemicals harmful to human health; the inability of American industry to provide jobs for . . . [millions] of would-be workers?

His second series of questions would revolve around industrial and political democracy. To what extent is it possible to involve workers in the decision-making process of huge corporations? Does lack of worker-participation give the workers a sense of alienation? Has it made them dependent wage slaves, however high their wages may be? Are workers encouraged to think of themselves as creative participants in the economic process? Does the financial power of huge corporations affect the workings of government? Are the "special interests" perceived as controlling government so completely that large sections of the population have become too apathetic or too cynical to vote?

CHAPTER 6

1 Sharpe, *Walter Rauschenbusch*, 59 ("physically commanding"). Rauschenbusch qtd. in ibid., 233: "When I got to New York City, I was asked to deliver a lecture before a group of about 500 distinguished people at the Hotel Astor." Note: In 1908, the Astor and the Waldorf were combined into the Waldorf-Astoria Hotel.

2 Rauschenbusch, *Christianity and the Social Crisis*, 217 ("submerged . . . fear"), 214 ("swept . . . hearts").

3 Sandoval-Strausz, *Hotel*, 4 ("mobility, transience, and anonymity").

4 Evans, *Social Gospel Today*, 66 ("mirrored . . . corridor"). Rauschenbusch's lecture at the hotel was doubly ironic because, in response to the notorious flaunting of wealth by the Bradley-Martin costume ball of 1897, which was held at the Waldorf-Astoria, he'd delivered a sermon condemning such extravagance (see Sharpe, *Walter Rauschenbusch*, 110). For a description of the Waldorf-Astoria lobby, see Kaplan, *When the Astors Owned New York*, 88.

5 Rauschenbusch, *Christianity and the Social Crisis*, 68 ("beating heart . . . Christian life"). In "Unless the Call Be Heard Again," 118, Joan Chittister calls attention to this aspect of Rauschenbusch's thought.

6 Rauschenbusch, *Christianity and the Social Crisis*, 68 ("personal religion"), 33 ("chiefly . . . common good").

7 Rauschenbusch, "Genesis of *Christianity and the Social Crisis*," 52 ("for the Lord . . . People," "dangerous"). Rauschenbusch's anxieties about the reception of *Christianity and the Social Crisis* are recounted in Minus, *Walter Rauschenbusch*, 157–58.

8 Minus, *Walter Rauschenbusch*, 132 ("wide forehead . . . smile," "Lincolnesque"). See also Sharpe, *Walter Rauschenbusch*, 59.

9 On Rauschenbusch's impact on listeners, see Evans, *Kingdom Is Always but Coming*, 201. See also Minus, *Walter Rauschenbusch*, 132. See Kaplan, *When the Astors Owned New York*, 89, on the velvet rope introduced by the Waldorf maître d'hôtel and its creation

of "an instant atmosphere of privilege and a social economy of scarcity." Dunlop, *Gilded City*, 135 ("that an individual . . . at it").

10 Rauschenbusch, *Christianity and the Social Crisis*, 220 ("social wrongs").

11 Qtd. in Evans, *Kingdom Is Always but Coming*, 66 ("rich, famous . . . and women"). H. G. Wells qtd. in Kaplan, *When the Astors Owned New York*, 88 ("bright hats . . . of costume"). Rauschenbusch, *Christianity and the Social Crisis*, 91 ("I am not . . . have lived"), 220 ("moral power . . . advance").

12 McKelvey, *Flower City*, 2–3 ("occasionally . . . post"), 12–13 (commercial flower nurseries).

13 Minus, *Walter Rauschenbusch*, 2 ("formidable"), 1–18 (background of the senior Rauschenbusch, Carl August Heinrich Rauschenbusch, D.D.). Sharpe, *Walter Rauschenbusch*, 20 ("grafted . . . antecedents"). Minus, *Walter Rauschenbusch*, 4 (August Rauschenbusch's antislavery views), 3 (August Rauschenbusch's baptism in the Mississippi). See also Sharpe, *Walter Rauschenbusch*, 19–23.

14 See Rauschenbusch, *Christianizing the Social Order*, 92–93, on objections to the Social Gospel ("the Kingdom idea") expressed by "older brethren" as "painfully upsetting. . . . All our inherited ideas, all theological literature, all the practices of church life seemed to be against us." See also Rauschenbusch, "Genesis of *Christianity and the Social Crisis*." See also Minus, *Walter Rauschenbusch*, 100–101.

15 Sharpe, *Walter Rauschenbusch*, 35 ("baptisms . . . imagination"), 31 ("gardens and houses"), 47, 49 ("artistic taste"), 27 (architect).

16 Fairbank, *Bright Land*, 4 ("Father was . . . universe"). On August Rauschenbusch's plan for Walter's education, see Dorrien, *Making of American Liberal Theology*, 2:75. Sharpe, *Walter Rauschenbusch*, 32 ("bad . . . from us"), 34 ("dyed . . . establishments"), 48 ("so intensely . . . earth of ours"). See also Sharpe, *Walter Rauschenbusch*, 25, 28.

17 Sharpe, *Walter Rauschenbusch*, 36 ("took me . . . pond"), 37 ("bathing beach," "à la Adam and Eve"), 38 ("great . . . swimming").

18 Ibid., 36 ("sexual morality"), 48 ("jewel . . . girl").

19 Ibid., 50 ("green," "violently"). Rauschenbusch qtd. in Evans, *Kingdom Is Always but Coming*, 26 ("How I long . . . caress").

20 Minus, *Walter Rauschenbusch*, 13–16 ("absolute submission," "not natural," "no Christian," "Poor Mrs. . . . alienation"). Sharpe, *Walter Rauschenbusch*, 42 ("solemn"), 39 ("wild bumble bee," "never been young"). On the Rauschenbusch family dynamic, see also Evans, *Kingdom Is Always but Coming*, 135–36, 236–37, 253.

21 Rauschenbusch, *Christianizing the Social Order*, 159 ("old-fashioned farm").

22 Rauschenbusch qtd. in Minus, *Walter Rauschenbusch*, 17 ("I am out . . . any longer"). Sharpe, *Walter Rauschenbusch*, 43 ("tender . . . citizenship"). Minus, *Walter Rauschenbusch*, 17 ("Very soon . . . souls").

23 For explanations of millennialism (and premillennialism and postmillennialism) in the context of Rauschenbusch's theological training, see Evans, *Kingdom Is Always but Coming*, 48–49, 117–19, 179–89, 225–26, 258–59.

24 Rauschenbusch, *Christianity and the Social Crisis*, 62–63 ("heavenly catastrophe . . . greater future"). See also ibid., 105–19.

25 Minus, *Walter Rauschenbusch*, 17 ("to do . . . missionary"). For an account of August Rauschenbusch's antislavery work, see ibid., 3–5.

26 Ibid., 46 ("image . . . self-sacrifice"). Sharpe, *Walter Rauschenbusch*, 53 ("rejoiced . . . conversions").

27 Rauschenbusch qtd. in Minus, *Walter Rauschenbusch*, 36–38 ("breezy and geniusy," "utterly fearless," "Christian evolutionist"). See also ibid., 61.

28 Walter Rauschenbusch to Munson Ford, June 30, 1886, qtd. in Sharpe, *Walter Rauschenbusch*, 59–60 ("old-fashioned . . . ugly," "decent flat," "homeless . . . population"). Rauschenbusch qtd. in Evans, *Kingdom Is Always but Coming*, 77 ("own master"). Rauschenbusch, *Christianity and the Social Crisis*, 304 ("peasants . . . market").

29 Rauschenbusch, *Christianity and the Social Crisis*, 304–5 ("day-nursery . . . expensive staff"), 298–99 ("physical . . . impaired").

30 Ibid., 305 ("procession . . . bruised").

31 Qtd. in May, *Protestant Churches and Industrial America*, 53 ("God has need . . . them"). See also ibid., 51–52.

32 Ibid., 56 ("over and over . . . deserved," "heavily-burdened neighbors"). Day, *Best of Clarence Day*, 383 ("incessant toil . . . good").

33 May, *Protestant Churches and Industrial America*, 53–60 ("ten hours' . . . condemnations").

34 Minus, *Walter Rauschenbusch*, 36–37 ("talked with Rauschenbusch . . . to him"). See also ibid., 61.

35 On workers' support for George, see Young, *Single Tax Movement in the United States*, 91–94.

36 Rauschenbusch to Ford, June 30, 1886, qtd. in Sharpe, *Walter Rauschenbusch*, 60 ("Anderson's . . . ante-room"). See also Minus, *Walter Rauschenbusch*, 61.

37 Rauschenbusch, *Christianity and the Social Crisis*, 177 ("amulets . . . statues"). For other passages critiquing Catholicism, see ibid., 45, 94, 143–45, 166, 205.

38 Rauschenbusch qtd. in Sharpe, *Walter Rauschenbusch*, 232 ("idea . . . religious sense"). Rauschenbusch to Ford, June 30, 1886, qtd. in Sharpe, *Walter Rauschenbusch*, 60 ("poor and downtrodden . . . Christ"). See also Sharpe, *Walter Rauschenbusch*, 61.

39 Rauschenbusch qtd. in Minus, *Walter Rauschenbusch*, 61–62 ("great audience . . . shout of joy"). See Rauschenbusch, *Christianizing the Social Order*, 91–92.

40 For the development and status of the Social Gospel and Rauschenbusch's acquaintance with the movement, see Dorrien, *Making of American Liberal Theology*, 2:77–79.

41 Rauschenbusch, *Christianity and the Social Crisis*, 186 ("State . . . ought to be").

42 Burrows and Wallace, *Gotham*, 1105 ("human river . . . HEN-RY GEORGE!"). See also Young, *Single Tax Movement in the United States*, 95–107.

43 For the range of Rauschenbusch's reading, see Sharpe, *Walter Rauschenbusch*, 65, 85.

44 Ely qtd. in Minus, *Walter Rauschenbusch*, 63–64 ("one-sided . . . social salvation"). See Ely, *Social Aspects of Christianity*, 149.

45 Ely, *Ground under Our Feet*, 36 ("tramping . . . on every hand"), 69 ("I became aware . . . dangerous").

46 Ibid., 66–67 ("crisis . . . 'as thyself'").

47 Ibid., 65 ("to do whatever . . . conditions"), 43 ("case . . . documents"). See also ibid., 60–61.

48 Ibid., 58 ("study . . . growth").

49   Ely, *Social Aspects of Christianity*, 15 ("Half of the time . . . slavery"). Ely wrote that the seminary curriculum had not, as yet, given sociology "that prolonged, concentrated attention which theology has received for thousands of years" and that the ministry was warped by its exclusive study of theology, which only led to dogma, dissension, and internecine hatreds (ibid., 86). Seminaries, he emphasized, ought to be "great leaders of thought in economic and social studies" (ibid., 17; see also ibid., 88). Ely, in addition, cited the need for work rules addressing "the labor of women under conditions which imperil the family," together with the need for children's playgrounds, for foster care for children of dysfunctional homes, and for "a juster distribution of wealth" (ibid., 74–77).

50   Rauschenbusch, *Christianity and the Social Crisis*, 250 ("take orders . . . their own shop").

51   Ibid., 250 ("habits of mind . . . paralyzed"), 75 ("That is the charm . . . curse"). 75.

52   Ibid., 250–51 ("class struggle").

53   Gladden, *Parish Problems*, 332 ("first and foremost . . . teaching").

54   Rauschenbusch, *Christianity and the Social Crisis*, 295 ("Water . . . their own class"). Day, *Best of Clarence Day*, 14 ("were all the right sort . . . conservative newspaper"), 17–18 ("mellow chants . . . deep colors").

55   Advertisement by J. & R. Lamb, Decorators and Furnishers for the Church, qtd. in *For the Right*, Oct. 1890, n.p. ("artistic side . . . interior"). Rauschenbusch qtd. in Sharpe, *Walter Rauschenbusch*, 48 ("nearest approach . . . erected"). Note: Rockefeller, a major contributor to the Rochester Theological Seminary, also supported Rauschenbusch's work and contributed to his family financially over many years. See Evans, *Kingdom Is Always but Coming*, 33, 51, 80–82. See also Minus, *Walter Rauschenbusch*, 59, 85, 96–97, 103, 115, 133–34, 140.

56   Rauschenbusch, *Christianity and the Social Crisis*, 301 ("courtly grace . . . society").

57   Ely, *Social Aspects of Christianity*, 77 ("actual dangers," "spread-eagleism," "deadly"). See also Rauschenbusch, *Christianity and the Social Crisis*, 324: "They [the ministers] may take a lively interest in municipal reform or public ownership, and yet view dubiously the efforts to create a fighting organization for labor or to end to the wages system."

58   See Rauschenbusch, *Prayers of the Social Awakening*, 55 ("For Women Who Toil"), 51 ("For Children Who Work"), 59 ("For Immigrants").

59   Ibid., 61 ("For Employers"), 63 ("For Men in Business"), 67 ("lords of industry").

60   Ibid., 65–66 ("For Consumers").

61   See Evans, *Kingdom Is Always but Coming*, 218: "The public response to *Prayers of the Social Awakening* was overwhelmingly positive. . . . Rauschenbusch was deluged by appreciative letters from across the country."

62   Walter Rauschenbusch, "The New Evangelism," *Independent* (London), May 12, 1904, 1055 ("new . . . synthesis").

63   Ely, *Social Aspects of Christianity*, 47–48 ("public robbery . . . public property"). Ely also wrote that the German state of Prussia purchased the private railways to prevent stock speculation, a purchase he regarded as "a strong argument for the nationalization of railways" (ibid., 22).

64   Qtd. in Burrows and Wallace, *Gotham*, 792 ("vicious . . . of the city"). For a concise

history of the planning for Central Park, see ibid., 790–95. See also Roper, *FLO*, and Fein, *Frederick Law Olmsted*.

65   *History of Public Works in the United States*, 225 ("nearly 370 . . . day").

66   Rauschenbusch, *Christianity and the Social Crisis*, 223–24 ("predatory interests . . . public schools"). See also ibid., 260–61, for a reference to "the first great election in Chicago in 1902, in which the people by referendum decided for municipal owner-ship of street railways and of the gas and electric lighting plants."

67   Rauschenbusch, *Christianizing the Social Order*, 344 ("even the child . . . not too full").

68   Ibid. ("When he begins . . . great corporation").

69   See ibid., 393–400, on Rauschenbusch's advocacy of municipal ownership of utilities, including water, parks, rail transit, electricity, and gas, as a force for social cohesion and Christian brotherhood.

70   Ely, *Social Aspects of Christianity*, 149 ("negative . . . Protestantism").

71   On excessive individualism in Christianity, see ibid., 150–53, 26–27. On the Twenty-third Psalm, see Day, *Best of Clarence Day*, 132.

72   Minus, *Walter Rauschenbusch*, 98 ("talk about . . . Christian men").

73   See Sharpe, *Walter Rauschenbusch*, 62, 65. See also Riis, *Making of an American*, 263–96.

74   Evans, *Kingdom Is Always but Coming*, 83–88, 133–35 (on *For the Right*). *For the Right*, Nov. 1889, n.p. ("reflect . . . things"). See "A Dinner Party in the Twentieth Century," reprinted from *Looking Backward*, in *For the Right*, Jan. 1890, 7–8.

75   Dietz qtd. in Minus, *Walter Rauschenbusch*, 99 ("Christ-like," "fearless").

76   *Bisno, Union Pioneer*, 198 ("spiritual lackeys of capitalism"). Rauschenbusch, "New Evangelism," 1058 ("under the . . . classes").

77   Qtd. in Minus, *Walter Rauschenbusch*, 84 ("sanctification . . . institutions"), 86 ("spa-cious . . . views"), 91 ("widened . . . non-Baptists"). For a fuller account of the origins of the Brotherhood of the Kingdom, see ibid., 84–93.

78   Rauschenbusch qtd. in ibid., 95 ("yearning . . . another"), 94 ("proud . . . us all"). Much of the Rauschenbusch poem is reprinted in Evans, *Kingdom Is Always but Coming*, 99. For Rother's background, see Evans, *Kingdom Is Always but Coming*, 86.

79   Sharpe, *Walter Rauschenbusch*, 33 ("lovely . . . for her").

80   McKelvey, "Walter Rauschenbusch's Rochester," 2 ("as the scholarly . . . Chris-tianity").

81   Qtd. in Minus, *Walter Rauschenbusch*, 101 ("great horror . . . workingman"), 135 (Rauschenbusch street address). See also Klos, *Rochester*, 33–34. Rauschenbusch, *Christianity and the Social Crisis*, 301–4 ("sacking . . . through fear").

82   Minus, *Walter Rauschenbusch*, 110 (Rauschenbusch's schedule of courses), 103–18 (Rauschenbusch's career in the seminary), 112 ("rich . . . Kingdom").

83   Rauschenbusch, *Christianity and the Social Crisis*, 301 ("very rich . . . poor"). On mod-ern industrial Rochester, see Hopkins, *Powers Fire-Proof Commercial*, 7; Shilling, *Roch-ester's Transportation Heritage*, 14; and Husted and Rosenberg-Naparsteck, *Rochester Neighborhoods*, 40–41, 83. The socioeconomic background of the late-nineteenth and early-twentieth-century Baptist, Methodist, and other Protestant ministries is repre-sented throughout Sinclair Lewis's thoroughly researched novel *Elmer Gantry*.

84 Rauschenbusch, *Christianity and the Social Crisis*, 301–4 ("fierce . . . mouth").

85 Commons, *Social Reform and the Church*, 14 ("preacher . . . contact"), 17 ("police court . . . almshouse"), 15 ("small library"), 19 ("wisely . . . dollars," "Sociology . . . religion"), 20 ("Theology . . . half").

86 Rauschenbusch's first years on the seminary faculty are recounted in Minus, *Walter Rauschenbusch*, 103–18.

87 See McKelvey, *Quest for Quality*, chaps. 1, 2, and 4.

88 Ibid., 36 ("almost . . . happening"), 40 ("appalling . . . fatalities"), 42 ("courteous cooperation . . . position").

89 See McKelvey, "Walter Rauschenbusch's Rochester," 6, 7, 12–13. Minus, *Walter Rauschenbusch*, 122 ("Rauschenbusch tasted . . . business"). See also Minus, *Walter Rauschenbusch*, 119–37.

90 Rauschenbusch, "Genesis of *Christianity and the Social Crisis*," 52 ("on social . . . People").

91 Rauschenbusch qtd. in Minus, *Walter Rauschenbusch*, 97 ("preach Christ . . . boldly").

92 For a discussion of the family problems exacerbated by Rauschenbusch's absences from home and by the deafness that isolated him from the ordinary conversation of his household, see Evans, *Kingdom Is Always but Coming*, 236–39, 273–76. Rauschenbusch, *Christianity and the Social Crisis*, 308–9 ("to elevate . . . but coming").

93 See Dorrien, *Making of American Liberal Theology*, 2:127: "Bruised by cold parental treatment in his youth, [Rauschenbusch] poured himself out in pursuit of his vision of society as a nurturing, cooperative family." Rauschenbusch, "Genesis of *Christianity and the Social Crisis*," 55 ("social movement . . . Christ").

94 West, "Can These Dry Bones Live," 231 ("most influential . . . immigration"). See also Evans, "Historical Integrity and Theological Recovery," 2: "Considering the complexities that confront churches at the beginning of the twenty-first century," the "basic theological premise for the social gospel—that Christianity must be rooted in faith-based communities committed to social transformation—is worthy of assessment." Raushenbush, foreword to *Christianity and the Social Crisis in the 21st Century*, xii ("Church's new enthusiasm . . . rights movement"). Note: The editor of this volume is the grandson of Walter Rauschenbusch and spells his name Raushenbush. For connections of the Social Gospel to the mid-twentieth-century civil rights movement, see Luker, *Social Gospel in Black and White*, 321: "Three decades after the death of Walter Rauschenbusch, the first important anthology of his work was edited by Morehouse College President Benjamin E. Mays. His student, Martin Luther King, Jr., was at the time experiencing an intellectual awakening in which Rauschenbusch played a significant role." Wallis, "What to Do," 345 ("theology . . . common good"). For an account of the potential for a new Social Gospel in "a post–religious right America," see Wallis, *Great Awakening*. See also Fitzgerald, "New Evangelicals." Rauschenbusch, *Christianity and the Social Crisis*, 412 ("At best . . . worthwhile").

CHAPTER 7

1 Wells-Barnett's breakfast and home work routines are described by her daughter, Alfreda Barnett Duster, qtd. in Sterling, afterword, 194–95.

2   "Girl Murdered; Body Mutilated," *Chicago Daily Tribune*, Nov. 10, 1909.

3   Wells-Barnett, *Crusade for Justice*, 65–66 ("old threadbare . . . women").

4   Qtd. in Schecter, *Ida B. Wells-Barnett*, 170 ("Jane Addams . . . Negroes"). Schecter explains, "The Negro Fellowship League [unlike Addams's Hull House] was not primarily a 'community of women reformers' . . . but [of] Christian worship, outreach, and moral instruction." See Wells, *Crusade for Justice*, 259, 276, 356, on Wells's admiration for Addams, collaboration with her, and help of Hull House to squelch proposals to racially segregate Chicago schools. Wells, *Crusade for Justice*, 196 ("consternation," hidden gun). See Wells, *Southern Horrors*, 70: "A Winchester rifle should have a place of honor in every black home, and it should be used for that protection which the law refuses to give."

5   See Wells, *Reason Why the Colored American*, 74, on Wells's definition of lynch law by the following quotation: "'Lynch Law,' says the *Virginia Lancet*, '. . . had its origin in 1780' in a combination of citizens of Pittsylvania County, Virginia, entered into for the purpose of suppressing a trained band of horse-thieves and counterfeiters whose well concocted schemes had bidden defiance to the ordinary laws of the land, and whose success encouraged and emboldened them in their outrages upon the community. Col. Wm. Lynch drafted the constitution for this combination of citizens, and hence 'Lynch Law' has ever been the name given to the summary infliction of punishment by private and unauthorized citizens." Davis, "John Lamar," 412 ("gigantic . . . muscles"), 422 ("creamy . . . sway").

6   *Chicago Daily Tribune*, Jan. 30, 1905, 7 (Marshall Field advertisement). See *Bookman*, Sept. 1908, 237–38, on "the success of Thomas Dixon's books, *The Leopard's Spots* and *The Clansman* [the latter of which, a novel] has sold two hundred thousand with a royalty of $40,000. The novels dealing with the negro question were dramatised by the author himself and produced under the title *The Clansman*. The play has made a sensational success . . . in three years." See also "Dixon's Novel on Grill," *Chicago Daily Tribune*, Dec. 24, 1895. See also "Drama Inspires Negro Lynching," *Chicago Daily Tribune*, Oct. 30, 1895, 4: "Bainbridge Georgia, Oct. 29 — Wrought up to a high pitch of anger against negroes by the presentation of Thomas A. Dixon's play, 'The Clansman,' last week, a mob of 300 men stormed the jail at midnight, took out Gus Goodman, a negro who had fatally shot Sheriff Stegall, and lynched him." See Wells, *Crusade for Justice*, 342: "*The Birth of a Nation* . . . has always been a sore spot with many of us here in free Chicago. [The film] won out in an injunction against the city and showed here for many weeks. There are many places in this country today which have never permitted a showing of *The Birth of a Nation*. And if the case had been properly managed here it would not have been shown in this city."

7   Wells, *Crusade for Justice*, 310 (baby carriages). "Cairo Mob Kills 2," *Chicago Daily Tribune*, Nov. 11, 1909, 1 ("refined," "elderly gray . . . black fiend").

8   "All Cairo Gloats over Lynchings," *Chicago Daily Tribune*, Nov. 12, 1909, 1 ("almost . . . neck," "mutilated," "little pile . . . carted away," "best citizens"). Qtd. in Schecter, 138 ("handed out as souvenirs"). "Law Blames Mob, Clergy Condones," *Chicago Daily Tribune*, Nov. 15, 1909, 7 ("lynchings . . . justice"). Following the lynching of James, the mob stormed the jail and lynched a white man, Henry Salzner, who was accused of killing his wife, then unsuccessfully attempted to seize another of the jailed black prisoners, Arthur Alexander, who was accused of complicity in the Pelley murder.

9   The verbatim language of the 1904 Illinois statute appears in Wells-Barnett, "How Enfranchisement Stops Lynching," 46. On the dismissal of Sheriff Davis, see Wells, *Crusade for Justice*, 310. On Edward Green, see Schecter, *Ida B. Wells-Barnett*, 142.

10 Wells-Barnett, "How Enfranchisement Stops Lynching," 46 ("With each repetition . . . country").

11 Wells, *Crusade for Justice*, 310 ("fruitless," "whitewash"). On the Appomattox Club, see Schecter, *Ida B. Wells-Barnett*, 139.

12 Wells, *Crusade for Justice*, 310–11 ("So it would . . . very strongly"). See Sterling, afterword, 194: According to Alfreda Duster, her father "loved stew and hash" and insisted on two or three meat dishes at each evening meal. "All Cairo Gloats," *Chicago Daily Tribune*, 1 ("inflamed . . . breast high").

13 Wells, *Crusade for Justice*, 255 ("arduous work"), 282 ("What It Means to Be a Mother"). For Wells-Barnett's civic work in Chicago, see McMurry, *To Keep the Waters Troubled*, 265–76.

14 Wells, *Crusade for Justice*, 311 ("do . . . refuse").

15 Ibid. ("important . . . will").

16 See ibid., 3: Wells-Barnett opens her autobiography with self-identification with Joan of Arc. See also Schecter, *Ida B. Wells-Barnett*, 32–33. Wells, *Crusade for Justice*, 62 ("I had bought a pistol the first thing after Tom Moss was lynched"), 241 (upon her marriage, "my people . . . seemed to feel that I had deserted the cause, and some of them censured me rather severely in their newspapers for having done so"), 255 (feminist Susan B. Anthony reproached Wells-Barnett for the maternity that "distracted" her from political work and produced a "divided duty"). A photograph of the Central Station waiting room appears in Downey, *Images of Rail*, 26.

17 Barnett qtd. in Schecter, *Ida B. Wells-Barnett*, 94 ("literally . . . White City" [italics added]).

18 See *Chicago World's Fair of 1893*, 103, on Colored People's Day, August 25, 1893, on which, "in the Choral Building, Frederick Douglass gave an address on 'The Race Problem in America,' Paul Laurence Dunbar read a poem he had written for the occasion, the Jubilee Singers performed spirituals, and the composer Will Marion Cook . . . presented selections from his opera *Uncle Tom's Cabin*." See Blackman, *Slavery by Another Name*.

19 Wells, *Reason Why the Colored American*, 46–137. For images of hangings, see ibid., 88, 91. McMurry, *To Keep the Waters Troubled*, 203 ("manned . . . Haitian Building"). See McMurry, *To Keep the Waters Troubled*, 199–205; Schecter, *Ida B. Wells-Barnett*, 94–97; and Rydell, editor's introduction, for the full account of the planning, printing, and distribution of the pamphlet (involving personal and collegial contentiousness and Wells's unsuccessful efforts to raise sufficient funds to produce the publication, as she wished, in several languages). See Alfreda Duster to Mrs. Mardus, Apr. 3, 1964, IBW, box 7, series 3, folder 11, referring to the "twenty thousand copies [of the pamphlet], a 'hard back book,' [which] were distributed," including those sent for three cents' postage by U.S. mail.

20 Douglass, introduction, 51 ("Negroes . . . advocate").

21 Wells, *Crusade for Justice*, 8 ("son . . . slavery").

22 Ibid. (James Wells's vote and move).

23   Ibid., 7 ("were sold . . . again"), 9 ("had been . . . famous cook"). For specifics of the skills of the slave kitchen, see Genovese, *Roll, Jordan, Roll*, 542–43, 545, 546.

24   See Sterling, afterword, 194. Wells, *Crusade for Justice*, 9 ("went along . . . Bible.").

25   Congressional civil rights legislation and amendments to the Constitution qtd. in Tindall and Shi, *America*, 706–9. Wells, *Crusade for Justice*, 9 ("anxious way . . . meant"). For the Civil War–era and Reconstruction-era political situation in Holly Springs and surrounding Marshall County, see McMurry, *To Keep the Waters Troubled*, 4–11. See Budiansky, *Bloody Shirt*, for an account of the lethal terrorism against freed African Americans and their white allies, 1866–76.

26   See McMurry, *To Keep the Waters Troubled*, 20–21, on the epidemic in Holly Springs and the Mississippi valley, including the city of Memphis.

27   Wells, *Crusade for Justice*, 16 ("When all . . . family").

28   *Memphis Diary of Ida B. Wells*, 75 ("old friend" identified as Mrs. Rachel Rather). Wells, *Crusade for Justice*, 17–18 ("stay . . . children"). Coppock, *Memphis Sketches*, 73 ("long-eared . . . mule"). Davidson, *"They Say,"* 50 ("for washing . . . clothes").

29   Wells, *Crusade for Justice*, 9 ("job . . . could").

30   The year of Wells's move to Memphis is disputed. McMurry, *To Keep the Waters Troubled*, dates the move at 1881, whereas Duster's introduction to Wells's *Crusade for Justice* gives 1882 or 1883. Wells, *Crusade for Justice*, 17 ("young, inexperienced . . . world's ways"). McMurry, *To Keep the Waters Troubled*, 13 ("missionary spirit . . . practical education"). See Wells, *Red Record*, 80–81, for Wells's deepest appreciation for "the heroism" of the "noblest, purest and best white women of the North, who felt called to a mission to educate and Christianize the millions of southern ex-slaves and for all the white northern women who came south to teach in the freedmen's schools."

31   McMurry, *To Keep the Waters Troubled*, 13 ("ideal . . . propriety"). See Wells, *Crusade for Justice*, 7: "My parents, who had been slaves and married as such, were married again after freedom came." It was important for Wells to report this. Bushman, *Refinement of America*, 290–91 ("delicacy," "taste," "refined virtues . . . God's law").

32   Bushman, *Refinement of America*, 329 ("no matter . . . study"), 283 ("cultivated people . . . polish"). Bushman adds, "In 1860, the Bureau of the Census considered books a sufficiently significant index of civilization to count the numbers of libraries in each state and the number of books they possessed" (283). See Wells, *Crusade for Justice*, 221–22, on her reading of Dickens. See *Memphis Diary of Ida B. Wells*, 21–2, 25, 51, on her reading of Sir Walter Scott, Charlotte Brontë, Louisa May Alcott, Victor Hugo, and sentimentalist Augusta Evans's *Vashti, or Until Death Do Us Part*, which she regarded as "pure" writing from a pure-of-heart "authoress." See also McMurry, *To Keep the Waters Troubled*, 23. The typical etiquette manual promoted the reading of fiction as a systematic exercise in self-improvement. See Wells, *Manners*, 478: "Begin with whichever characters you are interested in. Gather your materials about that person by examining all allusions to government, commerce, literature, science, and religion. . . . Fiction should have a place in our intellectual furnishing. . . . Read *Ivanhoe* . . . with a history at hand and look up historical allusions."

33   Thornton, *Handwriting in America*, 52–53 ("solidity . . . character"). DeCosta-Willis, editor's note, xxii ("large, well-formed letters"). Qtd. by DeCosta-Willis in *Memphis*

Diary of Ida B. Wells, 51 ("who handles . . . point"). See also Bushman, *Refinement of America*, 290, on the "high value . . . placed on conversation, penmanship, needle-work, and dancing." See *Memphis Diary of Ida B. Wells*, 44, on the importance of letters to Wells as indicated by her purchase of stationery on credit (i.e., at a point when she was short of cash).

34 See McMurry, *To Keep the Waters Troubled*, 17.

35 Davidson, *"They Say,"* 58 ("Up from . . . Negro America"). See also Coppock, *Memphis Sketches*, 64–65, and McMurry, *To Keep the Waters Troubled*, 18–22.

36 On Wells's devotional habits, see Davidson, *"They Say,"* 58–59. Wells, *Crusade for Justice*, 22 ("Negro Bishop"). DeCosta-Willis, introduction, 3 ("excited . . . hospitals"). McMurry, *To Keep the Waters Troubled*, 21–22 ("Mecca," discussion of the Memphis black middle class), 132 (Tennessee Rifles). See also Schecter, *Ida B. Wells-Barnett*, 39–42. See Hamilton, *Bright Side of Memphis*, for a limited retrospective assessment of the status of African Americans in Memphis in the 1880s.

37 Wells, *Crusade for Justice*, 22 ("watched the crowds"). See *Memphis Diary of Ida B. Wells*, 66: "The schoolboard [*sic*] paid two months [late, meaning May 16, 1885]." See DeCosta-Willis, introduction, 26, on Wells's Memphis boardinghouse locations.

38 Wells, *Crusade for Justice*, 31 ("distasteful," "never cared . . . teaching"). Willard, *Occupations for Women*, 262 ("guides . . . souls"). *Memphis Diary of Ida B. Wells*, 37 ("Friday [Jan. 30, 1886] was a trying day in school. I know not what method to use to get my children to become more interested in their lessons"). See DeCosta-Willis, introduction, 33, for a summary of Wells's classroom conditions in Memphis.

39 See Blum, *Victorian Costumes and Fashions*, 149–92, on women's fashion fabrics of the Gilded Age. *Memphis Diary of Ida B. Wells* records her purchases: 53 (shoes), 57 (gloves), 59 (dress goods), 61 (hat), 75 (shirtwaist), 59 (hair trimmed and sham-pooed), 61 (dressmaker). See also Beecher and Stowe, *American Woman's Home*, 353: "Every young girl should be taught to do the following kinds of stitch with propriety: Over-stitch, hemming, running, felling, stitching, back-stitch and run, buttonhole-stitch, chain stitch, whipping, darning, gathering, and cross-stitch."

40 Wells, *Crusade for Justice*, 23 ("recitations . . . poetry"). *Memphis Diary of Ida B. Wells*, 46–47 (her transition into journalism), 177 ("editress"), 181 "standard . . . woman-hood"). See *Memphis Diary of Ida B. Wells*, 177–89, for reprints of her "selected articles 1885–1888." See also McMurry, *To Keep the Waters Troubled*, 76–101. See *Historical Records of Conventions of 1895–1896 of the Colored Women of America*, IBW, box 9, series 15, folder F6, for Victorian terms of uplift appearing amply in the discourse of African American women's organizations of the era.

41 See Wells, *Crusade for Justice*, 22–23. See also McMurry, *To Keep the Waters Troubled*, 35. For a full discussion of Wells-Barnett's techniques of embodiment, see Piepmeier, *Out in Public*, 129–71.

42 T. Thomas Fortune qtd. by DeCosta-Willis in *Memphis Diary of Ida B. Wells*, 51 ("rather girlish . . . voice"), 31 (Wells's male correspondents).

43 *Memphis Diary of Ida B. Wells*, 98 ("base slanderous . . . life"), 125–26 ("iron"). For a full discussion of Wells's vulnerability in regard to her reputation, see Schecter, *Ida B. Wells-Barnett*, 15–17, and McMurry, *To Keep the Waters Troubled*, 50–75.

44 *Memphis Diary of Ida B. Wells*, 38 ("inevitable baby . . . babyhood"). Wells, *Crusade for Justice*, 80 ("society . . . married"). Marriage, in addition, would have restricted

travel opportunities, such as Wells's journey with her aunt and sisters in 1886, when she went west by train and, according to her *Memphis Diary*, marveled at sights along the way, including Colorado's Pike's Peak (91) and the Mormon Tabernacle in Salt Lake City (94). At San Francisco's Cliff House, she watched the Pacific "billows" and breakers and remarked that the salt foam looked like milk and the basking seals like "so many brown bags" (94). See *Crusade for Justice*, 24, on Wells's view that the California town of Visalia was "dull and lonely" and racially overwhelmingly white even though her aunt liked it, as did her sister Annie, both of whom remained permanently, whereas Wells returned to Memphis and once again enjoyed male escorts.

45 *Memphis Diary of Ida B. Wells*, 59–60 ("fits of loneliness . . . all my kind"). Wells's diary shows distinctly different colored inks. See IBW, box 9, series 15, folder F8.

46 *Memphis Diary of Ida B. Wells*, 34 ("was extremely dull . . . extreme"), 38 ("Went to service . . . pulpit").

47 Ibid., 106 ("consolation . . . just").

48 On Wells's expulsion from Shaw (Rust), see McMurry, *To Keep the Waters Troubled*, 13–14. *Memphis Diary of Ida B. Wells*, 78 ("darkest days . . . willfulness").

49 Mary Church Terrell qtd. in Richter, *Home on the Rails*, 50 ("My hands were clean . . . 'lady'"). The train incident is recounted in Wells, *Crusade for Justice*, 18–19.

50 Qtd. in Wells, *Crusade for Justice*, 19–20 ("Darky Damsel . . . this suit"). See Wells, *Southern Horrors*, 60: "The [Negro] race regardless of advancement is penned into filthy, stifling partitions cut off from smoking cars."

51 On Jim Crow, see Ronald L. F. Davis, "Creating Jim Crow: In-Depth Essay," *The History of Jim Crow*, <http://www.jimcrowhistory.org/history/creating2.htm>.

52 See Irons, *People's History of the Supreme Court*, 221–32, for a full account of *Plessy v. Ferguson*.

53 See *Memphis Diary of Ida B. Wells*, 178–84, for Wells's reprinted articles "Functions of Leadership" (1885), "Woman's Mission" (1885), and "A Story of 1900" (1885). Qtd. in McMurry, *To Keep the Waters Troubled*, 100 ("Princess of the Press").

54 Schecter, *Ida B. Wells-Barnett*, 70–75 ("hardening . . . leaders"). *Memphis Diary of Ida B. Wells*, 140–41 ("utterly discouraged . . . with them").

55 *Memphis Diary of Ida B. Wells*, 102 ("colored . . . to view," "dynamitic." Wells noted, "The only evidence" was "that the stomach of the dead woman contained arsenic & a box of 'Rough on Rats' was found in this woman's house, who was a cook for the white woman" (ibid.)

56 Ida B. Wells, "Functions of Leadership," *Living Way*, Sept. 12, 1885, reprinted in *Memphis Diary of Ida B. Wells*, 178–79 ("business establishments . . . employment"). Wells, *Crusade for Justice*, 48 ("sharply"), 47 ("best friends").

57 Wells, *Crusade for Justice*, 48 ("hostility"). For a personal reminiscence of the People's Grocery and the events of the lynching, see Fred L. Hutchins to Alfreda Duster, July 10, 1963, IBW, box 7, series 3, folder 11.

58 Qtd. in McMurry, *To Keep the Waters Troubled*, 133 ("crap den . . . hell"). Wells, *Crusade for Justice*, 48 ("pitched in . . . boy").

59 McMurry, *To Keep the Waters Troubled*, 132 ("over a hundred . . . negroes"). Wells, *Crusade for Justice*, 52 ("ringleader"). Qtd. in McMurry, *To Keep the Waters Troubled*, 133 ("Tell my people . . . here"). See also Schecter, *Ida B. Wells-Barnett*, 75–79, and McMurry, *To Keep the Waters Troubled*, 130–36.

60 Wells, *Crusade for Justice*, 47 ("changed . . . life"), 49 ("low dive . . . thugs"), 55 ("murdered . . . a dog"), 62 (Wells's pistol). A reproduction of the newspaper illustration of the lynched men appears in McMurry, *To Keep the Waters Troubled*, 134. Information on the probable model of Wells's pistol was provided by William Terrell Harrison.

61 McMurry, *To Keep the Waters Troubled*, 143 ("name . . . tirades"), 138 ("contributions . . . epidemic").

62 Wells, *Crusade for Justice*, 64 ("excuse . . . 'the nigger down'").

63 Ibid. ("opened," "eyes").

64 Wells-Barnett qtd. in McMurry, *To Keep the Waters Troubled*, 143 ("In whites' . . . rape"). Wells, *Crusade for Justice*, 66 ("Nobody in . . . their women").

65 Qtd. in McMurry, *To Keep the Waters Troubled*, 148 ("Lynch the author"). A threat of castration in the editorial shows the mistaken assumption that the author was male. Fortune qtd. by DeCosta-Willis in *Memphis Diary of Ida B. Wells*, 51 ("has no sympathy . . . trap").

66 Qtd. in Wells, *Southern Horrors*, 50 ("array . . . done"). *Tabulated Statistics and Alleged Causes of Lynching in the United States* is the subtitle of Wells's *Red Record*. See Wells, *Red Record*, 82–87, for her statistical compilation of lynchings, and 75 for her remark that "the statistics as gathered and preserved by white men, and which have not been questioned, show that during these years [1892–94] more than ten thousand Negroes have been killed in cold blood, without the formality of judicial trial and legal execution." Wells, *Southern Horrors*, 66 ("there is little difference . . . New South"). See Goldsby, *Spectacular Secret*, 46–48, 64–71, for a full account of Wells's exploitation of contemporary journalistic practices. See Royster, "To Call a Thing," for analysis of Wells's "rhetoric of defiance." See Schecter, *Ida B. Wells-Barnett*, 127, for an account of a lynching in Akron, Ohio, in 1900.

67 Wells, *Red Record*, 131 ("news gathered . . . white people").

68 Typescript of article qtd. in *Ladies Pictorial*, May 1893, IBW, box 8, series 7, folder 10, ("attractive . . . voice"). See Wells, *Southern Horrors*, 61, for Wells's view that educated African Americans were so revolted by the crime of rape that "they have too often taken the white man's word and given lynch law neither the investigation nor condemnation it deserved." Wells, *Crusade for Justice*, 265 ("trying to be first-class . . . abolished"), 264–65, 280–81 (Wells's critique of Washington's position). See also Wells, "Booker T. Washington."

69 Wells, *Southern Horrors*, 70 ("more the Afro-American . . . and lynched"). See Schecter, *Ida B. Wells-Barnett*, 63–70, 141–49, on Wells's difficult relationships with male and female black leaders and organizations and the racially charged dynamics of gender.

70 Wells, *Red Record*, 78 ("legislators . . . bishops"). Wells, *Southern Horrors*, 71 ("race of cut-throats . . . wild beasts"), 68 ("accomplices . . . breakers"), 61 ("cowards . . . whole country").

71 Willard qtd. in Wells, *Red Record*, 142 ("colored race . . . thousand localities"). See Wells, *Crusade for Justice*, 111–13, 151–52, 177–78, for a full account of the controversy with Willard.

72 Davis, *Spearheads for Reform*, 94 ("Many of the settlement . . . the Negroes"). See also ibid., 94–102. Strum, *Louis D. Brandeis*, 330 ("civil liberties . . . citizens"). Shaler

qtd. in Bannister, *Social Darwinism*, 191–92 ("old African . . . superior race"). See also Shaler, "Negro Question."

73 See Rauschenbusch, "Belated Races and the Social Problems," 259: "The Christian way out [of the social problems] is to take our belated black brother by the hand and urge him along the road of steady and intelligent labor, of property rights, of family fidelity, of hope and self-confidence, and of pride and joy in his race achievements." On racial "amalgamation," see Commons, *Races and Immigrants*. See Hamilton, *Exploring the Dangerous Trades*, 32, for her recollection of her mother "blaz[ing] out [at] the lynching of Negroes." See Hamilton qtd. in Sicherman, *Alice Hamilton*, 68 ("my little negress"). See Schecter, *Ida B. Wells-Barnett*, 84, on Wells's self-representation as "an educated, middle-class Southern woman of mixed racial ancestry" and "representative public figure" who "credibly told the truth."

74 Schecter, *Ida B. Wells-Barnett*, 89 (reproduction of "A Lecture" announcement in the *Washington Bee*, Oct. 1892). Wells's lecture "Lynch Law in All Its Phases" was presented at Tremont Temple in Boston, Feb. 13, 1893. A copy is on file in IBW, box 8, series 7, folder 8.

75 Wells's linkage to Paine is noted in Schecter, *Ida B. Wells-Barnett*, 85. See McMurry, *To Keep the Waters Troubled*, 169–87, on Wells's lectures in connection with her pamphlets.

76 Wells, *Crusade for Justice*, 209 ("Negro question . . . move them").

77 Ibid., 125 ("persistently denounced lynching," "regular paid correspondent"), 86 ("open door . . . wall"), 95 ("silent indifference").

78 Schecter, *Ida B. Wells-Barnett*, 99 ("London correspondent . . . activities"). *Chicago Inter-ocean*, Aug. 4, 1894, IBW, box 8, series 7, folder 10 ("British Emigrants . . . Lynching Ceases"). See Schecter, *Ida B. Wells-Barnett*, 91–94, 98–103, on Wells's speaking tours in Britain. See also McMurry, *To Keep the Waters Troubled*, 188–89. See Wells, *Crusade for Justice*, 125–200, for reprinted passages from her *Inter-ocean* dispatches and numerous British newspaper accounts of her lectures and her letters to British newspapers. *Times* (London) qtd. in Floyd D. Crawford, "Ida B. Wells: Some American Reactions to Her Anti-lynching Crusade in Britain," IBW, box 9, series 11, folder F2 ("to obtain . . . civilization").

79 "All Cairo Gloats," *Chicago Daily Tribune*, 1 ("ominous"). Wells, *Crusade for Justice*, 312 ("worthless . . . fellow"), 317 ("typewritten and worded").

80 Wells, *Crusade for Justice*, 316 ("blistering"), 315 ("mouthpiece").

81 Ibid., 315 ("Not a Negro . . . demand for reinstatement").

82 Ibid., 316 ("Negro ministers . . . Illinois").

83 Ibid., 317 ("Governor . . . to mob violence"), 318 "wonderful speech"), 319 ("terrific . . . no more"). See also ibid., 315–17, on the hearings conducted over a two-day period, including moments of contentiousness and sessions of fact-finding.

84 Ibid., 319 ("he had not . . . in Illinois"). See Schecter, *Ida B. Wells-Barnett*, 138–41, 290 n. 86, on a thwarted attempt by a Cairo mob within six weeks at another lynch murder.

85 Duster to Mardus, Apr. 3, 1964 ("dig dig dig"). See Wells, *Crusade for Justice*, 367–71, 383–95, on her subsequent investigations and activism. See also Wells-Barnett, *Arkansas Race Riot*. Wells, *Red Record*, 154–57 ("to disseminate . . . full rights of citizen-

ship"). Du Bois, "Postscript," qtd. in Thompson, *Ida B. Wells-Barnett*, 126 ("pioneer . . . conscience of the nation").

86 See Metress, *Lynching of Emmett Till*, for the national scope of the lynching and the trial in which the accused were swiftly found not guilty. See Jaspin, *Burn in the Bitter Waters*, for an account of racial "cleansing" in the United States, 1900–1920.

87 For postal card images, see Goldsby, *Spectacular Secret* (the cover illustration showing the site of Frog James's hanging in Cairo), and Davidson, *"They Say,"* 6. See also the online archive *Without Sanctuary*, <http://www.withoutsanctuary.org/>. The public television documentary series on the history of the civil rights movement *Eyes on the Prize* includes a TV network news clip showing Birmingham, Alabama, police chief "Bull" Connor ordering police dogs and fire hoses turned on civil rights activists in 1963.

88 See Tindall and Shi, *America*, 1312–14 ("most far-reaching . . . other accommodations"), 1353–54 ("attorney-general . . . or sex"). King, "Where Do We Go," 176 ("questions about . . . wealth").

POSTSCRIPT

1 Chapman, *Practical Agitation*, 17 ("All . . . experimental").

2 Santayana, *Life of Reason*, 383 ("progress . . . retentiveness"). Former secretary of labor Robert B. Reich, in *Supercapitalism*, 11, writes, "By the time Reagan came to power, the [U.S.] economy had already started to shift. Deregulation, for example, unleashed many of America's industries before Reagan took office. Small, profitable airlines, banks, and high-tech companies had already gained a foothold and were intent on bringing down regulatory barriers. The percentage of American workers belonging to labor unions was already declining. And the number of business lobbyists in Washington, D.C., had already begun rising."

3 See Anton Troianovski, "Most U.S. Unemployed Receive No Benefits," *Wall Street Journal*, July 29, 2008, A4. For a chronicle of banking deregulation from 1970 to 2008, see Prins, "Where Credit Is Due." In 2008, whistleblowers at the Federal Aviation Administration revealed lax aircraft inspections attributed to an ongoing collusive relationship between managers at Southwest Airlines and FAA supervisors who regarded the airline, not the flying public, as the agency's client. Fortunately, the disclosure prompted congressional hearings and the immediate cancellations of Southwest flights so that corrective inspections of fuselages for cracks in Southwest's Boeing 737 aircraft could be conducted. (Five aircraft showed the potentially dangerous cracks.) Newly recognizing its mission in protecting the safety of the flying public, the FAA ordered the inspection of the MD-80 fleet of American Airlines, which cancelled some 9,000 flights during April 2008 to inspect sheathed wiring in aircraft wheel wells, lest overheated wires cause fires in proximate fuel tanks. See Andy Pasztor, "Southwest's Cozy Ties Triggered FAA Tumult," *Wall Street Journal*, Apr. 3, 2008, A1, A11.

4 See Michael Lewis and David Einhorn, "The End of the Financial World as We Know It," *New York Times*, Jan. 4, 2009, <http://www.nytimes.com/2009/01/04/opinion/04lewiseinhorn.html>, p. 2 ("pyramid scheme," "required . . . gain"), p. 3 ("Rather . . . disguised it"). See also Lewis, *Panic*, a compilation of business journalists' pub-

lished warnings about the financial system's weaknesses from the late 1980s to the present.

5 Robert Pear, "Gap in Life Expectancy Widens for Nation," *New York Times*, Mar. 23, 2008, 14 ("'large and growing' . . . decades").

6 Silverstein, "Beltway Bacchanal."

7 Reich, *Supercapitalism*.

8 See U.S. Bureau of Labor Statistics, "Union Members in 2007," news release, Jan. 25, 2008, <http://www.bls.gov/news.release/union2.nro.htm>.

9 Tichi, introduction, 26 ("Between 1979 . . . in the U.S."). On pension and health care cutbacks, see Greenhouse, *Big Squeeze*. See Ellen E. Schultz and Theo Francis, "Companies Tap Pension Plans to Fund Executive Benefits," *Wall Street Journal*, Aug. 4, 2008, A1, A9. Frank, *Falling Behind* ("rising . . . class"). Pew Research Center, "Executive Summary" ("stuck . . . of polling"). Gosselin, *High Wire*. Kris Maher, "More People Pushed into Part-Time Work Force," *Wall Street Journal*, Mar. 8–9, 2008, A1, A6. See also "New Inequality," *Nation*.

10 Starkman, "Red Ink Rising," 14–15 ("1978 ruling . . . bread and butter").

11 Pew Research Center, "Executive Summary."

12 Newman and Chen, *Missing Class*. Bowe, *Nobodies*. See also Leonard Doyle, "Slave Labour That Shames America," *Independent* (London), Dec. 19, 2007, <http://www.independent.co.uk/news/world/americas/slave-labour-that-shames-america-765881.html>.

13 Hallinan, *Going up the River* ("prison nation"). See also Taibbi, "Jailhouse Nation." See U.S. Supreme Court rulings in *Parents Involved in Community Schools v. Seattle School District No. 1* (Seattle) and *Meredith v. Jefferson County Board of Education* (Louisville, Kentucky).

14 Rosen, "Supreme Court Inc.," 71, 40–41 ("ideological sea change . . . health and safety"). Rosen traces the history from 1971 of the proactive involvement of the U.S. Chamber of Commerce in bringing about a probusiness judiciary at the state and national levels. He writes, "Of 30 business cases last term [2006–7], 22 were decided unanimously, or with only one or two dissenting votes," and "several of the most important decisions were written by liberal justices. . . . In opinions last term, Ruth Bader Ginsburg, Stephen Breyer and David Souter each went out of his or her way to question the use of lawsuits to challenge corporate wrongdoing—a strategy championed by progressive groups like Public Citizen" (40).

On IRS accommodation of large corporations, see Lynnley Browning, "I.R.S. Scrutiny of Big Firms Plummets, Study Says," *New York Times*, Apr. 14, 2008, <http://www.nytimes.com/2008/04/14/business/14irs.html>: "The I.R.S.'s scrutiny of the nation's biggest companies is at a 20-year low, according to the study, conducted by Transactional Records Access Clearinghouse . . . a research group affiliated with Syracuse University." On the Justice Department's "deferred prosecution," see Eric Lichtblau, "In Justice Shift, Corporate Deals Replace Trials," *New York Times*, Apr. 9, 2008, A1: "In a major shift of policy, the Justice Department, once known for taking down major corporations [beginning with criminal indictments] . . . has put off prosecuting more than 50 companies suspected of wrongdoing. Instead, many companies, from boutique outfits to immense corporations like American Express, have avoided the cost and stigma of defending themselves against criminal charges with a so-called deferred prosecution, which allows the government to collect fines and appoint an outside monitor to impose internal reforms without going through a trial. In many cases, the name of the monitor and the details of the agreement are kept secret."

15 Forsberg qtd. in "Peace Action," *Wikipedia*, <http://en.wikipedia.org/wiki/Peace_Action> ("freeze . . . race").

16 On recent muckrakers and interviews with them on their development as writers, see Tichi, *Exposés and Excess*. Kozol, *Savage Inequalities*.

17 See Bina Venkataraman, "Amid Salmonella Case, Food Industry Seems Set to Back Greater Regulation," *New York Times*, July 31, 2008, A17. Steven Greenhouse, "$70 Million Effort Seeks New Safety Net for Workers," *New York Times*, July 31, 2008, A17 ("help build . . . vulnerable").

18 Sara Rimer, "In College, Brief Showers and a Green Conscience," *New York Times*, May 26, 2008, A1, A11 ("green conscience . . . economic issues"). See also the *New York Times*' "Education Life" special issue on ecological college and secondary school projects, July 27, 2008.

19 See the Coalition of Immokalee Workers' website, <http://www.ciw-online.org/>. From 1993, this coalition has organized a news media campaign, petition drives, public demonstrations, a documentary film, boycotts, a website, political outreach, and other means to secure a one-cent-per-pound increase in wages for Florida tomato field workers, whose manual labor provides these chains with tomatoes for a host of products. The coalition succeeded in getting McDonald's, Yum! Brands (owners of Taco Bell, Pizza Hut, and KFC), and Burger King to agree to a per-pound raise from forty-five cents per thirty-two-pound bucket of tomatoes to seventy-seven cents — a 40 percent pay boost — in a campaign begun in 1993 and still under way to enlist grocery store and other fast-food chains.

See "Fair Trade," *Wikipedia*, <http://en.wikipedia.org/wiki/Fair_trade>, on the fair trade movement goal "to deliberately work with marginalized producers and workers in order to help them move from a position of vulnerability to one of security and economic self-sufficiency." "United Students against Sweatshops," *Wikipedia*, <http://en.wikipedia.org/wiki/United_Students_Against_Sweatshops> ("works with NGOs . . . is produced").

20 Flowers, *American Dream and the Economic Myth*, 3 ("dominant myth"), 10–11 ("economic myth . . . capitalism").

21 Ibid., 5 ("bottom line . . . unconsciously"), 14 ("to create . . . might become").

22 On social entrepreneurs, see Bornstein, *How to Change the World*. Sam Dillon, "Two School Entrepreneurs Lead the Way on Change," *New York Times*, June 19, 2008, A15, A23.

23 Lathrop qtd. in Addams, *My Friend, Julia Lathrop*, 149 ("present time . . . defeat"). Kellogg, "Living Spirit of Florence Kelley," 8 ("tool marks . . . road").

BIBLIOGRAPHY

Ackerman, Kenneth D. *Boss Tweed: The Rise and Fall of the Corrupt Pol Who Conceived the Soul of Modern New York*. New York: Carroll and Graf, 2005.

Ackerman, S. B. *Industrial Life Insurance: Its History, Statistics, and Plans*. Chicago: Spectator, 1926.

Addams, Jane. "Chicago Settlements and Social Unrest." *Charities and the Commons*, May 2, 1908, 154–66.

———. *Democracy and Social Ethics*. 1902. Reprint. Urbana: University of Illinois Press, 2002.

———. *The Long Road of Woman's Memory*. 1916. Reprint. Urbana: University of Illinois Press, 2002.

———. *My Friend, Julia Lathrop*. 1935. Reprint. Urbana: University of Illinois Press, 2002.

———. "The Objective Value of a Social Settlement." In *Philanthropy and Social Progress*, 27–56. New York: Crowell, 1893.

———. "The Subjective Value of a Social Settlement." In *Philanthropy and Social Progress*, 1–26. New York: Crowell, 1893.

———. *Twenty Years at Hull-House*. 1910. Reprint. Edited by Victoria Bissell Brown. Boston: Bedford/St. Martin's, 1999.

Adkins, Sam, and M. R. Holtzman. *The First Hundred Years: The Story of Louisville Male High School*. Louisville, Ky.: Administration and Alumni of the Louisville Male High School, 1956.

Aldritch, Nelson W., Jr. *Old Money: The Mythology of Wealth in America*. New York: Allworth, 1996.

Alger, Horatio, Jr. *Adrift in New York* and *The World before Him*. Edited by William Coyle. New York: Odyssey, 1966.

———. *The Store Boy, or The Fortunes of Ben Barclay*. 1887. <http://www.authorama.com/the-store-boy-1.html>.

Amory, Cleveland. *The Proper Bostonians*. New York: Dutton, 1947.

Anderson, Paul Gerard. "'The Good to Be Done': A History of the Juvenile Protective Association of Chicago, 1898–1976." Ph.D. diss., University of Chicago, 1988.

Andrews, John B. "Phosphorus Poisoning in the Match Industry in the United States." *Bureau of Labor Statistics Bulletin 86*. Washington, D.C.: U.S. Government Printing Office, 1914.

Andrist, Ralph K., ed. *The American Heritage History of the Confident Years*. New York: American Heritage, 1969.

Ankenbruck, John. *The Fort Wayne Story*. Woodland Hills, Calif.: Windsor, 1980.

Applegate, Debby. *The Most Famous Man in America: The Biography of Henry Ward Beecher*. New York: Three Leaves Press, 2006.

Arne, Robert C. "William Graham Sumner, 1840–1910: His Life and Work." *Libertarian Heritage* 6 (1992), <http://www.libertarian.co.uk/lapubs/libhe/libhe006.pdf>.

Arter, Bill. "Ohio Columbus Barber." *Columbus (Ohio) Dispatch Magazine*, Oct. 13, 1963, 8–11.

Badger, R. Reid. *The Great American Fair: The World's Columbian Exposition and American Culture*. Chicago: Hall, 1979.

Baedeker, K[arl]. *Switzerland and the Adjacent Portions of Italy, Savoy, and the Tyrol: Handbook for Travellers*. Leipzig: Baedeker, 1889.

Baker, Ray Stannard. *Following the Color Line: American Negro Citizenship in the Progressive Era*. 1907–8. Reprint. New York: Harper and Row, 1964.

———. "The Problem of Race." In *The Conservation of National Ideals*, 71–98. New York: Revell, 1911.

Baltzell, E. Digby. *The Protestant Establishment: Aristocracy and Caste in America*. New York: Random House, 1964.

Bannister, Robert C. *Social Darwinism: Science and Myth in Anglo-American Social Thought*. Philadelphia: Temple University Press, 1979.

Barry, Bruce. *Speechless: The Erosion of Free Expression in the American Workplace*. San Francisco: Barrett-Koehler, 2007.

Basten, Fred E. *Great American Billboards: 100 Years of History by the Side of the Road*. Berkeley, Calif.: Ten Speed, 2007.

Bates, Roy M., and Kenneth B. Keller. *The Columbia Street Story*. Fort Wayne, Ind.: Board of Trustees of the Fort Wayne Public Library, 1975.

Bay, J. Christian. *The John Crerar Library 1895–1944*. Chicago: Directors of the John Crerar Library, 1945.

Beach, Bell. *Riding and Driving for Women*. New York: Scribner Sons, 1912.

Beckner, Earl R. *A History of Labor Legislation in Illinois*. Chicago: University of Chicago Press, 1929.

Beecher, Catherine E., and Harriet Beecher Stowe. *The American Woman's Home, or Principles of Domestic Science*. 1869. Reprint. Hartford, Conn.: Harriet Beecher Stowe Center, 1996.

Beer, Thomas. *The Mauve Decade: American Life at the End of the Nineteenth Century*. New York: Knopf, 1926.

Beers, Clifford W. *A Mind That Found Itself*. 1909. Reprint. Garden City, N.Y.: Doubleday, 1953.

Bellamy, Edward. *Looking Backward, 2000–1887*. 1888. Reprint. New York: Penguin, 1985.

Bellomy, Donald Cecil. "The Molding of an Iconoclast: William Graham Sumner, 1840–1885." Ph.D. diss., Harvard University, 1980.

Bernstein, Michael A. *A Perilous Progress: Economists and Public Purpose in Twentieth-Century America*. Princeton, N.J.: Princeton University Press, 2001.

Biographical Dictionary of American and Canadian Naturalists and Environmentalists. Edited by Keir B. Sterling. Westport, Conn.: Greenwood, 1997.

Birmingham, Stephen. *"Our Crowd": The Great Jewish Families of New York*. 1967. Reprint. Syracuse, N.Y.: Syracuse University Press, 1996.

Bisno, Abraham. *Bisno, Union Pioneer.* Madison: University of Wisconsin Press, 1967.

Blackman, Douglas A. *Slavery by Another Name: The Re-enslavement of Black Americans from the Civil War to World War II.* New York: Doubleday, 2008.

Blaug, Mark, ed. *Pioneers in Economics: Wesley Mitchell (1874–1948), John Commons (1862–1945), Clarence Ayres (1891–1972).* Brookfield, Vt.: Elger, 1992.

Blum, Stella, ed. *Victorian Costumes and Fashions from* Harper's Bazaar — *1867–1893.* New York: Dover, 1974.

Blumberg, Dorothy Rose. *Florence Kelley: The Making of a Social Pioneer.* New York: Kelley, 1966.

Boorstin, Daniel J. *The Americans: The National Experience.* New York: Random House, 1965.

Bornstein, David. *How to Change the World: Social Entrepreneurs and the Power of New Ideas.* New York: Oxford University Press, 2006.

Bowe, John. *Nobodies: Modern American Slave Labor and the Dark Side of the New Global Economy.* New York: Random House, 2007.

Bowen, Louise de Koven. *Growing Up with a City.* Urbana: University of Illinois Press, 2002.

Bowman, John R. *Capitalist Collective Action: Competition, Cooperation, and Conflict in the Coal Industry.* New York: Cambridge University Press, 1989.

Bradbury, Dorothy E. *Five Decades of Action for Children: A History of the Children's Bureau.* Washington, D.C.: U.S. Department of Health, Education, and Welfare, 1962.

Brandeis, Louis D. *Brandeis on Democracy.* Edited by Philippa Strum. Lawrence: University Press of Kansas, 1995.

———. *Brandeis on Zionism: A Collection of Addresses and Statements.* Washington, D.C.: Zionist Organization of America, 1942.

———. *Business: A Profession.* 1927. Reprint. Buffalo, N.Y.: Hein, 1996.

———. *The Curse of Bigness: Miscellaneous Papers of Louis D. Brandeis.* Edited by Osmond K. Fraenkel. New York: Viking, 1934.

———. *The Family Letters of Louis D. Brandeis.* Edited by Melvin I. Urofsky and David W. Levy. Norman: University of Oklahoma Press, 2002.

———. *"Half Brother, Half Son": The Letters of Louis D. Brandeis to Felix Frankfurter.* Edited by Melvin I. Urofsky and David W. Levy. Norman: University of Oklahoma Press, 1991.

———. *Letters of Louis D. Brandeis.* Edited by Melvin I. Urofsky and David W. Levy. 5 vols. Albany: State University of New York Press, 1971–78.

———. *Other People's Money and How the Bankers Use It.* Edited by Melvin L. Urofsky. 1914. Reprint. Boston: Bedford/St. Martin's, 1995.

———. "Wage-Earners' Life Insurance." 1906. Reprinted in Mason, *Brandeis Way,* 311–25.

———. "What Labor Can Learn from the McNamara Case." *American Cloak and Suit Review,* Jan. 1912, 237–38.

———. *Women in Industry: Decision of the United States Supreme Court in* Curt Muller vs. State of Oregon *Upholding the Constitutionality of the Oregon Ten Hour Law for Women and Brief for the State of Oregon.* 1908. Reprint. New York: Arno, 1969.

Bremmer, Robert H. *From the Depths: The Discovery of Poverty in the United States.* New York: New York University Press, 1967.

Briney, Melvile O. *Fond Recollection: Sketches of Old Louisville*. Louisville, Ky.: Louisville Times, 1955.

Brink, Carol Ryrie. *Caddie Woodlawn*. 1935. Reprint. New York: Aladdin, 1990.

Brooks, John Graham. *The Consumers' League: The Economic Principle upon Which It Rests and the Practicability of Its Enforcement*. Newton: Consumers' League of Massachusetts, 1898.

———. *The Social Unrest: Studies in Labor and Socialist Movements*. New York: Macmillan, 1903.

Brooks, Van Wyck. *New England: Indian Summer 1865–1915*. New York: Dutton, 1940.

Brown, Victoria Bissell. *The Education of Jane Addams*. Philadelphia: University of Pennsylvania Press, 2004.

Browne, Waldo. *Altgeld of Illinois: A Record of His Life and Work*. New York: Huebsch, 1924.

Budiansky, Stephen. *The Bloody Shirt: Terror after Appomattox*. New York: Viking, 2008.

Burrows, Edwin G., and Mike Wallace. *Gotham: A History of New York City to 1898*. New York: Oxford University Press, 1999.

Burt, Robert. *Two Jewish Justices: Outcasts in the Promised Land*. Berkeley: University of California Press, 1988.

Bushman, Richard L. *The Refinement of America: Persons, Houses, Cities*. 1992. Reprint. New York: Vintage, 1993.

Byington, Margaret F. *Homestead: The Households of a Mill Town*. New York: Charities Publication Committee, 1910.

Cameron, James. *A Time of Terror*. Baltimore: Black Classic Press, 1982.

Campbell, Helen. *Prisoners of Poverty: Women Wage-Workers, Their Trades and Their lives*. Boston: Roberts, 1889.

Carlebach, Michael L. *Working Stiffs: Occupational Portraits in the Age of Tintypes*. Washington, D.C.: Smithsonian Institution Press.

Caron's Directory of the City of Louisville for 1876. Louisville, Ky.: Caron, 1876.

Cashman, Sean Dennis. *America in the Gilded Age: From the Death of Lincoln to the Rise of Theodore Roosevelt*. 3rd ed. New York: New York University Press, 1993.

Casseday, Ben. *The History of Louisville from Its Earliest Settlement till the Year 1852*. Louisville, Ky.: Hull, 1852.

Chace, James. *1912: Wilson, Roosevelt, Taft & Debs — the Election That Changed the Country*. New York: Simon and Schuster, 2004.

Chambers, John Whiteclay II. *The Tyranny of Change: America in the Progressive Era, 1890– 1920*. 2nd ed. New York: St. Martin's, 1992.

Chapman, John Jay. *Practical Agitation*. New York: Scribner, 1900.

Chernow, Ron. *Titan: The Life of John D. Rockefeller, Sr.* 1998. Reprint. New York: Vintage, 1999.

The Chicago World's Fair of 1893: A Photographic Record. Text by Stanley Applebaum. Mineola, N.Y.: Dover, 1980.

The Child in the City: A Handbook of the Child Welfare Exhibit. Chicago: Blakely, 1911.

Chittister, Joan. "Unless the Call Be Heard Again." In Rauschenbusch, *Christianity and the Social Crisis in the 21st Century*, 117–21.

Clark, Sue Ainslie, and Edith Wyatt. *Making Both Ends Meet: The Income and Outlay of New York Working Girls*. New York: Macmillan, 1911.

Clarke, Michael Tavel. *These Days of Large Things: The Culture of Size in America*. Ann Arbor: University of Michigan Press, 2007.

Cleveland, Grover. *Good Citizenship*. 1908. Reprint. New Bedford, Mass.: Applewood Books, 1998.

Clymer, Jeffory A. *America's Culture of Terrorism: Violence, Capitalism, and the Written Word*. Chapel Hill: University of North Carolina Press, 2003.

Coleman, J. Winston, Jr. *Slavery Times in Kentucky*. Chapel Hill: University of North Carolina Press, 1940.

Committee on Industrial and Commercial Improvement. *The City of Louisville and a Glimpse of Kentucky*. Louisville, Ky.: Committee on Industrial and Commercial Improvement of the Louisville Board of Trade, 1887.

Commons, John R. *The Distribution of Wealth*. New York: Macmillan, 1905.

———. *Industrial Goodwill*. 1919. Reprint. New York: Arno, 1969.

———. *Institutional Economics: Its Place in Political History*. New York: Macmillan, 1934.

———. Introduction to *History of Labour in the United States*. Vols. 3 and 4. New York: Macmillan, 1935.

———. *Legal Foundations of Capitalism*. New York: Macmillan, 1924.

———. *Myself*. New York: Macmillan, 1934.

———. *Races and Immigrants in America*. 2nd ed. New York: Macmillan, 1924.

———. *Social Reform and the Church*. 1894. Reprint. New York: Kelley, 1967.

Commons, John R., and John B. Andrews. *Principles of Labor Legislation*. New York: Harper, 1916.

Continetti, Matthew. *The K Street Gang: The Rise and Fall of the Republican Machine*. New York: Doubleday, 2006.

Conwell, Russell H. "Acres of Diamonds." Temple University, n.d., < http://www.temple .edu/about/AcresofDiamonds.htm >.

Cooke, Maud C. *Twentieth Century Hand-Book of Etiquette, or Key to Social and Business Success*. Philadelphia: National, 1899.

Coppock, Paul R. *Memphis Sketches*. Memphis, Tenn.: Friends of Memphis and Shelby County Libraries, 1976.

Cornell, Stephen. *The Traders Ready Reckoner*. Hudson, N.Y.: Ashbel Stoddard, 1819.

Costin, Lela B. *Two Sisters for Social Justice: A Biography of Grace and Edith Abbott*. 1983. Reprint. Urbana: University of Illinois Press, 2003.

Coyne, Patrick, and Edward Moran. *A Bio-bibliography of Clarence S. Day, Jr., American Writer, 1874–1935*. Lewiston, N.Y.: Edwin Mellen Press, 2003.

Crews, Clyde F. *An American Holy Land: A History of the Archdiocese of Louisville*. Wilmington, Del.: Glazier, 1987.

Croly, Herbert. *Marcus Alonzo Hanna: His Life and Work*. New York: Macmillan, 1912.

———. *The Promise of American Life*. 1909. Reprint. Boston: Northeastern University Press, 1989.

Cromley, Elizabeth Collins. "A History of American Beds and Bedrooms, 1890–1930." In *American Home Life, 1880–1930: A Social History of Spaces and Services*, edited by Jessica H. Foy and Thomas J. Schlereth, 120–41. Knoxville: University of Tennessee Press, 1992.

Cronon, William. *Nature's Metropolis: Chicago and the Great West*. New York: Norton, 1991.

Cross, Gary. *An All-Consuming Century: Why Commercialism Won in Modern America*. New York: Columbia University Press, 2000.

Cruikshank, James A. *Canoeing*. New York: American Sports, 1913.

Danbom, David B. *"The World of Hope": Progressives and the Struggle for an Ethical Public Life*. Philadelphia: Temple University Press, 1987.

Darwin, Charles. *The Origin of Species*. 1859. Reprint. New York: Random House, 1993.

Davidson, James West. *"They Say": Ida B. Wells and the Reconstruction of Race*. New York: Oxford University Press, 2007.

Davis, Allen F. *Spearheads for Reform: The Social Settlements and the Progressive Movement, 1890–1914*. New York: Oxford University Press, 1967.

Davis, Rebecca Harding. "John Lamar." *Atlantic Monthly*, Apr. 1862, 411–23.

———. *Life in the Iron Mills*. Edited by Cecelia Tichi. Boston: Bedford, 1998.

Day, Clarence. *The Best of Clarence Day*. New York: Knopf, 1948.

DeCosta-Willis, Miriam. Editor's note to *Memphis Diary of Ida B. Wells*, xix–xxiv.

———. Introduction to *Memphis Diary of Ida B. Wells*, 1–16.

Deegan, Mary Jo. *Jane Addams and the Men of the Chicago School, 1892–1918*. 1988. Reprint. New Brunswick, N.J.: Transaction, 2005.

Deering, Richard. *Louisville: Her Commercial, Manufacturing, and Social Advantages*. Louisville, Ky.: Hanna, 1859.

De Kruif, Paul. *Microbe Hunters*. 1926. Reprint. New York: Harcourt, 1954.

Deland, Margaret. "The New Woman Who Would Do Things." *New Ladies Home Journal*, Sept. 1907, 17.

DeMause, Neil. "The Smell of Success." *Nation*, Dec. 4, 2006, 6–7.

Dembitz, Lewis N. *Jewish Services in Synagogue and Home*. 1898. Reprint. New York: Arno, 1975.

DePastino, Todd. *Citizen Hobo: How a Century of Homelessness Shaped America*. Chicago: University of Chicago Press, 2003.

Detzer, Karl. *Myself When Young*. New York: Funk and Wagnalls, 1968.

Devine, Edward T. *Social Forces*. New York: Charities Publication Committee, 1910.

———. *When Social Work Was Young*. New York: Macmillan, 1939.

Diner, Steven J. *A Very Different Age: Americans of the Progressive Era*. New York: Hill and Wang, 1998.

Diserens, Albert F. *Cultural Backgrounds of Fort Wayne since 1880*. N.p., 1956.

Dizikes, John. *Opera in America: A Cultural History*. New Haven, Conn.: Yale University Press, 1993.

Dorrien, Gary. *The Making of American Liberal Theology*. Vol. 1, *Imagining Progressive Religion, 1805–1900*. Louisville, Ky.: Westminster John Knox Press, 2001.

———. *The Making of American Liberal Theology*. Vol. 2, *Idealism, Realism, and Modernity, 1900–1950*. Louisville, Ky.: Westminster John Knox Press, 2003.

Douglas, Ann. *The Feminization of American Culture*. 1977. Reprint. New York: Avon, 1978.

Douglas, Emily. "The Forbes 400: When $1 Billion Isn't Enough." *Forbes*, Oct. 8, 2007, <http://www.forbes.com/free_forbes/2007/1008/034.html>.

Douglass, Frederick. Introduction to *Reason Why the Colored American*, in Wells-Barnett, *Selected Works*, 50–61.

Downey, Clifford J. *Images of Rail: Chicago and the Illinois Central Railroad*. Charleston, S.C.: Arcadia, 2007.

Dreiser, Theodore. *A Hoosier Holiday*. 1916. Reprint. Urbana: University of Illinois Press, 1997.

———. *Sister Carrie*. 1912. Reprint. New York: Modern Library, 1999.

Dryden, John F. *Addresses and Papers on Life Insurance and Other Subjects*. Newark, N.J.: Prudential Insurance Company of America, 1919.

———. *Careers for the Coming Men*. Newark, N.J.: Prudential Insurance Company of America, 1903.

Du Bois, W[illiam] E[dward] B[urghardt]. *The Souls of Black Folk*. 1903. Reprint. New York: Bantam, 1989.

Duis, Perry R. *The Saloon: Public Drinking in Chicago and Boston, 1880–1920*. Urbana: University of Illinois Press, 1983.

Dunlop, M. H. *Gilded City: Scandal and Sensation in Turn-of-the-Century New York*. 2000. Reprint. New York: HarperCollins, 2001.

Dunn, Jacob Piatt, and John Finley. "The Word 'Hoosier.'" *Indiana Historical Society Publications* 4, no. 2 (1895): 3–29.

Durrett, Reuben T. *The Centenary of Louisville*. Louisville, Ky.: Morton, 1893.

Eastman, Crystal. *Work-Accidents and the Law*. New York: Survey Associates, 1916.

Edwards, Wendy J. Deichman, and Carolyn De Swarte Gifford, eds. *Gender and the Social Gospel*. Urbana: University of Illinois Press, 2003.

Eggleston, Edward. *The Hoosier Schoolmaster: A Story of Backwoods Life in Indiana*. 1871. Reprint. New York: Grosset and Dunlop, 1913.

Elshtain, Jean Bethke. *Jane Addams and the Dream of American Democracy*. New York: Basic Books, 2002.

Elson, Ruth Miller. *Guardians of Tradition: American Schoolbooks of the Nineteenth Century*. Lincoln: University of Nebraska Press, 1964.

Ely, Carol. *Jewish Louisville: Portrait of a Community*. Louisville, Ky.: Jewish Federation of Louisville's Foundation for Planned Giving, 2003.

Ely, Richard T. *Ground under Our Feet: An Autobiography*. New York: Macmillan, 1938.

———. "The Hoosier Economist: John R. Commons." *People's Money*, Jan. 1936, 61–63, 88–89.

———. *An Introduction to Political Economy*. New York: Chautauqua Press, 1889.

———. *The Labor Movement in America*. New York: Macmillan, 1905.

———. "Pullman: A Social History." *Harper's New Monthly*, Feb. 1885, 452–66.

———. *Social Aspects of Christianity*. New York: Crowell, 1889.

Emerson, Ralph. *Abraham Lincoln: Personal Recollections of Abraham Lincoln by Mr. and Mrs. Ralph Emerson of Rockford, Illinois*. Rockford, Ill.: Wilson, 1909.

Emerson, Ralph Waldo. "Self-Reliance." 1841. Reprinted in *The Harper Single Volume American Literature*, edited by Donald McQuade, 537–54. 3rd ed. New York: Longman, 1999.

The Encyclopedia of Chicago. Edited by James R. Grossman, Ann Durkin Keating, and Janice L. Reiff. Chicago: University of Chicago Press, 2004.

The Encyclopedia of Louisville. Edited by John E. Kleber. Lexington: University Press of Kentucky, 2001.

Enstad, Nan. *Ladies of Labor, Girls of Adventure: Working Women, Popular Culture, and Labor Politics at the Turn of the Twentieth Century*. New York: Columbia University Press, 1999.

Epstein, Abraham. *The Negro Migrant in Pittsburgh*. 1918. Reprint. New York: Arno, 1969.

Evans, Christopher H. "Historical Integrity and Theological Recovery: A Reintroduction to the Social Gospel." In Evans, *Social Gospel Today*, 1–13.

————. *The Kingdom Is Always but Coming: A Life of Walter Rauschenbusch*. Grand Rapids, Mich.: Eerdman's, 2004.

————, ed. *The Social Gospel Today*. Louisville, Ky.: Westminster John Knox Press, 2001.

Fairbank, Janet Ayer. *The Bright Land*. Boston: Houghton Mifflin, 1932.

————. *Rich Man, Poor Man*. Boston: Houghton Mifflin, 1936.

————. *The Smiths*. Indianapolis: Bobbs-Merrill, 1925.

Fairchild, Fred Rogers. "The Factory Legislation of the State of New York." *Proceedings of the American Economic Association*, 3rd ser., 6, no. 4 (1905): 109–43.

Farrell, James J. *Inventing the American Way of Death, 1830–1920*. Philadelphia: Temple University Press, 1980.

Fein, Albert. *Frederick Law Olmsted and the American Environmental Tradition*. New York: Braziller, 1972.

Filler, Louis. *The Muckrakers*. 1939. Reprint. Stanford, Calif.: Stanford University Press, 1976.

Fink, Leon. *Progressive Intellectuals and the Dilemmas of Democratic Commitment*. Cambridge, Mass.: Harvard University Press, 1997.

Fishback, Price V. *Soft Coal, Hard Choices: The Economic Welfare of Bituminous Coal Miners, 1890–1930*. New York: Oxford University Press, 1992.

Fitch, John A. *The Steel Workers*. 1910. Reprint. Pittsburgh: University of Pittsburgh Press, 1989.

Fitzgerald, Frances. "The New Evangelicals." *New Yorker*, June 30, 2008, 28–34.

Fitzpatrick, Ellen F. *Muckraking: Three Landmark Articles*. Boston: Bedford/St. Martin's, 1994.

Flexner, Bernard. *Mr. Justice Brandeis and the University of Louisville*. Louisville, Ky.: University of Louisville, 1938.

Flowers, Betty Sue. *The American Dream and the Economic Myth*. Kalamazoo, Mich.: Fetzer Institute, 2007.

"Fort Wayne Medical Schools." *Indiana Medical History Quarterly* 3, no. 1 (1976): 55–67.

Fox, Richard Wightman, and T. J. Jackson Lears, eds. *A Culture of Consumption: Critical Essays in American History, 1880–1980*. New York: Pantheon, 1983.

Frank, Robert. *Richistan: A Journey through the American Wealth Boom and the Lives of the New Rich*. New York: Crown, 2007.

Frank, Robert H. *Falling Behind: How Rising Inequality Harms the Middle Class*. Berkeley: University of California Press, 2007.

Frazer, Robert. *The Making of the Golden Bough: The Origins of the Growth of an Argument*. New York: St. Martin's, 1990.

Friedman, Lee M. *Jewish Pioneers and Patriots*. 1942. Reprint. Plainview, N.Y.: Books for Libraries Press, 1974.

Fuller, Margaret. *The Great Lawsuit: Man versus Men, Woman versus Women*. 1843. Reprinted in *The Harper American Literature*, edited by Donald McQuade, 1:1178–1212. New York: Harper and Row, 1987.

Furner, Mary O. *Advocacy and Objectivity: A Crisis in the Professionalization of American Social Science, 1865–1905*. Lexington: University Press of Kentucky, 1975.

Gal, Allon. *Brandeis of Boston*. Cambridge, Mass.: Harvard University Press, 1980.

Galbraith, John Kenneth. *The Affluent Society*. Boston: Houghton Mifflin, 1958.

Genovese, Eugene D. *Roll, Jordan, Roll: The World the Slaves Made*. 1972. Reprint. New York: Vintage, 1976.

George, Henry. *Progress and Poverty: An Inquiry into the Cause of Industrial Depressions and of Increase of Want with Increase of Wealth; The Remedy*. 1879. Reprint. New York: Robert Schalkenbach Foundation, 1955.

German Workers in Chicago: A Documentary History of Working-Class Culture from 1850 to World War I. Edited by Hartmut Keil and John B. Jentz. Urbana and Chicago: University of Illinois Press, 1988.

Gerstle, Gary. *American Crucible: Race and Nation in the Twentieth Century*. Princeton, N.J.: Princeton University Press, 2001.

The Gilded Age in Fort Wayne, 1870–1900. Fort Wayne, Ind.: Public Library of Fort Wayne and Allen County, 1955.

Gilman, Charlotte Perkins. *Women and Economics: A Study of the Economic Relation between Men and Women as a Factor in Social Evolution*. 1898. Reprint. Berkeley and Los Angeles: University of California Press, 1998.

Ginger, Ray. *Altgeld's America: The Lincoln Ideal versus Changing Realities*. 1958. Reprint. New York: Franklin Watts, 1973.

Gladden, Washington, ed. *Parish Problems: Hints and Helps for the People of the Churches*. New York: Century, 1887.

———. *Ruling Ideas of the Present Age*. Boston: Houghton Mifflin, 1895.

———. *Tools and the Man: Property and Industry under the Christian Law*. Boston: Houghton Mifflin, 1893.

———. *Working People and Their Employers*. 1885. Reprint. New York: Arno, 1969.

Gladwell, Malcolm. *The Tipping Point: How Little Things Can Make a Big Difference*. 2000. Reprint. Boston: Little, Brown, 2002.

Glazier, Willard. *Peculiarities of American Cities*. Philadelphia: Hubbard, 1885.

Glowacki, Peggy, and Julia Hendry. *Images of America: Hull House*. Charleston, S.C.: Arcadia, 2004.

Goldmark, Josephine. *Fatigue and Efficiency: A Study in Industry*. New York: Survey Associates, 1913.

———. *Impatient Crusader: Florence Kelley's Life Story*. Urbana: University of Illinois Press, 1953.

———. *Pilgrims of '48: One Man's Part in the Austrian Revolution of 1848 and a Family Migration to America*. New Haven, Conn.: Yale University Press, 1930.

Goldsby, Jacqueline. *A Spectacular Secret: Lynching in American Life and Literature*. Chicago: University of Chicago Press, 2006.

Gollaher, David. *Voice for the Mad: The Life of Dorothea Dix*. New York: Free Press, 1995.

Gompers, Samuel. *Labor and the Common Welfare*. New York: Dutton, 1919.

———. *The Samuel Gompers Papers*. Edited by Stuart B. Kaufman. Vol. 5. Urbana: University of Illinois Press, 1996.

———. *Seventy Years of Life and Labor: An Autobiography*. 2 vols. 1925. Reprint. New York: Kelley, 1967.

Goode, James M. *Best Addresses: A Century of Washington's Distinguished Apartment Houses*. Washington, D.C.: Smithsonian Institution Press, 1988.

Gorrell, Donald K. *The Age of Social Responsibility: The Social Gospel in the Progressive Era, 1900–1920*. Macon, Ga.: Mercer University Press, 1988.

"Gospel of Paint." *McClure's*, Jan. 1, 1909, 20–21.

Gosselin, Peter. *High Wire: The Precarious Financial Lives of American Families*. New York: Basic Books, 2008.

Green, James. *Death in the Haymarket: A Story of Chicago, The First Labor Movement and the Bombing That Divided Gilded Age America*. New York: Pantheon, 2006.

Greenhouse, Steven. *The Big Squeeze: Tough Times for American Workers*. New York: Knopf, 2008.

Greenwood, Janette Thomas. *The Gilded Age: A History in Documents*. New York: Oxford University Press, 2000.

Grier, Katherine C. *Culture and Comfort: People, Parlors, and Upholstery, 1850–1930*. Rochester, N.Y.: Strong Museum, 1988.

Habenstein, Robert H., and William M. Lamers. *The History of American Funeral Directing*. Milwaukee, Wis.: Bulfin, 1955.

Hallinan, Joseph T. *Going up the River: Travels in a Prison Nation*. New York: Random House, 2001.

Hamilton, Alice. "The Cost of Medical Care." *New Republic*, June 26, 1929, 15–19.

———. *Exploring the Dangerous Trades*. 1943. Reprint. Beverly, Mass.: OEM Press, 1995.

———. "Forty Years in the Poisonous Trades." *American Industrial Hygiene Association Quarterly* 9, no. 6 (1948): 5–15.

———. "Industrial Diseases: With Special Reference to the Trades in Which Women Are Employed." *Charities and the Commons*, Sept. 5, 1908, 655–59.

———. *Industrial Poisons in the United States*. New York: Macmillan, 1925.

———. "Nineteen Years in the Poisonous Trades." *Harper's Monthly*, Oct. 1929, 3–14.

———. "State Pensions or Charity?" *Atlantic Monthly*, May 1930, 683–87.

———. "What Price Safety, Tetraethyl Lead Reveals a Flaw in our Defences." *Survey Mid-monthly*, June, 1925, 333–34.

Hamilton, G. P. *The Bright Side of Memphis: A Compendium of Information Concerning the Colored People of Memphis, Tennessee, Showing Their Achievements in Business, Industrial, and Professional Life and Including Articles of General Interest on the Race*. 1908. Reprint. Memphis, Tenn.: Lightning Source, 2003.

Handlin, Oscar. *American Jews: Their Story*. New York: Anti-defamation League of B'nai B'rith, 1976.

Hapgood, Norman. *The Changing Years: Reminiscences of Norman Hapgood*. New York: Farrar and Rinehart, 1930.

Hard, William, and others. *Injured in the Course of Duty*. New York: Ridgway, 1910.

The Harper American Literature. Edited by Donald McQuade. 2nd ed. Vol. 1. New York: HarperCollins, 1994.

"Harper's Index." *Harper's*, July 2008, 13.

Harriman, Florence Jaffrey Hurst. *From Pinafores to Politics*. New York: Holt, 1923.

Harris, Kristina. *Victorian and Edwardian Fashions for Women, 1840 to 1919*. Atglen, Pa.: Schiffer, 1995.

Harter, Lafayette G., Jr. *John R. Commons: His Assault on Laissez-Faire*. Corvallis: Oregon State University, 1962.

Hawfield, Michael C. *Fort Wayne Cityscapes*. Woodland Hills, Calif.: Windsor, 1988.

Highlights from the History of the John Crerar Library. Chicago: John Crerar Foundation, University of Chicago Library, 1989.

Hilkey, Judy. *Character Is Capital: Success Manuals and Manhood in Gilded Age America*. Chapel Hill: University of North Carolina Press, 1997.

History of Public Works in the United States, 1776–1976. Edited by Ellis L. Armstrong, Michael C. Robinson, and Suellen M. Hoy. Chicago: American Public Works Association, 1976.

Hochschild, Arlie Russell. *The Managed Heart: The Commercialization of Human Feeling*. Berkeley: University of California Press, 1983.

Hofstadter, Richard. *The Age of Reform: From Bryan to F. D. R.* 1955. Reprint. New York: Vintage, n.d.

———. *Anti-intellectualism in American Life*. New York: Knopf, 1963.

Holbrook, David W. "Florence Kelley." *Family*, Apr. 1932, 28–36.

Holbrook, Stewart H. *The Age of the Moguls*. Garden City, N.Y.: Doubleday, 1953.

Hoogenboom, Ari. *Outlawing the Spoils: A History of the Civil Service Reform Movement, 1865–1883*. Urbana: University of Illinois Press, 1961.

Hopkins, Alphonso. *The Powers Fire-Proof Commercial and Fine Art Buildings*. Rochester, N.Y.: Andrews, 1883.

Hopkins, Charles Howard. *The Rise of the Social Gospel in American Protestantism, 1865–1915*. New Haven, Conn.: Yale University Press, 1940.

Hopkins, Mary Alden. "This Matter of the Eight-Hour Day." *Century*, Jan. 1917, 346–60.

Horowitz, Daniel. *The Morality of Spending: Attitudes toward the Consumer Society in America, 1875–1940*. Baltimore: Johns Hopkins University Press, 1985.

Horowitz, Helen Lefkowitz. *Alma Mater: Design and Experience in Women's Colleges from Their Nineteenth-Century Beginnings to the 1930s*. 2nd ed. Amherst: University of Massachusetts Press, 1993.

House of Refuge. *Annual Reports of the House of Refuge, Louisville, 1872–1879*. Louisville, Ky.: Bradley and Gilbert, 1873–80.

Howard, H. B. "The Beifeld Cloak." *Printers' Ink*, Nov. 9, 1898, 46–47.

Howe, Frederic C. *The Confessions of a Reformer*. New York: Scribner, 1926.

Howe, Helen. *The Gentle Americans, 1864–1960: Biography of a Breed*. New York: Harper and Row, 1965.

Howe, M[ark] A. DeWolfe. *Boston: The Place and the People*. New York: Macmillan, 1903.

———. *A Great Private Citizen: Henry Lee Higginson*. Boston: Atlantic Monthly Press, 1920.

Howells, William Dean. "The Country Printer." In *Impressions and Experiences*. New York: Harper, 1896.

———. *Criticism and Fiction and Other Essays*. Edited by Clara M. Kirk and Rudolf Kirk. New York: New York University Press, 1959.

Hoy, Suellen M. "'Municipal Housekeeping': The Role of Women in Improving Urban Sanitation Practices." In *Pollution and Reform in American Cities, 1870–1930*, edited by Martin V. Melosi, 173–98. Austin: University of Texas Press, 1980.

Hull-House Maps and Papers. New York: Crowell, 1895.

Husted, Shirley Cox, and Ruth Rosenberg-Naparsteck. *Rochester Neighborhoods*. Charleston, S.C.: Arcadia, 2000.

Indiana: A Guide to the Hoosier State. Compiled by members of the Writers' Program of the Works Projects Administration of the State of Indiana. New York: Oxford University Press, 1941.

Irons, Peter. *A People's History of the Supreme Court: The Men and Women Whose Decisions Have Shaped Our Constitution*. 1999. Reprint. New York: Penguin, 2000.

Jackson, Charles O., ed. *Passing: The Vision of Death in America*. Westport, Conn.: Greenwood, 1977.

James, Henry. *The American Scene*. 1907. Reprint. Bloomington: Indiana University Press, 1968.

James, William. "The Energies of Men." In *Essays on Faith and Morals*, 216–37. New York: Meridian, 1962.

Jaspin, Elliot. *Burn in the Bitter Waters: The Hidden History of Racial Cleansing in America*. New York: Basic Books, 2007.

Jenks, Jeremiah W. *The Political and Social Significance of the Life and Teachings of Jesus*. New York: International Committee of Young Men's Christian Associations, 1906.

John B. Andrews Memorial Symposium on Labor Legislation and Social Security, Memorial Union, the University of Wisconsin, Nov. 4 and 5, 1949. N.p.: n.d.

Johnson, Charles B. *Illinois in the Fifties, or A Decade of Development, 1851–1860*. Champaign, Ill.: Flanigan-Pearson, 1918.

Johnson, Ronald N., and Gary D. Libecap. *The Federal Civil Service System and the Problem of Bureaucracy: The Economics and Politics of Institutional Change*. Chicago: University of Chicago Press, 1994.

Johnson, Tom. *My Story*. New York: Huebsch, 1911.

Johnston, J. Stoddard. *Memorial History of Louisville from Its First Settlement to the Year 1896*. Vol. 1. Chicago: American Biographical, 1896.

Johnston, Robert D. *The Radical Middle Class: Populist Democracy and the Question of Capitalism in Progressive Era Portland, Oregon*. Princeton, N.J.: Princeton University Press, 2003.

Jones, Mary Harris. *Autobiography of Mother Jones*. 1925. Reprint. Mineola, N.Y.: Dover, 2004.

Joseph Beifeld and Company. *Beifeld Catalogue: Crash and Duck Skirts, 1899*. N.p.: n.d.

Kagan, Robert. *Dangerous Nation: America's Place in the World from Its Earliest Days to the Dawn of the Twentieth Century*. New York: Knopf, 2006.

Kaplan, Justin. *When the Astors Owned New York: Blue Bloods and Grand Hotels in a Gilded Age*. New York: Viking, 2006.

Katz, Irving. "Henry Lee Higginson vs. Louis Dembitz Brandeis: A Collision between Tradition and Reform." *New England Quarterly* 41, no. 1 (1968): 67–81.

Keating, Ann Durkin. *Invisible Networks: Exploring the History of Local Utilities and Public Works*. Malabar, Fla.: Krieger, 1994.

Kelley, Florence. *The Autobiography of Florence Kelley: Notes of Sixty Years*. Edited by Kathryn Kish Sklar. Chicago: Kerr, 1986.

———. "Congestion and Sweated Labor." *Charities and the Commons*, Apr. 4, 1908, 48–50.

———. *First Special Report of the Factory Inspectors of Illinois on Small-Pox in the Tenement House Sweat-Shops of Chicago*. Springfield, Ill.: Rogers, 1894.

———. "Hull House." *New England Magazine*, July 1898, 550–66.

————. "The Illinois Child-Labor Law." *American Journal of Sociology* 3, no. 4 (1898): 490–501.

————. *Modern Industry in Relation to the Family, Health, Education, Morality.* New York: Longmans, Green, 1914.

————. "The Need of Theoretical Preparation for Philanthropic Work." 1887. Reprinted in *Autobiography of Florence Kelley*, 91–104.

————. "On Some Changes in the Legal Status of the Child since Blackstone." *International Review* 13 (Aug. 1882): 7–98.

————. *Some Ethical Gains through Legislation.* 1905. Reprint. New York: Macmillan, 1910.

————. *Third Annual Report of the Factory Inspectors of Illinois for the Year Ending December 15, 1895.* Springfield, Ill.: Hartman, State Printer, 1896.

————. *What Women Might Do with the Ballot: The Abolition of Child Labor.* New York: National Woman Suffrage Association, 1911.

————. *Women in Industry: The Eight Hours Day and Rest at Night Upheld by the United States Supreme Court.* New York: National Consumers' League, 1916.

————. *The Working Child.* Chicago: Hollister, n.d.

Kelley, Nicholas. "Early Days at Hull House." *Social Science Review* 28 (1954): 424–29.

Kelley, William. *Speech of Hon. William Kelley of Pennsylvania on Protection to American Labor.* Washington, D.C.: Congressional Globe Office, 1866.

Kellogg, Paul U. "The Living Spirit of Florence Kelley." *Survey Mid-monthly*, Jan. 1940, 5–8.

————. "The Pittsburgh Survey." *Charities and the Commons*, Jan. 2, 1909, 517–26.

Kessler-Harris, Alice. *Gendering Labor History.* Urbana: University of Illinois Press, 2007.

————. *In Pursuit of Equity: Women, Men, and the Quest for Economic Citizenship in 20th Century America.* New York: Oxford University Press, 2001.

Keyes, Emerson. *A History of Savings Banks in the United States from Their Inception in 1816 down to 1874.* 2 vols. New York: Rhodes, 1876–78.

King, Martin Luther, Jr. "Where Do We Go from Here?" In *I Have a Dream: Writings and Speeches That Changed the World*, edited by James Melvin Washington, 169–79. San Francisco: HarperSanFrancisco, 1992.

King, Moses. *King's Handbook of Boston.* Cambridge, Mass.: King, 1879.

King, William McGuire. "The Biblical Base of the Social Gospel." In *The Bible and Social Reform*, edited by Ernest R. Sandeen, 59–84. Philadelphia: Fortress Press; Chico, Calif.: Scholars Press, 1982.

Kingsley, Charles. *Cheap Clothes and Nasty.* 1850. Reprint. *A Web of English History*, n.d., <http://www.historyhome.co.uk/peel/economic/sweat.htm>.

————. *The Water-Babies.* Illustrated by Linley Sambourne. 1863. Reprint. Ann Arbor, Mich.: University Microfilms, 1966.

Kisseloff, Jeff. *You Must Remember This: An Oral History of Manhattan from the 1890s to World War II.* San Diego, Calif.: Harcourt Brace Jovanovich, 1989.

Klos, Lloyd E. *Rochester: A Resident's Recollection.* Interlaken, N.Y.: Empire State Books, 1987.

Knight, Louise W. *Citizen: Jane Addams and the Struggle for Democracy.* Chicago: University of Chicago Press, 2005.

Kozol, Jonathan. *Savage Inequalities: Children in America's Schools*. 1991. Reprint. New York: Harper, 1992.

Kraut, Alan M. *The Huddled Masses: The Immigrant in American Society, 1880–1921*. Arlington Heights, Ill.: Harlan Davidson, 1982.

Krentz, Christopher. *Writing Deafness: The Hearing Line in Nineteenth-Century American Literature*. Chapel Hill: University of North Carolina Press, 2007.

Kurlansky, Mark. *The Big Oyster: History on the Half Shell*. 2005. Reprint. New York: Random House, 2006.

Ladd-Taylor, Molly, ed. *Raising a Baby the Government Way: Mothers' Letters to the Children's Bureau, 1915–1932*. New Brunswick, N.J.: Rutgers University Press, 1986.

Lambert, Josiah Bartlett. *"If the Workers Took a Notion": The Right to Strike and American Political Development*. Ithaca, N.Y.: ILR Press, 2005.

Lang, Amy Schrager. *The Syntax of Class: Writing Inequality in Nineteenth-Century America*. Princeton, N.J.: Princeton University Press, 2003.

Lappe, Frances Moore. *Getting a Grip: Clarity, Creativity, and Courage in a World Gone Mad*. Cambridge, Mass.: Small Planet Media, 2007.

Lathrop, Julia C. "The Background of the Juvenile Court in Illinois." In *The Child, the Clinic, and the Court*, 290–97. New York: New Republic, 1925.

———. "The Children's Bureau." *American Journal of Sociology* 18, no. 3 (1912): 318–30.

———. "The Cook County Charities." In *Hull-House Maps and Papers*, 143–61.

———. Introduction to *The Delinquent Child and the Home*, by Sophonisba Breckinridge and Edith Abbott, 1–10. New York: Russell Sage Foundation, 1917.

———. *Suggestions for Institution Visitors*. Chicago: Public Charities Committee of the Illinois Federation of Women's Clubs, 1905.

Lears, T. J. Jackson. *No Place of Grace: Antimodernism and the Transformation of American Culture, 1880–1920*. New York: Pantheon, 1981.

LeHaye, Tim F., and Jerry B. Jenkins. *Left Behind: A Novel of the Earth's Last Days*. Wheaton, Ill.: Tyndale House, 1995.

Levine, Lewis. *The Women's Garment Workers: A History of the International Ladies' Garment Workers' Union*. New York: Huebsch, 1924.

Lewis, David Levering. *W. E. B. Du Bois*. Vol. 1, *Biography of a Race, 1868–1919*. New York: Holt, 1993.

———. *W. E. B. Du Bois*. Vol. 2, *The Fight for Equality and the American Century, 1919–1963*. New York: Holt, 2000.

Lewis, Michael, ed. *Panic: The Story of Modern Financial Insanity*. New York: Norton, 2009.

Lewis, Sinclair. *Elmer Gantry*. 1927. Reprint. New York: Signet, 1970.

———. *Free Air*. New York: Harcourt, Brace, 1919.

Lief, Alfred. *Brandeis: The Personal History of an American Ideal*. Harrisburg, Pa.: Stackpole, 1936.

Lindenmeyer, Kriste. *A Right to Childhood: The U.S. Children's Bureau and Child Welfare, 1912–46*. Urbana: University of Illinois Press, 1997.

Linn, James Weber. *Jane Addams*. 1935. Reprint. Urbana: University of Illinois Press, 2000.

Lippmann, Walter. *A Preface to Morals*. 1929. Reprint. New York: Time-Life Books, 1964.

Lloyd, Henry Demarest. *Men: The Workers.* 1909. Reprint. New York: Arno, 1969.

———. *Wealth against Commonwealth.* 1894. Reprint. Englewood Cliffs, N.J.: Prentice-Hall, 1963.

Lombardi, John. *Labor's Voice in the Cabinet: A History of the Department of Labor from Its Origin to 1921.* New York: Columbia University Press, 1942.

Louisville Information. Louisville, Ky.: Standard, 1921.

Louisville Past and Present: Its Industrial History. Louisville, Ky.: Joblin, 1875.

Low, Seth, and Richard Ely. "A Programme for Labor Reform." *Century,* Apr. 1890, 638–51.

Lubove, Roy. "John A. Fitch, *The Steel Workers,* and the Crisis of Democracy." In *The Steel Workers,* by John A. Fitch. 1910. Reprint. University of Pittsburgh Press, 1989: vii–xiv.

Lugan, Gregory A., Dennis Domer, and David Mohney, eds. *Louisville Guide.* New York: Princeton Architectural Press, 2004.

Luker, Ralph E. *The Social Gospel in Black and White: American Racial Reform, 1885–1912.* Chapel Hill: University of North Carolina Press, 1991.

Lundin, Jon W. *Rockford: An Illustrated History.* Tarzana, Calif.: American Historical Press, 1996.

Lytle, Mark Hamilton. *America's Uncivil Wars: The Sixties Era from Elvis to the Fall of Richard Nixon.* New York: Oxford University Press, 2006.

Mack, W. W., ed. *600 Ways to Sell Life Insurance.* New York: Underwriter, 1925.

Mackin, Anne. *Americans and Their Land: The House Built on Abundance.* Ann Arbor: University of Michigan Press, 2006.

MacLean, Annie Marion. "Two Weeks in Department Stores." *American Journal of Sociology* 4, no. 6 (1899): 721–41.

Mandel, Bernard. *Samuel Gompers: A Biography.* Yellow Springs, Ohio: Antioch Press, 1963.

Marchand, Roland. *Creating the Corporate Soul: The Rise of Public Relations and Corporate Imagery in American Big Business.* Berkeley: University of California Press, 1998.

Markowitz, Gerald, and David Rosner. *Dying for Work: Workers' Safety and Health in Twentieth-Century America.* Bloomington: Indiana University Press, 1987.

Marling, Karal Ann. *Merry Christmas: Celebrating America's Greatest Holiday.* Cambridge, Mass.: Harvard University Press, 2000.

Marsh, George Perkins. *Man and Nature, or Physical Geography as Modified by Human Action.* 1864. Reprint. Edited by David Lowenthal. Cambridge, Mass.: Harvard University Press, 1965.

Marten, James, ed. *Childhood and Child Welfare in the Progressive Era: A Brief History with Documents.* New York: Bedford/St. Martin's, 2005.

Mason, Alpheus Thomas. *Brandeis: A Free Man's Life.* New York: Viking, 1946.

———. *The Brandeis Way: A Case Study in the Workings of Democracy.* Princeton, N.J.: Princeton University Press, 1938.

Matteucci, Marco. *History of the Motor Car.* New York: Crown, 1970.

Matthews, Shailer. *The Messianic Hope in the New Testament.* Chicago: University of Chicago Press, 1905.

Maurice, Frederick Denison. *Reconstructing Christian Ethics: Selected Writings.* Edited by Ellen K. Wondra. Louisville, Ky.: Westminster John Knox Press, 1995.

May, Henry. *Protestant Churches and Industrial America*. 1949. Reprint. New York: Octagon, 1977.

McGerr, Michael. *A Fierce Discontent: The Rise and Fall of the Progressive Movement in America*. 2003. Reprint. New York: Oxford University Press, 2005.

McGovern, Charles F. *Sold American: Consumption and Citizenship, 1890–1945*. Chapel Hill: University of North Carolina Press, 2006.

McIlwaine, Shields. *Memphis Down in Dixie*. New York: Dutton, 1948.

McKelvey, Blake. *Rochester: The Flower City, 1855–1890*. Cambridge, Mass.: Harvard University Press, 1949.

———. *Rochester: The Quest for Quality, 1890–1925*. Cambridge, Mass.: Harvard University Press, 1956.

———. *Snow in the Cities: A History of America's Urban Response*. Rochester, N.Y.: Rochester University Press, 1995.

———. "Walter Rauschenbusch's Rochester." *Rochester History* 14, no. 4 (1952): 1–27.

McMurry, Donald L. *Coxey's Army: A Study of the Industrial Army Movement of 1894*. Boston: Little, Brown, 1929.

McMurry, Linda O. *To Keep the Waters Troubled: The Life of Ida B. Wells*. New York: Oxford University Press, 1998.

Melosi, Martin V. *Garbage in the Cities: Refuse, Reform, and the Environment, 1880–1980*. College Station: Texas A&M University Press, 1981.

Melville, Herman. "Bartleby, the Scrivener: A Tale of Wall Street." 1853. Reprinted in *Harper American Literature*, 2nd ed., 1:1953–78.

Menand, Louis. *The Metaphysical Club: A Story of Ideas in America*. New York: Farrar, Straus, and Giroux, 2001.

Metress, Christopher, ed. *The Lynching of Emmett Till: A Documentary Narrative*. Charlottesville: University of Virginia Press, 2002.

Milkis, Sidney M., and Jerome M. Mileur, eds. *Progressivism and the New Democracy*. Amherst: University of Massachusetts Press, 1999.

Miller, Donald L. *City of the Century: The Epic of Chicago and the Making of America*. New York: Simon and Schuster, 1996.

Miller, William. *The Art of Canvassing: How to Sell Insurance*. 1894. Reprint. New York: Spectator, 1913.

Mintz, Steven. *Huck's Raft: A History of American Childhood*. Cambridge, Mass.: Harvard University Press, 2004.

———. *Moralists and Modernizers: America's Pre–Civil War Reformers*. Baltimore: Johns Hopkins University Press, 1995.

Minus, Paul M. *Walter Rauschenbusch: American Reformer*. New York: Macmillan, 1988.

Mitchell, Alexander D. *Washington Then and Now*. San Diego, Calif.: Thunder Bay Press, 2000.

Montgomery, David. *Citizen Worker: The Experience of Workers in the United States and the Free Market during the Nineteenth Century*. Cambridge: Cambridge University Press, 1993.

———. *The Fall of the House of Labor: The Workplace, the State, and American Labor Activism, 1865–1925*. New York: Cambridge University Press, 1987.

Mooney, James E. *John Graham Brooks, Prophet of Social Justice*. Worcester, Mass.: Davis Press, 1968.

Morantz-Sanchez, Regina. *Sympathy and Science: Women Physicians in American Medicine.* Chapel Hill: University of North Carolina Press, 1985.

More, Ellen Singer. *Restoring the Balance: Women Physicians and the Profession of Medicine.* Cambridge, Mass.: Harvard University Press, 1999.

Morison, Samuel Eliot. *One Boy's Boston, 1887–1901.* 1962. Reprint. Boston: Northeastern University Press, 1983.

Morn, Frank. *"The Eye That Never Sleeps": A History of the Pinkerton National Detective Agency.* Bloomington: Indiana University Press, 1982.

Morris, Edmund. *The Rise of Theodore Roosevelt.* 1979. Reprint. New York: Modern Library, 2001.

Mosley, Walter. *Workin' on the Chain Gang: Shaking Off the Dead Hand of History.* New York: Ballantine, 2000.

Moss, David A. "Kindling a Flame under Federalism: Progressive Reformers, Corporate Elites, and the Phosphorus Match Campaign of 1909–1912." *Business History Review* 68 (Summer 1994): 244–75.

Moyers, Bill. "For America's Sake." *Nation*, Jan. 22, 2007, 11–17.

Mumford, Lewis. *The Brown Decades: A Study of the Arts in America, 1865–1895.* 1931. Reprint. New York: Dover, 1955.

Nathan, Maud. *Once upon a Time and Today.* New York: Putnam, 1933.

Nelson, C. Hal, ed. *Sinnissippi Saga: A History of Rockford and Winnebago County, Illinois.* N.p.: Winnebago County Illinois Sesquicentennial Committee, 1968.

———. *We, the People of Winnebago County.* Mendota, Ill.: Winnebago County Bicentennial Commission, 1975.

The New Gilded Age: The New Yorker *Looks at the Culture of Affluence.* Edited by David Remnick. 2000. Reprint. New York: Modern Library, 2001.

"The New Inequality." Special issue, *Nation*, June 30, 2008.

Newman, Katherine S., and Victor Tan Chen. *The Missing Class: Portraits of the Near Poor in America.* Boston: Beacon Press, 2007.

New York Legislature. *Report of the Joint Committee of the Senate and Assembly of the State of New York Appointed to Investigate the Affairs of Life Insurance Companies.* Albany, N.Y.: Brandow, 1906.

Nicholson, Meredith. *The Hoosiers.* New York: Macmillan, 1916.

Noble, David W. *The Paradox of Progressive Thought.* Minneapolis: University of Minnesota Press, 1958.

———. *The Progressive Mind, 1890–1917.* Chicago: Rand McNally, 1970.

Nord, David Paul. *Communities of Journalism: A History of American Newspapers and Their Readers.* Urbana: University of Illinois Press, 2001.

O'Donovan, Edmond. *The Merv Oasis: Travels and Adventures East of the Caspian during the Years 1879–80–81.* 2 vols. London: Smith, Elder, 1882.

Oliver, Thomas, ed. *Dangerous Trades: The Historical, Social, and Legal Aspects of Industrial Occupations as Affecting Health, by a Number of Experts.* New York: Dutton, 1902.

———. *Diseases of Occupation: From the Legislative, Social, and Medical Points of View.* New York: Dutton, 1909.

Oppel, Frank, ed. *Tales of Gaslight New York.* Secaucus, N.J.: Castle, 1985.

Oppenheimer, Mark. "The Queen of the New Age." *New York Times Magazine*, May 4, 2008, 60–65.

O'Reilly, John Boyle. *Athletics and Manly Sport*. Boston: Pilot, 1890.

Ornelas-Struve, Carole M., and Frederick Lee Coulter. *Memphis, 1800–1900*. Edited by Joan Hassell. New York: Powers, 1982.

Paper, Lewis J. *Brandeis*. Englewood Cliffs, N.J.: Prentice-Hall, 1983.

Parsons, Kermit Carlyle. *The Cornell Campus: A History of Its Planning and Development*. Ithaca, N.Y.: Cornell University Press, 1968.

Paxson, Mary. *Mary Paxson: Her Book, 1880–1884*. Bedford, Mass.: Applewood, n.d.

Perrin, W. H., J. H. Battle, and G. C. Kniffen. *Kentucky: A History of the State*. Louisville, Ky.: Battey, 1886.

Perry, Arthur Latham. *Elements of Political Economy*. 1865. Reprint. New York: Scribner, 1869.

———. *Introduction to Political Economy*. New York: Scribner, 1880.

———. *Political Economy*. New York: Scribner, 1888.

Perry, Bliss. *Life and Letters of Henry Lee Higginson*. Boston: Atlantic Monthly Press, 1921.

"Personal Account." *Harper's*, Feb. 2007, 16.

Pew Research Center. "Executive Summary." *Inside the Middle Class: Bad Times Hit the Good Life*. Apr. 9, 2008. <http://pewsocialtrends.org/pubs/706/middle-class-poll>.

Piepmeier, Alison. *Out in Public: Configurations of Women's Bodies in Nineteenth-Century America*. Chapel Hill: University of North Carolina Press, 2004.

Polacheck, Hilda Satt. *I Came a Stranger: The Story of a Hull-House Girl*. Edited by Dena J. Polacheck Epstein. 1989. Reprint. Urbana: University of Illinois Press, 1991.

Polikoff, Barbara Garland. *With One Bold Act: The Story of Jane Addams*. Chicago: Boswell, 1999.

Ponce de Leon, Charles L. *Self-Exposure: Human-Interest Journalism and the Emergence of Celebrity in America, 1890–1940*. Chapel Hill: University of North Carolina Press, 2002.

Prins, Nomi. "Where Credit Is Due." *Mother Jones*, July–Aug. 2008, 38–43.

Quinn, D. A. *Heroes and Heroines of Memphis: Reminiscences of the Yellow Fever Epidemics That Afflicted the City of Memphis during the Autumn Months of 1873, 1878, and 1879*. Providence, R.I.: Freeman, 1887.

Rand McNally & Co's New Ideal State and County Survey and Atlas. Chicago: Rand McNally, 1911.

Rauschenbusch, Walter. "The Belated Races and the Social Problems." *Methodist Quarterly Review*, Apr. 1914, 252–59.

———. *Christianity and the Social Crisis*. 1907. Reprint. Louisville, Ky.: Westminster John Knox Press, 1991.

———. *Christianity and the Social Crisis in the 21st Century: The Classic That Woke Up the Church*. Edited by Paul Raushenbush. New York: HarperOne, 2007.

———. *Christianizing the Social Order*. New York: Macmillan, 1912.

———. *For God and the People: Prayers of the Social Awakening*. Boston: Phillips, 1910.

———. "The Genesis of *Christianity and the Social Crisis*." 1913. Reprinted in *Rochester Theological Seminary Bulletin*, Nov. 1918, 51–53.

———. *Prayers of the Social Awakening*. 1910. Reprint. Boston: Pilgrim Press, 1925.

———. *The Social Principles of Jesus*. New York: Association Press, 1923.

———. *A Theology for the Social Gospel*. Nashville: Abingdon, 1917.

———. "Unto Me." Boston: Pilgrim Press, 1912.

Reich, Robert B. *Supercapitalism: The Transformation of Business, Democracy, and Everyday Life*. New York: Knopf, 2007.

Renehan, Edward, Jr. *Dark Genius of Wall Street: The Misunderstood Life of Jay Gould, King of the Robber Barons*. New York: Basic Books, 2005.

Rice, Alice Hegan. *Calvary Alley*. Toronto: Briggs, 1917.

———. *The Inky Way*. New York: Appleton-Century, 1940.

———. *Mrs. Wiggs of the Cabbage Patch*. 1901. Reprint. Lexington: University Press of Kentucky, 2004.

Richter, Amy G. *Home on the Rails: The Railroad and the Rise of Public Domesticity*. Chapel Hill: University of North Carolina Press, 2005.

Riding and Driving: A Handbook of Valuable Information on Man's Most Faithful Friend—the Horse. New York: Street and Smith, 1891.

Riis, Jacob A. "The Children of the Poor." *Scribner's*, May 1892, 531–56.

———. *How the Other Half Lives*. 1890. Reprint. New York: Dover, 1971.

———. *The Making of an American*. 1901. Reprint. New York: Macmillan, 1913.

———. *Theodore Roosevelt: The Citizen*. 1903. Reprint. Washington, D.C.: Johnson, Wynne, 1904.

Riley, James Whitcomb. *The Complete Poetical Works of James Whitcomb Riley*. Garden City, N.Y.: Doubleday, 1941.

Rodgers, Daniel T. "In Search of Progressives." *Reviews in American History* 10, no. 4 (1982): 113–32.

———. *The Work Ethic in Industrial America, 1850–1920*. Chicago: University of Chicago Press, 1978.

Rokicky, Catherine M. *James Monroe: Oberlin's Christian Statesman and Reformer, 1821–1898*. Kent, Ohio: Kent State University Press, 2002.

Roper, Laura Wood. *FLO: A Biography of Frederick Law Olmsted*. Baltimore: Johns Hopkins University Press, 1973.

Rosen, Jeffrey. "Supreme Court Inc." *New York Times Magazine*, Mar. 16, 2008, 38–45, 66, 71.

Rosenberg, Simon, and Peter Leyden. "The 50-Year Strategy: Beyond '09: Can Progressives Play for Keeps?" *Mother Jones*, Nov.–Dec. 2007, 63–66, 92.

Rosner, David, and Gerald Markowitz. *Deadly Dust: Silicosis and the Politics of Occupational Disease in Twentieth-Century America*. Princeton, N.J.: Princeton University Press, 1991.

Rourke, Constance. *Audubon*. New York: Harcourt, Brace, 1936.

Roy, Andrew. *A History of the Coal Miners of the United States*. Columbus, Ohio: Trauger, n.d.

Royster, Jacqueline Jones. "To Call a Thing by Its Right Name: The Rhetoric of Ida B. Wells." In *Reclaiming Rhetorica: Women in the Rhetorical Tradition*, edited by Andrea A. Lunsford, 167–84. Pittsburgh: University of Pittsburgh Press, 1995.

Ruegamer, Lana. "'The Paradise of Exceptional Women': Chicago Women Reformers, 1863–1893." Ph.D. diss., Indiana University, 1982.

Rutherford, Malcolm. "Wisconsin Institutionalism: John R. Commons and His Students." Working paper, University of Victoria, Canada, 2005, <http://web.uvic.ca/~rutherfo/Commonsandhisstudentslong.pdf>.

Rydell, Robert W. Editor's introduction to *The Reason Why the Colored American Is Not in the World's Columbian Exposition*, xi–xlviii. Urbana and Chicago: University of Illinois Press, 1999.

Samuels, Warren J., ed. *The Founding of Institutional Economics: The Leisure Class and Sovereignty*. London: Routledge, 1998.

Sandoval-Strausz, A. K. *Hotel: An American History*. New Haven, Conn.: Yale University Press, 2007.

Sangamon County Alms House, Buffalo — Inmate Record: Sangamon County Poor Farm. Vol. 1, April 1875–August 1888. Springfield, Ill.: Sangamon County Genealogical Society, 1994.

Santayana, George. *The Life of Reason, or The Phases of Human Progress*. 1905–6. Reprint. Amherst, N.Y.: Prometheus, 1998.

Schapiro, Mark. *Exposed: The Toxic Chemistry of Everyday Products and What's at Stake for American Power*. White River Junction, Vt.: Chelsea Green, 2007.

Schecter, Patricia A. *Ida B. Wells-Barnett and American Reform, 1880–1930*. Chapel Hill: University of North Carolina Press, 2001.

Schivelbusch, Wolfgang. *Three New Deals: Reflections on Roosevelt's America, Mussolini's Italy, and Hitler's Germany, 1933–1939*. New York: Holt, 2006.

Schlereth, Thomas J. *Victorian America: Transformations in Everyday Life, 1876–1915*. 1991. Reprint. New York: HarperCollins, 1992.

Schneider, Mark. *Boston Confronts Jim Crow, 1890–1920*. Boston: Northeastern University Press, 1997.

Schneider, Samuel. *Three Economics Professors Battle against Monopoly and Pricing Practices: Ripley, Fetter, and Commons*. Lewiston, N.Y.: Edwin Mellen Press, 1998.

Schocket, Eric. *Vanishing Moments: Class and American Literature*. Ann Arbor: University of Michigan Press, 2006.

Schorman, Rob. *Selling Style: Clothing and Social Change at the Turn of the Century*. Philadelphia: University of Pennsylvania Press, 2003.

Schwantes, Carlos A. *Coxey's Army: An American Odyssey*. Lincoln: University of Nebraska Press, 1985.

Sears, Roebuck and Co. Catalogue, 1897. Reprint. Philadelphia: Chelsea House, 1968.

Sears, Roebuck and Co. . . . Consumers Guide. 1900. Reprint. Northfield, Ill.: BDI Books, 1970.

Sellers, Christopher C. *Hazards of the Job: From Industrial Disease to Environmental Health Science*. Chapel Hill: University of North Carolina Press, 1997.

Sergeant, Elizabeth Shepley. "Toilers of the Tenements." *McClure's*, July 1910, 231–48.

Serrin, William. *Homestead: The Glory and Tragedy of an American Steel Town*. 1992. Reprint. New York: Vintage, 1993.

Shaler, Nathaniel Southgate. *The Autobiography of Nathaniel Southgate Shaler, with a Supplementary Memoir by His Wife*. Boston: Houghton Mifflin, 1909.

———. *The Citizen: A Study of the Individual and the Government*. New York: Barnes, 1904.

———. "The Negro Question." in Shaler, *Citizen*, 220–35.

———. "Science and the African Problem." *Atlantic Monthly*, July 1890, 36–45.

Sharpe, Dores Robinson. *Walter Rauschenbusch*. New York: Macmillan, 1942.

Shilling, Donovan A. *Rochester's Transportation Heritage*. Charleston, S.C.: Arcadia, 2003.

Shoemaker, Linda Morse. "Jane Addams and the Settlement House Movement." Ph.D. diss., State University of New York, Binghamton, 2001.

Sicherman, Barbara. *Alice Hamilton: A Life in Letters.* Cambridge, Mass.: Harvard University Press, 1984.

Silverstein, Ken. "Beltway Bacchanal: Congress Lives High on the Contributor's Dime." *Harper's,* Mar. 2008, 47–53.

Sinclair, Upton. *The Jungle.* 1906. Reprint. Edited by Virginia Eby. New York: Norton, 2003.

Sklansky, Jeffrey. *The Soul's Economy: Market Society and Selfhood in American Thought, 1820–1920.* Chapel Hill: University of North Carolina Press, 2002.

Sklar, Kathryn Kish. *Florence Kelley and the Nation's Work: The Rise of Women's Political Culture, 1830–1900.* New Haven, Conn.: Yale University Press, 1995.

———. "Hull House in the 1890s: A Community of Women Reformers." *Signs* 1, no. 4 (1985): 658–77.

Smucker, Donovan E. *The Origins of Walter Rauschenbusch's Social Ethics.* Montreal: McGill-Queen's University Press, 1994.

Snyder-Haug, Diane. *Antique and Vintage Clothing: A Guide to Dating and Valuation of Women's Clothing 1850–1940.* Paducah, Ky.: Collector Books, 1997.

Spears, Timothy B. *Chicago Dreaming: Midwesterners and the City, 1871–1919.* Chicago: University of Chicago Press, 2005.

———. *100 Years on the Road: The Traveling Salesman in American Culture.* New Haven, Conn.: Yale University Press, 1995.

Stafford, Hanford Dozier. "Slavery in a Border City: Louisville, 1790–1860." Ph.D. diss., University of Kentucky, 1982.

Stalson, J. Owen. *Marketing Life Insurance: Its History in America.* 1942. Reprint. Homewood, Ill.: Irwin for the McCahan Foundation, 1969.

Standiford, Les. *Meet You in Hell: Andrew Carnegie, Henry Clay Frick, and the Bitter Partnership That Transformed America.* New York: Crown, 2005.

Starkman, Dean. "Red Ink Rising: How the Press Missed a Sea Change in the Credit-Card Industry." *Columbia Journalism Review,* Mar.–Apr. 2008, 14–16.

Starr, Paul. *The Social Transformation of American Medicine.* New York: Basic Books, 1982.

Stead, William T. *If Christ Came to Chicago.* 1894. Reprint. Chicago: Chicago Historical Bookworks, n.d.

Stebner, Eleanor Joyce. "The Women of Hull House: A Study in Spirituality, Vocation, and Friendship." Ph.D. diss., Northwestern University, 1994.

Steiner, Michael J. *A Study of the Intellectual and Material Culture of Death in Nineteenth-Century America.* Lewiston, N.Y.: Edwin Mellen Press, 2003.

Steigerwalt, Albert K. *The National Association of Manufacturers, 1895–1914: A Study in Business Leadership.* Ann Arbor: Bureau of Business Research, Graduate School of Business Administration, University of Michigan, 1964.

Sterling, Dorothy. Afterword to *Memphis Diary of Ida B. Wells,* 191–99.

Stilgoe, John R. *Metropolitan Corridor: Railroads and the American Scene.* New Haven, Conn.: Yale University Press, 1983.

Stimson, F. J. "Democracy and the Laboring Man." *Atlantic Monthly,* Nov. 1897, 605–20.

Storrs, Langdon R. Y. *Civilizing Capitalism: The National Consumers' League, Women's*

Activism, and Labor Standards in the New Deal Era. Chapel Hill: University of North Carolina Press, 2000.

Strasser, Susan. *Satisfaction Guaranteed: The Making of the Mass Market*. New York: Pantheon, 1989.

Stromquist, Shelton. *Re-inventing "the People": The Progressive Movement, the Class Problem, and the Origins of Modern Liberalism*. Urbana: University of Illinois Press, 2006.

Strong, Josiah. *The New Era, or The Coming Kingdom*. New York: Baker and Taylor, 1893.

———. *Our Country: Its Possible Future and Its Present Crisis*. New York: American Home Missionary Society, 1885.

Strum, Philippa. *Brandeis: Beyond Progressivism*. Lawrence: University of Kansas Press, 1993.

———. *Louis D. Brandeis: Justice for the People*. New York: Schocken, 1984.

Suffern, Arthur S. *The Coal Miners' Struggle for Industrial Status*. New York: Macmillan, 1926.

Sullivan, Mark. *Our Times*. Vol. 1, *The Turn of the Century*. 1926. Reprint. New York: Scribner, 1971.

Sumner, William Graham. *War and Other Essays*. New Haven, Conn.: Yale University Press, 1911.

———. *What Social Classes Owe to Each Other*. New York: Harper, 1883.

Taibbi, Matt. "Jailhouse Nation." *Rolling Stone*, Aug. 24, 2006, 38.

Tamarkin, Elisa. *Anglophilia: Deference, Devotion, and Antebellum America*. Chicago: University of Chicago Press, 2008.

Tapp, Hambleton, and James C. Klotter. *Kentucky: Decades of Discord, 1865–1900*. Frankfort: Kentucky Historical Society, 1977.

Tarbell, Ida M. *The History of the Standard Oil Company*. 2 vols. New York: McClure, Phillips, 1904.

Teitelbaum, Gene. *Justice Louis D. Brandeis: A Bibliography of Writings and Other Materials on the Justice*. Littleton, Colo.: Rothman, 1987.

Thernstrom, Stephen, Ann Orlov, and Oscar Handlin, eds. *The Harvard Encyclopedia of Ethnic Groups*. Cambridge, Mass.: Harvard University Press, 1980.

Thompson, Mildred I. *Ida B. Wells-Barnett: An Exploratory Study of an American Black Woman, 1893–1930*. Brooklyn, N.Y.: Carlson, 1990.

Thornbrough, Emma Lou. *Indiana in the Civil War Era, 1850–1880*. Indianapolis: Indiana Historical Bureau and Indiana Historical Society, 1965.

Thornton, Tamara Plakins. *Handwriting in America: A Cultural History*. New Haven, Conn.: Yale University Press, 1996.

Thurston, John H. *Early Days in Rockford: Reminiscences, Sporting, and Otherwise*. Rockford, Ill., 1891.

Tichi, Cecelia. *Embodiment of a Nation: Human Form in American Places*. Cambridge, Mass.: Harvard University Press, 2001.

———. *Exposés and Excess: Muckraking in America, 1900/2000*. Philadelphia: University of Pennsylvania Press, 2004.

———. Introduction to Bellamy, *Looking Backward*, 7–28.

———. *Shifting Gears: Technology, Literature, Culture in Modernist America*. Chapel Hill: University of North Carolina Press, 1987.

Tindall, George Brown, and David E. Shi. *America: A Narrative History*. 3rd ed. New York: Norton, 1984.

Tobey, James A. *The Children's Bureau: Its History, Activities and Organization*. Baltimore: Johns Hopkins Press, 1925.

Todd, Alden L. *Justice on Trial: The Case of Louis D. Brandeis*. New York: McGraw-Hill, 1964.

Trachtenberg, Alan. *The Incorporation of America: Culture and Society in the Gilded Age*. New York: Hill and Wang, 1982.

Twain, Mark, and Charles Dudley Warner. *The Gilded Age*. 1873. Reprint. New York: Grosset and Dunlap, 1915.

"Two Nice Men." *Time*, May 8, 1939, 17.

Uchitelle, Louis. *The Disposable American: Layoffs and Their Consequences*. New York: Knopf, 2006.

Unger, Irwin. *The Greenback Era: A Social and Political History of American Finance, 1865–1879*. Princeton, N.J.: Princeton University Press, 1964.

Unger, Nancy C. *Fighting Bob La Follette: The Righteous Reformer*. Chapel Hill: University of North Carolina Press, 2000.

Urofsky, Melvin I. *Louis D. Brandeis and the Progressive Tradition*. Boston: Little, Brown, 1981.

———. "Louis D. Brandeis, Progressivism, and the Money Trust." In Brandeis, *Other People's Money*, 1–40.

———. *A Mind of One Piece: Brandeis and American Reform*. New York: Scribner, 1971.

U.S. Congress. Senate. Committee on the Judiciary. *Hearings before the Subcommittee of the Committee on the Judiciary, United States Senate, Sixty-Fourth Congress, First Session on the Nomination of Louis D. Brandeis to Be an Associate Justice of the Supreme Court of the United States*. Feb. 1916. Washington, D.C.: U.S. Government Printing Office, 1916.

U.S. Department of Labor. *Report on Conditions of Woman and Child Wage-Earners in the United States*. Vol. 19, *Labor Laws and Factory Conditions*. Washington, D.C.: U.S. Department of Labor, n.d.

———. Bureau of Labor Statistics. *Conciliation, Arbitration, and Sanitation in the Dress and Waist Industry*. Bulletin of the U.S. Bureau of Labor Statistics, no. 145. Washington, D.C.: U.S. Government Printing Office, 1914.

U.S. Industrial Commission. *Report of the Industrial Commission on the Relations of Capital and Labor Employed in the Mining Industry*. Vol. 12. Washington, D.C.: U.S. Government Printing Office, 1901.

Van Riper, Paul P. *History of the United States Civil Service*. Evanston, Ill.: Row, Peterson, 1958.

Views of Louisville since 1766. Edited by Samuel W. Thomas. Louisville, Ky.: Courier-Journal Lithographing, 1971.

Vincent, Henry. *The Story of the Commonweal*. 1894. Reprint. New York: Arno, 1969.

Violette, Ralph. *Images of America: Fort Wayne, Indiana*. Charleston, S.C.: Arcadia, 2000.

Wald, Lillian D. *The House on Henry Street*. 1915. Reprint. New Brunswick, N.J.: Transaction, 1991.

———. *Windows on Henry Street*. Boston: Little, Brown, 1934.

Walker, Charles Rumford. "The Twenty-Four-Hour Shift: A Chapter in Steel III." *Atlantic Monthly*, Dec. 1922, 45–51.

Wallis, Jim. *The Great Awakening: Reviving Faith and Politics in a Post–Religious Right America.* New York: HarperOne, 2008.

———. "What to Do." In Rauschenbusch, *Christianity and the Social Crisis in the 21st Century,* 341–46.

Warren, Louis S. *Buffalo Bill's America: William Cody and the Wild West Show.* New York: Knopf, 2005.

Watson, Bruce. *Bread and Roses: Mills, Migrants, and the Struggle for the American Dream.* New York: Viking, 2005.

Watterson, Henry. *The Editorials of Henry Watterson.* New York: Doran, 1923.

———. *"Marse Henry": An Autobiography.* 2 vols. 1919. Reprint. New York: Beekman, 1974.

Waugh, Joan. *Unsentimental Reformer: The Life of Josephine Shaw Lowell.* Cambridge, Mass.: Harvard University Press, 1997.

Waugh, Norah. *The Cut of Women's Clothes, 1600–1930.* London: Faber and Faber, 1968.

Webb, Ross. *Kentucky in the Reconstruction Era.* Lexington: University Press of Kentucky, 1979.

Weinberg, Arthur, and Lila Weinberg, eds. *The Muckrakers.* 1961. Reprint. Urbana: University of Illinois Press, 2001.

Weinstein, Cindy. "How Many Others Are There in the Other Half? Jacob Riis and the Tenement Population." *Nineteenth-Century Contexts* 24, no. 2 (2002): 195–216.

———. *The Literature of Labor and the Labors of Literature: Allegory in Nineteenth-Century American Fiction.* Cambridge: Cambridge University Press, 1995.

Wells, Ida B. "Booker T. Washington and His Critics." *World Today* 6 (1904): 518–21.

———. "A Conserving Force." In *Conservation of National Ideals,* 17–45. New York: Revell, 1911.

———. *Crusade for Justice: The Autobiography of Ida B. Wells.* Edited by Alfreda M. Duster. Chicago: University of Chicago Press, 1970.

———. "Lynch Law in America." *Arena,* Jan. 1900, 15–24.

———. *The Memphis Diary of Ida B. Wells.* Edited by Miriam DeCosta-Willis. Boston: Beacon Press, 1995.

———. "The Northern Negro Woman's Social and Moral Condition." *Original Rights,* Apr. 1910, 33–37.

———. *The Reason Why the Colored American Is Not in the World's Columbian Exposition.* In Wells-Barnett, *Selected Works,* 46–137.

———. *A Red Record.* In Wells, *Southern Horrors and Other Writings,* 73–157.

———. *Southern Horrors: Lynch Law in All Its Phases.* In Wells, *Southern Horrors and Other Writings,* 49–72.

———. *Southern Horrors and Other Writings: The Anti-lynching Campaign of Ida B. Wells, 1892–1900.* Edited by Jacqueline Jones Royster. Boston: Bedford, 1997.

Wells, Richard A. *Manners: Culture and Dress in the Best American Society.* Springfield, Mass.: King, Richardson, 1891.

Wells-Barnett, Ida B. *The Arkansas Race Riot.* Chicago: Wells-Barnett, 1920.

———. "How Enfranchisement Stops Lynching." *Original Rights,* June 1910, 42–53.

———. "Our Country's Lynching Record." *Survey,* Feb. 1, 1913,: 573–74.

———. *Selected Works of Ida B. Wells-Barnett.* Compiled by Trudier Harris. New York: Oxford University Press, 1991.

West, Cornel. "Can These Dry Bones Live?" In Rauschenbusch, *Christianity and the Social Crisis in the 21st Century*, 231–34.

Westbrook, Robert B. *John Dewey and American Democracy*. Ithaca, N.Y.: Cornell University Press, 1991.

Wharton, Edith. *The Custom of the Country*. 1913. Reprint. New York: Macmillan, 1987.

Who Built America? Working People and the Nation's Economy, Politics, Culture, and Society. Vol. 2. New York: Pantheon, 1992.

Wiebe, Robert H. *The Search for Order, 1877–1920*. New York: Hill and Wang, 1967.

Wiernik, Peter. *History of the Jews in America*. 3rd ed. New York: Hermon Press, 1972.

Wilkinson, Bruce. *The Prayer of Jabez: Breaking Through to the Blessed Life*. Sisters, Ore.: Multnomah, 1971.

Willard, Frances E. *Glimpses of Fifty Years: An Autobiography of an American Woman*. Chicago: Women's Temperance Publication Association, 1889.

———. *Occupations for Women*. New York: Success, 1897.

Williams, Caroline. *Louisville Scenes*. Garden City, N.Y.: Doubleday, 1970.

Williamson, Harold Francis. *Northwestern University: A History, 1850–1975*. Evanston, Ill.: Northwestern University Press, 1976.

Wischnewetzky, Florence Kelley. *An Address in Memory of Thomas Paine*. Pittsburgh: Truth, 1889.

———. *Our Toiling Children*. Chicago: Women's Temperance Publication Association, 1889.

Woods, Robert A., and Albert J. Kennedy, eds. *Handbook of Settlements*. 1911. Reprint. New York: Arno, 1970.

Woodward, C. Vann. *The Strange Career of Jim Crow*. 1955. 2nd rev. ed. New York: Oxford University Press, 1966.

Woodworth, Benjamin S. "The Practice of Medicine in the Fort Wayne Area." 1889. Reprinted in *Indiana Medical History Quarterly* 3, no. 1a (1977): 4–6.

Wright, Carroll D. *The Battles of Labor*. New York: Jacobs, 1906.

Wright, George C. *Life behind a Veil: Blacks in Louisville, Kentucky, 1865–1930*. Baton Rouge: Louisiana State University Press, 1985.

Wyckoff, Walter A. *The Workers: An Experiment in Reality*. Vol. 1, *The East*. New York: Scribner, 1897.

———. *The Workers: An Experiment in Reality*. Vol. 2, *The West*. New York: Scribner, 1901.

Yater, George H. *Two Hundred Years at the Falls of the Ohio: A History of Louisville and Jefferson County*. Louisville, Ky.: Filson Club, 1987.

Yochelson, Bonnie, and Daniel Czitrom. *Rediscovering Jacob Riis: Exposure Journalism and Photography in Turn-of-the-Century New York*. New York: New Press, 2008.

Young, Arthur Nichols. *The Single Tax Movement in the United States*. Princeton, N.J.: Princeton University Press, 1916.

Young, Charles P., ed. *Cornell in Pictures: 1869–1954*. Ithaca, N.Y.: Cornell University Press, 1954.

Young, J[ohn] P[reston], ed. *Standard History of Memphis, Tennessee*. Knoxville, Tenn.: Crew, 1912.

Zelizer, Viviana. *Pricing the Priceless Child: The Changing Social Value of Children*. Princeton, N.J.: Princeton University Press, 1985.

ACKNOWLEDGMENTS

The onset of the second Gilded Age prompted this project, which took shape from questions raised in the privileged setting of a yearlong seminar at the Robert Penn Warren Center for the Humanities at Vanderbilt University in 2005–6. Director Mona Frederick provided our interdisciplinary group with wide-ranging opportunities for our weekly discussions of feminist authority, and throughout the year the notion of preparing profiles of Progressive Era figures became plausible in challenging exchanges with Brook Ackerly, Karen Campbell, Vivien Fryd, Holly McCammon, Benita Roth, Melissa Snarr, Ronnie Steinberg, and Barbara Tsakirgis.

Civic Passions gained incalculable momentum from my residency as the chair of modern culture at the Library of Congress John W. Kluge Center in the spring of 2006 and 2007. The cordiality of director Carolyn Brown and spirited engagement of Mary Lou Reker have been—and continue to be—great gifts. Mary Lou first recognized (and demonstrated and promoted) the visual dimensions of this project, and Carolyn has probably forgotten her observation, which proved to be crucial to the chapter on Julia Lathrop, on Malcolm Gladwell's remarks on "connecters" in *The Tipping Point*. Acquaintance with Patricia Sullivan in adjacent offices at the Kluge Center went far to validate this project, especially in regard to the chapter on Florence Kelley. I appreciate help also from Robert Saldini, Jane Sargus, and Joanne Kitching. The book benefited from Library of Congress staff in the Reference Department, the Geography and Map Division, the Rare Book and Special Collections Division, the Manuscript Division, the Copyright Office, and especially the Prints and Photographs Division, where Jeffrey Bridger helped me locate elusive images and patiently reviewed the copyright status of numerous photographs. I thank Mark Lewis of the Photoduplication Service for help with a complicated order.

Other libraries and archives proved crucial for *Exiting the Gilded Age*, and I thank the helpful professionals at the Allen County (Indiana) Library, the John J. Burns Library (Boston College), the Filson Historical Society, the Fort Wayne Historical Society, the Joseph Regenstein Library (University of Chicago), the Howard Colman Library (Rockford College), the University of Illinois at Chicago Library, the Schlesinger Library (Harvard University), the Louis D. Brandeis School of Law Library (University of Louisville), the Louisville (Kentucky) Free Public Library, and the Warshaw Collection (Smithsonian National Museum of American History).

Research and writing were aided immeasurably on and off the Vanderbilt campus. Academic leave was facilitated by Dean Richard McCarty of the College of Arts and Science, and, as ever, I am thankful to the William R. Kenan Charitable Trust for supporting my work. The Bodacious writers' group listened to draft passages and made invaluable suggestions. I thank J. T. Ellison, Janet McKeown, Peggy Peden, Mary Richards, Del Tinsley, and J. B. Thompson. On campus, as always, the Vanderbilt University librarians were most helpful and of good cheer, from the front desk to the annex and the interlibrary loan service. I thank Peggy Earheart, Deborah Lilton, Marilyn Pilley, and Janet Thomason. Thanks also to Janis May of the Department of English.

Along the way, conversations with colleagues, family, and acquaintances contributed greatly to *Exiting the Gilded Age*. These include "Peets" moments on the Caltech campus with Cindy Weinstein, and Thadious Davis's suggestion that the youth of the Progressives must be emphasized. The serendipitous conversation with attorney Abby Cohen on a cross-country flight made another contribution when Abby called an important title to my attention. Three days of research in Louisville with Julia Harrison were enormously helpful and productive, as were Julia's suggestions on the draft of the chapter on Louis Brandeis. I appreciate valuable discussions with Wendy Martin, Amy Lang, and Julie Abraham. I also thank Terry and William T. Harrison for their encouragement and hospitality and William (Billy) for information on firearms (useful in the discussion of Ida B. Wells-Barnett). I appreciate the goodwill of Winston Harrison and of Claire and Uri Grezemkovsky.

The process of publication brings its own appreciation to editors and external reviewers. Sian Hunter, senior editor at the University of North Carolina Press, was receptive to the idea of the book, gave it focused attention at every point, solicited outside reviews that proved immeasurably helpful, and streamlined the final version with her editorial pencil. The project editor, Paul Betz, guided the manuscript toward publication, and Anna Laura Bennett showed superb skills as copyeditor. Courtney Baker produced an elegant design. I also thank the Press's director, Kate Torrey, for her support. The close scrutiny of external reviewers Professor Daniel Horowitz and a second historian (whose identity is confidential) cannot be sufficiently credited, but I say to both of them: thank you.

My debt is great to the few who agreed to read and critique drafts along the way. Neither Ann Covington nor Teresa Goddu has a minute to spare from her schedule, but both consented to read draft chapters and offer frank suggestions. Both responded promptly time after time, and their contributions are present throughout *Civic Passions*. Bill Tichi, always the first reader, had the woeful task of sending preliminary chapters back to my drawing board because biographical summaries lack the vibrancy of narrative. He has spent untold hours reading, editing, talking about, and listening to matters relevant to this book—and insisting on its significance. To him: gracias!

INDEX

Gerstle, Gary, 289 (n. 3)

Gilded Age: first Gilded Age, xi–xviii, 4, 6, 7, 9, 156, 207, 224, 279, 281; second Gilded Age, xi–xviii, 9, 276–81. *See also* Twain, Mark

Gladden, Washington, 71–72, 221, 226

Gladwell, Malcolm, 93

Goldman, Emma, 93

Goldmark, Alice (Mrs. Louis D. Brandeis), 178

Goldmark, Josephine, 123, 156, 162, 192, 201

Gompers, Samuel: American Federation of Labor, 18, 84–85, 132, 152, 225

Gould, Jay, 15, 23

Grady, Alice H., 167, 186, 196–98, 199–200

Grant, Ulysses S., 171

Green, Edward, 245

Griffith, David W.: *Birth of a Nation*, 243

Guild, Curtis, 202

Halleck, Henry, 171

Hallinan, Joseph, 282

Hamilton, Agnes, 47

Hamilton, Alice, xvi, 6, 26, 74, 114–15, 120, 137, 144, 278; as industrial toxicologist, 30–40, 55–56; as Hull House resident, 33, 52; education, 37, 44–46; Harvard professorship, 40; writings of, 40, 52–53; early years, 41–44

Hamilton, Allen, 41, 42–43

Hamilton, Edith, 32, 44

Hamilton, Gertrude, 43, 50

Hamilton, Montgomery, 36

Hanna, Marcus (Mark), 85–86

Hard, William, 50, 192

Harriman, Edward H., 15, 168, 169

Harriman, Mrs. J. Borden, 147

Haymarket riot, 21, 102, 152

Hearst, William Randolph, 16

Hendricks, Francis, 169

Herbert, Victor, 1

Higginson, Henry Lee, 179, 186, 197, 203

Higginson, Mrs. Henry Lee (Ida), 179

Hine, Lewis W., 135

Holden v. Hardy, 152

Holmes, Oliver Wendell, 175, 176, 185, 203

Hooper, W. W., 258

Howe, Mark DeWolfe, 187

Howells, William Dean, 138

Hughes, Charles Evans, 169

Hull, Charles J., 98

Hull House. *See* Addams, Jane

Hull House Maps and Papers, 136

Hume, David, 86

Hyde, James Hazen, 167–68, 178

Immigration, xiii, 21, 77; and tenement housing, 100–101; and neighborhoods, 103–4, 146; diseases of, 108, 210. *See also* Labor

Iyenaga, Toyokichi, 66

Jacobi, Mary, 142, 143

James, Henry, 147

James, William, 149, 156

Jim Crow, 3, 268. *See* Wells, Ida B.

Johnson, Tom, 4

Kelley, Caroline Bonsall, 139, 140

Kelley, Florence, xvi, 6, 7, 27, 76, 107, 120, 123, 187, 201, 268, 278, 279, 283, 284, 285; and Chicago smallpox outbreak, 108–9; as Illinois state factory inspector, 124–25, 143; as Crerar Library staff member, 124–28, 138; education, 133, 136–37; socialist politics of, 137–38; as National Consumers' League general secretary, 147–63; as NAACP member, 150; work in *Muller v. Oregon* ("Brandeis brief"), 158–60. *See also* Wischnewetzky, Florence Kelley

Kelley, John, 139

Kelley, Margaret, 139, 147, 161

Kelley, Nicholas, 139

Kelley, William, 129, 132, 137

Kellogg, Paul, 76, 87, 123, 147, 153

Kenney, Mary, 6, 187

King, Martin Luther, Jr., 205, 273–74

Kingsley, Charles, 50; *Cheap Clothes and Nasty* and *The Water-Babies*, 44

Parks, Rosa L., 273

Pelley, Anna, 241, 243, 244

Pendleton Act, 119

Pitt, William, 74

Pittsburgh Survey, 62, 78–84. *See also* Commons, John R.

Plessy v. Ferguson: and Wells, Ida B., 260

Powers, Johnny, 116, 118

Pugh, Sarah, 149

Pulitzer, Joseph, 16

Pullman, George, 7

Progressive Era, 4, 9

Progressives: youth of, xvi, 5–6; critique of, 5; programs of, 5, 9, 275–76; geographic origins of, 6; fact seeking of, 7; in twenty-first century, 282–88. *See also* Brandeis, Louis D.; Commons, John R.; Hamilton, Alice; Kelley, Florence; Lathrop, Julia Clifford; Rauschenbusch, Walter; Wells, Ida B.; Wells-Barnett, Ida B.

Rauschenbusch, August, 212; Rochester Theological Seminary professorship, 216

Rauschenbusch, Emma, 217

Rauschenbusch, Walter, xvi–xvii, 6, 26, 71, 205, 284; *Christianity and the Social Crisis*, 205, 206–9, 237–38; Social Gospel of, 205–12, 221, 234–39; and Rochester, N.Y., origins of, 207, 212–13; ministry in New York City (Hell's Kitchen), 210, 217–18, 231–32; education, 213–14, 215, 217; Christian conversion of, 215; eschatological doctrine considered by, 215–16; as Brotherhood of the Kingdom founder, 233; marriage and family, 233–34; Rochester Theological Seminary faculty appointment, 234–36, 237–38

Rauschenbusch, Winifred, 234

Reagan, Ronald, 276

Ricardo, David, 86

Riis, Jacob, 23–24, 46

Ritchie v. People, 133

Ritchie v. Wayman, 159–60

Roberts, John (U.S. Supreme Court chief justice), 280

Rockefeller, John D., xi, xiv, 1, 6, 17, 23, 226, 278; Standard Oil Co., 24

Roosevelt, Theodore, 9, 14, 50, 136, 203

Rother, Pauline, 233

Russell Sage Foundation, 62, 77, 120, 192

Ryan, Thomas Fortune, 168

Santa Clara County v. Southern Pacific Railroad, 19

Santayana, George, 275, 276

Sargent, John Singer, 1

Schiff, Jacob Henry, 167–68, 169

Schlosser, Eric, 282

Scripps, E. W., 16

Shaler, Nathaniel Southgate, 180, 186, 188, 201; as Union army officer, 180; *The Citizen: A Study of the Individual and the Government*, 184–85, 198–99, 203

Sheppard-Towner Act, 121, 162

Sinclair, Upton, 7, 50; *The Jungle*, 35, 84

Smith, Adam: *Wealth of Nations*, 86

Smith, Mary Rozet, 139

Social Darwinism, 59, 66, 91. *See also* Commons, John R.; Spencer, Herbert

Social Gospel. *See* Ely, Richard T.; Rauschenbusch, Walter

Social Security Act of 1935, 88

Sousa, John Philip, 1, 3

Spencer, Herbert, 58, 63, 64

Starr, Ellen Gates, 99, 103, 106

Steffens, Lincoln, 50, 281

Stewart, A. T., 1

Stewart, Henry, 261

Storey, Morefield, 248

Stowe, Harriet Beecher, 101, 116; *Uncle Tom's Cabin*, 112

Strong, Josiah, 105, 221

Strum, Philippa, 204

Sullivan, Louis, 142

Sullivan, Mark, xv, 25

Sumner, William Graham, 58–60, 68, 71

Swift, Gustavus, 7, 132

Taft, William Howard, 54, 90

Tarbell, Ida M., 25, 50, 281

Taylor, Frederick Winslow, 202